THE GOOD NEWS ACCORDING TO MATTHEW

THE
GOOD
NEWS
ACCORDING TO
MATTHEW

Eduard Schweizer

TRANSLATED BY DAVID E. GREEN

JOHN KNOX PRESS
Atlanta

© 1975 John Knox Press   74- 3717
Printed in the United States of America 2-14-77

CONTENTS

INTRODUCTION

1

The first difference to strike the eye between this Gospel and the Gospel of Mark is its greater length. Closer examination reveals the difference to be even more noteworthy, because most of the stories that also occur in Mark are recounted much more briefly in Matthew (see the introductory discussion of 8:1-4). Most of the expansion therefore is due to new material, in particular the introductory infancy narratives and above all the interpolation of major discourses of Jesus. It would thus be reasonable to suppose that Matthew was less concerned with the historical events of Jesus' life than with his teaching. The answer, however, is not that simple: Matthew's purpose is in fact to make not only Jesus' own words but also his actions authoritative for the Christian community. On this point he is actually more skeptical than Mark (see the excursus on 7:13-23 [§3]). Furthermore, the many references to Scripture scattered through the Gospel are meant to show that the historical events of Jesus' life fulfill all the promises of salvation made by God. Miracle stories, of course, are introduced not for their factual character, but for their significance to the community; but this is not to deny that they happened—only those things that actually occurred in the life of Jesus or his disciples could have any import for the community. That community was not interested in fabrications, but in the realities that would affect its members. In other words, only the actual facts of history can affect the present (see the commentary on 8:23). We must wait until the end of our study to understand the whole of the evangelist's intent—which was theological rather than historical. But on the question of whether his account is true, see the Introduction to *The Good News According to Mark*, §5.

2

In chapters 3–4 and 12–28, Matthew follows Mark almost without exception. Although he interpolates considerable additional material, he presents the individual sections in exactly the same sequence as Mark, often using nearly identical words (e.g., 15:32-39; 16:24-28). Matthew clearly represents a further development of Mark, rather than the other way around; for three examples among many, see 14:13 (introductory remarks); 19:1; 20:22. The logical conclusion is that Matthew was acquainted with the Gospel of Mark.

The additional material includes numerous sections in which there is considerable verbal agreement between Matthew and Luke (e.g., 3:7-10). It is noteworthy that these sections, too, occur in roughly the same order. The sequence is preserved even when Matthew and Luke insert these sections at different points in the Markan narrative. In both, for instance, the message of John the Baptist is followed by the account of Jesus' temptation, then the sayings of the Lukan Sermon on the Plain (which all also appear in the Matthaean Sermon on the Mount), and the healing of the servant of the Roman officer, although Matthew places the Sermon on the Mount immediately after the call of the first disciples, while Luke first narrates the entire section Mark 2:1–3:19, which Matthew keeps for later, and although Luke appends the healing of the servant directly to the Sermon on the Plain, whereas Matthew interpolates the healing of the leper from Mark 1:40-45, recounted earlier by Luke.

These observations can hardly be explained except by the two-source theory (see the introductory comments on Mark 1): according to this theory, Matthew was acquainted not only with Mark but also with a Sayings Source, abbreviated "Q" (see the introductory remarks on 4:1-11). By and large, Q contained only sayings or conversations of Jesus (see the introductory remarks on 8:5-13). Since the Markan material and Q material, each considered independently, exhibit the same sequence through extensive sections, but not in combination, we cannot be dealing with a common tradition in which the two were already associated. In other words, we do not have to consider a proto-Matthew, i.e., an earlier form of our Matthew, or a Mark already augmented by the Q material. Since the discovery of the

Gospel of Thomas, which is of relatively late date and records the words of Jesus in markedly altered form, we have been certain that there were collections containing only sayings of Jesus. Such collections of "words of the wise" stand directly in the line that we meet in Proverbs and the Wisdom of Solomon. In content, too, the Sayings Source continues this older tradition (see the excursus on 23:24-39), except that it has taken on a markedly eschatological tone. Attention is focused, for example, on the still awaited coming of Christ; but Good Friday (see 23:37 and the introductory remarks on 4:1-11) and Easter (see the discussion of 11:27) have also left their mark. It is quite likely, furthermore, that the community that read Q was also familiar with the Good Friday and Easter narrative as part of their liturgy, just as in Jewish tradition, after the Old Testament achieved its final form, instruction and historical narrative continued on independently as two distinct strands of tradition.

3

Of course this two-source schema is still too simple; in particular, it does not explain why Matthew 5–11 departs so strikingly from the sequence of Mark. In the introductory comments on 4:17–11:30, it is suggested that, for example, the sayings contained in the Lukan Sermon on the Plain (Luke 6:20-49) had already been supplemented in the Matthaean community and altered for purposes of catechism, and that something similar may have taken place with several accounts of Jesus' acts. In chapters 3 and 4, for instance, Matthew follows Mark but adds material from Q; furthermore, in sections that appear in both Mark and Q, he follows Mark while occasionally adopting the words and sequence of Q. With similar license, in the Sermon on the Mount and his collection of the acts of Jesus, he may have allowed himself to be influenced by a "catechism" current in his community.

Neither is it reasonable to suppose that all the material common to Matthew and Luke simply derives from Q. In cases such as the parable of the feast (22:1-10; Luke 14:15-24), where neither the wording nor placement is the same although we are dealing with the same parable, such a supposition is very dubious. Under these circumstances an oral tradition is conceivable, which has developed the material differently; of course, some of the differences may be due to

Jesus' having told the same parable more than once in different ways.

Furthermore, Mark may have been available to Matthew and Luke in a wording that does not correspond precisely to our text. Minor alterations can occur in manuscript copies; for example, there is a group of manuscripts of Acts that at several points provide a different, somewhat longer text, something like a revised edition. This might explain minor agreements between Matthew and Luke against Mark (besides chapters 8–9, see, for example, the discussion of 26:75).

What is more important, Matthew must not be pictured as a modern scholar, copying Mark precisely and consciously considering every modification. Obviously he is freely recounting the narratives before him, influenced by the style that sayings of Jesus or narratives took in his community, possibly even in its liturgy. Nevertheless, his changes, which were often made unconsciously, exhibit a theological development. His rendition of Mark should not be pictured too mechanically, although the precisely retained structural sequence is conceivable only on the basis of a written copy; at the same time, careful attention must be paid to what is left out, added, or modified. Often it is precisely these unconscious reformulations that betray a shift of emphasis and understanding. Therefore in passages that have a Markan parallel, the commentary that follows will presuppose a familiarity with the Markan text and will emphasize only the changes Matthew has made. In addition, in treating these passages we will leave aside important questions of their historical basis and of pre-Markan accounts. That is, our approach will not be that of tradition history, but of redaction history (see the introduction to *The Good News According to Mark,* §§ 2 and 3).

4

In the middle of the second century, Papias records: "Matthew collected the sayings [*logia*] in the Hebrew tongue, but each man translated them as he was able." The term "sayings" suggests discourses; but it is possible he also had narratives in mind, just as the English expression "Word of God" encompasses both. Of course this passage cannot refer to our Gospel, which is certainly not simply a translation from Hebrew or Aramaic. Besides which, the prehistory of Matthew, discussed in §§ 2 and 3, eliminates the idea of its being a firsthand report by an eyewitness (Matt. 9:9), and some of its quotations fit the text only in the Greek translation of the Bible. No, the differences between the Gospels cannot be accounted for by so simple an explanation as different translations.

But Papias' statement does indicate four things: (a) In the middle of the second century the differences between the Gospels presented a problem. (b) Our Gospel was associated with Matthew, the disciple of Jesus mentioned in 9:9. (c) No one ventured to ascribe to Matthew the entire Gospel as we have it; instead, they credited him with a Hebrew or Aramaic prototype. (d) This prototype was probably limited to some or all of the sayings of Jesus contained in Matthew. Neither can Q have been compiled by Matthew the tax collector called by Jesus, because the Q material is itself far from homogeneous and presupposes, for example in the temptation narrative with its use of the title "God's Son," a considerable period of theological reflection. The tradition, even at this early date, is exceedingly uncertain—as is shown by the common retailing as factual of such miraculous legends as the one, recounted by the same Papias, of how the daughters of Philip restored a dead man to life (see the discussion of Mark 16:18). The only possibility left, as the change of the name "Levi" (Mark 2:14) to "Matthew" (Matt. 9:9) itself suggests, is that Matthew the tax collector was a familiar figure in the community that stands behind our Gospel, and that certain accounts of Jesus, which can no longer be singled out, may have been ascribed to him.

5

The content of the Gospel permits us to draw certain conclusions. It must undoubtedly be dated some time after A.D. 70 (see the introductory remarks on 22:7). Since the Markan tradition was already familiar and had undergone some changes, and since learned Scriptural disputations, like those that took place after A.D. 70, may be assumed alongside earlier material, a date in the early eighties may tentatively be proposed. As the place of origin, Syria is still the most likely possibility. On the one hand, an association with Palestinian Judaism and its interpretation of the Law is clearly discernible; on the other hand, a full recognition of the gentile world and the admission of pagans into the post-Easter community are accepted facts. The destruction of Jerusalem plays some role; but it was not experienced firsthand, and the exodus of Christians from Jerusalem is perceptible only in the tradition borrowed from Mark, not in Matthew himself. Furthermore, the mention of persecution by pagan officials and the implied preaching to all nations (10:18) would suggest an area outside Palestine. The Gospel of John, by contrast, mentions persecution only by the Synagogue. Of course, Matthew's reference could have originated inside Palestine: Galilee, for example (see 4:15), is not out of the question.

But Syria is suggested by the major role assigned to Peter, especially his authoritative interpretation of Jesus' commands as referring to new situations (see the discussion of 16:19); for according to Acts 12:17 Peter had left Jerusalem. He was certainly in Syrian Antioch, as we know from Galatians 2:11 ff. He was probably also in Corinth (1 Cor. 1:12; cf. 3:22; 9:5), but Greece (and Asia Minor) can hardly be considered as a possibility, because the nature of the Matthaean community is very different from the Pauline community or the community in Asia Minor, which we know from other documents (see the excursus on 7:13-23), and because there is a total lack of references to Paul or Pauline statements.

The Jewish background is plain. Jewish customs are familiar to everyone (see the discussion of 15:5); the debate about the Law is a central question (see the discussion of 5:17-20), and the Sabbath is still observed (see the discussion of 24:20). The dispute with the Pharisees serves primarily as a warning to the community (see the introduction to chapters 21–25); but a reference to leading representatives of the Synagogue is not far below the surface. Above all, the method of learned interpretation of the Law, which "looses" and "binds," was still central for Matthew and his community (see the discussion of 16:19; 18:18). Preservation of sayings such as 23:2-3, which support the continued authority of Pharisaic teaching, and above all the special emphasis placed on the requirement not to offend those who still think in legalistic terms (see the discussion of 17:24-27), show that dialogue with the Jewish Synagogue had not yet been broken off. On the other hand, a saying like 27:25 shows that the Christian community had conclusively split with the Synagogue, even though hope for the conversion of Jews was not yet totally dead.

The community in which Matthew lived exhibits a highly individual nature, found elsewhere only in the Didache, presumably likewise in Syria, at a somewhat later stage of development (see the excursus on 7:13-23). This community still shows strong links with the historical Jesus; it insists on a literal transmission of his instructions, shows a definite ascetic bias, and has a high esteem for ethical demands, learned Scriptural interpretation, and charismatic authority. These characteristics are probably typical of the Syrian church as a whole, not just one small group within it. Either possibility is conceivable; but the presence of the Didache and the fact that our Gospel was accepted relatively early by the church as its primary book suggest the whole church rather than a part. The evangelist therefore was probably a Jewish Christian of the Syrian church.

6

For most of the sections not already discussed in my commentary on Mark, I have retained the threefold organization of introduction, detailed exegesis, and conclusion. The first discusses the history of the tradition; the third recapitulates the theological content in summary. Unless otherwise stated, references elsewhere in the commentary refer to the detailed exegesis. New Testament quotations, except as emended to bring out a particular meaning, are from *The New Testament in Today's English,* published as *Good News for Modern Man,* replacing Schniewind's translation used as the basis for the German edition. For present purposes, precision and close following of the Greek text are more important than elegance or modernity, which are important for liturgical or private reading. Old Testament quotations are from the King James Version (marked KJV) or the Revised Standard Version (marked RSV). The scholarly grounds for certain unusual hypotheses cannot be given here. I have published much of the relevant material in various places, and hope to assemble the articles later in a single collection.

7

If I may dedicate this attempt to understand Matthew to the Faculty of Protestant Theology at the University of Vienna, it is as a small token of gratitude for the honorary doctorate conferred on me by the University of Vienna at their request. It may be that a community that has survived for centuries as a minority, suffered persecution, often left home and kindred to follow Jesus, and preserved its identity underground, without officials, and without theological training understands the message of this Gospel for our own day especially well, and better than I.

8
BIBLIOGRAPHY

Scholarly Commentaries: Adolf von Schlatter, *Der Evangelist Matthäus*, 6th ed. (Stuttgart: Calwer Verlag, 1963); Walter Grundmann, *Das Evangelium nach Matthäus*, 2d ed., Theologischer Handkommentar zum Neuen Testament, vol. 1 (Berlin: Evangelischer Verlag, 1971); Pierre Bonnard, *L'Evangile selon Saint Matthieu*, 2d ed., Commentaire du Nouveau Testament, vol. 1 (Neuchatel: Delachaux & Niestlé, 1970).

Popular Expositions: Julius Schniewind, *Das Evangelium nach Matthäus*, 12th ed., Das Neue Testament Deutsch, vol. 2 (Göttingen: Vandenhoeck & Ruprecht, 1968); Josef Schmid, *Das Evangelium nach Matthäus*, 5th ed., Regensburger Neues Testament, vol. 1 (Regensburg: F. Pustet, 1965); Krister Stendahl, "Matthew," in *Peake's Commentary on the Bible*, ed. Matthew Black (London: Thomas Nelson & Sons, 1962).

Monographs: Wolfgang Trilling, *Das wahre Israel: Studien zur Theologie des Matthäusevangeliums*, 3d ed. (Munich: Kösel-Verlag, 1964); Reinhart Hummel, *Die Auseinandersetzung zwischen Kirche und Judentum im Matthäusevangelium*, 2d ed. (Munich: Chr. Kaiser Verlag, 1966); Ernst Haenchen, *Der Weg Jesu*, 2d ed. (Berlin: Alfred Töppelmann, 1968); Günther Bornkamm, Gerhard Barth, and Heinz Joachim Held, *Überlieferung und Auslegung im Matthäusevangelium*, 6th ed. (Neukirchen: Neukirchener Verlag, 1970), English translation: *Tradition and Interpretation in Matthew* (Philadelphia: The Westminster Press, 1963); Georg Strecker, *Der Weg der Gerechtigkeit: Untersuchungen zur Theologie des Matthäus*, 3d ed. (Göttingen: Vandenhoeck & Ruprecht, 1971); Krister Stendahl, *The School of St.*

Matthew and Its Use of the Old Testament, 2d ed. (Lund: C. W. K. Gleerup, 1968); M. Jack Suggs, *Wisdom, Christology and the Law in Matthew's Gospel* (Cambridge, Mass.: Harvard University Press, 1970); W. D. Davies, *The Setting of the Sermon on the Mount* (Cambridge: The University Press, 1963).

Rabbinic sources are cited from (Hermann Strack and) Paul Billerbeck, *Kommentar zum Neuen Testament aus Talmud und Midrasch,* 5th ed. (Munich: Beck Verlag, 1969). When not otherwise indicated, the passages will be found in volume one under the verse in question.

The Qumran texts are found in Eduard Lohse, *Die Texte aus Qumran* (Munich: Kösel-Verlag, 1964) and are translated in Theodor Herzl Gaster, *The Dead Sea Scriptures,* 2d ed. (Garden City, N. Y.: Doubleday & Co., 1964) and Geza Vermes, *The Dead Sea Scrolls,* 2d ed. (New York: Heritage Press, 1967). 4QDb (on CD xv, 15-17) will be found in Josef Tadeusz Milik, *Dix ans de decouverts dans le desert de Juda* (Paris: Les Editions du Cerf, 1957), English translation by J. Strugnell, *Ten Years of Discovery in the Wilderness of Judea* (Naperville, Ill.: Alec R. Allenson, 1959). The other Jewish texts are contained in Robert Henry Charles, *The Apocrypha and Pseudepigrapha of the Old Testament in English* (Oxford: The Clarendon Press, 1913).

For a discussion of the questions usually dealt with in introductions, see the concluding section of the introduction in my commentary on Mark.

The Apostolic Fathers are most readily available in the Loeb Classical Library or in Robert McQueen Grant, *The Apostolic Fathers* (New York: Thomas Nelson & Sons, 1964–68). The apocryphal gospels can be found in Montague Rhodes James, *The Apocryphal New Testament,* 5th ed. (Oxford: The Clarendon Press, 1953) and Edgar Hennecke, *Neutestamentliche Apokryphen,* vol. 1, 3d ed. (Tübingen: J. C. B. Mohr, 1959), English translation: *New Testament Apocrypha* (Philadelphia: The Westminster Press, 1963).

The use of a synopsis, like Kurt Aland, *Synopsis of the Four Gospels* (Stuttgart: United Bible Societies, 1973), which contains both the Greek original and its English translation, is almost indispensable.

I wish to express my gratitude to the Stiftung für wissenschaftliche Forschung of the University of Zürich for a grant enabling me to undertake research in Palestine.

I
THE COMING OF JESUS
1:1–4:16

Matthew differs from Mark (and John) in that, like Luke, he tells of Jesus' birth and childhood. His purpose is to show from the very outset, even before Jesus begins his ministry, that he is speaking of the one in whom God's promises are fulfilled (see 1:18-25, excursus) and whom the nations long for (see 4:12-16, conclusion). Like Mark, Matthew tells of John the Baptist, the baptism of Jesus, his temptation, and his trip to Galilee; but he supplements the account by adding material from Q, the Sayings Source. This stresses even more the call to repentance and the impending judgment (see 3:7-12, exegesis), and at the same time limits the chances that Jesus will be misunderstood as a political revolutionary (see 4:1-11, conclusion). In 3:14-15, an addition unique to Matthew, there is sounded for the first time the important Matthaean theme of the new meaning given to righteousness by Jesus.

Jesus, the Goal of God's History (1:1-17)

¹This is the genealogy of Jesus Christ, who was a descendant of David, who was a descendant of Abraham.

²Abraham was the father of Isaac; Isaac was the father of Jacob; Jacob was the father of Judah and his brothers. ³Judah was the father of Perez and Zerah (their mother was Tamar); Perez was the father of Hezron; Hezron was the father of Aram; ⁴Aram was the father of Amminadab; Amminadab was the father of Nahshon; Nahshon was the father of Salmon; ⁵Salmon was the father of Boaz (Rahab was his mother); Boaz was the father of Obed (Ruth was his mother); Obed was the father of Jesse; ⁶Jesse was the father of King David.

David was the father of Solomon (his mother had been Uriah's wife); [7]Solomon was the father of Rehoboam; Rehoboam was the father of Abijah; Abijah was the father of Asaph; [8]Asaph was the father of Jehoshaphat; Jehoshaphat was the father of Joram; Joram was the father of Uzziah; [9]Uzziah was the father of Jotham; Jotham was the father of Ahaz; Ahaz was the father of Hezekiah; [10]Hezekiah was the father of Manasseh; Manasseh was the father of Amos; Amos was the father of Josiah; [11]Josiah was the father of Jehoiachin and his brothers, at the time when the people of Israel were carried away to Babylon.

[12]After the people were carried away to Babylon: Jehoiachin was the father of Shealtiel; Shealtiel was the father of Zerubbabel; [13]Zerubbabel was the father of Abiud; Abiud was the father of Eliakim; Eliakim was the father of Azor; [14]Azor was the father of Zadok; Zadok was the father of Achim; Achim was the father of Eliud; [15]Eliud was the father of Eleazar; Eleazar was the father of Matthan; Matthan was the father of Jacob; [16]Jacob was the father of Joseph, the husband of Mary, who was the mother of Jesus, called the Messiah.

[17]So then, there were fourteen sets of fathers and sons from Abraham to David, and fourteen from David to the time when the people were carried away to Babylon, and fourteen from then to the birth of the Messiah.

[In this and all subsequent extracts, divergences from *Good News for Modern Man* are the author's.]

The very fact that Matthew begins with a genealogy of Jesus reveals something of his individuality. Mark, it is true, also begins with an Old Testament reference; but he can do no more than proclaim this connection between prophecy and fulfillment; Matthew attempts to demonstrate it from history. The genealogy does not agree with that of the Old Testament, either Hebrew or Greek (cf. in particular 1 Chron. 2:1-15; 3:5-16).

[3-4] The Greek Bible lies behind the form "Aram"; according to the Hebrew text of Ruth 4:19 and 1 Chronicles 2:9-10, he is called "Ram" (which, in the Greek text of 1 Chron. 2:9, is the name of a brother of Aram). [9] Between Uzziah and Jotham (vs. 9) three generations have dropped out, probably because a manuscript of the Greek Bible contains the sequence Uzziah—Joash—Amaziah—Uz-

ziah—Jotham at 1 Chronicles 3:11-12, and someone's eye skipped from the first "Uzziah" directly to the second. [11] Jehoiakim (608-597) and his son Jehoiachin (597, after spending three months of his reign in captivity [2 Kings 24:6 ff.]) have been fused into a single figure, perhaps because in the Greek Bible both are called "Jehoiakim" (2 Kings 24:6). [12] The designation of Zerubbabel as the son of Shealtiel is likewise found only in the Greek translation of 1 Chronicles 3:17-19; in the Hebrew original, he is called the son of Pedaiah (but cf. the Hebrew text of Hag. 1:1 and Ezra 3:8; 5:2). All this suggests that the genealogy was assembled on the basis of the Greek Bible.

[17] The entire genealogy is probably the product of a kind of learned Christian exegesis (see the discussion of 13:52) that was current even before Matthew. From Adam to Abraham, three times seven generations were reckoned (Luke 3:34-38; a somewhat different set is found in 1 Chron. 1:1-4, 24-27); when six times this number are reckoned from Abraham to Jesus, the result is that the Messiah appears after nine "weeks of years" after Adam, at the beginning of the tenth (see the excursus following Luke 2:38), or—reckoning from Abraham—at the beginning of the seventh, the "sabbath week." No hint of such calculations remains in Matthew. The Hebrew letters (which are also used as numerals) of the word "David" add up to fourteen (vs. 17); but this may be accidental, since fourteen also represents twice seven, the "sacred" number. The genealogy from Abraham to David comprises fourteen members, counting Abraham, and from David to Jehoiakim likewise fourteen, but only thirteen from Jehoiakim to Jesus. Since, however, ancient reckoning always includes the first and last elements of a series, we must probably understand the sequence as follows: from Abraham to David, fourteen; from David (counted a second time) to Josiah, the last free king, fourteen; from the first king of the captivity, Jehoiakim, to Jesus, fourteen.

Luke 3:23-38 has a totally different genealogy comprising eleven times seven (from Abraham eight times seven) generations. The two cannot be harmonized. Even if, contrary to Luke 3:23 and all common usage, the Lukan parallel is considered a genealogy of Mary, this would not explain why Matthew traces Shealtiel and Zerubbabel (vs.

12) back to David by way of Solomon, while Luke goes by way of Nathan and totally intermediate links. He must have been familiar with another list not preserved in this form within the Old Testament. Precisely because these genealogies are not meant as records of historical data, we must inquire all the more vigorously into what Matthew is trying to say.

[1] The importance the evangelist attaches to this statement is shown not only by its place at the beginning of the entire Gospel, but also by the superscription, modeled after Genesis 5:1 (cf. 2:4). Since the term "genealogy" is used in the broad sense of "family history" in Genesis 6:9; 37:2, some have wanted to understand the superscription as merely a haphazard naming of Jesus' forebears. But that would be a strange use of the term; and, since David and Abraham are mentioned in verses 1 and 17, these two verses define the stress of the genealogy, and it is implied that the story of Jesus, to be told in what follows, is not merely the genetic but the logical outcome of God's history as recounted in this opening section.

[17] The purpose of this genealogy is revealed by verse 17: all history is in God's hands; since the election of Abraham, history has been moving toward Jesus as its goal. Of course this is not historical proof (see the discussion of vss. 9 and 11 above); it is the community of believers stating that in Jesus the God who guided the history of Abraham and David and gave them special promises (Gen. 17:4-8; Gal. 3:16; 2 Sam. 7:12-16; John 7:42; Heb. 1:5) has had a personal encounter with men, fulfilling all that went before. [2, 11] Verse 2 mentions the brothers of Judah, verse 11 the brothers of Jehoiachin. Thus the history of all Israel—the twelve tribes and the many-branched dynasty of David after the Babylonian captivity—falls within the author's purview. [8, 10] The use of the form "Asaph" instead of "Asa," "Amos" instead of "Amon," probably calls to mind the psalmist (Psalms 50 and 73–83) and the prophet, and may be meant to suggest that Jesus fulfills the prophecies of both, the psalms and the prophets.

[3, 5-6] It is striking that the familiar matriarchs Sarah, Rebecca, and Leah are omitted, along with other women mentioned in the Old Testament. Matthew singles out the minor women—Tamar, Rahab,

Ruth, Bathsheba—those who were not celebrated, to reveal something of the strange righteousness of God, which does not choose what is great in the eyes of men. Even more striking is the mention of Rahab, although the Bible says nothing of her marriage. What do these four women have in common? It might be suggested that all of them, rightly or wrongly, were suspected of adultery (Gen. 38:14-18; Josh. 2:1; 2 Sam. 11:1-5; Ruth 3:7-15). Is this meant to exalt the power of God, who can raise even those of humble or disreputable origin to positions of the highest honor, as Josephus (*Ant.* v. 337) says with respect to Ruth and David? Is it even perhaps intended to excuse the notorious tale of how Mary bore Jesus? But Jewish tradition lauds the "righteousness" of Tamar (Gen. 38:26), the actions of Rahab (cf. also Heb. 11:31; James 2:25), and Ruth as ancestor of the Messiah; and in the case of Bathsheba, only David is ever blamed. In addition, Mary is introducted into the genealogy quite differently, not following the pattern "X was the father of Y and Z (their mother was A)," but without mention of the man: ". . . who was the mother of Jesus." Probably all four are mentioned because they are aliens. Pre-Christian Jewish writings (and possibly Ruth 4:12?) term Tamar an alien; Joshua 2:1; 6:25 do the same for Rahab. Ruth is a Moabite (Ruth 1:4, 22 and *passim*). Bathsheba is not mentioned by name but is introduced as "Uriah's wife" because she became an alien through her husband, who always appears in the Bible as "the Hittite" (e.g., 2 Sam. 11:3). If so, the four women are meant to prefigure God's activity—to culminate in Jesus (28:19)—that will embrace not only the Jews but all gentiles as well.

[18] The statement of verse 18 that Jesus was not physically the son of Joseph does not lessen the importance of the genealogy for Matthew; for "if someone says, 'This is my son,' he is so attested" (Jewish legal dictum, Baba Bathra 8.6). The crucial point is legal recognition, not biological descent. So, too, engagement, though clearly distinct from marriage, is the crucial action legally. Bereaved, an engaged woman is a widow. An engaged woman who consorts with other men is guilty not of fornication but of adultery. Since Joseph is legally Mary's husband, Jesus is his son, provided he does not contest the existing marital status and the child born within it. Verse 20, also,

calls Joseph, not Mary, a descendant of David. For a Syriac translator this was not enough. He writes: "Joseph, to whom Mary, the virgin, was betrothed, was the father of Jesus." But since verse 18 is retained and Mary is referred to expressly as a betrothed virgin, unless we have merely a mechanical accommodation to the preceding verses, we can only be dealing with the notion that it is precisely Mary's legal husband who is the "father." The Syriac translation also appends in verse 21: "she will give birth to *your* son" (similarly in vs. 25). Many other corrections have been undertaken upon this passage. Some, for example, have found the phrase "husband of Mary" startling and have corrected it to read "to whom Mary was engaged" or "to whom Mary, the virgin, was engaged, who was the mother of Jesus."

To the modern mind, the genealogy of Joseph and the virgin birth present stumbling blocks; difficulties arise from a reckoning that counts David twice (but not Josiah), as well as the failure of the names to agree with the Old Testament, not to mention the lack of any historically verifiable sequence of generations. This reveals all the more clearly that the question is not whether we consider it true that from Abraham to Jesus there were the forty-two or fifty-six generations listed in Matthew and Luke, or even that Shealtiel was the descendant of both Solomon and his stepbrother. What we have is the evangelist's testimony to his faith; his purpose is to tell us that God began his history with his people in the election of Abraham, and in Jesus, despite all the opaque, dubious, and sinful actions of men, he has brought it to its goal. Whether we can affirm this faith, not the historical accuracy, is the question put to us by our text.

Immanuel (1:18-25)

[18]This was the way that Jesus Christ was born. His mother Mary was engaged to Joseph, but before they were married she found out that she was going to have a baby by the Holy Spirit.[19]Joseph, her husband, was a man who always did what was right; but he did not want to disgrace Mary publicly, so he made plans to break the engagement secretly. [20]While he was thinking about all this, an angel of the Lord appeared to him in a dream and said: "Joseph, descendant of

David, do not be afraid to take Mary to be your wife. For it is by the Holy Spirit that she has conceived. [21]She will give birth to a son and you will name him Jesus—for he will save his people from their sins."

[22]Now all this happened in order to make come true what the Lord had said through the prophet: [23]"The virgin will become pregnant and give birth to a son, and he will be called Immanuel" (which means, "God is with us").

[24]So when Joseph woke up he did what the angel of the Lord had told him to do and married Mary. [25]But he had no sexual relations with her before she gave birth to her son. And Joseph named him Jesus.

(Vs. 21—Ps. 130:8; Ps. Sol. 17:26. Vs. 23—Isa. 7:14; 8:8, 10.)

1

In verses 22-23, Matthew uses a reflective quotation (i.e., one in which there is reflection on the fulfillment of the Old Testament in Jesus) to interpret the story of verses 18-21. Eleven more such quotations introduced by similar formulas appear in Matthew, if one includes 2:6, spoken by the chief priests and teachers of the Law, and 13:14-15, which uses a slightly different formula and has its content already given in Mark. The quotation always follows the narrative. In other words, we are not dealing with an illustration of Scripture by reference to contemporary events, like that practised by the Jewish monks of Qumran, but the reverse: the present story of Jesus is illuminated on the basis of previous Scripture—the focus is not on an old formula but on a recent life.

The question arises whether the quotations Matthew uses were available in a kind of collection. The introduction was certainly formulated by Matthew himself. He alone uses the word for "talk" or "say" employed here (in 3:3, for example, in contrast to Mark, who uses a form of "write"). Furthermore he alters the introduction in those cases where he wants to avoid ascribing terrible things to God's purpose (cf. the commentary on 2:17; 27:9). In 21:4-5 he has interpolated such a quotation into a narrative where none had been before; like the concluding verse (see §2 below), the introductory verse therefore is probably Matthew's own. The quotations follow neither the

Greek nor the Hebrew Bible. Only two correspond precisely to the Greek text: 1:23, even to the substitution of "they will" for "you will" (as used by Matthew in vs. 21!); and 13:14-15, even to the omission of a minor word. Since in 1:23 the Greek version speaks clearly of a "virgin," whereas the Hebrew text mentions only a (married or unmarried) "young woman," the Greek-speaking community must have had some part in at least this passage. Since, however, other quotations in Matthew, to the extent that they do not derive from Mark, contain mixed forms and in part free renderings of Old Testament texts, there is no solid evidence for a collection containing precisely these twelve quotations. In fact, there was probably no such collection, because 2:15, 18; 27:9-10 are incomprehensible without the accompanying narrative. Therefore if Matthew himself was not the first to append them (2:15, 18, 23), they were at best only vaguely associated with the story. The exception is the quotation in 27:9-10, which had long shaped the tradition of how Judas met his end (see commentary on that passage). Furthermore, these quotations appear almost exclusively in sections that do not occur in Mark. This means that neither was there a fixed collection nor did Matthew himself locate all of the quotations. It is easiest to suppose that Christian study of Scripture linked Old Testament texts with stories about Jesus in various stages, and that Matthew gave special emphasis to these twelve by means of his introductory formula. Why?

2

With four of the Old Testament quotations, Matthew characterizes Jesus as the prophetic revealer of God's secrets (13:13-16, 35) and as the silent healer endowed with God's authority (8:17; 12:17-21).

Two quotations stress the obedience of a disciple. In 1:24 there occurs an "execution formula" that is reminiscent of the Old Testament: "So when Joseph woke up he did what the angel of the Lord had told him to do." Similarly in 21:6 we read after a reflective quotation: "So the disciples went ahead and did what Jesus had told them to do" (there is an echo in 26:19). In both cases the quotation is introduced by the words "(All) this happened to. . . ." Both depict an overly literal fulfillment of the quotation: Joseph refrains from sexual intercourse in order that Mary may not only "conceive" but also "give birth" as a virgin, and the disciples bring Jesus two donkeys to sit on. In other words, Matthew was emphasizing obedience to the very letter. The last quotation (27:9-10), conversely, describes the remorse of a disobedient disciple.

3

The other five quotations (2:6, 15, 18, 23; 4:15-16) may to some extent already have been associated with Matthew's stories; they describe the journeyings of Jesus from Bethlehem through Ramah to Egypt and thence—the point of Matthew's greatest interest—to Nazareth and Capernaum. Matthew's purpose is undoubtedly to throw into sharp relief Jesus' charismatic ministry in word and deed, as well as the obedient discipleship this ministry demands. May the travels of the young Jesus also have been important to him as representing the fate of the disciple, who travels about as a wandering prophet (see 7:13-23, excursus), even though these quotations only follow Jesus to the beginning of his ministry?

It is striking that the miracle of the virgin conception is not told, but presupposed. It is therefore familiar to Matthew as part of the tradition of his community, probably oral. The expression for "become pregnant" and the formulation in the first part of verse 21 derive from the Old Testament quotation. Matthew probably phrased much of his material quite freely, and only verses 18-20 are likely to have been what was repeated over and over again in the community. Here there also appears the expression "in a dream," which turns up four more times in chapter 2 (elsewhere only in 27:19).

Joseph is portrayed in terms similar to those used in contemporary Jewish circles to depict the father of Moses (cf. the commentary on 2:13-23): "God . . . came to him while he was asleep: . . . 'This son will . . . deliver the people of the Hebrews from the bondage of the Egyptians' " (Josephus, *Ant.* ii. 212, 16); "and the spirit of God came over Mary [the sister of the unborn Moses] by night, and she beheld a vision in a dream: . . . 'Go and say to your parents: That which will be born of you . . . , I shall do signs through him and deliver my people.' " (Pseudophilo, *Ant.* ix. 10)

In addition, Matthew must have had in his sources the explanation of the name of Jesus, comprehensible only in Hebrew. The association of the quotation Isaiah 7:14 with the story of Jesus' birth probably also antedates Matthew, since it seems to be presupposed in Luke 1:31 as well. Finally, Matthew was presumably familiar with Jewish insinuations about Mary. Now how does he go about shaping the material he had before him?

[18] Neither the conception (1:18) nor the birth (2:1) of Jesus is recounted directly, but only their consequences: the embarrassment of Joseph in the one case, of Herod in the other. This shows that Matthew is stressing the points that Jesus was born in Bethlehem (2:1 ff.) and through the operation of the Holy Spirit—these probably to answer attacks on Jesus' dubious birth out of wedlock and in Nazareth (rather than Bethlehem). He is saying simply that this birth was intended and brought to pass by God, and that Jesus is in this sense God's son (on 1:22, see also 2:13-23, introduction). Not until Luke (1:35) is it appropriate to ask whether the Spirit plays something like the role of a father ("for this reason the holy child will be called the Son of God"). In any event, this reference to the Holy Spirit distinguishes the birth of Jesus from many similar stories (cf. the excursus below on the virgin birth).

In the Old Testament the Spirit of God is already associated with God's creative force, which produces life (Ezek. 37:9-10, 14; later Judg. 16:14; Syr. Bar. 21:4; 23:5; cf. John 3:5-6; 6:63; 2 Cor. 3:6). In the New Testament the Spirit refers to the presence of God, which characterizes Jesus throughout his entire life and ministry (Mark 1:10, 12; Matt. 12:18, 28; Luke 4:14, 18; 10:21; John 3:34; 7:37-39; 14:16-18). Thus the Christian community adopted the Old Testament notion of God as the actual creator of all life, who alone can give children. This notion is already illustrated by the miracles that befall the wives of the patriarchs (Gen. 18:10-12; 25:21; 29:31; 30:2, 22-23). This explains why Matthew 1:18 is so restrained about the miracle of this birth, and makes not the slightest reference to any notion of a divine lover.

[19] In contrast to the account in Luke, in Matthew Joseph plays an important role. For Matthew his "doing what was right" can hardly mean his fidelity to the Law (Deut. 22:20-21), but his compas-

sion (25:40; 10:41;). "Secretly" does not mean that Joseph wanted to break the engagement stealthily, but rather "without bringing charges," which strictly speaking might have led to a death sentence.

[20] The Bible speaks of "angels" to express the idea that God intervenes concretely in our lives, addresses us, sets us on a new course, etc. In the New Testament, less and less emphasis is placed on the miraculous element in the appearance of an angel (cf. the commentary on Mark 16:5); Paul even declares that the words of his gospel are incomparably more important and trustworthy than any angel, who might actually be the Devil in disguise (Gal. 1:8; 2 Cor. 11:14). In Matthew, too, there is no trace of the speculations found in Jewish writings about all the various classes of angels in heaven. The angel simply represents God on earth, and his instructions are utterly uncomplicated and tied to the realities of life. The form of address "descendant of David" shows that legal fatherhood alone is all that matters: as the acknowledged son of Joseph, Jesus is a descendant of David (see the commentary on 1:18). This is more important to Matthew than the virgin birth.

[21] The same is true of the name bestowed by God, which is given more stress than the birth itself. The name is emphasized by the sentence's structure, ". . . will give birth to a son and you will name him . . . ," which follows the Greek text of Isaiah 7:14 (vs. 23; cf. Gen. 17:19) exactly. Of course "Jesus" is a common Jewish name. Even his name, therefore, does not set Jesus apart from his fellow men; he is truly a man, not a demigod. "Jesus" is the Greek form of "Joshua," and is so used in the Greek translation of the Old Testament. Etymologically the name probably means "Yahweh (is) salvation"; but in the New Testament period all that was still heard was the echo of "save" (or "deliver"), and thus also of "savior" (or "deliverer"; Luke 2:11; Acts 5:31; 13:23; Phil. 3:20; John 4:42; 1 John 4:14; and in post-Pauline epistles). This etymology applies only in Hebrew; but Matthew presupposes knowledge of it without providing a more detailed explanation. Jesus is to "save his people"—in Matthew, as generally among the Jews, his "people" always means "Israel"; this inclusive salvation was expected not only of God, but also at times of the messiah. Jesus' ministry is therefore not directed merely to a few devout souls, a group distinguishing itself from others, but to the

entire nation (see the commentary on 2:2). What is new is Matthew's express mention of "sins" as that from which people are to be saved (cf. Ps. 130:8). The forgiveness of sins (see the commentary on Mark 1:4) is a central concept even in the Old Testament, because man's critical need consists in his separation from God. In the New Testament, too, the entire message can be summarized thus; but there are documents in which the expression never occurs, because the Bible never uses "salvation" in a merely negative sense.

[23] Thus a positive statement is made at once: salvation consists in "God's being with us." It is true that the quotation (see the excursus above) does not quite fit the context, which is speaking of "Jesus" rather than "Immanuel." But for Matthew "salvation" (from sins) is identical with God's being with men. Isaiah 7:14 speaks of a birth in the time of King Ahaz. But the period immediately following is depicted in such glowing colors that it can only be described by the word "*Immanu-El*," "with us God" (Isa. 8:8, 10). Even in Isaiah, then, we find something like an expectation of a messianic age, only he expects it in the immediate future. Under certain kinds of illumination, a series of mountain ranges may be perceived as a single chain, without any suspicion of how many valleys lie between the first slope and the highest visible ridge; in like manner the prophets see God's saving work in the immediate and in the distant future as a single act. When Matthew finds this prophecy fulfilled in the birth of Jesus, he is right, not in the sense that precisely what Isaiah expected has come true—Isaiah expected something different and sooner—but in his sense of the continuity of God's providence, operating coherently from the past and on into the future.

The Virgin Birth of Jesus. In the case of the Christmas story and the associated narratives it is especially difficult to realize that the true miracle of Jesus' birth does not lie in the various details and ephemeral legends. Matthew and Luke both bear witness to this miracle in the manner appropriate to their belief in Jesus as Christ. Their accounts are therefore largely in agreement in what they are really trying to say, but are historically irreconcilable. According to Matthew, Jesus was born in the time of Herod the Great (in other words, prior to 4 B.C.). As we know from historical sources, the first census in Judaea (not in the entire Roman Empire) was not ordered until A.D. 6/7; further-more, Quirinius (Luke 2:2) did not become governor of Syria until A.D. 6, though of course he may have held another position previously. More important, according to Luke Jesus' parents move from Nazareth to Bethlehem before his birth, while according to Matthew they do not move to Nazareth until later (see the commentary on 2:23). In addition, Matthew recounts nothing that is found in Luke's narrative, and vice versa. Even the message of the angel comes to Joseph in Matthew and to Mary in Luke, so that the only points of agreement between the two are the fact that Jesus was born of a virgin in Bethlehem and the names of his parents were Joseph and Mary.

Bethlehem as the place of Jesus' birth and the prophecy of his birth by a virgin were already given to the Christian community by their Bible, the Greek Old Testament. Naturally the Christians thought in terms of the ideas of their period. It was assumed of many great men at the time, from Plato to Alexander, that they had been born without human father. The fact of such a birth therefore did not single Jesus out as unique, it simply placed him in the company of all the great men of the age.

More important than the idea of Mary's virginity therefore are the points that distinguish the birth stories of the Gospels from these other accounts. In them a god is presented as mating with a woman or virgin. Of course this is not pictured in gross bodily terms. The god approaches the woman in the water or as a stroke of lightning; about A.D. 100, the Greek writer Plutarch even speaks of the Egyptian belief in a kind of divine generation through the "power" or the "spirit" of God (cf. Luke 1:35), which may be thought of in similar terms as the creation of the world. But even here the spirit is clearly the medium through which the generative power of the god operates. This is out of the question in the Gospels, if only because "spirit" is of feminine gender in Hebrew, neuter in Greek.

Hellenistic Judaism in Egypt comes somewhat closer, evincing stories similar to those in the Gospels, but having to do with the Old Testament patriarchs. Philo, who is still thinking only in metaphorical and allegorical terms, writes, for example: Scripture "has Sarah become pregnant when God . . . looks upon her . . ."; "God opened her [Leah's] womb—but the opening of the womb appertains to the husband"; "Rebecca becomes pregnant by him whom she had implored [i.e., God]"; "Moses . . . finds . . . Zipporah pregnant, certainly not by a mortal" (*Cherubim* 45-47).

Whether a virgin birth is possible is a question only a modern would ask; virgin birth was an accepted notion to men of the New Testament period. By no means, therefore, should a man's faith be judged by whether or not he thinks a miracle like this is possible, the less so because the virgin birth plays such an infinitesimal role in the New Testament. It is nowhere described; only the Annunciation is mentioned in Matthew 1 and Luke 1. Neither Matthew nor Luke returns to the subject, not even in the course of the Christmas story proper. According to Mark 3:21, Jesus' mother, who thinks him mad, appears to have no inkling of the promises made by the angel. No other document, above all none of the many summaries of the faith in a formula, hymn, or sermon in the New Testament, mentions the virgin birth.

Neither John nor Paul exhibits any knowledge of it. John 1:13 even says about *all* who believe, that they "were born, not of blood nor of the will of the flesh, nor of the will of man, but of God" (RSV), without saying anything similar about Jesus; the statement in John 6:42 that Jesus is Joseph's son is never contradicted. Paul's use of the phrase "son of a human mother" for Jesus in Galatians 4:4 is merely the usual Jewish expression emphasizing the wretchedness and weakness of man, and therefore makes a point of *not* distinguishing Jesus from other men.

In fine, even in Matthew 1 the virgin birth is quite peripheral, while what the evangelist is trying to express in these terms is something else: that it is the personal God, the Lord of Israel's history, that acts in this birth. Therefore he begins with the genealogy and lays so much stress on the naming of Jesus.

In the first place, therefore, the story of a birth without a human father, even the idea of God's creative power that performs an act of generation, was widespread outside the Christian community. And in the second, the idea did not signify much more than that a certain person was given to the world by God. In Matthew, the significance of Jesus' birth is much more clearly indicated in the name God gives him. This naming signifies that now the one has been born in whom

God himself dwells among men (Immanuel), and who thus will be the salvation of his people (Jesus). The importance of Jesus' (subsequent) life, not his birth, is the reason for placing such stress on the obedience of Joseph, who, in the light of God's great promise, can give up his previous moral principles and fulfill God's command literally. The focus of the story therefore is not the physical, biological process, but the theological watershed. The biology did not appear unique to Matthew and his contemporaries, and, like all the rest of the New Testament, Matthew assumes that Jesus had younger brothers and sisters (12:46; 13:55-56; 1 Cor. 9:5); only until Jesus' birth does Joseph refrain from sexual intercourse (vs. 25). The focus is God's offer, in Jesus, of salvation to man, and man's response in obedience.

What the text asks is therefore not whether we can consider a virgin birth physically possible, but the same question put by Mark in his statement that Jesus was sent by God, by John in his statement that the Word became a human being (1:14), by Paul in his use of the term "Son of God" (Gal. 4:4): whether in this birth we can see God's own and unique intervention for man's salvation. And if this is the case, then we can also say what this story of the virgin birth is further meant to say: that this birth stands not merely as one among many in the long series of millions of births, that it took place not merely through the creative will or drive of a man, but through God's own will as creator.

Homage to the King of the Universe (2:1-12)

[1]Jesus was born in the town of Bethlehem, in the land of Judea, during the time when Herod was king. Soon afterwards some men who studied the stars [astrologers] came from the east to Jerusalem [2]and asked: "Where is the baby born to be the king of the Jews? We saw his star when it came up in the east, and we have come to worship him." [3]When King Herod heard about this he was very upset, and so was everybody else in Jerusalem. [4]He called together all the chief priests and the teachers of the Law and asked them, "Where will the Messiah be born?" [5]"In the town of Bethlehem, in Judea," they answered. "This is what the prophet wrote:

⁶"You, Bethlehem, in the land of Judah,
    Are not by any means the least among the rulers of
    Judah;
For from you will come a leader
Who will guide my people Israel.' "

⁷So Herod called the visitors from the east to a secret meeting and found out from them the exact time the star had appeared. ⁸Then he sent them to Bethlehem with these instructions: "Go and make a careful search for the child, and when you find him let me know, so that I may go and worship him too." ⁹With this they left, and on their way they saw the star—the same one they had seen in the east—and it went ahead of them until it came and stopped over the place where the child was. ¹⁰How happy they were, what gladness they felt, when they saw the star! ¹¹They went into the house and saw the child with his mother Mary. They knelt down and worshiped him; then they opened their bags and offered him presents: gold, frankincense, and myrrh.

¹²God warned them in a dream not to go back to Herod; so they went back home by another road.

(Vs. 2—Num. 24:17. Vs. 6—2 Sam. 5:2; Mic. 5:1 [5:2 in modern translations]. Vs. 11—Isa. 60:6 [cf. Ps. 72:10, 15].)

This story has no direct connection with the preceding one. But like the earlier one, its interest is not biographical. The birth of Jesus at Bethlehem during the reign of Herod is only mentioned in passing (vs. 1). The account has two major emphases.

The first is the struggle between King Herod and the newborn king. It is reminiscent of that between Pharaoh and the baby Moses (cf. also Heb. 3:1-6), especially because contemporary Jewish traditions told how an Egyptian scholar of the priestly class or certain astrologers had predicted the birth of the coming savior of Israel, whereupon Pharaoh and all the Egyptians were very upset and summoned all the astrologers in Egypt (Josephus, *Ant.* ii. 205–206, 215; Midrash Exod. rabba 1; Jerusalem Targum on Exod. 1:15). As in 1:18-25, we have here a stratum of tradition that emphasizes the parallels between Moses and Jesus. The motif of the homage offered by the astrologers is of different origin. While 1:18-25; 2:13-15, 19-23 speak of Joseph and have him taking an active part in the narrative, here we read only of the child and Mary (vs. 11; also 2:13, 14, 19, 21 with the child mentioned first). One is reminded of the story of Balaam, who was a kind of seer and had visions, came from the east, and saw the star (the messiah) rise out of Jacob (Num. 23:7; 24:3-4, 15-17). An historical event may also have influenced the development of the story. In A.D. 66, astrologers from Persia in the company of King Tiridates came to Nero at Naples because of certain prophecies in the stars, to worship him as king of the universe in the west and then return by another route. It may be supposed that the journey of the astrologers to Bethlehem was first recounted for its own sake.

According to verse 9, the miraculous star led them to the house of Joseph, so that their conference with Herod is in fact unnecessary. And on the other side, Herod in the present story is absurdly trusting; why doesn't he send his soldiers or at least a confidant to Bethlehem with the astrologers instead of counting on their returning and reporting to him? It is possible, though not demonstrable, that there was another story told about Herod, to the effect that, as in the Moses tradition, scholars prophesied the birth of a coming king on the basis of Micah 5:1-3 (vs. 6), with the result that Herod and all Jerusalem became terribly upset and the events of verses 13 ff. took place. Matthew was probably the first to link the two traditions; he would then have framed the reference to the dream in verse 12 after the model of 1:20 and above all 2:22. If so, verse 16 must also derive at least in part from Matthew. Typical of Matthew are the expressions "so, in this way" (vss. 7, 16, 17) and "go back, leave" (vss. 12, 13, 14, 22). Thus Matthew strikes a contrast between the pagans who are ready to accept the king of the universe and the Jewish king who refuses to accept him. The relationship between Israel and the gentiles is one of Matthew's central concerns.

[1] As the introduction shows, he also has an interest in Bethlehem as the place of Jesus' birth. [6] The quotation from Micah 5:1, 2 was already interpreted messianically by the Jews; in popular Aramaic translations, the term "messiah" is actually introduced. On the other hand, the phrase "in the land of Judah" occurs in neither the Hebrew nor the Greek text. [1, 5] It may derive from Matthew

himself, who anticipates it in Verse 1. But there are other changes as well. The misreading of a single Hebrew letter has resulted in the translation "not by any means the least" where the Old Testament reads the opposite, "the least." The same holds true for "rulers," misread for "thousands," introducing in turn the related term "leader." The last line suggests Micah 5:3, 4, but derives its actual wording from the promise to David in 2 Samuel 5:2. Since Matthew nowhere else draws on the Hebrew text, this probably took place before him. Matthew may have consciously divided chapter 2 into five sections (1-6, 7-12, 13-15, 16-18, 19-23), each ending with a Biblical quotation.

[1] The birth of Jesus is mentioned only in passing. According to 2:22, the "Herod" of verse 1 is undoubtedly Herod the Great (for a discussion of the historical difficulties, see the excursus following 1:18-25). Thus Jesus' birth is dated in 7 B.C., for which a special conjunction of stars can be calculated that might appear as a single large star, as is here assumed. Whoever puts more confidence in the Lukan data must disagree with Matthew and date Jesus' birth A.D. 6/7 on account of the tax enrollment and the governorship of Quirinius. Matthew knows nothing of any journey to Bethlehem (see the comments on vs. 23). Astrologers are not kings; this conclusion, as well as the idea that there were three of them, was derived later from Psalm 72:10, 15; Isaiah 49:7; 60:3, 6, 10 and the fact that there were three gifts (Matt. 2:11). Astrologers were highly esteemed, but also felt to be sinister (the same term occurs in a derogatory sense in Acts 13:6, 8; and 8:9 is very similar). The east was not only the home of astrology, but also of a robust Judaism. Around A.D. 50, for example, a Babylonian prince was converted to Judaism.

[2] Expectation of a universal king who would inaugurate the golden age was current at the time; it originated primarily in the east. In Numbers 24:17 (see the introductory section above) the messiah himself is referred to as a star; in CD vii. 19 the eschatological Teacher of Righteousness is referred to in the same way. The Testament of Levi 18:3 says of the messiah: "His star will rise in the heavens." The phrase "king of the Jews" (see also 27:37) places the newborn infant in opposition to "King" Herod (vs. 1) from the very beginning, as does

the desire of the foreign visitors to "worship" him. The word refers to prostration in the presence of the king or God, and often means "worship" in the literal sense. Thus the universal significance of Jesus is stressed from the very outset. His power is shown even before he appears in public. [3] Herod's terror and his struggle against the idea of a messiah depict the general situation accurately. Herod's most vulnerable point was his Edomite origin (Gen. 36:19; Mal. 1:2-5); he therefore feared any messianic movement because it might dispute his right to his throne. The mention of "everybody else in Jerusalem" underlines the danger.

[4] Herod's "calling together" the chief priests and teachers of the Law is merely Matthew's way of introducing the quotation; it is historically almost inconceivable, since there were severe tensions between the two groups. [5] Bethlehem, the city of David, was also expected to be the birthplace of the messiah. [6] Matthew emphasizes this point by introducing the quotation. [7] Incredibly, Herod fails to send soldiers along at once—the narrator is doing a bit of scrambling —[8] instead he gives hypocritical instructions to the astrologers. [9] Jewish stories frequently tell how a cloud stood over the place where Abraham was to sacrifice Isaac. Thus the star does not point the way to Bethlehem—which the astrologers would easily have found—but to the house of Joseph. [10] The astrologers' joy is powerfully portrayed and is important to the narrator: "How happy they were, what gladness they felt" (cf. Luke 2:10). [11] The gifts are royal gifts (Ps. 72:10-11, 15; 45:7-9; also Isa. 60:6; Song 3:6). Myrrh is the resin of an Arabian shrub and produces a pleasant aroma, like frankincense. There is a common symbolic interpretation: gold for the king, incense for the God, myrrh for him who is to die (Mark 14:3, 8; 15:23; John 19:39); but even the Old Testament parallels cited above argue against such an interpretation. [12] Once again a dream plays a crucial role (see the introduction to 1:18-25). Return by another road (1 Kings 13:9) is necessary in the present context on account of Herod.

When we inquire into the message of the text, we must distinguish between its present form and the ancient account, which establishes a conflict between the newborn Jesus and King Herod like the Old Testament clash between Moses and Pharaoh. In this account Jesus is depicted as a new Moses, sent by God to be the savior of his people but threatened from the very beginning by those in worldly authority. It is true that Jesus is worshiped as king of the universe, unlike Moses; and the alien figures suggest that the shepherd of God's people Israel (vs. 6) will also lead all the other nations of the earth as well (25:32; 28:19). He is acknowledged by those who know nothing of God beyond what the silent stars tell. Nevertheless, despite their royal gifts, they remain ambiguous figures, while all the recognized authorities, civil and ecclesiastical, reject Jesus. Thus both his royal dignity and Israel's rejection of him are prefigured, and it will soon be evident that Bethlehem, the city of the messiah, will not shelter him for long.

From Bethlehem to Nazareth via Egypt (2:13-23)

[13]After they had left, an angel of the Lord appeared in a dream to Joseph and said: "Get up, take the child and his mother and run away to Egypt, and stay there until I tell you to leave. Herod will be looking for the child to kill him." [14]So Joseph got up, took the child and his mother, and left during the night for Egypt, [15]where he stayed until Herod died.

This was done to make come true what the Lord had said through the prophet, "I called my Son out of Egypt."

[16]When Herod realized that the visitors from the east [the astrologers] had tricked him, he was furious. He gave orders to kill all the boys in Bethlehem and its neighborhood who were two years old and younger—in accordance with what he had learned from the visitors about the time when the star had appeared.

[17]In this way what the prophet Jeremiah had said came true:

[18]"A sound is heard in Ramah,
The sound of bitter crying and weeping,
Rachel weeps for her children,
She weeps and will not be comforted,
Because they are all dead."

[19]After Herod had died, an angel of the Lord appeared in a dream to Joseph, in Egypt, [20]and said: "Get up, take the child and his mother, and go back to the country of Israel, because those who tried to kill the child are dead." [21]So Joseph got up, took the child and his mother, and went back to the country of Israel.

²²When he heard that Archelaus had succeeded his father Herod as king of Judea, Joseph was afraid to settle there. He was given more instructions in a dream, and so went to the province of Galilee ²³and made his home in a town named Nazareth. He did this to make come true what the prophets had said, "He will be called a Nazorite." (Vs. 15—Hos. 11:1. Vss. 17-18—Jer. 31:15. Vs. 20—Exod. 4:19. Vs. 23—Judg. 13:5; Isa. 11:1; 53:2.)

Here, too, the quotations that come true are striking (cf. the excursus on 1:18-25). The careful way in which Matthew introduces them is shown by the way in which verse 17 avoids the formula "to make come true," in order to escape any suggestion that God willed the slaughter of the infants (the only other similar instance is 27:9). Only in two quotations does the Gospel of Matthew ascribe a saying directly to the "Lord": 1:22 and 2:15. Both speak of the "son" Immanuel or "my [God's] Son." Elsewhere in the chapter Matthew (probably unconsciously) uses the term "child" and avoids "son" with reference to God. This demonstrates the importance he attaches to the mystery of Jesus' divine sonship.

All three quotations, together with the preceding one in verse 6 (Bethlehem) and the following one in 4:15-16 (Galilee), have one element in common: they contain place-names. In the two just mentioned, it is clear that the crucial point is precisely this geographical reference. But in 2:23 as well Matthew associates a change of residence with a quotation that does not even come from the Old Testament, although the evangelist may have thought it did. The importance of geographical changes may also account for the quotation in verse 15: it is put after a short section which contains the first mention of Egypt, rather than after verse 20, which speaks of God's calling the child back. On the other hand, why wasn't the quotation incorporated into the narrative as early as verse 13? The most likely explanation for this tardy placement is that the narrative was already familiar to the evangelist in either oral or written form, and he interpolated the corresponding quotation at the end of each appropriate minor section. This also helps explain why the passage contains texts from the prophets, which are more appropriate to the story as it stands, rather than texts from Exodus, in which the evangelist had a greater interest.

Matthew probably thought of Ramah as a stopping place on the flight into Egypt, where the family could still hear the cries of the victims. The stress on these geographical data is probably meant to suggest that the life of the Son of God himself is destined to be a life of homeless wandering, such as will also be characteristic for his disciples (see the excursus on 7:13-23 [§§2 and 7]).

In verse 15 we can probably already hear echoes of Christian Scriptural exegesis. Only the Hebrew text reads thus; the Greek speaks of "his [Israel's] children." On the other hand, the use of Hosea 11:1, which refers to the entire people of Israel, may have been made possible by the statement that occurs only in the Greek text of Numbers 24:7-8: "God brings him [the messiah] out of Egypt."

The same applies to verse 23; its use reflects Christian exegesis. Most likely we are to think of Judges 13:7 (cf. 13:5 and 16:17): "You will become pregnant and give birth to a son [Samson]; . . . he will be a Nazirite of God." Another manuscript reads at this point "a holy one of God," and Mark 1:24 (cf. also John 6:69) shows that "Nazorite" or "Nazarene" and "holy one of God" were once felt to be equivalent. Many scholars have attempted to explain the *o*, which is linguistically not impossible, by suggesting that in Hebrew, where originally only the consonants were written, the word *nazir* later had the vowels of the word *qadosh* ("holy") inserted into it, just as the vowels of *edonai* ("lord") where written over the consonants of "Yahweh," producing the form "Jehovah." Others have suggested the Hebrew terms for "watchmen" (Jer. 31:6), "prince" (Gen. 49:26), "shoot" (Isa. 11:1, etc.), and "preserved [by God]" (Isa. 49:6), which have a similar sound. In any case, we are dealing with Christian exegetical tradition. Even the vague form "what the prophets had said" shows that Matthew does not know the precise passage, but probably considers the brief statement a genuine quotation.

The story itself is reminiscent once more of the story of Moses, especially as told by Josephus (*Ant.* ii. 205 ff., 210 ff., 254 ff.): a priestly scholar in Egypt announces to the king the birth of a deliverer; the king is afraid of him and orders all male children killed. The father of Moses, terribly worried by the impending birth, is comforted in a dream by God and the birth takes place painlessly. For three months his parents keep the infant at home and then set him adrift on the Nile. There are also echoes of Moses' flight and return to Egypt after the death of the king who was persecuting him (Exod. 2:15–5:1). Later Jewish teachers tell of a rabbi who fled to Egypt with Jesus when King Jannaeus (104–78 B.C.) gave orders to have all the scholars slain; there, the story goes, Jesus learned Egyptian magic. This might go back to a vague awareness that the Christians spoke of a flight to Egypt. It is certainly not based on precise acquaintance with Matthew 2, for Joseph is not a learned rabbi and Jesus is not yet old enough to receive tutelage from Egyptian magicians. Probably nothing more than vague memories of Christian stories lies behind this Jewish tradition.

The basis of the account is therefore most likely a story of Jesus' birth, naming, persecution, escape, and return—largely parallel to the early life of Moses. Characteristic is the part played by a dream in reaching a decision, mentioned five times (1:20, 2:13, 2:19, 2:12, 2:22). Portions of 2:13-14 reappear, in exactly the same words, in 2:20-21. Joseph is throughout the focus of attention. Matthew himself composed the introductions in 2:13 and 2:19 (like 2:1 and 1:18); he probably also introduced quotations into his narrative, some of which had been linked even before him with the flight to Egypt (2:15) and the designation of Jesus as a Nazorite (2:23).

[13] As in 1:20, the "angel of the Lord appearing in a dream," who in the Old Testament speaks for God in the first person, determines all that follows. In a way the angel represents the incarnate operation of God. [14] Here, too, Joseph is the center of attention. His obedience is shown once more (cf. the commentary on 1:25) in his following the angel's command to the letter: "Joseph got up, took the child and his mother, and left during the night for Egypt" (as also in vss. 20-21).

The flight to Egypt shows once more the discrepancy between the power of the reigning king and the humility and impotence of the coming king of the universe. He appears as the passive object rather than the active subject of history; but in fact he dominates the entire course of events. [15] By "God's son" Hosea means Israel. Matthew transfers the reference here to Jesus, and suggests that the deliverance the Messiah brings will be as astonishing as the deliverance from Egypt (see above).

[16] Herod's calculated cruelty has become proverbial. He ordered the execution of three of his sons; and at his burial one member of every family was to have been slain so that the nation might truly mourn (Josephus, *Ant.* xvii. 181). Josephus, who deliberately compiles these acts of cruelty, makes no mention of any slaughter of infants; that argues against the historical truth of this particular outrage.

[18] According to Judges 19:13 (cf. 1 Sam. 1:1), Ramah is located to the north of Jerusalem. This agrees with the statement of 1 Samuel 10:2 that Rachel was buried at the boundary between Benjamin and Ephraim and with the mention in Jeremiah 31:18 of Ephraim, whose territory is located north of Jerusalem. Genesis 35:16-19 locates the site more precisely as lying between Bethel and Ephrath. Here and in 48:7 a later hand has identified Ephrath with Bethlehem, which lies south of Jerusalem, on account of Micah 5:1, 2, where Bethlehem is also called Beth-ephrathah. Rachel's tomb has been pointed out there ever since the fourth century of the Christian era.

[19-20] The command to return parallels precisely the command to flee in verse 13. This is the only place where we find the phrase "country of Israel" in the New Testament, an expression adopted once more by the modern state of Israel. The plural in "those who tried to kill the child" is striking. Perhaps we are dealing with an echo of the parallel in Exodus 4:19: "And the LORD said to Moses, . . . 'Go back to Egypt; for all the men who were seeking your life are dead.' "

[22] After Herod's death, his kingdom was divided among his three sons, of whom Archelaus was the most feared. Matthew attaches particular importance to the fact that the move to Nazareth also took place at the command of the angel. [23] The expression "he made his home" and the fact that Joseph is commanded in a dream to move to Nazareth are unambiguous: according to Matthew, Jesus' parents lived not in Nazareth but in Bethlehem. With this move to Nazareth in Galilee, once more confirmed by a quotation from the prophets, we reach the climax of the story.

Looking back on the first two chapters, we can see how the community tried in various ways to express the uniqueness of Jesus.

The genealogy represents him as the descendant of David promised by God, who at the same time fulfills the entire history of Israel since the call of Abraham. The stories that follow see in him the savior of Israel who surpasses even Moses. In addition, he is associated with texts that represent him as the one promised by the prophets. In the genealogy and infancy narratives Joseph holds stage center, taking the role that the tradition of the virgin birth suggests should be Mary's. Mary is the focus of attention only in the account of the homage of the astrologers, where we also find the motif of the king of the universe. Matthew is able to draw upon all these statements without taking any special interest in the Mosaic or Davidic parallels. What matters to him is the unique status of Jesus, whose significance for all the nations is probably alluded to by the mention of the four women in the genealogy.

He is interested at the same time in Jesus' function as a forerunner: something of his nomadic life, his call, and his protection by God will be reflected in his disciples (see the excursus on 7:13-23). This explains the evangelist's interest in the geographical series Bethlehem–Ramah–Egypt–Nazareth (–Capernaum). The first chapters therefore determine the "dimension" in which the reader must see Jesus. It is not just his actions in his ministry that make him the deliverer of Israel. He is already "Jesus," Immanu-el and Son of God, from the very beginning: forced to wander from place to place, at enmity with the world whose king he is, but guided by God himself.

John the Baptist (3:1-6)
Cf. Mark 1:2-6; Luke 3:1-6

[1]At that time John the Baptist came and started preaching in the desert of Judea. [2]"Turn away from your sins," he said, "because the Kingdom of heaven is near!" [3]John was the one that the prophet Isaiah was talking about when he said:
"Someone is shouting in the desert:
'Get the Lord's road ready for him,
Make a straight path for him to travel!' "
[4]John's clothes were made of camel's hair; he wore a leather belt around his waist, and ate locusts and wild honey. [5]People came to him from Jerusalem, from the whole province of Judea, and from all the

country around the Jordan River. ⁶They confessed their sins and he baptized them in the Jordan.

(Vs. 3—Isa. 40:3. Vs. 4—2 Kings 1:8; Isa. 66:24.)

Matthew passes at once to John the Baptist and the baptism of Jesus. He has nothing to tell us about the interim, which according to Luke 3:23 lasted nearly three decades. At first he follows Mark (q.v.; on the overall structure of our Gospel, see §2 of the Introduction). [3] Since two chapters of stories about Jesus precede, the quotation from Isaiah 40:3 does not function as a superscription to the entire Gospel (as in Mark 1:2-3), but is only one citation among many. It is therefore not introduced until after verses 1-2 and has no special introduction emphasizing it as a fulfillment (see the excursus on 1:18-25). [1] Thus the "desert" in verse 1 is no longer directly associated with the quotation; in other words, it is no longer the "desert" of God's planned salvation announced in the Old Testament. Matthew defines it geographically as "the desert of Judea." In the introduction (vs. 1), which is his own composition, Matthew uses the title "the Baptist," which Mark does not employ until 6:25. [4] He also begins by describing the Baptist, a more logical order. It is clear once again that Matthew is more interested in geographical and historical data, because these show John to be the returned Elijah (11:14; 17:13), while Mark's primary aim was to tell how the message was first proclaimed and the effect it had.

[2] It is true that Matthew, like Mark, mentions the Baptist's message as early as verse 2; but instead of "the baptism of repentance for the forgiveness of sins," we have the statement "Turn away from your sins [cf. the commentary on Mark 1:4], because the Kingdom of heaven is near!" (cf. the discussion of vs. 8). Thus the Baptist's message becomes more a moral summons to "turn away from sin" (the root meaning of the Old Testament word for "repent"). This is also shown by Matthew's association of the forgiveness of sins not with John but with the Last Supper of Jesus (26:28). To be sure, John is the one who proclaims "the right path to take" (see the discussion of 21:32; cf. vss. 7-12); but primarily he is the prophet of God's eschatological hour. Men are to turn from their sins because the Kingdom

of God is near; it is only God's coming to men that makes it possible for men to come to God. Matthew's use of the expression "Kingdom of heaven" may be connected with Jewish aversion to employing the name of God. Probably, however, there is more behind it: according to 28:18, all power and authority in heaven and earth are given to Jesus. Thus Matthew can also speak of the Kingdom of the Son of Man (see the discussion of 13:41; 16:28; 20:21). "Kingdom of heaven" suggests both God and Christ as the Lord. Jesus is Lord, but he does bear some resemblance to the Baptist. His appearance is announced in the same way as John's (vss. 1 and 13 contain the same comparatively rare verb); and above all, his message sounds like John's (4:17; cf. 3:10 with 7:19; also 13:30 with 3:12 and 12:33; 23:33 with 3:7). But Matthew also states that the Baptist is "more than a prophet" (11:9). And one must note that the message of the Baptist is immediately qualified by the quotation (vs. 3) as a promise, while the same message from the mouth of Jesus is characterized by another quotation (4:14-16) as the promise's fulfillment. Furthermore, Matthew states clearly that John has reservations about baptizing Jesus (see the discussion of 3:14-15) and Matthew identifies the Baptist more clearly than the tradition does with Elijah, who is understood to be the forerunner of the messiah (11:14; 17:13; cf. also the discussion of 11:12-13).

The differences between Matthew and Mark are thus determined by the addition of chapters 1 and 2. These make it clear that in Jesus a man has come through whom God intends to make his prophetic promises come true. The section dealing with the Baptist must therefore be devoted less to this purpose than to recounting the beginning of Jesus' ministry. The call to repentance becomes central and on this point Jesus and the Baptist agree. But the gift of forgiveness comes only from Jesus; [6] the story of the Baptist goes no further than confession.

Against Smugness (3:7-10)
Cf. Luke 3:7-9

[7]When John saw many Pharisees and Sadducees coming to him to be baptized, he said to them: "You brood of snakes—who told you

that you could escape from the wrath of God that is about to come? [8]Bear the fruit that is true to repentance. [9]And do not suppose you can excuse yourselves by saying, 'Abraham is our ancestor.' I tell you that God can take these rocks and make descendants for Abraham! [10]The axe is ready to cut the trees at the roots; every tree that does not bear good fruit will be cut down and thrown in the fire."

(Vs. 7—Gen. 3:1.)

Except for the introduction in verse 7 and certain minor changes ("fruit"/"fruits" in vs. 8; "do not suppose"/"don't start saying" in vs. 9), the Baptist's message agrees word for word with Luke 3:7-9. This means that both reproduce the Sayings Source Q (cf. §2 of the Introduction) without modification. This may also be the source of the statement that the Baptist preached in "the country around the Jordan River" (Matt. 3:5=Luke 3:3).

In his introduction to this section, however, Matthew makes a distinction within Israel: the wrath of God is directed not against all of Israel as in Luke, but against the "Pharisees and Sadducees" (cf. the discussion of Mark 12:18). It is strange to find these mutually hostile groups comprehended under a single rubric (also in 16:1, 6, 11-12). But in Matthew's time there were no longer any Sadducees; people remembered only that in the time of Jesus they constituted the other group of devout Israelites. Since at least verse 11 and possibly even verse 9 seems to apply to all Israel, and since it is not easy to think, in the light of 21:25, 32, that "many Pharisees" came to be baptized, Luke is probably more accurate historically. This is confirmed by the fact that in 16:1-12, too, Matthew introduces "Pharisees and Sadducees" four times into the Markan text. These introductions simply reflect a different theological estimate of Israel: Luke sees the Baptist impugning Israel as a whole, while prior to 27:25 Matthew draws more of a distinction between the obedient and disobedient within Israel (and also within his own community; cf. 7:19 =3:10). In other words, both evangelists record John's words unchanged, but they interpret them very differently by providing different introductions. (The fact that Q contained the Baptist's message shows that it was understood as being part of the gospel even before the time of the evangelists [cf. Acts 10:37 ff.; 13:24-25; Mark 1:1 ff.; John 1:6-8, 19-27].)

[7] Both Old and New Testaments take the wrath of God's coming judgment seriously (Amos 2:4 ff.; Wis. 5:19 ff.; 1 Thess. 1:10); and it is particularly the devout who are terrified out of their smugness. "Brood of snakes" also occurs in Isaiah 11:8; 14:29; 30:6; in each case only a single Hebrew word is used, so that it is not merely descent from snakes that is emphasized (cf. Jer. 46:22). But so vitriolic a metaphor used as a term of address is very striking and is almost without parallel, although CD xix. 22 speaks of the "dragon's venom and viper's poison" of the unfaithful Israelites.

[8] All the security in ritual is overthrown; what matters is not the fact, but the "fruit" of baptism. "His guilt is not taken away by rites of atonement, nor can he be cleansed by waters of purification; he cannot be sanctified in lakes and rivers, nor can he be purified in any water of washing. . . . unclean he remains as long as he despises the ordinances of God . . . . By his subjection to all the laws of God will his flesh be purified . . . . Then he will find acceptance in the presence of God through pleasing rites of atonement." So we read in the rule of the Jewish monks (1QS iii. 4-12), even though the many pools still visible among the ruins there show vividly how important these ritual washings or baptisms were. The Baptist is even prone to discourage baptism; he is not after cheap success with hosts of the baptized whose hearts are not renewed. The metaphor of "fruit" is typically Biblical: fruit is what "grows" out of a fundamental disposition of the heart; it is not something that can simply be "done" (cf. the discussion of 7:16-18). The Baptist's preaching summons men to "do" something, but in full knowledge that this can only be "true" of radical repentance, accompany it, grow out of it. What matters is not a list of isolated "works" subject to evaluation, but an entire life in which God is taken so seriously that he determines what is positive and negative, what is strong and what is weak (cf. the discussion of 16:27).

[9] This means first of all that people surrender their false securities, especially religious securities. The merits and intercession of the "fathers," especially Abraham, were an important matter to contem-

porary Judaism, for they guaranteed the covenantal grace God had granted to Israel. This attitude is correct in realizing that we are dependent in every moment on what God has given us, that therefore it is only God's faith.~lness that sustains our lives. But all this loses its validity as soon as God's gift is seen as a secure possession rather than something to be received anew each day.

All religion attempts to constrain God by means of magic, ritual, amulets, as well as by sacrifice, prayers, and sacraments, or, as here, by scrupulous fulfillment of the Law. John here sets such attempts at nought. God will not be constrained; even election does not mean that man has God at his disposal. This is said without detracting from the assurance of the election itself; any new "children" God raises up will be joined with Abraham, God's elect (cf. also Rom. 9:7 ff.; Gal. 3:7; 4:22 ff.; most profoundly worked out in Gal. 3:16, 29: only "in Christ" can anyone be the child of Abraham).

Whether there is an echo here of Isaiah 51:1-2, the image of Abraham as the "rock" (or "stone") from which Israel derives, is debatable; but in any case the image of stones is well chosen, because in Aramaic the words for "stones" and "children" sound almost identical, and stones are the best way of depicting someone who is dead and bears no fruit. The enigmatic statement of 2 Esdras 6:8 that in the eschaton the genealogy will go only "from Abraham to Abraham" is perhaps meant to signify just this, that at that time a new people will be raised up for Abraham by God. But the message of the Baptist declares that this is no longer a matter of descent but of God's free creative act, which can bring into being what does not exist (Rom. 4:17).

[10] Therefore God's coming judgment has already overtaken those who feel secure. There is no way a man can sit back and observe, thinking he still has a long time and can safely put off the question of God.

This confronts us with the difficulty of how salvation is to be known, of what the proper fruit is. All we see at first is the shattering of every illusion, of all false security, of all "boasting," as Paul puts it. But this is itself one aspect of the saving event described in the following verses.

The One to Come (3:11-12)
Cf. Mark 1:7-8; Luke 3:15-18

[11]"I baptize you with water to show that you have repented; but the one who will come after me will baptize you with the Holy Spirit and fire. He is much greater than I am; I am not good enough even to carry his sandals. [12]He has his winnowing-shovel with him, to thresh out all the grain; he will gather his wheat into his barn, but burn the chaff in a fire that never goes out!"

Verse 11 follows the account in Mark; but it reverses the order, speaking first of baptisms and then of rank. And to the account of baptisms Matthew adds the phrase "and fire." Both changes are also found in Luke. Verse 12, with very minor alterations, also occurs in Luke. This shows that both verses were probably in Q, from which both Matthew and Luke got them. In verse 11, Luke follows Mark more closely ("One who is much greater than I is coming. I am not good enough even to untie his sandals . . ."). In Luke, therefore, or even earlier, the form in Mark and that in Q were accommodated to each other. In any case, the account in Q is somewhat fuller than that in Mark.

[11] Matthew adds "to show that you have repented." As in verse 8 (see above), Matthew understands baptism as a summons to do what is right. Matthew's conception is thus quite different from the baptism with Spirit and fire which John associates with the messiah. The Baptist was probably thinking of the judgment that was to come with "wind [another meaning of the Greek word that also means 'spirit'] and fire" (cf. the discussion of Mark 1:8). The same may even be true of Q. In some manuscripts, Luke 3:16 does not add the word "Holy" to "Spirit" (or "wind"), and Q makes almost no other mention of the Spirit (Matt. 4:1 in a different sense; perhaps also 12:32).

[12] Thus the message of judgment in verse 12, which is not easily squared with the Christian picture of Jesus, probably derives from the Baptist himself. Whether he meant it to refer to God or the messiah is uncertain (see the discussion of Mark 1:7-8). Its preservation in Q and not in Mark shows how much Q thought of Jesus as the messiah

coming in judgment. But anyone who has truly heeded verses 7-10 has already undergone God's judgment, and thus belongs on the side of "bearing fruit." In threshing, grain is tossed into the air; the heavier kernel falls to the ground while the wind blows the chaff away, so that it can then be burned. Thus the image of judgment, which winnows by wind and fire.

"The fire that never goes out" (Isa. 34:10; 66:24) no longer fits the image; here we are dealing with the notion of the Last Judgment. This interweaving of symbol and what is symbolized is characteristic of apocalypticism, with its interest in the imminent end and attendant cosmic catastrophes. To the Christian community, of course, the everlasting fire would suggest Jesus' earthly ministry; but for Q and for Matthew that ministry was a sign of the end (see the discussion of 9:37-38). Jesus in fact initiated the Last Judgment; by his example and exhortations he separated the fruit from the chaff (see the discussion of vs. 8). But for the Baptist at this point, Jesus' ministry is still in the future: he is merely predicting. How the people reacted to this gauntlet from the Baptist is no longer recounted (but see vs. 6): Matthew's purpose is simply to pass the message on to his readers; he expects them to respond on their own. The community that hears the Gospel is to tremble in fear of being mere chaff. It must realize that God's judgment—that is, God's way of seeing their lives—is inescapable and constant.

Jesus Is Baptized, Fulfilling God's Requirements (3:13-17)
Cf. Mark 1:9-11; Luke 3:21-22

[13]At that time Jesus went from Galilee to the Jordan, and came to John to be baptized by him. [14]But John tried to make him change his mind. "I ought to be baptized by you," John said, "yet you come to me!" [15]But Jesus answered him, "Let it be this way for now. For in this way we shall do all that God requires." So John agreed.

[16]As soon as Jesus was baptized, he came up out of the water. Then heaven was opened to him, and he saw the Spirit of God coming down like a dove and lighting on him. [17]And then a voice said from heaven, "This is my own dear Son, with whom I am well pleased."
(Vs. 17—Ps. 2:7 [2 Sam. 7:14]; Isa. 42:1.)

[13, 16-17] Verses 13 and 16-17 correspond to the account in Mark, except that Matthew tells his story more "objectively" (see the discussion of Mark 1:9-11). This is in line with prophetic style. "Then heaven was opened to him, and he saw" repeats precisely the expression of Ezekiel 1:1, and the Spirit "coming down on him" is found in 2:2. The phrase about a voice from heaven occurs also in a Jewish apocalypse, echoing Ezekiel 1:28; 2:1 (Syr. Bar. 13:1). No distinction is made between an "objective" event and the mere content of a vision (cf. Rev. 4:1 with 19:11). The direct address emphasizes God's transcendence even more: only when the heavens actually open is God accessible to man. The statement that Jesus came up out of the water "as soon as he was baptized" is somewhat strange; here we have only an echo of the Markan text, which is more logical.

[14-15] In verses 14-15 Matthew has interpolated a discussion about the baptism of Jesus (see the comments on vs. 11). We do not know whether there was a tradition of this conversation before Matthew; be that as it may, the solution offered in verse 15 corresponds completely to Matthew's way of thinking and was probably formulated in these terms by Matthew himself. Verse 14 clearly expresses the problem that Jesus' baptism presented to the community. John cannot have spoken the words given to him here. If he recognized who Jesus was, why didn't he cease baptizing and become a disciple? Furthermore, John 1:31-34 states that John did not recognize Jesus until the descent of the Spirit (see also the discussion of vs. 17).

Matthew is more interested than Mark in the historical juxtaposition of the community of Jesus and the disciples of John, and therefore also in the correct teaching about Christ. He therefore states the actual problem involved in the baptism of Jesus: can Jesus Christ subordinate himself to John? **[15]** Jesus' reply, "Let it be this way for now," determines for the moment what John will do. And in essence, "doing all that God requires" is Matthew's deepest concern (see 5:17-20). But what is meant by "all that God requires"?

The Righteousness of God. The Greek and Hebrew terms for "what God requires" are usually translated as "the righteousness of God." In the Old Testament this term does not mean some standard by which God metes out the reward and punishment appropriate to human actions. Neither does it refer to an attribute, but rather to conduct that "does justice" to another's needs. Thus God's deeds on behalf of Israel are called "acts of righteousness" (Judg. 5:11; Mic. 6:5). His righteousness is without exception salvation for his people (Isa. 4:5; Ps. 22:31; 40:10; 69:28; etc.), which of course includes judgment upon Israel's oppressors. This is what righteousness requires because it corresponds to God's covenant and brings to his people what they may expect on the basis of this covenant.

In the Psalms in particular, despite a flood of accusations against God, it is maintained that his righteousness will be demonstrated gloriously at the eschaton; and the famous thematic statement at the beginning of Romans (Rom. 1:16-17) sounds like a recapitulation of the hope expressed in Psalm 98:2-3 (KJV): "The LORD hath made known his salvation: his righteousness hath he openly shewed in the sight of the heathen. He hath remembered his mercy and his truth [fidelity] toward the house of Israel: all the ends of the earth have seen the salvation of our God." God's righteousness is therefore God's salvation. Therefore the messiah is called "the LORD is our righteousness" (Jer. 23:6; 33:16 RSV; cf. Isa. 11:1-4; Ps. Sol. 17:31; 18:7-8). Such goodness and righteousness goes forth from God to man (Ps. 36:10; Isa. 61:11). There it is to flourish (Ps. 11:7; 33:5; Isa. 61:8-10), not remain hidden in his heart (Ps. 40:10); God's people are to keep his Law and righteous requirements upon earth (Ps. 119:106, 121); righteousness from heaven corresponds to fidelity upon earth (Ps. 85:12).

At Qumran, also, the two are associated (1QS xi. 10-18). God's righteousness is vindicated against all others (1QH xii. 31; viii. 2); none is righteous beside him (1QH iv. 30-31; xii. 19; vii. 17). God's creative adherence to his covenant (1QH xv. 14-15; vii. 15-20) judges the disobedient and vindicates the "lowly of spirit" (1QH xiv. 3), so that for them God's righteousness means mercy (1QH xiv. 3), so that for them God's righteousness means mercy (1QH xi. 18, 31), forgiveness, and deliverance (1QH ix. 13-23; xi. 7-9; xvii. 20), because man becomes righteous only through God's righteousness (or mercy) (1QH iv. 37; xiii. 17); then he will shun all unrighteousness and live a righteous life (1QH xiv. 26). The two aspects are brought together beautifully in Isaiah 56:1 (RSV): "do righteousness, for soon my salvation [my righteousness] will come." At the same time, this passage shows that the righteousness of God, like the Kingdom of God (Matt. 4:17), represents an approaching force in Jesus' message (the Greek uses the same verb, "is near"). God will one day reveal universal righteousness (1QH xiv. 16). In the Testament of Dan 6:10, devotion to the righteousness of God, which leads to eternal salvation, means renunciation of all injustice, and in some manuscripts the righteousness of God is equated with fulfilling the requirements of God's Law.

If, then, we follow the Old Testament in understanding the righteousness of God as the power of love seeking to carry the day on earth and win men's hearts, we can no longer make a sharp distinction between God's actions with respect to men and the human actions that spring from God's. The question is only one of emphasis.

In Matthew (see the discussion of 5:6), 5:20 undoubtedly refers to human actions according to the norm of what God's righteousness requires; the same is probably true in 3:15; 21:32. The question remains open in 5:10. In 6:33, on the other hand, the "righteousness of God" appears as a parallel to the "Kingdom of God," and is therefore probably to be understood as a gracious gift, given by God in his mercy. The same is probably also true for 5:6. In 6:10 God's Kingdom and God's will stand side by side; both are gifts to be besought, but the doing of God's will by men is included.

In our passage the doing of God's will is certainly intended. In the Old Testament and above all in the Judaism of the last two centuries before Jesus, doing God's will consisted mainly of humble acceptance by the righteous man of the suffering imposed on him by God. With the Pauline statement about being "born under the Law" (Gal. 4:4 RSV), Matthew shares the picture of Jesus as devoted obediently to the furtherance of God's will rather than himself; unlike Paul, however, Matthew speaks of Jesus' willing acceptance of God's command, which far transcends the written Law. Paul explains the lowliness and suffering of Jesus as the consequence of the Law, to which Jesus became subject; Matthew sees in lowliness an act of conscious obedience by Jesus. Both share the conviction that the Law is God's Law, but as such does not by itself lead to salvation. For Paul, its abuse by men has transformed it into an evil power to which Jesus also falls victim (Gal. 3:13) in order to deliver men from it; for Matthew, Jesus overcomes the Law by identifying himself with the sinner who comes forward to be baptized. He thus exemplifies a "righteousness" far transcending the legalism spoken of here and in 5:20, and establishes this innovative righteousness as the righteousness of God.

[17] Jesus, according to Matthew, is quite aware of his unique dignity as he comes to be baptized. But the reader, too, is aware of his uniqueness (1:18, 20, 23; 2:15). Thus his divine sonship (see the discussion of Mark 1:11 and the excursus on Mark 15:39) is not bestowed on him here, but rather is simply proclaimed—in the presence of John and the community: "This is [no longer, as in Mark, 'You are'] my Son." Matthew also stresses the fact that God's Spirit is upon the life of Jesus from the very beginning (1:18, 20), though without eliminating the possibility of God's sending his Spirit upon Jesus at the beginning (3:16) and repeatedly in the course of his ministry (12:18, 28), as well as upon his disciples (10:20).

Retrospective consideration of chapter 3 shows that the Sayings Source Q emphasizes primarily the call to repentance, the proclamation of judgment, and the puncturing of smugness. The greater man to come differs from the Baptist only in that he will baptize with the fire that will consume all the chaff. Matthew himself adopts this accent and assimilates the preaching of Jesus to the preaching of the Baptist. At the same time Matthew demonstrates more explicitly than Mark how what was prophesied comes true in the form of concrete history in the Baptist and in Jesus, but in such a way that we find in the former a preparation, in the latter a fulfillment. Both concerns appear in the story of Jesus' baptism: Jesus' superiority to the Baptist consists precisely in the fact that, by subjecting himself humbly and willingly to baptism, he does" all that God requires," fulfilling all righteousness.

The Temptation of Jesus (4:1-11)
Cf. Mark 1:12-13; Luke 4:1-13

[1]Then the Spirit led Jesus into the desert to be tempted by the Devil. [2]After spending forty days and nights without food, Jesus was

hungry. ³The Devil came to him and said, "If you are God's Son, order these stones to turn into bread." ⁴Jesus answered, "The scripture says, 'Man cannot live on bread alone, but on every word that God speaks.' "

⁵Then the Devil took Jesus to the Holy City, set him on the highest point of the Temple, ⁶and said to him, "If you are God's Son, throw yourself down to the ground; for the scripture says,

'God will give orders to his angels about you:
They will hold you up with their hands,
So that you will not even hurt your feet on the stones.' "

⁷Jesus answered, "But the scripture also says, 'You must not put the Lord your God to the test.' "

⁸Then the Devil took Jesus to a very high mountain and showed him all the kingdoms of the world, in all their greatness. ⁹"All this I will give you," the Devil said, "if you kneel down and worship me." ¹⁰Then Jesus answered, "Go away, Satan! The scripture says, 'Worship the Lord your God and serve only him!' "

¹¹So the Devil left him; and angels came and helped Jesus.

(Vs. 2—Exod. 34:28. Vs. 4—Deut. 8:3. Vs. 5—Ezek. 8:3. Vs. 6—Ps. 91:11-12. Vs. 7—Deut. 6:16. Vs. 8—Deut. 3:27; 34:1. Vs. 10—Deut. 6:13; 5:9.)

The story of Jesus' temptation, which Luke presents in similar form, diverges greatly from the very brief account in Mark. All they have in common is Jesus' being led by the Spirit, his temptation by Satan or the Devil, the forty days, and the service of the angels. According to Mark, Jesus is tempted by Satan and served by angels throughout the entire period; according to Matthew and Luke, this does not take place until Jesus has fasted for forty days. This version therefore probably derives from Q, although all Q probably contained was the dialogue between the Devil and Jesus with a brief introduction (see 8:5-13, introduction). The unique verb for "lead (up)" used by Matthew may also derive from Q, since Luke 4:1 also speaks of Jesus' being "led."

The sequence of the second and third temptations differs in Matthew and Luke. The order in Matthew is certainly original, because there the two first temptations begin in the same way ("If you are God's Son . . ."); not until the third does Satan drop his disguise and demand to be worshiped. Possibly Luke understood the statement "You must not put the Lord your God to the test" (Matt. 4:7 = Luke 4:12) as demanding that Satan no longer tempt Jesus, intending to finish the matter. At the same time, Luke's sequence brings Jerusalem in at the end: Satan leaves Jesus in Jerusalem "for a while" (Luke 4:13), where he will wait for him until the time of his Passion (Luke 22:3; but 22:28 refers to earlier temptations).

The reference to Jesus as Son of God appears to presuppose Jesus' baptism and the voice from heaven (3:17). If so, Q began like Mark with John's announcement of Jesus, Jesus' baptism, and his temptation. Mark says that in Jesus Adam's disobedience is healed and Paradise is restored; Q presupposes that Jesus is God's Son and merely reflects on how to understand his sonship.

It is hard to imagine that Jesus told his disciples in detail about one of his experiences and that only a brief note about it was preserved in Mark. Since the question of divine sonship plays hardly any role in Jesus' discourses (see the excursus "Son of God" on Mark 15:39), and since throughout the entire section the Greek translation of the Old Testament is quoted, the tradition of the community was probably limited originally to the bare fact of Jesus' temptation (cf. Heb. 2:18; 4:15; also 11:17). This temptation the community read in the light of its Bible, especially Deuteronomy. All Jesus' responses (Deut. 6:13, 16; 8:3) derive from the chapters that contain the fundamental creed of Israel, which every devout Jew recites daily: "Hear, O Israel, the Lord our God is the only Lord, and you shall love the Lord your God with all your heart, with all your soul, and with all your strength." (Deut. 6:4-5) This is precisely the point of all three temptations.

Only the first and second are introduced by the phrase "If you are God's Son . . . ," only in the second does the Devil cite Scripture. **[8-10]** The third temptation was probably the first to be formulated, because here the conflict is presented most openly, and the rejection of Satan refers directly to the first commandment (Deut. 5:6-7), the central tenet of all Israel's obedience.

In the earliest period the community had to make clear to themselves and their Jewish contemporaries why Jesus did not become the expected national messiah who was to achieve world dominion for Israel. As was noted concerning Jesus' birth, visitors, persecution, and flight, a likeness was seen very early between Jesus and Moses—and this made the issue of political salvation all the sharper. [3-4] In addition, there was an active expectation that in the day of salvation the miracles of Israel's journey through the desert would be repeated, e.g. the provision of manna (Exod. 16:15-36) or the parting of the Jordan River (Joshua 3; prophesied and attempted by Theudas [**Acts 5:36**] in A.D. 44, as recounted by Josephus, *Ant.* xx. 97). Here, of course, there is more emphasis on the contrast between Jesus and Israel, but the similarity to Moses can be noted once more (see below).

[5-7] The second temptation has undergone the most extensive development. Here we find what almost amounts to a disputation such as might have taken place among Jewish and Christian students of Scripture. The use of the temple as the site of the disputation may be associated with contemporary expectations (see the discussion of vs. 5 below). It is conceivable that Psalm 91 was drawn upon, because verses 11 and 13 of it speak of the service of angels and of the wild beasts (cf. also Deut. 8:15) that cannot harm the believer—in other words, what Mark 1:13 says of Jesus. The community would then have been maintaining that in Jesus the fulfillment of Psalm 91:10-13 and the restoration of the Paradisal situation had come to pass.

But as the first temptation implies, Jesus would not heed the demand to perform some miracle to bring Paradise about; instead, he relied completely on God. The fantastic and self-seeking claims of hellenistic miracle-mongers—like the claim of Simon (Acts 8:9-10) that he could fly through the air over the city gate (Acts of Peter 4) —may have been what this second temptation story was working against. Jesus is anything but a miracle-worker of this sort. The first temptation is strikingly similar to the Johannine account of the feeding of the multitude, with its temptation to perform a bread miracle (John 6:31), to perform miraculous signs of any sort (6:30), and to claim the power of earthly nationalism (6:15). The written tradition in its final form (as fixed by Q?) is a composite. It derives from a community which used the Septuagint, applied the title "Son of God" to the earthly Jesus, and opposed any view of him as a mere magician.

[1-11] All this became immediately relevant once more in the 60s, when the Zealots summoned Israel to revolt against Rome. As in the Maccabean wars, Israel was to vanquish the Roman Emperor and trust in God's miracles, which would make the temple at Jerusalem the center of the world and give Israel terrestrial dominion. The miracles of the Mosaic period would be repeated and manna would fall from heaven. It was to oppose such programs that the community framed the collection of Jesus' sayings which we call Q, placing at its front the Baptist's call to repentance and the story of Jesus' temptation. If this is correct, then the community was addressing itself clearly and precisely to the political problems of the day. From the commandment to obey only one God (Deut. 6:4-5), it drew a conclusion precisely opposite to that of its revolutionary contemporaries: the Zealots urged violence and worldly power, the community, submission, worldly death, and otherworldly life.

[1] The introduction was framed by Matthew after the pattern of Mark 1:12, but even more clearly than in Mark Matthew emphasizes that the Spirit of God leads Jesus directly into temptation. **[2-4]** New elements include the forty days of fasting, the temptation to turn stones into bread, and Jesus' response quoting Deuteronomy 8:3. The way taken by Jesus is described as being parallel to the way of Israel: "the LORD your God . . . led you . . . forty years in the wilderness, that he might humble you, testing you to know . . . whether you would keep his commandments, or not. And he . . . let you hunger and fed you with manna . . . that he might make you know that man does not live by bread alone, but . . . by everything that proceeds out of the mouth of the LORD." (Deut. 8:2-3 RSV) We also read in verse 5 that God's purpose is to discipline Israel "like a son."

In the course of the Old Testament but above all in later Judaism Satan comes to replace God as the source of temptation (cf. 2 Sam. 24:1 with 1 Chron. 21:1). According to Jubilees 17:16, the Devil instigated God to tempt Abraham (Gen. 22:1); and according to Jubilees 48:2 it is not God (Exod. 4:24) but the Devil who attacks Moses. In the Christian narrative, too, Satan replaces God in the Old Testament account. The community knew that a starving Israel murmured against God and refused to obey him (Exod. 16:2-4; Ps.

78:18-32); as Son of God, Jesus, unlike Israel, had the power to get bread for himself, just as Satan insinuated; but he remained obedient and answered Satan with the very response that, according to Deuteronomy 8:3, Israel was supposed to learn. Not only did he thereby allow himself to be disciplined "like a son" of God, but proved himself to be *the* Son of God while at the same time fulfilling the example of Moses, who during Israel's desert wanderings took God's side against the murmuring people. Moses himself, according to Exodus 34:28, was "forty days and forty nights" (Matt. 4:2; not in Luke 4:2) with the Lord, ate no bread (very similarly put in Luke 4:2; less clearly in Matthew), drank no water, and wrote down God's words. This, not some penitential fast of forty days on the part of Adam (Life of Adam 6), furnishes the most immediate parallel.

The problem of Evil. The idea of the Devil creates difficulties. Matthew conceives him as a visible person; as in 28:18, when speaking of the risen Lord, he adds a phrase that he alone uses: he (here, Jesus) "drew near and said . . . ." As elsewhere in the New Testament, Satan is neither described nor introduced as the lord of hell. In Matthew, too, he is heard; nothing is made of seeing him. We can no longer conceive him in visual terms as Matthew could. In the wake of witchhunts, pogroms, or racism we still speak of "forces" that can rule a whole nation. Modern talk of the power of the individual or collective unconscious demands rather than eliminates precise analysis of causes, and precise analysis is an important attitude; but so is the Biblical experience, expressed in the mythological image of the Devil, that evil can fall upon individuals or whole groups, overwhelm them and overpower their ability to make rational judgments.

James 1:13, 14 is very modern in stating that there is no temptation that does not derive from a desire within. But the possibility that this can grow and develop into a more than personal force, which the individual or even the entire group is helpless to control, is described in almost all the documents of the New Testament through the image of the Devil. But the call to resist him, not to mention James 1:13, shows that this is not simply an "explanation" of evil, relieving man of responsibility.

The problem is considered even more profoundly when, as in 1

Corinthians 10:13 and probably also Matthew 6:13, God is himself seen as the source of temptation (cf. Gen. 22:1; Exod. 16:4; etc.), when indeed the very same action can be ascribed now to God, now to Satan (see the discussion of vss. 2-4). In similar fashion Matthew 4:1 says that God himself leads Jesus to the Devil (cf. the mythological conception of Satan as the servant of God in Job 1:6-12; 2:1-6). This avoids an erroneous exaggeration of the Devil's role, as though all temptation were evil in itself. It is even stated that evil itself remains in God's hand (cf. Amos 3:5-6).

It may be God's will to lead us into conflict with evil. This is linked with God's creation of man in partnership, giving him freedom for both good and evil. In no other way could God be loved and glorified; only a free creature can do this, never one constrained by force. A child can be forced to kiss a person, but love is in the kiss only when the child is fully free to refuse. Therefore the father in the parable of Luke 15:11-32 does not call the police to bring the younger son home or his servants to fetch the elder to the banquet, but at the end of Jesus' story stands helplessly outside, appealing only with words of love. Love is not unquestioning endorsement; it must be subject to doubt, it demands decisions, it is aware of change, and itself changes. A God who invariably granted man his wishes would be a machine. So not only good but also evil, also Satan, is God's agent, but in such a way that Satan remains subject to him who, in the deepest sense of the word, is good to man. These considerations may be grounds for affirming our darker nature (see Matt. 26:47-56, conclusion); our evil impulses will not be denied, we must understand and admit we feel them, so that they don't express themselves despite us, and so we can constructively pursue the desire they represent.

The temptation for Jesus is to misconstrue divine sonship as the power to do miracles. [4] Jesus' answer, however, reveals that he depends not on his own powers, but on those of God for everything. The early church's confession of Jesus as "true God" is thus far from meaning he can perform miracles and somehow has God under his control; quite the contrary: it means that he can hear and obey God totally, leaving everything to him—in other words, that he is also "true man." He identifies himself expressly with the "man" of the quotation.

[5] In the second temptation, too, Matthew probably envisions a literal removal to the "highest point" of the temple. The Greek word can mean "little tower" or "parapet" and sounds almost like the word for "wings" in Psalm 91:4. Of course there is no earthly mountain like that described in verse 8, and the same holds true for Revelation 21:10. A sharp line is maintained—just as we perceive it today— between experiences that take place in the physical world and those that take place in the spirit or mind (cf. also 2 Cor. 12:2; Rev. 21:10; 1:10).

Ever since Ezekiel 47:1 ff. and similar prophecies, God's eschatological miracles had been expected at the temple. Rabbinic sources, albeit of unknown date, say: "Our teachers taught that when the king the messiah is revealed, he will come and stand on the roof of the sanctuary" (Billerbeck). Psalm 91, quoted by Satan, was used as a temple psalm and occasionally associated with Israel's desert wanderings.

Once again Satan presupposes Jesus is God's Son, and hopes that he will see his sonship as the power to perform miracles. But the temptation is increased: now the Devil cites Scripture and apparently calls on Jesus to trust in God. He practically turns religious. Is he not after all demanding that Jesus take the Bible seriously and discover its direct application to his position?

But really, no. The reliance on Scripture is not to be for the glory of God, but rather the glory of Jesus, the man who is to demonstrate his great faith. What the "venture of faith" really is, and what it is not—that must be examined in every case. God's "no" to a prayer can be just as much an experience of God as a miraculous "yes." But the Devil is after a miracle, so that man may become lord of God and compel him to act through the power of his faith.

[6] But of course, that would destroy faith and substitute blackmail. Jesus refers once again to a passage from Deuteronomy (6:16), which recalls the murmuring of the Israelites when they were tormented by thirst at Massah. While Israel despaired of God because it did not experience a miracle, Jesus knows that faith holds even when miracles do not happen. Thus Q contains a hint of what the Passion narrative recounts. In 27:40 we read once more: "If you are God's Son . . . ." On the cross Jesus is once more "up high," very

concretely, and once more he refuses to "throw himself down." In this identical situation he once more lets God be fully God, although he can only feel forsaken by God; and he dies, without any visible miracle, in final unity with God's will as "Son of God" (see the discussion of Mark 15:34, 39). Thus the cross will be the final answer to Satan.

[8] The third temptation, too, begins with something like a change of scene (see the discussion of vs. 5). In like fashion Moses was led up to a high mountain to see "all the land"—indeed, according to rabbinic interpretation, the whole earth (Deut. 34:1-4). The expression "all the kingdoms of the world" occurs in a similar vision of Baruch (Syr. Bar. 76:3). But in the case of Moses it is God who allows him to see this, and he dies without being able to lay his hand on it. [9] Jesus, however, is offered dominion over the entire world; he could take possession of all he surveys if he wanted. Thus the temptation hits the direct sore. The lord of the world by virtue of power stands face to face with the lord of the world appointed by God. The theme of chapter 2 is taken up once more. Doesn't the Devil in fact rule in this world? Isn't any other conclusion simply naive optimism? Isn't one forced to use the means of the Devil if one wants to bring any kind of order into the world? Now, of course, the disguise has been dropped; now what is demanded is apostasy from God, and Jesus can only dismiss Satan with finality (cf. 16:23).

[10] In 17:1 and 28:16-18 Jesus will once more stand upon a mountain, but as the real ruler of the world, who does not receive his sovereignty at the hands of the Devil and does not exercise it through a balance of terror and violence. Jesus, too, thinks in sober and realistic terms—not, however, those of the Devil, but of God. In Psalm 2, a royal psalm, God says, "Ask of me, and I will make the nations your heritage, and the ends of the earth your possession." (vs. 8) This is the principle followed by Jesus. [11] Thus Satan is vanquished; now, as Matthew probably borrows from Mark 1:13, God's angels serve Jesus. But this victory is depicted in restrained terms, with no suggestion of any visible divine triumph.

The question whether the three temptations took place historically in just this way and whether Jesus told his disciples about them or not is unimportant (see the discussion of vs. 3). The crucial point is the unique way in which the question of God is posed. We encounter God, the community is saying, in Jesus, that is, in the man who totally renounced the temptation to use God for his own purposes and entrusted his entire life and death to God. We encounter the "true God" in the one who rejected the superhuman temptation to "be like God" (Gen. 3:5), to have power and score successes, the one who proved himself to be "true man." This happened at some time in the life of Jesus, and our section simply concentrates it into a few hours. It is likely that Q, amid the turmoil of Jewish revolt against Rome, began his account with this story; and it puts a challenge precisely as fierce to us today. Will we invoke God's authority for our own goals, to be achieved through tactics and violence, or will we allow ourselves to be won by him for the true humanity, which took form in the life of Jesus—that is the real question posed by this narrative.

The best summary of it is found in the chapter about the Grand Inquisitor in Dostoevsky's *Brothers Karamazov*. The temptation that besets the church is success; it is gained when the church rules over man, depriving him of decisions that he is not mature enough to make. Perhaps the accent is shifted a little because Matthew 4 places less stress on the question of how the Messiah—or the church acting in his name—is to gain power over others, than on the more modest question, which applies to every man, of how man comes to certainty of God and learns to obey him. What Jesus demonstrates is less his messianic office than his "religious devotion"; more precisely, in proving himself to be true man—ruling out the assurances and guarantees, accepting the treachery of freedom—he is Messiah and Son of God. Dostoevsky's black satire on a church dominated by the success-ethic follows.

In the course of history this point has been variously stressed. At first, in the contentions with Jewish expectations, it was maintained that Jesus had rejected all political power (the third temptation). Later, more emphasis was laid on his trust in God: unlike the people of God during their desert period, Jesus in his did not complain—and indeed rejected food that would only glorify himself (the first temptation). Finally, actual discussions with Jewish scholars came to be reflected in the formulations of the second temptation. As in chapter 2, Jesus in the first temptation appears as a superior parallel to Moses and the generation of the exodus. But this, a purely theological conclusion, took on political significance when the Zealots summoned the people to revolt against the might of Rome. By recalling the Baptist's denunciation of origin-proud Jews, and also the story of the third temptation, the community unambiguously remained aloof from the Jewish Zealots.

But by the time of the evangelist this was no longer an active question. The catastrophe of the year 70 and the fall of Jerusalem had put an end to revolt. Matthew was free to elaborate the theme of trust in God, which mattered to him as the prime quality of discipleship. Trust in God means renouncing all guarantees. Jesus' status and miraculous powers mean nothing (or worse) if he is not prepared to give them up (the second temptation). In this sense Matthew 27:40 is already in view.

Jesus Moves to Galilee (4:12-16)
Cf. Mark 1:14-15; Luke 4:14-15

[12]When Jesus heard that John had been put in prison, he went away to Galilee. [13]He left Nazara and went and lived in Capernaum, a town by Lake Galilee, in the territory of Zebulun and Naphtali. [14]This was done to make come true what the prophet Isaiah had said:
> [15]"Land of Zebulun, and land of Naphtali,
> In the direction of the sea, on the other side of Jordan,
> Galilee of the gentiles!
> [16]The people who live in darkness
> Saw a great light.
> On those who live in the dark land of death
> The light shone."

(Vss. 15-16—cf. Isa. 8:23; 9:1.)

The imprisonment of John and Jesus' move to Galilee are taken over from Mark. Matthew, however, makes a point of the transfer from Nazareth (2:23) to Capernaum (see the excursus on 1:18-25). [13] Verse 13 is in Matthew's style and was probably inserted here by him. In Mark (1:21), Capernaum is not mentioned until after the call of the disciples (1:16-20=Matt. 4:18-22), and then only as a place where Jesus exercised his ministry, not where he lived. Matthew therefore is placing special emphasis on Capernaum, obviously because Nazareth is not located in the territory mentioned by the prophets. It is striking that here, as in Luke 4:16, we have the form "Nazara," whereas 2:23 and 21:11 use the form "Nazareth." May this form possibly derive from a tradition, found otherwise only in Luke, that Jesus was spurned in Nazara? Such a rejection might explain why Jesus moved to Capernaum with his family (John 2:12), so that only his (married) sisters stayed in Nazareth (Mark 6:3). The further details about Capernaum undoubtedly derive from the Isaiah quotation (vss. 15-16).

In order to make the agreement clear from the outset, Matthew in verse 13 employs the very words of the prophet he intends to cite. The text is a free rendering of portions of Isaiah 8:23–9:1. The Hebrew word *galil* ("region") is also rendered as "Galilee" in the Septuagint; the word "live" occurs in neither the Hebrew nor the Greek text; "saw" follows the Hebrew, not the Greek; and the conclusion may have been influenced by Isaiah 58:10. The quotation must have come to Matthew from the tradition; since much from Isaiah is omitted in verse 15, it is hard to see why Matthew would have included the particular phrase "on the other side of Jordan," which crops up in verse 25 in another context.

[12] Matthew does not say whether the imprisonment of the Baptist is the reason for Jesus' return (cf. the discussion of 14:13) or merely coincides with it. He may have in mind that the end of John's ministry is God's signal to him to replace John and bring his work to fruition. "He went and lived" uses the same expression as 2:23, and it is expressly stated that it is Nazareth he left; so we are dealing with his last change of residence, in which the prophecy comes true.

[14] Once again the quotation is appended directly to the geographical name, rather than being kept until after verse 17, where the second half of the prophet's quotation would have fit in very well. Matthew apparently is concerned with the route taken by Jesus on his journeys (see the excursus to 1:18-25). [15-16] The quotation itself, especially the included portion of verse 16, states that in Jesus is God's final fulfillment of all prophetic hopes, and, what is more, he has come in the despised "land of the gentiles."

This brings the Gospel's introductory section to a close. Jesus' move to "Galilee of the gentiles" demonstrates God's amazing initiative toward those who had never even been considered. Like the four women in the genealogy and the astrologers in the birth narrative at the beginning of this section, the gentiles stand at its end. At the same time this conclusion points toward what is to come. The example of Jesus' leaving the city of his youth and going to those who live in darkness is an ideal for whoever would be his disciple (cf. 4:18-22; 5:14).

II

THE MESSIAH:
HIS MESSAGE, MINISTRY,
AND DISCIPLES
(4:17–11:30)

In describing the beginning of Jesus' ministry, his preaching, and the call of his disciples (4:17-22), Matthew continues to follow Mark, as he has done since 3:1, albeit with expansions from Q and additions of matter he considers important such as 3:14-15; 4:13-16. From 12:1 on he once again follows the thread of Mark. It is striking that he does not do so in chapters 5–11.

Now it is clear that in chapters 5–7 Matthew seeks to present Jesus as the messiah in his message, in chapters 8–9 as the messiah in his ministry. He therefore repeats 4:23 word for word in 9:35 (without "all over Galilee"), thus furnishing a framework for this two-part intent.

The reason for inserting chapter 10 is likewise clear. In Q the Sermon on the Plain (or Sermon on the Mount) is followed by the story of the Roman officer at Capernaum (Matt. 8:5-13 = Luke 7:1-10) and the inquiry of the Baptist (Matt. 11:2-6 = Luke 7:18-23). Here Jesus cites his miracles in his replies. Matthew therefore places the miracles beforehand, in chapters 8–9; he even adds the healing of two blind men and a deaf-mute although he has no proper occasion to do so (see the discussion of 9:27-34), only because in 11:5 Jesus tells the Baptist's disciples to say to their master what they have seen: "the blind can see . . . , the deaf hear . . . ." But Matthew does not place this reply to the Baptist directly after the miracles: he first inserts chapter 10 because he wants to make the point that the same authority to perform miracles is also given to the community (see the discussion of 9:35 and 10:8). Jesus' response to the disciples of the Baptist is thus also the response of the community to adherents of the Baptist in the period of the evangelist. Jesus' authority can still be seen at work in the Christian community. It answers all doubting questions.

All that follows are some further sayings about the Baptist (11:7-19) and two sections calling for decision (11:20-30). Then, in 12:1, Matthew returns to the Markan narrative. Thus the large-scale structure is clear, but this does not clear up all the problems.

[Chapters 5–7] Chapters 5–7 contain major sections that also appear in the Lukan Sermon on the Plain. Although Matthew interpolates much other material, the sections that parallel the Sermon on the Plain come in the same sequence. These are the Beatitudes (5:3-12 = Luke 6:20-26), the commandment to renounce force and love one's enemies (5:38-48 = Luke 6:27-36), the requirement not to judge (7:1-5 = Luke 6:37-42), the reference to the tree and its fruit (7:15-20 = Luke 6:43-45), and the concluding parable with its warning against pleading "Lord, Lord" (7:21-27 = Luke 6:46-49). Only one verse (Luke 6:31) has Matthew taken out of sequence (7:12), and that for quite specific reasons.

This parallel sequence can only be explained on the assumption that all these sections were available in writing to both evangelists in this very order, that is, in Q. But why, then, do the two evangelists differ so much in their wording of these sections? Even when he is following Mark, Matthew permits himself to be influenced by the formulation of Q and includes sections taken directly from it (see the discussion of 3:7-12). Would we not expect him to follow the same procedure here? Perhaps the sections of the Sermon on the Plain mentioned above were used for instruction by the Matthaean community, expanded by the addition of other material, and occasionally altered in wording, just as today passages from the Bible may be collected in a devotional manual and at the same time translated into modern English. According to this theory, Matthew borrowed the Sermon on the Plain from Q in the expanded form with which he was familiar, at the same time (as in 3:14-15) inserting additional material and adding his own commentary.

Important sections not belonging to Q probably existed before their appearance in Matthew: the first two anitheses, and probably also the third and fourth (5:21-22, 27-28 [29-30, 33-37]); the teaching concerning the three good works (6:2-6 [7-8], 16-18); and perhaps also the metaphor of the two ways (7:13-14). It is reasonable to suppose that something like these sections were associated with those from the Sermon on the Plain and used in the community.

[Chapters 8–9] The collection of Jesus' deeds is harder to explain. In the individual stories of chapters 8–9, Matthew's dependence on Mark or Q is still clear. But their sequence is totally different. The healing of the leper (8:1-4) follows Mark 1:40-45; this is followed by the story of the Roman officer at Capernaum, which in Q follows immediately upon the conclusion of the Sermon on the Plain/Mount. In 8:14-17 Matthew goes back to Mark 1:29-37, then in 8:18-34 and 9:18-26 presents the section Mark 4:35–5:43. In between (9:1-17) come the disputes with the scholars and Pharisees, which we find in Mark 2:1-22. This raises the question, why should Matthew diverge so radically from Mark at this precise point, quite unlike his technique from 12:1 on?

All we can do is make certain conjectures. Some facts are significant. The saying about the narrow gate (7:13), the declaration of judgment upon those who call on the "Lord" at the Last Judgment but have done evil (7:23), and the threat against Israel, which will be excluded while the gentiles flood in (8:11-12) occur in the same sequence in Luke 13:23-29. In Matthew they are linked with the conclusion of the Lukan Sermon on the Plain and the story of the Roman officer at Capernaum, which follows directly in Q. In all three cases there is significant verbal disagreement between Matthew and Luke. Might this mean that the collection used for instruction in the Matthaean community extended beyond the conclusion of the Sermon on the Plain, encompassing the following story, and that in both places a tradition was used (it was also in Q [Luke 13:23-29]), that attempted to explain the rejection of Israel?

A second observation may be made. Shortly after the above sequence are the sayings addressed to two would-be followers (8:19-22); these have been incorporated into the story of the storm on the lake. This story clearly follows Mark 4:35-41, but exhibits minor points of agreement with Luke (see 8:18-27, introduction). Of course one must not attach too much importance to this, as 12:47 (q.v.) and 14:13 (q.v.) show; but here there are many points of agreement not found in Mark. Is it possible that even before Matthew the sayings about the decision to follow Jesus were associated with the story of the storm as an illustration? Might this have been part of the community tradition just mentioned?

The third observation is that there are minor agreements between Matthew and Luke, as against Mark, in passages that show Jesus' controversy with Judaism. For example, 9:1-17. All these stories are clearly didactic. Jesus' acts serve merely to illustrate the discussion with Israel: the story of the Roman officer leads up to the threat against Israel; the story of the storm on the lake shows what it means to follow Jesus, a course from which the teacher of the Law shrinks back; the healing of the paralytic gives the lie to the teachers of the Law who doubt Jesus' authority to forgive sins; the call of Levi and the discussion about fasting distinguish Jesus and his disciples from the Pharisees. Matthew 8:1-4 may also have been a part of this cluster: Jesus accepts the leper whom Israel casts out, and he emphasizes the difference with an allusion to Moses and a warning to the priests. In this passage, too, there are points of agreement with Luke. The same may even hold true for 9:32-34 (cf. Luke 11:14-15).

Is it possible then that the Matthaean community already made use of a collection of Jesus' sayings and acts that concentrated on the dispute with Israel? Whether or no, it is obvious that Matthew followed the healing of the leper (8:1-4 = Mark 1:40-45) with that of Peter's mother-in-law (Mark 1:29-34) because the appended list of healings made it possible to insert the quotation which shows Jesus to be the fulfillment of prophetic hopes (Matt. 8:14-17). That list can only be included at this point, since the encounter with the Roman officer took place while Jesus was still on the road to Capernaum, whereas Peter's house is located in Capernaum (Mark 1:21, 29). Following the story of the storm on the lake (8:23-27) Matthew inserts the healing of the Gadarenes (8:28-34), with which it is closely associated in Mark; the verse marking the transition to the next section of the collection before him (9:1) is still clearly influenced by this story ("Jesus got into the boat [cf. Mark 5:18], went back across the lake [cf. Mark 5:21] . . ."). The continuation, with the restoration of the dead girl to life (9:18-26), he placed at the end as a climax, to be followed only by the brief account of the healing of two blind men and a dumb man, which he needed for 11:5, thus concluding with the final divorce between Jesus' supporters and opponents. Those who "follow" Jesus, acknowledging him to be the "Son of David" because "their eyes have been opened according to their faith" so that they become missionaries, thus stand in emphatic contrast to the Pharisees, who accuse Jesus of being in league with demons. Of all the miracle stories in Mark 1–5, the only one not included is the healing of the demoniac (Mark 1:23-28), because Matthew invariably cites only one instance of each type (cf. 8:28-34).

[Chapters 5–7] However this structure is to be explained, its theological significance for Matthew is overwhelming. That he begins his Sermon on the Mount, as Luke begins his Sermon on the Plain, with the Beatitudes shows his awareness that only God's promise of grace and mercy, which of course evokes right conduct on the part of man, can stand at the beginning. Then in Matthew follow the sayings about what it means to be a disciple (5:13-16), and above all the exposition of the "better righteousness" of the disciples in contrast to that of the Pharisees in their observance of Mosaic Law (5:17-20).

In this contrast we find the major concern of Matthew and his community. This can be seen from the fact that Matthew sets forth the command to love your enemy by means of antithesis—as a contrast between the Old Testament commandments and the new ethics of Jesus. Further, whereas Luke puts this command right after the Beatitudes, in Matthew it does not appear until 5:43-48, as the climax of six other antitheses. In addition, all of chapter 6 describes this new ethics of Jesus as freedom and distinguishes it from all legalistic religion. Thus the summons to love God takes its place alongside the summons to love one's neighbor, and is contrasted with Jewish narrowness (6:1-18) and gentile greed (6:19-34). Goodness and mercy are demanded of the community in 7:1-6, because it is only the goodness and mercy of God that open the way to the Kingdom of God in prayer (7:7-11). Matthew's separate treatment of the Golden Rule (7:12) shows how important it is to him. It in fact means that love for one's neighbor is *the* solution to the whole problem of the Law.

All that remains is the section that Matthew borrows from the Sermon on the Plain (7:1-6, 15-20, 24-27 = Luke 6:37-49), but with a new emphasis: the warning against false prophets within the Christian community, who seek to lead men astray from this active love (7:7-14,

21-23, 28-29). This is the point of the parable that concludes the Sermon on the Plain (7:24-27=Luke 6:47-49). In a similar way, the community is admonished against false prophets (twice) after the dispute with Israel in chapters 21–25 (see the introduction to this section).

[Chapters 8–9] The faith of the gentiles, which puts Israel to shame (8:5-13), already formed a part of Q. Just as Jesus' revision of the Law (5:21 ff.) was prefaced by a declaration of his faithfulness to it (5:17-20), so now his praise of gentiles is prefaced by his demonstration of loyalty to the rites of Moses (8:4). The teaching of what it means to follow Jesus and its illustration by the storm (8:18-27) distinguishes Jesus' disciples from the teacher of the Law. The preceding section describes following Jesus as "waiting on him [no longer 'them,' as in Mark 1:31]" and depicts Jesus as fulfilling a prophetic promise (8:14-17). Perhaps the evangelist also felt that the important point about the healing of the demoniacs, which follows, was the distinction between the men who were healed, who address Jesus as "Son of God," and the inhabitants of the city, who beg him to leave (8:28-34). In any case the conflict with Israel is the theme of 9:1-17. The raising of the dead girl (9:18-26), which constitutes the climax, depicts Jesus once more as a Jew faithful to the Law (see the discussion of 9:20); and the two concluding sections, which already look ahead to 11:2-6, distinguish the followers of Jesus, who believe in him, from the Pharisees, who reject him.

A. PROLOGUE
4:17-25

The Call to Discipleship (4:17-22)
Cf. Mark 1:14-20

[17]From that time Jesus began to preach his message: "Turn away from your sins! The Kingdom of heaven is near!"

[18]As Jesus walked by Lake Galilee, he saw two brothers who were fishermen, Simon (called Peter) and his brother Andrew, catching fish in the lake with a net. [19]Jesus said to them, "Come with me and I will

teach you to catch men." [20]At once they left their nets and followed him.

[21]He went on and saw two other brothers, James and John, the sons of Zebedee. They were in their boat with their father Zebedee, getting their nets ready. Jesus called them; [22]at once they left the boat and their father, and followed Jesus.

[17] Matthew starts off with Mark's account of the beginning of Jesus' ministry, if only because the call of the disciples must precede the Sermon on the Mount, in which they appear as a special group of listeners. Matthew first appends to the quotation in verses 15-16 Jesus' call to repentance, using the phrase "from that time," which is peculiar to him. The quotation as combined with Jesus' announcement shows that it is in his preaching that the light shines on those who dwell in darkness. Further, this combination of quotation with Jesus' words shows that it is no longer the forerunner who speaks but the fulfiller, although the message he preaches is identical in wording with that preached by the Baptist (see the discussion of 3:2). The omission of Mark's double reference to the Good News is theologically significant (see the excursus on 7:13-23 [§3]). The two stories of the call of the two pairs of disciples are markedly similar to each other; we read in both 4:18 and 4:21 that "he saw two (other) brothers," and in both 4:20 and 4:22 that "they left . . . and followed him." This emphasizes the exemplary nature of what is happening. That Zebedee is sitting in the boat is stated at once (rather than as afterthought, as in Mark), making the abruptness of the sons' departure even bolder.

[18] More important are two other differences from Mark. Simon is introduced from the very beginning as "Peter," probably because the readers know him by this name. In other words, Matthew no longer says that Jesus himself gave him this name (Mark 3:16). His rock-like nature, which is important to Matthew, is not created by what Jesus says; Jesus simply confirms it (see the discussion of 16:19). Is this connected with the fact that all the names occurring twice in the list of disciples (Simon, James [10:2-4]; cf. Judas [Luke 6:16]) are associated with an epithet? A related point is Matthew's omission of any special appointment of the twelve (see the discussion of 10:1).

Even more crucial is Matthew's emphasis on the motif of "following" Jesus. [22] Not only does he repeat in verse 22 the word "follow," which had already become a technical term; he also states that the disciples "at once" left their boat and their father (in Mark 1:20 it is Jesus' call that comes immediately).

All this means that the light announced in verse 16 of the quotation is Jesus' *call* to repentance. There is no way to attain salvation through adoption of a theological formula, bypassing repentance. But repentance, as the call of the first disciples shows, is a gift. It is the following of Jesus, who leads and is always the initiating agent, but who in this very way sets men in motion. The true help that comes from God consists in his taking men and their actions seriously, incorporating them into his own operation.

The Messiah Teaches and Heals (4:23-25)
Cf. Mark 1:39, 28; 3:7-8

[23]Jesus went all over Galilee, teaching in their synagogues, preaching the Good News of the Kingdom, and healing people from every kind of disease and sickness. [24]The news about him spread through the whole country of Syria, so that people brought him all those who were sick with all kinds of diseases, and afflicted with all sorts of troubles: people with demons, and epileptics, and paralytics—Jesus healed them all. [25]Great crowds followed him from Galilee and the Ten Towns, from Jerusalem, Judea, and the land on the other side of the Jordan.

The juxtaposition of the Messiah's words and actions in chapters 5–7 and 8–9 is anticipated in this summary introduction, verse 23 of which is repeated in 9:35. The survey, composed by Matthew, is strongly reminiscent in verse 23 of Mark 1:39, in verse 24 of Mark 1:28, 34, and in verse 25 of Mark 3:7-8 (see below). The last parallel is interesting because the summary of Jesus' acts in Mark 3:7-13 concludes with Jesus going up a "hill" (as in Matt. 5:1). Mark tells how a crowd assembles and Jesus heals the sick and possessed, then climbs a hill and chooses the twelve disciples. Matthew eliminates the choice of the twelve (see the excursus on 7:13-23 [§1]) and proceeds directly to the discourse in chapters 5–7, thus making it the "Sermon on the Mount." Luke inverts the order, first telling how the twelve are chosen on the hill; then the people congregate and Jesus heals the sick after coming down, so that the discourse that follows, which contains the nucleus of the Matthaean Sermon on the Mount (see the introduction to 4:17–11:30), becomes the "Sermon on the Plain." Both accounts succeed in having the sermon that follows addressed to the crowd (Matt. 4:25; Luke 6:17), although both single out the "disciples" at the beginning (Matt. 5:1; Luke 6:20). The sequence in Q probably ran: the crowd gathers by the lake, Jesus goes up the hill, Jesus addresses the disciples alone. By means of omission or transposition, Matthew and Luke have expanded the circle of listeners to include the whole crowd (see the discussion of 5:1).

[23] From Mark 1:39 Matthew once more borrows the mention of Galilee, a place he finds significant (see the discussion of 4:13-16). But he goes beyond Mark in stressing Jesus' journeying about (also mentioned in Mark 6:6), a point never made about any other Jewish prophet or teacher (cf. the excursus on 1:18-25 [§3]). While Mark reports Jesus as "preaching in the synagogues," Matthew seems to distinguish "teaching in their synagogues" from "preaching the Good News of the Kingdom" (see the excursus on 7:13-23 [§3]); is he trying to suggest that Jesus first taught Israel assembled for worship in "their" (cf. the discussion of 7:29; 10:17) synagogues and only afterwards preached his special message "in the streets" (22:9-10; cf. also the discussion of 10.5-6)? Matthew associates "teaching" with synagogue, Law, and ethical admonition, "preaching" with the Good News and the Kingdom of God. Therefore in 13:1-3 he no longer calls the parables "teaching," as does Mark 4:1-2. None of the discourses of Jesus whose content is recorded is set in a synagogue or even in a house (unlike Luke 4:16-28). Apart from the eschatological discourses (Matthew 24–25; perhaps also 17:24 ff.), they are not even pronounced in cities or villages but on a hill, in the open countryside, on the shore, wherever Jesus is to be found.

The omission of the healing of demoniacs, as mentioned in Mark 1:39, is due only to the omission of the exorcism that precedes in Mark (see the end of the introduction to 4:17–11:30). Exorcisms are recounted in 4:24; 8:16 and elsewhere (on the omission of Mark 9:38-40, see the discussion of Matt. 18:6).

[24] Especially noteworthy is the mention of Syria; perhaps it is

the homeland of the evangelist. It is not totally out of the question that Matthew actually wrote *synoria* ("region"), as attested by one late manuscript, which would represent the meaning of Mark 1:28, and that this was misread as *syria.*

For the rest, the content of the verse for the most part agrees with Mark 1:28 and 34, except that the latter does not mention "troubles" and "epileptics and paralytics." This lengthy catalog of illnesses and sufferings shows vividly that Matthew wants to make sure this aspect of Jesus' ministry is not underestimated. He will return to this point in chapters 8–9. [25] Matthew's omission of the demons who confess Jesus to be the Son of God (Mark 3:11) is understandable. It is not demons but disciples who are prepared to follow Jesus and recognize him as the Son of God (14:33; 16:16; but also 8:29).

What, then, are the points Matthew is trying to make before he unfolds Jesus' ministry in word and act? Jesus' activity is in "Galilee of the gentiles," where no one would have expected it; the call to discipleship is to a life of preaching and charismatic assistance conformable to Jesus' own; Jesus' healing is through the power of God; and the effective ministry of Jesus lies beyond Galilee, reaching into the homeland of the evangelist and (?) the community that reads his book.

B. JESUS' MESSAGE
5:1–7:29

Jesus as Teacher (5:1-2)

¹Jesus saw the crowds and went up a hill, where he sat down. His disciples gathered around him, ²and he began to teach them.

[1] While the "hill" (see 4:23-25, introduction to 4:23) and the "disciples" may have been mentioned in the tradition, both Matthew and Luke emphasize that the discourse is addressed to the whole crowd (see 4:23-25, introduction); this is stressed once more by Matthew 7:28-29. Undoubtedly the Sermon on the Mount is an ethics of discipleship. Sayings concerning discipleship are introduced immedi-

ately after the Beatitudes, and the disciple is required to exhibit a righteousness superior to that of the Pharisee. Nevertheless, anyone who allows Jesus to call him to God is a disciple, and so the Sermon on the Mount is addressed to the whole crowd. This is also why it includes those sayings of Jesus that liberate men from the agonies of legalism and summon them to the carefree existence of the birds and flowers. On the other hand, such freedom for everyone cannot be allowed to weaken Jesus' requirement of love for one's neighbor; when disciples of Jesus teach in such a way that active love grows cold, then they are false prophets, whose house will collapse under the assault of God's judgment (see the discussion of 7:15).

God's Partiality Toward the Poor (5:3-12)
Cf. Luke 6:20-26

> [3]"Blessings on the poor in spirit,
>   for theirs is the Kingdom of heaven!
> [4]Blessings on those who mourn,
>   for they will be comforted!
> [5]Blessings on the humble,
>   for they will inherit the earth!
> [6]Blessings on those who hunger and thirst for righteousness,
>   for they will be satisfied.
> [7]Blessings on the merciful,
>   for they will find mercy!
> [8]Blessings on the pure in heart,
>   for they will see God!
> [9]Blessings on those who make peace,
>   for they will be called sons of God!
> [10]Blessings on those who are persecuted for righteousness,
>   for theirs is the Kingdom of heaven!

[11]Blessings on you when men insult you, and persecute you, and tell all kinds of evil lies against you because you are my followers. [12]Be glad and happy, because your reward is great in heaven. This is how men persecuted the prophets who lived before you."

(Vss. 3-4—Isa. 61:1-2. Vs. 10—1 Pet. 3:14. Vs. 11—1 Pet. 4:14.)

1

Beatitudes or blessings are found even in the Old Testament. They occur primarily in wisdom literature, and declare those "happy" who conduct their lives according to the rules of wisdom (e.g. Ecclus. 25:7-10). But they also occur in the Psalms, often pronounced as a greeting to arriving pilgrims (Ps. 84:5-6, 12; 128:1). Series of woes or curses are found in the prophets (Isa. 5:8-23), but beatitudes or blessings occur at most in doublets (Ps. 84:5-6 etc.; somewhat more elaborated in Ecclus. 25:7-10). With the exception of the Greek text of Ecclesiastes 10:16-17, they are never associated with woes. Both, however, are found in the proclamation of the Law, where the contrasted terms are "blessed" and "cursed" (Deut. 27:15 ff.; 28:1 ff., 15 ff.). The collocation in Matthew of nine, in Luke of four beatitudes supplemented by a corresponding series of woes suggests a further development of the form, like that found in Jewish literature of the time of Jesus dealing with the imminence of the eschaton (e.g., Slavonic Enoch 42 and 52).

2

In the Old Testament, beatitudes in the second person are rare. Not until the Jewish apocalyptic literature just mentioned do we find an example resembling the sayings of Jesus as recorded in Luke 6:20-21: "Blessings on you elect and righteous, for glorious will be your lot!" (Eth. Enoch 58:2) In the New Testament, however, the second person is found elsewhere as well (Matt. 13:16; 16:17). We may assume this was the form Jesus used, for the saying in Matthew 5:11-12 is likewise formulated in this way, although the preceding eight Beatitudes have already been recast into the usual third-person form. This shows that Luke 6:20-21 has preserved the ancient form, using direct address. In this special time of God's favor, distinguished from any other by the ministry of Jesus, the Beatitudes are addressed directly to those now standing in Jesus' presence. We are no longer dealing with rules formulated in the third person, valid for every man in every age, but with the direct promise of salvation to all who can hear.

3

All the Old Testament and Jewish examples mention the recipient of the blessing in a relative or participial clause: "Blessings on him who lives in such a way," or "Blessings on the man living in such a way." Only the quotation from Ethiopic Enoch already mentioned comes anywhere close to the sayings of Jesus. In the original form (Luke 6:20-21), Jesus proclaims blessings on all who are poor, who hunger, who weep, without the addition of any conditions that men must first fulfill.

4

Old Testament wisdom speaks of the earthly happiness that will be granted the blessed; later on, those who will live to see the coming age of salvation are called blessed. With the exception of Ethiopic Enoch 58:2, Jesus' Beatitudes are totally new in taking a future blessing and declaring it as right now present.

5

All that has been said applies also to the rather infrequent blessings found in Greek literature. They, too, do not occur in series, and are usually phrased in the third person, the common form being "Blessings on him who . . . !" As a rule these are wisdom aphorisms intended to show the way to earthly happiness. Only in the mystery religions are they sometimes used to indicate a broader type of blessing or salvation.

Thus the blessings pronounced by Jesus differ from their prototypes. No longer are there conditions to be met before someone can be called blessed. The question is not really raised as to who will receive blessings, but rather how it is with all those on this earth who are poor, who hunger, who weep. For all those poor enough to have ears to hear, Jesus promises blessings, and with an authority that establishes future fulfillment in the present. Therefore the Beatitudes are formulated as direct address, in the second person. Divorced from this presence of Jesus' authority and the hearing it evokes, considered as universally applicable rules saying that everyone who is badly off now will be all the better off hereafter, the Beatitudes would be untrue.

But when Jesus' promise goes forth and is heard, the person who receives it is made new and whole, because in Jesus' blessing the future Kingdom of God has come upon him.

[11-12] The last Beatitude differs markedly from the others. It is much longer, is formulated in the second person, and presupposes persecution of the disciples. They, rather than Jesus (as in 23:37; but cf. 23:34) are compared to the prophets. This Beatitude has therefore been subject to later expansion, although it already appears in Q (Luke 6:22-23).

[2-10] The other eight Beatitudes comprise two groups of four, which agree even with respect to the number of words in each. The second group extols more highly the actions of men rather than the mere fact of their suffering. The first, second, and fourth Beatitudes appear in similar form in Luke 6:20-23, which means they already formed part of Q.

[4] Matthew has assimilated the second to Isaiah 61:2-3: "mourn" instead of "weep," "be comforted" instead of "laugh." This also explains why Matthew places this Beatitude second, whereas Luke places it third: Isaiah 61:1 begins with the proclamation of joy to the poor, and adds comfort for those who mourn in verse 2. The first two Beatitudes are therefore looked upon as fulfilling the prophetic promises and are assimilated to the Biblical wording. In other instances, also, Isaiah 61:1-3 played an important role in the community of Jesus (Luke 4:18-19; cf. Matt. 11:5; possibly James 4:9-10); it may have been suggested in this case also because it is immediately preceded (Isa. 60:21) by the same statement as that made here in verse 5. All this must antedate Matthew, for the corresponding curse in Luke 6:25 combines both forms: "they will mourn and weep," and the promise of comfort has left its mark on the first curse, in Luke 6:24. The saying was therefore current in two forms before both Matthew and Luke. It is also possible to account for these observations by the reverse course of development: two muted echoes of Isaiah 61:2, accidentally separated, cropped up first in the two curses that now constitute Luke 6:24 and 25; when brought together in Matthew 5:4, the echo of Isaiah 61:2 became plain, and the sayings were once again made positive— blessings parallel to Isaiah 61:1 and 2. This explanation, however, is most unlikely.

That means that the curses are a later development than the assimilation of this Beatitude to the Old Testament text (see below). The curse in Luke 6:26 also is formulated in a way that exhibits similarities to Matthew 5:11, but not to the corresponding blessing in Luke 6:22: "speak well of you" (Luke 6:26) and "tell all kinds of evil (lies) against you" (Matt. 5:11). If this is not accidental, at the time when the curses (like Luke 6:26) were being formulated there may have been a variant current that was closer to the Matthaean form. It is conceivable that Jesus framed his words with conscious reference to Isaiah 61, and that this echo was dropped by Luke except in the curses; but the assimilation to Isaiah 61 is more likely a later elaboration, like the Old Testament influences in verses 5 and 8, the details of verse 3, and probably also the formulation in the third person.

It is more difficult to reach conclusions about the five Beatitudes not found in Luke. [5] The promise to the humble might be merely a variant of the promise to the poor; both words are almost identical in Aramaic. In Syriac manuscripts, where this is also true, this Beatitude follows the first directly, probably for this very reason. The second clauses are identical in content, for the earth that the humble will inherit is none other than the Kingdom of heaven, since the latter is to be realized on the new earth.

The promises in the Psalms have undoubtedly been very influential: Psalm 37:11 in verse 5, Psalm 24:3-4 in verse 8. And the development of the other Beatitudes as well can probably be accounted for on the basis of Psalm texts. Psalm 37 played an important role in the community of the "poor," in the Jewish community at Qumran (4QpPs 37). Here we find the themes of hungering and being satisfied linked with the theme of righteousness (vss. 19 and 12 [cf. Matt. 5:6]), the theme of righteousness linked with that of mercy (vs. 21 [cf. Matt. 5:7]), and the theme of inheriting the earth (vs. 22 [cf. Matt. 5:5]). And in the blessing of Aaron (Num. 6:25-26) God's countenance, mercy, and peace are juxtaposed (cf. Matt. 5:7-9). Mark 9:50 may have set its stamp on verse 9, and verse 10 is a shorter form of the material in verses 11-12.

Undoubtedly the three Beatitudes in Luke 6:20-21 are the earliest. At least the first and probably all three go back in their paradoxical form to Jesus himself. For only issuing from his mouth, only on the assumption that it is God himself who is speaking, are these words comprehensible. In the second and third, the "now" (lacking in the first) that strongly contrasts the dark present with the glowing future, has been added as an afterthought, probably by Luke himself (cf. 16:19-31). In Matthew, the change to the third person (see the excursus on the Beatitudes above, §2) and the assimilation to Isaiah 61:2 (see the discussion of vs. 4 above) go back to the community. [6] The addition of "righteousness" corresponds to Matthew's prevailing interests (vss. 10, 20; 6:33); and the expansion of "hunger" to "hunger and thirst" is an assimilation to Old Testament language (Ps. 107:9; Isa. 49:10; 65:13; Amos 8:11; cf. John 6:35). [3] The expansion of "poor" to "poor in spirit" is also a later gloss; according to Matthew 11:5, the words of which go back to Isaiah 61:1, Jesus preaches his good news simply to the poor without further qualification.

We may ask whether the five Beatitudes that do not occur in Luke represent a variant that likewise concluded with a promise to the persecuted (Matt. 5:10; Luke 6:22). It is far more likely that the original three Beatitudes were supplemented by the addition of others derived from Psalm quotations or Jesus' own words. It is possible that the first group of four was formed first by the interpolation of verse 5; the subjects in each case begin in Greek with the letter *p*. Later, perhaps, a group of seven was formed, without verse 10, because a pattern based on sevens appears to crop up occasionally in the pre-Matthaean tradition.

The evangelist would then finally have composed verse 10 on the basis of verses 11-12. The Greek form "persecuted" expresses even more strongly than verse 11 a situation already come to pass, thus indicating in any case the post-Easter period. The theme of righteousness is important to Matthew (see the discussion of 5:20), and the repeated promise of the Kingdom of heaven from the first Beatitude completes the structure. The theme of this last Beatitude is already provided by verses 11-12, but becomes more pressing in Matthew's own period, as 10:15-39 shows. Furthermore, the catchword "persecute," which both Beatitudes have in common, appears only in the version of Matthew, not that of Luke. The language of the later Beatitudes is that of the later Christian community; cf. 1 Peter 3:4 (tranquility); 2:10 (mercy); 1:22 (purity of heart); 1:8 (seeing God);

3:11 (Matt. 5:9); 3:14 (Matt. 5:10); 4:14 (Matt. 5:11); 4:13 (Matt. 5:12).

Did the curses in Luke (see the excursus on the Beatitudes above, §1) form part of the sayings from the very beginning? Matthew, it might be argued, left them out because he is more concerned with instructions for proper conduct than with prophetic repudiation. But several facts undercut the idea that the curses are early. First, they do not appear in Luke until after 6:22-23, in other words, after the highly elaborated promise to those who are persecuted, which is certainly a later supplement. Then too, they are not really appropriate to a discourse addressed to disciples, so that Luke has to start all over again in verse 27. And last, they presuppose the alteration of the Beatitude addressed to those who weep (see the discussion of vs. 4 above). The curses thus constitute a kind of interpretation of the original sayings, stating expressly to whom they are addressed and to whom not.

[11] In the promise to the persecuted, Matthew, who thinks only in terms of defamation, appears to set forth an earlier stage of development than Luke, who already presupposes the expulsion of the Christians from the synagogue. It is possible that both variants go back to a single Aramaic original. This might explain the differing forms taken by the concluding phrase. In this case Matthew would have taken "who were before you" as referring to the prophets, while Luke thought it referred to the persecutors and therefore translated it as "for so their fathers [those who were before you] did to the prophets." The reading "for righteousness' sake," which occurs only in a few manuscripts, is probably a secondary borrowing from verse 10; the same manuscripts omit the gloss "falsely," probably as being obvious when someone is being persecuted "for righteousness' sake."

Thus the first three Beatitudes in the form of Luke 6:20-21 (without the "now") probably go back to Jesus. Even before Matthew, they were expanded in Q by the addition of an extended Beatitude addressed to those who are persecuted for Jesus' sake (Luke 6:22-23). There was an accretion of similar sayings, based especially on echoes of Old Testament passages (Matt. 5:5, 7-9 and 10). Finally, they were interpreted in two ways: either by a series of curses identifying those to whom the Beatitudes did not apply (Luke 6:24-26) or by more precise identification of those to whom they did (Matt. 5:3, 6). It is possible that Matthew took what had originally been a series of seven, added one element, and transformed the whole into two series of four, at the same time appending a conclusion that was theologically important to him (Matt. 5:10). For the theological significance of this development, see the conclusion below.

[3] At the time of Jesus, the term "poor" is never used in a merely figurative sense, independent of social class. But as early as Isaiah 61:1 the terms "poor" and "brokenhearted" or "broken in spirit" are juxtaposed (cf. Prov. 16:19; 29:23; Ps. 34:19). In the Judaism of Jesus' time "poor" had also become a kind of title of honor for the righteous (Ps. Sol. 5:2, 11; 10:7; 15:1; 18:2 [first centuryB.C.]), because it was an important mark of righteousness and devotion to accept in faith the difficult way of God and not resist. At the time of Deutero-Isaiah, "poor" was still a term applied to all Israel, deprived of its own land and living among aliens; in the centuries that followed, the social class of the poor began to apply this term to themselves as distinct from the upper classes. Thus "poor" and "righteous" became largely parallel concepts (Ecclus. 13:17-18; 4QpPs. 37 ii. 8-11; CD xix. 9). Finally, at Qumran we find a formula most closely resembling the one in Matthew: "poor [or 'humble'] of spirit" (1QM xiv. 6-7); these are people who "have knowledge of God," and he "gives firm stance to those whose knees are weak and upright posture to those whose backs are broken," so that they may "walk perfectly" (cf. Matt. 5:48).

It is no longer possible to distinguish clearly whether "poor in spirit" means that they are poor because the Spirit of God has made them so or because their human spirit feels thus. The terms they apply to themselves, "the poor of grace," "the poor of your redemption," "the poor who have accepted the time of tribulation" (1QH v. 22; 1QM xi. 9; 4QpPs. 37 ii. 9-10) are open to both interpretations. In Matthew, we should probably translate it "poor with respect to spirit," the immediate reference being the human spirit, as in the parallel formula "pure with respect to their heart" (vs. 8). But as in Mark 14:38 (=Matt. 26:41) and in Psalm 51:12 the (willing) spirit of man is to be identified with the Holy Spirit given by God (Ps. 51:11). Matthew's choice of "spirit" rather than "soul" or "heart," terms abundantly familiar to him, or circumlocutions like those in 6:4, 6, 18 shows that he is still aware of this connection. Probably he has in mind people whose outward circumstances force them to look to God for everything, but who also receive from God the gift of the spirit (faith) to look to him for everything. As at Qumran, this has nothing to do with a submissiveness that no longer ventures to act (see vss. 13-16).

Jesus' original promise is addressed simply to the "poor." Any suggestion that man must first do something is avoided. Salvation is promised to all the poor, not just to those who are aware of their condition or accept it humbly. God is on the side of all of them, taking the part of the wretched just as the judges of the Old Testament did. They are all under the King's protection and are the objects of his mercy because it is God's royal prerogative to uphold the powerless. How paradoxical this Beatitude is becomes all the more striking. The poor are to be happy simply because someone, who is as poor as they are, tells them to be—without altering their circumstances a jot. Scarcely the most compelling of statements. And the only reason Jesus can give them is to say that theirs is the Kingdom of God. Which, of course, is in the future, and in fact all the reasons Jesus gives are cast in future form.

But Jesus is not simply a fanatical dreamer, using enthusiastic religiosity to gloss over poverty, misery, and hunger. He is well aware that everything depends on God's redeeming these pledges. But as Jesus speaks them—because of the quality of his love in speaking —the future Kingdom approaches, therefore his hearers are already "saved," assured of God's care. Therefore, of course, everything also depends on the fact that God's authority stands behind Jesus; without it, he would be ridiculous. Jesus' view is that *every* kind of defect, every lack, is poverty in the eyes of God; and so his promise is made to anyone who can hear him, for the very act of listening presupposes some need that takes God's promise seriously. The hearer who listens knows his need, and repents it.

The theme of repentance has already been sounded—in the Baptist's onslaught against smugness, and in the temptation narrative, which in Q precede the three Beatitudes. Whoever can hear Jesus' promise bids farewell to certainty, not only in outward wealth but also in spiritual treasure of the Pharisaic kind (3:7-12). Undoubtedly Jesus' promise to the poor is made without qualification; undoubtedly, too, its truth depends on its being spoken by one in whom God himself has suddenly entered the world. Thus these Beatitudes fall into the class of most of the New Testament beatitudes, which depict the unique eschatological age that dawns in Jesus (Matt. 11:6; 13:16; also 16:17; Luke 1:45; 12:37-43; cf. a kind of modification in Luke 11:27/28; for Judaism, see §1 of the excursus above on the Beatitudes).

Only to one who can hear the Beatitudes and hear in them his own lack do they make sense: such a person knows very well that being poor necessarily means being "poor in spirit." By his amendment of the phrase Matthew has made a most significant change—his version points out the danger of thinking that poverty is an honor. Poverty is not a virtue; it should no more be boasted about by the poor than despised (and upheld) by the rich. Matthew has been more insightful about what Jesus said than Luke, who merely translates Jesus' dictum literally into Greek. In Luke the statement becomes simply the legalism that in heaven all conditions are reversed, so that the poor become rich and the rich poor. Matthew, by contrast, has retained the point that this saying becomes true only when the mystery takes place that the Old Testament calls an event of the "Spirit." A modern Jewish philosopher, Martin Buber, has said that the words of the Bible must never be isolated from the situation in which they were spoken; this applies with special force to the words of Jesus. Only in the emotional transaction occurring between Jesus and his hearers do his words become true. Matthew wished to derail the mere mechanical response to Jesus' words (the assumption of poverty as a ticket to heaven), so he added the phrase "in spirit," to emphasize the inner quality of Jesus' appeal.

[4] Blessings are pronounced on those who mourn, not those who mourn their sins, as the rabbis say. According to Matthew one hates sin and forsakes it; one does not mourn it. Neither, however, is there any reference to those who mourn the damnation of unbelievers, as a later Christian document suggests (Syr. Didascalia v. 14. 22). According to Matthew, one calls on unbelievers to hear, but understands the judgment threatened against them also as a warning against oneself.

As in Isaiah 61:2, all kinds of misery are meant, whether physical or psychic in origin (cf. Ps. 126:5; Rev. 7:17). Once more, in other words, it is stated that God is present where he is needed. This, too, is not a universal rule, like the aphorism that trouble teaches men to pray. Indeed, that is counter to all experience: more frequently, trouble teaches men to curse, complain, grow bitter, or persecute. As a general maxim, it is simply wrong. Those who mourn very often are not comforted.

The way Matthew understands it may be seen from 9:15: only in the presence of Jesus is it true to say that mourning is overcome. This was the meaning in the pre-Matthaean tradition, which was shaped by the messianic passage Isaiah 61:1-2 (see the discussion of vs. 4 above). In later Judaism the messiah was even called the "comforter" on account of this passage; but Matthew 5:4, like Isaiah 12:1; 49:13; 51:3, 12; 52:9; etc., expects the comfort from God himself. Once more the statement is a direct address, a promise calling for belief, seeking a hearing that is something more than mere taking cognizance, as of a mathematical postulate or a universally valid proverb. The statement becomes true for whoever will let Jesus tell him that in this very moment God is becoming reality, just as the prophets expected in God's eschaton. In the Lukan recension, reinforced by the interpolation of "now," lurks once more the misapprehension that a universally applicable rule is being stated about how all suffering in this world will be compensated by reward in the next. Matthew runs in danger of the opposite misunderstanding, that men must first show by their attitude that they are worthy of salvation; this is the error suggested by James 4:9-10, where "mourning" means a kind of moral humility (cf. also the discussion of Matt. 9:15).

[5] The third Beatitude refers to the "humble." The Greek world, too, extolled the humility of wise men and rulers. This humility, as Plato says of Socrates, is true divinity. Jewish writers who were educated in Greek culture, like Philo and Josephus, borrowed this idea; but in Palestine, too, there circulated anecdotes depicting the humility of Rabbi Hillel (shortly before Jesus). But in Jesus this attitude is not like the wisdom of a philosopher or ruler seeking to avoid hubris, presumption. In the language of Jesus, the word can hardly be distinguished from "poor." It has echoes of "insignificant, lowly," and may perhaps best be rendered "powerless." It has nothing to do with

weakness: but the strength these powerless ones have is derived from love rather than fear.

The term "humble" occurs in this sense only in Matthew (11:29; 21:5, applied to Jesus) and 1 Peter 3:4. Matthew looks upon Jesus himself as the true example of such "humility." What is meant is that the poor and those who mourn, on whom blessings are pronounced in the first two Beatitudes, are also those who are powerless—they do not have power, but they do not need it, for, resting their entire hope on God, they attempt not to overbear others but to serve them. This variant of the first Beatitude (see introduction) accordingly exhibits a more markedly catechetical interest from the very outset; it is meant to exhort the community to live as if Jesus' promise—that they will inherit the earth—had already come true. They should serve one another according to the rule of love, without regard to any consequences of reward or punishment.

The promise of possessing or inheriting the earth (the land) referred in the Old Testament first to the land of Canaan (Gen. 17:8), then to the whole earth, which will one day be the site of God's Kingdom (cf. also James 2:5-6). But God's dwelling place is heaven; men are appointed to earth. From these two notions there developed in Israel two distinct expectations for the future. On the one hand, there was hope for an earthly kingdom in which God himself would reign and all the nations would serve Israel or be absorbed into her. It is worth stressing that we are not dealing merely with political wish-fulfillment, but with a world transformed by God, and thus in a sense "transcendent" (Isa. 65:17; 66:22; 2 Pet. 3:13). On the other hand, there was the hope of being taken up bodily into heaven, as was vouchsafed Enoch and Elijah. The two ideas are really not very far apart, and therefore occur in juxtaposition in both verses 3 and 5. Both notions express something important in Biblical thought. On the one hand, God's future will not negate his creation; what he has created and done in history will be brought by him to a significant goal. On the other hand, this will not be the result of human efforts and historical processes, but will be entirely God's doing. It follows that both the Old and the New Testament are deeply interested in what is taking shape on this earth: God is controlling history, and God will bring his Kingdom about in the events on this earth. Therefore our Gospel closes with authority given to Jesus "in heaven and on earth" (28:18), and the Matthaean community prays that God's will be done "on earth as it is in heaven" (6:10).

[6] In Luke 6:21 blessings are pronounced on the hungry and they are promised satisfaction. In Matthew, however, as in Old Testament passages, we find "hunger and thirst" (see the discussion of vs. 6 above). This is not a major difference, but the addition of "for righteousness" (see the excursus on 3:15) is. This term, which does not occur at all in Mark, is used seven times by Matthew; Luke uses it only once (1:75), in a psalm with marked Old Testament affinities, to characterize the promised divine age. The evidence therefore suggests that Matthew added the expression.

The Old Testament frequently uses "hungering" and "thirsting" as metaphors for yearning after God's word (Amos 8:11), mercy (Isa. 55:1-2, 7), and presence (Ps. 42:3). The poor and lowly are promised that their hunger will be satisfied (1 Sam. 2:5; Ps. 107:36-41; 146:7); in the Judaism of Jesus' period (Psalms of Solomon and Testaments of the Twelve Patriarchs) hunger is interpreted as God's beneficent chastisement. According to Baruch 2:18, only the "soul that hungers" can extol God's glory and righteousness. Of course Jesus does not commend a particular group of the devout or even those who hunger for social justice, as in Luke. The Beatitude is an expression of salvation, inviting all to hear, and bringing those who do hear within the circle of God's salvation. On the basis of 5:20, we may say that Matthew was mainly interested in bringing God's righteousness to practical fruit in his community. When, therefore, he came to a saying that spoke of "hungering" (and "thirsting"), he added the catchword "righteousness."

Against the Old Testament background, this refers first of all to yearning for the coming Kingdom and the righteousness of God that will be realized in it: hungering for righteousness means a longing for the one who will bring justice to those suffering from violence (Ps. 146:7, associated with the "kingship" [="Kingdom"] of God in vs. 10), an appeal for "new heavens and a new earth, where righteousness will be at home" (2 Pet. 3:13). But even though Matthew urged the establishment of this righteousness by the disciples, still, as a Jew dieted on the Old Testament he could hardly forget that the real fulfillment of righteousness will be God's eschatological act. This is described as the satisfaction of hunger. Jesus, who spoke of eating and drinking at the banquet table in the coming Kingdom (22:1 ff.; Luke 22:30), was not so much worried that such hopes would be understood too literally as that they would pale into a commonplace and no longer bring joy.

[7] A call to be merciful is also found in the Sermon on the Plain (Luke 6:36; cf. the discussion of Matt. 5:48) and in even briefer form in 1 Clement 13:2 and Polycarp 2:3: "Show mercy that you may receive mercy" (cf. James 2:13). This means that traditional material used, for example, in instruction, has here been cast in the form of a Beatitude.

For Matthew, mercy is the focal point of Jesus' message, which shows what it means to fulfill the Law (see the discussion of 5:17-20; 9:13; 12:7; 25:31-46). Mercy has been forgotten by the Pharisees (23:23; unique to Matthew). It is not limited to generosity in almsgiving. Luke 6:36 maintains that all human acts of mercy derive from God's mercy. This is true above all in Jesus' parable of the unforgiving servant (Matt. 18:23-24). The important point to Matthew, however, is the statement that no one can count on God's mercy who does not himself show mercy (18:35; likewise James 2:13). That is Matthew's commentary on the Lord's Prayer (see the discussion of 6:14-15). Thus the fifth Beatitude resembles the statement that human mercy triumphs over God's judgment (James 2:13) and the rabbinic statement that the heavens have mercy on him who in turn shows mercy to men. The Greek word for "merciful" occurs only here and in Hebrews 2:17 (applied to Christ) in the New Testament, but occurs frequently in the Greek Old Testament. Thus we catch sight once more of a Jewish community, familiar with the term, behind the Gospel of Matthew.

[8] As 1 Timothy 1:5 and 2 Timothy 2:22 show, Christian exhortation also made good use of the Old Testament term "pure heart." Just as Matthew contrasts mercy to the purely outward performance of cultic acts (9:13; 12:7), so Judaism saw purity of heart in obedience to God rather than ritual sacrifice. Passages such as 1 Samuel 15:22; Isaiah 1:10-17; Jeremiah 7:3-7 led to the demand for circumcision of the heart in contrast to the purely ritual circumcision of the cult

(Deut. 10:16; 30:6; Jer. 4:4; 9:25-26; 1QS v. 4; 1QpHab xi. 13 [1QH xviii. 20?]; Rom. 2:29; cf. also Ezek. 11:19). As a rule, of course, pure hands and a pure heart are mentioned side by side, as in Psalm 24:3-5 (cf. also 51:10), which lists the conditions to be fulfilled for admittance by those who wish to climb the mountain of the Lord and stand in the holy place (i.e., the Temple); the pure heart is described as meaning that the person in question is not embarked upon a course of evil and does not deceive his neighbor.

The heart is therefore not only the seat of the emotions but also a person's innermost being, which shapes his entire life, often unconsciously. A similar view is found at Qumran (cf. the discussion of 3:8). What Matthew has in mind is thus a "simple" (6:22; Rom. 12:8) heart, set on God—what he elsewhere calls "faith" (see the discussion of 14:31), and what Paul calls innocence and purity (2 Cor. 1:12; Phil. 1:10; 2:15). This can apply to one's attitude toward women (Matt. 5:28), toward money (6:21-22), or toward one's own words (5:37). It stands in contrast to the outward purity brought about by cultic means (23:26). Thus verse 8 calls into question all the cultic practices of the Jews and of the gentiles, with their sacrifices and propitiations (cf. the discussion of Mark 7:15). And, as the location of it between verses 7 and 9 shows, it has to do essentially with conduct toward one's neighbor.

The vision of God, which at present is impossible to man (Isa. 6.5), is promised for the eschatological age, when unclouded communion will be established between God and man (Rev. 22:4; 1 Cor. 13:12); such is now granted only to the angels (Matt. 18:10). To see God as he is is what faith hopes for (1 John 3:2). It comprehends everything that men call salvation, life, glory. Furthermore, God is mentioned explicitly here only in verses 8–9; in all the other Beatitudes, in line with the practice of Judaism in Jesus' period, there is merely a veiled suggestion of God as the unnamed author of the promise.

[9] In verse 9, too, we have traditional material from Christian preaching in the background. In James 3:18, in precise tally between act and reward, peacemakers are promised peace. A similar blessing, associated with a curse, also occurs in Jewish tradition (Slav. Enoch 52:11-13). This is the only occurrence of the noun "peacemaker" in

the Bible (the verb is found in Prov. 10:10; Col. 1:20). It refers to men who are not only peaceful, but "make peace" (a rabbinic expression). In the Judaism of the period, the call to make peace is as important as the law of love is in the New Testament. Shortly after the destruction of the Temple, Johanan ben Zakkai, the foremost rabbi of that period, promised the salvation that could formerly be obtained only by a sacrifice at the altar to whoever made peace. "Peace" is the everyday form of salutation, and in the Old Testament it encompasses all God's benefits. Whoever has peace is at peace with God. "Prince of Peace" is one of the titles of the messiah (Isa. 9:6); and Isaiah 52:7, which speaks of God's messenger proclaiming peace, was interpreted messianically by Judaism, probably as early as the time of Jesus. It is important not to idealize these peacemakers; they do not always prevail in the midst of violence.

Sons of God. The peacemakers are promised they will be God's sons. Jesus spoke of "the Father" and "my Father" (cf. the discussion of Mark 14:36 and 15:39), and probably also on occasion of "your Father." This is by no means an unheard-of usage, either for Jesus or for the Old Testament and Judaism. What is new is the distinction between "my Father" (referring to Jesus) and "your Father." Jesus never includes himself with all men in a common "our Father"; for even Matthew 6:9 is limited to the disciples, whom Jesus is teaching to pray in this fashion. There is, however, no occurrence of "my Father" in Mark, and "your Father" appears only in Mark 11:25, in a form strikingly reminiscent of Matthew. Both are infrequent in Q as well ("my Father" in Matt. 11:27 and possibly Luke 22:29; "your Father" in Matt. 5:48; 6:32; just possibly in Luke 12:32). Luke and above all Matthew use both expressions side by side, without confusing them. In any case, Jesus primarily addressed God as his own Father (Mark 14:36); that he should teach his disciples, following his lead, to address God as their father, is unheard-of.

The Bible refers to people as sons or children of God only with great reserve. Except for Paul and John, it is universally maintained that divine sonship is a gift that will only be granted at the Last Judgment, for eternal life (cf. Hos. 1:10, cited in Rom. 9:26-27; Jub. 1:24-28). According to Revelation (21:7), the believer will one day be what the exalted Christ is now, God's Son (2:18). Then Psalm 2, which speaks of the Son of God, will apply to him as it now applies to Christ (Rev. 2:26-28).

The first three Gospels speak of divine sonship in the same way. Only in the saying about loving one's enemies (Matt. 5:44-45), is there the suggestion that this miracle can take place on earth if a person grows into total obedience and becomes like God in his actions (see the discussion of the passage). This is in fact the only place in the first three Gospels where the terms "Father" and "sons" are even used together (elsewhere only with reference to God and Jesus: Mark 13:32; Matt. 11:27, and parallels). Matthew is fond of adding the phrase "in heaven" to the term "Father," thus recalling the miraculous aspect of this form of address—a miraculous aspect which is underlined in Mark, in Q, and in Luke's special material by the rarity of the term "Father" (see the discussion of Matt. 6:9). Matthew stresses the uniqueness of Jesus' sonship in 1:18-25 (cf. 2:15), and again in 14:33; 16:16 (cf. 4:3 and 11:27=Q).

Down to the time of Matthew, then, Jesus and his disciples still stand within the tradition of the Old Testament, where consciousness of the unmerited covenant, granted as a gift of God's grace, inhibits the use of the term "Father," which was employed by the neighboring peoples to express something like an obvious relationship between God and men on the basis of creation. Like Isaiah and Jeremiah, the evangelists see in it the miracle of God's mercy and forgiveness. For similar reasons, John distinguishes the "children" of God (1:12) from the one "Son"; and Paul makes it clear that only through faith in Jesus and participation in his Spirit do we become sons (Gal. 4:4-7; Rom. 8:3, 14-17). Thus Matthew 5:9, too, refers unambiguously to the miracle of communion with God that is to be granted the peacemaker at the Last Judgment through God's authoritative word, which transforms him ("will be called").

[10] That the persecuted are among God's favorites is widely stressed in the Judaism of Jesus' time. Psalms that speak of the sufferings of the righteous contain this idea (Psalm 22; also 34:19-20; more clearly in Wis. 2:10-20; cf. the discussion of Matt. 27:43). First Peter 3:14, which speaks of suffering "for doing what is right," and 4:13-14,

where the key words "blessings," "insult," "be glad," and "be happy" (Matt. 5:11-12) occur, show that a statement like that in Matthew 5:10 or 11-12 was familiar in various forms. In contrast to verse 6, "righteousness" occurs here without the article, perhaps because the writer has in mind the various forms of expression in which "righteousness" becomes concrete (see the excursus on 3:15). The promise of the Kingdom of God concludes the entire series, as it began it in verse 3. Thus all eight Beatitudes are permeated by God's "yes" to those who are dependent on him and wait for him, a "yes" that becomes reality in each Beatitude because of Jesus' presence, although the visible fulfillment of the promise rests solely in God's hands and will not be realized until the coming of his Kingdom.

[11] This final and much more detailed promise is a late inclusion; by it, Matthew specifies just where Jesus' promise becomes a reality: it becomes a reality right now, in the community, in the very teeth of oppressors. The use of the second person anticipates the transition to verses 13–16. The passage reflects a period when the community was still only the victim of verbal abuse (physical abuse came later). But Jews considered defamation extraordinarily vicious; the rabbis thought it as evil as idolatry, fornication, and the shedding of blood all put together. Its victim lost his place in the community and hence, under the circumstances of that day, almost the possibility of staying alive. Here, too, there is no idealization; we are not dealing with martyrdom, which can be transfigured by legend. Once again the passage extols not the strong, who, to the admiration of all, heroically defend their faith, but those who are defamed and go down to ignominious defeat. Of course there is the mincing addition that this holds only if the defamation is untrue. The same reservation appears in 1 Peter 2:19-20; 4:15-16 (see also the discussion of verse 10), and goes back to bad experiences the community had had with impostors going under the guise of the Christian faith (see the discussion of 7:15-29).

[12] What is implied in the "blessing" formula is here described more pointedly as being "glad and happy," and is thus removed from the purely religious sphere. This makes it clear how concretely the hearing and acceptance of Jesus' promise is supposed to affect one's

life. Here again we are not dealing with some profound spirituality reserved for those who are religious, but with wholeness of heart (see the discussion of vs. 8). The heart is to live from Jesus' words, and all its utterances are to take on a radiance; not in the sense of modest contentment, which knows there is more happiness in a cottage than a palace, but in the sense of clear and critical hope. This hope is faith that God's future is the goal of human life.

On the idea of reward, which is mentioned quite unashamedly, see the discussion of 20:1-6 and Mark 9:41. The comparison with the fate of the prophets does not mean that only the twelve, as opposed to ordinary disciples, are being addressed, but just the opposite: every disciple of Jesus to whom verses 13-16 apply is a prophet of God. Joel 3:1-2; Jeremiah 31:34; Isaiah 54:13 (=John 6:45) predicted God's reward in the eschaton; what was merely a wish in Numbers 11:29, namely that all of God's people were prophets, is now fulfilled (see the excursus *Prophets* on 7:13-23). Their fate is the violent fate of the prophets. That their reward awaits them "in heaven" means that God has undoubtedly so determined (2 Esdras 7:83; 13:56; cf. Eth. Enoch 108:10).

The formal uniqueness of Jesus' Beatitudes has already been made clear (see excursuses 1 and 4 on 5:3-12). There is a striking absence of any injunction to observe the Law, after the manner of the Pharisees, or to observe the cult, after the manner of the Sadducees. This is reminiscent of similar statements found in wisdom literature. What is dissimilar is the repeated emphasis on things eschatological. The only formal parallels are found in a blessing which refers to God's age of salvation (Eth. Enoch 58:2; see above). But the Beatitudes differ even here, for the salvation Jesus promises in the Beatitudes is not only future but present. Of course by pronouncing the Beatitudes, Jesus does not rob God of his place: God's own action will bring the Kingdom, comfort, inheritance, satisfaction. But Jesus speaks with the authority of God and promises joys on this every day to whoever can hear his words in inward application.

The original Beatitudes of Jesus extolled neither a particular religious attitude, for example devout submissiveness, nor a particular class; poverty is not glorified, the proletariat is promised no victory.

All depends on a particular event: Jesus' promise must be heard. Not simply those who seek God, but rather those who need God can hear this and are made happy in the promise of Jesus. In a way totally unexpected, expectations surrounding the coming of the messiah are fulfilled. Jesus does not simply turn expectation into wealth; rather, he endorses the waiting upon God that lets God remain God and therefore expects real fulfillment from his act to come. But Jesus is so firmly convinced of this coming God that he calls on men to hear and enter now into his assurance and thus be saved. Anyone who cannot hear God's call in Jesus' words can see this only as the delusion of a fanatic. But whether those Jesus calls are poor inwardly or outwardly, consciously or unconsciously, deservedly or undeservedly, willingly or unwillingly—that he leaves quite open, allowing them all.

More precise definitions came later. Q, like Matthew, underlined the significance of conversion that comes through hearing; Luke, on the other hand, with his "now," emphasized the fact that it is people who are really poor, hungry, and mourning that are addressed. Through additions to the first three Beatitudes and the inclusion of an additional five, Matthew stressed the inward attitude of those described and the resulting conduct. He maintained the position that Jesus' words are meant to be heard, to enter into the hearts of men, and to place their stamp on the entire lives of those who hear. Although he tinkered with Jesus' words more than Luke, Matthew remained more faithful to the message, which is concerned with outward acts as reflecting inward change (see the second section of the discussion of vs. 3 above).

Discipleship (5:13-16)

[13]"You are the salt of the earth. But if salt loses its taste, how can it be made salty again? It has become worthless, so it is thrown away and people walk on it. [14]You are the light of the world. A city built on a hill cannot be hid. [15]No one lights a lamp to put it under a bowl; instead he puts it on the lampstand, where it gives light for everyone in the house. [16]In the same way your light must shine before people, so that they will see the good things you do and give praise to your Father in heaven."

The saying about salt and the saying about the lampstand are also preserved elsewhere in different forms: the former in Mark 9:50 and Luke 14:34-35, the latter in Mark 4:21 (see the introduction to Mark 4:21-25) and Luke 8:16. The sayings have been assigned different positions. As pointed out in the commentary on Mark, the metaphors salt and light no doubt referred originally to Jesus' message, perhaps even to Jesus himself. The later application to the disciples is a frequently observed phenomenon (see the discussion of 16:23). This holds true even for Mark 9:50 ("Have salt in yourselves"); and according to Luke 14:33, the even more closely related saying in Luke 14:34-35 also refers to the disciples. Matthew makes the point explicit by bringing the two sayings together and adding brief introductions that mention the disciples directly: "You are the salt of the earth. . . . You are the light of the world . . . ." A Roman author states that there is nothing so necessary as salt and son; in Israel the Law can be described as salt and as light. This shows how appropriate the juxtaposition is. In parallel fashion, Mark 9:49-50 associates fire and salt.

[13] In form, Matthew 5:13 is closer to Luke 14:34-35; in contrast to Mark 9:50, both Matthew and Luke contain the expression "loses its taste" instead of "loses its saltness" (possibly because the Aramaic original was not translated precisely). In addition, Luke and Matthew both have the passive form "be made salty," and above all both have the addendum that speaks of discarding salt that has lost its savor.

[14-15] The saying about the lampstand was probably associated with that about the city on a hill even before Matthew; otherwise it would hardly be likely to interrupt the sequence of light and lampstand. In one papyrus and in the Gospel of Thomas (32) this saying appears with the additions that this city is strongly fortified and therefore cannot fall. That might suggest an early linkage of this metaphor with the eschatological prophecy that Mount Zion would "stand fast" and be higher than all other mountains, that instruction would go forth from it and that all nations would come to it because God's glory would serve as a light and a flaming fire (Isa. 2:2-5; 4:5-6; 60). Later, in this theory, the mountain came to be applied to the community of Jesus, which is firmly grounded and shall not fall (cf. 16:18). But all three variants speak only of *a* (not *the*) city upon *a* (not *the*) mountain or hill.

The association of the saying about the city with the one about the lampstand in the Gospel of Thomas suggests the two were thought of together before Matthew; on the other hand, Thomas may have derived his passage from Matthew. It is hard to determine the original form of the lampstand saying. Matthew mentions only the bowl; Mark 4:21 contains the later expansion "bowl or . . . bed," which Luke 8:16 has changed to "jar or . . . bed" and Luke 11:33 to "hiding place" (cf. "hide" in Luke 8:16) and "bowl." Strangely, therefore, Luke's version in 11:33 is closer to Mark's than to his own first use of the saying in (Luke) 8:16. In addition, both Lukan recensions agree in beginning with "No one lights a lamp and . . ." and in concluding with "that people may see the light as they come in." This last is reminiscent of the closing formula in Matthew 5:16, while 5:15 has the version similar to Luke's second one (11:33): "It gives light for everyone in the house." Only Matthew 5:15 contains the motif of lighting the lamp. Matthew accordingly interprets the saying thus: No one lights a lamp only to cover it again immediately with a bowl (used to extinguish lamps without making smoke). Whether this was the earliest form or represents a later development can hardly be determined. Perhaps the original form ran something like this: "No one places a lamp [or: 'No one lights a lamp and places it'] under a bowl, but on a lampstand." The meaning was clarified in two ways: on the one hand, by saying that the lamp then shines through the whole house or for everyone who enters; on the other, by images of hiding. **[16]** The summary, which incorporates the key word "light" from the Matthaean introduction (vs. 14), was probably formulated by Matthew, showing how he interprets the metaphors.

[13-16] In Matthew, the "earth" (vs. 13) and the "world" (vs. 14) simply refer to the totality of mankind (vs. 16). This is much like the Old Testament use of the term "earth" (Gen. 11:1; Matt. 10:34; Luke 12:49); the Greek-speaking community usually adopts the term "world" (as in Wis. 6:24; 10:1; 14:6; Mark 14:9; Matt. 13:38; 18:7; 1 Cor. 1:27-28). It is clear that according to Matthew the disciples are light (and salt) in their good works, but in such a way that these very works call attention not to themselves but to their Father in heaven (vs. 16). Three times the impression the disciples ("you," "your") make on the earth, the world, mankind is emphasized; but the response does not lead back to the disciples, but to their "Father in heaven." Perhaps we may see in the structure a deliberate Matthaean parallel to 16:17-19. The blessings conferred in the Beatitudes, to which Matthew adds the suggestion that the disciples are prophets (vss. 11-12), are followed, as in chapter 16, by recognition of their new character ("You are . . .") and a new commission (vss. 13-15 / 16). The traditional use of "salt" and "light" as symbols for the Law and God's covenant (see the discussion of vss. 13 and 14) suggests that the commission be interpreted as meaning that as God's prophets and Jesus' disciples they are to proclaim to the world their master's new interpretation of the Law and live according to it themselves (see §3 of the Retrospect).

[13] At the same time, there are overtones of a contrast between what is small and insignificant, and its great effect. What is the pinch of salt when compared to everything else, the flour and other ingredients? What are *you* (strongly emphasized in the Greek)—the poor, those who mourn, who hunger, who wait for God—in comparison to an entire world? Nevertheless the introduction talks of the world-remaking significance of this salt. Startling in its very commonplace, salt as a metaphor has behind it a rich growth of allusion—from the rabbinic likeness of the Law to salt, hence salt as a sign of God's covenant (Lev. 2:13; Num. 18:19; 2 Chron 13:5; cf. Acts 1:4, which reads literally that the risen Lord "took salt" with his disciples), and hence the purifier of sacrifices (Exod 30:35; Ezek. 16:4; 43:24) or whatever is spoiled or polluted (2 Kings 2:20 ff.), to simply the idea that food without salt is unappetizing (Job 6:6). These allusions would hint the foreignness of Jesus' disciples to the world, so that the disciples are seen not as gently influencing the world but as persevering even under persecution, or even if sacrificed completely (like the sacrificial salt of the cult, Mark 9:49!). This may distinguish the salt saying from the lamp saying, which places more emphasis on the active role played by the light; but this is not certain.

Attempts have been made to remove the paradox from the image of "saltless salt." Some have suggested translating "How can it (the earth) be made salty again?" This is completely impossible for Mark 9:50 and Luke 14:34, and almost so for Matthew 5:13, since only salt is mentioned both before and after. Others have suggested foreign substances in Palestinian salt, which remain behind when the salt is dissolved by moisture, or sheets of salt used by bakers and then discarded after a while when burned through. This is as absurd as attempts to take the edge off the saying about the beam in the eye (see the discussion of 7:3-5) or the camel going through the eye of a needle (see the discussion of Mark 10:25; other similar images are found in Matt. 6:3; 8:22). When a rabbi at Rome ridicules the question—what could make salt salty if it has lost its taste—by quipping, "The after-birth of a mule" (mules are sterile), it merely shows how well the daring images used by Jesus have done their work (see the discussion of 7:3).

It is possible that the saying of Jesus at one time attacked Israel as salt that had lost its taste. In this case, the sayings about the lamp and the city on a hill at one time called on Israel to be in fact what it claimed to be: the prophetical light of the nations and the city of Zion, towering above the world and attracting it.

[14] The imagery of light and lamps is used in the Old Testament for God (Ps. 18:28; Mic. 7:8; Isa. 60:1-3), in the rabbinic milieu for Israel, the Law, or the Temple, as well as individual great scholars (cf. Rom. 2:19), and in Matthew for Jesus (4:16). All this suggests that it is not the disciples who are to shine, but rather the Father in heaven, who is to shine through them. In Isaiah 42:6 the Servant of God as a covenant with one nation and a light to all others, points in the same direction. If the prophetic hopes for Zion in the eschaton stand in the background of the saying about the city on a hill (see above), that would also indicate special emphasis on the presence of God.

[15] To light a lamp only to place it at once under a bowl, in other words to extinguish it, is absurd. The lamp is there to give light to "everyone in the house"—the house in Palestine, as a rule, consisting of a single room. Once more the mission of the disciples to "all" is underlined.

In the context of Jesus' parables, the lampstand refers to Jesus' preaching (Mark 4:21 = Luke 8:16); in the context of Jesus' glorification and the saying about the sign of Jonah (Luke 11:33) it refers to Jesus himself (or possibly, if taken with vs. 34, the inner light of men). Matthew can hardly have had another meaning in mind, although he makes the saying refer to the disciples. To him they are, as it were, transparent, and reveal the light of the one who stands above them and gives all that they are. **[16]** So of course, the saying means something different from the cliché about not hiding your light under a bushel. What is rendered visible is not the man himself but only the "Father in heaven" (see the discussion of vs. 9). If works are truly good and not evil, they reveal their true agent (see the discussion of 6:1-4). But even this does not suffice; such works are to be done within the purview of "people," not within the seclusion of a brotherhood— so that all people may encounter God.

Thus the Beatitudes, which place so much emphasis on the poverty and the dependence upon God of those addressed, are here protected against misinterpretation. Jesus' disciples are not to wallow in inferiority complexes, withdraw from the world, and let it go its arrogant way. Even if the company of disciples is no more than a handful of salt to a mountain of flour, they are called upon to perform their works, so that their God, who is strong and rich and powerful, may permeate the world. On the one hand, Jesus says to each of his disciples, "You [already] are . . . ." This sets them apart from the Old Testament people, who are told, "[if you do certain things] You *shall be* to me a royal priesthood and a holy tribe." On the other, he throws the disciples a challenge—to *be* salt and to *be* light, and that to all the world. Without the challenge, Jesus' metaphors would engender only isolationism and arrogance. The disciples are to be a church that retains firm contours and is far from identical with the world, but they are still a "church for the world."

Jesus, Fulfillment of the Law (5:17-20)

[17]"Do not think that I have come to do away with the Law or the prophets. I have not come to do away with them but to fulfill them. [18]Amen, I tell you this: until heaven and earth pass away, the least point or smallest stroke of the Law will not pass away until all takes place. [19]So, then, whoever omits even one of these least commandments and teaches others to do the same will be called least in the Kingdom of heaven. But whoever obeys the Law and teaches others

to do the same will be great in the Kingdom of heaven.—[20]I tell you then, that you will be able to enter the Kingdom of heaven only if your righteousness is far greater than that of the teachers of the Law and the Pharisees."

[18] The saying about the inviolability of the Law down to the smallest stroke is preserved in similar terms in Luke 16:17: "It is easier for heaven and earth to disappear than for the smallest detail of the Law to be done away with." These were the words of a strict Jewish Christian community seeking to maintain absolute obedience to the letter of the Law, probably in opposition to a more liberal interpretation such as those represented by Stephen (cf. Acts 7:48 ff.; 8:1) and later by Paul (Gal. 2:2-6, 11-16; Acts 15).

The form "Amen, I tell you . . . will not . . . until . . ." is typical of statements concerning the eschaton and recurs frequently (cf. Mark 13:30; 14:25; Matt. 10:23; 5:26; John 13:38; Mark 9:1). "Amen" at the beginning of a sentence probably derives from the usage of Greek-speaking Judaism; of course this does not rule it out for Jesus, since much Greek was spoken in Palestine. In any case, it occurs only in his discourses, and one single doubtful passage (Test. Abr. A 8) might be influenced by them. If this is not the case, the community added the "Amen" later in order to express, as in Jeremiah 28:6, that Jesus spoke in full accord with the will of God and full obedience to it.

Presumably the saying originally concluded an eschatological discourse such as Mark 13:30-31 and was formulated according to the same pattern: "Amen, I tell you this: no point or stroke of the Law will pass away until (all) this takes place." The form in Luke 16:17, likewise dependent on Mark 13:30-31, was given to the saying as soon as it came to be transmitted alone, outside the context of the eschatological discourse. Because the phrase "until all this takes place" was now incomprehensible, the statement in Mark 13:31 about heaven and earth passing away was thought of. In this way the formulation of Luke 16:17 came to stress the importance of the Law even more. The Sayings Source, which throughout softens Jesus' criticism of the Law (Luke 11:42 conclusion), incorporated the statement in something like this form. Matthew, too, has dropped the association with an eschatological discourse, but he still knows the original conclusion. He must therefore give it a new interpretation. The Law does in fact remain in force down to its last letter, but it is only really fulfilled through Jesus and his community (see below).

[19] There is added a saying that makes a similar point. The threat that anyone who breaks "the least" commandment "will be called least in the Kingdom of heaven" is probably formulated this way only for the sake of parallelism; what is meant is probably not a place, however lowly, in the Kingdom of heaven, but in fact exclusion from it. The description of the punishment in words as close as possible to those used for the transgression is typical of such threats of judgment (cf. 1 Cor. 3:17). These probably go back to prophets in the primitive Christian community (see the excursus on 7:13-23, §2), who, with their announcement of imminent judgment, laid down the norms the Spirit of God imposed on his community, using the parallelism that had appeared already in the admonitions of wisdom literature.

First Corinthians 5:5 and Acts 5:5, 10 prove that such authoritative declarations of judgment could occasionally be followed by the death of the sinner, as may still be observed in Africa today. This suggests that verse 19, which is not typical of Matthew, was associated with verse 18 even before Matthew incorporated it. Just as according to verse 18 not the least point must drop from the Law, so according to verse 19, not even the least commandment can be ignored. This is made even more likely by the observation that what is mentioned is "omission," that is, assumption that a commandment does not apply in particular situations (see the discussion of 16:19), not "doing away with," as in verse 17. This schema, which combines a major thesis beginning with "Amen, I tell you this . . ." and two conditional sentences, usually antithetical, is found elsewhere in similar form (pre-Matthaean in 6:2-3, 5-6, 16-17; probably composed by Matthew in 12:31-32; 18:3-5, 10-14, 15-18).

If the saying about the "least place" were taken literally, it would mean gradation: transgression of the great commandments would exclude the transgressor from heaven, transgressions of the minor ones would merely reduce his status. Such a notion would have been completely alien to the Judaism of Jesus' time. To the conflict of the community over Law we find a distant parallel in the so-called Apostolic Decree (Acts 15:20, 28-29), which requires that the gentiles observe only the most fundamental requirements of the Law, though without suggesting any gradation assigned them in the Kingdom of heaven. The idea of ranking in heaven based on fidelity to the Law was one peculiar to the Syrian church. Paul, for example, did not authorize even the Apostolic Decree, diluted though it is compared with our passage from Matthew (5:19). Acts 21:25 and Galatians 2:6 show that Paul was not involved in any such edict; and 1 Corinthians 8:1 ff.; 10:23 ff.; and Romans 14:1 ff. All indicate that it was unknown to him, because he never mentions it even though he is discussing the very question of meat offered to idols.

[17] Matthew himself probably framed the first sentence as an introduction to this controversy. In exactly the same way, in altering the saying preserved in Luke 12:51, he added his own introduction in 10:34-35, "I have come to . . . ." It is possible that in 5:17 Matthew was softening—by making negative—the positive assertion by Jesus that he had come to bring the Law to fulfillment. At that time, such a positive assertion would have provoked instant and unquenchable outrage. However this may be, the evangelist follows an opposite line and emphasizes the permanence of the Law. From the very outset, therefore, he sets himself against an erroneous viewpoint that he obviously had much experience with, namely, that lawlessness was permissible because Jesus had supplanted the Law.

The formula "the Law and the prophets" (here "or" is used because a negation precedes) is a typically Matthaean idiom. It is not found in Palestinian Judaism; but it does occur in Greek-speaking Judaism (2 Macc. 15:9; 4 Macc. 18:11), and may have been suggested to Matthew in this case by Luke 16:16 (vs. 18 = Luke 16:17). In 7:12 and 22:40 Matthew repeats this phrase in an emphatic position and gives it quite a bit of theological weight. It is noteworthy that he speaks not only of the Law, as do the traditional sayings he is working with, but also of the prophets (see the discussion of vs. 18).

[20] Verse 20, finally, with its emphasis on "righteousness" (see the discussion of vs. 6), its opposition to the teachers of the Law and Pharisees, and its reference to the Kingdom of heaven, is Matthew's own composition. It summarizes the preceding verses and provides the superscription for the antitheses to follow, and in fact for the entire Sermon on the Mount.

[17] This statement attacks the suggestion that Jesus intends to "do away with" the Law and the prophets, that is, abrogate them. But what does "fulfill" mean? When Matthew, in contrast to verse 18 (and 19), but as in 7:12 and 22:40, adds the prophets to the Law, the addition is conceivable only because he sees a theological thread running through history that continues from them down to Jesus. "Fulfill" therefore has the meaning it has in 1:22 and all the introductions to Old Testament quotations: in Jesus there has come true what the Law and the prophets only announced. In him has come the fullness that was intended in them but not attained. But how is this to be taken? Undoubtedly we are to think of the teaching of Jesus cited in 5:21 ff., in which there becomes visible what the Law and the prophets were trying to say.

For Matthew, however, there is no right teaching that does not include doing. The Pharisees are accused of teaching but not doing what they teach (23:3), and it has just been said that Jesus' disciples are to teach the world by doing good works (5:16). In this sense also, according to 3:15, Jesus "fulfilled" all righteousness by his action of submitting humbly to the baptism of John. Verse 19 above all suggests that Matthew includes the doing of the Law in his use of the word "fulfill" (see discussion). "Fulfill" in the sense of "do" is also found, albeit rarely, in Greek Judaism (for example in Phil. associated with the Law in Rom. 13:8; cf., however, the greater emphasis on action in Gal. 5:14-15).

[18] On the use of "Amen" at the beginning of a sentence, see the discussion of verse 18 above. The common formula "until heaven and earth pass away" itself implies a certain limitation. The words of Jesus, of course, will *not* pass away, but will survive into the new world of the Kingdom of God (24:35 = Mark 13:31); but this interpretation still does not solve the riddle of this verse. How can Matthew state that not a letter of the Law, not even one of the decorative strokes added by the devout copyist, is to pass away as long as the earth endures, if Jesus breaks the Sabbath (12:8), rejects Mosaic legislation on divorce (5:31-32), and abrogates the dietary laws (15:11)?

For Matthew, "until all takes place" can no longer signify the arrival of the events heralding the eschaton, because that would only be repeating what has already been stated at the beginning of the sentence. Except in 24:34 (= Mark 13:30), "take place" always refers in Matthew to the realization of a promise within the life of Jesus (1:22; 21:4; 26:56) and is always equated with "come true" or "be fulfilled." This is how Matthew understood it in this passage as well. Now the Greek word for "until" must often be translated "in order that"; such is clearly the case in 14:22 and 26:36 (= Mark 6:45; 14:32); cf. Luke 13:8; 17:8. One of the best ancient manuscripts even distinguishes between these two forms of "until." This means that Matthew incorporates the strict Jewish-Christian saying that none of the Law will pass away until the end of the world, but he interprets the saying to mean that everything intended by the Law must really take place, must really be fulfilled.

But where does this take place, where is it fulfilled? In the teaching and ministry of Jesus and in his band of disciples, which continues his teaching and ministry. What Matthew means becomes clear when one sees that he takes up the expression "the Law and the prophets" once more in 7:12 and declares that the Golden Rule, treating others as one would be treated by them, "is" in fact the Law and the prophets. Matthew deliberately places this statement here as the conclusion of Jesus' entire teaching in the Sermon on the Mount (see the discussion of 7:12); in fact, therefore, he is saying that the entire Law, every point and every stroke of it, is contained in the commandment to love one's neighbor, as expounded by Jesus in his teaching and ministry. This is confirmed by the observation that Matthew adds this commandment in 19:19, equates it explicitly in 22:39 with the commandment to love God, states in 22:40 that on these two commandments the entire Law and the prophets "depend," and in 9:13 and 12:7 interpolates the statement that God desires "mercy and not sacrifice." In similar fashion Paul, too, can consider love of one's fellow men to be fulfillment of the Law (Rom. 13:8-10). According to Romans 8:4, the righteous demands of the Law are fulfilled "in us"; Paul does not say either "for us" or "through us," because he is thinking of the operation of the Spirit.

[19] What, then, are "these" commandments, even the "least" of which must not be omitted? Probably the saying at one time was set in a context in which the reference was clear. As adopted by Matthew, it probably refers to the commandments taught by Jesus, which fol-

low. [20] The summary requires more of Jesus' disciples than of the Pharisees. It does not mean they are to adopt a greater number of commandments and prohibitions—Matthew in fact reduces all the commandments to one, the double commandment to love God and one's fellow man. Jesus means that people must think in terms of a new and far more comprehensive righteousness. It must nevertheless be remembered that the righteousness of the Pharisees is not denied; they are not simply turned into devils. It is only that disciples of Jesus must go a step further, a crucial step. Matthew speaks of "entering" the Kingdom of heaven as Psalm 24 speaks of entering the sanctuary and the commandments that must be fulfilled as the precondition, or as Isaiah 26:2 speaks of righteousness as a requisite for admittance.

The crucial point of this section is not to misunderstand Jesus' message: it is a call to take the Law seriously, to take God's will seriously. The Pharisees practised a magnificent obedience: in addition to all their taxes, they donated ten percent of their income, down to the last penny, to charity; they let themselves be butchered defenselessly rather than make light of God's gift of the Sabbath; they suffered the most horrible forms of martyrdom not to surrender their Bible; they knew that life is truly human only when God is more important than anything else. Nothing is said to ridicule their obedience. Obedience must not be made easy, God must not be devalued. But what is expected of Jesus' disciples is something even more: the mighty, luminous, unmistakable discipleship referred to in verses 13-16. They are to be the "oaks of righteousness" spoken of in Isaiah 61:3, because in them the righteousness of God becomes a dynamic force and, through them, righteousness pervades the world. But, more important, Matthew and Paul speak of "love." This, however, requires more than a new teaching: it is made possible only by God's own act, as is suggested by talk of *God's* righteousness or the Law written by God on men's hearts (cf. the discussion of vs. 22 and the excursus on Mark 3:1-6). According to Matthew, this act of God is Jesus. Therefore he does not speak simply of Jesus' new teaching, but of fulfillment of the Law. He means that Jesus himself does what he teaches, and thus makes it possible for his disciples to do God's will, learning by his example.

The New Righteousness (5:21-48)

If we start by examining the antitheses, we note that the first two (vss. 21 and 27) refer to two of the Ten Commandments (those against killing and adultery), strengthening them by declaring that the commandment is already transgressed by anger or a lustful glance. In the case of the fourth (vs. 33), this reference is not so clear; but the prohibition against oath-breaking might refer to misuse of God's name, and perhaps also to the admonition against false witness, because the sequence "Do not kill; do not commit adultery; . . . do not bear false witness" also occurs in Matthew 19:18 (=Mark 10:19). The commandment to love one's neighbor (Matt. 19:19) would then correspond to the final two antitheses, verses 38 and 43 (cf. Rom. 13:9; Did. 1:2). The admonition against oath-breaking also occurs in a Hellenistic Jewish document alongside many other admonitions (Phocylides 16), and in Greek authors. Jesus' general admonition gains its pregnant meaning from the positive statement about the "Yes" or "No" of the disciples (vs. 37). This alone alludes to interpersonal relationships, which are central to all the other antitheses. But this statement already occurs in a more primitive form in James 5:12 (see below), and without any contrast to the Old Testament.

The situation is similar with the fifth antithesis. Here, too, the brief summons "Do not resist one who wrongs you" derives its meaning from the examples cited. It, too, occurs, along with the final antithesis, in the Sermon on the Plain in Luke 6:27-36, but not formulated in opposition to the Old Testament. The same is true of the parallel to the third antithesis in Luke 16:18. While the first two anitheses strengthen two of the Ten Commandments, the third, fifth, and sixth abrogate Old Testament regulations (but not one of the Ten Commandments). Of course this holds true only for the form found in Matthew. In the case of the divorce antithesis, the contrast was already established by Mark 10:2-12 (=Matt. 19:3-12), although it was unknown to the Q saying (Luke 16:18). In the summons not to resist, the contrast was furnished by the principle of "An eye for an eye," which does not, however, quite suit the context; in the final antithesis, the statement "Hate your enemies" could only derive from the argument that the Old Testament commandment mentions only one's "neighbor" as an object of love. The fourth antithesis occupies a middle ground. It does not state a direct opposition, but abolishes the practice described, namely the use of harmless oaths; in addition, one of the Ten Commandments may be in the background.

What may we conclude from these observations? The most likely conclusion is that antitheses one and two were formulated first (by Jesus?). The second, which cautions against adultery, was later expanded by the third, which deals with the commandment requiring a notice of divorce. This antithesis, based on one of Jesus' sayings (Mark 10:9), was formally assimilated to the second, although with an abbreviated introduction ("It was also said"). Only in these three cases is a relative clause used. The fourth antithesis was added as a reformulation of a familiar saying of Jesus, to which verse 37 and James 5:12 bear witness, perhaps associated from the very outset with a total renunciation of oaths (vs. 34), not merely perjury.

Finally, Matthew (or the community before him?) linked the four antitheses with the sayings about nonresistance and love for one's enemies; the formulation of the fourth antithesis provided a model for the appending of the fifth. The fourth, with its "also" and repetition of "men were told in the past," refers back to the first; this may indicate that it constituted a kind of conclusion before the association with the sayings of the Sermon on the Plain. In Leviticus 19:12-18 and 24:14-22, the prohibition of perjury and hatred and the commandment against blasphemy are associated with the principle of "an eye for an eye, a tooth for a tooth"; this association may have paved the way for appending the last two antitheses. Matthew thus deliberately places in the emphatic concluding position Jesus' call to love one's enemies. All the other antitheses lead up to it as the climax. In Q, as in Luke 6:27, it probably followed the Beatitudes immediately (note the catchwords "hate" [Luke 6:22, 27], "persecute" [Matt. 5:10-12, 44], and "sons" [Matt. 5:9, 45], as well as the similarity in content of Matt. 5:7, 9-11 to the command to love one's enemies; of course this argument is convincing only if Matthew is dependent on an expansion of Q in which these verses were included).

[38-48] The evolution can best be traced in the last two antitheses. In Luke 6:27-36, the saying about not taking vengeance and the one

about loving one's enemies are interwoven, both in a form markedly different from that in Matthew. The latter, in verses 27-28 and 32-36, is in the plural; the former, which interrupts abruptly in verses 29-30, is in the singular. Verse 32 clearly picks up verse 27 once more. This shows that both sayings once circulated independently, although they are already found together in Q's Sermon on the Plain. The first was probably understood as a specific illustration of the second and was thus interpolated.

Matthew cites the two sayings in sequence and at the same time casts them in antithetical form. That this is a subsequent development can still be seen from Matthew 5:39; the Matthaean introduction uses the second person plural, as do all the antitheses ("But now I tell you"); the saying itself, however, is in the second person singular. The two sections are bridged by the general admonition "Do not resist one who wrongs you" (literally "the evil one"), which may be addressed to an individual or to all.

[31-32] In the case of the third antithesis, the saying preserved in Luke 16:18 furnished the model; it refers to the current practice of giving notice for a divorce (Mark 10:4 = Matt. 19:7). First Corinthians 7:10 also implies that Jesus prohibited divorce, though without mentioning the regulation about written notice, which was no longer relevant. Once again, it is hard to determine where the earliest version of this saying is preserved. The addition of "except for adultery" in Matthew 5:32 and 19:9 must be charged to the account of Matthew or his community's tradition. On the other hand, the Matthaean expression "making her commit adultery" reproduces the Jewish understanding; since in Matthew 19:9 Matthew does not depart from Mark, at this point he may have been familiar with an earlier form of the saying.

[39-42] The saying about not taking revenge also still exhibits its Semitic form in Matthew (see the discussion of vs. 40), while the Lukan parallel appears to be an abridgment in line with Hellenistic thought. The example of military requisitioning (see the discussion of vs. 41 below) may have lost its point outside of Palestine (and Syria), and was therefore dropped by Luke, although it is also possible that it was added (in Q?) during the period of high tension with Rome. In addition, Matthew has preserved the exemplary nature of the instruc-

tions better than Luke (see the discussion of vs. 42), and the saying about lending may also have belonged here originally (see the discussion of vs. 42). The occurrence of this rare word only in Matthew 5:42 and Luke 6:34-35 may indicate that Luke, too, knew this saying in the context of the commandment not to resist, because in verses 34 and 35 he summarizes nonresistance by an exhortation to "lend."

[43-48] The saying about loving one's enemies is particularly characteristic of Jesus. The saying was current in various versions. Romans 12:14 combines "persecute" (Matt. 5:44) with "bless/curse" (Luke 6:28). A papyrus knows of the form "pray for your enemies," which mixes the first and second injunctions in Matthew 5:44. The same statement appears in Didache 1:3, Luke 6:28, and in Justin, at the beginning of the second century, with additional fragments of the Lukan recension and the "But now I tell you" of the Mathaean recension. It is striking that the expression "Love your enemies," which both Matthew and Luke place at the beginning in identical words, is not found in any other sayings except for a subordinate clause in 2 Clement 13:4. For the most part it is praying for your enemies and loving those who hate you that are mentioned. When the first two evangelists are compared, they exhibit only three points of agreement: the idea that love towards those who love you is nothing exceptional, the mention of "reward," and the reference to God's nature. Luke 6:35-36 is explicit about God's mercy (cf. the discussion of Matt. 5:7); Matthew 5:45 simply implies the idea of God's mercy by referring to the one who causes his sun to shine and his rain to fall "on bad and good people alike" (this sequence also occurs in 22:10, probably a Matthaean interpolation). In both, this reference to God's goodness is associated intimately with the promise that the disciples shall become sons of God. Whether the reference to the creator (Matt. 5:45), which belongs more in the context of wisdom instruction, or to the God who acts mercifully (Luke 6:35-36) is earlier can hardly be determined.

The concluding admonition to be merciful (Luke 6:36) goes well with the continuation in Q "Do not judge . . . Do not condemn . . ." (Luke 6:37); and since Matthew has inserted the requirement of perfection also in 19:21, verse 48 may derive from him. The name of God, too, appears in both in the form that is typical of them ("the Most

High" only in Luke; "your Father in heaven" in Matthew). In short, in verses 46-48 only the general train of argument is fixed; the wording is still very free. All we can say, then, is that the expanded recension of Luke, especially ⁺he repetition of the commandment in 6:35 (cf. 6:27), is a later development. In his last antithesis Matthew more likely contains the original wording.

On the other hand, Luke's version appears to be less affected by local concerns than Matthew's. The mention of "greeting" as an example in Matthew 5:47 (not found in Luke) has a strangely weak effect alongside the comprehensive "love" of verse 46, whereas "doing good" (Luke 6:33) describes the "love" in concrete terms and therefore fits better. "Tax collectors" and "pagans" (Matt. 5:46-47) are appropriate to a Jewish Christian milieu (18:17). Jesus, it is true, never idealized tax collectors or pagans; but if the saying does go back to him, we should sooner expect "sinners," as in Luke 6:32-33.

[21] Even in Matthew alone we can observe the process by which the sayings of Jesus underwent further development and exegesis. Jesus' first antithesis probably ended with verse 22a, and one might ask whether 21b formed a part of the saying in the beginning; it is introduced by "Anyone who . . . ," like the additions in 22b and c, rather than by "Whoever . . . ," as in 22a. In verses 31-32, also, the second expression may well go back to the formulation of Q (Luke 16:18), the first to the free rendering of Matthew or his predecessor. The progression is strange: the series of offences and the series of punishments are both illogical, since "Raca" and "Fool" are roughly synonymous (see the discussion below), and hell is something totally different from the judgment of the Council. "Fool" might simply be the Greek translation of "Raca"; in this case the saying involving "Raca" would have developed first as an illustration of "being angry," while a later hand would have added the saying involving "Fool" in order to bring in the fires of hell. Verse 22c also differs from the preceding two statements in that there is no mention in it of the "brother." In the punishments, "judgment" (vs. 22a) must once have meant God's final sentence. In conjunction with the references to the Council (vs. 22b) and hell (vs. 22c), it now probably refers to a local tribunal, although the term always designates only a sentence or punishment, never a judicial agency. All these expansions take on

meaning only as polemic against the hair splitting of the teachers of the Law.

[23-26] Above all verses 23-26 must have been added later as specific examples of conduct; they are in the second person singular. Nothing is said about the person going to offer sacrifice being angry with his brother; on the contrary, the fact that his brother holds a grudge against him shows that this summons to forgive belongs in a totally different context. The subject matter is extremely important to Matthew, as 6:14-15; 18:21 ff. show. He therefore incorporates a variant of these latter sayings at this point. Whether the saying implies that the sacrificial cult is still going on, and therefore goes back to the time of Jesus or the primitive Christian community at Jerusalem remains uncertain. The situation depicted in fact corresponds more closely to the Old Testament than to the time of Jesus, when only the priest offered sacrifice at the altar. The final admonition is a variant on the same theme. It is not impossible that both sayings were associated even before Matthew, for the word for "settle the matter" in the Lukan recension (12:58) is almost the same as that for "make peace" in the first saying (Matt. 5:24). It is therefore possible that the second saying, in a version even closer to Luke and probably understood literally, was associated with the first before Matthew adopted it and formulated it in somewhat more general terms.

Jesus may have used the advice of verses 25 and 26 as a parable to call men to repentance before the fast approaching divine judgment (as in Luke 12:58-59). Matthew interprets it as an admonition to make peace speedily in a dispute. In the description of the judicial process (vs. 25), Roman terminology is adapted to the Palestinian environment ("police"); in the next verse, on the other hand, a Roman coin is mentioned, while otherwise the wording is practically identical with Luke 12:59. Are we to conclude that verse 25, which differs appreciably in wording from Luke 12:58, was an earlier addition, supplemented by Matthew following Q? In any case, Matthew shows in these additions the significance the words of Jesus had in the life of the community. They presuppose a human closeness like that found in the community of Jesus ("brother" in vss. 23-24).

[29-30] Here, the second antithesis (vss. 27-28) has appended to it the saying about taking out one's eye or cutting off one's hand. The saying (vss. 29-30) differs from 18:8-9 (=Mark 9:43-48) in using the second person singular. That "life" is no longer mentioned as the opposite of "hell" shows that Mark 9:43, 47 preserves the more vigorous and probably earlier form.

[33-37] The fourth antithesis is especially interesting because James 5:12 still preserves it in a form that mentions only oaths, not vows. This form is also closest to that cited by the early Christian fathers in their writings, and is therefore probably the most primitive. Since only oaths are mentioned in the Old Testament commandment, verse 33 b is certainly a later elaboration; the teachers of the Law were primarily concerned with vows. Forbidding all vows cannot be the meaning here; for when Jesus interposes that it would be better not to make any vows at all, it can hardly be his intent to forbid promises made to God, but rather the use of oath formulas on every conceivable occasion.

When vows are the topic of discussion, as in Matthew 23:16-20, Jesus' point is that the vow must in fact be carried out. This eliminates the detailed explanation in verses 34 b, 35, and 36, which resembles Matthew 23:16-22; such material derives from debates to define which vows have really been made to God, and are therefore irrevocable. Furthermore, only in this antithesis are Scriptural passages cited in support of Jesus' position, and cited precisely according to the Greek Bible; even "Jerusalem" appears in its Greek form. These details therefore derive from Greek-speaking Jewish Christians. Swearing by "heaven" and "earth" is mentioned in rabbinic sources as well as in other authors such as Philo (*Special Laws* ii. 5). In any event these expansions are illogical; in the face of the radical demand for a plain "yes" or "no," it makes no sense to point out that even the less perilous oath formulas make reference to the divine name. The final verse thus also refers to statements emphasized by an oath. James 5:12 states that every "yes" must always be merely a "yes," every "no" a simple "no"; the Matthaean statement is open to misinterpretation as a recommendation that a "yes" or "no" be twice repeated, as certain rabbis also advised, instead of an oath. Finally, the direct command in James 5:12, "Do not swear," is more primitive than the indirect form in Matthew ("I tell you not to swear"). The threat of "judgment" (James 5:12) against anyone who is untruthful is a kind of parallel to Matthew 5:22*a* in the first antithesis and may confirm the reference to God's judgment there as well.

a. Teaching about Killing (5:21-26)

²¹"You have heard that men were told in the past, 'Do not kill; anyone who kills will be brought to judgment.' ²²But now I tell you: whoever is angry with his brother will be brought to judgment; anyone who says to his brother, 'Raca' will be brought before the Council; anyone who says, 'You fool!' will be consigned to the fires of hell.

²³"So if you are about to offer your gift to God at the altar and there you remember that your brother has something against you, ²⁴leave your gift there in front of the altar and go at once to make peace with your brother; then come back and offer your gift to God.

²⁵"If a man brings a lawsuit against you and takes you to court, be friendly with him while there is time, before you get to court; once you are there he will turn you over to the judge, who will hand you over to the police, and you will be put in jail. ²⁶Amen, I tell you, there you will stay until you pay the last penny."

(Vs. 21—Exod. 20:13.)

[21] The Greek text might also be translated "Men of the past said"; but in the New Testament the rare impersonal passive ("it is said") always introduces a divine utterance, and, almost always, a Scriptural quotation. The "men of the past" are therefore the Sinai generation, to whom the Mosaic Law was given by God. The Decalogue does not state that anyone who kills will be brought to judgment, but the statement is often made elsewhere in the Mosaic Law (Exod. 21:12; Lev. 24:17; Num. 35:16 ff.; Deut. 17:18 ff.; cf. Gen. 9:6). What Jesus says in the original antitheses is by no means unprecedented in Judaism (cf. also Lev. 19:18; Eccles. 7:9; Prov. 15:1; Ecclus. 10:6; 28:7; Did. 3:2). The rabbinic statement that whoever hates his neighbor is to be counted with those who shed blood comes very close to it (Billerbeck, under Matt. 5:22 G). [22] We are in fact dealing here with a reinforcement of the Law, whose purpose is to explain the Law's fundamental aim.

What is unprecedented is the phrase "But now I," with strong emphasis on the "I," which places the "I" of Jesus in parallel to the veiled name of God in the phrase "men were told." This surpasses any other possible messianic claims; the temporal difference between "men were told in the past" and "now I tell you," this very day, must also be noted. This must go back to Jesus himself; it is unprecedented in Judaism, and in the early Christian communities Jesus' opposition to the Law was either mitigated or, as in Paul, reinterpreted from the perspective of the crucifixion—in either case it was totally lost to view. Here we can see that God's revelation can never be simply a collection of tenents, embodied in a legal code and used when occasion warrants; God's revelation is rather an emergence from the self, exfoliating mysteriously and at its own moments.

In the antitheses and other sayings of Jesus it is made clear that there is no longer a sharp line between willing and acting. Wishing to kill is as bad as killing; what is needed is a new heart, created by God (Jer. 31:33; cf. the discussion of Mark 3:1-6). James 1:20 may contain an echo of this saying: "Man's anger does not help to achieve God's righteous purpose" (cf. Matt. 5:20). The crucial point is that attention is no longer focused on us, and our striving to be beyond reproach, but on the *other* person, and how his living is whittled away by our conduct, even if only by an angry heart. This shift from personal righteousness to the protection of one's fellow men is characteristic of the antitheses; it can even be observed in the additions made by the evangelist.

"Judgment" refers to God's final judgment (see above). The objection that its meaning would then differ from its meaning in verse 21 is untenable, for carrying out a death sentence according to the Law of Moses is the same as executing God's final judgment. The Pentateuch does not think in terms of a judgment after death, and God's judgment can only be performed in this world. Of course when the continuation was added with its mention of the Council (the Sanhedrin or supreme judicial body in Palestine), the meaning of the first "judgment" was restricted to that delivered by a local authority. The result was the sequence: local judge—Council—judgment of God (see above), imitating the Pharisaic teaching in which all particular cases are precisely defined so as to distinguish minutely between more and less serious offences and the punishments appropriate.

"Raca" is probably an inaccurate rendering of a Hebrew term for "blockhead" or "fool," although the rendering "braggart" has been suggested on the basis of a Greek etymology. The remarkable gulf between the final threat of hell and the two that precede might be explained by the observation that "fool" is mainly applied to the godless (Ps. 14:1; 94:8; Isa. 32:5-6; Deut. 32:6; Jer. 5:21); the meaning would then be that whoever interferes with someone else's human relationships becomes subject to human judgment, but whoever interferes with another's relationship to God becomes subject to wrath divine. Of course such an explanation renders the whole procedure ridiculous: under such rules the whole administration of justice would collapse, for where would there be enough courts to carry out all these trials? On the problem of hell, see the discussion of Mark 9:47 and 48.

[23] Matthew added what follows (23-26) in hopes his community would realize in daily life the purpose for which Jesus' words were spoken. He felt they must be coaxed to keep coming back to the words of Jesus and prevented from inscribing them in gold letters on the walls of their churches as high ideals without actually living by them. Matthew's characteristic emphasis—on one's fellow man instead of the cult (9:13; 12:7; 23:25-26), the basic thrust of which goes back to Jesus himself (Mark 7:15)—leads him to the imagery of offering sacrifice, which throws his message into clearer relief than even the imagery of prayer in Mark 11:25. Even the Day of Atonement could not atone for sins against a neighbor unless the person first made peace with that neighbor (Billerbeck on vs. 24, B 2). Now the Pharisees taught that a sacrifice could be interrupted, but only for ritual reasons—to interrupt it simply on account of a neighbor would be inconceivable, because its purpose, for them, was above all the offering of a pure and unsullied ritual. When a cultic act is stopped for the sake of one's brother, as Jesus requires, cultic ideology has been fundamentally overcome.

[24] On the other hand, worship can never be reduced to love for one's fellow man; the latter is rather a prerequisite for the former. This is the point made by the conclusion of the verse.

[25] The following admonition, too, can only be taken literally, and was probably so understood by those who appended it. Here, however, "before you get to court" is represented in the Greek text only by the general expression "on the way" without the more precise addition of "to the court" (Luke 12:58).

[26] The solemn "Amen, I tell you" at the beginning of the concluding sentence is also disconcerting: as a rule it singles out eschatological events. And in 18:34 a formulation very similar to verse 26 is used in a parable with an eschatological purpose—to describe the final pronouncement of God's judgment, when there will be no chance whatever of paying everything down to the last penny. In Luke 12:59, too, the statement is so understood, as the context shows. Since Matthew repeatedly underlines his references to God's impending judgment (22:13; 24:51; 25:30, 46), he was probably thinking of God's final judgment here as well. Neither would a literal interpretation of "paying" be appropriate here, since there has been no prior mention of debts. In this case "on the way" simply means "during a man's lifetime," and Matthew is referring to any conflict with an opponent who might some day file a complaint before God. There is no notion of any expiation in Purgatory; as in 18:34, the point is to emphasize that one can never settle accounts with God (see the discussion there). And so the admonition calls on the hearer to seize the chance for a fruitful encounter with his brother, granted by God's grace. We are not dealing with the possibility of making compensation—verse 26 makes that impossible—but with personal reconciliation despite all inflicted wrongs, for some of which there is no making amends.

b. Teaching about Adultery (5:27-30)

[27]"You have heard that it was said, 'Do not commit adultery.' [28]But now I tell you: anyone who looks at a woman and wants to possess her is guilty of committing adultery with her in his heart.

[29]"So if your right eye causes you to sin, take it out and throw it away! It is much better for you to lose a part of your body than to have your whole body thrown into hell.

[30]"If your right hand causes you to sin, cut it off and throw it away!

It is much better for you to lose one of your limbs than to have your whole body go off to hell."
(Vs. 27—Exod. 20:14.)

[28] The second antithesis also deals with one of the Ten Commandments. The common Greek term actually means "injuring her adulterously." This shows how the purpose here is to protect the rights of the woman. The tenth Commandment, with its prohibition against desiring a neighbor's wife, points in the same direction as the saying of Jesus; and the recollection of God's marriage to Israel (Hos. 2:4–3:1) leads in Malachi 2:10-16 to a call for fidelity, albeit only towards a Jewish wife. Other passages exhibit a totally different tendency. Job 31:1; Ecclesiasticus 23:4-5; 26:9-11; Psalms of Solomon 4:4-5; The Testament of Issachar 7:2 know that even a look can be adulterous, and rabbis say the same thing. But it is always the woman who is considered a danger to the man—such a danger that the devout man will shut his eyes when a woman approaches, preferring to stumble rather than sin, neither speaking to her nor even extending his hand.

Marriage law was based on this conception. Only a married woman committed adultery by becoming sexually involved with a single man or a gentile; a married man involved with a woman committed no adultery. Of course male philandering was opposed by devout Jews; but it did not stand on a par with adultery committed by a woman. This shows how totally the law expressed the man's point of view; even when men went beyond the law of marriage and sought to avoid all forms of unchastity, it was not because the woman had rights, but because she was dangerous. Therefore total ascetic renunciation of sexual union had its place within Judaism, for example at the Qumran monastery. The Old Testament nevertheless considers sexual union to be God's creation and a natural act in accord with his purposes.

Jesus, too, was familiar with this idea (19:4-6); but his concern was to tell people that there is something far greater, which must not be endangered by man's natural desires (19:10-12), namely, the life and the rights of the woman (5:28). We are certainly meant to think not only of the woman who is endangered at the moment, but also of a future wife. This is why there is no admonition against the danger of looking at a woman, but rather against looking at her with desire, and ignoring the holiness of *her* desires. It thus becomes clear that adultery always takes place "in the heart," and is not subject to legal definition and judgment. Adultery in the heart can accompany outward hypercorrectness; purity of heart can accompany acts that are outwardly dubious and condemned by society.

[29-30] The expansion states that it is better to lose one's right eye or right hand than to be cast whole (on "body," see the discussion of 10:28) into hell (see the discussion of Mark 9:47-48). This already points in another direction, and derives, as Mark 9:43-48 shows, from another context (see above). Matthew has tried to make these sayings refer to adultery by bringing in the mention of the eye first ("looks at" in vs. 28) and omitting the mention of the foot, although a Jewish tractate mentions hand, foot, eye, and heart in this context and also speaks of cutting off the hand. But even the restriction to the right eye and the right hand shows that the saying does not really belong with verse 28. Above all, it calls attention away from the neighbor who might be injured, focusing it instead on one's own fate at the last judgment.

On the other hand, the members of the community are enjoined by these words not merely to repeat the teachings of Jesus but to live by them. Even though the obedience of discipleship—in contrast to the Jewish idea—does not earn special merit in the eyes of God, but is the natural way of living that comes automatically to the disciple, men must still be called to it. This summons can be acted upon rightly only when Jesus' conduct toward the woman taken in adultery (John 8:1-11; cf. Luke 7:47) is not forgotten.

c. Teaching about Divorce (5:31-32)
Cf. 19:18; Mark 10:11-12; Luke 16:18

[31]"It was also said, 'Anyone who divorces his wife must give her a written notice of divorce.' [32]But now I tell you: if a man divorces his wife, except for unchastity, he is guilty of making her a cause of

adultery; and the man who marries a divorced woman drives her to adultery."

(Vs. 31—Deut. 24:1.)

[31] The next legal section does not refer to any of the Ten Commandments, but to the procedure laid down in Deuteronomy 24:1-4. Its original purpose was precisely the same as Jesus' purpose in verse 28: protection of the woman. But it increasingly became a gimmick in the hands of the man, permitting him to enter into a temporary marriage, sometimes only for a single day, thus in effect giving him sexual license. Thus once again the woman became an object, that is, the property of her husband, which he could give away or acquire. The Old Testament conditions and procedural regulations, which are not cited here, restrained the tendency but did not overcome it entirely.

[32] Jesus' antithesis unambiguously attacks and abrogates an Old Testament commandment. This is true, of course, only if we follow Luke 16:18 or Mark 10:11 in omitting the interpolation "except for unchastity," which goes back to Deuteronomy 24:1, albeit in rabbinic wording. By means of this addition, the saying of Jesus is once again assimilated to the position of the strictest teachers of the Law. Even before Jesus, Shammai opposed Hillel, for whom a burned dinner furnished sufficient grounds for a notice of divorce, by stating that only infidelity on the part of the wife was sufficient grounds. The form without this addition (Luke 16:18; Mark 10:11; cf. 1 Cor. 7:10) undoubtedly goes back to Jesus. The Matthaean addition is comprehensible on the basis of the practice of his community.

The clear and unambiguous statement of Jesus in Mark 10:9 (=Matt. 19:6), "What God has joined together, man must not separate," is first of all reformulated as a legal dictum, "The man who divorces his wife and marries another commits adultery against his wife" (Mark 10:11). In the Hellenistic world women were also prohibited from divorcing their husbands (1 Cor. 7:10-11), but at the same time an exception was made for mixed marriages with unbelievers (vss. 12-16). Finally the prohibition against remarriage for both parties was appended (Luke 16:18; Mark 10:11-12). First Corinthians 7:15 allows for the dissolution of the marriage, though not, of course, if both parties know they are bound by God's word. The crucial point is that according to 1 Corinthians 7:12-16 only the non-Christian party has the right to decide whether or not to divorce. This means, in contrast to some legalism that supposes literal fulfillment of Jesus' words is enough, that the rights of the other party, in this case in fact the non-Christian, are once more strictly maintained. If he or she wishes a divorce he or she must be given the freedom to do so; if not, likewise. The Matthaean addition represents the last link in this chain of development. "Unchastity" probably means continued infidelity rather than a single instance of adultery. Now of course a marriage in which one of the parties, adamant against all communication, lives continuously in intimate association with a third party can no longer be considered a marriage. But the insertion forbidding unchastity, if this is to be taken as a legal dictum, cannot be considered as absolute. The very infidelity of one of the parties can, for example, bring about a crisis in a marriage that has settled into boredom, a crisis in which both may once more communicate with one another and thus find the way back together. This is rendered impossible if one of the parties bases his right to a divorce on Matthew 5:32. He would then be missing the chance, given him by God, of recognizing the failure on his part that has driven his partner to infidelity and miss the chance of doing something about it.

Catholic exegetes in particular have attempted to square this passage with the teaching that marriage is indissoluble. Other translations are linguistically impossible: "Anyone who divorces his wife for any reason, even unchastity," or "Anyone who divorces his wife—and even for unchastity divorce is not allowed—. . . ." If unchastity is interpreted as a symbol for idolatry, as in the Old Testament, which is certainly impossible in this context, only a mixed marriage could be dissolved; but in direct contradiction to 1 Corinthians 7:12-16, the right to decide would be given to the Christian partner. Another way out, in the case of one party's unchastity, would be not to permit divorce, but to tolerate a second marriage. This might be viable in practice, but certainly does not correspond to the teaching of Jesus.

Our verdict on this addition must be different if the addition was aimed at the community's converts. According to the so-called Apostolic Decree (Acts 15:20; see the introductory remarks to 5:19), the gentiles who were received into the community were required to observe the same laws as those observed by resident aliens in Israel (Lev. 17:10; 18:26): they had to refrain from idolatry (17:8-9; 18:21; 20:1-6), from eating blood (17:10-12), and from eating meat not kosher (17:13). In addition, they were required to abstain from "unchastity" (the word used here is not found in Leviticus 18). According to Leviticus 18:6-20, this includes not only adultery, which is mentioned in the final verse, but above all, along with the unusual sexual persuasions to be detailed in verses 22 ff., consanguineous marriage. Does the Matthaean addition thus preserve a glimpse of the way the early Christian community received converts, requiring a gentile coming to be baptized to dissolve his marriage in case his wife was within the prohibited degrees listed in Leviticus 18? Might this be the "one ground" on which, according to Matthew 19:9, marriage may be dissolved? It has even been suggested that the saying about self-mutilation refers to this sacrifice of a spouse (19:12; cf. 19:9). If this is the case, it would of course represent another invasion of the freedom of the community of Jesus by a legalism every bit as bad as the requirement of circumcision (Gal. 2:3-4; 5:2-3).

This in turn raises the question whether missionaries who, with the best of intentions, have introduced the absolute requirement of monogamy into the polygamous structure of Africa have not acted in exactly as legalistic a way. This interpretation is not impossible; but it runs counter to the spirit of both Jesus' saying in verse 28 about putting a woman in danger through a look of desire and the addition made by the community in verses 29-30, both of which think of adultery as a surrender to unconcerned desire.

It is not likely that "unchastity" was understood in some totally extraordinary sense, the less so because it was not given any unusual meaning in the so-called Apostolic Decree. So we are probably left with the usual interpretation. It is supported by the context both here and in 19:3-12, where the more likely translation in verse 9 almost excludes any other interpretation. The wording "making her a cause of adultery" derives from typically Jewish sensibility. It presupposes what is stated in Mark 10:4 ff. but not here: that both, despite the divorce, constitute an indissoluble entity; therefore the first marriage is not really dissolved until the divorced woman remarries (cf. also 1 Cor. 7:11). Nevertheless the more simple formulation in Mark 10:11 (=Matt. 19:9) may correspond more closely to Jesus' concern. The case of remarriage is discussed by the second statement in Matthew 5:32, which places responsibility for the adultery on the second man. In Luke 16:18, the correspondence between the two statements is better than in Matthew 5:32 (two participles). Whether this represents the earlier form or a later assimilation cannot be determined.

Once more, then, Jesus attacks the self-satisfaction of the man who holds that everything is fit and proper provided only that all the rules regulating the notice of divorce have been observed. Once more Jesus takes as his target all attempts at self-legitimation and legalization of sin. Once more he takes into his protection primarily the helpless party, the woman who is thus driven into adultery. The danger in the exception Matthew makes for the case of unchastity does not reside in the exception itself. Precisely for the sake of the other party divorce can sometimes be the better solution. The rub is that this ruling gives the man but not the woman the right to decide on divorce, so that he can once more salve his conscience with the feeling that his conduct has been proper. The exception, that is, supposes the man to have rights and the woman to have none. It allows him to inflict injustice on her under the semblance of legality. In the final analysis, all we can say is that under certain circumstances two people must go the way of divorce, experiencing God's forgiveness, because the other way would be even more culpable. But on the whole question, see the concluding remarks on Mark 10:1-12.

d. Teaching about Oaths (5:33-37)

[33]"You have also heard that men were told in the past, 'Do not swear a false oath,' but rather 'do what you have sworn to the Lord to do.' [34]But now I tell you: do not swear at all, neither by heaven, because it is God's throne, [35]nor by the earth, for it is the stool for his feet, nor by Jerusalem, for it is the city of the great King. [36]Do not even swear by your head, for you cannot make a single hair black or white. [37]Just say: Yes, yes, No, no; anything else you have to say comes from evil."

(Vs. 33—Exod. 20:7; Lev. 19:12; Num. 30:3; Deut. 23:22; Ps. 50:14. Vss. 34-35—Isa. 66:1. Vs. 35—Ps. 48:3; 99:5.)

[33] With verse 33 we probably return to exposition of the Ten Commandments (see the introductory remarks). The positive addition, to the effect that one must carry out what one has sworn to do, is cited from other passages (Num. 30:3; Deut. 23:22-24; Ps. 50:14). Now for Judaism oaths play an important part in vows; but there is also the oath insisting that one knows nothing of a certain matter or that one is innocent, as well as the oath administered to a suspect to make him tell the truth (26:22; John 9:24). The continuation (vss. 34-37) therefore limits the discussion to certain cases and is an interpretation of the original saying of Jesus.

[34-35] This catalogue was suggested by the question, much debated among teachers of the Law, of what oaths are really binding (cf. 23:16-22). Any invocation of the deity, of course, held one to the oath, and so the trifling distinctions that the legalists arrived at are made to look ridiculous: a simple appeal to Scriptures (Isa. 66:1; Ps. 48:3), which the teachers of the Law accept as their only authority, unmasks the various circumlocutions—swearing by heaven, by the earth, or by the city of Jerusalem—as invocations of God himself. But of course this is not the actual import of Jesus' saying. One might now conclude that all that matters is avoidance of the moderately dangerous words, the ones that might involve mentioning the name of God, rather than total renunciation of oaths (as James 5:12 correctly understood). [36] The argument takes a different course in the final member. A person's inability to change a single hair at will—there is obviously no thought of hair-dye, which was also used in that period —shows that he, and all that he is, remains totally dependent on God. This is a maxim of wisdom instruction, met with again in such sayings of Jesus as 6:27, 30. It is appropriate in the context of the preceding example because it shows that God eventually enters the picture even when one invokes one's own head.

[37] A contrast is drawn with the simple Yes and No that obviate oaths because they are spoken in total honesty. In Slavonic Enoch 49:1 a repeated Yes or No is recommended as a substitute for an oath, and it is possible that the saying of Jesus was already reduced to such

a recommendation. The original meaning, attested by James 5:12 and the church fathers, is undoubtedly that every Yes must be simply Yes, every No simply No. The brief concluding clause is linguistically obscure: is the intention to reject excessive swearing, or is *everything* besides a simple Yes or No denounced? It is also uncertain whether it is evil or the Evil One that is spoken of. In Matthew 13:19 the Evil One replaces Satan (Mark 4:15), whom John 8:44 terms the father of all lies, and Matthew also uses "the Good One" as a term for God (19:17); nevertheless, "evil" is the more likely translation.

Rejection of swearing is nothing new (cf. Hos. 4:15, an early example). The Greek, especially the Phythagoreans, as well as Jews with a Hellenistic education (Eccles. 9:2; Ecclus. 23:9-11; Philo) know of such a prohibition. The important point is that Matthew 5:37 cuts the ground from under an ideology that attempts to fulfill God's commands by means of precise and exhaustive casuistry instead of honest concern for others. The saying frees men from the painstaking discrimination between innocuous formulas and those that use God's name or tacitly include it—a distinction that can never be defined precisely. Above all, it frees men from the even more painstaking attempt to justify themselves, in their own eyes and in the eyes of others. Philo says the best course would be to be so truthful that whatever one says could be counted as an oath, the next best would be to swear truly. Such resignation and compromise are foreign to Jesus, as well as any new legalism that would only force men to speak more cautiously than before. The point of what Jesus says is freedom from introspection, from concern for one's own perfection or imperfection, and freedom to live a life that is totally devoted to one's neighbor. When human discourse is debased so that under certain circumstances Yes can mean No and No Yes, community is destroyed.

e. Teaching about Nonresistance (5:38-42)
Cf. Luke 6:29-30

[38]"You have heard that it was said, 'An eye for an eye,' and 'A tooth for a tooth.' [39]But now I tell you: do not resist someone who does you wrong. If anyone slaps you on the right cheek, offer him the left

cheek, too. ⁴⁰And if someone takes you to court to sue you for your shirt, let him have your coat as well. ⁴¹And if anyone forces you to go a mile, go two miles with him. ⁴²Give to anyone who asks you; and if someone wants to borrow something, do not turn away from him." (Vs. 38—Exod. 21:24-25; Lev. 24:19-20.)

[38] "An eye for an eye . . ." is a legal dictum found not only in Exodus 21:4; Leviticus 24:20; Deuteronomy 19:21 (elaborated), but at the foundation of all judicial systems. Originally it was intended to restrict unrestrained blood vengeance (Gen. 4:23-24); but in the course of time it came to be used chiefly to make one's own claims prevail. At the time of Jesus, to be sure, monetary damages had replaced revenge, though the propriety of this was contested.

[39] Jesus, on the contrary, calls on men to forgo all resistance. The association of this saying with the Old Testament dictum is probably facilitated by the fact that the Greek word represented by "re-" (sistance) in the New Testament is the same as that represented by (an eye) "for" (an eye) in the Old. Whether the object is taken as neuter ("evil") or as masculine ("the evil one," i.e., "one who does you wrong"), the association with verse 37 on the one hand and with verses 43-48 on the other shows that one must not do evil and must also not simply stand to one side when it befalls others (cf. also vss. 21-32). Jesus does not erase all distinctions between those who are good and those who are evil; what he does reject is the stance that will only show love toward those who are considered good.

It is possible that Matthew has in mind primarily "resistance" in a court of law, because he incorporates typical legal disputes in his examples. The word is used in this sense in Deuteronomy 19:18 and Isaiah 50:8 in the Greek Bible. In the same section (Isa. 50:6) we find the same two words used in verse 39 for "offering the cheek." Is Matthew thinking of the suffering servant of God described in the Isaiah passage? In rabbinic law, to deliver retribution by a blow with the back of the hand, which is thought to be especially degrading, is considered twofold compensation. Matthew may therefore have in mind the disciples who were so struck for being heretics. But perhaps this, too, is just a random example, as in verse 29.

[40] In verse 39 a reference to contemporary legal practice is possible; in the following example it is certain. The two words "shirt" and "coat" are employed exactly opposite to the way they are employed in Luke. In Luke, the image is that of a robber who first tears off someone's coat; in Matthew, we have a legal adversary who is after the shirt because according to Israelite law the coat, being both an article of clothing and a covering for the night, is not distrainable. In Exodus 22:25-26 God himself promulgates this law, which is meant to protect the poor. Jesus' unprecedented statement that it is better to surrender everything and go through life naked than to insist on one's legal rights is grounded on an absolute trust in God, who shows mercy to those who are in need.

[41] In the third example, we are dealing with the legal right enjoyed by the Roman occupation forces to compel a Jew to go along as a guide or porter. The term translated as "force" is a technical word for requisitioning by civil or military authorities, and is applied in 27:32 to Simon from Cyrene, who is forced by the Romans to carry Jesus' cross to the place of execution. As in that case, individuals probably demanded such services often, even contrary to precise legalities. Jesus' saying here may have had certain precursors in the Sayings Source because it is the precise opposite of what the Zealots advocated doing in their revolutionary sedition against the Romans (see the discussion of 4:1-4). The saying of Jesus neither affirms nor rejects the right of requisitioning; that is simply a fact, like rain or drought. Jesus' concern again is to destroy self-consciousness, here the self-pity of the persecuted. He recommends going two miles rather than just the required one for precisely this reason; when the *victim* determines how far he will go, he has control—he is no longer subjugated, he is superior.

[42] The final example corresponds to an admonition already inculcated by Deuteronomy 15:7-11, and involves a different situation. Here we are no longer dealing with "evil" forces that are not to be resisted. The rabbis distinguish between objects such as an ax or sickle, whose use is "asked for" (Billerbeck on vs. 43, 2*a*), and money, which is "borrowed" (Billerbeck on vs. 42, 2). Or perhaps a contrary distinction may be involved between "asking" that does not consider return and "borrowing" that does. The form of the Greek verbs shows that Matthew is thinking of examples that arise in particular situations, whereas Luke 6:29-30 states universally valid rules. This holds true even more for chapter 95 of the Gospel of Thomas, where loans at interest are prohibited.

The Greek sage Diogenes is also said to have given his shirt as well to someone who demanded his coat; in this case, however, we are dealing with the ideal of the self-sufficient sage who understands how to live without coat or shirt. Rabbis, too, call on men to exhibit ready complaisance, but almost always have in mind the demands or, above all, the chastisements imposed by God, in other words, the meritorious and propitiatory acceptance of suffering (Billerbeck on vs. 39 A).

In the case of Jesus, we find once more a clear emphasis on the other person. Jesus is concerned with the fragile and perpetually vulnerable social bond, which so often through the use of force or even mere legal coercion erupts into bitterness, counterforce, and thence into catastrophe. Therefore one must never under any circumstances adopt the style of one's opponent, not even to gain a worthwhile end, however obvious may be the universal principle, which even crops up in Jewish tradition, "If one seeks to slay you, anticipate his design and slay him" (Billerbeck on vs. 39 A). The use here of the second person singular instead of plural is not accidental: the decisions involved are the most intensely personal. On the basic question of renouncing force, see the excursus following 7:29, especially *a.* 3 and *c.* 4.

f. Teaching about Love for Enemies (5:43-48)
Cf. Luke 6:27-28, 32-36

[43]"You have heard that it was said, 'Love your neighbor' and hate your enemy. [44]But now I tell you: love your enemies, and pray for those who persecute you, [45]so that you will become the sons of your Father in heaven. For he makes his sun to shine on bad and good people alike, and gives rain to the righteous and the unrighteous. [46]For what is your reward if you love only the people who love you? Don't even the tax collectors do that? [47]And if you speak only to your friends, have you done anything out of the ordinary? Don't even the pagans do that? [48]You must be perfect, just as your Father in heaven is perfect."
(Vs. 43—Lev. 19:18. Vs. 48—Lev. 19:2.)

[43] With the call to love one's enemies we reach the climax. The summons to hate one's enemies does not occur in so many words in the Law. The principle "Love your neighbor" (Lev. 19:18), to be sure, was always interpreted so as to apply to fellow Israelites, not to aliens. This is understandable under primitive circumstances, in which one can hardly see beyond the limits of one's own tribe or nation. Love was also expressly commanded toward any resident alien, by God himself (Lev. 19:33-34; Deut. 10:18-19); but later this requirement came to be restricted to those who within a year asked for reception into the religious community through circumcision and obedience to the entire Law. Even love for one's enemy is extolled (1 Sam. 24:19), and demanded in certain circumstances of everyday life, e.g. in dealing with cattle (Exod. 23:4-5) or emergencies (Prov. 25:21-22). But the Old Testament also contains the psalms of vengeance (cf. Ps. 137:7-9; 139:21-22), although the hatred there is not directed against a personal enemy, but against those who rebel against God and his ordinances.

These two strands are continued in the time of Jesus. Even before Jesus a rabbi had advised loving all men and bringing them to the Law; and rabbis had also attacked envy, evil impulses, and hatred (Aboth i. 12; ii. 12-13). On the other hand, total devotion to God and strict observance of his laws led in the Qumran community to the commandment "love all that he has elected, and hate all that he has cast aside," and "love all the sons of light . . . and . . . hate all the sons of darkness" (1QS i. 3-4, 9-10; but cf. x. 17b, 18). Statements can also be found among the teachers of the Law directed against those who are not learned in the Scriptures and therefore do not obey all the commandments: "Anyone who gives his daughter in marriage to someone from the common people is like one who binds her in chains and sets her before a lion." "Greater is the hatred with which the common people hate the disciples of the learned than the hatred with which idolaters hate the Israelites, and their womenfolk hate them even more than they." (Billerbeck on 5:43, under 3) As in all militant movements, what is meant is not hatred directed against the individual personally, but hatred of godlessness or capitalism or communism or whatever is being cast in the role of devil, a hatred that uncompromising battle seems to demand.

[44] This is precisely the attitude Jesus here attacks. In this form the statement is unparalleled and unprecedented in Jesus' time. Jesus demolishes all the fences into which men would confine love of neighbor. He expressly includes those who are battling against us at the very moment; persecution has probably influenced Matthew himself. Whereas Luke 6:27-28 speaks in general terms—hatred, cursing, mistreatment—Matthew's mention of "persecute" shows that he is thinking in very realistic terms—about the instinctive dislike for punishment of one's body, not just ideological or racial difference.

Both Matthew and Luke speak of prayer for one's enemies. This shows on the one hand that love must not remain a mere feeling, but must issue in action; when one's hands are tied in persecution, the greatest and most important action may well be prayer. This goes beyond the Old Testament, which makes no mention of prayer for those who do not share a bond of nature or common history. On the other hand, it shows that such love can be realized only when one places oneself truly in the presence of God and opens oneself to help. It is thus a blessing, not a definable achievement for which one might claim merit.

[45] This is especially clear in Matthew, because the reason for not claiming merit follows immediately—loving one's enemies is God's doing, like rain and sunshine. The development in this antithesis (vss. 45-48) goes far beyond the brief original statements in the other ones. This probably means that the verses (45-48) are sayings of Jesus which from the beginning (like Luke 6:27-36) belonged with the sayings about love of enemies and nonresistance, but not with the Matthaean antitheses. Matthew probably thinks of them as concluding all the antitheses, and therefore makes them apply fundamentally to all.

The reference to the God who rules in his creation (vs. 45) is already to be found in wisdom literature. Even there it is by no means a self-evident principle. Unlike the Jewish witnesses, Matthew mentions not only the rain, which is usually beneficent in Palestine, but also the scorching sun. The former is mentioned by Job's false friend Eliphaz (Job 5:10), while Job himself counters by blaming natural catastrophes on God (9:7, 24). Among the Greeks similar statements serve to illustrate the indifference of the gods toward men. The philosopher Seneca, roughly contemporary with Jesus, who otherwise takes an optimistic view of nature, knows that "the sun also rises for criminals and the seas stand open for pirates," although he goes on at once to qualify his words. When he goes on to conclude that we, like the gods, should do good to those who fail to show gratitude, thus coming very near Jesus' statement, he means by "the gods" nothing more than the forces of nature, to which a man should adapt himself. The reference to the creator thus really only helps those who know, on the basis of God's entire history with his people, that he is indeed well disposed towards "bad and good, righteous and unrighteous" (note the chiasmus).

Matthew does not speak expressly of God's goodness like Luke 6:35-36 or even of God's acts of mercy like Paul (Rom. 5:5-10); but he, too, knows how Jesus snatched the saying about the sun and rain from the realm of unbelief (Job 9:5-7, 16-18) and based his summons to love one's enemies upon it. Jesus is asserting that we are not really men until we learn to love not only good people but also evil ones, the unrighteous as well as the just, communists and capitalists, those who are normal and those who are degenerate, the emotionally mature and the emotionally disturbed. Therefore Jesus does not state that we are sons of God, but calls on us to become sons (see the excursus on 5:9).

[46] The natural man acts otherwise, as do "tax collectors" and "pagans." As in the Beatitudes (vss. 3-12), when Jesus addresses someone God's grace and mercy become real—for Jesus confronts the listener knowing full well what he is, and accepting him, loving him, so. Only by receiving that kind of love does the listener know what Jesus sees everywhere: God actively loving even his enemies. Only on this basis can there be love that is not simply a natural reaction to the love of someone else, not merely self-love in some strangely transformed shape, but love that really centers on the person loved.

[47] Greeting others plays an important role among the rabbis, and being the first in speaking to another is a mark of special honor. The Greek text uses the word "brothers," referring not only to members of the same family, but mainly to members of the same (religious) community. Persecution by those outside the community, already alluded to in verse 44, gives the example a special poignancy.

[48] Summing up, Jesus bases his call on a reference to the God who is perfect (Luke 6:36: "merciful"). In the Greek Old Testament, this term is used to translate a Hebrew concept that refers to what is whole, intact, undivided. Thus the Old Testament can say that someone lives "perfectly" (i.e., totally, indivisibly) with the Lord in his heart (1 Kings 8:61; 11:4; 15:3, 14). The term "perfect" is used in a somewhat different sense at Qumran; there it has become a description which the community applies to itself, referring to its way of life totally devoted to God's Law, although of course with the knowledge that this way of life is always a gift from the Lord himself (1QS i. 8-13; 1QH iv. 30-32).

In Matthew, too, it refers to devotion to God, not to the flawlessness of a rounded personality brought to the utmost pitch of perfection. That would in fact represent a defection from such total devotion to God. In Matthew devotion to the Law plays a role similar to that played at Qumran, but in Matthew such devotion means doing right, not being holy (1QS viii. 20; CD xx. 2, 5). It is understood in the same sense in James 1:4; 3:2. Unlike the Qumran sect, in fact unlike the Old Testament and all Judaism, Jesus calls God perfect not because God is aloof and totally unlike man, but precisely the reverse: God is totally, undividedly devoted to man; he is faithful to his covenant; he is totally given to those he loves. The statement is prefigured on the one hand by Leviticus 19:2: "You will be holy, for I, the Lord your God, am holy"; and on the other by Deuteronomy 18:13: "You will be perfect before the Lord your God." Matthew maintains that man is not inherently perfect, but can become so. Of course the formulation, both in Greek and in Hebrew, includes the promise "You will be" as well as the summons "You must be." God thus resembles a mold, for man's clay to conform to: cf. 7:7-11 and perhaps even 22:20-21, where man, the image of God, is to render himself over entirely to God. The same point is made with theological language in 1 John 4:19 (cf. 10): only those loved by God can love.

Thus the conclusion and sum of all the antitheses is this statement of the favor which God shows man. The greater righteousness demanded by Jesus of his disciples (vs. 20) is the wholeness of heart that does God's will and stops inquiring after areas not prescribed by God's commandment. Such wholeness, however, is a miracle, a gift, and is granted only to whoever becomes once more one of God's children (18:3).

Elsewhere, such wholeness is at best a hope, expressed for the coming Kingdom; Jesus' desire is to bring his disciples along into his undivided relationship to the Father. As stated in verses 13-16, the disciples are to be shining examples of the coming Kingdom to the world. They are only signs, not the Kingdom itself; but they are truly signs of God's sovereignty and grace. And just as in the promises of salvation in verses 3-12, everything depends on the fact that it is Jesus who makes these pronouncements with the authority of God. This is made clear by his use of "But now I tell you," with its emphatic first person, alongside the words spoken by God himself to his people through Moses. The actual content of Jesus' message is nothing unprecedented. Almost all his sayings have parallels in Judaism; only the call to love one's enemies cannot be found in the same blunt terms. What is unprecedented is this "But now I," which itself shows that here we are not dealing with a further elaboration of certain points in God's Law, but with something utterly new.

What is this thing that is so new? First of all, Jesus' total overthrow of legalistic thinking. Jurists like P. Noll state the consequences of Jesus' message and actions for our modern legal theory: (1) Law must serve man, not some abstract theory. (2) Law must not be inflexible, but must be interpreted to fit the specific situation. For example, damages are no longer fixed and predetermined; the severity of the punishment to the guilty party must be weighed, so that a rich man pays more than a poor man for the same wrong. The reasons for the act must also be weighed, whether the accused's "heart" was in what he did or whether it took place out of negligence. (3) The "general clause" (for Jesus the law of love) carries more weight than the particular stipulations, so that the latter must be corrected to agree with the former. (4) Law takes weakness (human sin) into account, and transcends the ideology that absolutely distinguishes good from evil; law must actively help men in a world not always good. As regards divorce, for example, law should restrain it, but at the same time make it possible, decent, and fair. (5) Above all, there is to be no discrimination against the outsider, the alien; God's own decree on behalf of the disestablished demands protection of the weak.

(6) Law itself therefore must be critical of any tendency to make the existing order absolute.

If, however, it is true that an angry thought, a covetous glance, a legal divorce, a protestation that goes beyond a simple Yes or No, a blow struck in self-defense, or hatred of an enemy is a departure from God's will, then righteousness is beyond calculation and no one can claim to be perfect. And even if one were clear of all the other debts, the debt of love remains. Anyone who would maintain that he has loved perfectly, to the utmost limit, would in the very claim be revealing the absence of love (Rom. 13:8). Jesus simply rejects the question of how one can become righteous in God's eyes by focusing attention on the human heart: the heart can be totally devoted to God and God's will (i.e. to righteousness) only when it is genuinely devoted to other men. What matters is not my righteousness in the eyes of God; what matters is my brother, whose life is restricted by the wrath in my heart; the woman, whose rights are imperiled by my narcissistic lust; society, rendered mute and fearful by my fears; the enemy, whose bitterness is only intensified by my hatred.

This perspective was well appreciated by the Christian community and Matthew, who sought to indicate by his additions how men could and must live in the real world on the basis of Jesus' sayings. Of course there was danger involved: he could have become lost once more in a wilderness of casuistic regulation. Gratefully, he avoided reducing Jesus' summons to mere high ideals, to be venerated and ignored.

Sometimes it is more important that the oppressed are actually helped, that the imperiled bonds of society are maintained, than that the motives of the one helping or maintaining be absolutely pure. But one must not lose sight of Jesus' fundamental point: only the man who learns to place his confidence entirely in God can also learn to renounce his own security and thus encounter his neighbor openly. And when he encounters his neighbor thus—with the compassion of God himself—he will no longer need to kill in order to live; no longer need to destroy his neighbor's marriage and freedom in order to experience supposed sexual fulfillment; no longer need to guard his heart with half-truths or oaths; no longer maintain his cause by vengeance—by returning blows or going to court—or carry the day for his own party by vilifying the enemy. This is not the same thing as the righteousness demanded by Paul. No condemnation of good works is to be found in Matthew; on the contrary, God expects them. But the affinity between Paul and Matthew must not be overlooked either. It is also Paul's desire that God's righteousness make itself felt in human actions, in the life of the community and of the world itself. And conversely, Matthew is aware that only one who has become the son of God—who shows God's favor to all men in all that he does—can receive the title of righteousness, which is greater than that of the teachers of the Law. True righteousness requires a whole and undivided heart, which belongs first to one's neighbor and thus also to God (see the excursus following 7:29).

Righteousness before God (6:1-18)

[1]"Be careful not to perform your religious duties in public so that people will see what you do; otherwise you will not have any reward from your Father in heaven.

[2]"So when you give alms, do not make a big show of it, as the hypocrites do in the synagogues and on the streets, so that people will praise them. Amen, I tell you, they have their reward in full. [3]But as for you, when you give alms, do it in such a way that your left hand will not know what your right hand is doing, [4]that your almsgiving may be in secret. And your Father, who sees what you do in secret, will reward you.

[5]"And when you pray, do not be like the hypocrites! They love to stand up and pray in the synagogues and on the street corners so that everyone will see them. Amen, I tell you, they have their reward in full. [6]But as for you, when you pray, go to your room and close the door, and pray to your Father, who is in secret. And your Father, who sees what is in secret, will reward you.

[7]"But when you pray, do not use a lot of meaningless words, as the pagans do, who think that God will hear them because they have so much to say. [8]Do not be like them; your Father already knows what you need before you ask him. [9]This, then, is how you should pray:

Our Father in heaven: may your holy name be honored; [10]may your Kingdom come; may your will be done on earth as it is in heaven.

[11]Give us today our bread for the coming day. [12]Forgive us the wrongs we have done, as we have forgiven the wrongs that others have done us. [13]Do not bring us into temptation, but deliver us from evil.

[14]"If you forgive others, your Father in heaven will also forgive your wrongs. [15]But if you do not forgive the wrongs of others, then your Father in heaven will not forgive you.

[16]"And when you fast, do not put on a sad face as the hypocrites do. They go around with a hungry look so that everyone will see that they are fasting. Amen, I tell you, they have their reward in full. [17]But as for you, when you fast, anoint your head and wash your face, [18]so that others cannot know you are fasting, but only your Father, who is in secret. And your Father, who sees what is in secret, will reward you."

(Vs. 6—Isa. 26:20; 2 Kings 4:33.)

[2-6, 16-18] Initially we can distinguish three sayings concerning almsgiving, prayer, and fasting, which constitute the three most important demonstrations of religious devotion in Judaism (Tob. 12:8: "Give with fasting, alms, and righteousness"; cf. Acts 10:31). The three are constructed in precisely the same way, repeating the same words: "When you . . . , do not . . . as the hypocrites do . . . (in the synagogues) . . . , so that everyone will see them. Amen, I tell you, they have their reward in full. But as for you . . . when . . . (to your Father) . . . who is in secret. And your Father, who sees what is in secret, will reward you." (In the protasis, it is true, the second person singular [vs. 2], which always appears in the apodosis, alternates with the second person plural [vss. 5, 16], which is also characteristic of the introduction [vs. 1] and the interpolation [vss. 7-15]. The fact that prayer is the subject of verses 7-8 probably accounts for the assimilation to the second person plural. In addition, the plural is much more strongly suggested by the following phrase, "like the hypocrites," than by the longer phrase in verse 2, "as the hypocrites do.")

The close of each of the three sayings resembles passages from wisdom poetry (cf. Ecclus. 17:15; 23:19; 39:19); but something more is suggested by the prophetic "Amen, I tell you" (see the introductory remarks on 5:17-20, discussing vs. 18) and the clear allusion to God's eschatological judgment, which appears only rarely in the wisdom literature. Matthew undoubtedly was using material already extant, as even his use of the unaccustomed phrase "your Father" shows. Throughout these sayings it appears in the singular, whereas everywhere else Matthew uses only the plural form (with the addition of "in heaven," except in 6:8; 10:20, 29).

[7-15] Had Matthew been composing this passage freely, he would probably have transferred the section on prayer to the end, because to it he appends the Lord's Prayer and some additions. The Lord's Prayer is also found in Luke 11:1-4 (see below), while the other sayings have no parallel in the other Gospels. It is introduced by a saying directed against long prayers, which corresponds in form to verses 31-32: "Do not (babble) as the pagans do . . . , for your Father knows (what/that you) . . . need." Matthew may in fact have composed this introduction on the model of verses 31-32, or merely framed it in this particular form; of course, an original saying of Jesus may have influenced the form of verses 31-32 in Q, or both sayings may have been pronounced in similar form by Jesus himself; the evidence is insufficient to decide the question. Appended to the Lord's Prayer we find a saying about mutual forgiveness, the positive portion of which appears also in Mark 11:25 (with the phrase "your Father in heaven," unique there in Mark); the negative portion is appended by some manuscripts in Mark 11:26. Since the wording does not agree precisely even in the first half, it was probably already familiar to Matthew in this fuller form. He omits it in the parallel to Mark 11:25, but frames a similar statement independently at the end of the parable of the unforgiving servant (18:35).

[1] Can the three sections dealing with almsgiving, prayer, and fasting go back to Jesus himself? The introduction is Matthew's own. The phrase "be careful" occurs in the New Testament only in Matthew and in Luke 20:46 (it does appear elsewhere, but always with a noun, "watch out for . . .": Matt. 7:15; 10:17; 16:6, 11). Performance of religious duties ("righteousness") is one of his major themes (vss. 6, 10, 20, and many other places). The phrase "so that people will see what you do" appears likewise in 23:5; the reference to a reward is taken from the three sayings (vss. 2, 5, 16). "Your Father in heaven" is typically Matthaean (see above).

The rest can hardly derive from Jesus, for the contrast between being seen by men and being seen by God does not suffice. The Pharisee in the parable found in Luke 18:9-14 likewise desires to be seen by God alone. He, too, prays "apart by himself," offers sacrifice and fasts only in the sight of God. In addition, Jesus categorically rejects fasting as an exercise of devotion (Matt. 9:15 = Mark 2:19). The supposition that these three sayings are spoken to outsiders, and the Beatitudes and ethical injunctions (ch. 5) to the disciples, does not suffice. Or is Jesus' radically new message not addressed to outsiders? Nevertheless, echoes of Jesus' voice can be heard behind this passage, for each of the three sections exhibits some truly radical formulation.

[3] If the left hand must not know what the right hand does, a man cannot desire to present what he does before God; in the presence of God he cannot know the good he has done, as the discourse concerning the judgment of the world shows (25:31-46). [7-8] And if the Father already knows what we need before we ask, then all *performance* of prayer, which trusts in special human effort, in other words "babbling," loses its meaning. [17] The admonition to anoint one's head and wash one's face when fasting is strange; it actually recommends donning a mask to give the opposite effect. But it is reminiscent of a far more radical saying of Jesus, which states that where the bridegroom is there can be no fasting, only feasting (9:15).

All this suggests that behind the section stand three sayings of Jesus which may have belonged together from the very outset as defining his attitude toward the three major forms of Jewish piety; in a vividly impressive way they rule out what is always uppermost in the thoughts of the devout person of all periods: his achievement in the eyes of God. The single citation of Scripture in verse 6 may point to replacement by a more radical saying of Jesus, contained in verse 7. The distinction between what is done for show and what is done in secret, to receive commendation only from God, not from men, is also found in Paul (Rom. 2:28-29). There, too, it is associated with statements rooted in Jewish piety which had been expressed even before the time of Jesus—statements that men must allow God to circumcise their hearts, not merely their flesh (Deut. 10:16; 30:6; Jer. 4:4; Ezek. 44:7, 9; cf. the discussion of Matt. 5:8). In Paul, too, we find a statement reminiscent of our passage: the true Jew, who is a "Jew in secret," i.e., in his heart, receives his praise from God and not from men. But Paul, too, following Jesus, sees the contrast in much more radical terms than do the Old Testament passages and the Jewish statements: he stresses that such devotion can only be given by God's "spirit," and can never be attained by obedience to the "letter" of the Law.

It is clear, then, that the Christian community was familiar with the idea of a "secret" devotion addressed only to God, not to men, and this idea was associated with certain statements made by reformed Judaism. But the voice of Jesus was not forgotten. The paradoxical metaphors in Matthew have the same point that Paul makes: the man who really places his confidence in God renounces all righteousness that can be judged by men, even by the agent himself; he thus escapes the notion of any accomplishment that would earn reward in the eyes of God.

The situation would be different if the late manuscripts were correct in adding "(reward you) openly" at the end of each section. In this case we might think of a Hebrew or Aramaic basis, similar to Proverbs 25:21-22, making the point that God will not bring our acts to their fulfillment until the Judgment, when all secrets will be revealed (Col. 3:1-4). But both this reading and this exegesis remain extremely dubious; it might apply at most to a preliminary stage that can no longer be reconstructed. Thus we may distinguish three strata: a saying of Jesus that can no longer be determined in detail; a threefold admonition about true devotion, shaped by the community when it was still firmly rooted in Judaism; and the redaction by Matthew himself. We must distinguish the concerns of each of these three stages.

a. The Three Acts of Devotion (6:1-6, 16-18)

[1] The theme, according to the Matthaean introduction, is human "righteousness," the performance of "religious duties." Matthew uses this term to include almsgiving, prayer, and fasting, i.e., the good works that, according to Jewish belief, go beyond the demands of the Law, earn a special reward, atone for transgressions of the Law, or even benefit others at the Last Judgment if they exceed what is re-

quired of the person himself. Obviously the performance of such good works is not wrong, nor is the expectation of reward at God's Last Judgment (cf. the discussion of 20:1-6 and Mark 9:41); what is wrong is the attention paid to the esteem of other men. Matthew 23:5 expresses a similar thought. At the conclusion of this section we shall consider how much truth there is in this position.

[2] The first saying deals with works of charity. The immediate reference is to alms, but any act of charity toward another is included. Judaism had an exemplary system of charity, regulated by the community on the basis of taxes imposed on all; private charity was also copious. Tobit 1:3 and Ecclesiasticus 7:10 both urge charity. Especially nice is a rabbinic statement that modesty, compassion, and charity belong together, all deriving from God's own act (Billerbeck IV, 538-39 [a]; I, 346[2]; and the discussion of 6:3-4).

The word for "hypocrite" was originally the term for an actor playing a specific role. The Greek Bible uses it as a term for the godless; the Pharisaic Psalms of Solomon (4:7, 25) apply it to the Sadducees, whom the Pharisees considered worldly; in the second century of the Christian era a Jewish rabbi states that nine tenths of the world's hypocrisy is concentrated in Jerusalem (Billerbeck on 23:13, A 1). The word "hypocrite" does not automatically imply subjective dishonesty; it can refer to self-delusion as well as pretense to others. In our verse, however, the practice of Jewish piety is raked in such horrible terms that conscious deception is probably meant.

In the synagogue the amount donated and the name of the donor were announced, and it is possible that at one time trumpets called attention to a large gift. That may have been exceptional, but the description corresponds to universal practice, even in the Christian church, where institutions bore (and still bear) the name of the donor endowing them. But in the Judaism of the period we also hear voices saying that almsgiving must remain as hidden as a man's hip, that it would be better to give nothing than to embarrass the recipient with a gift (third century of the Christian era). In fact, then, the saying does not propose anything more than a reform, one which might have been possible even within Judaism. This is shown by the formula "They have their reward in full," which is the standard formula on a receipt, corresponding to "I have received (payment)." Precise reward was, in fact, the belief of Judaism: a man either receives his reward in this life, for instance in the form of honor and esteem among his fellow citizens, and then has no further expectations, or else he forgoes that reward, even accepting suffering and disgrace for the sake of God, and may expect heavenly reward in return. Only in acts of charity is there sometimes hope for both: the capital remains invested in heaven while one already enjoys the interest upon earth. Once more, we shall consider the truth of this position at the conclusion of our discussion.

[3] The saying about the left hand that must not know what the right hand is doing presents an arresting and impressive metaphor, far transcending this schema. Of course the anatomy of our brain prevents the right hand from doing anything that is not under the control of the same central nervous system as controls the left hand. And so the paradox (see the discussion of 5:13) is one of the enigmatic sayings that points to the miracle of a new (John 3:3 ff. would say "reborn") kind of man. If a man's left hand no longer knows what is being done, then his heart, which might expect a reward for it, also does not. Here is accomplished the breakthrough that eliminates all thought of measuring one's achievements so as to claim an appropriate reward, from other men or even from God.

[4] But this raises the question of how to interpret the saying about the Father who sees what is in secret. It may mean merely that what is done is known only to God and to the agent himself—who does what he does with an eye to recompense from God. Or it may mean actions that are radically secret, actions of which the agent himself is unaware, which he never computes for profit. We shall discuss this question in our summary on verses 1-18. That the second reading is not out of the question is shown by the phrase "*your* Father," which occurs only here in the first three Gospels; it recalls sayings of Jesus in which "reward" means not merely the wages earned for a certain amount of work, but also an outright gift, of love (see the discussion of 20:1-16).

[5] The second saying deals with prayer, which was a vital force in Judaism, engaged in with devout frequency: unison prayer in Temple and synagogue as well as private prayer, fixed liturgical prayer as well as free prayer born of the moment. The psalms of the Old Testament as well as those newly composed at the time of Jesus

demonstrate the vigor with which the Jews could pour out their hearts in prayer. Once more the conduct of the "hypocrites," though censured, is easy to understand. Fixed times of prayer had been developed, and wherever one was, they were observed simply by turning toward the Temple in Jerusalem and praying; similar practice can be observed among Moslems today. Prayers were said aloud only during public fasts; at other times they were whispered, and it was recommended that one retreat as much as possible into a corner. Of course, being seen at prayer might stimulate others. Nevertheless, the "others" induced by such devotion are as little likely to have their mind on *their* prayers as the one is who consciously sets the example. His prayer is addressed not to God but to them, theirs not to God but to the hope of gaining merit in God's eyes. Such exercises in preening and bribery are denounced in the Judaism of that period (cf. the discussion of vss. 7-8).

[6] The worshiper is advised to go into the small storeroom attached to the house—the only room provided with a door. The wording has been assimiliated to the Greek translation of Isaiah 26:20, which speaks of the flight out of Egypt (but cf. 2 Kings 4:33); the storeroom is nevertheless almost a proverbial term for a place where one cannot be seen. The storeroom, of course, is mentioned merely as an example, not as the only possibility—Jesus, for instance, prays by himself on a hillside (14:23), and communal prayer is endorsed in 18:19-20. What matters is "wholehearted" devotion to God without concern for other men or one's own convenience. It is of course not guaranteed by the proper choice of a place to pray. The significant point of the example is the choice of a totally ordinary room, not a quiet corner in the Temple or the synagogue.

[16] Fasting is discussed in corresponding terms. Officially, the only fast is the Day of Atonement, when eating, drinking, bathing, and anointing with oil are forbidden; fasting is also associated with extraordinary acts of corporate penance when disaster strikes. But fasting was also widely practised at that time on an individual and voluntary basis (9:14; Luke 18:12). In the Greek text, the words represented by "a hungry look" and "everyone will see" involve a pun; the first expression is quite strong, so that one might suppose they "disfigure" their appearance so that others will take notice. But

since the word was chosen for its phonetic similarity, a freer translation is presumably justified. Men are in fact so perverted that they can
take pleasure in the pain of their own penance and look with satisfaction on their sorrow for sins. True and false fasting must be clearly
distinguished; what matters is the inward concern true repentance,
not outward actions. Judaism has been aware of this principle—
genuineness—since Isaiah 58:5 ff. (cf. Jer. 14:12; Zech. 7:5 ff.; Joel
2:12), and a similar approach appears in the attitude toward baptism
at Qumran (cf. the discussion of 3:8). [17] At heart, then, the passage
seems to be saying nothing new. But paradoxically, it calls on men,
when they fast, to anoint their heads and wash their faces—in other
words, to act as if going to a feast. And in this we find an echo of what
is characteristic of Jesus' preaching: true repentance is joy, an anticipation of the exultation the eschaton will bring (9:15; 13:44; 22:1-10;
Luke 15:7, 10, 22-24). [18] Once more, then, we must face a question:
does the passage mean that we are not to "be seen" fasting by men,
but only by God; or is joy being proclaimed far more radically, a joy
that can only rejoice in God's great goodness, not fast to deserve it?
Even in the latter case, of course, fasting would not be prohibited; it
can even be recommended when a man wants to participate in something far greater than eating and drinking, something that requires a
certain openness of the senses (4:2; 1 Cor. 7:5).

b. The Lord's Prayer (6:7-13)
Cf. Luke 11:1-4

[7] A new note, equally radical, is sounded in verses 7-8. Using
a word found nowhere else, these verses warn against using "a lot of
meaningless words," that is, against prayer that would gain a hearing
from God by its own efficacy, by sheer quantity. The pagans are
singled out here because the pagans of this period no longer knew who
the true God really was. They therefore joined together a variety of
names or terms for God. As the magical papyri still attest, this led to
the construction of endless lists so that the correct name of God might
not be omitted during the incantation. Similar developments can be
observed within Judaism; the Eighteen Benedictions, to be recited
three times each day, became quite elaborate. Once again, the attack

on long prayers says nothing new; it can be found in Ecclesiasticus 7:14 and Ecclesiastes 5:1-2, and some of the rabbis also recommend brief prayer.

[8] The second sentence is the crucial one. Once again a mere literal interpretation, reducing the number of words, would not represent any gain. We read that Jesus prayed through entire nights (14:23-25 = Mark 6:46-48; Mark 1:35); Paul speaks of continuous prayer (Rom. 12:12; 1 Thess. 5:17); and Jesus himself, according to 7:7-11; Luke 11:5 ff.; 18:1 ff., inculcates perseverance in prayer. What matters is how the worshiper thinks of his prayer—whether, as the contemporary Roman philosopher Seneca puts it (Ep. xxxi. 5), he seeks "to weary the gods," or whether he takes God's promise in Isaiah 65:24 seriously: "Before they call I answer; while they are yet speaking I will hear." (RSV) Thus prayer becomes totally a gift of God and ceases to be an action performed deliberately to achieve a goal or support a claim. Jesus' purpose is not to take the gift of prayer away from men, as his own example shows; but he releases them from having to make a special effort to guarantee access to God. He turns prayer once more into children's conversation with their father.

The Lord's Prayer is found in a rather different form in Luke 11:2-4. It is astounding how little legalism the early Christians showed in transmitting the words of Jesus. Even so central a text as this is reshaped with relative freedom, adapted to local usage, and elaborated. The community had no sacred texts in the sense of ones that had to be repeated without the slightest change. The Lord's Prayer is therefore not the letter of the law; it is an aid to prayer, a guide to be followed without being bound to this or that precise wording. Mark and John (and Paul) omit it entirely. Even in Greek, however, the Matthaean and Lukan forms are undoubtedly based on a common original, as is indicated by the very rare adjective modifying "bread," which appears in both versions.

The most striking difference is the omission in Luke of the third petition. This petition is therefore a later accretion, probably based on the prayer of Jesus in Gethsemane. Only in Matthew (26:42) is the Gethsemane petition expressed in the same words as in the Lord's Prayer, and that in a verse reformulated by Matthew from Mark (put differently in Matt. 26:39 = Mark 14:36).

It is further noteworthy that in many manuscripts the petition in Luke 11:2 is replaced by the sentence "May your Holy Spirit come upon us and purify us"; still other manuscripts read "May your Kingdom come upon [or 'to'] us," which probably represents an echo of this variant. As far as we can see, a prayer for the Holy Spirit occasionally replaced the first petition. Probably we are dealing with words that were spoken in the course of baptism; similar prayers are found in early Christian texts outside of the Lord's Prayer, into which they probably found their way from the original setting.

There appear three petitions in Matthew, two in Luke; in Greek they follow in parataxis, each concluding with the emphatic "your." This can only be represented in English by beginning each with "(May) your." There follow three additional petitions dealing with our bread, our wrongs, and our temptations. In Luke, God is addressed simply as "Father"; in Matthew, the term of address is a form current in Judaism, expanded by the addition of "our" and "in heaven." The third petition, not found in Luke, differs from the first two in being elaborated by the addition of "on earth as it is in heaven." A further addition has been made by Matthew to the last petition ("but deliver us from evil"). We thus find expansions in the address, after the first two (second person singular) petitions, and after the last petition. This suggests the prayer originally began with the brief address "Father" followed by two second person singular petitions in parallel and then two longer parallel first person plural petitions, concluding with a third short petition expressed emphatically. The three final petitions, which go beyond the lapidary initial petitions (to which quite similar parallels are found in Jewish prayers), are linked with "and," while the first two petitions stand in parataxis.

The concluding doxology "Yours is the kingdom and the power and the glory for ever" appears only in later manuscripts of Matthew. The community probably used this formula, which goes back to 1 Chronicles 29:11-13, as a response to the prayer spoken by the leader, thus affirming it. In Judaism it was customary to make such free or liturgically prescribed responses to prayers; we may therefore assume that some such doxology, in variable form, was pronounced from the very beginning.

Luke's version, to go now into details, replaces the "today" of the petition for bread with "daily," and also changes the form of the verb so as to suggest repeated giving. There are also other suggestions of reworking in Luke: he uses a more common term for "sins" in the petition for forgiveness and a different wording in the apodosis—"for we, too, forgive whoever wrongs us." Matthew is thus closer to the original form in specific details, Luke in overall form.

Didache 8:2-3 prescribes recitation of the Lord's Prayer three times a day in the Matthaean form. Since the Didache uses "heaven" and "wrong" in the singular rather than the plural, it probably did not borrow the prayer directly from Matthew but from the liturgical practice of the community. In addition, the prayer of Jesus is probably attested in a Latin translation as early as the end of the first century. There is a five-by-five magic square that can be read upwards, downwards, from left to right, and from right to left, always yielding the same text. The hidden formula we are intended to find presumably reads "Pater noster A O" (twice repeated), Latin for "Our Father, A[lpha] and O[mega]" (cf. Rev. 1:8).

[9] To address God simply as "Father" without further addition, as is done in Luke 11:2, is without parallel in Palestinian Judaism at the time of Jesus (see the discussion of 5:9 and Mark 14:36). Jesus' gift to his disciples is the spirit behind this bold way of addressing God. Luke still senses the miracle of this form of address; according to Luke 11:1, the disciples plead for this prayer and receive it from Jesus. The Matthaean community expressed its sense of wonder at this gift by adding "in heaven," so that the form of address "our Father" would never be taken for granted. We are no longer so impressed by what the Old Testament considers as examples of God's omnipotence: thunder resounding, lightning flashing and mountains smoking, the earth trembling, clouds pouring forth and the sea raging (Exod. 19:15-19; Judg. 5:4-5; Hab. 3:8 ff.; Ps. 77:17-19). But the miracle of being able to say "Father" is if anything made all the greater by the modern worshiper's sense of the hugeness of the universe, in which not only he but his whole earth is only a speck among millions. Prayer must always remain worship and adoration, in which there lives something of the worshiper's awe at God's mercy. In the Old and the New Testaments, when men encounter God they fall to the ground as though dead, and only the miracle of being told "Do

not fear" permits them an encounter with God (Ezek. 1:28; Matt. 28:5, 10; Luke 1:13; Rev. 1:17). Precisely because the ability to call God "Father" has become so devalued today, it is imperative that we hear the early Christian community reminding us that he is "in heaven." The use of "our" reminds the community that no worshiper stands alone (cf. also the discussion of vss. 14-15).

Not until we know God's name can he really become God for us, that is, cease to be a mysterious unknown power and become a person with significance for our lives, helping us and challenging us. Something similar can take place when we suddenly discover who it is we have been talking to, unaware of his identity. The history of God with Moses and Israel begins with the naming of his name; his name is in a sense a sign of the covenant between him and Israel (Exod. 3:13-15; 6:2-8). But to men of antiquity a name meant even more; it had voodoo power. Whoever knew the name of his enemy had him in his power and could destroy him, for instance by inscribing this name on a tablet then boring a hole through it (cf. the discussion of Mark 1:24). Above all, according to the Old Testament, God dwells among his people in his name. His word and spirit emphasize God's concern for the people; his name implies his presence. Just as a herald or judge proclaiming the formula "in the name of the king" can make the law and power of the king a present reality, so that, decked with the king's authority and power, he can decree the king's message or execute the king's justice, so God's name is pronounced when-ever his message is proclaimed (Gen. 4:26; 12:8). God's name, written on a piece of paper together with a curse and dropped into the water, can bring sickness and suffering to a guilty woman who drinks the water (Num. 5:21-24).

The petition that God's name be honored or "hallowed" is also rooted in the Old Testament. Ever since Isaiah 40:25; 43:15; etc., "the Holy One" has been a name of God. God's name is to be honored as holy upon earth through those who are his people, but it is God's people who repeatedly desecrate his name (Lev. 22:32; Deut. 32:51), so that he must intervene himself and honor his own name, profaned by men (Isa. 29:23-24; 48:11; 52:5-6; Ezek. 36:23-27; Ps. 79:9). Isaiah 30:27 states, "The name of the LORD comes from afar" (RSV); the Greek translation seeks to stress that this takes place repeatedly, and adds "through many ages." It is therefore not surprising to read in the third petition of the Jewish Eighteen Benedictions: "You are holy and your name is holy." Most closely related, however, is the first petition of the Kaddish, which was pronounced as the conclusion of synagogue worship and often at the end of other prayers: "May his name be glorified and honored as holy in the world, which he created according to his will." This petition from the Kaddish shows that the first two petitions in the Lord's Prayer are in fact the same: God's holy name will be "honored" (hallowed) when (and because) his Kingdom comes. It is God himself, therefore, who honors his name. The Lord's Prayer also expresses this notion indirectly by its use of the passive. The Greek verb form implies an action that takes place only once; the petition therefore looks for a final fulfillment in which God will be all in all (1 Cor. 15:28), and in which every knee will bow in honor of God the Father in heaven, on earth, and under the earth, and every tongue confess that Jesus Christ is Lord (Phil. 2:10-11).

But the Old Testament background shows how that which will one day be perfect also comes into being now among God's people. In addition, the community knows that the name of God has already become present reality in Jesus. Matthew, who begins the Sermon on Mount, following the Beatitudes, with sayings about discipleship using the metaphors of salt, a lamp, and a city on a hill, is therefore undoubtedly thinking of the realization of this petition in Jesus himself and his band of disciples, who represent proleptically what is to come (cf. the discussion of 18:20). This anticipation of eschatological fulfillment passes increasingly into the background as time goes by. Thus we read in Didache 10:2: "We thank you, holy Father, for your holy name, which you have caused to lodge in our hearts"; and in 1 Clement 59:2-3 (cf. 58:1) this petition becomes a prayer for the church's mission.

[10] With reference to the second petition, see the treatment of the Kingdom of God in the discussion of Mark 1:15. The second petition of the Kaddish (see the discussion of vs. 9) reads: "May he establish his Kingdom in your lifetime and in your days and in all the ages of the whole house of Israel soon and in the near future." Thus what is referred to is the final establishment of the Kingdom of God, to be expected "soon." All that follows is a doxology and an Amen. But we

do not know whether and above all in what form this prayer was used in the time of Jesus. As in the Lord's Prayer, the Kaddish honors God's name in its first petition, and supplicates his sovereignty in its second. The same sequence is observed at the accession of a king to the throne. This second petition therefore certainly refers to the time when "the world has become the kingdom of our Lord and of his Messiah, and he shall reign for all eternity," when "salvation and power and sovereignty belong to our God" (Rev. 11:15; 12:10; etc., the author's translation).

But on this point Jesus differed from his contemporaries: although he held fast to this hope for the future, he also promised the Kingdom to men in the immediate present, clothing it with reality; indeed he sees it coming upon men in his own mighty acts (Matt. 12:28). Thus whoever prays for the coming of this Kingdom prays also for the establishment of Jesus' authority, which is at work in the words and deeds of his disciples and is already causing "Satan [to] fall like lightning from heaven" (Luke 10:17-18). Thus in the second petition the worshiper is praying that Jesus will become reality in his own time and in his own life; at the same time, however, he is also longing for the coming of that time when "every tear shall be washed away from their eyes and there shall be no more death or suffering or crying or pain, because the old things have passed away" (Rev. 21:4, the author's translation).

The third petition is not meant fatalistically, here or in 26:42. God's will is done where men carry it out, just as God's Law is "done" where men carry out its precepts (5:18), or as in Jesus' entire ministry there "comes true" what was prophesied (1:22; 2:6, 15, 17, 23; 3:3; 4:14-16; 8:17; 12:17-21; 13:14-15, 35; 21:4-5, 42). Therefore all the Gospels speak of doing God's will (7:21; Mark 3:35; Luke 12:47-48; John 7:17), and according to the last of these passages, only the person who does God's will can be persuaded of the truth of Jesus' message. This third petition of Matthew's of course implies that God's will will be fulfilled perfectly only on the day when every knee will bow; but it also expresses better than the first two the idea that God's will is carried out all the time by the action of his people, even those who serve without knowing it (Isa. 10:5-6, etc.; Acts 4:27-28; cf. the discussion of Mark 14:10). There is no direct parallel to this in Jewish prayers. This triumph of God's will is also referred to by the phrase "on earth as it is in heaven." God's wish, which is accepted as accomplished among the angels, is also to be realized among men. To put it in modern terms: in the universe as a whole it is taken for granted that everything follows its own proper course, under the control of an ordering power; this is also to be realized among men, who violate this order. To be human means to accept responsibility under God's mandate and according to his will (Gen. 1:26-28); and we are praying here simply that man will become human. The anticlimactic structure of this prayer itself makes the point: it moves in reductive sequence from the large concerns of God to our own needs and problems. Thus we pray, and following after Jesus, we discover: precisely when we concern ourselves with God—his name, his Kingdom, but most of all his will—will our needs be met, and met better than by any amount of concern for ourselves. An affluent society has found this lesson all too painful.

[11] With the fourth petition our own needs are mentioned. The prayer is not overconcerned with spirituality; the bread we need each day is taken seriously, as it is throughout Jesus' life. Not only does he heal the sick and quiet tempests, he also feeds the hungry with real bread and real fish (14:13-21; 15:32-39). Even in the Old Testament the image of a banquet was used to portray fulfillment of the eschaton (Isa. 25:6 ff.); Jesus himself adopts this imagery (8:11; 22:1-10; cf. 11:19). There is nothing more striking about the early Christian community than this fact: its only practise in any way resembling those of a "cult" is a meal, a full meal than can satisfy hunger. That shows how seriously Jesus and his band of disciples take the body and its needs.

The yearing for a new earth, where righteousness will be at home (2 Pet. 3:13), has deep roots in the community of Jesus. Our understanding of this petition, to be sure, depends on the unusual adjective modifying bread, of uncertain etymology. Even today scholars cannot decide whether it refers to "necessary" bread, "today's" bread, or bread "for the coming day" (the morrow, or, when the prayer was spoken at an early hour, the same day). The last interpretation remains the most likely, because an Aramaic translation of Matthew so interprets it, and Matthew himself naturally set the sentence down in the form used by his community in prayer.

It has therefore been suggested that the choice of so obscure a word indicates that what is being prayed for is the bread of the coming Kingdom, the heavenly bread of eschatological fulfillment, in other words, the bread "of the (eschatologically) coming day." This remains unlikely for three reasons: first, Jesus paid close attention to earthly needs and their alleviation; second, the next petition, and probably the one following, refer unambiguously to this world, where men wrong each other and must find again the path of reconciliation; and third, if the plea were eschatological the word "our" would be out of place. Furthermore, wine and fat meat—not bread—are characteristic of the eschatological banquet. Bread, of course, did find its way into the Lord's Supper, but in only one passage (Luke 14:15-24) is "bread" used as a comprehensive term for food at a feast (cf. Acts 2:42). At most we might suppose, analogously to the first petition, that we are praying for the living bread of the coming Kingdom and at the same time for the bread we need in the present. But is this really likely? A banquet with wine, or even the bread of the Lord's Supper consumed within the community, could be a sign of the coming glory; so much is clear. But can one petition include both this coming glory and at the same time the crust eaten daily? And so the petition probably means: grant that we may lie down to sleep, not with a sense of abundance or surety against hard times, but simply without despair, knowing the coming day has been provided for.

Neither does such a prayer contradict Jesus' call to abandon all concern for the morrow (vs. 34); it entrusts this concern to the one who alone can really provide for us. "Bread" includes everything that man really needs; his occasional need for banqueting and celebration is shown by Jesus himself when he institutes the Lord's Supper for his community with bread and wine. The Lord's Supper was understood as a symbol of the eschatological banquet (Mark 14:25; Luke 22:16-18, 30), and when the words were translated into Greek a recollection of that end banquet may have led to the rare word that includes ambiguously both the morrow and the day that will one day come. Here, too, the worshiper does not pray for himself alone but for the brethren, for "our" bread. Once again there is no direct parallel in Jewish prayers, apart from the ninth of the Eighteen Benedictions: "Sanctify for us, Lord, this year . . . and satisfy the world from the bounty of your goodness."

[12] Forgiveness is the point of Jesus' entire ministry: it was Jesus after all who incurred derision as a "friend of tax collectors and sinners" (11:19), who called Matthew to be his disciple (9:9), who promised the Kingdom to pagans—theretofore excluded from society with God (8:11-12)—and who restored the leper ostracized by God's people (8:4). But is this not something that takes place once and for all? Isn't the petition for forgiveness appropriate only in the mouth of one who still stands far off from Jesus? The problem would be solved if we were able to think only in terms of God's Last Judgment, the fulfillment of forgiveness all at once, here and now; but at least the apodosis speaks of something that happens day by day. We may note that unlike Luke, who speaks of "sins," Matthew speaks of "wrongs" or "debts," and that this is the earlier term. The forgivness granted once and for all is thus to include all those actions, words, thoughts, and feelings of ours by which we have hurt or ignored others (cf. the excursus on 18:18). Our relationship to God can be healthy only when our relationship to men is love; and both the earliest effort and latest fruit of love is forgiveness.

Even though the Greek from "we have forgiven" may be based on an Aramaic sentence in which present and past cannot be distinguished, a mere prayerful resolve was never intended, but rather the action that is really performed at the very moment the worshiper pronounces this petition. The Matthaean form has preserved this meaning more clearly than the Lukan, where the statement we "have forgiven" probably signifies only the acts of forgiveness the worshiper has performed in the past, not those he is now (in the prayer) performing.

Any misunderstanding that God's forgiveness can be earned by our actions is exploded by the parable of the workers paid the same for unequal work (20:1-16). But on the other hand, as 5:23-24 shows, mere good intentions are not enough. Whether the petition here goes back to Jesus or only to the post-Easter tradition, the interruption of the rhythm shows the importance of the supplementary clause. So important to the community was a readiness to forgive that a summons to forgive was incorporated into their prayer, where it is actually out of place. Neither does it occur in the corresponding petition of the Eighteen Benedictions: "Forgive us, our Father, for we have sinned;

pardon us, our King, for we have offended; you are pleased to forgive and to pardon" (sixth petition). More apposite is the Day of Atonement, when the statement is recited from God's Law that atonement with God comes only to him who has already been reconciled with his fellow men.

[13] The final petition is not easy to understand. Does God lead men into temptation? On this question, see the excursus on 4:3. It would not lessen offence to understand the petition in strictly eschatological terms, in other words, to think only of the one great temptation that is to come over the world shortly before the end (as according to many Jewish expectations, and also according to 24:21-22 = Mark 13:19-20). But the absence of the article, the fact there is no mention of "the" one great temptation, argues against this interpretation.

It is noteworthy that Jesus prays to be kept from temptation; the devout Jew would pray instead for God to test him so that he might demonstrate his total obedience. Thus Psalm 60:6 is interpreted in Judaism as follows: "You give temptation to those who fear you, that they may be exalted" (Billerbeck on 4:1 A). In the seventh petition of the Eighteen Benedictions we read only: "Look upon our misery and guide our cause and deliver us for your name's sake," which corresponds to the second half of our verse, but not the first. Whoever prays the Lord's Prayer is not outstandingly pious, not a religious superstar; he does not ask God for opportunity to prove his faith, but asks not to be put to the test. He does not, of course, require that God take from him the great and onerous gift of freedom, but he does ask to be kept from those situations in which a wrong decision might almost force itself on him.

If the second half of the petition refers not only to evil but to the Evil One, as 13:19 suggests, the double statement discussed above is especially striking: God wills temptation, and yet it is the Evil One whom we encounter in temptation. Here at the end of the prayer a yearning makes itself heard, a yearning for that world in which this dichotomy, affecting our entire life, will vanish. What is to be realized now in one particular temptation—deliverance from evil or the Evil One—will reach its fulfillment when communion with God is fully realized, in his coming Kingdom. It will be characterized by the fact that what now takes place fragmentarily in our experience of God will one day be the *whole* reality of life: nothing opposed to God will come between God and man. What is already true in Jesus will be realized in all mankind: the unity of man's will with that of God. The familiar doxology is already found with two of its three components ("power and glory") in Didache 8:2 (see the introductory comments on vss. 9-13). With this formula the worshiper claims the prayer once more as his own.

[14] Matthew appends by way of explanation a sentence whose first, positively formulated half is already found in Mark 11:25. That Matthew borrows it from tradition is shown by the fact that he uses the traditional word for "trespasses," not the word used in the Lord's Prayer. Tradition had already associated this saying with prayer. [15] Matthew further emphasizes the saying by repeating it in negative form; the idea appears again in negative form in 18:35: if you do not forgive others God will not forgive you. The negative repetition in 6:15 adapts this passage to the schema of two contrasting conditional sentences already noted in 5:19. The second sentence is artfully joined to the first: in the second, the expression "your wrongs" comes in the subordinate clause that begins the sentence; in the first, it comes in the concluding main clause.

Matthew's appending of this particular commentary to the Lord's Prayer shows how concerned he was that God's will actually be done in the Christian community, above all where the spirit of brotherhood was endangered. The gift of being able to address God as Father, which far surpasses anything one might dare to ask; the great hope that one day God's name, God's Kingdom, God's will would be victorious; even the pain of hunger, sin, and temptation—none of these concerned Matthew and his community as much as forgiveness between men. This says much about how God becomes reality to men: not simply by their having a proper understanding of God, to be used in obedient recitation of prescribed commandments. Just as love does not become reality until it "reaches" another, stirring him and setting its stamp on him, so God's forgiveness cannot become reality until it takes effect in men. Thus the summons to forgive is also a statement of how to receive God's forgiveness.

Jesus' parable in 18:23-34 emphasizes the disparity between God's infinitely great forgiveness and our forgiveness. But the saying in Luke

17:4 = Matthew 18:21-22 shows the limitlessness of even our forgiveness. Mark 11:25 takes our forgiveness and links hope for God's forgiveness to it; and Matthew 6:14 so strengthens this association that God's forgiveness appears almost as a consequence.

[9-13] Behind the entire section we can make out the ministry and message of *Jesus* most clearly in the prayer he gave his disciples. In large measure the individual petitions are not new; his prayer, nevertheless, is totally new because it concentrates with such pregnant brevity on precisely these petitions. Here we no longer find a prayer for the increase and triumph of the community, not to speak of the annihilation of enemies. The simple invocation "Father" is itself unprecedented, depending in everything upon God's power and goodness while at the same time remaining dignified—neither abject nor clubby. What follows is a way of learning to live in the perspective of the future. In the Jewish Eighteen Benedictions this emphasis does not appear until the second half, and is even then conceived very much in terms of a restoration of the past. Jesus sets his mind primarily on God and his coming Kingdom, and he illuminates the present in that light. Thus prayer becomes "faith in action" and ceases to be a meritorious duty to be performed. It is a liberating expression of oneself before God, upon whose coming the worshiper waits.

Jesus' prayer revolves around the great concerns of God, but in such a way that from the outset God is seen as concerned with man. God's name is blessed now, his Kingdom begins to come now, his will is done now in that men receive their bread from him (and thus are free to share it), men are forgiven (and thus are free to forgive others), men are delivered from evil (and thus are free to deliver others from it). Thus Jesus' exemplary prayer prevents us from misconstruing piety as our good work—piety comes as God's doing, not through efforts of ours. This point is made even more emphatic by the three paradoxical sayings about the father who hears before we speak (vss. 7-8), the left hand that does not know what the right hand is doing (vs. 3), and the fasting that turns into feasting in the presence of Jesus (vs. 17).

It was incumbent on the community not to preserve the words of Jesus with slavish accuracy but rather to make additions to them to keep them from being misinterpreted. [9-13] The addition of "in heaven" prevents the invocation "Father" from being taken lightly. The petition that God's will be done is borrowed from Jesus' own experience. The petition for deliverance from evil recalls the eschatological perspective and the end of salvation.

[2-6, 16-18] More dubious is the tripartite schema into which Jesus' sayings have been incorporated in the community. The community was concerned (rightly) that the good works of Judaism—almsgiving, prayer, and fasting—should not simply be forgotten. Without prayer there can be no life with God, the poor must be helped, and even fasting was found necessary in certain cases on behalf of service to others (2 Cor. 11:27; 1 Cor. 9:27). The familiar Old Testament anithesis between religion that springs from the heart and religion for outward show furnished a useful schema to distinguish the idea of faith in action from mere religious activity.

[1] Matthew uses the term "righteousness" to summarize the trinity of true charity, prayer, and fasting; this is the righteousness required of the disciples according to 5:20. The assumption is that one does this not to be seen by men but in expectation of reward from God. But the reward God gives is contained in the demand he makes: God demands that men love one another from the heart to obtain his love (9:13), but when men love one another from the heart, that *is* God's love. But to be able to love, one must also be able to forgive. Whence Matthew's heavy stress on forgiveness: to obtain God's love, the community had to embody that love, and to love they had to be able to forgive. [14-15] Matthew makes clear throughout his Gospel (esp. ch. 18) how brotherhood was endangered in the community by rivalry and dispute. He was, indeed, so concerned with the problem of forgiveness that he took a statement that does not appear until later in its Markan context, and appended it to the Lord's Prayer to lend it extraordinary emphasis, at the same time assimilating it in form to the prophetic utterances which expressed divine law in the community.

Teaching about Possessions (6:19-34)
Cf. Luke 12:33-34; 11:34-36; 16:13; 12:22-31

[19]"Do not save riches for yourselves here on earth, where they can be destroyed by moths and eaten away and where robbers break in and

steal. ²⁰Instead, save riches for yourselves in heaven, where they cannot be destroyed by moths or eaten away, and where robbers cannot break in and steal. ²¹For your heart will always be where your riches are.

²²"The lamp of the body is the eye. If your eye is clear, your whole body will be full of light; ²³but if your eye is bad, your whole body will be in darkness. So if the light in you is darkness, how terribly dark it will be!

²⁴"No one can be a slave to two masters; for either he will hate one and love the other, or he will be loyal to one and despise the other. You cannot serve both God and money.

²⁵"This is why I tell you: do not be worried about the food and drink you need to stay alive, or about clothes for your body. After all, isn't life worth more than food? And isn't the body worth more than clothes? ²⁶Look at the birds flying around: they do not plant seeds, gather a harvest, and put it in barns; your Father in heaven takes care of them! Aren't you worth more than birds? ²⁷Which one of you can add a yard to the length of his life by worrying about it?

²⁸"And why worry about clothes? Look how the wild flowers grow; they do not work and do not spin. ²⁹But I tell you that not even Solomon in his splendor had clothes as beautiful as one of these flowers. ³⁰It is God who clothes the wild grass—grass that is here today, gone tomorrow, burned up in the oven. Won't he be all the more sure to clothe you? How little faith you have! ³¹So do not start worrying: 'Where will my food come from? or my drink? or my clothes?' ³²These are the things the heathen are always concerned about. Your Father in heaven knows that you need all these things. ³³Instead, be concerned above everything else with his Kingdom and with what he requires, and he will provide you with all these other things. ³⁴So do not worry about tomorrow, for tomorrow will worry about itself; it is enough that each day has its own troubles."

This entire section, which deals with the requirement of wholeness, especially in material things, is also not found in the Sermon on the Plain, which picks up once more with 7:1 = Luke 6:37. But all the statements about not worrying (vss. 25-34), apart from the concluding Matthaean verse, occur also in Luke (12:22-31), as do the sayings about inner light and serving two masters (Matt. 6:22-24), albeit in different settings (Luke 11:34-35; 16:13). In the first part, the sayings about riches in heaven and about the heart that is bound to riches are also in Luke, although they are placed after the other warnings about worrying (Luke 12:33-34 following 22-31 = Matt. 6:25-34). The order in Matthew differs because his verses 1-18 concern the difference between rewards given by men and rewards given by God, so the saying about riches in heaven rather than upon earth follows beautifully. The idea of rewards evidently brought to Matthew's mind the saying about the heart's being where one's riches are; this saying he then explicated by the two following ones, which depict "simplicity" of heart, i.e., sole and total devotion to God alone. This was Matthew's interpretation in verse 1 of the prior section (6:1).

The extensive agreement in wording between this section and passages in Luke makes it very likely that Matthew derived all this material from Q. It is striking that Matthew follows the structure in Luke for the Sermon on the Plain/Mount exactly, but not the wording, whereas precisely the reverse obtains here (cf. the introductory comments on 4:17–11:30). Luke 12:13-34 is a discourse on the dangers of wealth, which is introduced by the parable of the rich fool, from Luke's special material, and this passes in verse 35 into an eschatological discourse. If Luke added this special material on his own, then in Q the "do not be worried" of Luke 12:22 originally stood next to the "do not be worried" (about what to say in defense) of Luke 12:11 and the image of the thief (Luke 12:39) next to the same key word in verse 33. The latter verbal association is certainly pre-Lukan. Not only is it interrupted by the special material in Luke 12:35-38, but the association is clear only when one assumes that the saying about the thief was originally transmitted in the form preserved by Matthew, in which the "breaking in" corresponds precisely to the "breaking in" of Luke 12:39. This shows that, as in the case of the Lord's Prayer, Matthew has preserved the actual wording better, but has probably altered the structure independently.

[19-21] It is likely the first three verses were not always linked. The saying about the heart that will be where the riches are is in the second person singular, while the other two sentences are in the plural. And, correspondingly, the word for "riches" is in the singular

in verse 21, but in the plural in verses 19-20. Luke 12:33-34 changed both in the interests of uniformity. He also stated his interpretation at the very outset (vs. 33a): "Sell all your belongings and give the money to the poor." Matthew, on the contrary, elaborates verse 20, introducing two double members into the subordinate clause ("destroyed by moths and eaten away"—"not break in and steal"), where Luke uses one noun with each verb, and precedes the whole with an antithesis formulated in parallel terms. It is possible that in elaborating verse 20, Matthew used the rare word for "destroy" as an echo of the same word in 5:18, replacing the commoner word found in Luke 12:33. This means that Matthew 6:21, which reads almost identically in both Gospels, was once transmitted independently.

To say that "riches" bind our hearts is not simply to distinguish transitory riches from eternal ones. It is also to criticize the man who tries to lay up riches in heaven by acts of devotion. Its terseness makes it easily conceivable as a saying of Jesus, although we have no idea in what context it was originally spoken.

[19] The translation "eaten away" is a makeshift; the Greek word, which is not found in Luke, can refer to both the worms that eat wood, making chests and boxes fragile, and to rust, which pierces iron coffers. The Greek word translated "break in" refers to digging; it may suggest forcing a hole through a wall (of the house, as in 24:43, or more likely the storeroom, where it would be less easily observed) or just digging up what is buried. [20] The rabbis, too, spoke of riches in heaven, meaning good works credited to a man's account (cf. also the discussion of vs. 1). Movements that preached and practised renunciation of personal property, such as the Qumran community, did not speak of riches in heaven. It all depends on how the phrase is understood, for a man can be just as selfishly and greedily devoted to riches stored up in heaven as to earthly riches.

[21] In this verse nothing is said of reward, credited to a man's account or the like; all we hear is a warning against setting one's heart on earthly treasures. But we also find here no teaching about the way to riches in heaven; here we are asked where our hearts are. Thus there stands behind Jesus' statement the call to purity and wholeness of heart, as found already in 5:8 and 5:28; 7:21; 12:34 with various

concrete interpretations. Ultimately, then, the riches in heaven can be only the Kingdom of heaven itself, not specific rewards for specific acts.

[22-23] The idea in what follows is ambiguous. Does the statement mean that the eye betrays what the person is like inwardly, or that the eye either transmits light to the body or leaves it in darkness? If the former, the train of verses 19-21 suggests that an evil eye, as Jewish statements put it, betrays ill will and meanness (Billerbeck on 20:15). This would be in accord with the rabbinic statement that a good heart gives rise to a good look, an evil heart to an evil look (Aboth ii. 12-13), and with Hellenistic usage, according to which "simple" can also mean "generous." The final brief statement, however, shows that more is intended than mere knowledge of a man's heart through the look in his eye.

It is better, therefore, to understand the passage in the second sense: a simple eye admits God's light into the entire body; an evil eye causes terrible darkness of heart. This is in accord with the usage of the Testaments of the Twelve Patriarchs, where "simplicity of soul" or "uprightness of heart" can "behold" life rightly, whereas "evil eyes" fall victim to the temptations of the world and pervert the Lord's commandments (Test. Iss. 4:6; cf. the saying about the eye that leads astray in Matt. 5:28). This fits the context, which is discussing the total devotion of a man's heart and of his service to God rather than to the world (vss. 19-21 and 24-25). The passage is therefore saying that, just as a man's entire life is shrouded in darkness when his eye is blind, so too is a man's life dark when he no longer looks toward God, but allows himself to be distracted by his earthly riches.

[24] This is confirmed and emphasized by the metaphor of the two masters, which is reproduced (except for the omission of "servant") word-for-word as in Luke 16:13. "Slave" is not a metaphor in the strict sense—Matthew no longer says, "No servant" (Luke 16:13), but "No one"—what we have is a universally applicable statement, which at the end is applied directly to the listeners and their relationship to God and money. What the devout Jew says in prayer daily must be realized in daily life: there is only one God. Whoever would serve him cannot have other masters as well. "Hate" and "love" do not refer primarily to feelings and emotions, but to a decision in favor of one

party or another (cf. the discussion of 10:37 and Luke 14:26); this fact is emphasized here by the paraphrase "be loyal to one and despise the other." In Jewish usage, "money" or "mammon" has no bad connotations; the contrast is therefore all the more striking. The saying deals with property in general, not with property acquired by evil means or used for evil purposes. The only legitimate question is whether property is to be served or to serve (and for what).

[25-34] Undivided devotion to God and his Kingdom (vs. 33), not to earthly goods, is urged once more in the following section, which like Luke 12:22-31 constitutes a single unit. [25] The word translated "life" actually means "soul" (cf. the discussion of 10:28). Here it does not stand in contrast to "body," but as a synonymous variant. The conclusion drawn is not quite clear, but presupposes that body and life are given us by the creator. The argument proceeds from the major to the minor, concluding that the one who created the body and life will surely also take care of food and clothing. The first statement is thus formulated as an obvious wisdom saying, but it makes sense only on the premise that God is considered first as the creator of the body and life, and second as a gracious creator, faithful to his creation. In other words, it presupposes that men take seriously God's grace and mercy as shown forth in Jesus' entire ministry and preaching, grace and mercy that are anything but obvious apart from Jesus.

[26] The same holds true for the images drawn from nature (see the discussion of 5:45). Jesus is far from being romantic about nature; he does not paint idyllic pictures and ignore nature's brutality (vs. 30; 7:6,15; 10:29; 24:28). "Birds flying around" (literally "birds of heaven") is a typically Jewish expression; perhaps Jesus mentioned the unclean "crows" (Luke 12:24) and the weeds ("wild flowers" or "lilies" in vs. 28; cf. vs. 30) to emphasize that God takes care even of them. Matthew substitutes "your Father in heaven" for "God" (Luke 12:24; but cf. 12:28 = Matt. 6:30) in order to emphasize God's hiddenness, and thus the faith that is needed to believe these words —a faith which Jesus here is conferring. Thus the point is not a call to be self-sufficient, as in a similar saying of one of the Hellenistic philosophers (Seneca, *Remed. fort.* 10), or a statement that men are to undergo greater tribulation than the beasts on account of sinfulness, as in a similar Jewish saying, but a summons to trust God with

a whole and undivided heart. We are not to worry, because worry drives out joy and makes action impossible, and God is encountered in acts. The choice is therefore not between action and passivity, but between two different kinds of action.

[27] The next verse was probably already an interpolation in Q (but see the introductory remarks on 12:11). It interrupts the context, which is expatiating on the proper attitude toward food and clothing (vs. 25). Its content also differs: it is not a summons to place confidence in God, but an allusion to the senselessness of worrying. The image (adding a "yard" to one's life) refers not to height of body but to length of life, as Matthew's addition of "single" makes clear: a yard, even a single yard, added to a man's stature would be astonishing; while a yard, meaning a short space of time, added to one's years would not be much of an accomplishment—yet worrying cannot add a "single" one. "Yard" is also used elsewhere as a metaphor for a short space of time. As a self-evident truth this statement has lost some of its point: in our age human life can be extended significantly, if necessary even by heart transplants; but as a reference to the limits set by God for every life it raises very serious questions about human efforts to extend life, which, to be sure, fight against the tragedy of impending death, but which also worsen the tragedy of a death that will not come.

[28] Verse 28 returns to the context; the transition has been improved in Luke. Matthew juxtaposes man's labor in the fields and woman's labor in the home. [29] Without engaging in either, the wild flowers surpass even Solomon, whose luxury is proverbial. [30] The very weakness of wild flowers emphasizes their faith: they grow to beauty unfailingly despite tempest, sickle, and their inborn evanescence. Yet man, who grows stronger and lives longer, rattles out his life worrying over survival. Jesus' hearers are therefore expressly called away from their "little faith," which looks upon God only with a divided heart, while still paying attention to much else (cf. the discussion of 14:31 and 17:20). [31] The conclusion takes up once more the question of food and clothing (thus only in Matthew); [32] the response is strongly reminiscent of verses 7-8, warning against the attitude of the "heathen," i.e., natural man. God is therefore far from being some kind of universal principle, deducible through observation

of nature. True, God does manifest himself in the processes of nature, whereby man lives. But God is also distinct, and he shows that distinctness by also manifesting himself in the ministry and preaching of Jesus. And the life that that ministry speaks of—life in the coming Kingdom—is more important than any life that nature supports. [33] Therefore the entire section leads up to this summons: devote your life to the Kingdom of God.

What does this mean? In the first place, the Kingdom of God (see the excursus on Mark 1:15) is something in the future; thus man's life is carried beyond the point where he cannot add a single yard, and set in the framework of God's future. But when this happens, the future becomes lord over man here and now, so that in his future perspective there is already realized something of God's Kingdom, i.e. God's sovereignty over man. What man really is in his inmost being is determined by his end, by what he "seeks." When Matthew mentions God's righteousness, "what God requires," alongside God's Kingdom, he probably has in mind the exercise of God's righteous judgment (as in Test. Dan 6:10 and 1QS xi. 12), judgment which will ultimately be revealed at the end of all things. But just as God's Kingdom is already making its appearance, so too is God's righteousness. Both are present in Jesus' ministry, and Jesus' disciples are brought into both (cf. the excursus on 3:15).

[34] In a conclusion he probably composed himself, Matthew once more summarizes the entire section. Once again he takes up the admonition of verse 31 and summons men to a freedom that comes from taking a first step even when the second and third are not yet in view.

Thus the entire section puts the question between worldly-wise subsistence and childlike life—between the man who ruins his life out of worry for food and clothing, and the one who takes God seriously, the God who created both body and life. The statements bear a marked resemblance to wisdom dicta that should be obvious to everyone, but to act on such wisdom requires more than a little faith. In understanding that the life of faith is realized in man's ability to live the present day confidently, free from worry about tomorrow, Matthew understood well what Jesus was trying to say. The terseness of many of the sayings reflects the radical nature of the liberation with which Jesus would set us free to live our lives; for true life comes only when life is received as a gift and can therefore be lived in fundamental confidence.

Teaching about Judging Others (7:1-6)
Cf. Luke 6:37-42

[1]"Do not judge others, so that you will not be judged; [2]for you will be judged in the same way you judge others, and it will be measured out to you with the measure by which you measure. [3]Why, then, do you look at the speck in your brother's eye, and pay no attention to the log in your own eye? [4]How dare you say to your brother, 'Please, let me take that speck out of your eye,' when you have a log in your own eye? [5]You hypocrite! Take the log out of your own eye first, and then you will be able to see and take the speck out of your brother's eye.

[6]"Do not give what is holy to dogs; and do not throw your pearls in front of pigs—they will only trample them underfoot and turn and attack you."

[1] With 7:1 we pick up the Sermon on the Plain once more. Matthew passes from the theme of total devotion to God, with its concomitant freedom from self, to that of relationships toward our fellow men. The first saying is familiar to Luke (6:37) in a more fully developed form, which may derive from Jesus. [2] The saying about the "measure" was already associated with that about judging in Q; Luke interprets it as referring to almsgiving, an important subject for him, and expands it accordingly by the addition of other sayings, while in Matthew it appears directly linked to verse 1 by means of a transitional saying (vs. 2a).

The principle of "measure for measure," already familiar in Judaism, appears also in Mark 4:24. It was therefore probably at one time known independently and given various applications: Mark 4:24 applies it to the new knowledge that is continually given to anyone who hearkens to Jesus' words; Luke 6:38 applies it to reward for generosity; Matthew applies it to the judgment by which anyone who judges will be judged. The addition in Mark 4:24 (my

translation)—"it will be added to you" (using the same verb as
Matt. 6:33)—points originally to a judicial setting (Matt. 25:29).
One might even think in terms of what was originally a double saying: "Do not judge others, so that you will not be judged; for . . ."
(vs. 2a); and "Do not condemn others, so that you will not be condemned" (Luke 6:37b); "for . . ." (vs. 2b).

[3-5] The image in Luke 6:39 of the blind leading the blind interrupts the context in both form and content. In Q, too, therefore, the
image of the speck and the log must have constituted the immediate
continuation of the warning against passing judgment with its appended reference to the principle of "measure for measure." The very
paradoxicality of the image (see the discussion of Matt. 5:13) suggests
that it goes back to Jesus. Perhaps he used it on some occasion to warn
against the judgmental attitude that reproached him for associating
with tax collectors and prostitutes. In this case the saying would not
have denied the difference between the righteous and unrighteous, the
"speck," but it would have shown that the difference was so small
when seen by the perfect righteousness of God that all human passing
of judgment would be laughable.

Jesus' saying probably encompassed only verse 3. The wording of
verse 4 varies in the tradition; and the verse also contains a Hellenistic
idiom, "let me." Verse 5, at least in its second part, deals with another
subject (see below).

[6] The last sentence is Matthaean special material and probably
derives from a strongly Jewish Christian heritage (see below). An
Aramaic original has therefore been proposed: "Don't bedeck the
dogs and don't hang pearls on the snouts of pigs," which is reminiscent of the saying about the beautiful but immoral woman who is like
a gold ring in the snout of a sow (Prov. 11:22).

[1-2] Strictly speaking, the first and second sentences are contradictory. Did Jesus take the radical approach of forbidding all judging
(vs. 1), while the community, in which it became necessary at times
to reprimand, stood for judging as generously and carefully as possible
(vs. 2)? But the second sentence can be taken in another sense. Anyone
who recalls that God will measure out to him with the measure he
uses toward his fellow men should be so terrified as to forgo judging
entirely. In commercial contracts on pre-Christian papyri there oc-

curs a technical idiom "with the measure by which you have measured out to me." It means that the very same balance or yardstick has been used for the goods received as for what has been given in exchange. Jesus may have used the familiar contractual clause to emphasize the seriousness of the warning, since the rabbis applied it to the Last Judgment of God (Billerbeck on 7:2 B).

And of course, the first sentence is more than a mere admonition not to endanger the social bond. It means that we are lost as long as we live at all by the categories of weighing, measuring, and classifying. This goes well beyond Jewish statements that are formally similar: "Do not judge your neighbor until you are in his shoes" or "Whoever passes lenient judgment on his neighbor will be judged leniently" (Billerbeck on 7:1 and 7:2 A 1). We are dealing once more with the radical restatement of a current principle. On the judicial office, see the excursus following 7:29, c. §3.

[3-4] It is certain the deliberately grotesque image of the log in one's own eye is meant in a radical sense. It was therefore mocked by a Jewish rabbi (cf. the discussion of 5:13): "I would be surprised if there were anyone in this generation who would accept rebuke. If one were to say to him, Take the speck out of your eye, he would reply, Take the log out of your own eye." This may reflect a misuse of Jesus' saying. Did Christians reply to the Pharisees in this vein? If so, we can see that even literal repetition of a saying of Jesus does not prevent it from being transformed into its exact opposite.

[5] Verse 5, of course, which contains the hostile word "hypocrite" (see the discussion of 6:2), appears to condone the practise of brotherly rebuke. But while such a rebuke is countenanced elsewhere (18:15-18), it can hardly have belonged to Jesus' original teaching here. Jesus speaks with this kind of absoluteness only when he wishes to concentrate all his force on a point—here, the obduracy of the man who always considers his own actions right and the actions of others wrong. In another situation, faced with another need, Jesus can say the opposite.

[6] The concluding statement is hard to interpret. Since 15:26-27, like the rabbis, compares the heathen to dogs, and since the pig is an unclean animal for Jews and plays an important role in intercourse with the heathen, as well as being used as a symbol for heathen Rome,

there is much to suggest that the saying was shaped by a Jewish Christian community—still living strictly according to the Law—and was intended to attack the gentile mission. What is "holy," that is, the sacrifice offered to God, must not be tossed to the dogs, as the rabbinic regulation maintains. Pigs to which pearls are thrown become enraged discovering they cannot eat them and attack the man who offers them. Thus in the opinion of this community, the gentiles to whom the gospel is preached might turn against their missionaries, attack their legalism, reject circumcision and sumptuary laws and purity regulations, and finally "dismember" Israel. In the Pseudo-Clementines rec. iii. 1 this saying was still being used by strict Jewish Christians to attack those who joined the Catholic Church.

Matthew, however, does not take it in this sense (28:19), as is indicated by the context in which he puts it. Perhaps he is trying to say that there are situations in which one of the brethren is no longer willing to listen, in which it is pointless to waste words on him, in which it is better to treat him "like a tax collector or heathen" (18:17). In 2 Peter 2:22 apostates are also likened to dogs and pigs. In our text, however, there is no "but" to mark a contrast with what precedes. Perhaps Matthew merely means to stress more strongly the holiness of God's word and commandments, which should not simply be exposed to mockery. There is certainly no suggestion that some dogmas should be reserved for advanced Christians only. The saying is nevertheless interpreted this way even in Didache 9:5 (cf. 10:6): the Lord's Supper should not be discussed with outsiders. Although there is a kind of precedent in Exodus 29:33, this idea is most closely related to the thought of Hellenistic religious cults, which attempt to protect their "holy treasure" from the profane world; it has nothing to do with the thought of Jesus.

Once again we can see a movement within the brief section. Jesus himself probably intended radical liberation from all the categories to which we would assign others and above all ourselves. When we realize that we no longer have to judge, that is, assign people to higher or lower positions, then we will no longer judge ourselves—no longer be judged, and we will be able to stand confidently and fully before the judgment of God. God nevertheless takes what we do so seriously that he looks upon it and will not forget it; this does not contradict what has been said, but rather gives it full weight. The same holds true for 1 Corinthians 3:12-15, which states that no one will be condemned even if his works are consumed by the fire of judgment, precisely as in Matthew 5:45 or 20:1-16.

But only someone who is truly aware that he is standing in the sight of God can speak in this fashion. As a general maxim from which God might even be omitted if necessary, it is open to all kinds of abuse, as the rabbinic quotation shows, particularly on the part of those who invoke Jesus' authority. It is possible to take the literal words of Jesus quite seriously and still falsify them completely, subjecting others to judgment rather than oneself. Only the man who knows the "log" of his own guilt can understand Jesus' grotesque image. What was understood in a quite specific situation when expressed so radically was incorporated by Matthew into a Gospel addressed to many men, living in various situations. No attempt was made to make Jesus' image less exaggerated, and no one who really heard it and took to heart the blindness of his own log could misunderstand it. But something had to be added for the community and what was in fact taking place in it: the man who has truly applied this saying of Jesus to himself is in a position then to point out the speck to his brother and see to it that God's word and will do not "go to the dogs." Of course in this case, too, the pithy saying of Jesus must be kept in mind to keep the community from drowning out the clear note of gospel with ecclesiastical discipline and brotherly censure.

Teaching about the Joy of Prayer (7:7-12)
Cf. Luke 11:9-13; 6:31

[7]"Ask, and you will receive; seek, and you will find; knock, and the door will be opened to you. [8]For everyone who asks will receive, and he who seeks will find, and the door will be opened to him who knocks. [9]Would any of you who are fathers give your son a stone when he asks you for bread? [10]Or would you give him a snake when he asks you for fish? [11]As bad as you are, you know how to give good things to your children. How much more, then, will your Father in heaven give good things to those who ask him!

[12]"Do for others what you want them to do for you, for that is the Law and the prophets."

[12] This entire section derives from Q, where the last verse was already associated in the Sermon on the Plain with the summons to love one's enemies (Luke 6:31). Matthew deliberately transferred it to this context, adding that it represents the entire import of "the Law and the prophets." What 5:17 announced ("Do not think that I have come to do away with the Law or the prophets. I have not come to do away with them but to fulfill them.") is fulfilled in this summary of Jesus' discourse. That discourse began with the Beatitudes and sayings on discipleship, and leads, here, to the Golden Rule—all this being Jesus' exposition of the Law; and, with the repetition of the word "prophets," the discourse ends (7:13-27) with warnings against false prophets in the community. We are thus dealing with a quite conscious composition on the part of the evangelist.

The initial verses deal with prayer, as the final sentence makes clear. It is striking that Matthew did not place them in the context of 6:5-15, the more so because in Luke 11:9-13 they appear as an appendix to the Lord's Prayer. Now James 1:5 interprets the introductory saying as a reference to praying for true wisdom, and the words "seek" and "find" at Qumran are characteristic of the search for the hidden wisdom of God (see below). Does Matthew therefore have in mind the wisdom that is needed to judge one's brother? This is suggested by 18:18-20, where the promise that a common prayer will be heard is associated with the circumstance that one of the brethren has sinned and the community must "bind" or "loose" according to Jesus' words. This problem was of great concern to Matthew (see the discussion of 13:24-30; 18:15-18; and the introductory remarks on chapters 21–25).

Nevertheless the examples cited in verses 9-10, as well as the general term "good things" (but see below) in verse 11, clearly point beyond this special case. We can conclude, therefore, that Matthew put this section here first because of its bearing on verse 5b (taking the speck out of your brother's eye), but also with an eye to its much more general sense. Perhaps we hear an echo of the intimate connection between love for God and love for one's neighbor, which Matthew also understands as a summary of the entire Law and the prophets (22:37-40; cf. the discussion of 5:18), although this particular saying refers only to God's love for us, not ours for him. Perhaps there is also a reference back to the Lord's Prayer, to emphasize that such fulfillment of the Law and the words of the prophets is possible when God grants it.

[7-8] The saying about asking repeats the wording of Luke 11:-9-10. The Qumran Manual of Discipline begins with the statement that God must be sought with all one's heart and soul; those who do not seek after knowledge of what is hidden or study God's Law do not stand within God's covenant (1QS i. 1-2; v. 8, 11). Matthew 6:33 also summons men to seek the Kingdom of God and the righteousness of God. Jeremiah 29:13-14 already promised that those who search for God will find him. The image of knocking on a door and having it opened is associated by the rabbis with study of the Law and its interpretation, as well as with the prayer for God's mercy (Billerbeck on vs. 7 C); in Jesus' parable it is associated with the Kingdom of God and its banquet (25:10-11; cf. the introductory comments on 7:21-23).

The statement cannot be transformed into instructions for an unfailing magic ritual. There is still presupposed the asking described in the preceding sections and summarized in the Lord's Prayer. This asking is always a supplication; the fact the seeker is promised to find in no way means he can coerce God. Jesus' clear statement in 6:7-8 eliminates this possibility. But Jesus does not make the point didactically; he is not concerned about the chance of being misunderstood by someone with no idea what prayer is, who would transform the gift into an instrument for his own designs. In fact, Jesus' very unguardedness here shows the importance he attaches to prayer: he is not concerned that his hearers might misuse it, only that they have it. His emphasis is exclusively on the joy of prayer. The unboundedness of this joy (unboundedness is even suggested by the phrase "*everyone* who") Jesus makes striking and dramatic by the parable: what is stressed is the certainty that the request will be granted.

[9-11] Since a fish—some eel-shaped species is meant—resembles a snake and a round piece of bread resembles a stone, this is probably the original image; the substitution of a scorpion and an egg (Luke 11:12) destroys the image. On "would any of you," see the discussion of 12:11. Human maliciousness is here simply presupposed. This is extremely sobering in the face of the widespread romantic belief that

man is innately good and need only be left to himself with as few restrictions as possible for everything to improve. But the statement is also provocative because in the same breath this same man is expected to be capable of good. Such insight into man's maliciousness, far from producing resignation, leads to an attitude that is unillusioned but hopeful and active. The two statements can be reconciled only when man is viewed in his relationship to God, who alone is truly good (19:17).

Only so can one understand the deepest nature of one's own maliciousness: separation from God. And one can understand what one's good deeds nevertheless signify: that in the love of every earthly father for his children there lives something of the Father from whom all fatherhood on earth is named (Eph. 3:14-15). Only thus is Jesus' argument from minor to major convincing. If even (sometimes malicious) earthly fathers fulfill the wishes of their children, he who is truly Father and never malicious will surely do so. Isaiah 49:15, which draws the same conclusion from the love shown by mothers, is aware that there are earthly mothers who neglect their children. Thus there can also be earthly fathers who give their sons stones instead of bread. But because God infinitely surpasses all fatherhood or motherhood, it is true to say that one can see his love reflected in the love of earthly fathers or mothers. The "good things" that God gives us probably include everything mentioned in the Lord's Prayer. Or are we to assume that Matthew is thinking of insight into God's will, just as the rabbis see in the Law the first of the three "good gifts" of God? At this point Luke speaks of the Holy Spirit, to whom he attaches great importance; but Jesus' metaphor is not so spiritual as to exclude, for example, bread for tomorrow.

[12] The so-called Golden Rule is stated in negative form by an Athenian as early as the fourth century B.C.: "Whatever angers you when you suffer it at the hands of others, do not do it to others" (Isocrates, *Nicol.* [*Cypr.*] 61). Other instances are admittedly nothing more than worldly wisdom to the effect that anyone who wants to live in peace should not attack others. From this source the saying first infiltrated Greek-speaking Judaism. Even before Jesus, Rabbi Hillel stated as a fundamental principle: "Whatever is displeasing to you do

not do to your neighbor; that is the entire Law, and everything else is interpretation." There is no evidence for the positive form in this period; the advice given the ruler in the Hellenistic Jewish Letter of Aristeas (207), "If you . . . want all good to befall you, do the same to your subjects," remains within the framework of worldly wisdom. Slavonic Enoch 61:1 is hard to date and might represent Christian editing.

Presumably, then, Jesus himself gave the saying its present terse and universal form. It can no longer be understood as self-centered advice, for what a man desires for himself is usually limitless, and the requirement of doing that for others represents the most radical of summons to love one's neighbor. In this form the saying states that it does not take scholarly expertise to know what we should do for our neighbors. A man usually knows what he himself would like. His naive egoism is once again taken for granted. We find suggestions of this interpretation in Ecclesiasticus 34(31):15, in certain expositions of Leviticus 19:18 (Jerusalem Targum), and in other Jewish statements. Matthew undoubtedly saw in this saying a variant of the law of love, for by the addition of "that is the Law and the prophets" he brackets this rule with 5:17 and at the same time places it alongside 22:39-40 (see the discussion of 5:18).

The wish behind the Golden Rule is common. The Roman emperor Alexander Severus, who worshiped both Christ and Alexander the Great, inscribed it in golden letters on the wall of his chamber at the beginning of the third century. The difficulty is, how do we receive the strength to *act* accordingly? In Matthew the discussion of prayer precedes. That discussion, in turn, proceeds from the Old Testament assumption that God has first spoken to man. Therefore it is not the human attitude of asking and seeking that is lauded; the emphasis is on God's action, on his love—and the conclusion is that man becomes truly man only when he makes that kind of love the basis of his life. The man who has thus been set free does not need legal texts to lay down the details of how to live perfectly. In sober awareness of human wickedness, above all his own, he can open himself to receive from the true Father the gift of doing for his neighbor what he would like his neighbor to do for him (vss. 11-12).

Dangers of Discipleship (7:13-23)
Cf. Luke 13:23-24; 6:43-44, 46; 13:26-27

[13]"Go in through the narrow gate, because the gate is wide and the road easy that leads to perdition, and there are many who travel it. [14]The gate is narrow and the way is hard that leads to life, and few people find it.

[15]"Watch out for false prophets; they come to you in the skins of sheep, but on the inside they are fierce wolves.—[16]By their fruits you will know them. Can one gather grapes from thorns or figs from thistles? [17]A good tree bears good fruit, while a poor tree bears evil fruit. [18]A good tree cannot bear evil fruit, and a poor tree cannot bear good fruit. [19]Any tree that does not bear good fruit is cut down and thrown into the fire. [20]So you will know them by their fruits.

[21]"Not everyone who calls me 'Lord, Lord,' will enter into the Kingdom of heaven, but only those who do what my Father in heaven wants them to do. [22]When that Day comes, many will say to me, 'Lord, Lord! In your name did we not speak prophetically and by your name did we not drive out demons and by your name did we not perform many miracles?' [23]Then I will say to them, 'I never knew you, "away from me, you who practise lawlessness"!' "
(Vs. 22—Isa. 14:12-15. Vs. 23—Ps. 6:8.)

In the concluding section of the Sermon on the Mount, Matthew's hand is especially clear in structuring the material. The Golden Rule has just referred back to the beginning of the discussion about the problem of the Law (5:17). [13] In 7:13 the phrase about "entering" the Kingdom of heaven (5:20), which served as a superscription for the whole discussion, is taken up once more; it will appear again in verse 21. Thus after the Golden Rule has stated in summary how the Law is not abolished but fulfilled through Jesus, there follows a severe warning to the community about God's judgment, characteristic of Matthew (cf. the discussion of 13:40-43, 49-50 and the introductory remarks on chapters 21–25).

This warning was suggested by the conclusion to the Sermon on the Plain, which ends with the parable of the tree and its fruit, the warning about saying "Lord, Lord," and the parable of the house built on rock (Luke 6:43-49). But how does Matthew develop this theme? First he introduces a saying about the narrow gate through which one must "enter." This saying, in a different form, is found also in Luke 13:23-24, where it is closely associated with a warning about God's judgment. [15-20] Then Matthew follows the conclusion of the Sermon on the Plain with its reference to the tree and its fruit (vss. 16-20), but in such a way that the warning is made to refer specifically to false prophets (vs. 15). This verse is probably Matthew's own composition (cf. the discussion of "be careful" in the introductory remarks on 6:1) and describes the false prophets as appearing in the community under the guise of "sheep."

[16-18] But he has also reconceived the image of the tree and its fruit, taken from the Sermon on the Plain. Surprisingly, the actual parallel does not appear until 12:33-35. In contrast to that passage (12:34-35), here all references to false teaching are omitted, and the emphasis on false ethical conduct is increased. In the Greek text, the singular of "fruit" is kept only in verse 19; everywhere else (in contrast to Luke 6:43-44=Matt. 12:33) it is replaced by the plural. Since the situation is precisely the contrary in Matthew 3:8 (alongside Luke 3:8), Matthew is probably referring here quite deliberately to particular good or evil deeds. This is certainly suggested by reference to the "good" rather than the "healthy" tree and the "evil" instead of the "poor" fruit (cf. 5:45; 22:10; also 7:11). This is emphasized in verse 19 by repetition of the Baptist's harsh word of judgment (see the discussion of 3:2) about the tree that is cut down and tossed into the fire because it does not bear good fruit (3:10). Verse 20 takes the conclusion back to the introduction (vs. 16), referring again to false prophets.

[21-23] The addition of the statement that not everyone who says "Lord, Lord" will "enter into the Kingdom of heaven" associates verse 21 closely with the theme of the entire Sermon on the Mount (5:20) and with the warning that introduces this section (7:13). The phrase "do what my Father in heaven wants them to do" (literally "do the will of my Father in heaven") probably also goes back to Matthew and is meant to recall the petition of the Lord's Prayer added in his

community (6:10; cf. also 21:31). Even more significant is the use of an expression drawn from the complaint against the false prophets in Jeremiah 14:14; 27:15 to refer to those who are turned away at the Last Judgment. Thev are fully credited with having driven out demons and performed miracles, i.e. probably healings. Those already under discussion since verse 15 are therefore probably still the target. They are condemned with a curse deriving from Psalm 6:8, which comes from the parable of judgment associated in Luke 13:25-27 with the saying about the narrow gate, which is also reminiscent of Matthew 25:1-12. The term "lawlessness" is unique to Matthew. It appears once more in 24:12, where it is interpreted as meaning that the false prophets have cooled the love for one's neighbor—which for Matthew is the whole of the Law and the prophets. The same expression occurs also in Paul in contexts markedly eschatological. After this warning against false prophets, Matthew inserts the concluding parable of the Sermon on the Plain (vss. 24-27).

Prophets, Wise Men, Teachers, and the Righteous in the Matthaean Community

1

Matthew 23:34 states that Jesus will send "prophets and wise men and teachers." It is therefore clear that we are dealing with men who function within the Christian community. In contrast to Mark 3:-13-14, Matthew says nothing about Jesus' selection of the Twelve, but he does probably know of their special mission (10:1, 5-42). Only in this latter passage (10:2) do we find the term "apostle," which in Greek actually means "emissary" and is once used by the Septuagint for a prophet (1 Kings 14:6). But in this same passage they are described in more detail as prophets, righteous men, and disciples (10:40-42). The Twelve are thus singled out as the first disciples of Jesus; they are promised a special place in the coming Kingdom (19:28). But just as the authority granted Peter among them "to bind and to loose" (16:19) is likewise granted to all members of the community (18:18), so that Peter stands for any disciple of Jesus, so the Twelve are mentioned here only as examples of all the disciples "sent as emissaries" by Jesus (cf. the discussion of 8:23). Therefore the "prophets, wise men, and teachers" mentioned in 23:34 may be taken as referring to all disciples without restriction, not merely, say, to those sent particularly to the Jews.

2

Matthew 7:22-23 condemns prophets who prophesy and perform miracles in the name of Jesus but do not observe God's law. The problem of false prophets played an important role in early Christianity. Several criteria are given by which they may be judged: whether they really confess Jesus as Lord and serve the good of the community as a whole (1 Cor. 12:1-3, 7); whether they confess the orthodox faith that Jesus came in the flesh (1 John 4:2); above all, their general ethical conduct (Matt. 7:16; later Did. 11:7-12, with precise regulations); their relationship to the community (Hermas, *Commandments* xi. 7-16, in combination with the preceding criterion); whether they agree with Paul (so-called 3 Cor. i. 2-5; iii. 34-39); whether what they prophesy comes to pass (Ps. Clem., *Hom.* ii. 6-11). Until well into the second century, then, this problem was not resolved in the early church.

But Matthew is far from being opposed in principle to charismatics, i.e. men enabled by the Spirit of God to prophesy and perform miracles. The very warning against false prophets must imply that there are true prophets within the community. This is presupposed in 5:12, and explicitly stated in 10:41 and 23:34. They probably proclaimed God's law to the community and told the sinner of coming judgment (see the introductory remarks on 5:19). Even more important is the statement made in 10:1: the charismatic deeds of Jesus continue on in the community of Jesus and are God's signs that the Old Testament prophecies have been fulfilled (cf. the introductory remarks on 4:17–11:30). The presence of charismatics is also attested by 9:8; 10:24-25; 17:20. The mighty acts of Jesus are also emphasized (see the discussion of 8:17; 11:20; 12:15-21, 28, 31-32; 14:14, 35; 19:2; 21:14-16); in fact, Matthew may well describe Jesus as the prototype of the wandering prophets (see the excursus on 1:18-25). It is certain in any case that in the Matthaean community there are prophets who wander from place to place, as 10:41 shows.

3

With them are associated in 23:34 wise men and teachers. The wise man first appears as a teacher in Ecclesiasticus 21:13-17 (cf. 24:33). Now 13:52 also presupposes that there are teachers of the Law who are "instructed for the Kingdom of God," in other words, are disciples of Jesus and therefore "wise." According to 16:19 the duty of a teacher of the Law is entrusted to Peter, and according to 18:18 it is entrusted to all members of the community: they are to declare with an authority that condemns or releases for all eternity what Scripture says about the ethical situations at hand (cf. the discussion of 18:18).

What has redefined Scripture for this kind of use is the instruction, along with the unique presence, of Jesus (cf. the discussion of 5:17-20 and 28:18-20). This redefinition of Scripture is a redefinition of life, and is always to take its pattern from Jesus' service and Jesus' teachings. Matthew wishes to stress that the focus of his message—including his ethical message—is always Jesus; and for this reason, instead of using the term "gospel" alone (as used by Mark), he uses the phrase "gospel of the Kingdom [of God]," to recall his message's uniqueness. This phrase occurs at two especially important points: first, to introduce the Sermon on the Mount, which presents Jesus' new teaching (4:23), and second, to conclude Jesus' acts of authority, which demonstrate his conduct toward those who suffer (9:35). Twice Matthew adds *"this* gospel [of the Kingdom of God]" (24:14; 26:13, italics added) to reemphasize that there is no gospel other than that proclaimed by the earthly Jesus. Twice he omits the word "gospel" entirely, so that only Jesus or his name is referred to, not a "gospel" that might be thought of apart from him (16:25; 19:29). Matthew therefore looks askance at any post-Easter proclamation made in the name of Jesus but no longer oriented by his commandments and his life (cf. the discussion of 7:28-29). Thus the true wise men and teachers are those who authoritatively interpret Scripture for new situations and problems, but who also follow his teaching and live by his model.

4

The righteous stand alongside prophets, wise men, and teachers of the Law. Matthew's combination of "prophets and righteous men" (13:17; 23:29) is also typical of the Old Testament. There it refers primarily to martyrs who, following in the footsteps of the prophets, bore practical witness to God. They closely resemble the teachers and wise men who, according to Jewish thought, became the intellectual witnesses on God's behalf in the period when prophecy ceased. According to 10:41, however, there are also righteous men in the community of Jesus; in fact, according to 13:43, 49; 25:37, 46 all those whom God accepts at the Last Judgment are righteous. The first passage (13:43) is based on a quotation from Daniel 12:3, where the "intelligent" (Greek text) or "teachers" are those "who convert many to righteousness" (cf. also Dan. 11:33, 35). In Ethiopian Enoch the righteous are those who will stand at the Last Judgment, in chapters 72–82 probably the members of a group living by an especially strict rule; in the Jewish monastic community at Qumran, all members are called "sons of righteousness," while the "intelligent one" or "teacher" holds a special office.

5

Alongside prophets and righteous men, 10:42 mentions "the least of these" and "followers" or "disciples." The first expression is found already in Mark 9:42 (cf. also the introductory remarks on Mark 9:41) and is thus pre-Matthaean. Matthew 23:8-12 forbids the use of honorifics in the community of Jesus; only he who is "little" is truly great in the eyes of God. Thus the terms prophet, wise man, teacher, and righteous man probably designate those possessed of certain gifts for service in the community: preachers moved by the Spirit, counselors in certain situations and problems, interpreters of Scripture in the light of Jesus' teachings, and men who bear witness on Jesus' behalf primarily through their actions. In principle, however, none is superior to the others; they are all "little ones." Conversely, every disciple is called to all these forms of service. In chapter 18, which regulates the life of the community, as elsewhere in the Gospel of Matthew, there is no mention of any office. One can only make out that this gift or that is given in greater measure to this or that particular person (cf. also the introductory remarks on 24:45-51). All these forms of service clearly stand in unbroken succession to the prophets (cf. 22:3-4; 23:34 alongside 37), wise men, teachers, and righteous men of the Old Testament, who in turn likewise do not represent special offices, but are instead men sent by God and endowed for special forms of service, who carry out to a special degree the functions expected of and promised to all.

6

This community therefore knows nothing of the order of elders, nor that of bishops and deacons; neither are they familiar with the whole profusion of spiritual gifts listed in 1 Corinthians 12. Matthew 23:8-12 may indicate that a need for established office is already making itself felt, perhaps because of abuses on the part of prophets (7:22-23). Matthew's community differs from the strict Jewish Christians in not requiring literal obedience to the Law and in showing less interest in Jesus' family, who are leaders in the community, than in Peter, who is open to the gentile mission. At the same time, it differs from the Pauline communities in its devotion to Jesus' commandments and his exemplary life, refusing to let them take second place to any post-Easter proclamation of Christ. Love for one's neighbor and a kind of ascetic obedience are required of Matthew's community (this is implied by 1 Cor. 7:7; Paul's conduct was more stringent than that in his communities). Matthew's is a community in which many Old Testament elements survive, and which still lives off the period in which there was no division between Judaism and the disciples of Jesus. The notion of the prophets as servants of God derives ultimately from Amos (3:7) and also became central in the Revelation to John (10:7; 11:18).

7

Much that can be observed here lives on in the community we find in the Didache, which probably comes from Syria; the Didache even begins with sayings from the Matthaean Sermon on the Mount (cf. the excursus following 7:29 b §7). It continues with a long series of admonitions intended to turn men away from the path leading to death and set them on the way leading to life. This document likewise shares with the Gospel of Matthew the baptismal formula, the Lord's Prayer, the demand for perfection which had already appeared at Qumran, and the warning against the false prophets of "lawlessness"—the sheep who turn into wolves. Faith means primarily obedience and the ardent expectation of the coming of the Lord (Did. 16). In Didache 11:7 there appear wandering prophets who speak in the Spirit and must be given liberty to do so; the problem of false prophets comes up and is solved in thoroughly reasonable fashion (11:8 ff.; 16:3). Teachers, too, are for the most part still wandering teachers, if they are in fact to be distinguished from the prophets (13:1); but one can see how prophets are beginning to disappear (13:4) and be replaced by bishops and deacons. Obviously these wandering prophets are without property and unmarried.

Here, then, we find a type of community very different from that in Paul, where the prophets are settled, where in fact all residents of the community should be prophets (Rom. 12:4; 1 Cor. 12:4; 14:1-4). But in Syria, well into the second century, indeed in many movements well into the fourth century, there survives an independent Christianity of the poor and homeless who live in ardent expectation of the coming Lord. They frequently renounce marriage, wine, and flesh meat. And they believe, every bit as seriously as Matthew, that evil can be at work in a disciple of Jesus alongside the divine Spirit. Here Christianity is much more a "way" than a doctrine; the doctrine is understood as directions for proceeding along the road that demands renunciation of the world in imitation of the unmarried, poor, and homeless Jesus.

Probably the Gospel of Thomas (discovered in 1945/46), many of whose ascetic sayings are alien to Jesus, is a product of this church. The Pseudo-Clementine Epistles (I. xii. 1-2; II. i. 3) still refer to men and women living together while abstaining from sex, wandering through the countryside individually or in groups, visiting the faithful, driving out demons, assembling the brethren and preaching gospel to them without rhetorical skill, trusting only in the Spirit. In the apocryphal Acts of the Apostles, likewise composed in the third century, the apostles are also described as wandering prophets who heal the sick and drive out demons. The recently found and yet unpublished Apocalypse of Peter (Naghammadi Codex VII/3, p. 79, 19-30) is the first direct witness to a church typically Matthaean. It is the church of "the little ones" fighting against those "who let themselves be called bishop and also deacons, as if they had received authority from God, who recline at table after the law of places of honor" (cf. Matt. 23:6-10; 18:10). In this church there is a mystical strain, subject to heavenly visions and prophetic insights, and an ascetic trend, condemning wealth and concupiscence (p. 71, 14 and 75, 15). Much of this style of Christianity, which remained characteristic of Syria, was incorporated later into the monastic movement, where the distinction already drawn in Didache 6:2 between the perfect, who bear the entire yoke of the Lord, and the profane, who only do what cannot be avoided, becomes paramount. Questionable as such a distinction is (and Matthew certainly doesn't authorize it; cf. the discussion of 19:21), a vigorous and fruitful power of renunciation issued from this current of Christian thought, and continued through the centuries. Thus not only Paul but also Matthew and his community have remained to this day a source of unrest in the life of the church.

[13-14] In Luke 13:23-24 the image is that of entering through the narrow door; the context suggests entering a banquet hall and so the statement that this door is narrow does not really fit (Luke 13:25 therefore mentions only a closed door, so that it doesn't matter whether it is narrow or wide). The image is opaque in Matthew because it has been confused with the image of the two ways. There are manuscripts that mention the door in the first clause, drop the metaphor, and only later speak of the ways; but this is probably a later adjustment. The two-ways schema is widespread in the Greek and Jewish worlds. It symbolizes man's ethical decision between good and evil, and is therefore appropriate to Matthew, whose image we should probably think of as a city, the city of God, with its gates. The sequence suggests that the narrow and wide ways begin within the gates; the images must still, however, be taken merely as allegorical symbols, e.g. the gate standing for teaching, the way for ethical conduct. Thus one must either assume that the sequence is to be pictured in reverse order, the wide way leading to the wide gate of hell (cf. the discussion of Mark 9:47-48), the narrow way leading to the narrow

gate of the city of God; or, more likely, that we are simply dealing with a double image, both parts of which have the same meaning (cf., for example, vss. 9-10; 13:31-33).

The Didache begins: "There are two ways, one leading to life and one to death, and great is the difference between the two ways"; there follows a series of sayings from the Sermon on the Mount. The schema of two ways, already found in Jeremiah 21:8 (cf. Deut. 11:26), found frequent employment, especially for catechesis. Thus 2 Esdras, roughly contemporary with Matthew, speaks of the narrow access to the heavenly city, running along the brink of the abyss, only wide enough for a single man (7:7-8). This shows the close connection between the way and the entrance (in Matthew the "gate"). Our saying does not exhibit any of this allegorical elaboration, nor does it admonish each individual to obey the Law. The less common image of the gate (Jesus' own?) has its primary setting in the Temple liturgy, where the righteous (Ps. 118:19-20) or the Lord himself (Ps. 24:7-10) enter. It is probably in this light that the Matthaean community understood the image. In 5:8 there was already an echo of the Temple liturgy from Psalm 24.

The suggestion that only a few can "find" the narrow gate is clearly associated with the saying (cf. "seek" in Luke 13:24). Matthew is not thinking in terms of any divine predestination, and certainly not of God's dooming the multitude of mankind to hell. How the "entering" through the narrow gate, to which men are here called, is to take place has already been explained in 5:20, and what follows here is merely the admonition to do so now, to accept the invitation. But the use of the term "find" (unlike the summons to "do your best" in Luke 13:24) sustains the point made by verses 7-11, that the giving to those who ask and the opening of the door to those who knock are always gifts, whose miraculous nature is underlined by mention of the "few."

[15] The appearance of false prophets at the eschaton is presupposed in 24:11-12. Since Matthew substitutes this material for sayings about the persecution of the community, which he already anticipates in 10:17-22, he is clearly making a distinction between the present age, in which the community suffers persecution, and the eschatological age, when it is generally expected that false teachers will appear (1 Tim. 4:1; 2 Tim. 3:1-8; 1 John 2:18-19; Jude 18). But

our passage also means that what will take place at the eschaton is now appearing proleptically.

A flock of sheep is a frequent image for the community (Num. 27:17; Ps. 100:3; Matt. 9:36; 18:12-14). The image of wolves is apposite; it is used in the Old Testament to symbolize the gentiles (Jer. 5:6) or the faithless leaders of Israel, who deceive the people like the false prophets associated with them (Ezek. 22:27-28; Zeph. 3:3-4; cf. also Prov. 28:15). It is also used in Matthew 10:16 and John 10:12 to represent opponents of the community; above all Acts 20:29 refers to false teachers thus. Their greedy ferocity is also mentioned in Ezekiel 22:27; and Didache 11:6, 12 and Hermas, *Commandments* xi. 12 likewise state that the false prophet can be recognized by his demand for payment. These "wolves" appear in "skins of skeep." The image is supported by the fact that prophets wore clothes made of skin (2 Kings 1:8; Zech. 13:4; see the discussion of Mark 1:6). False prophets, according to the image, appear as members of the community and probably believe they really are (clearly so in vs. 22). This shows how concerned Matthew is that what was once said against those outside the community be understood now as a warning to the community itself (cf. the introductory comments on chapters 21–25; also 7:24-27; 13:36-43, 49-50; 18:23-35; 20:11-16; 22:11-14; 24:45-51; 25:1-46).

[16-18] When we return to the Sermon on the Plain (Luke 6:-43-45), the image changes from sheep to crops; this image is likewise commonly used for God's people (Isa. 5:1-7; 61:3; Jer. 2:21; Matt. 15:13). Two metaphors whose collocation may well be original (and go back to Jesus?) constitute the basis of the passage: first, that of the good tree which produces only good fruit and the poor tree which produces only poor, and second, that of the thorns that cannot bear figs and the thistles (Luke: thorn bushes) that cannot bear grapes. The images stress the connection between the nature of the tree and the fruit it bears. There is no parallel in Judaism, but it is consistent with Jesus' call to surrender oneself to God "wholeheartedly." Fruit is not brought forth as an action apart from the heart of the doer. Conversion must be radical, must proceed from the root, and is therefore not simply an action to be performed. Jesus attaches utmost importance to his words and actions, and he frankly expects to produce a revolutionary change in men—for example, in the tax collectors at his table

or in those who accidentally overhear him (Mark 2:17; 3:34). It is in this sense of a transformed heart producing a transformed life (conduct) that we should also understand the image in Luke 6:45 = Matthew 12:34-35 ("a good man brings good things out of his treasure of good things").

The emphasis at the conclusion of the Sermon on the Plain is still on the invitation to open oneself to this healing of one's whole being and not to rest content with an outward "Lord, Lord"; the nature of the warning is emphasized by the reference in Matthew 12:36 to the judgment that threatens every useless word. The image in James 3:11-12 moralizes: a tongue that praises God can no more bring forth evil than a good spring can produce bitter water, a fig tree olives, or a grapevine figs. Another interpretation, however, is already found in Luke 6:44a. Starting with the idea that the fruit is characteristic of the tree and therefore the action is characteristic of the inner man, Luke stresses the difference between a purely outward ritual, which says nothing about true conversion, and an inward change of heart (cf. Matt. 3:7-10). This suggests the possibility of recognizing the tree by means of its fruit. This is exemplified in Judaism by the testimony of good works before the judgment of God; in Matthew 7:16-20, it has become the dominant note in the conflict with the false prophets, as the verses of the introduction and conclusion show (16a, 20—these were composed by Matthew himself, albeit modeled on the saying in Q = Luke 6:44).

[15-20] The same purpose can be seen behind the transposition vis-à-vis Luke 6:43-44, for it is easier to determine whether we are dealing with a grapevine or a thorn bush (vs. 16) than to determine whether a tree is sound or not (vss. 17-18). The double restatement of Luke 6:43 in verses 17-18 points in the same direction. This line of interpretation is characterized by the change to adjectives more markedly ethical in meaning and to the plural "fruits." In Galatians 5:19, 22 Paul distinguishes clearly between the works of the flesh and the fruit of the spirit. The latter represents something that has developed as a single whole, not an achievement nor yet an obvious quality, in contrast to works, which can be tallied and judged. Luke 6:43-45 and Matthew 12:33-35 both betray an awareness that what the new man brings forth is a single "fruit," a totality and wholeness of life

(cf. the discussion of 3:8). Matthew 7:15-20, on the contrary, is thinking of the diverse actions of the false prophets, which indicate their nature. **[19]** And finally, there is a blunt reminder of the all-examining judgment of God, once again strongly underscored by an echo of the Baptist's message (cf. the discussion of 3:2,10).

[21-23] In its short Lukan form, "Why do you call me, 'Lord, Lord,' and don't do what I tell you?" (Luke 6:46), this saying may go back to Jesus. In that context, "Lord" would refer to the polite form of address, used when speaking to a rabbi, among others. In Matthew, however, the next verse clearly refers to the exalted Lord the Last Judgment. This is indicated by the phrase "when that Day comes," which goes back to the Old Testament expectation of the Day of the Lord (Amos 5:18, 20; Joel 2:1; etc.), which in the New Testament becomes the Day of the Son of Man (Luke 17:24) or of the Lord (Christ) (1 Thess. 5:2). Both the Old and the New Testaments occasionally speak merely of "the Day" (Mal. 3:19 **[4:1]**; 1 Thess. 5:4; 1 Cor. 3:13; Heb. 10:25) or "that Day," as here (Luke 10:12; 2 Tim. 1:12,18). Since Matthew reserves "Lord" as a form of address to those who believe in Jesus, it is clear that he associates with it the full weight of what it means to confess Jesus as "Lord." Thus he is clearly thinking of Christians (this is also indicated by the false prophets' use of the name of Jesus in working their miracles). Matthew is probably thinking of a liturgical acclamation or brief expression of faith such as "Jesus is Lord" (1 Cor. 12:3), which the person making the confession might think would also assure his relationship to Jesus at the Last Judgment.

This interpretation implies the post-Easter development of the Christian community and its worship. And this of course means that the very community for which Matthew is writing his Gospel is being urgently cautioned against neglecting the will of God. Here for the first time Matthew has Jesus speak of "his" Father (cf. the discussion of 5:9), perhaps precisely because in the next verse Jesus appears as judge, i.e. as authorized representative of the Father. It is in this context that the Father-Son relationship appears in sharpest relief (cf. the discussion of 10:33 and 11:27). The phrase "I never knew you" is to be understood against the background of the Old Testament, where "know" can express the most intimate of human relationship (see the discussion of 11:27).

[23] In the Old Testament, "lawlessness" means doing what is forbidden by the Law; circles with a pronounced eschatological bent later came to apply it to attacks of Satan at the eschaton (cf. 2 Thess. 2:3, 7; 2 Cor. 6:14). For Paul, "lawlessness" describes the actions of the man who is a slave to sin, the Law, and death (Rom. 4:6-7; 6:19). For Matthew the original Old Testament meaning is probably primary, although he is probably also thinking that such acts will multiply at the eschaton; in his eyes, however, what the Law forbids is the cooling of love for one's neighbor (24:12; cf. the discussion of 5:18). Prophecy, and the performance of exorcisms and miracles, are not necessarily suspect—no more so than is confession of Jesus as Lord. But when anyone neglects the command to love his neighbor, he alienates himself from the Lord of the Last Judgment. Therefore even the Pharisees, who slavishly observe the Law, can be full of "lawlessness" (23:28).

This section began with the image of the two ways. In quite similar terms Hellenism speaks of Hercules at the crossroads, where the figure of virtue seeks to win him down one road, the figure of vice down the other. Astonishingly, however, Matthew turns his attack on his own community. Therefore he cannot present the two ways in such simple terms. "Lord, Lord" is heard not only along the narrow way but also along the wide, and spiritual gifts like prophecy, exorcism, and the power to perform miraculous healings are likewise found in both places. The rabbis say, "Whoever has made [done] the words of the Law has gained the life of the coming age" (about 20 B.C.; Billerbeck IV. 820). Matthew has no such easy prescription. He learned from Jesus that one can observe all the precepts of the Law, never kill anyone, phrase a letter of divorce correctly, and still be guilty in the eyes of God. He can only speak of the will of the heavenly Father. And he knows that only a tree that is sound from the root up can bring forth good fruit. On this matter see the excursus following 7:29

What Hearing Really Means (7:24-27)
Cf. Luke 6:47-49

²⁴"So then, everyone who hears these words of mine and does them will be like a wise man who built his house on the rock. ²⁵The

rain poured down, the rivers flooded over, and the winds blew hard against that house. But it did not fall, because it had been built on the rock. 26But everyone who hears these words of mine and does not do them will be like a foolish man who built his house on the sand. 27The rain poured down, the rivers flooded over, the winds blew hard against that house, and it fell. What a terrible fall that was!"

This parable also constitutes the conclusion to the Sermon on the Plain, but Luke's wording agrees only slightly with Matthew 7:24-27. The Lukan text envisions two houses next to a river, the foundation of one reaching down to rock, that of the other not; Matthew, on the contrary, envisions two houses, one on the rock of a mountainside, the other on the sand of the valley. The detailed description of the foundation, and the expansion of the introduction in the first verse are probably Lukan additions, while the introductory formula "will be like" in Matthew probably goes back to an earlier collection of parables (see the introductory comments on 13:24). Matthew presumably found the parable not only in Q but also, slightly varied, in the tradition of his own community.

[24] The subject matter is the words of Jesus, emphasized by the emphatic "mine." Matthew goes beyond Luke 6:47, adding "these" to identify Jesus' words explicitly as the Sermon on the Mount; cf. "this gospel" in the excursus to 7:13-23. This distinguishes Jesus' parable from similar rabbinic parables. There a man who "has done many good works and learned much about the Law" (in contrast to one who has done only the latter) is compared to a man who builds his foundation out of stone and his walls out of adobe, and not the other way around. Elsewhere it is stated that where actions are stronger than knowledge it is like a tree whose roots are strong and keep the tree from being uprooted. Matthew underlines the importance of actions and their connection with Jesus' words by speaking of "doing," five times in verses 17-19 and twice more in verses 21-22. The false prophets, too, he condemns only on account of what they do, not what they say. Just as Old Testament bodies of law conclude with the offer of a blessing for good actions and a curse for bad (Lev. 26:3-45; Deut. 28; 30:15-20; cf. the excursus on Matt. 5:3-12 [§1] and 7:13-14), so here the listener at the conclusion is asked to decide.

The future form "will be like" indicates that only the Last Judgment will reveal the difference between the two houses. Thus with reference to 7:22 one may also recall that the difference between the two houses is not visible at first, so that the one built without rock for its foundation can look just as solid as the one built on rock, perhaps more so. **[25]** The imagery of the Judgment is reminiscent of the Deluge (cf. 24:37-39), and even more directly of the prophetic image of whirlwind and cloudburst that demolish whatever cannot stand before God (Ezek. 13:10-16; cf. also Ecclus. 22:16-18). The waters may "fall" upon the house, but the house does not "fall." **[26-27]** The opposite happens to the one who builds on sand; the fall of his house is "terrible," as the concluding phrase of the parable emphatically states: in other words, it will be final. Thus the Sermon on the Mount ends with a warning about the impending Judgment that demonstrates the hopelessness of the man who hears Jesus' words but does not do them.

The durability of the one house and the collapse of the other are not ascribed to the strength or weakness of the walls, as in the rabbinic parable, nor even to the careful laying of a foundation or its lack as in Luke, but only to the site chosen for a location. Thus everything depends on where a man "settles" with his "house," i.e. his life. We are reminded of Paul's saying about the one foundation on which alone it is safe to build (1 Cor. 3:11). Unlike Paul, however, Matthew is not thinking of Jesus' death and resurrection as the seat of all salvation, but of Jesus' *teaching* as presented in "these words" of the Sermon on the Mount (cf. the discussion of vss. 28-29). He goes on to state explicitly that the man who has merely heard these words has not built upon them, but only the man who does them. Unlike 1 Corinthians 3:11, Matthew 16:18 refers to Peter as the "rock"; this is precisely because he transmits and interprets "these words" authentically to the community. Of course the contrast must not be exaggerated.

Verse 22 shows that no act, however imposing, can guarantee salvation if it is not based on the foundation of Jesus' teaching. The image of the fruit makes the same point: only when a man is totally devoted to God, from the root up, can his actions be "good fruit." Matthew in particular is well aware that for Jesus word and deed are one. At the beginning of the Sermon on the Mount, everything centers

authority

on Jesus' authoritative promise of salvation to those who stand in need of God; and here at the conclusion it is once again "these words of mine" that are the only foundation stone. Of course it is important that they be heard. But just as a man does not really hear music until it sets him in motion, so a man does not really hear Jesus' words until they are transformed into action and permeate his entire being. Thus we see once more that here stands someone who makes a far greater claim than any prophet. In his words God himself makes his appearance. The man who really hears them is brought by Jesus into God's new Kingdom, because the man who hears them acts, changes, and is therefore a new being.

Conclusion (7:28-29)
Cf. Mark 1:21-22; Luke 7:1; 4:32

28When Jesus had finished saying these things, the crowd was amazed at the way he taught. 29For he taught like one with authority, and not like their teachers of the Law.

[28] The conclusion shows once more how Matthew interprets the Sermon on the Mount. The formula in verse 28a is probably patterned after a phrase that was already present in Q (Luke 7:1). But Matthew once more refers pointedly to "these" words of Jesus (see the discussion of vs. 24). This is the formula he uses to conclude all the major discourse sections (11:1 after the sending of the Twelve; 13:53 after the parables; 19:1 after instructions for the community; 26:1 after the eschatological discourse). Some scholars have attempted to divide the Gospel into five sections, parallel to the five Books of Moses, each concluding with such a discourse; but the introductions to chapters 5-11 and 21-25 show that the units Matthew considers basic do not coincide with the boundaries defined by this scheme. In all the other cases this ending formula marks a transition to what follows and (except in 26:1) goes on to speak of Jesus' departure; here, however, it is conceived only as a conclusion to the Sermon on the Mount. Matthew does not continue the narrative until 8:1.

[28-29] Apart from the fact that Matthew still refers explicitly to the crowd (see the discussion of 5:1-2) and calls the teachers of the Law "their [the Jews'] teachers of the Law," emphasizing that they

are no longer the teachers belonging to the Christian community (see the excursus on 7:13-23 [§3] and on 10:17), the sentence agrees verbatim with Mark 1:22. The interesting point, however, is the position of this verse. In Mark, the statement about the crowd's amazement at Jesus' mighty words follows directly upon the call of the disciples (=Matt. 4:18-22). Mark does not even state that Jesus taught (Mark 1:39, 28, 34; 3:7-13) until after he has said that the people were astonished at the teaching (1:22). Matthew, on the other hand, withholds his statement of the crowd's response until after he has given not only the report that Jesus did teach (Matt. 4:23–5:1) but the whole substance of that teaching.

This change is based on a totally different theological perspective. Mark "proclaims" to his readers that in Jesus God's authoritative Word has taken on reality, but he does not give any evidence before making this assertion. For Mark this is the witness of faith, simply beyond demonstration. Matthew, by contrast, presents the entire Sermon on the Mount and only afterwards speaks of the authority of Jesus' teaching. Thus he bases this judgment of faith on the content of Jesus' message, which the reader can now judge for himself. Here we can see once more what has already been indicated by his use of the term "gospel"; cf. the excursus on 7:13-23 (§3). Matthew is skeptical about any post-Easter proclamation that God entered the world in Jesus which does not also contain the substance of Jesus' teaching —for Matthew, to believe that God came in Jesus necessitates that you will do his teaching, otherwise it is not belief.

The Sermon on the Mount

a. The problem

The most difficult question posed by the Sermon on the Mount is whether its demands can be fulfilled. Are we not dealing simply with lofty and admirable ideals that founder on the realities of life?

1

Ever since the Middle Ages, the Catholic Church has distinguished between the commandments binding on all Christians and the "evangelical counsels" meant only for a narrower group. They are accepted by those who decide to dedicate their lives to God and to this end withdraw from the world into the life of the cloister. There poverty, chastity, and obedience are possible. It is undoubtedly true that in the common life of a small group a signpost can be set that will be helpful to a far larger circle. Jesus himself called a series of men away from their families and professions and lived with them a life devoted to the will of God. But the problem cannot be resolved in this way; the Sermon on the Mount is not directed merely to the disciples in the narrower sense (cf. the discussion of 5:1-2). Jesus' teaching is addressed to everyone; no one can be a disciple of Jesus and do anything less than all he demanded.

2

In opposition to this approach, Luther spoke of the "two kingdoms." It would be impossible, for example, to conduct a trial on the basis of the rules laid down in the Sermon on the Mount; but this does not mean that only in a withdrawal from the world is it possible to live by Jesus' commandments. According to the doctrine of the two kingdoms, one must distinguish between what the disciple of Jesus is obligated to do by virtue of his office, e.g. as judge, and what is required of him in his personal life. Since the order of the family, the church, and the state is willed by the Creator, one must act in these contexts according to their appropriate rules; e.g. one must condemn a thief to prison as an enemy of the state, but refuse to take vengeance for a wrong suffered in the personal realm. According to this theory, the requirements laid down by Jesus are not legislation to be followed literally in every situation—according to Matthew, for example, Jesus himself launches a violent counterattack against the charges of the Pharisees (22:15-23, 33). But in truth, there is not the slightest hint of any realm where the disciple is not bound by the words of Jesus; the realm of the family has been explicitly discussed in the sayings about adultery and divorce, the state in the sayings about revenge and love for enemies.

3

Then is the left wing of the Reformation correct—and hence all the movements down to the present that interpret the Sermon on the

Mount as a realizable social program? Undoubtedly the demands of the Sermon on the Mount are really meant to be fulfilled; but through all that Jesus says there sounds the call to faith, and faith can only grow in total liberty. One can hardly demand by legislation (i.e., force) that everyone act lovingly, and expect the love, or the faith, behind their actions to be genuine. This difficulty of imposing Jesus' ethics on people either engenders a hostility toward civilization, like that we may observe in Tolstoy or even more clearly in Friedrich Neumann, who finds in Palestine a way of life not yet under the sway of technology, the "world of Jesus," and seeks to revive the past in the backward perspective of romanticism; or, for those who insist on the practical establishment of order, it leads to a system founded on the power of the state, whose beginning is not altruism but force, and whose end is at best equity, at worst tyranny.

4

Must we then admit, with Albert Schweitzer, for example, that Jesus intended men to follow the Sermon on the Mount literally, but that this can be done only as long as men are convinced that the end of the world is imminent? In the brief interim remaining, in which there can be no thought of civil order or of rearranging society, men could concentrate all their efforts on leading lives pleasing to God. Now the Sermon on the Mount refers (rarely) to the coming Kingdom of God and bases the precepts of Jesus on that idea. But there is no suggestion of imminence; on the contrary, marriage and the family are discussed positively, with even fewer reservations than in 1 Corinthians 7. In addition, the Sermon on the Mount is especially aware that the coming Kingdom of God is now becoming reality.

5

Must we then follow Wilhelm Herrmann and to an extent also Rudolf Bultmann in interpreting the words of Jesus merely as a call to a new way of looking at the world, apart from consideration of whether the actual deeds are possible? This approach, too, makes an important point. Jesus in fact repeatedly starts with the outward act in order to probe the heart that lies behind the act: even in a proper marriage the heart can commit adultery; even without the slightest physical violence the angry heart can kill. But this approach fails to recognize the way the Sermon on the Mount expressly calls on men to act in certain ways, without allowing any loopholes.

6

Does this mean that our only recourse is to follow Lutheran orthodoxy, for example, in understanding the Sermon on the Mount as a judgment because it cannot be fulfilled, a judgment that confronts the hearer with his sin so that only Jesus' death on the cross can solve the problem for the sinner? One might put the matter in more modern and cautious terms, with Guardini, for example: the Sermon on the Mount is indeed the breakthrough of the new life of which the prophets spoke; but in the rejection of Jesus one can see how little it has been accepted. Only in defeat, in death on the cross, according to Guardini, can Jesus bring men back to God, so that the church here receives its commission to act as advocate for man's weakness and offer man the possibility of a life with God. In this interpretation it is still clear that the antitheses, for example (5:21-48), are designed to explode any complacency the hearer has about his devoutness. But we are still faced with the fact that the Beatitudes, and all the teaching that follows—even the eschatological sections—make not the slightest reference to any atoning death of Jesus, yet they explicitly require of men an attitude of mercy, of purity of heart, of peacemaking, and of acceptance of persecution, as well as the very concrete actions that issue from this attitude.

7

Should we then be content, like Eduard Thurneysen, for example, to interpret the Sermon on the Mount merely as a self-proclamation of Christ, bringing before the eyes of men the only one who fulfills all the requirements? Perhaps this redirecting of our attention from what man does to what Jesus is doing in the Sermon furnishes the best aid to understanding; the words are incomprehensible apart from the man who speaks them. But this does not help the interpreter around the difficulty that, apart from the phrase "but now I tell you" in the antitheses, the text scarcely mentions the speaker explicitly. And in any case, Jesus is demanding not a confession of faith—this is what a self-proclamation by him would imply—but a *life* of faith, the realization of his words in action.

b. The various answers in the Sermon on the Mount

Probably we will not make any further progress until we take seriously the observation that the Sermon on the Mount is not a discourse delivered by Jesus but a veritable chorus of voices, some bearing the stamp of Jesus, the others assembled by the evangelist to form a single whole that makes certain specific points.

1

The passages in which we unmistakably hear Jesus' voice constitute a summons to faith, an invitation to a total trust that takes the "Father" as the absolute center, and that experiences all of life as a gift. Thus, knowing that the Father is aware of our needs frees us from anxiety and keeps us from treating prayer as a good work (6:31-32, 7-8). Jesus' promise of salvation bestows God's saving presence on the poor, on those who mourn, on those who hunger, not primarily on those who bear everything in an exemplary fashion (5:3-6). Jesus' antitheses set men free from all scrupulous introspection through which they would use the commandments to determine how perfect or how sinful they have been (5:21-48). When the left hand no longer knows what the right hand does (6:3), there is no room for the relentless presumption that stands in dread of losing the perfection attained, nor for the equally relentless self-depreciation that wallows in feelings of inferiority. When a man is finally relieved of the duty of judging, classifying, and evaluating others (7:1-5), he can also stop classifying himself—stop going around in circles like a dog chasing his tail, perpetually attached to his own merits or sins.

Of course, Jesus' words are a summons to a way of life. The grotesque notion of a faith that is purely intellectual, totally divorced from real life with its feelings and emotions, its words and gestures, its actions and suffering, is surely not the notion of Jesus. Rather, it is a real way of life, but based on joy, in which even the fasting required for service is turned into feasting (6:17). It is therefore primarily an act of prayer (6:9-13), but brief, so that it can never be confused with a meritorious act of devotion (6:7): it is nothing more or less than a training for life with the Father. Therefore the first two clauses in the Lord's Prayer focus on him, on his name and his Kingdom. The man who is thoroughly familiar with this way of praying knows as well that his bread has been seen to and his wrongs forgiven, and that temptation would consist in diverting his attention from the Father to his own sinlessness or sin. The most important realization, attested by Jesus' own words, is the fact that there is one who, by promising us salvation with authority, sets us free to live (cf. the concluding remarks on 5:3-12). His speaking seeks after hearing, and where this hearing becomes reality, there is the new heart to which salvation is promised. This is the eschatological salvation referred to already by the prophets: there is one who promises us salvation with the authority of God, and we may believe the promise, because we change. That is the law written on the heart, which need no longer be taught in formulas and lives only on the knowledge that God has forgiven his people and given himself to them (Jer. 31:33-34).

2

A community still devoutly attached to Judaism was bedeviled by the question of whether or not the message of Jesus nullified God's Law. The community realized it would be a total misunderstanding to think of Jesus merely as someone offering men a sinecure. Jesus called men not to less but to more than the letter of the Law. Indeed, it was this community that produced such interpretations as the one that Jesus' call does not abolish the least point or smallest stroke of the Law, and that whoever mitigates one of the least commandments will be least in the Kingdom of heaven (5:18-19). This holds the line against any negligence of Jesus' strict requirements, which would also be a negligence of God's goodness. But it is absolutely vital that the Law be understood in Jesus' sense as an invitation to faith, not as the embodiment of what a man must do to be eligible for salvation. Therefore the warning against disobedience becomes perverted the moment it is divorced from the promise of Jesus; Matthew can incorporate it only with his own interpretive addition (5:18).

3

But even had there been no traditional interest in observing the Law to its letter, it would still have been essential for the community of Jesus to live by his words. To understand Jesus' radical sayings about alms, prayer, and fasting as simply saying they could be dispensed with would have been a fundamental misconstruction. But following the example of Jesus, the community approached such practises theologically, taking heed of the sayings of the prophets about a religion of the heart as opposed to a religion of token performance. Those sayings also appear in Stephen and Paul, in the catchwords "circumcision of the heart" and "Holy Spirit" (Acts 7:51; Rom. 2:29). There was always a danger of spiritual pride, as Paul well knew, and the convert was always to remember—and pay heed to—Jesus' sayings about a new heart, to render impossible any complacency or hopes for approval by God (e.g. Phil. 3:3-14). But on the other hand, there was also a danger of carelessness, and the convert was also expected to remember that though Jesus unmasked the "hypocrites" whose goal was approval from the crowd, his disciples were still expected to practice almsgiving, prayer, and fasting—but from the heart (6:2-6, 16-18).

4

The Sermon on the Plain in Q (roughly Luke 6:20*b*-23, 27-38, 41-49) was already organized around Jesus' sayings about loving one's enemies and not judging. It dealt expressly with prescriptions that included all men, not just one's own brethren. Therefore reference is not made to the perfect God, as in Matthew, but to the loving God, who sets his stamp on the way his community is to live (Luke 6:36; Matt. 5:48). In the relatively short Sermon on the Plain, the Beatitudes and the saying about the good fruit that can only derive from a good tree receive increased importance. Further, the Sayings source associates the good-fruit-good-tree image with the Baptist's harsh words against race-proud Jews, and it places the Sermon on the Plain between the account of Jesus' temptation and that of the healing of the Roman officer's servant—all of which depreciates the "righteousness" of formality and tradition, and extols the true righteousness, of a heart genuinely trusting in God and acting accordingly. The Sayings Source apparently arose as a polemic against the Zealots, i.e. against a revolutionary group that, presuming on God's assistance, wanted to drive out the Roman occupation troops by force; and that Q did arise in so tumultuous an atmosphere shows how seriously it (and Luke) took Jesus' warning against works that remain purely external and do not involve the heart.

There is not a trace in Q about the validity of the Law or even of Jewish devotional practices such as appear in Matthew. Neither has any reference to the gift of the Lord's Prayer and of life without anxiety been incorporated into the Sermon on the Plain, although Q is familiar with this material. The Sermon on the Plain is primarily concerned with the true community possible among men who have been made radically whole through the promise of Jesus and who can thus abandon hatred and judgment.

5

There is evidence suggesting that the Sermon on the Plain had already been expanded in Matthew's community before he included it, although the details are very uncertain. Most likely is the extension of the Beatitudes to form a series of seven, with increased emphasis on the attitude men are to have (5:7-9). Likewise pre-Matthaean are the original antitheses, which make the Law more rigorous (5:21, 22 a, 27-28, 33-34, 37), and the tripartite structure of religious duties (6:2-6, 16-18). The former probably go back to Jesus, the latter to the catechetical interests of the community. Matthew follows the sequence of the Sermon on the Plain almost without exception and adopts its placement in the Sayings Source; but he diverges quite markedly from its wording and incorporates other material from Q almost word for word in his Sermon on the Mount: this observation can best be explained by the hypothesis that he was also familiar with the Sermon on the Plain in an expanded form used by his community.

If the sections just mentioned (5:21, 22a, 27-28, 33-34, 37; 6:2-6, 16-18) were included in this pre-Matthaean version, then the community was already reading the Sermon on the Mount primarily in terms of controversy over the Law. The solution to that controversy was relatively simple: Jesus did not abolish the Law but only interpreted it in such a way as to emphasize the will of God actually expressed in it. The hostility toward the Pharisees (6:2-6, 16-18) was probably directed against the Judaism that was consolidating its position in the years following the fall of Jerusalem. No fundamental questions were raised about the Pharisees per se, but they were accused of inconsistency in terms similar to those found in 23:2-4 and above all in 23:5. Perhaps the antitheses were also expanded at this stage by material placing the disquisitions of the Pharisees in an ironic light (5:22b, 29-30[?], 33b-36).

6

Matthew (cf. the excursus on 7:13-23 and the retrospective summary at the end of the commentary) was upset by a tendency toward "lawlessness" that threatened to cheapen God's grace. The most serious threat, practically eschatological in nature (24:11-12), was presented by the false prophets; their danger lay not in their false teaching but in their false actions. The community, he said, had to resist "to the end" the coldness of heart that caused licentiousness. Matthew took on his opponents emphatically and in a kind of postscript made the whole Sermon on the Mount refer to the need for action (7:15-27). For this reason he also emphasized Jesus' approval of God's Law (5:17-20). He could not rid himself of anxiety that the community of Jesus would understand their new life in a way all too new. The community might forget that God also seeks his people in the Law. Matthew stressed repeatedly, therefore, that what is demanded of the disciples is not less but more than what the Pharisees and teachers of the Law do.

Matthew is certainly not Paul. Aware as he is of Jesus' total upending of the Law (the secondary antitheses make this clear: 5:31-32, 38-40), he nevertheless maintains that the Law can bring God's commandments to fulfillment—if used in the service of love for one's fellow man. Wisdom literature maintained that only wisdom could give knowledge of the commandments and bestow perfection (Wis. 9:6, 9-10); but according to Matthew, in Jesus there appeared a wisdom (see the excursus on 23:34-39) that teaches men what God *really* intended by his Law. Matthew's solution of the question is to summarize the entire Law in Jesus' call to love.

This also accounts for the only change he makes in the order of the Sermon on the Plain, changing the position of the Golden Rule so that it and 5:17-20 constitute the framework surrounding the sayings about the new and greater righteousness. Matthew is well aware that it is only because of the love Jesus himself showed that his disciples are able to love in the way that fulfills the Law. And it is in this sense—the ability of love alone to keep the Law's spirit—that he interprets the traditional sayings about "fulfilling" the Law, and fulfilling its every stroke and line (5:17-18). Thus the call to renounce all vengeance and love one's enemy constitutes the high point of Jesus' treatment of the question of the Law (5:38, 39 a, 43, 44 a).

This focus on the good of others also shows up in Matthew's interpretation of the Lord's Prayer, which emphasizes the unconditional obligation to forgive anyone who wrongs us (once again not merely our "brothers"). But even the passages that deal with the preservation and restoration of community among men and call for definite actions (5:23-26; the addition in 5:32) point in the same direction. Matthew is concerned that love be concretely acted upon within the community and beyond its confines. Therefore having stated the radical commandment of Jesus he goes on to provide practical guidance (cf. also the concluding remarks on 26:47-56).

Neither did he forget that according to Jesus' will the community is never called to achieve its own perfection, but to establish a sign for all. Thus he begins with the sayings about the disciples' being the salt of the earth, the light of the world, and a city on a hill (5:13-16), and strengthens his community to meet the persecution to follow when it practises his preaching (5:10). Matthew knows throughout what the only source of the strength is that enables the community to live such a life. From other parts of Q he borrowed material for the Sermon on the Mount: not only the Lord's Prayer (6:9-13), but also the sayings about the good God who will more certainly requite a need than any human father (7:7-11) and the statements meant to set men free from greedy amassing of wealth and from anxiety (6:19-34).

In a certain sense the Lord's Prayer marks the center of the Sermon on the Mount; the first three petitions are developed in the sections that precede, the last three in the sections that follow (6:19-34; 7:1-12, 13-23). Since, however, the Lord's Prayer has been interpolated into a preexisting tripartite schema on the basis of the catchword "pray," and since 7:13-23 is primarily a postscript insisting on action, we can probably say no more than that Matthew learned from Jesus, and especially from the Lord's Prayer, to place the great concerns of God ahead of the wishes and needs of men. A deliberate parallelism of structure between the Sermon on the Mount and the five Books of Moses is hardly likely. The first book (God blesses his people that they may be a blessing for all) has been compared to Matthew 5:3-16, the second (God gives the Law) to 5:17-48, the third (God teaches the proper way to worship) to 6:1-18, the fourth (God preserves his people) to 6:19-34, and the fifth (judgment by the divine word and the offer of life or death) to 7:1-27. But the parallels are very dubious.

Matthew's most important contribution is undoubtedly his composition of the Sermon on the Mount and his incorporation of it into his Gospel. He thus presented Jesus as the "Messiah of the Word" and made it clear than one can understand and live what is said here only as a disciple of Jesus, brought by him to share in his total devotion and obedience to God. The astonishing freedom with which he arranged and reshaped his material is an outstanding sign of the liberation that he himself experienced through his encounter with this Lord (cf. the discussion of the "gospel" in §3 of the excursus on 7:15-23).

7

Finally, the Syriac Church Order, for instance, shows how one can misunderstand the Sermon on the Mount as a simple and obvious wisdom discourse, divorce it from its center, and thus falsify it. "Love those who hate you" is now merely a clever maxim, concluding: "and you will have no enemies." The statement "Do not demand it back" is grounded on common experience with debtors who show no prospect of repaying: "for you cannot succeed." "He will not get out until he has paid the last penny" is now applied to the dishonest recipient of alms. To the command "Give to everyone who asks you" is added: "Your alms may sweat in your hand until you know to whom you should give them" (Did. 1:3-6). Similar clever maxims dealing with how one should manage one's life were composed by a Jew as "sayings of the righteousness of the holy God" and ascribed to the Greek poet

Phocylides (cf. for instance i. 2-3, 7, 11, 14-17, 22, 32-34). Didache 6:2 also belongs with this type of saying, exhorting the man who finds he cannot be perfect at least to do all that he can, as do the statements in 8:1-2 to the effect that one should not fast like the hypocrites on Monday and Thursday but rather on Wednesday and Friday and should not use a Jewish formula when praying but rather the Lord's Prayer.

c. The truth of the Sermon on the Mount

1

All of this discussion merely poses the question of truth and does not answer it. How does the situation actually stand? Which of these various voices is the one that must not be ignored? But even this question does not state the critical problem, for the very variety in the transmission and interpretation of Jesus' sayings shows unmistakably that a legalistic formula that lays down the rules for all time can never be the answer. We may cite examples to illustrate this point. We never read that Jesus retired into his chamber to pray, as 6:6 recommends, only that he prayed in the presence of all the people or alone upon a hillside (14:19, 23). Neither was Jesus content merely to remain silent when he was arrested and brought into court (26:55; John 18:23). The same is true of his disciples (Acts 16:37 ff.; 22:25-28; 25:10-11). When attacked by the Pharisees, far from turning the other cheek, Jesus counterattacked so vigorously that people have asked whether Jesus loved the Pharisees and prayed for them or even made any attempt to understand them. Jesus probably received invitations from the Pharisees and wanted to engage them in dialogue (Luke 7:36-50; John 3:1-13). He could agree with one of the teachers of the Law and state that he was not far from the Kingdom of God (Mark 12:34), and he had friends among members of the Council (Mark 15:43). But it cannot be denied that Jesus also criticized these groups bitterly.

But this very example raises the question of truth. The meaning of this criticism depends on the question of who utters it and in what context he does so. The material of the Gospels was assembled at a time when the community of Jesus and Pharisaic Judaism were coming to a parting of the ways and both groups were struggling for their very existence. New anti-Pharisaic sayings came into being and earlier sayings received new interpretations. The extent to which this was justified or historically inevitable remains in question. Jesus himself bitterly criticizes many other groups within his nation, and in this criticism his struggle on behalf of his fellow men and his love are expressed. Therefore the fundamental considerations are more important. It would often be easier not to dispute with others and simply remain silent instead of helping to clarify the points of contention. It might be easier merely to turn the other cheek to a child that strikes in rage than to resist and try to help the child grow through a conversation that demands emotional involvement. It is often easier just to give a beggar something than to find time for him. To live like the birds of the air and the lilies of the field can be an expression of faith, but it can also be simple laziness; 2 Thessalonians 3:6 ff. (cf. 1 Thess. 4:10 ff.) is already aware of this problem. In each of these instances one must determine what represents the service of love concretely towards someone else and what represents evasion; literal fulfillment of the law of Jesus can no more relieve us of this decision than literal fulfillment of the Law of Moses. This point is made by the fact that the community again and again used new approaches to find out what Jesus' instruction meant in actual practice.

2

This is the most important point to be made in answering the enormous questions associated with the Sermon on the Mount. What does it mean not to resist evil when I receive my draft notice? Does it mean that I comply without resisting, or does it mean that, in order to avoid being forced to resist as a soldier, I resist the draft? Does it mean that I must not resist an evil system that exploits the poor and the weak, and thus participate in exploitation, or does it mean that I must in fact resist so as not to participate? Idealistic movements seeking to set up a kingdom of peace on earth after the model of the Sermon on the Mount have sometimes brought about an increase of violence in order to achieve a noble goal. Examples can be cited from Jan Matthys in Münster to Stalin. And on the other side, carelessness that has not offered prompt resistance to irresponsible luxury or an inequitable system or the persecution of a minority cast in the role of devils has led to immeasurable suffering. Again, examples can be cited from the period of the French Revolution through the decades of industrialization in Europe with its child labor down to the eruption of anti-Jewish pogroms.

What is required of the Christian community? The Sermon on the Mount calls it to faith, in all its strata. This means that it must really expect the answer to come from its Lord, not from within itself. It is thus called to pray, and initially also to wait and listen. The likelihood that the sermon on the Mount arose in part to denounce the violence of first-century revolutionaries ought to remind us to be suspicious whenever we are called upon to use violence in achieving a noble or supposedly noble end.

Initially, at least, and above all in the Sermon on the Mount, it is required that we face suffering and persecution, and not strike out. Of course the boundaries are not always so well defined that we can invariably keep our hands clean. In the Gospel of Matthew it is Pilate who wants to wash his hands clean of the matter, not the highly suspect and equivocal Jesus. A band of disciples who only suffer and offer passive resistance nevertheless exert a pressure that is a form of violence. And when Jesus drove men from the Temple and attacked the Pharisees with bitter animosity, he was making at least symbolic use of violence. Matthew himself calls upon the community not to remain silent when a brother falls into sin but rather to reprove him and if necessary even treat him as a tax collector or a heathen (18:-15-18). There can be circumstances in which we owe it to a person not to give in to him until he has been brought back from his evil.

Above all, there will always be situations in which members of the same community are called by God to arrive at different decisions. A man fulfilling his military service may, in Switzerland in 1940, for example, be seeking to preserve not only his own life but thousands of refugees from a terrible death. At the same time another man must refuse military service, even in the same situation, in order to warn against any kind of jingoism. Jesus refused to identify either with the revolutionary Zealots or with the politically conservative Sadducees or with the Pharisees who were inclined to retreat from political life.

Thus there is no simple formula that could prescribe the stance of the community for all time.

3

The problem is intensified when we consider affairs of the state. A judge who acquitted all the accused without distinction would be saddling himself with a heavy responsibility. He could be handing over thousands to onslaught and murder. On the other hand, he cannot simply hide behind the notion that he is carrying out an official function and must act according to the laws of his office. The official who sent millions of Jews to their deaths without hesitation in accordance with the laws prevailing under National Socialism was rightfully condemned, even if he had been a model husband and father in his personal life. A judge, too, must fulfill the requirements of love. He must even be prepared to suffer consequences if he feels he must acquit an accused criminal contrary to the regulations of his office. He is, in short, delegated to protect from the unrestricted right of the stronger, and to love, everyone he can—whether it be society, endangered by a criminal, or a "criminal," imperilled by society's unjust code.

In this example a single individual can still to some extent trace the consequences of his actions; the decision becomes more difficult when a man must consider economic measures, labor regulations, and real estate values. Here the community of Jesus has a special interest in getting experts, who can only work together as a team, to help them see and answer the question of what love means in concrete terms. The commandment to love the individual who confronts me must be weighed against the commandment to love the multitude who need a certain order to protect them. There is no escaping the conflict. What Jesus expects of his disciple is courage: he expects the vigorous investment of his love, not the innocence that always stands on the sidelines.

4

Life in faith is never a ready answer to every question. Whenever the community tried this approach, it met with failure. It is surprising, and to some shocking, that Jesus spoke out bluntly against unethical practices in family law, but never suggested framing new laws; that he denounced the killing that begins with an angry heart, but never forbade military service; that he advocated the "yes" that needs no oath to support it, but had nothing to say on the question of swearing an oath required by the state; that he called on men to love their enemies, but took no position on behalf of either the Zealots or the political conservatives; that he praised the way the birds and flowers live, but did not try to change contemporary labor laws or even reform the institution of slavery; that he warned against wealth, but did not attack the economic system. Of course there have been disciples of Jesus who understood that his words demanded action, e.g. the struggle of the Methodists and Baptists against slavery in the eighteenth century.

But the limitations of all concrete efforts must be noted. Had Jesus established a new system of family or labor law in Palestine, it would be long outmoded and vanished; above all, in a different situation it would have proved to be as wrong as what it replaced, and under certain circumstances more dangerous. The law of the medieval church against interest, inspired directly by the Sermon on the Mount (cf. the discussion of 5:42), meant that only the Jews could make commercial loans, with results that were totally pernicious. Jesus did not lay out any programs, because programs can only be put into effect by threat of punishment. The goal of Jesus' ministry was the renewal of men's hearts, that they might act not by virtue of constraint but through the freedom that comes from faith. The law, which functions through constraint, stands in the way of this very freedom. Of course there are situations in which constraint must be used for the sake of those who are suffering.

5

The central concern of Jesus is the call to faith, faith that shows itself in the concrete way the believer lives. This is what gives the additions to the antitheses in 5:23-26 their point. The important thing is not for a man to attain perfection, not even for him to realize that he has failed to attain perfection. The important thing is for him to be free for God and thus at the same time for his fellow man who needs him. He may set up signs for this purpose. He will be ready to draw personal as well as political and economic conclusions, and at the same time be open to the realization that something for which he may have struggled his entire life is no longer good and must therefore be abandoned or changed.

6

In 1946/47, the World Council of Churches, meeting at London and Bossey, emphasized obedience within the community, obedience as a sign to the world; in 1954 at Evanston it emphasized better righteousness within the world as a foretaste of the coming Kingdom of God, in 1961 at New Delhi the role of the Christian community as light of the *world,* and in 1968 at Uppsala the concrete political and economic responsibility of the community. The Sermon on the Mount urges men to draw practical conclusions; at the same time, it must be clearly maintained that love springing from faith can never become a program. In political and social movements it must remain the salt and light that stings and illuminates, must repeatedly swim against the current and proclaim the one whose own ministry was not accommodated to any program, who eliminated in advance the possibility of defining who is friend, who enemy.

C. JESUS' MINISTRY
8:1–9:38

Jesus Makes a Leper Clean (8:1-4)
Cf. Mark 1:40-45; Luke 5:12-16

[1]Jesus came down from the hill, and large crowds followed him. [2]Then a leper came to him, knelt down before him, and said, "Sir, if you want to, you can make me clean." [3]Jesus reached out and touched him. "I do want to," he answered. "Be clean!" At once he was clean from his leprosy. [4]Then Jesus said to him, "Listen! Don't tell anyone, but go straight to the priest and let him examine you; then offer the sacrifice that Moses ordered, to prove to everyone that you are now clean."

(Vs. 4—Lev. 13:49; 14:2-32.)

Matthew abbreviates the narrative section markedly. He reduces the miracle stories as a whole to about 55% of their compass in Mark, while shortening the narratives that display Jesus as the Christ by only about 10% and the narratives associated with controversies by 20% on the average. In the miracle stories, his concern is Jesus' encounter with men. The description of the healing is always much abbreviated, with compensatory emphasis on discussion of faith (e.g. 9:20-22, where only Jesus and the woman are involved; 8:13; 15:21-28; cf. also the introductory comments on 18:1-15). We find the same phenomenon here. On the question of miracles, cf. the excursus on Mark 4:35-41.

[1] Verse 1 links the story with the Sermon on the Mount. The crowds (5:1a) are represented as witnesses not only to Jesus' words but to his deeds. Perhaps the verse is also intended to suggest a return to the world of pain and suffering.

[2] The Greek text of verse 2 begins "And behold," imitating the language of the Bible, because it is God's history that is here recounted. This formula, elsewhere in the Gospel, calls special attention to the healing of the paralytic, the woman with a hemorrhage, and the dumb demoniac (9:2, 20, 32), as well as—especially important to Matthew—the peril of the disciples (8:24), the confession of the Son of God (8:29), the driving of the demons into the herd of swine (8:32; cf. 34), the protest of the teachers of the Law (9:3), and the arrival of the tax collectors (9:10). It does not appear with the healing of the blind, on which Matthew lays such weight because of 11:4-5 (cf. 20:30), nor above all with the restoration of the dead to life. It is therefore wrong to speak of a systematic usage, even though Matthew likes using the idiom to emphasize something that seems important to him.

In the Old Testament, "come and kneel down" frequently refers to cultic adoration, and Matthew frequently uses the first term to describe the respectful approach of people to Jesus (used 41 times for others who come to Jesus, usually showing respect; only twice used for Jesus himself: 17:7; 28:18; cf. the discussion of 8:25; 9:18; 15:25). The desperate need of the sick man is no longer emphasized as in Mark, only his manner of approach which shows deference to Jesus. Deference is emphasized by the word "sir" or "lord"; this term is notable, because Matthew adds it despite his tendency to abbreviate, and because he never uses it except in the speech of those who believe in Jesus (cf. 8:6; 15:22; 17:14; 20:30-31). The request is therefore already an example of worship in faith, which expects everything from the omnipotence of the "Lord."

[3] The healing is described as tersely as possible, in terms corresponding precisely to the words of Jesus. The parallelism between "came to him, knelt down before him, and said" and "reached out his hand and touched him and said" in the Greek text is unusual. Was it already present in the tradition Matthew was drawing on? Jesus' anger is omitted (Mark 1:43), as well as the reference to his pity (Mark 1:41). The human side of Jesus takes a back seat to his divine omnipotence.

[4] The final verse is not meant to confirm the miracle, but to present Jesus as an Israelite faithful to the Law (5:17). The command to keep silent (Mark 1:44) Matthew retains—and that he does so is striking since his introduction made the whole crowd a witness to the event. The command to keep silent appears once more in 9:30 at the end of the miracle narratives, along with the disobedience to the command corresponding to Mark 1:45. Matthew probably intends to emphasize the humility of Jesus as the servant of God who neither cries out nor proclaims his propaganda in the streets (cf. the discussion of 12:15-21 and 8:17).

Unlike Mark, Matthew uses this story to call men to worship the "Lord" whose help is given in answer to every petition brought to him. Jesus' obedience to the Law is stressed here more than in Mark, but so is the way Jesus breaks through those petrified religious codes that can only exclude a leper, not heal him. Thus the healed leper becomes a witness against official Israel, as the next section will confirm. He also becomes a witness against the reader, asking him if *he* can open himself enough to God (in Jesus) to break down walls (even those of religion).

The Faith of the Roman Officer (8:5-13)
Cf. Luke 7:1-9; 13:28, 29; 7:10

⁵When Jesus entered Capernaum, a Roman officer met him and begged for help: ⁶"Sir, my servant is at home, sick in bed, unable to move, and suffering terribly." ⁷"I will go and make him well," Jesus

said. [8]"Oh no, sir," answered the officer. "I do not deserve to have you come into my house. Just give the order and my servant will get well. [9]I, too, am a man under the authority of superior officers, and I have soldiers under me. I order this one, 'Go!' and he goes; and I order that one, 'Come!' and he comes; and I order my slave, 'Do this!' and he does it." [10]Jesus was surprised when he heard this, and said to the people who were following him, "I tell you, I have never seen such faith as this in anyone in Israel. [11]But I tell you this: Many will come 'from the east and the west' and will sit down at the table in the Kingdom of heaven with Abraham, Isaac, and Jacob. [12]But the sons of the Kingdom will be thrown out into the darkness outside, where they will cry and gnash their teeth." [13]And Jesus said to the officer, "Go home, and what you have believed will be done for you." And the officer's servant was healed that very hour.

(Vs. 11—Isa. 49:12; 59:19; Mal. 1:11; Ps. 107:3 [cf. Isa. 2:2-3; 43:5].)

[5-10] The words of the officer and of Jesus in verses 8-10 agree almost word for word with Luke 7:6-9, except that in verse 7a Luke adds a comment in his typical style. In the rest of the narrative, however, there is no agreement except for the term "officer" and the place: "entered Capernaum" (vs. 5). According to Luke the officer does not come at all but merely sends his friends, who, however, say the same words that Matthew assigns to the officer. Obviously both versions cannot be true in a historical sense. In addition, Matthew describes the patient as being unable to move, while Luke describes him as being at the point of death without specifying the disease. Furthermore, according to Luke the officer first sends some elders who persuade Jesus to come before the friends are sent to meet him; Matthew knows nothing of any of this. Matthew 8:6 speaks of the officer's "boy," a term that could mean either "servant" or "son"; Luke speaks unambiguously of the "servant," although in the request of the officer (Luke 7:7) he uses the same word as Matthew 8:6, 8. John 4:46-54, where the sick "son" of the royal official at Capernaum is healed at a distance, is probably likewise an outgrowth of this story dating from a period in which the question of Jew or gentile was no longer so acute. It is clear, then, that Q contained only the dialogue

in verses 8-10, probably with a kind of title mentioning the sickness of the "boy" of the "officer at Capernaum."

[11-12] A fundamental saying has been interwoven into the Matthaean account. In connection with the story of the exemplary gentile Jesus speaks of gentiles sitting at the eschatological banquet, the exclusion of Israel, and the subsequent crying and gnashing of teeth. Luke 13:28-29 preserves the same saying in reverse order, perhaps because there it is appended to the condemnation in 13:27. The saying presumably was often repeated, now in one form, now another. But the reference to the gentiles is not appropriate to the Lukan context, and the application of the preceding condemnation (Luke 13:27) to the Jews (vs. 26) is more likely due to Luke himself than to an earlier tradition. Thus even before Matthew, and possibly from the very beginning, the saying belonged to our narrative (cf. the introductory discussion of 4:17–11:30). It may go back to Jesus himself (see the discussion of vs. 11) and may well have been uttered under circumstances like those described here. **[13]** Matthew himself composed the saying about the healing that corresponds to belief (vs. 13; cf. the excursus on miracles at Mark 4:35-41). The similarity in content to 15:21-28 is striking; we hear of healings at a distance only in the case of gentiles.

The officer is to be thought of as a Syrian gentile in the service of Rome. So much stress is placed on his faith that even his request is a mere statement, leaving it fully up to Jesus what he will do. Verse 7 might be read as a question; probably, however, it is to be taken as an expression of Jesus' openness and authority. There follows the statement that led Calvin to comment that this officer had been healed by God before his servant was healed by Jesus. It is an expression of sober awareness of where the speaker stands before God. In Palestine a Jew would never enter a gentile house, because it would render him unclean. And as a gentile, the officer has no plea to enter before God like those who say, "Abraham is our ancestor" (3:9); but his very awareness of this is the new way of thinking that signalizes repentance (3:8). Jesus' readiness to respond overwhelms the officer, just as God's irruption into the life of the prophet reveals his situation to him at a stroke: "Lord, I am a man of unclean lips" (Isa. 6:5; cf. Luke 5:8).

Astonished by Jesus' firm confidence, the officer is open to expect everything from him, even what is apparently impossible. Thus what he says expresses both his awareness of his own emptiness and the daring leap that counts concretely on the power of God.

The Greek text rendered "under the authority of superior officers" actually reads "under commanding force," a strange expression. There are Syriac translations that render it as "with the power to give orders," and it has been suggested that we are dealing with a misunderstood Aramaic text. But we have no idea whether there ever was such a text, and the Syrians are probably only trying to avoid the notion that Jesus might be subject to any higher power. But this is precisely what the officer is trying to say. This leaves the question open of how this superiority to Jesus might be correctly expressed. Or are we to understand that Jesus, who has no superior, is all the more entitled to give orders? In either case the saying reveals a faith that God acts in as matter-of-fact and concrete a way as the officer does in his world.

Jesus' suprise shows that faith, when it really occurs, always partakes of the miraculous. Jesus does not reject the officer's trust in what he says; he does not even direct attention away from himself, as do prophets and apostles, and even angels (Acts 3:12; 14:15; Rev. 19:10). On the contrary, he states that this is an expression of "great faith." This shows that faith is not simply assent to a specific doctrine, although it can certainly include such assent, but, if genuine, faith always expresses itself in vital terms. Therefore Jesus can say that he has never found such faith in "anyone in Israel" (the expression is unique to Matthew), although hardly anyone in Israel doubted the existence of God and many were of the opinion that obedience to God ranked higher than anything else.

Verse 11 promises the Kingdom of heaven to such faith. This presupposes the hope, widespread in Israel since Isaiah (2:1-5), that the nations would come streaming in to Zion (Tob. 13:11; 14:6-7; Eth. Enoch 90:30-36), but not the vision of a community comprising gentiles and Jews, for which Stephen's group laid the groundwork (Acts 11:19-20) and for which Paul gained general acceptance. Instead of the Temple of Zion, the text speaks of participation in the heavenly banquet (mentioned in the Old Testament only in Isa. 25:6), because it is no longer thinking in terms of an earthly kingdom. What is new and unprecedented, although hinted at by such prophetical sayings as Micah 3:12; Amos 3:2; 9:7, is the notion that this will not take place for the glory of Israel, to be made somehow greater by the inclusion of the nations, but that Israel is threatened with exclusion from the Kingdom of God. Only Acts 28:25 ff. and above all Romans 9–11 (albeit coupled with hope in 11:24-25) are comparable.

The "sons of the Kingdom" are those who actually belong to the Kingdom; the Jew speaks in similar terms of "sons of the city," "sons of the Law," etc. Matthew takes the threat also as a warning against his own community, even though its members are now "sons of the Kingdom" (cf. the introduction to chapters 21–25); this is shown in other places by the application of the image in verse 12 to everyone (13:42, 50; 22:13; 24:51; 25:30). It is impossible to determine whether "crying and gnashing of teeth" merely represent oriental gestures of remorse, rage, and horror, or go back to the idea that the place of damnation is "hot as fire and cold as snow" (Eth. Enoch 14:13). The darkness outside is an image complementary to that of the banquet: the banquet represents a sense of being at home with God and in his world; the darkness means separation. According to the final verse, what matters to Matthew is not the miracle as such, but the correspondence between faith and its fulfillment (similarly in 9:29; 15:28); the reference to the precise hour is also an addition from Matthew's hand in 9:22 and 17:18.

Did this story actually take place as told? We do not know for sure; but the danger for us today lies not so much in thinking that such an event is impossible as, strangely enough, in thinking that it is not only possible but is the main point. Indeed, we are familiar with psychosomatic paralysis that is suddenly healed; and in the religions of Eastern Asia, for example, there are authentic instances of healing at a distance. That Jesus was a "charismatic" able to effect bodily healing cannot be doubted and is an important point. That power, however, is not absolutely unique, and the significance of his deeds does not reside in these apparently supernormal occurrences. On the contrary: if we take the miracle as the crucial question, we entirely miss the point Matthew is trying to make.

From the beginning the story is a warning against the complacency of those who claim the succession of Abraham, and a praise of the man who, on the contrary, lives his faith, in the problems and necessities of everyday life. The warning is reinforced by the saying in verses 11-12 and in Q by being associated with the critical sayings of the Sermon on the Plain, to which were added, perhaps even before Matthew, the antitheses against merely literal obedience to the Law and the dispute with the Pharisees in 9:1-17. Matthew is familiar with the decades-old view that the gentiles will stream to Jerusalem, and he therefore shows the gentiles trooping to Jesus, not out of respect for tradition but because of his words and deeds, in the Sermon on the Mount and the ten miracles that follow, and his power that lives on in his community. The story shows that faith may indeed be alive as practical confidence in concrete situations of need, but that it is also far more than this, that it brings miraculous salvation, and brings it above all to the man who knows he has done nothing to deserve it and never can. The warning in this story may be especially urgent in an age when Africans and Asians in the community of Jesus may well be called on to show to "Christian" Europe what Christian life really is.

The Healing at Peter's House (8:14-17)
Cf. Mark 1:29-34; Luke 4:38-41

¹⁴Jesus went to Peter's home, and there he saw Peter's mother-in-law sick in bed with a fever. ¹⁵He touched her hand; the fever left her, and she got up and began to wait on him. ¹⁶When evening came, people brought to Jesus many who had demons in them. And Jesus drove out the spirits with a word and healed all who were sick. ¹⁷He did this to make come true what the prophet Isaiah had said, "He himself took our illnesses and carried away our diseases."
(Vs. 17—Isa. 53:4.)

[14] On the sequence see the introduction to 4:17–11:30. The account of the healing of Peter's mother-in-law (Mark 1:29 calls her Simon's mother-in-law; cf. the conclusion of the introduction to Matt.

16:17-19) is much abbreviated. It is the only healing in which Jesus acts totally on his own initiative (according to Mark 1:30 the disciples point out that she is sick). **[15]** Throughout this passage, in fact, we find only Jesus and the sick (cf. the introduction to 8:1-4). Jesus' "going to her" (Mark 1:31) is omitted (see the discussion of 8:2). According to Mark she is helped up by Jesus; here she stands up by herself when she is healed, demonstrating Jesus' complete success. Her waiting on "him" (not "them" as in Mark) underlines the idea of discipleship. All actions, all of life are to center on Jesus alone.

[16] That the people waited until evening to bring their sick made sense in Mark, because the evening marked the end of the Sabbath so that the sick could be carried; in Matthew this reason is omitted. According to him this day begins with 5:1 and is of course no longer a Sabbath. He also abbreviates Mark's general reference to the crowd and the healings. Instead he expressly underlines the "word" (8:16) of Jesus as the means by which he overcame demons. The statement that Jesus healed "all" who were sick also goes beyond Mark, according to whom "all" came and "many" were healed.

[17] Above all, however, he appends the Isaianic saying about the servant of God. No longer as in Mark is Jesus recognized by the demons and confessed to be the "Holy One of God" (Mark 1:24, 34); strictly speaking his identity is not even revealed through his miracles; according to Matthew it is Scripture that identifies Jesus' miracles as God's activity and Jesus himself as the servant of God. This is the only explicit citation of Isaiah 53 in the Gospels. It is striking that the passage from Isaiah is interpreted not as referring to Jesus' suffering and exaltation (as in Acts 8:32-33; cf. 1 Pet. 2:22-25). Rather—contrary to all Jewish interpretations, and contrary also to the Greek Old Testament, which speaks of "sins"—the Isaiah passage is seen as predicting Jesus' acts of healing. What was originally understood as "taking upon himself" and "bearing" is interpreted by Matthew as "taking away" and "bearing off," since the words can also have that meaning. As is apparent once again in 12:16-21, Matthew sees the acts expected of the messiah—the quiet, inconspicuous, propaganda-free righteousness—primarily in Jesus' healings (cf. 8:17). The man who comes with the authority of God performs his ministry on behalf of outcasts. In speaking of "our" illnesses, Matthew probably has in mind the community in which Jesus' ministry is continued (cf. also the excursus on 1:18-25).

Discipleship Under Test (8:18-27)
Cf. Mark 4:35-41; Luke 8:22-25; 9:57-60

[18]Jesus noticed the crowd around him and ordered his disciples to go to the other side of the lake. [19]A teacher of the Law came to him. "Teacher," he said, "I am ready to go with you wherever you go." [20]Jesus answered him, "Foxes have holes, and birds have nests, but the Son of Man has no place to lay his head." [21]Another man, who was a disciple, said, "Sir, first let me go back and bury my father." [22]"Follow me," Jesus answered, "and let the dead bury their own dead."

[23]Jesus got into the boat, and his disciples went with him. [24]Suddenly a fierce storm hit the lake, so that the waves covered the boat. But Jesus was asleep. [25]The disciples went to him and woke him up. "Save us, Lord!" they said. "We are about to die!" [26]"Why are you so frightened?" Jesus answered. "How little faith you have!" Then he got up and gave a command to the winds and to the waves, and there was a great calm. [27]Everyone was amazed. "What kind of man is this?" they said. "Even the winds and the waves obey him!"

On the sequence see the introduction to chapters 4:17–11:30. This section is the most impressive instance of how a miracle story can be given a new function. Verse 18 picks up the introduction to the story of the storm from Mark 4:35, 36a ("go to the other side of the lake," "crowd"). Matthew, or perhaps even the tradition before him, changed the Greek word meaning "cross over" into one meaning "go (away)" to link up with the same word at the end of verse 19 (=Luke 9:57). Likewise verse 21 now speaks of "one of the disciples," Jesus' command "follow me" (cf. vs. 19) has been inserted after verse 22, and the same two expressions are repeated in verse 23, contrary to Mark, in order to show quite clearly that the story to come describes this very "following" of the disciples. As in 8:5-13, the conversation between the two disciples and Jesus is found in almost the same words in Luke (9:57-60), while the surrounding material differs markedly; Luke also adds a third instance.

[18] Are we then to understand that Jesus' order to cross the lake is issued to all and that only those who obey this call to follow are really "his disciples"? Apart from 5:1, where the term derives from tradition, this is the first mention of the disciples, and not until 10:1 is there any mention of the Twelve. Is this passage then meant to replace the omitted calling of the Twelve (Mark 3:17-19), and be a watershed separation between the ones who follow Jesus and those who do not? But verse 21 implies that there were already disciples (those mentioned in 4:18-22?). Or is Jesus seeking to evade the great enthusiasm of the crowd and consciously adopt his role as servant of God (vs. 17)?

[19] Only in Matthew is the inquirer called a "teacher of the Law." Is Matthew thinking how hard it will be in his own time for Jewish teachers of the Law to become disciples of Jesus? As almost everywhere in the New Testament, to "follow" is conceived very concretely and is associated directly with Jesus' decision to depart. "Wherever" underlines the universal application of this decision to follow Jesus. [20] Jesus makes no attempt to capitalize on his success and attract as many adherents as possible. On the contrary he frightens off those who are enthusiastic about him (cf. the discussion of Mark 5:19) by referring to the demands that will be made. Anyone who wishes to follow after him must renounce all forms of security.

Absolute freedom, even of the mind, must be preserved. Enthusiasm stirred up by eloquence or successful healings must not develop into constraint. It has been suggested that the saying was originally a general proverb describing the uncertain fate of men in contrast to animals, who at least have holes and nests; but this is very unlikely, since it would apply only to times of war and distress. Even less likely is the suggestion that in the animals we have abusive terms for Edomites (Herod; cf. Luke 13:32) and Romans, to whom Israel, deprived of its rights, is being contrasted.

The saying presumably is meant to insist on the uncertainty of the road taken by Jesus and his followers. The Son of Man is Jesus himself in his earthly wanderings, devoid of all middle-class security (see the excursus on the Son of Man at Mark 8:27-33). Thus to follow Jesus is in fact to step forth into insecurity, because the one in whom God comes to men has no home among men; they fail to recognize him.

Therefore the follower of Jesus is promised nothing more than the opportunity to join the Son of Man in his insecurity and share his fate. This is precisely the meaning of entrance into communion with God, and only there is it possible to learn the blissful freedom from anxiety spoken of in 6:25-34; 10:26-31; and 16:25-26.

[21] The expression "another man, who was a disciple" is strange. Elsewhere Matthew appears to equate the "disciples" with the Twelve. In Matthew only those who believe in Jesus address him as "Lord" or "Sir"; the teacher of the Law just mentioned merely calls him "teacher." Finally, the word "first" shows that the inquirer assumes from the outset that he will later depart with Jesus. The only possible conclusion is that Matthew means "another man, one of the disciples." The fact that the inquirer is referred to as a disciple makes the request clear without the necessity for a preceding offer to follow Jesus (as in vs. 19) or a command of Jesus (as in Luke 9:59). As Luke 9:59 shows, the saying had already assumed fixed form before it was more clearly defined to whom it was addressed.

Judaism places extraordinary emphasis on the obligation to bury the dead; only the High Priest and the Nazirite dedicated to God are prohibited from touching a corpse, even that of their own father, because their "consecration" is more important (Lev. 21:11; Num. 6:6-7). In 15:4 Jesus vigorously defends the commandment to honor one's father and mother. There, however, the point is evasion of God's commandment through artificial interpretation; here it is evasion of God's presumptive decree, which negates even the commandment of Law. [22] Jesus' curt response might be interpreted as meaning that men who do not hear the call of God are in fact dead because there is life only in following Jesus and in communion with God (16:25-26). Probably, however, it is only a shocking image like that of the log in the eye (see the introductory comments on 7:3-5), meant to get the listener's attention by means of tension.

The dead can be left in charge of the dead now that life itself is present and awaits men in following Jesus. The burial cult loses its meaning when God breaks into the world. When something new comes into the world so that death loses its central position and power, freedom is created. It restores meaning to life by transforming it into a voyage with Jesus into communion with God. That a disciple appears here as the questioner merely shows that this communion must be achieved repeatedly. The saying is reminiscent of 1 Kings 19:20, where Elisha asks only to say goodbye to his father and Elijah's apparently indifferent answer, "Go back again," moves him at once to offer sacrifice and follow.

[23] Unlike Mark, Matthew describes the boarding of the ship as the "following" of the "disciples"; as in 14:24, the ship has become a symbol for the band of disciples, the community of Jesus (cf. the discussion of 13:16-17). Of course Matthew is of the opinion that the incident took place as described; but besides being historical the event is also exemplary and reveals what holds true for Jesus' disciples throughout the ages. **[24]** The Greek text reads "And behold"; cf. the discussion of 8:2. The Greek term for the storm actually means "tremor"; its use here is striking, although it does occasionally refer to a storm at sea (Mark uses "gale"). The narrator probably selects this rare word because it also occurs in descriptions of the catastrophes to come at the eschaton, among which persecution of the Christian community has an important place (24:7; cf. 27:54; 28:2; Rev. 6:12; 8:5; 11:13, 19; 16:18). The clipped form of the second half of this verse makes Jesus' imperturbability all the more evident. **[25]** Like Luke but unlike Mark, Matthew says that the disciples "approach" Jesus (cf. the discussion of 8:2). Their cry "Save us, Lord" is reminiscent of the cry with which the community calls on its Lord to save.

[26] In his response Jesus accuses the disciples of fright or cowardice (also in Mark 4:40) before stilling the storm; they are also accused of having little faith (see the discussion of 13:16-17). Both expressions also describe the community. This is further suggested by the use of the present tense in Greek for Jesus' response. What is described is failure of faith in a concrete situation despite all their affirmation of God in principle. Once again, Matthew's brevity accentuates the authority of Jesus; the calm comes suddenly just as the storm did (vs. 24).

[27] The reference to "everyone's" amazement ("fear" in Mark 4:41) at the calming of the storm is striking. Mark 4:36, it is true, mentions other ships, but Matthew omits this detail. Is Matthew, like Mark 4:41, thinking of the disciples and emphasizing how even though they know who Jesus is they remain mere men with far too little trust in God (1 Cor. 3:1-3)? This is possible; but more likely Matthew shifts subjects because the disciples know Jesus and therefore would not ask this question about what kind of man he is.

To follow Jesus is thus to attend a pilgrim school of discipleship, in temptation and persecution, where one receives solider instruction than within the walls of a college (Bengel). The blunt demands of Jesus at the beginning summon men to that poverty in which they can really hear for the first time his promise of salvation and his invitation. But anyone who follows the Son of Man into insecurity experiences God's intervention in very practical terms. He will of course be subject to periods in which his faith grows small, when he will see nothing more than chance in everything; but he may always be recalled once more to the right way by his Lord and restored to faith.

Jesus' Authority Over Demons (8:28-34)
Cf. Mark 5:1-20; Luke 8:26-39

[28]Jesus came to the territory of the Gadarenes, on the other side of the lake, and was met by two men who came out of the burial caves. These men had demons in them and were so fierce that no one dared travel on that road. [29]At once they screamed, "What do you want with us, Son of God? Have you come to torment us before the right time?" [30]Not far away a large herd of pigs was feeding. [31]The demons begged Jesus, "If you are going to drive us out, send us into that herd of pigs." [32]"Go," Jesus told them; so they left and went off into the pigs. The whole herd rushed down the side of the cliff into the lake and they were drowned. [33]The men who had been taking care of the pigs ran away and went to the town, where they told the whole story, and what had happened to the men with the demons. [34]So everyone from the town went out to meet Jesus; and when they saw him they begged him to leave their territory.

(Vs. 29—1 Kings 17:18.)

This story is much shorter than its parallel in Mark. Gadara has replaced Gerasa (see the discussion of Mark 5:1). The one demoniac has become two, as in 9:27 and 20:30. Here, too, the influence of Biblical language can be felt ("and behold" occurs in vss. 29, 32, 34; see the discussion of 8:2). The account of the demoniac's conduct has been omitted, as have the dialogues between Jesus and the demons about their name, between the residents of the city and the healed demoniac, and between Jesus and the man who is prepared to follow him. The effect is to throw Jesus' victory over the demons (vss. 29-32) into sharper relief. Matthew distinguishes more clearly than Mark between the singular "the . . . herd rushed down" and the plural "they [the demons] were drowned." Possibly the peculiar formulation of verse 33 ("told the whole story, and what had happened to the demoniacs") is also meant to stress that the really important point is the destruction of the demons rather than the healing, which is not even described. The demons' charge that Jesus has come to torment them "before the right time," i.e. before the Last Judgment (vs. 29), shows that with Jesus the eschaton has already dawned (12:28). But the city, which comes out "to meet Jesus" (only Matt. 8:34) as one would go to meet a high-ranking personality (John 12:13) or the Judge of the world (Matt. 25:31-32) does not recognize this. The people do not see the victory over the demons; they see Jesus, not the healed demoniac as in Mark 5:14-15, and, afraid, they beg him to go away. It is a hostile and rejecting amazement that concludes this story. There is no longer any hint of mission to the gentiles after this episode (cf. Mark 5:20) —even the heathen expression "Son of the Most High God" (Mark 5:7) is eliminated. Jesus is sent only to Israel (cf. the discussion of 10:5-6).

Authority to Forgive Sins (9:1-8)
Cf. Mark 2:1-12; Luke 5:17-26

¹Jesus got into the boat, went back across the lake, and came to his own town. ²Some people brought him a paralyzed man, lying on a bed. Jesus saw how much faith they had, and said to the paralyzed man, "Courage my son! Your sins are forgiven." ³Then some teachers of the Law said to themselves, "This man is blaspheming." ⁴And Jesus knew what they were thinking and said, "Why are you thinking such evil things? ⁵Is it easier to say, 'Your sins are forgiven,' or to say, 'Get up and walk'? ⁶I will prove to you, then, that the Son of Man has

authority on earth to forgive sins." So he said to the paralyzed man, "Get up, pick up your bed, and go home!" [7]The man got up and went home. [8]When the people saw it, they were afraid, and praised God for giving such authority as this to men.

Verse 1 was composed by Matthew himself as a transitional verse; he made use of material from the preceding story. In his view Capernaum is Jesus' own city (4:13), i.e. his place of residence. Minor points of agreement with Luke can be discerned (vss. 2, 4-7; see the introduction to 4:17–11:30), as well as the use of Biblical language in verses 2-3 (see the discussion of 8:2). The narrative has once again been markedly abbreviated; above all there is no longer any mention of the incident's location inside a house or the concomitant feature of having the sick man let down through the roof (Mark 2:1-4). This of course takes away the evidence of these people's special faith (vs. 2 = Mark 2:5). Thus the story concentrates much more on the question of whether the Son of Man has authority to forgive sins; the connection between faith and healing, elsewhere stressed by Matthew, is pushed into the background (see the discussion of 8:1-4).

The charge of blasphemy in verse 3 is perhaps even more important for Matthew than for Mark, because he expressly repeats it in the context of Jesus' trial (26:65), where Jesus also refers to himself as the Son of Man (vs. 64; but cf. also Mark 14:64, 62). Verses 1-2 thus serve merely to introduce the controversy, which is made explicit in verse 3 (cf. the introductory remarks on vss. 9-13). Verse 4 speaks of Jesus' fundamental knowledge, not just his momentary recognition as in Mark. The most interesting point, however, is the alteration of the conclusion, the amazement at the "God who gives such authority to men," put in the style of a panegyric. Matthew has the Christian community in mind and possibly for this reason omits Mark 2:7b. What the people find astonishing is that what is possible only for the Judge of the world is here taking place (vs. 6, as in 16:19; 18:18): a mere man is daring to summon others back to union with God (cf. the discussion of 9:35). As is true throughout until 27:25 (cf. the discussion of 9:32-34), Matthew draws a clear distinction between the crowd, which is amazed (vs. 8; Mark 2:12: "all"), and the teachers of the Law, who think "evil things" (vs. 4; not in Mark).

Eating with Sinners (9:9-13)
Cf. Mark 2:13-17; Luke 5:27-32

⁹Jesus left that place, and as he walked along he saw a tax collector, named Matthew, sitting in his office. He said to him, "Follow me." Matthew got up and followed him. ¹⁰While Jesus was having dinner at his house, many tax collectors and sinners came and joined him and his disciples at the table. ¹¹Some Pharisees saw this and said to his disciples, "Why does your teacher eat with tax collectors and sinners?" ¹²Jesus heard them and answered, "People who are well do not need a doctor, but only those who are sick. ¹³Go and find out what this Scripture means, 'I do not want animal sacrifices, but mercy.' I have not come to call the righteous, but sinners."

(Vs. 13–Hos. 6:6 [1 Sam. 15:22; Isa. 1:10-17; Ps. 40:7-8; Mic. 6:6-8].)

The account largely follows Mark. But there are some changes: in the preceding story Matthew mentioned only the teachers of the Law, because the charge of blasphemy for professing to forgive sins is typical of them; in this section he mentions only the Pharisees, who condemn social intercourse with tax collectors and sinners; and in the next, he mentions only the disciples of John, who take issue with the unascetic way of life of the community. Thus there is more emphasis on the issues under dispute than on the parties advancing them. Nevertheless, verse 10 singles out tax collectors and sinners for special praise (using the Biblical "it came to pass" and "behold" in the Greek text), because, in their faith, they "came" to Jesus.

[9] The substitution of "Matthew" for the name "Levi" is significant. With very few exceptions, double names are found only where a Greek name stands alongside an Aramaic name, or a descriptive epithet ("Cephas" = Peter = Rock) alongside the name proper. Neither is the case here. Thus we are dealing with a change of names probably due to the fact that Levi does not appear in the list of the Twelve. The story itself is recounted in so terse and exemplary a fashion that in a sense it applies to all who follow after Jesus (cf. the

discussion of 8:23). Therefore Matthew states in the Greek text that Jesus saw "a man," and only afterwards gives his name. But for this Gospel only the Twelve are "disciples" in the time of Jesus, so the man who is called must be one of them. Matthew is referred to in 10:3 as the "tax collector" to reaffirm that the man called here is one of the Twelve. On the question of the authorship of the Gospel, see section 4 of the Introduction.

[11] Even more important is the addition of the prophetical quotation stating that God desires mercy and not sacrifice. That it is also inserted in the discussion concerning the Sabbath, which follows directly in Mark but does not occur until later in Matthew (12:7), is striking. Were both stories perhaps used as illustrations of this saying even before Matthew? The saying itself played an important role in Judaism following the destruction of the Temple, which spelled the end of the sacrificial cult. In any event, the introduction in verse 13 is a typically Pharisaic formula, in which "go" is a Biblical idiom and not to be taken literally. But at the same time, the statement is in accord with Matthaean theology (cf. the discussion of 5:18), which considers love of one's neighbor to be true fulfillment of the Law. Therefore this particular statement, with its call for mercy, was selected from many similar statements, and the story became more markedly a controversy with Pharisaic (legalistic) Judaism. In the Greek text, the last sentence begins with a causal "for," emphasizing that the banquet of Jesus and his community is a fulfillment of this prophecy (see the discussion of 12:8), an act of eschatological worship in which the will of God is done.

Freedom from Religious Duties (9:14-17)
Cf. Mark 2:18-22; Luke 5:33-39

[14]Then the followers of John the Baptist came to Jesus, asking, "Why is it that we and the Pharisees fast often, but your disciples don't fast at all?" [15]Jesus answered, "Do you expect the guests at a wedding party to be sad as long as the bridegroom is with them? Of course not! But the time will come when the bridegroom will be taken away from them, and then they will go without food.

[16]"No one patches up an old coat with a piece of new cloth,

because such a patch tears off from the coat, making an even bigger hole. ¹⁷Nor does anyone pour new wine into used wineskins. If he does, the skins will burst, and then the wine pours out and the skins will be ruined. Instead, new wine is poured into fresh wineskins, and both will keep in good condition."

[14] Form and content agree with Mark, but the typically Matthaean "then" connects the whole passage more closely with the dinner given for the tax collectors. In addition, it is only the disciples of John who now make inquiry (see the introduction to vss. 9-13), perhaps because they can still be won over, while this is no longer true of the Pharisees (cf. 11:2-19; 14:1-12; 21:32). [15] As in Luke 5:34, the repetition in Mark 2:19b is omitted; [17] at the conclusion we also find minor points of agreement with Luke. Matthew alone states that the new wine and the new wineskins will be kept "in good condition." [15] Instead of "fast" Matthew writes "be sad" (as in 5:4); above all he writes in the apodosis only "then they will go without food," omitting "on that day" (Mark 2:20). The whole period of the Christian community after the death of Jesus is once more a time of fasting. Therefore Matthew was also able to incorporate 6:16-18 into his Gospel.

Thus in Matthew the problem of old versus new emerges even more clearly than in Mark. In fact Jesus and the primitive community continued by and large to take a conservative position within Jewish life and its worship. Fasting was not required of everyone, but was practised only by particularly devout groups. Matthew is nevertheless aware that in Jesus something fundamentally new has dawned, something that revolutionizes all earlier forms of religiosity. Matthew 6:16-18 at least gave a hint of this revolution: fasting is no longer a meritorious exercise. It might be a natural and genuine expression of "sadness" by a man aware of his separation from God, and it might at the same time allow him the silence for fellowship with God (cf. also 1 Cor. 7:5). But Matthew, unlike Paul, has not thought this idea through to its conclusion. Both ideas stand in juxtaposition independent of each other: fasting can still be practised in the community, but it is something totally new, not comparable in any way to the old fasting of John's disciples and the Pharisees.

Jesus' Authority Over Sickness and Death (9:18-26)
Cf. Mark 5:21-43; Luke 8:40-56

[18]While Jesus was saying this to them, a Jewish official came to him, knelt down before him, and said, "My daughter has just died; but come and place your hand on her and she will live." [19]So Jesus got up and followed him, and his disciples went with him. [20]A certain woman, who had had severe bleeding for twelve years, came up behind Jesus and touched the edge of his cloak. [21]She said to herself, "If only I touch his cloak I will get well." [22]Jesus turned around and saw her, and said, "Courage, my daughter! Your faith has made you well." At that very moment the woman became well. [23]So Jesus went into the official's house. When he saw the musicians for the funeral, and the people all stirred up, [24]he said, "Get out, everybody! The little girl is not dead—she is just sleeping!" They all started making fun of him. [25]As soon as the people had been put out, Jesus went into the girl's room and took hold of her hand, and she got up. [26]The news of this spread all over that part of the country.

This story is about a third shorter than its Markan parallel. It is striking that in contrast to verse 22, verses 23-25 make no mention of any summons to faith or in fact of any words spoken by Jesus to the girl at all (Mark 5:36, 41). Matthew omits such words again in 20:34 (though cf. 9:29). As in Luke 8:44, the woman merely touches the tassels of Jesus' robe. In contrast to the Markan account, the official's daughter is dead even before her father comes to make his request; this emphasizes the miracle of his faith; according to Luke 8:42 she is at the point of death. The interpolation of the healing of the woman with a hemorrhage makes sense only in Mark, because the child dies while this is taking place; this probably represents the earlier form.

[18] The crossing in the boat (Mark 5:21) has already been mentioned in 9:1-8. By the initial words of verse 18 and the addition of verse 19, according to which Jesus "got up" from the meal, Matthew forges an intimate link with verses 14-17, perhaps because what follows is a demonstration of the presence of the "bridegroom." The

supplicant is referred to in general terms as an official, a word that might designate either a Jew or a gentile; but flute players ("musicians," vs. 23) seem to have been employed only in Jewish households (see the discussion of Mark 5:38 and Josephus, *Bell. Jud.* iii. 437). His name, Jairus, is no longer mentioned. The introductory phrase "and behold" in the Greek text together with the reference to the official's "coming and kneeling" (cf. the discussion of 8:2) emphasize the significance of Jesus: men in deep distress, even confronted with the death of a daughter, have faith in Jesus' power.

[20] The mention of the tassels depicts Jesus as a Jew faithful to the Law (see the discussion of 23:5). [21] In Mark the woman's approach from behind Jesus is occasioned by the crowd's surrounding him; in the briefer version of Matthew the shyness of the woman, who dares do no more than touch the tassels from behind (cf. 14:36), receives greater emphasis. [22] There is also more stress on the words with which Jesus promises her healing because of her faith. In the first place, they appear, emphasized by "Courage," directly after the expression of her faith. In the second place, Matthew says that the woman "became well" only after Jesus spoke to her. Faith in the healing to be found in Jesus, Jesus' promise of salvation to those who have faith, and the actual event of healing and salvation are all intimately associated.

[23-25] The restoration of the official's daughter to life is also reported much more briefly; Jesus' Aramaic call to arise (Mark 5:41; likewise 7:34; cf. 7:11 = Matt. 15:5), which could easily be mistaken for a magic formula, is omitted. On the other hand, musicians, characteristically part of Jewish mourning ritual, are mentioned. [26] Instead of a command to remain silent as in Mark 5:43 (cf. the excursus on the messianic secret at Mark 1:34), we find here a statement more resembling Mark 1:28, which Matthew omits: the news of Jesus' mighty acts spreads all over "that part of the country" (the narrator no longer resides there). On the problem of raising the dead, see the excursus on Mark 5:21-43.

Everything else that is typical of a miracle story is omitted. The only purpose of the section is to show what faith is and what faith can experience.

Jesus Heals Two Blind Men and a Dumb Man (9:27-34)

[27]Jesus left that place, and as he walked along two blind men started following him. "Have mercy on us, Son of David," they shouted. [28]When Jesus had gone indoors, the two blind men came to him and he asked them, "Do you believe that I can do this?" "Yes, sir!" they answered. [29]Then Jesus touched their eyes and said, "May it happen, then, just as you believe!" [30]And their eyes were opened. Jesus spoke harshly to them, "Don't tell this to anyone!" [31]But they left and spread the news about Jesus all over that part of the country.

[32]When the men had left, some people brought to Jesus a man who was dumb because of a demon. [33]As soon as the demon was driven out, the man started talking. Everyone was amazed. "We never saw the like in Israel!" they exclaimed. [34]But the Pharisees said, "It is the chief of the demons who gives him the power to drive them out."

[27] Verse 27 agrees to a large extent with the narrative in 20:29-34. The order not to call Jesus Son of David, which causes the blind men to cry out even louder (20:31), [30-31] appears here in 9:30-31, albeit in altered form, and is markedly reminiscent of Mark 1:43, 45, which were omitted in 8:1-4. [28] The change of location, so that the miracle takes place indoors, paves the way for Jesus' command to keep the event secret. [29] The reference to the faith of those who are healed, omitted in 20:33, corresponds to Mark 10:52. [28] Jesus' inquiry about their faith strongly emphasizes the idea; but what is most striking is that the content of their faith is indicated by means of a "that I can do this" clause. Apart from John, we find this idiom only in Mark 11:23-24; Romans 6:8; 10:9; 1 Thessalonians 4:14; and Hebrews 11:6. Faith is a confidence manifested in every action of life, not just intellectual assent (James 2:19).

Matthew is trying to fill what he felt to be a gap (Jesus' answer in 11:5 also mentions the blind and dumb; cf. the introduction to 4:17–11:30). He uses the Markan account of the healing at Jericho but transfers it to the vicinity of Capernaum, drawing on motifs from that account as well as on the verses he omits from the healing of the leper (Matt. 8:1-4 = Mark 1:41-45). The important element is the conversation between the blind men and Jesus, transferred to the privacy of the house. Jesus' special position has been hinted at by the call of the first disciples (4:18-22), the faith of the Roman officer (8:9-10), the sayings about the Son of Man (8:20; 9:6), the images of the doctor and the bridegroom (9:12, 15), and Jesus' mighty acts; it has been represented in the story of Jesus' birth and the flight into Egypt, by the story of his baptism and temptation, and above all by Matthew's references to fulfillment of the Old Testament; here Jesus is described for the first time as the "Son of David," i.e. the messiah. But at this very point Jesus withdraws into the house and demands that nothing be said about the healing. Blindness is one of the most terrible scourges of the Near East. The Old Testament hopes for healing from blindness in the coming age of salvation (Isa. 29:18; 35:5), and Deutero-Isaiah appears also to consider the healing of blindness as a sign of God's sovereign power (42:7; cf. 61:1; Luke 4:18). This will be spoken of further in connection with Matthew 16:13-28.

[32-34] The healing of the dumb man that follows also paves the way for 11:5. The Greek word can refer to a man who is deaf, dumb, or both; verse 33a excludes the first possibility. The blind and dumb are mentioned together in Isaiah 29:18; 35:5. This section, too, has a parallel (Matt. 12:22-24). As the accusation in verse 34 shows, this section belongs, like the parallel account in Luke 11:14-15, in the discussion about Beelzebul. It is noteworthy, however, that it is our passage rather than Matthew 12:22-24 that agrees to a large extent with the wording of Luke, except that the catchword "Beelzebul" is missing; in the other cognate to Luke's version (Matt. 12:24 = Luke 11:15) that word does appear.

Once again material common to Matthew and Luke appears in a different place, presumably on the basis of pre-Matthaean tradition (see the introduction to 4:17–11:30). Apart from the introduction, which tells how the dumb man is brought to Jesus, the only point unique to Matthew is the reference to the hostility of the Pharisees and the recognition of Jesus on the part of the people in 9:33, which uses Biblical language to suggest to the reader the uniqueness of what is happening ("We never saw anything like it in Israel!"). Here this summarizes the effect of Jesus' deeds in chapters 8-9 (on this double use of material cf. also the discussion of 9:8; 12:22-24; 21:14-16).

The charge "It is the chief of the demons who gives him the power to drive the demons out" occurs in the same words in Mark 3:22; Matthew 9:34; 12:24; and Luke 11:15. The detailed account of the incident takes quite different forms, but this statement impressed itself on the memory. Even here there breathes a hint of the uniqueness of what is taking place in Jesus; perhaps, despite its hostility, it is closer to the truth than the more modern attempt to remove all the difficulties by explaining everything as the happy coincidence of psychic states in the healer and the person he heals, as though this coincidence were not itself a unique miracle bestowed by God.

The healing itself is not described; the only important point is the distinction between the people, who at least are amazed and remain open to the significance of Jesus, and those who bluntly reject him. Thus we reach the conclusion, but also the transition to what is coming.

The radical nature of Jesus' demands has been made clear, both in the Sermon on the Mount and to those following Jesus, whom he invites to venture into the storm. So, too, have Jesus' mercy and pity toward the poor and oppressed, both in the Beatitudes and in his many healings. These healings illustrate the power of the faith he awakens. When Jesus encounters someone he awakens him to faith, thus setting him free to venture into insecurity and to expect everything from the one who gave him faith. How this invitation is extended to all, particularly the reader of the Gospel, is shown by the next chapter.

From Jesus to the Community (9:35-38)
Cf. Luke 10:1-2; Mark 6:6, 34

[35]So Jesus went around visiting all the towns and villages. He taught in their synagogues, preached the Good News of the Kingdom, and healed people from every kind of disease and sickness. [36]As he saw the crowds, his heart was filled with pity for them, because they were worried and helpless, like sheep without a shepherd. [37]So he said to his disciples, "There is a great harvest, but few workers to gather it

in. ³⁸Pray to the owner of the harvest that he will send out more workers to gather in his harvest."
(Vs. 36—Num. 27:17; 1 Kings 22:17.)

[35] Since verse 35 and the first words of verse 36 are identical with 4:23; 5:1, the two passages constitute the framework surrounding the presentation of Jesus as the messiah in word and deed (see the discussion of 4:23). The only difference is that the phrase "all the towns and villages" replaces "all over Galilee," as in Mark 6:6*b*, which like this passage directly precedes the sending of the Twelve. At the same time the verse lays the groundwork for their mission, since what is given to the disciples—authority (10:1)—corresponds precisely to the final words, which describe Jesus' own authority and his power to heal. Thus Matthew inserts the sending forth of the disciples here because he wants to show that the power and authority of Jesus to perform miracles, to which 11:5 will return, is also given to the community (cf. the discussion of 9:8; 10:25; 12:31-32).

[36] Verse 36 agrees to a large extent with Mark 6:34, but the saying about the sheep without a shepherd (Num. 27:17; Ezek. 34:5; cf. Matt. 10:6) is almost proverbial. Matthew's omission of it in 14:14 (=Mark 6:34) shows that he recognized it to be the same saying. [37-38] What Jesus says to his disciples, however, is identical with Luke 10:2 (except for the transposition of two words); in Luke it stands as an introduction to the discourse Jesus delivers to the disciples before sending them forth (see the discussion of Matt. 10:1), here it is still an independent unit. The transition to another tradition can be seen also in the total change of imagery. Only the notion of "gathering" unites the two images. Elsewhere in his parables Jesus speaks of the harvest at the Last Judgment (see below); but he can also see the beginnings now of what will one day take place in the Kingdom of God (cf. the discussion of 12:28).

[35] The important point to Matthew is that the power and authority of Jesus illustrated in chapters 5–9 continue on in his community. [36] This continuity can only be explained by Jesus' pity (see the discussion of 20:34), which sees the distress of Israel. The image suggests a flock that is tormented and almost totally exhausted, or is

at least being led astray and neglected by careless shepherds (Zech. 11:16; Ezek. 34). **[37-38]** This desperate situation is the time of God's harvest. When men reach the limit of their abilities, God will intervene and perform his great deeds. Therefore the disciples are not simply pressed into service, but are called on to pray. Man cannot create the new situation that is necessary; God alone will choose his messengers. Therefore prayer is needed. Elsewhere the harvest symbolizes God's Last Judgment (Isa. 9:2-3; 27:12; Hos. 6:11; Joel 4 [3] :13; Matt. 3:12; 13:8, 39-40; etc.); those who labor at the harvest are the angels, who gather men in for condemnation or ultimate salvation (13:41; 24:31). The saying of Jesus, however, implies that this angelic harvest will be begun by men, who go out into the world and proclaim the name of Jesus.

D. Jesus' Disciples
10:1–11:30

The Mission of the Disciples (10:1-16)
Cf. Mark 3:14-19; 6:7-11; Luke 6:13-16; 9:1-5; 10:3-12; Acts 1:13

¹Jesus called his twelve disciples together and gave them authority over unclean spirits, to drive them out, and to heal every disease and every sickness. ²These are the names of the twelve apostles: first, Simon (called Peter) and his brother Andrew; James, the son of Zebedee, and his brother John; ³Philip and Bartholomew; Thomas and Matthew, the tax collector; James, the son of Alphaeus, and Thaddaeus; ⁴Simon, the Canaanite, and Judas Iscariot, who betrayed Jesus.

⁵Jesus sent these twelve men out with the following instructions: "Do not go into any gentile territory or any Samaritan towns. ⁶Go, instead, to the lost sheep of the people of Israel. ⁷Go and preach, 'The Kingdom of heaven is near!' ⁸Heal the sick, raise the dead, make the lepers clean, drive out demons. You have received without paying, so give without being paid. ⁹Do not carry any gold, silver, or copper money in your pockets; ¹⁰do not carry a bag for the trip, or an extra

shirt, or sandals, or a staff. A worker should be given the food he needs. [11]When you come to a town or village, go in and look for someone who is willing to welcome you, and stay with him until you leave that place. [12]When you go into a house say, 'Peace be with you.' [13]If the people in that house welcome you, let your greeting of peace remain; but if they do not welcome you, let your greeting of peace remain; but if they do not welcome you, then take back your greeting. [14]And if some home or town will not welcome you or listen to you, then leave that place and shake the dust off your feet. [15]Amen, I tell you, on the Judgment Day God will show more mercy to the people of Sodom and Gomorrah than to the people of that town! [16]Listen! I am sending you just like sheep to a pack of wolves. You must be as cautious as snakes and as gentle as doves.[11]
(Vs. 16—2 Esd. 5:18.)

The discourse addressed by Jesus to the disciples he is sending forth is preserved in two forms. In Luke the two forms are distributed over chapters 9 and 10. The first follows Mark 6:7-13 for the most part and refers, like it, to the sending of the Twelve; the second is associated by Luke with a sending of 70 or 72 disciples. Matthew combined both recensions in a discourse addressed to the Twelve. We have already come across the initial words of the second recension in Matthew 9:37. Possibly even before Matthew various sayings of Jesus on the same theme were brought together, as happens, for example, in the Gospel of Thomas. For a discussion of the historical problems, see the excursus on Mark 6:7-13.

Verses 5-6 are hard to reconcile with Jesus' openness to Samaritans and gentiles (Luke 10:33; John 4:4 ff.; 8:48; Matt. 8:11), and would apply at most to a single mission during the time of Jesus. More likely the saying goes back to a group within the primitive Christian community that maintained that only those who became Jews through circumcision could be accepted into the community (cf. the discussion of Gal. 2:1-10; Col. 2:10-11; Tit. 1:10). Later the saying came to be understood as representing a temporal sequence: first Israel, then the gentile world would receive God's word (see below).

[1] The introduction follows Mark. The juxtaposition of two different traditions is shown by the fact that a prayer to God to

send workers (9:38) is hard to reconcile with their being sent at once by Jesus. In addition, Jesus could hardly have "called together" (= Mark 6:7) the disciples, who were already standing around him. At the conclusion of the verse Matthew equates the authority of the disciples with that of Jesus (see the discussion of 9:35).

[2-4] The list of the Twelve is traditional (cf. the introductory comments on 4:23-25). As in Luke 6:14, Andrew is placed directly alongside his brother (cf. the discussion of 4:18); in addition, Matthew is referred to as a tax collector (cf. the discussion of 9:9). Additions always appear in the second member of the pairs that make up the list, and therefore the order of Thomas and Matthew was reversed.

[5-6] Then follows a saying found only in Matthew. It comes in the same place as does the saying about sheep among wolves in Luke 10:3. Did Luke find it between 10:7 and 10:8 but omit it (cf. the echoes of Luke 10:9 in Matt. 10:7-8)? It probably derives from the period in which a strict Jewish Christian community expected an influx of gentiles seeking to be incorporated into Israel, but did not expect to go on a mission to gentiles. [7] That the command to proclaim the nearness of the Kingdom of God derives from the Q recension (Luke 10:9) can be seen from the fact that it is associated in both passages [8] with instructions to heal the sick. Matthew, however, expands these instructions markedly to conform to Jesus' just-accomplished acts (see below).

[10-11] The sayings about what the disciples are to take along once again follow Mark 6:8-10, but have been reformulated to agree with the stricter recension in Luke 10:4, no longer allowing "sandals," which are expressly permitted by Mark 6:9. The statement that the worker should be given what he needs as well as the mention of the city derive from the version used in Luke 10:7-8; the exhortation to remain in the house that offers hospitality, on the other hand, derives from Mark 6:10. In Matthew, verses 9, 10a, and 10b now appear together, whereas they were separated in Luke 10:4, 7; this probably led Matthew to change "wages" to "food" so as to avoid any contradiction. The phrase about the greeting of peace remaining upon the house belongs once more to the other discourse (Luke 10:6). [13] Then follows the conclusion of the first section (Mark 6:11), the

mention of the city and the Greek word for "dust" deriving from the tradition used in Luke 10:11. The closing threat against the city, which appears in Luke 10:12, is expanded by the image of the sheep among wolves (Luke 10:3), and the snake-dove saying, unique to Matthew. Mark 6:12 and 6:30, the departure and return of the disciples, are omitted (cf. the discussion of 11:1).

[1] Matthew never recounts the appointment of the Twelve; he simply presupposes this inner circle here, where it appears for the first time; before this he has only described the call of five disciples (4:18-22; 9:9). Through the medium of these men's words, Jesus is to continue his progress through the world. Their authority is "given" them by him. It is neither the derivative authority of the teacher of the Law, who can only repeat and interpret, nor the direct authority of the inspired prophet. [2] Whether Matthew already calls the Twelve "apostles" (Greek for "emissaries") is not certain, because a Syriac translation reads "disciples" at this point; nevertheless "apostles" is also found at the corresponding place in Luke (6:13; cf. Mark 6:30 and the excursus before Mark 6:7-13). Matthew is probably thinking of the Twelve as prototypes of all the wandering apostles of his own period, as the instructions that follow clearly indicate (see the discussion of 8:23).

The addition of "first" to Peter probably refers only to his position in the list, not to some special primacy. He occupies a distinctive place in Matthew's community, although this need not mean special dignity or even a particular office (cf. the concluding remarks on 16:13-20). [3-4] The express mention of the "tax collector," who worked for the Romans, alongside the "Zealot" Simon, who fought against them (cf. the discussion of Mark 3:18), underlines the fact that Jesus cannot be made to fit any preconceived schema.

[5-6] The command to avoid both Samaritan and gentile territory contradicts not only Acts 8:5, 26 but also Matthew 28:18-20. Even if the statement is based on an Aramaic sentence reading, "Do not go to the gentiles and do not enter the province of Samaria," the bluntness of the prohibition is striking. The Greek text says literally not to go by the "way" of the gentiles. Generally the way to a gentile settlement was to be avoided only during idolatrous festivals, and then

only if it led nowhere else (Billerbeck on vs. 5 A). By this saying, Matthew is trying to show that it is not God who abandons Israel, but that the gentile mission becomes necessary after Israel has said no to Jesus (cf. the introductory remarks on chapters 21–25 and the discussion of 12:15-21; 27:25; also Isa. 49:5-6; Acts 13:46-47; 28:23-28; Rom. 9–11; John 10:16). That God wishes to bring his lost sheep to pasture, seek those who have gone astray, and send his servant to be their shepherd is already stated in Ezekiel 34:16, 23 (cf. also the discussion of Matt. 15:24).

At the same time, Matthew maintains the position that the gentile Christian community does not simply replace Israel (see the discussion of 21:43). The significance of Jesus for all peoples is already suggested in 2:1 ff.; 4:15(?); 12:18-21; and above all 8:11 ff.; 15:21 ff.; but salvation was first offered by Jesus exclusively to Israel (cf. the discussion of 15:24) until Israel finally refused (27:25). Matthew is always aware that the same fate faces his own community if it does not remain faithful (cf. the introductory remarks on chapters 21–25 and the discussion of 19:28).

The Samaritans are also rejected by the rabbis (*pace* Rabbi Akiba [d. A.D. 135]; Billerbeck on vs. 5 B 1; and Ecclus. 50:25-26) on account of gentile influences and a cult that developed apart from the rest of Judaism (cf. Ezra 4:1-5). They are probably Israelites who had not been taken captive to Babylon but who had lived in association with the heathen occupation forces and intermarried with them (for a different view, cf. 2 Kings 17:24-28). The lost sheep of Israel are those who belong to the new people mentioned in 21:31-32, 43.

[7] Preaching is here mentioned for the first time, while authority to heal was mentioned in the first verse. Both of course go together (chapters 5–7/8–9). There is no more thought of preaching without the authority that confirms it than there is of miracles without the words that explain what is taking place. The Kingdom of God is said to be near, so near that salvation or judgment is already at hand (vss. 12-14). There is no explicit call to repent (4:17), perhaps because the disciples, unlike Jesus (and John the Baptist, 3:2), are identified with the sinners, perhaps because the offer of salvation is to receive primary emphasis.

[8] The ministry of the disciples is conceived in terms as close as

possible to the ministry of Jesus; in fact the sentence that mentions the raising of the dead and the cleansing of lepers already looks forward to 11:5, and the injunction to "heal the sick" also means healing the blind, lame, and dumb, as Jesus has just done. The command freely to give the gift that has been freely received has an important place in primitive Christianity (2 Cor. 11:7; cf. 1 Cor. 9:3-18; also the discussion of Mark 6:10). This is also shown by the frequent exhortations to hospitality (Rom. 12:13; 1 Tim. 3:2; Tit. 1:8; Heb. 13:2; 1 Pet. 4:9), which is likewise implicit here.

[10-11] Poverty gives the disciple the freedom to accept help. Paul's refusal to accept compensation shows how concerned he was that his message remain credible (1 Cor. 9:11-12; 1 Thess. 2:9; Phil. 4:10-17). Passages like 1 Corinthians 9:14; 1 Timothy 5:18 (cf. already Num. 18:31 and Deut. 25:4 = 1 Cor. 9:9; 1 Tim. 5:18) reveal how important such instructions were for the early Christians. In a land where snakes abounded it was almost impossible to do without sandals and a staff; the requirement may go back to a cultic prohibition against entering the courtyard of the Temple with staff and shoes, knapsack and dusty feet. [9] In its earliest form, the saying probably forbade the disciples to "provide for" these things (see the introduction to Mark 6:7-13).

[12-13] The very real effect a word can have is shown by the idea that "peace" comes upon a house and remains there simply by virtue of a common form of greeting, "Peace be with this house" (thus in Luke 10:5). But the conception is not magical; only where the greeting is warmly responded to—that is what is meant by "if the people in the house welcome you," or, in Greek, using a favorite expression of Matthew's, "if the house is worthy"—does peace come upon the house. In this saying we can sense an impressive conviction that the blessing promised to those who believe in the preaching of the disciples is a very real quantity: in the disciples' words God himself visits men, comes to them, or departs from them. The content of their message is summarized in the word "peace," which is also the common formula of greeting. It is all the more apparent that the messenger's personal authority and integrity must be believed in if his preaching is actually to bring salvation and judgment and not just remain a theological lecture.

[11, 14] The city, logically, is mentioned before the entering of the house and after the departure from it; but the words that bring salvation or judgment are spoken between individuals within the house, and only thus does the message come to the entire city. [15] The reference to the most terrible judgment that could be cited underlines the warning. Gomorrah is usually mentioned in the same breath as Sodom (Isa. 1:9 = Rom. 9:29; Jude 7; 2 Pet. 2:6); it is not found in Luke 10:12 because Genesis 19 speaks only of the crimes of the Sodomites, mentioning Gomorrah only as the name of another city near Sodom.

[16] The saying about sheep among wolves makes a good transition to the passage predicting persecution (vss. 17-39). The metaphor occurs in both Jewish (2 Esd. 5:18) and Greek literature. The band of disciples is not a safe haven for sheep; they must venture out not only into insecurity but even into defenselessness. Suffering becomes an important function of Jesus' band of disciples. Of course the final saying of our section also warns against deliberately seeking martyrdom. The caution of the disciples is to consist not in clever diplomatic moves but in the purity of a life that is genuine and wears no masks. Nevertheless, the possibility of flight (10:23) or of reasonable defense, given by God himself (vss. 17 ff.), remains.

In itself, a system of regular compensation is better than dependence on unregulated gifts; but salaries would promote a sense of security counter to Matthew 6:25 ff. and to the instructions here, and could make the disciples' message less credible. Of course neither system can guarantee the disciples from anxieties or from mercenary suspicions. But the message must shine forth in visible terms if the preaching of it is to retain credibility. Such concrete embodiment is all the more important if the Word is to have the incomparable power that this passage imputes to it: only Isaiah 45:23; 55:11 credit it with as much. Men have debated whether unbelievers also receive the body and blood of Christ in the Lord's Supper—to their condemnation rather than to their help. From the perspective of this passage, one could say that the principle does hold true for God's Word: when it is truly and credibly proclaimed, it brings God's peace to a house, but when a house rejects the Word all smiles cease. "Post-Christian" man is a different man from the heathen, to whom the Word of Jesus has not yet come. The message of the nearness of the Kingdom of God is conceived in such realistic terms that the disciples actually bring it in their words rather than merely telling about it. So serious, however, is the rejection of this call to God that all the terrible perversions ascribed to the Sodomites pale to insignificance beside it.

Coming Persecutions (10:17-25)
Cf. Mark 13:9-13; Luke 12:11, 12; 6:40

[17]"Watch out for men, however! They will arrest you and take you to court, and they will whip you in their synagogues. [18]You will be brought to trial before rulers and kings for my sake, to tell the Good News to them and to the gentiles. [19]When they bring you to trial, do not worry about what you are going to say or how you will say it; when the time comes, you will be given what you will say. [20]For the words you speak will not be yours; they will come from the Spirit of your Father speaking in you. [21]Men will hand over their own brothers to be put to death, and fathers will do the same to their children; 'children will turn against their parents' and have them put to death. [22]Everyone will hate you, because of me. But whoever holds out to the end will be saved.

[23]"When they persecute you in one town, run away to another one. Amen, I tell you this: you will not finish your work in all the towns of Israel before the Son of Man comes.

[24]"No disciple is greater than his master; no slave is greater than his lord. [25]A disciple should be satisfied to become like his master, and a slave like his lord. If the head of the family is called Beelzebul, the members of the family will be called by even worse names!"
(Vs. 21—Mic. 7:6.)

[17-22] The sayings about suffering occur in almost exactly the same words in the eschatological discourse in Mark 13:9-13. The only differences are the warning against men in the introduction and a few other minor changes. In verse 19 we can still hear an echo of the earlier form of the saying used in Luke 12:11 ("what or how"; the

manuscripts do not all agree). **[18]** Between verses 18 and 19 the sentence "and the gospel must first be preached to all peoples" (Mark 13:10) has been omitted; it is more appropriately kept until the eschatological discourse in Matthew 24:14. Since the manuscripts did not include any punctuation, the phrase "and to all peoples" in Mark 13:10 could easily be attached to the preceding sentence, resulting in the Greek text of Matthew 10:18 (= Mark 13:9), "as a witness to them and to (all) peoples." Matthew 24:14, "as a witness to all peoples," is similar.

[23] The reference to the end in verse 22 leads to the interpolation of a saying about the coming of the Son of Man, which is unique to Matthew and hard to interpret. It is noteworthy that the form of the sentence, as well as the verb forms, corresponds to Luke 12:11 (= Matt. 10:19). Did the saying once form part of that context, which speaks of persecution in Jewish cities, and was it then omitted by Luke? Or did Matthew add the saying about the Son of Man and assimilate it to verse 19?

It was on this saying that Albert Schweitzer based his hypothesis that Jesus expected the Kingdom of God to arrive even before his disciples returned and thus experienced his first disappointment. But the composite nature of the missionary discourse (Schweitzer considered the whole of it more or less historical) makes this ingenious suggestion untenable. Schweitzer supposed that in his Transfiguration Jesus revealed to his three trusted disciples the messianic secret, which Peter betrayed to the other disciples at Caesarea Philippi, although the Gospels tell the story in the opposite order. According to Schweitzer, the crucifixion was Jesus' last and greatest disappointment, since it was his purpose to bring about the Kingdom, at first in company with his disciples, later through his own vicarious suffering. This entire edifice collapses upon the realization that the structure of our Gospels is largely the work of each individual evangelist (see the discussion of 11:12).

Verse 24 is found in similar form in the Sermon on the Plain (Luke 6:40), but also in John 13:16; it was probably current as an independent saying. It links the fate of the disciples with that of Jesus, drawing for illustration on the blasphemous identification of Jesus with Beelzebul (9:34; 12:24, 27), which Matthew apparently considered important.

All of these sayings would be more appropriate to an eschatological discourse (Mark 13:9-13) than Jesus' missionary discourse. In any case nothing had previously been said about any mission of the disciples to their families or about persecution; neither are trials before rulers and kings conceivable in Palestine at the time of Jesus. [17] As far as we can tell from historical evidence, actual persecutions appear to have taken place only in the Diaspora.

"Men" appear from the very outset as enemies of Jesus' messengers. As in 12:9; 13:54; 23:34, Matthew no longer speaks merely of "synagogues" (Mark 13:9) but of "their [the Jews'] synagogues." Israel, which whips the messengers of Jesus in its synagogues, is no longer for Matthew the people of God, but an alien people (cf. the discussion of 7:28-29). There is no warning, however, about exclusion from the synagogue (John 9:22; 12:42; 16:2), probably because the community in the time of Matthew no longer fell under jurisdiction of the synagogue, and so had no dealings with it. The mention of "courts" ("councils" or "sanhedrins"; the only other occurrence of the term is Mark 13:9) may point to the period after the destruction of Jerusalem, when the single Council or Sanhedrin at Jerusalem had ceased to exist. That the disciples of Jesus will suffer in bearing witness before all the nations is emphasized. [20] The Spirit is referred to as "the Spirit of your Father," a new expression. However much the disciples are left in a state of insecurity, they can still have a sense of ultimate security such as they could not find anywhere else in the world.

[23] The saying about the coming of the Son of Man is appended to the promise that he who holds out to the end (of the world) will be saved (Mark 13:13). The remarkable statement that the Son of Man will come, as the Greek text puts it, before the disciples have finished going through all the towns of Israel, was probably at first intended as a word of comfort to them in their flight, but here it is made to refer to their entire preaching commission, as suggested by the term "finish." It is reasonably certain that the saying originated in a period when the end was considered close at hand and the Christian mission was limited to Palestine, a situation like that behind verses 5-6. The failure of this ex-

pectation was not felt as a problem until relatively recently (cf. the discussion of Mark 9:1). In the early church, parties that denied the divinity of Jesus never appealed to this saying or others like it. But how was it taken by the community in which the gentile mission had already begun? The juxtaposition of "synagogues" and "rulers and kings" (vs. 17) suggests missionary efforts not only to the gentiles but also to the Jews throughout the Roman Empire— which of course is to be an object lesson for Israel (Rom. 11:11-12). Either effort would have led to persecution, especially at the hands of the Jews. Verse 23 means, then, that there will be no end —either to the mission to Israel or to the persecution with which Israel hounds Christians from city to city.

[24] Unlike the metaphor of teacher and pupil, that of the servant or slave and his lord suggests the Old Testament use of "servants of God" as a term of honor for the prophets, and possibly even the eschatological Servant of God (Isaiah 53). Certainly, the use of "Beelzebul" as an insult is possible only within the realm of Judaism, the more so because it is based on a pun, since "Beelzebul" means "head of the family." If Jesus' disciples are his household, his family, it is logical that they will be hit with the same insults that have already been directed at the head of the family. The Beelzebul slur probably shows that charismatic healings and exorcisms are continuing in the community (see the discussion of 9:34) and that the community is therefore subject to the same attacks as Jesus himself.

Why does the discussion of persecution appear here rather than in the eschatological discourse (24:4 ff.)? Matthew even includes an eschatological verse from Micah (7:6) and a saying about the coming of the Son of Man. But, though his wording agrees with Mark, whose discourse is eschatological, Matthew uses a different arrangement, so we may assume his point is different, namely that persecution is a normal part of life for the disciple. The idea that Jesus and his disciples would share the same fate is basic. It appears in a quite different way in Romans 6:1 ff., associated with baptism, and in John 15:1 ff. associated with the discourse about the vine and its branches. In verse 20 of the latter passage the saying about the slave and his master (Matt. 10:24) is likewise interpreted as referring to the persecution that awaits the disciples. Perhaps it best reveals to us today the meaning of Jesus for his disciples. Whoever dares to follow Jesus joins him in a fate that will invariably resemble his. Solidarity with Jesus in suffering and abuse is a central token of discipleship. Jesus always remains the master, the head of the family; the disciple remains his slave, a member of his household. The very uniqueness of the path Jesus takes is what makes it possible for others to accompany him along part of it. The sense of humor Jesus shows in his pun also makes following him easier—it holds in wry balance his sense of the irreparable nature of pain and, at the same time, pain's end.

Discipleship in Confession (10:26-33)
Cf. Luke 12:2-9

[26]"Do not be afraid of men, then. There is nothing covered that will not be uncovered, and nothing hidden that will not be made known. [27]What I am telling you in the dark you must repeat in the light, and what you have heard in private you must tell from the housetops. [28]Do not be afraid of those who kill the body but cannot kill the soul; rather be afraid of God who can destroy both body and soul in hell. [29]Can't you buy two sparrows for a penny? Yet not a single one of them falls to the ground without your Father's consent. [30]As for you, even the hairs of your head have all been counted. [31]So do not be afraid; you are worth much more than sparrows! [32]Whoever confesses publicly that he belongs to me, I will do the same for him before my Father in heaven. [33]But whoever denies publicly that he belongs to me, then I will deny him before my Father in heaven."

This whole section is found in the same sequence in Luke 12:2-9, albeit with many differences in wording. This means it is a collection of sayings intended to allay fear, a collection current in various forms before Matthew and Luke incorporated it. Up to this point the sections in Matthew that do not occur in Mark or any other place in Matthew, but do occur in Luke have appeared in roughly Luke's sequence. The same applies to 11:21-27; 12:22-45. Exceptions (8:-11-12, 19-22 and sections of the Sermon on the Mount) have had their explanation. Our section, however, varies from the Lukan parallel in both its order and wording. Perhaps besides forming part of Q it was also used independently for instruction, and was incorporated by Matthew (or Luke) in this independent form.

[26] The first saying is found in similar form in Mark 4:22; it may at one time have referred to Easter or to the Judgment when everything hidden will be revealed, or it may have been meant to comfort the oppressed by stating that the present hiddenness of the Kingdom of God will give place to a glorious revelation. Alongside Luke 8:17 (=Mark 4:22), Luke 12:2 contains our saying in a version related to Matthew 10:26. Luke probably understands it as a judgment against the Pharisees (cf. 12:1 and the new beginning in 12:4a). Matthew takes a different approach. By means of his introduction he links the saying with the preceding material and interprets it as an exhortation to fearless preaching (cf. the discussion of 11:27). [27] Therefore Matthew also changes the passive in verse 27 (Luke 12:3: ". . . will be heard in the light . . . will be proclaimed from the housetops"), which, like the parallel form in verse 26, originally referred to the onset of God's judgment or revelation; and he addresses the saying instead directly to the disciples: their proclamation is to be public, not like his discourses delivered within the restricted circle of disciples. The Gospel of Thomas contains two versions of the same saying (5, 6). The one refers to God's judgment, before which nothing can remain hidden; the other thinks in terms of increasing religious knowledge within the individual.

[28] The next saying, too, was preserved in various forms; only Matthew distinguishes the "soul" from the body. Since Luke also eliminates the notion of a soul that survives death in 9:24-25 and Acts 2:27, 31, he has probably made changes here. On the other hand, he has preserved an idiom typical of Q: "Indeed I tell you. . . ." [29] In the saying about the sparrow the price varies; perhaps the great devaluation of silver under Nero intervened between the earlier form in Matthew and the later form in Luke, or they were cheaper by the dozen. Under Domitian, price control set a ceiling price of about five cents apiece. The more general conclusion in Luke probably represents a later softening of the objectionable statement that ascribes suffering and death to God's will. [30-31] In the interpretation Matthew diverges from Luke through the addition of "your" and "you"

to emphasize the contrast. The saying about the hair interrupts the continuity and probably represents a later example added to the collection before it was incorporated by Matthew and Luke. The rabbis were also aware that God's mercy extends even to a nest of birds, but they differed from Jesus and denied the extension of that mercy to men, who have an obligation to obey (Billerbeck III 398-99).

[32-33] The saying about confessing the Son of Man, however, has a complicated history of transmission (cf. the discussion of Mark 8:38). Probably the direct "I" in Matthew is an attempt to attest more strongly the identification of Jesus with the coming Son of Man, already mentioned in 10:23. This is a matter of dispute, however; it is possible that both sentences were originally formulated in the passive like Luke 12:9, so that one tradition made the meaning clear by inserting "I," the other by inserting the "Son of Man," or even that Jesus himself formulated the saying in the first person. Luke 12:9 and Mark 8:38 both mention "angels" of God—they are usually mentioned with the phrase "Son of Man"—so Matthew himself probably substituted "my Father in heaven" for "angels"; it is a favorite expression of his.

[26-27] Throughout the entire section it is Matthew's purpose to impart confidence to the community of disciples, who are to confess Jesus publicly before men largely hostile. Therefore he has Jesus exhort his disciples directly to proclaim their message in public. [28] Verse 26, originally an admonition to be cautious, is boldly transformed into the opposite. Limits are set to the fear of men. Similar statements are found in the rabbinic writings: the killing performed by a king of flesh and blood is not an eternal killing, but the killing performed by the King of all kinds is; he kills for this age and the age to come. In the Matthaean form of the saying there might be a glimpse of the Greek distinction between immortal soul and mortal body, which had penetrated into Hellenistic Judaism (Wisd. 16:13-15; 4 Macc. 13:13-15; 14:6), except that the second half of Matthew's verse states that body and soul can perish in hell. In the Old Testament, "flesh" and "soul" both always designate man as a whole, but under different aspects. This applies for the most part to the New Testament as well, where the word "body," for which there is no Hebrew equivalent, can replace "flesh." "Flesh" depicts man primarily as dependent

on God, subject to sickness and death; "body" refers more to man's outward appearance. As a rule, "soul" should be translated as "life," because the term designates man as a living being subject to various fates. That "body" and "life" are two sides of man, not two parts, is demonstrated by 6:25 (cf. also the discussion of Mark 8:35).

Here, therefore, it is probably better to interpret the saying as meaning that men cannot kill life itself, real life; only God can destroy the body and the life given it. Undoubtedly God is meant; according to Jewish belief only he condemns, never the devil. Probably Matthew, like the Old Testament and most of the New Testament, simply cannot conceive of life apart from the body. But the death of the earthly body is not the end of life, because God will give man a new body which will live in God's Kingdom or be cast into hell. It remains unclear how much Hellenistic Jewish notions may have influenced the language and possibly also the thought of this passage and whether Matthew is speaking of "destruction" or "perdition" (the word can mean both), that is, the end or simply an eternal state of torment in hell. Jewish teachers as early as the time of Jesus supposed, for example, that body and soul are destroyed after twelve months in hell (Billerbeck IV 1180-81). Matthew is not primarily concerned, however, to depict the state after death but to call men to be without fear in this life, because there is only one who deserves to be feared, namely God himself.

[29-31] Fear of God, however, is the same as trust in him (Ps. 33:18; cf. the discussion of Mark 4:41); it is nothing more or less than the total devotion of one's life to him who, as Matthew makes clear, seeks to be a Father to his children. Fear is therefore not anxiety, which is often irrational, but a carefully considered and rational avoidance of the only thing that can really cause harm, namely, a loss of devotion to God or to men. Misfortune at the hands of men is really in the hands of God, like the fall of a sparrow, and only appears dreadful if a man lacks trust.

[32-33] These statements are given their ultimate weight by Matthew's having Jesus speak of God as his Father. Thus it is made clear that through him, the Son, the disciples also become sons of God (vs. 29) because he lets them participate in his communion with the Father (cf. the excursus on 5:9). Jesus is more than an example and model

belonging to the past; he is the one through whom the entire conduct of the disciples, their sufferings and their fidelity as well as their failures, take on the character of the eternal and will one day be present before God himself (cf. the discussion of Mark 8:38). Thus it is already suggested that the fear of God, which bestows fearlessness toward men, lives through the death and resurrection of Jesus, because in Jesus it is made clear for all time that those who kill the body cannot separate men from God himself and from real life.

This section derives its force from the fact that it does not try to sketch an illusory picture of a kindly God. Sparrows fall to earth and disciples of Jesus are slain, and Jesus never says that it hardly matters. What these sayings assert is that God is indeed God, that he is above success and failure, help and isolation, weal and woe, holding them in hands that Jesus says are the hands of the Father. He can say this because he himself addresses God as his Father, and does so throughout his entire life and in his death. Therefore he knows and can say with authority that after the death of the body God, and fullness in life, await the disciple who confesses Jesus.

Discipleship and the Cross (10:34-39)
Cf. Luke 12:51-53; 14:26-27; 17:33; Mark 8:34-35

³⁴"Do not think that I have come to bring peace to the world; no, I did not come to bring peace, but a sword. ³⁵I came to set men 'against their fathers, daughters against their mothers, daughters-in-law against their mothers-in-law; ³⁶a man's worst enemies will be the members of his own family.'

³⁷"Whoever loves his father or mother more than me is not worthy of me; whoever loves his son or daughter more than me is not worthy of me. ³⁸Whoever does not take up his cross and follow in my steps is not worthy of me. ³⁹Whoever tries to gain his own life will lose it; whoever loses his life for my sake will gain it."
(Vss. 35-36—Mic. 7:6.)

Once more we find three sayings brought together that Luke puts in three different places and in somewhat different words. The first and second have the catchwords "father and mother" in common, while the second half of the second saying is already associated with the third saying in Mark 8:34-35. **[34]** The formula "I have come" (see the introductory remarks on 11:19) is repeated three times in Matthew 10:34-35; it occurs only once in Luke, who also uses a different Greek word that he is especially fond of. But the same word as that used by Matthew also occurs in Luke 12:49 ("I have come to light a fire"). Verse 34*b* may go back to Jesus, but the saying was expanded even before Matthew and Luke used it, probably through the addition of a question like Luke 12:51*a,* and Matthew has elaborated it even more (cf. the discussion of 5:17). The Lukan term "division," however, looks like a weaker substitute for the Matthaean "sword."

The Old Testament quotation from Micah 7:6 found in both Matthew and Luke does not follow either the Greek or the Hebrew Old Testament precisely. The final clause is omitted in Luke; otherwise he exhibits a more fully developed version, stating correctly in an interpolated phrase that we are dealing with five persons, since mother and mother-in-law are in fact one and the same. **[37]** In the following saying Luke probably retained the Aramaic word "hate," while Matthew renders more accurately "love more than me." "Be worthy" and "be a disciple" (Matthew/Luke) could also derive from two almost identical Aramaic words. Only in Luke are a man's wife, brothers, and sisters included in the list. A similar saying of Jesus occurs in Matthew 19:29 = Mark 10:29-30.

[38-39] Verses 38 and 39 are parallels to Mark 8:34-35, where the different forms of discipleship are discussed. Matthew is fond of the expression "be worthy." In verse 39, the Greek text actually reads "find," rather than "gain," which is not really appropriate; it is probably only a pedantic assimilation to the same verb in the concluding clause. "For my sake" is not found in Luke 17:33 (or John 12:25). The uncompromising terms in which discipleship is presented here mean that this saying probably harks back to Jesus himself, and the very lack of any reference to his own person is typical of him (see the discussion of Mark 8:35). Otherwise Luke has assimilated the saying to the language of the Greek Old Testament, and John to the Greek antithesis between "this world" and "eternal life."

[34] The messiah has been awaited as Prince of Peace ever since Isaiah 9:6; 11:1 ff. When battle is mentioned, it is the heathen he defeats in order that Israel may find eternal peace (Ps. Sol. 17:21-31). The "breath of his mouth" may be enough (2 Esd. 13:10-11), or he may come only after the battles are over (rabbinic literature; likewise 4QFlor. i. 10-13?). Jewish eschatological documents likewise link family strife with general wars (Jub. 23:14-17), albeit only as a prelude to the messianic kingdom of peace. Since Luke also associates this saying with eschatological material, it is clear that more is involved here than teaching individuals to have such trust in God that they accept all of life's reverses with stoic equanimity; God's acts are thought of as convulsing the entire world (Greek: "earth").

What is new for Jewish expectations is that the messiah himself brings such strife. This appears even more clearly in Matthew because he interpolates the saying into his missionary discourse; simple adherence to Jesus can set a family at variance. Whether the sword is merely a symbol of strife, as it is taken in Luke 12:51 (cf. Heb. 4:12), or, more likely, a symbol of persecution and martyrdom (Matt. 10:28), the subject matter is the strange presence of the Kingdom of God, spoken of in Matthew 11:12. In strife and tribulation, when the disciples appear to be abandoned by God to the world struggling against him, the way is paved for God's Kingdom. God's Kingdom has never been the peace of the false prophets who cry, "Peace, peace!" while avarice and meanness lay waste the earth and transform God's good creation into its opposite (Jer. 6:14; etc.); neither, however, is it the "holy war" of the devout who take the field to conquer their oppressors with the mighty support of God. The sword is not in the hands of the disciples, but of their opponents. But the disciples know that it is Jesus himself who brings the sword, that by perishing and thus bearing witness to him they will conquer—with a victory such as he himself gained on the cross (vss. 38-39).

[37] Jesus does indeed call upon his disciples to love their families (5:27 ff.; 19:1 ff.), to honor father and mother (15:3 ff.), but it is absolutely clear this must not stand in the way of obedience to God (cf. the discussion of 8:21-22). The word for "love" is therefore not the same word used for love of neighbor (i.e., love of God), but a verb more suggestive of family ties. In this sense Qumran extolled Levi,

since he left father and mother for the sake of the priesthood (Deut. 33:8-11; 4QTest. 15-17).

[38] Thus the summons to confess Christ, indeed to be ready to surrender one's life, is pronounced without reservation. The saying is not yet associated with Jesus' own way of the cross, as it is in 16:21 ff. = Mark 8:31 ff. and John 12:24 ff., because the first announcement of the Passion will not come until after the confession of Peter; but the association is present for Matthew in his use of the catchword "cross" (see the discussion of Mark 8:34; cf. also Matt. 10:24-25). [39] The paradox of the last sentence is sharpest in Luke 17:33, where "for my sake" is omitted. There, of course, it stands in the context of flight in the face of the Last Judgment, whereas elsewhere it is associated, correctly, with Jesus' call to discipleship (also in John 12:25). The remarkable statement that a man will find his life in giving it away, in the tranquility that does not seek desperately to hold onto it, in readiness to accept suffering and death, is true only when a man knows the mystery of the Kingdom of God as incarnate in Jesus.

God's Presence in the Disciples (10:40–11:1)
Cf. Mark 9:37, 41

[40]"Whoever welcomes you, welcomes me; and whoever welcomes me, welcomes the one who sent me. [41]Whoever welcomes a prophet because he is a prophet will receive a prophet's reward; and whoever welcomes a righteous man because he is a righteous man will receive a righteous man's reward. [42]And whoever gives even a drink of cold water to one of the least of these my disciples because he is my disciple, Amen, I tell you, he will not lose his reward."

[11:1]When Jesus finished giving these instructions to his twelve disciples, he left that place and went on to teach and preach in their cities.

At the end of the discourse Matthew returns once more to the missionary situation. The first saying is related to Mark 9:37, which, however, like Matthew 18:5, speaks of welcoming a child, not a disciple. The last saying corresponds fairly closely to Mark 9:41. It can be shown that Matthew 10:42 represents the earlier form, and that this was linked even before Mark with Matthew 10:40=Mark 9:37, probably in the form "one of these little ones," which Matthew rightly interprets as referring to the disciples, whereas Mark makes it refer to the children (see the introduction to Mark 9:41-50 and the excursus on Matt. 7:13-23 [§5]). The circumlocution "the one who sent me" as a way of designating God occurs in Mark 9:37=Luke 9:48, as well as in Luke 10:16, and is there used in an address to the disciples. It is typically Johannine (cf. the parallel in John 13:20), except that in John a different Greek verb is always used for the participle. The hypothetical original form of the saying in verse 40 could very well go back to Jesus. The same might hold true for verse 42, with the further stipulation "because he is my disciple" being a later accretion. Verse 41 was not associated with verse 42 from the beginning, as can be seen from the fact that the "reward" in verse 41 is "a prophet's reward" or "a righteous man's reward"; this being the case, the "reward" of verse 42=Mark 9:41 should be called "a disciple's reward." All the important terms in verse 41 are taken from verse 40 ("welcome") and 42 ("because he is a . . ."). This means that verse 41 was almost certainly composed later, when the community came to include wandering prophets and "righteous men" as well as missionaries proper (see the excursus on 7:13-23; also 13:17; 23:34-35).

[40] Like verse 12, this verse states that in Jesus' messenger Jesus himself, and with him God, enters the life of whoever welcomes him. [42] There is no emphasis on any particular duty; even a drink of water will not be forgotten in the presence of God (see the discussion of Mark 9:41). [41] Behind these sayings, but above all behind the middle one, we can glimpse the church in which Matthew lives: wandering missionaries, prophets, and righteous men, who presumably have authority to teach the commandments of God and their interpretation by Jesus, move from one congregation to another, often despised and persecuted, always dependent on hospitality, and bringing with them the living Word of God that sets its stamp on their lives (cf. the excursus on 7:13-23). [11:1] The concluding saying corresponds to 7:28; but here Matthew stresses that we are dealing with instructions delivered to the twelve disciples. Unlike Mark 6:12, 30; Luke 9:10 (10:17), Matthew says nothing about the actual mission. Of

course he also assumes that the disciples obeyed; but he is concerned above all to show that the authority given then to the Twelve and their experience of it continues on today among all Jesus' disciples (cf. the discussion of 8:23).

Thus Matthew concludes the entire discourse, showing his community that it still has the authority of Jesus. It is surprising how little material has crept in dealing with doctrine, cult, and organization (cf. also the discussion of 18:1–20:16). This is due not simply to Matthew's fidelity to the situation in which he has set this discourse, for he also included sayings that apply only to the situation of the later community (e.g. vss. 17-25). What is more important is that the church is still understood as discipleship, as a pilgrimage always ready to bear witness to Jesus, but also possessed of authority to heal and prophesy.

The Presence of the Promises (11:2-6)
Cf. Luke 7:18-23

²When John the Baptist heard in prison about Christ's works, he sent some of his disciples to him. ³"Tell us," he had them ask Jesus, "are you the coming one or should we expect someone else?" ⁴Jesus answered, "Go back and tell John what you are hearing and seeing: ⁵the blind can see, the lame can walk, the lepers are made clean, the deaf hear, the dead are raised to life, and 'the poor receive the Good News.' ⁶How happy is he who does not find me a stumbling block!" (Vss. 5-6—Isa. 35:5-6; 29:18-19; 61:1.)

In quoting the words of Jesus, Matthew 11:2-19 agrees almost totally with Luke 7:18 ff. Here the arrangement of Q is once more adopted, going from the words of the Baptist to the Sermon on the Plain/Mount and the conversation with the officer at Capernaum. The introduction is Matthew's own, especially the unusual expression "Christ's [or: 'the Messiah's'] works" (see the introductory remarks on 11:19). It is much shorter than Luke's version, but agrees with it in the question asked by the Baptist. Luke speaks of *two* disciples of the Baptist and does not mention his being in prison, though he has already reported that imprisonment in 3:20. In verse 4 hearing is placed first, and the preaching of the Good News does not appear until the end of verse 5; this gives it greater emphasis. The obvious reason for placing the episode here is that it interprets what is happening in Jesus' own person (chapters 5–7 and 8–9) as well as in his community (chapter 10); cf. the introductory discussion of 4:17–11:30. The cleansing of lepers and the raising of the dead, not found in Isaiah, may have been added in Q because of what Jesus is reported to have done. The miracles are typical of the prophets (1 Kings 17:17-24; 2 Kings 4:18-37; 5). Thus this passage may go back to a community that saw in Jesus the eschatological prophet and appealed to such sayings of Jesus as 12:28. Thus the passage is important as another allusion in support of Matthew's abiding theme—that Jesus conforms precisely to Old Testament hopes of the redeemer.

It is very doubtful that, if this exchange actually took place, it did so in just these words. Could the Baptist, who was expecting a judge to come with fire and whirlwind, probably God himself (cf. the discussion of Mark 1:7-8), have framed such a question? On the other hand, adherents of the Baptist, who (at first) looked upon him as the messiah, were asking just such questions about Jesus even in the time of Matthew; in this section Matthew is merely pointing out to them the evidence of the Holy Spirit's work in the Christian community. But according to 3:11 the Baptist himself referred in vague terms to "the coming one," leaving open the question whether this would be God himself (Mal. 3:1; Zech. 14:5), coming to judgment, or one who would inaugurate the eschaton at God's behest (Ps. 118:26 = Mark 11:10; Dan. 7:13 = Mark 13:26; 14:62; Hab. 2:3 = Heb. 10:37; Ps. 40:8 = Heb. 10:7; cf. also the discussion of Mark 1:7-8). If the Baptist saw in Jesus at baptism something like the fulfillment of his still vague hope for the one yet to come, his question would be historically possible; for it is likewise hard to imagine that the Christian community merely invented the doubt expressed by the Baptist, whom they considered the most important witness on behalf of Jesus. All that we can safely conclude is that the question of the Baptist must antedate Q, because Q sees Jesus and John fighting the same campaign.

[2] The Greek text reads literally, "through his disciples," a striking construction probably to be explained on the basis of an Aramaic original. More important is the phrase *"Christ's* works" (see the introductory remarks on 11:19). This is the Christian community speaking, making the ultimate claim about all that has gone before. [3] But Matthew can also understand the Baptist's question. Jesus' lowliness, which sometimes lands his messengers in prison, does lead to doubts. Open and inquiring doubt was taken very seriously by the community. The very security of disbelief as well as that of orthodoxy is probed deeply by the New Testament, to see whether it still contains an openness to faith (cf. the discussion of Mark 8:29, 33 and the concluding remarks on Mark 4:41). If faith is not simply assent to a proposition but life with God, then it can live only by increasing and decreasing, in experiences that strengthen or endanger it.

[4-5] Jesus' response is striking. No miracles were expected of the messiah. The Baptist, it is true, is asking about "the coming one," thinking perhaps of the return of Elijah (cf. the discussion of vs. 10 and the introduction to Mark 9:9-13). Then miracles would happen, and prophets appearing at the time of Jesus held up the prospect of such miracles to their adherents. Jesus' response, however, goes beyond that idea, and incorporates the words of Isaiah 35:5-6 (cf. 29:18-19). The eschaton announced by the prophets is not about to dawn; in the actions of Jesus it *has* dawned. It is noteworthy that there is no mention of any punishment of the nations, associated with the promises in Isaiah 34; 61:5-7 (cf. 29:15, 20). And the cleansing of lepers (cf. only Num. 12:10 ff.) and resurrection of the dead go beyond the promises of the prophets and Jewish expectations (but see above). The emphasis on the greatest blessing brought by Jesus, the proclamation of joy to the poor (cf. Matt. 5:3 ff.), is unprecedented. This was not understood by later copyists who removed this promise from the end of the sentence and placed it earlier.

For Jesus, however, miracles are not the point; what is most important in his ministry is what is least pretentious—his message of love and hope. Certainly his miracles are signs of authority (see the discussion of 9:35 and the excursus on Mark 4:35-41; also John 5:36; 10:25, 38; 14:11; 2 Cor. 12:12). But never are they unequivocal: they evoke faith, but also doubt and even total rejection. Thus it is clear that his deeds truly open their meaning only to the person who can hear. [6] This is expressly stated by the concluding sentence. Jesus' response does not eliminate an act of faith on the part of the inquirer; on the contrary, it calls him to such an act of faith, because faith must always be a man's own personal response and can never be the mere mechanical repetition of what has just been said. John's impending death raises doubts in his mind; very soon (12:14) Jesus will deliberately take the same path.

If the community preserved the words of Jesus in verses 4-6, it was probably to answer such questions as the community of the Baptist was still putting to them. With this saying the Christian community was trying to help those who heard Jesus' message but did not know whether to believe it. In a very similar way a preacher might use this section today. Verses 5-6 are important for our reading of the Old Testament. They are not put forward as irresistible proof. The hearer's doubts are taken seriously—so seriously that only his own spontaneous faith can answer them, not some explanation formulated for him by someone else. It is not the man stricken by doubts who stumbles but the man no longer stricken by the question of Jesus, the man who immerses himself in the everyday round. It might well be asked whether we have forgotten how to take seriously our experiences of God's power. But they must not be paraded as proofs, as certain tracts do, for in fact they prove nothing. Faith is proved in their absence: only to those who have become poor is the promise given. Nevertheless according to Jesus' own words such an experience is an indication that in him and therefore in his disciples God has arrived, and this was the goal foreseen by the prophets. A band of disciples that is no longer a stumbling block but also no longer proclaims the message of joy to the poor would no longer be Jesus' disciples.

The Extraordinary Presence of the Kingdom of God (11:7-19)
Cf. Luke 7:24-35; 16:16; Mark 9:11-13

[7]While John's disciples were going back, Jesus spoke to the crowds about John: "What did you go out into the desert to see? A reed

bending in the wind? [8]What did you go out to see? A man dressed up in fancy clothes? People who dress like that live in palaces! [9]What did you go out to see? A prophet? Yes, I tell you, much more than a prophet! [10]For John is the one of whom Scripture says: 'Behold, I am sending my messenger ahead of you,' 'to prepare the way for you.' [11]Amen, I tell you, among those born of woman there has never been any man greater than John the Baptist; but he who is least in the Kingdom of heaven is greater than he.

[12]"From the time John preached his message until this very day the Kingdom of heaven has suffered violent attacks, and violent men try to seize it. [13]All the prophets and the Law of Moses prophesied until the time of John; [14]and if you are willing to accept their message, John is Elijah, whose coming has been predicted. [15]Listen, then, if you have ears!

[16]"Now to what can I compare this generation? They are like children sitting in the market place. One group shouts to another, [17]'We piped to you, but you did not dance! We sang funeral songs but you would not beat [your breasts]!' [18]John came, and he fasted and drank no wine, and everyone said, 'He has a demon in him!' [19]The Son of Man came, and he ate and drank, and everyone said, 'Look at this man! He is a glutton and a drunkard, a friend of tax collectors and sinners!' God's wisdom, however, is shown to be true by its results."

(Vs. 10—Mal. 3:1; Exod. 23:20.)

The tradition incorporated in the preceding episode (Q) is still being followed. Verses 7-11 and 16-19 agree almost word for word with Luke 7:24-28 and 31-34. In between the two parts Luke inserts an account that abruptly interrupts the discourse, telling how the people reacted during the period of John's baptismal ministry, already far in the past. **[12-15]** The sayings in Matthew 11:12-13, which are difficult to interpret, appear in different and more comprehensible form in Luke 16:16. Luke also omits the identification of the Baptist with returning Elijah (vss. 14-15), in contrast to Mark 9:11-13. Did Luke find verses 12-15 in his prototype and replace them? Or did Matthew and Luke fill out the narrative differently, because verse 16 signals a new beginning? Matthew corrects a kind of limitation implicit in verse 11*b* by inserting his new beginning, "From the time John preached his message . . ."; John thus belongs within the period of the Kingdom of God (cf. the discussion of vss. 12-13 and of 3:2). This may also explain why the reference to the time of preparation does not come until second in verse 13, the reverse order from that found in Luke 16:16.

The obscure verse 12 very early ceased to be understood. Probably Luke ran across it in an innocuous form associated with sayings about the Law and the prophets and their new interpretation by Jesus (Luke 16:16-18; Matt. 5:17-18, 32) and therefore omitted it from this passage. This applies also to the statement that, although John is greater than any prophet, not just Jesus but everyone in the Kingdom is greater than John (vss. 9, 11). Verse 10 was added by the community; as a rule Jesus quotes loosely and not in such a way that the Old Testament passage can be compared precisely to what is happening now, as was done in the learned exegesis at Qumran and in the early community of Jesus.

[16-19] Verses 16-19 are subject to some uncertainty on formal grounds. Elsewhere Jesus tells parables without going on to interpret them (cf. the discussion of Mark 2:23 and 4:1-9). Verses 18-19 therefore remain questionable, if only because of the word used for "demon," which comes from literary Greek. And on the other side, the theological question of who is meant by the "Son of Man" remains unsettled. It has been suggested that the use of the past tense looks back on Jesus' completed ministry, so that the saying must have been formulated by the Christian community. This argument is not convincing, however, since the formula also expresses Jesus' own sense of his mission (see the introduction to the excursus on Mark 8:27-33). In any case the subject matter of Jesus' preaching is accurately reproduced, and since it would be hard to understand the parable without reference to the Baptist and Jesus, only the form (or tense) of the saying appears to have been changed (the Son of Man "came"). The idea that the two men's work is the same, and the sense of mission that sees God working in the present (vs. 19*c*)—these are strongly typical of Jesus himself.

[19*c*] The concluding clause, "God's wisdom, however, is shown to be true through all its children," refers in Luke 7:35 to those who

accept John and Jesus. There is no mention of them in the parable, however. Probably we are dealing with a conclusion composed as part of the Sayings Source, whose affinity with wisdom literature also appears elsewhere (see the excursus on Matt. 23:34-39), intended (without "all") to describe John and Jesus as sons or children of wisdom, i.e. her obedient messengers. Luke 7:35 refers to disciples of Jesus (vs. 28b); Matthew 11:19 reinterprets: ". . . by its results [lit.: 'works'],'' wording perhaps suggested by the phonetic similarity of the Aramaic terms for "children" and "works." Since "Christ's works" were already mentioned in verse 2, these two phrases frame the entire section (see the discussion of vs. 19).

[16] With regard to details, the double introduction to the parable in Luke 7:31 corresponds to what is also observed in Luke 13:18, 20 (cf. Matt. 13:31, 33). The shorter form is probably the earlier (Matt. 11:16a). [18] In verse 18, also, Matthew preserves the more primitive short form, which corresponds to the parallel in verse 19 = Luke 7:34, while Luke 7:33 states it more precisely: John did of course eat and drink (locusts and honey; Mark 1:6 = Matt. 3:4), but not bread and wine.

[7] The very first saying takes the question posed by Jesus about faith and repeats it for all to hear. The hearer too must be questioned and cannot comfort himself with the thought that he is not in the same boat as the imprisoned Baptist. Jesus asks, Just what does this pilgrimage to the Baptist mean—this wave of religion sweeping over Israel? Of course such a question could be asked only while the movement was still going on. In combination with verse 8 the "reed" should probably be taken symbolically (cf. 1 Kings 14:15; 3 Macc. 2:22): it is a kind of weather vane that points first in one direction, then in another, and moves with every breeze. [8] The "fancy clothes" are not intended to signify some royal messiah expected by the people; they are merely the opposite of what John was found wearing. Jesus is saying that when the people went out they must have known that they were not running after a weather vane or follower of fashion, that they would not find the fulfillment of their dreams but rather the difficult path taken by the Baptist and by Jesus himself: in other words, not the theology of grandeur but the theology of the cross.

[9] By their own admission they went out to see a prophet; but Jesus makes the crucial point that they saw much more than this. [10] Malachi 3:1 speaks of preparing the way before God ("before me"); the second person, which also occurs in Mark 1:2, is found in Exodus 23:20 in a related statement that Jewish scholars placed alongside the passage from Malachi. According to Malachi 3:1 "the angel of the covenant will come" as well as God, and in a postscript (3:23 [4:5]) the angel or messenger who is to prepare the way for God is identified with Elijah. This is the sense in which the passage was understood in the time of Jesus: Elijah will prepare the way for God before he comes to judgment (thus still in Luke 1:16-17; see the discussion of Mark 1:2). But one might also see the messiah in the angel of the covenant who comes with God. In this sense the saying was undoubtedly applied to the Baptist even before Mark and Matthew (see the discussion of Mark 1:6 and 9:9-13). Thus Jesus suggests that with the Baptist the age has come that will fulfill all the expectations of the prophets, while the Christian community emphasizes that the Baptist is only Jesus' precursor, correctly stressing that the Baptist is "more" not because he holds a higher office than any prophet but because he stands on the threshold of the fulfillment.

[11] In its Matthaean form, verse 11 follows directly from verse 9; the verb used to mean "there has never been" is used only of religious figures like the prophets. "Those born of woman" simply refers to men in contrast to God or his angels (Gal. 4:4; Job 14:1; 1QH xiii. 14; xviii. 12-13, 16, 23; 2 Esd. 4:6; 7:46). In the second half of the sentence, "the least" (literally: "the lesser") cannot refer to Jesus as the one coming after. Who would understand that, especially in conjunction with the phrase "in the Kingdom of heaven"? It is not Jesus who is being contrasted with the Baptist, but the whole of the Kingdom. Then, of course, it is clear that we cannot be dealing with "small" and "great" in the usual sense. The disciples of Jesus belong by nature among the "least" (10:42). That is precisely what makes them greater than the greatest of all those born of woman. Lowliness is the sign of the new age. If John is "more" than all the prophets, it is because he stands on the threshold of this new age; therefore, even the least of those who stand beyond the threshold is greater than he. Behind this saying lurks the extraordinary certainty that in Jesus

there exist not only a greatness and dignity surpassing those of the Baptist himself, but there exists also the whole Kingdom of God. Without this assumption, the preceding words would be meaningless.

[12] Verse 12 might be translated "does violence" instead of "has suffered violent attacks"; it would then mean that the Kingdom is ushered in with violence. The word for "violent men" is extremely unusual, and its meaning can only be derived from comparison with similar Greek formations; these, as well as three post-Christian passages in which it occurs, all have pejorative sense. The word for "seize" actually means "take by force"; its only other occurrence in Matthew is in 13:19, where it refers to the actions of the Devil. The suggestion that it should be understood in the good sense as the violent struggle of a passionate faith is almost out of the question, as is the interpretation that the Kingdom is being "vigorously pursued" by God.

Albert Schweitzer interpreted the saying to mean that Jesus himself wanted to inaugurate the Kingdom by force, first through fanning the flames of revolt, then through his own Passion (see the introductory remarks on 10:23). This could well apply to the program of the Jewish legalists and above all the attempts of the Zealots (cf. the end of the introduction to 4:1-11), but not to the Sermon on the Mount or to sayings like Matthew 11:27-29, or in fact to any of Jesus' acts. At most it might be possible that Jesus' opponents termed him and his disciples "violent men" because they interfered in areas that were supposedly the preserve of the Law and obedience to it. But in this case Jesus would have had to use the word in quotation marks, so to speak, and who would have understood what he was saying? Thus all the evidence suggests that Jesus is in fact declaring the presence of God's Kingdom, but also that it is being assaulted and trampled under foot by men. The presence of the Kingdom, which was expected to bring victory and triumph and the solution to every problem, stands itself under the sign of the cross; it means oppression, harassment, suffering.

[13] But what is meant by "from the time John preached his message" (literally: "from the days of John")? Verse 13 appears to reckon John still among the prophets: unlike Luke 16:16, it mentions

the Law after the prophets and associates it with the concept of "prophecy." This would mean that the Kingdom of God begins after John. Elsewhere, however, Matthew uses the idiom "from . . ." in such a way as to include the following term, in this case the Baptist (23:35; 1:17; 2:16; 27:45). This fits with the observation that in verses 18-19 Jesus speaks of himself and the Baptist together (cf. 21:31-32), that verse 9 concedes John to be "more than a prophet," and that Matthew himself brackets John and Jesus, while distinguishing them clearly as forerunner and fulfiller (see the discussion of 3:2). But isn't the situation different in verse 11?

The contradiction can probably be resolved by assuming that God's Kingdom refers to an event that announces itself in the opposition to John, his imprisonment and execution; it becomes present for whoever has ears to hear (vs. 15) and eyes to see in the ministry of Jesus, his preaching, actions and death; and it will be visible to all and fulfilled in the glory to come (cf. 13:1-50). For Jesus, as for Matthew, both are important: the activity of the Kingdom of God commences with the Baptist, but only Jesus himself makes it present for those who have ears to hear. A similar perspective can be seen also in numerous early Christian communities: they placed the Baptist at the beginning of their summaries of the faith (Acts 10:37; 13:24); they began all four Gospels with him; and they understood the fate of Jesus and his disciples as standing directly in the line of the persecuted prophets (cf. Matt. 14:5 and 21:26 with 21:46; also 5:12; 23:29-36 and 21:36-37).

[14] As early as verse 10 it is suggested that John the Baptist is Elijah; Mark 9:13 also states this. To be sure, not all the primitive communities accepted this equation, as Mark 9:4 and above all John 1:21 show. But Matthew's point in 11:14 is not so much that John the Baptist is Elijah as that with the Baptist something new, God's great turning point, has come. [15] The call to listen, which always follows a decisive passage (also appended to Matt. 13:43; cf. also Rev. 2:7, etc.; 13:9), here underlines the identification of John with Elijah, mainly because this idea became important in debates with the Baptist's disciples, who saw in their master a messianic figure. The call to listen also sets the call to repent, in the following verses, apart from the sayings about the Baptist, thus lending them more weight.

[16-19] The concluding parable talks about children who want to

play wedding or funeral but cannot get their friends to dance or lament with them. It is not likely that the picture is of two groups who cannot agree—the one wanting to play wedding, the other funeral. **[18-19]** The application shows that the same children suggest the one, then the other, without getting any response. The natural interpretation is that John proffered the way of asceticism, Jesus the way of freedom, but the people refused to take either. **[16]** If the introduction in verse 16 is taken literally, it is not John and Jesus but the men of "this generation" who are the children looking for playmates. One might then think in terms of people wanting to sit comfortably on the sidelines as spectators while the others have to dance to the piping of the flute or go through wild lamentations to its music. This would mean that they expected John to dance, Jesus to lament, while they themselves stood apart as critical observers, determining that their expectations had not been fulfilled. Since, however, parables are often introduced imprecisely (cf. the discussion of 13:45, for example), both interpretations are possible. The first one is the more likely.

[19] The charge of eating and drinking leveled against Jesus shows what an impression his "no" to all religious observances and his dinners with tax collectors made on people (cf. Luke 15:1-2). **[16]** The "Son of Man" and "this generation" are often mentioned in the same passage (Mark 8:38; cf. the discussion of Matt. 12:39-40). Strictly, of course, the passage is referring to the generation living in Jesus' day; but the point is the contrast between *all* men and the Son of Man, whom they do not understand (the Greek text speaks of "men" and the "Son of Man" in vs. 19, as well as 9:6-8; Mark 2:27-28; 9:31).

[19c] The last clause, in which the wisdom of God suddenly appears, is difficult. Taken alone, the statement refers to both John and Jesus. Several points in the passage are typical of Jesus: the way in which he brackets the work of the Baptist with his own, his reserve regarding all titles of honor, and his sense of mission seeing God's wisdom at work in the present. This applies also to the Lukan recension, according to which it is wisdom's "children," i.e. those who understand her, that "prove her true" (Greek: "justify"; cf. the use of this verb with the same meaning in Luke 7:29; Rom. 3:4-5; 1 Tim. 3:16). The nature of faith is to show God aright, to let him be God. For the majority of men, however, the statement of Ethiopian Enoch

42:2 applies: "Wisdom came to make her dwelling among the children of men, and found no dwelling place" (similarly Ecclus. 24:6-22). Matthew, however, speaks of "works" or "results," interpreting the saying from the perspective of verse 2. He thus equates the works of God's wisdom with the works of Jesus (see the excursus on 23:34-39). The preposition translated "by" is striking; some scholars, thinking in terms of Aramaic influence, have suggested rendering it "in contrast to" (her children the Israelites, Luke 7:35) or "in view of (her results)." The same preposition, however, occurs in the Greek text of Isaiah 45:25 in the sense of "by, through."

In retrospect what stands out is the cryptic saying about the presence of God's Kingdom as an object of violence, hatred, and attack. The passage must have been leading up to this statement from verse 2 on, and what follows is Jesus' call not to be under any illusions about sitting on the sidelines as an uninvolved spectator. Anyone looking for a trendie or weather vane to guide him, in order to be left in peace with all wishes gratified, has certainly found the wrong man in the Baptist. But anyone who allows the call of Jesus to take hold of him will discover that John is indeed greater than all the prophets, because in him the new world of God commences, and that the least in the Kingdom—attacked, resisted, and suppressed by men—will be even greater than John.

Warning Against Unbelief (11:20-24)
Cf. Luke 10:12-15

²⁰Then Jesus began to reproach the towns where he had performed most of his miracles, because the people had not turned from their sins. ²¹"How terrible it will be for you, Chorazin! How terrible for you too, Bethsaida! If the miracles which were performed in you had been performed in Tyre and Sidon, long ago people there would have put on sackcloth and sprinkled ashes on themselves to show that they had turned from their sins! ²²But I tell you, on the Judgment Day God will show more mercy to the people of Tyre and Sidon than to you! ²³And as for you, Capernaum! You want to be lifted up to heaven? You will be thrown down to hell! If the miracles which were performed in you

had been performed in Sodom, it would still be in existence today! [24]But I tell you, on the Judgment Day God will show more mercy to Sodom than to you!"

(Vs. 23—Isa. 14:13, 15.)

Verses 21-23*a* are found in almost identical words in Luke 10:-13-15. This continues the Sayings Source, which Matthew has been following since 11:2. In Luke, much Mark and special Lukan material comes between Luke 7:18-35 (= Matt. 11:2-19) and our passage; from the Q tradition Luke includes only the section dealing with discipleship (9:57-60), which was already used in Matthew 8:19-22 to illustrate the stilling of the storm and the missionary discourse, which follows immediately and was included (with Markan material) in Matthew 10:7-16. The immediate continuation of our Q passage follows in Matthew 11:25-27; Luke merely interpolates his editorial statement about the return of the seventy. In Q, then, these verses were appended directly to the missionary discourse, or more precisely to the saying about Sodom in Luke 10:12 = Matthew 10:15. That Matthew found them there can be shown.

While Luke 10:12 reads "on that day" and 10:14 "at the Judgment," Matthew combines the two expressions and writes in both verse 22 and verse 24, "on the Judgment Day." Above all, he has added a sentence about Capernaum in verse 23*b* that corresponds precisely to the ones about Chorazin and Bethsaida, except that it now refers to Sodom, because he appends to it the verse used by Luke in verse 12. In other words, Matthew gives to the traditional curse upon Capernaum (vs. 23*a*), which is stated in general terms in Luke 10:15, a searing force by bringing in a reference to Sodom. Verses 21-22 might well be Jesus' own words: Chorazin is never mentioned elsewhere, Bethsaida only in passing. One would be more likely, however, to expect it at the end of Jesus' ministry, since he does not leave Galilee until Matthew 19:1. Since, however, Matthew and Luke incorporate the saying at different points, we really know nothing about where or when it was spoken.

[20] The introduction is Matthew's own composition. He stresses

that Jesus' miracles should lead men to repent, and emphasizes the point once more by taking Jesus' threat against the city that rejects the *preaching* of his disciples and applying it to Capernaum, which did not truly understand Jesus' *acts* (see the discussion of 9:35 and 11:5-6). **[21-22]** Tyre and Sidon were notoriously profligate heathen cities (Isa. 23; Ezek. 26-28; Joel 3[4]:4); even in them, however, Jesus' ministry would be better understood (cf. 12:41-42; 8:11-12). The wearing of sackcloth and sprinkling of ashes on one's head are signs of mourning (Dan. 9:3). **[23-24]** The threat of judgment is aimed particularly at Capernaum, which is Jesus' own town (9:1). The threat, originally pronounced against Nebuchadnezzar (Isa. 14:13-15; cf. Ezek. 26:20 and 28:2, 8), was probably provoked by the pride which citizens of Capernaum took in having the famous prophet Jesus in their midst: they felt merit in being associated with him, but ignored to live by his preaching. Whether the first clause is read as a question or as a negative statement, it presupposes in any case the notion that Capernaum could be lifted up to heaven; all the more terrible then is its threatened fall, which Matthew throws into caustic relief by his reference to Sodom (see the discussion of 10:15). In the Lukan context this saying is spoken to comfort the rejected disciples; Matthew incorporates it in a judgment discourse (cf. Matt. 11:16-27).

The Presence of Salvation (11:25-30)
Cf. Luke 10:21-22

²⁵At that time Jesus said, "Father, Lord of heaven and earth! I thank you because you have revealed to the unlearned what you have hidden from the wise and learned. ²⁶Yes, Father, this was done by your own choice and pleasure.

²⁷"My Father has given me all things. No one knows the Son except the Father, and no one knows the Father except the Son, and those to whom the Son wants to reveal him.

²⁸"Come to me, all of you who are tired from carrying your heavy loads, and I will give you rest. ²⁹Take my yoke and put it on you, and learn from me, for I am gentle and humble in spirit; and you will find

rest for your souls. [30]For my yoke is easy to carry, and my burden is light."

(Vss. 28-30—Ecclus. 51:23 ff.; 24:19. Vs. 29—Jer. 6:16.)

Three sayings are brought together here, the first two of which appear in almost the same words in Luke 10:21-22 (cf. the discussion of Matt. 11:20-24); even the introductory formula "at that time" is common to both Gospels, albeit phrased in Luke's own way in Luke 10:21. The third saying, promising rest to the weary, is not found in Luke; since it is cited independently in the Gospel of Thomas, it probably circulated on its own and was associated with the other two sayings by Matthew or one of his sources. But even the first and second sayings can hardly have belonged together from the outset, for in the first God is addressed directly and in the second he is spoken of in the third person. Furthermore, although the first saying addresses the Father as Jesus often does, it differs from the second in not having anything to say about the special ministry of *Jesus*. Neither can the giving of "everything" in verse 27 refer back to the revelation of verse 25. Verse 27 may possibly be a later elaboration and interpretation of verses 25-26. Or were the sayings combined only because the catchwords "Father" and "reveal" appeared in both?

Furthermore, verses 25 and 28-30 have close parallels in Ecclesiasticus 51, in other words in wisdom literature, while verse 27 does not. But Ecclesiasticus 51 does exhibit the same sequence as this passage: thanksgiving to the Father (vss. 1-12), revelation of wisdom (13-22), and the call to accept a beneficent yoke (25-30). All three sayings likewise share an interest in the ones who receive revelation, those who are "unlearned" and "burdened." This might have led Christian exegetes—Matthew or his predecessors—studying the wisdom writings to bring the three sayings together; Matthew is the first Gospel to identify Jesus clearly with wisdom (see the discussion of vss. 28-30)—an identification understandable in view of Matthew's stress on the *teachings* of Jesus.

The original context of the sayings remains uncertain; the content of the revelation in verse 25 must once have been something specific. It is even more difficult to determine whether the sayings go back to Jesus himself. Their background in the Old Testament and Judaism is clear (see below), and the implied polemic against the teachers of the Law in the first and last sayings would be appropriate to a saying of Jesus, as would a certain similarity to the Beatitudes addressed to the poor (5:3, 5). There are also points of contact with Daniel, where the "wise" are mentioned. More difficult is the contrast between the terms "Father" and "Son," used absolutely, in the middle saying (see below).

[25] The beginning recalls the prayer of that other Jesus, Jesus Sirach, who begins (Ecclus. 51:1): "I thank you, Lord and King . . . ." But here the Jesus of Christianity praises God for his failure. The Jewish Qumran sect also places great emphasis on the obscurity of God's mysteries: "You have hidden the source of insight . . ." (1QH v. 25-26); ". . . unheeded and unrecognized remains the seal of his mystery" (viii. 10-11); it is known only to members of the group, and they "faithfully conceal the mysteries of knowledge" (1QS iv. 6). Such notions are already present in the Old Testament (Isa. 29:14 = 1 Cor. 1:19; Ps. 8:2 = Matt. 21:16; Ps. 19:8; 116:6; 119:130; Wisd. 10:21; cf. Isa. 53:1-3) and are borrowed by Paul (1 Cor. 1:26) and John (1:10-13). The background is once again Jewish wisdom speculation, which is typical of Q. The negative statement, appended in typical Semitic fashion only by means of the conjunction "and," goes even further: the promise is not given to the wise and learned, but to the "unlearned" (literally "immature"). As the Old Testament passages show, this is not an absolute contradiction, but it is a shift of emphasis. The religious tradition of Qumran is similar: "My eye beheld wisdom, hidden from men of knowledge" (1QS xi. 6); "Praise be to you, Lord, . . . you have . . . not despised the most lowly, . . . you are with the wretched . . . , to raise up . . . the poor . . . [by your] grace" (1QH v. 20-21). The Old Testament insight that God is on the side of the poor and oppressed leads to an understanding of faith as poverty before God in the sense of expecting everything of him. This attitude also helps explain the term "the least of these" applied to the disciples (see the discussion of 10:42).

. [26] God's "pleasure" is his gracious elective will, as promised in the angels' Christmas hymn to "men of his pleasure." The Qumran sect is also familiar with the idea that revelation means election (1QS xi. 15-18; 1QH x. 27 ff.; xiv. 12-15, 25). Jesus, however, differs from the Qumran theology and perhaps also from Q: he is not speaking of special eschatological secrets, but of the full knowledge of God spoken of in the next verse. The humble and poor to whom this knowledge is granted are not those who fulfill the Law in exemplary fashion, but those to whom verse 30 promises an easy yoke and a light burden. For what God reveals in Jesus is not merely new insight into Scripture but his way of dealing with men, his righteousness as Isaiah 56:1 and Romans 1:16-17 put it, his arm as Isaiah 52:10 puts it, or his finger as Luke 11:20 states. A new note is struck, not heard in the opening words of the Sermon on the Mount; what was promised to the poor there is understood here as present fact in Jesus. In Jesus God breaks through into the world, the God before whom a man cannot be wise or rich, but also need not be, because he can dare to surrender himself totally to him, can expect everything from him, and live without anxiety.

[27] One set of manuscripts reads in the opposite order: "No one knows the Father except the Son, and no one knows the Son except the Father." This makes the transition to the last clause difficult, however. Above all, that is the usual Greek and also Gnostic view: it is the Father who is unknown; the distance of the invisible God is the real problem, to which the Son brings the solution. In this saying, however, the situation is reversed: the one who is truly unknown, whom no one but the Father understands, is Jesus—whom even the Baptist doubts (vss. 2-3), whom his own home town rejects (vss. 20-24), but who can still (vs. 25) give thanks for this failure. The same point is made by Matthew 16:17 and Galatians 1:16: it is God who reveals his Son to men.

"Knowledge" is not primarily an intellectual process; in the Old Testament it refers to election (Amos 3:2: "You only do I know of all the families of the earth"), to a man's choice of his wife, and to the sexual act. In Greek the words for "know" and "beget" are related, as are "kin" and "ken" in English. Here, too, we are to think of a personal bond. The Greeks at the time of Jesus spoke of the mutual knowledge of God and man; but the boundary between the two becomes blurred, because the Greeks understood God as a force of nature with which man can feel himself one. The New Testament learned from the Old that there can be true knowledge of God only when he knows us (Gal. 4:9; 1 Cor. 8:2-3; 13:12; cf. Exod. 33:12-13; 1 Kings 8:39, 43). Thus the Father's elective love for the Son furnishes the basis on which the Son in turn knows the Father and can reveal him to others.

In the time of Jesus interest in things eschatological was rising, and with it an attention to those who had insight into the end—such insight was thought to be knowledge of God, and hence characteristic of God's favorite (1QpHab vii. 2-5; 2 Esd. 4:21 ff.; especially Eth. Enoch 60:1-3, 10). Thus at Qumran, election, knowledge of God, and revelation are all linked (1QS iv. 22; cf. 1QH xviii. 23-24), and the Old Testament itself looks forward to knowledge of God at the eschaton. The land will then be filled with the knowledge of God (Isa. 11:9); he will be known personally to everyone in the nation (Isa. 52:6), from the least to the greatest (Jer. 31:33-34). This is the background against which we must understand our saying.

Totally new is the exclusiveness with which only one, the Son, is chosen by God to know him. We do not, however, find the statement of the mystic, "The Father knows no one except the Son," but rather, "No one knows the Son except the Father." That is the danger, that no one will recognize him. The saying might be taken as a parable: only a father can know his son, and only a son can know his father.

The saying may derive from Jesus himself. The allusion to his own special status would be in line with his other statements. On the other hand, as a realistic parable the saying is not really convincing—even in that period men were better known to their wives or even good friends than to their fathers. What is more, the introduction and above all the concluding clause, which no longer speaks of the "son" in metaphorical terms, are hard to reconcile with the idea that the saying is an aphorism.

It is very likely that the saying was formulated after Jesus' death and refers to the eschatological age, which he inaugurated. This interpretation is the more plausible because "Son" and "Father" used as absolute terms (as here) also appear elsewhere in sayings referring specifically to the eschaton (Mark 13:32; 1 Cor. 15:28). The close resemblance of our saying to several about wisdom or the Logos (see the discussion of vss. 28-30), often understood as the "Son" of God, suggests that the "Son" expression (here and elsewhere) comes from wisdom literature, which was, of course, thoroughly eschatological. This theory is also supported by the beginning of the saying, "My Father [or possibly, as in several good manuscripts, 'the Father'] has given me all things," which sounds like a saying more appropriate to the risen Lord (28:18), and is once again formulated in the language of eschatology (Dan. 7:14).

For Q this was probably a central saying. Like Galatians 1:15-16, it described the crucial Easter experience of the community: what happened on Easter was like the revelation of the Son of Man to the elect in Ethiopian Enoch 48:7 and 62:7. Now a small group of the elect knows the Son of Man, to whom all power is given (28:18); but he will be revealed to the world as a whole at the Last Judgment.

What is new is the conclusion to which the saying leads: the Son himself (and his disciples: see 10:26 and 28:19-20) will reveal this mystery. Even as the unrecognized Son he is the Lord of the universe, God's elect. But only God truly knows this, and conversely only the Son has insight into what God has done. It is only through the Son that men can gain insight into God's plan and so be incorporated into his sonship. Later John will frequently make the same point (3:35-36; 5:19-26).

[28-30] The final saying is closely related to Ecclesiasticus 51:-23-27; cf. also 6:24-31. In both texts the yoke of wisdom is associated with the promise of rest. Now in Judaism wisdom was identified with Law (Ecclus. 24:23). The rabbis also spoke of the Law as the yoke of the Kingdom of God, which men must put on (Billerbeck on vs. 29 A b. c). Matthew is probably glancing at this idea, especially the individual commandments of Pharisaic legalism, which were impossible to fulfill (23:4; cf. Acts 15:10).

Up to now we have heard that God (vs. 25) or the Son (vs. 27) will reveal the hidden wisdom of God; now Jesus calls all men to himself to give them final "rest." Hence he is no longer simply the bearer of the wisdom of God: he in fact becomes that wisdom. Like him, wisdom calls out, "Come to me, you unlearned" (Ecclus. 51:23). It is only Matthew who records this identification of Jesus with wisdom (see the excursus on 23:34-39). The "yoke" should probably be pictured not just as the ordinary yoke that a laborer lays across his shoulders with containers on both ends, but as the yoke imposed by the victor on the vanquished (e.g. Jer. 28:10-14). Thus a cuneiform inscription reads: "He sent all through a yoke without pause," i.e. his military conquests were unceasing. This is also the sense intended by Sirach; moreover, Sirach calls on men to bow their necks beneath the yoke of the Law in order that they may find rest when their labor is finished—their burden will be brief compared to their reward. Jesus says, however, that it is not toil and labor that lead to rest, but following after him who is as gentle as if humbled—following not after a conqueror but one who apppears conquered (cf. the discussion of 21:5). Because Jesus is himself among those who are tired and burdened, he can inspire the disciple to follow his life of total openness to God and thus attain true peace (see the discussion of 10:13), as verse 29 states, borrowing from Jeremiah 6:16.

The purpose of the three sayings is to assert God's divinity. That only the Son reveals this divinity means that we cannot plumb the nature of God, but can speak truly of him only when we see him from the perspective of Jesus as the one who is God in his giving and loving. There is no God per se; there is only the God who extends himself to the Son and his sons.

At the same time, however, the point is maintained that we do not have the Son at our disposal, like a regular monthly check we can count on. Who the Son is we do not know; only the Father knows. Whether we picture him as the soul's bridegroom or a social reformer, we are picturing him in our own likeness. This is also demonstrated by the long history of his representation in art. The path to God passes through poverty, immaturity in our understanding, burdens imposed on our souls. The poor, the immature, and the burdened are promised that they will attain what no learning and no successful activity can attain: the quiet in which a man can understand his life as God's gift and be free for real service to God and to his neighbor.

Perhaps Matthew was **aware** of the relationship between these sayings and the last verses of his Gospel. As in 11:27, the risen Lord declares that all power in heaven and earth has been given to him (28:18); as the disciples are called to come in 11:28, they are called to go forth into the world (28:19); and as they are to learn from him (11:29), so they are to teach (28:19; the Greek words derive from the same root: "learn to be disciples"/"make disciples"). Here (11:29) peace is promised to them; later (28:20) the presence of Jesus is promised until the end of the world. Thus chronologically Jesus occupies the middle ground between Jewish wisdom teachers who call men to the Law (Ecclus. 51; cf. 24; Prov. 1:20 ff.; 8:1 ff.) and later Christians who borrow this saying (Gospel of Thomas 90) or frame similar sayings themselves (Odes of Solomon 33), but in doing so offer men freedom from the material world through the heavenly knowledge given to the initiate. Jesus' own subject matter is quite different: he is speaking of discipleship, which gives men freedom from the Law and the criteria by which the world judges, thus placing them in the service of the world.

III

JESUS CONFRONTS HIS OPPONENTS
12:1–16:12

Here Matthew follows the structure of Mark 2:23–8:26; but he omits the selection of the Twelve (Mark 3:13-19; see the discussion of Matt. 10:1), the statement of Jesus' family that he is mad (Mark 3:20-21), the previously recounted miracles (4:35–5:43), the mission of the disciples, likewise already recounted (6:6-13), the return of the disciples (6:30-31; see the conclusion of the introductory remarks on Matt. 10:1-16), and the healing of a blind man at Bethsaida (Mark 8:22-26), probably because two other healings of the blind have already been recounted. Matthew elaborates the Beelzebul discussion by including material from Q, as well as the demand for a sign, the saying about the sign of Jonah, and the warning against apostasy (Matt. 12:38-45). Matthew presents these three sections at a later point than Q, who places them right after a passage corresponding to Matthew 11:20-27. Q may have, like Luke (11:9-13), prefaced the Beelzebul section with a passage that Matthew uses earlier (Matt. 7:7-11), as part of the discussion of prayer.

Matthew's use of a variety of Q material (12:32-35) to interpret the saying in 12:31 about blasphemy against the Spirit shows how he understands the saying. This continues the friction between Jesus and the people, which was hinted at in the doubts of the Baptist (11:3) and came into full view in 11:16-24. In the following chapters leading up to Peter's confession, the immature and burdened become more and more sharply distinguished from the mass of the people. As in Mark, we find first a chapter of parables, where Matthew's editorial work is especially significant, destroying the unity of the parables assembled in Mark 4, all of which deal with seed and harvest. Matthew's replacement of the parable of the seed growing by itself, whose point is not to his taste, with that of the weeds is still appropriate to Mark's framework.

But in the very next parable, Mark's parable of the mustard seed, we can see the altering influence of the Q recension: as in Q, the mustard seed parable has the parable of the yeast appended to it (13:31-33), and this changes its significance. In what follows the new note comes through clearly. At the conclusion of the parables which parallel Mark, Matthew recalls the one about the weeds and explains its significance (13:36-43) and then appends three additional parables all linguistically similar to the parables of the mustard seed and yeast in Q. This can best be explained by the hypothesis that Matthew found these two parables in Q but was also familiar with them in association with the other three in an oral or written collection. The resulting division into parables for the people (13:1-33) and for the disciples (13:36-52) is not justified by the text, since verses 10-23 are also spoken to the disciples and verses 40-50 do not differ from the parables spoken to the people. It is possible that the parable of the weeds belonged to a special collection (cf. the introductory remarks on 13:24-30). Finally a parabolic saying about a homeowner is appended (13:52). From 14:1 on Matthew follows Mark throughout, only altering details, though often in highly characteristic fashion; as usual, Matthew at times truncates the Markan account (e.g. 14:3-12), or enriches it with new episodes (14:28-31; cf. 15:23-24).

The New Interpretation of the Law (12:1-8)
Cf. Mark 2:23-28; Luke 6:1-5

¹Not long afterward Jesus was walking through the wheat fields on a Sabbath day. His disciples were hungry, so they began to pick heads of wheat and eat the grain. ²When the Pharisees saw this, they said to Jesus, "Look, your disciples are doing what they are not allowed to do on the Sabbath!" ³Jesus answered, "Have you never read what David did that time when he and his men were hungry? ⁴He went into the house of God and they ate the bread offered to God, even though they were not permitted to eat that bread, only the priests. ⁵Or have you not read in the Law that every Sabbath the priests in the Temple actually break the Sabbath, yet they are not

guilty? ⁶But I tell you, there is something here greater than the Temple. ⁷Scripture says, 'I want mercy and not sacrifice.' If you really knew what this means, you would not condemn people who are not guilty. ⁸For the Son of Man is Lord of the Sabbath."

(Vs. 3—1 Sam. 21:3-6. Vs. 4—Lev. 24:5-9. Vs. 5—Num. 28:9. Vs. 7 —Hos. 6:6 [1 Sam. 15:22; Isa. 1:10-17; Ps. 40:7-8].)

Although Matthew has already introduced the conflict about fasting, this is the first time he associates it with the conflicts about the Sabbath (Mark 2:23–3:6), possibly because the Sabbath of Judaism is considered to foreshadow the great rest promised by God for the eschatological age; for Jesus, the eschatological day will be feasting not fasting (cf. 9:14-15). The creation story in Genesis 1:1–2:3 leads up to the Sabbath, which even there was probably understood as a symbol of the world to come, which would be "all Sabbath." It is therefore possible that Matthew uses the opening words "Not long afterward" (Greek: "At that time") to refer to the promise of rest given in 11:29.

He basically follows Mark, but with significant changes. [7] It is easy to understand why he added Hosea 6:6 in verse 7. The principle that God wants mercy rather than sacrifice would have kept Jesus' opponents from condemning him. [1] This agrees with the addition of the remarks that the disciples "were hungry" and therefore "began to eat," as Mark had already said of David and his group. Since Matthew also added this quotation from Hosea in 9:13, this new interpretation probably goes back to him. In addition, the statement that the Son of Man is Lord of the Sabbath, which is already found in Mark, is now linked directly to verse 7 by the addition of "for," as in 9:13. The Christological basis of the principle in Hosea 6:6 is therefore important to Matthew. For this reason he also had to follow Luke in omitting the statement of Mark 2:27 that the Sabbath was made for man, not the reverse. It would have been out of place in this context and would probably have seemed to Matthew an all too liberal interpretation of God's Law.

[7] Because Jesus has come to call sinners and to reinterpret the Law according to the principle of mercy, meals with tax collectors and

freedom from the Sabbath law are possible. The rabbis speak of the Law, sacrifice, and acts of love as the three pillars that together bear up the world (Billerbeck on 9:13 B); Matthew thinks of acts of love as the eschatological fulfillment of the other two. He does not mean merely that mercy is an acceptable substitute when the other two are impossible, or even that the enlightened mind recognizes the others to be senseless, but that mercy excels the others and therefore abrogates them in case of conflict. This is Jesus' new interpretation of the Law and the cult in eschatological fulfillment.

[5] Verse 5 also presents an argument, based on the Law, alongside the argument based on Biblical history. Several words in this sentence appear only rarely in Matthew. Furthermore, the principle in verse 7 is really in disagreement with verse 5, which probably therefore represents a different attempt, already found in Matthew's sources, to deal with the problem of the Sabbath. Perhaps it was at this stage that Mark's comment about David's needing the bread (Mark 2:25) was lost, since it would actually have suited Matthew's purpose. This of course presupposes that Matthew had access to an altered text of Mark in his community. [6] However that may be, the argument does not really become effective until verse 6: "There is something here greater than the Temple." We may have here an isolated saying of Jesus, especially because this obscure statement does not refer directly to Jesus as that which is greater but rather to the Kingdom of God that comes through him.

We can discern three stages in the answer to the question of the Sabbath, which was a matter of serious concern to the early Christians. As early as Mark, steps had been taken toward the idea that the Law is God's gift to man. The story of David served to illustrate this insight (see the discussion of Mark 2:23-28). The saying about the Son of Man as Lord of the Sabbath (Mark 2:28) led to a theological argument: if it is true that in Jesus something has come "greater than the Temple," then he and his band of disciples at least enjoy the privilege granted the priests, who perform their work on the Sabbath. Matthew incorporates this argument, but he defines more precisely what it means to say something great has come: it has come, to his way of thinking, through the new interpretation of the Law by Jesus, who places mercy above all cultic regulations. By a very minor change in the text of verse 1 (saying the disciples were hungry), Matthew gave point to his theme that mercy transcends legalism: love must allow where Law forbids. This debate over the question of the Sabbath helps us today to understand what God's Law is and what the freedom is which Jesus alone could bring: Freedom places men under an obligation to love and therefore can never become irresponsibility.

Goodness Transcends the Law (12:9-14)
Cf. Mark 3:1-6; Luke 6:6-11; 14:5

[9]Jesus left that place and went to one of their synagogues. [10]A man was there who had a crippled hand. There were some men present who wanted to accuse Jesus of wrongdoing; so they asked him, "Is it permitted to cure on the Sabbath?" [11]Jesus answered, "What if one of you has a sheep and it falls into a well on the Sabbath? Will you not take hold of it and lift it out? [12]And a man is worth much more than a sheep! Therefore it is permitted to do good on the Sabbath." [13]Then he said to the man, "Stretch out your hand." He stretched it out and it became well again, just like the other one. [14]But the Pharisees left and made plans against Jesus to kill him.

Once more Matthew follows the text of Mark. But in place of Jesus' question whether it is permitted to do good on the Sabbath (Mark 3:4), Matthew substitutes the positive statement, which he supports after the fashion of a rabbinic legal decision through comparison with other Sabbath regulations. A very similar substitution is placed in Jesus' mouth in Luke 14:5 on the occasion of another Sabbath healing. The form in Luke 14:5 may be based on an Aramaic pun (son/ox/well). Of course not only Jesus spoke Aramaic; so did the earliest community, which had a great interest in Sabbath regulations. The arguments, presented in rabbinic style, are more what one would expect from the community than from Jesus himself; but Jesus' freedom from all legalism and above all his consequent intervention on behalf of others is well attested. The introduction, "What if one of you has . . ." (also in Luke 14:5), appears to go back to him, since there are no contemporary parallels, whereas the expression is frequent in sayings attributed to him, especially as an introduction to a parable (6:27=Luke

12:25; 7:9=Luke 11:11; Luke 11:5; 14:28; 15:4; 17:7).

[9] Matthew links this episode closely with the preceding one by assigning it unequivocally to the same day. Thus Hosea's saying about mercy, fulfilled through the Son of Man, serves also to introduce the principle stated in verses 11-12. On the phrase "to one of their synagogues," cf. the discussion of 4:23. The Greek text of verse 9 begins "And behold"; cf. the discussion of 8:2. The descriptive details found in Mark 3:3-5 are omitted, and [10] the entire episode is transformed into disputation comprising a question and Jesus' reply. [11] Jesus' almost automatic assumption that the Law permits a man to rescue his sheep from a well contradicts the rabbis and Essenes (CD xi. 13-14). They allow men to be rescued only when they are in peril of their lives; in the case of animals, the most that is allowed is assisting them to escape by themselves. [12] Presumably this principle was still in force in the time of Jesus and the early community. The reference to the dignity and value of every individual decides the question. Man can be seen in this light only from the perspective of faith in his creator. A human being is always more important than property, even a poor man's only sheep. Here, as in verse 7, the appeal is to mercy. The statement that it is permitted to do good on the Sabbath, which is borrowed from Mark, is now expressly introduced as the logical conclusion; it is so abbreviated that it can apply universally to any conceivable case in the life of the community. [13-14] The end of the episode follows Mark, though with the omission of the Herodians, who are hard to define (Mark 3:6).

It becomes clearer here than in Mark that Jesus' very actions have the nature of words, i.e. have something to say to men of all periods. They set men free from all legalism, but show him engaged in a responsibility toward his fellow men greater than any law could impose.

The Charismatic Servant of God (12:15-21)
Cf. Mark 3:7-12; Luke 6:17-19

¹⁵When Jesus heard about it, he went away from that place; and many people followed him. He healed all the sick, ¹⁶and gave them orders not to reveal him, ¹⁷to make come true what was spoken through the prophet Isaiah, who says:

¹⁸"Here is my Servant, whom I have chosen,
    the one I love, with whom I am well pleased.
I will put my Spirit on him,
    and he will proclaim justice to the nations.
¹⁹He will not argue or shout,
    nor will his voice be heard in the streets.
²⁰He will not break off a bent reed,
    nor put out a flickering wick
until he brings justice to victory.
    ²¹And in his name will the nations hope."

(Vss. 18-21—Isa. 42:1-4.)

[15-16] Everything found in verses 15-16a occurs in Mark in the corresponding sequence. Mark merely recounts in more detail the influx of people from everywhere in Palestine and surrounding countries (already mentioned by Matthew in 4:24-25), and the healings that lead to the confession of the Son of God on the part of demons. Instead, verse 15, like 8:16, states that Jesus healed "all," not merely "many." The readying of a boat, which is quite unsuitable for Jesus' healings, is omitted (see the discussion of Mark 3:7-12). The "following" of the crowd (also mentioned in Mark 3:7) may be intended as a deliberate contrast to the Pharisees, who are plotting Jesus' death (vs. 14; see the discussion of 27:25).

[17-21] The addition of a long quotation (cf. the excursus on 1:18-25) from Deutero-Isaiah is significant. Verses 18-20 present a text that agrees with neither the Hebrew nor the Greek Bible, nor yet with any known targums, i.e. translations into the vernacular, which often explicate the text by changes and additions. Echoes of other passages (Isa. 26:8; 50:10; Hab. 1:4) might explain some phrases; but "beloved" is associated in the Old and New Testaments almost exclusively with "son" (daughter, brother), never with "servant" (cf. only Col. 1:7). Thus we may have here a Christian Greek targum that assimilates the text to the story of Jesus' baptism. [21] The last sentence derives undoubtedly from a different hand, for here the text agrees precisely with the Greek Bible. It is probably Matthew's addition.

Matthew does not introduce the quotation to prove that Jesus is the messiah, but to stimulate reflection. It is the longest quotation in his Gospel, and therefore especially noteworthy. **[21]** Through his addition of the last sentence Matthew represents Jesus as the hope of all peoples. Further, he completely omits Mark's description of the crowd and its provenance (Mark 3:8; it appeared in Matt. 4:24-25), because that mentions only Israelites, and Matthew's concern here is all peoples. On the other hand, the quotation talks of the "messianic secret"—which Jesus has just urged upon the crowd (vs. 16)—and this secrecy comes right after the first inkling of a plot to kill Jesus (vs. 14). So it would appear that Matthew is urgently foreshadowing, first, Jesus' death, and second, the hope which that death will open for all nations (cf. John 12:20-24).

[18] Because the quotation is so strongly reminiscent of the voice of God and the gift of the Spirit at Jesus' baptism, it is particularly well suited to represent Jesus' major purpose. When one considers that the word for "servant" can also mean "child" (see the discussion of 8:5-13), the echo of Jesus' baptism becomes even clearer. **[20]** What is stated, then, is that the hope of all nations (as in vs. 18) consists in God's establishment of his justice throughout the entire earth. **[19-20]** It is the justice of one who does not spout propaganda or destroy what is weak. In the face of all messianic expectations, the text emphasizes what Jesus does *not* do. Since the "flickering wick" is undoubtedly a metaphor representing a lamp about to go out, the image of a bent reed fits the context better than that of a staff bent to signify the death sentence, which may have been the original meaning of the phrase in the Old Testament. Despite its totally different language and theology, this passage is remarkably reminiscent of Paul's proclamation of the righteousness of God which seeks to establish itself on earth among all the nations. Behind both modes of expression stands the knowledge of what the preceding section already suggested: God's justice seeks men out and intervenes on their behalf, on behalf of their dignity and their rights. For this reason it is not a shattering judgment but a supportive justice, under which victory goes to the one whose purpose is not to carry the day for his own cause but to intervene on behalf of the weak.

The Hardness of Men's Hearts (12:22-37)
Cf. Mark 3:22-30; 9:40; Luke 11:14-23; 12:10; 6:43-45

²²Then some people brought a demoniac to Jesus who was blind and dumb. Jesus healed the man, so that the dumb man could speak and see. ²³The crowds were all amazed. "Could he be the Son of David?" they asked. ²⁴When the Pharisees heard this they replied, "He drives out demons only through Beelzebul, the ruler of the demons."

²⁵Jesus knew what they were thinking and said to them, "Any kingdom at variance with itself is devastated. And any town or family that is at variance with itself will fall apart. ²⁶So if Satan drives out Satan, he is at variance with himself; how will his kingdom endure? ²⁷You say that I drive out demons through Beelzebul. Well, then, through whom do your followers drive them out? Therefore they will be your judges. ²⁸But if I drive out demons through the Spirit of God, then God's sovereignty has come among you!

²⁹"Or how can someone break into a strong man's house and take away his belongings unless he ties up the strong man first? Then he can plunder his house. ³⁰Anyone who is not for me is against me; anyone who does not help me gather is scattering.

³¹"Therefore I tell you: men can be forgiven any sin and any blasphemy; but whoever blasphemes against the Spirit will not be forgiven. ³²Anyone who says something against the Son of Man can be forgiven; but whoever says something against the Holy Spirit will not be forgiven, neither in this age nor in the age to come.

³³"To have good fruit you must have a healthy tree; if you have a poor tree you will have bad fruit. For a tree is known by the kind of fruit it bears. ³⁴You brood of snakes, how can you say good things when you are evil? For the mouth speaks what the heart is full of. ³⁵A good man brings good things out of his treasure of good things; a bad man brings bad things out of his treasure of bad things. ³⁶I tell you this: on the Judgment Day everyone will have to give account of every useless word he has ever spoken. ³⁷For by your words you will be justified, and by your words you will be condemned."

[22-30] At first Matthew in the main follows Mark. Unlike Mark, however, he does not begin with the accusation by Jesus' opponents, but, like Luke 11:14-15, first cites the occasion, the healing of a demoniac. He has already told the same story in 9:32-34. [22-24] In both passages he merely reports that the sick man was brought to Jesus and that the Pharisees (in Mark 3:22 the teachers of the Law, in Luke 11:15 some of the people) made their accusation. Did the question of miracles figure in the dispute with Pharisaic Judaism in the time of Jesus?

The same word is used for "demoniac" in both Matthaean passages; it is not used in either Mark or Luke. What is new is the statement that the sick man is also blind and the question about the Son of David (cf. the discussion of 15:22; 21:9, 15). [24] This catchword appeared in 9:27, but not in 9:32-34. Here the name "Beelzebul" appears (see the discussion of 10:25), which also appears in the two other Gospels but was omitted in 9:34. [27] It does not reappear until verse 27; Satan appears in the intervening passage. In the earliest form of this episode, verse 27 was therefore probably the response to the accusation in verse 24. In Luke 11:18b we see the transition from one tradition to the other. [25-26] In the intervening section, first Mark 3:25 and then 3:23 became associated with appropriate formulations from Q (cf. the introductory remarks on 10:1-16).

[28] Verse 28 is probably a later addition to the argument in verse 27; in the present context, one could argue with equal cogency that God's Kingdom has arrived in the exorcisms of the Pharisees' disciples (cf. the discussion of vs. 45). Here, however, Jesus declares that the Kingdom of God has arrived in him; later, when linked with the Beelzebul charge, this declaration was expanded by the argument in verse 27. Here as elsewhere Matthew borrows heavily from Q (Luke 11:15-20); but verses 25b-26a are reminiscent of the wording in Mark 3:25 and 23b.

[29] Verse 29 agrees almost word for word with the shortest version in Mark 3:27. It proves that Luke 11:14-23 was already in fixed form in Q. Although Matthew cites it in the shorter recension of Mark, he does not, like Mark, append it to verse 27 (=Mark 3:26), but to the place where the closely related verses Luke 11:21-22 stand, and then in verse 30 Matthew immediately adds the concluding state-

ment of Luke 11:23 (cf. also the introductory remarks on vss. 43-45).

[31-32] In the saying about blasphemy against the Spirit, Matthew combines the Markan recension with the one used in Luke 12:10. An Aramaic original has been postulated, understood by some as: "Any blasphemy committed by the children of men will be forgiven" (vs. 31a = Mark 3:28), and by others as: "Anyone who blasphemes against the Son of Man will be forgiven" (vs. 32a = Luke 12:10a). This was then followed by the saying about blasphemy against the Spirit. This theory is possible, but cf. the introductory remarks on Mark 3:20-35. In any case the saying in the recension of verse 32a came into being in the post-Easter community (see below).

[33-35] There follows a section that also appears in the Sermon on the Plain (Luke 6:43-45). We have already met it in 7:16-20, albeit in another form. Matthew introduces it once more because, while dealing with the idea of confession, he mentions for the first time sinning in speech. Therefore Matthew takes the catchword "say," which does not appear until the end in Luke (6:45), and uses it in verse 34, underlining its significance by means of the hostile epithet "brood of snakes," which he takes over from the preaching of the Baptist (3:7). In similar fashion he inserted a saying of the Baptist (3:10) in 7:19. On the identification of Jesus' message with that of the Baptist, see the discussion of 3:2 and the introductory remarks on 11:7-19. Verse 33, whose content was already incorporated in 7:17 from Luke 6:43, is now introduced in better Greek. Luke 6:44b (figs from thistles, etc.) he omits because it has already appeared in 7:16. That a tree is known by its fruit is repeated here literally and in somewhat different form in 6:20-21; the sayings that refer to speech (Luke 6:45) appear only here in verses 34-35.

[36] Finally Matthew appends still another independent saying on the same theme and follows it [37] with a second, similar saying, which, as the change from second person plural to second person singular shows, was not originally associated with the first. It is no longer possible to determine to what extent Matthew combined the two recensions and to what extent they had already influenced each other and become linked in the course of transmission. The schema of verses 31-32 (see the introductory remarks on vs. 19) derived from a combination of Mark (vs. 31) and Q (vs. 32); the term "say against"

corresponds to Matthew 5:11. The construction of Luke 12:10, however, with the first sentence beginning "Anyone who . . ." and the second sentence appended by means of a participle and "but," has been assimilated to the preceding verses, not originally part of the passage, which speak of confessing or (unforgivably) denying the Son of Man.

[22] By the use of "then," one of his favorite words, but above all through his choice of the verb "he healed the man" (instead of "the demon was driven out"), Matthew deliberately links this healing with the acts of Jesus described in verse 15, to which the quotation about the Servant of God refers. [23] This is made even clearer by the addition of the question asked by the crowd; for "Son of David" naturally means the promised eschatological king, who is described in Ezekiel 34:23; 37:25 as the Servant of God. By his deeds Jesus shows himself to be the long expected Servant of God, the promised "Son" of David, whose father, according to 2 Samuel 7:12 ff., will be God himself. The crowd is amazed, as Matthew puts it with a word he does not use elsewhere, because they cannot account for their previous lack of faith. [24] This can only be countered with the charge of magic, an accusation that Jewish sources also make against Jesus. According to Matthew, it is directed primarily against the confession of Jesus as Son of David.

[25] The words about the kingdom, which appear in Mark 3:24 as well as in Luke 11:17 (Q), are expanded by Matthew through the insertion of "town" between "kingdom" and "family." Beelzebul is thus thought of in terms of a "kingdom," that is, a sovereign power that takes the field against God's work in Jesus, who is likewise conceived as a power, the "Kingdom of God," and engages it in inevitable combat. [26] This is underlined by the powerful image of driving out Satan. [27] Exorcism was also practised in Judaism (Acts 19:13; Josephus, *Ant.* viii. 45-49; cf. *Bell. Jud.* vii. 185). The Greek text speaks of "your sons," in the sense of membership in a group (as in 8:12 and elsewhere); here it means the disciples of the Pharisees; in Luke, following a different introduction in 11:15, it refers simply to the Israelites.

[28] The saying that follows is one of the most amazing in the

Gospels: God's Kingdom has already come among those who see the acts of Jesus. In 1 Thessalonians 2:16, the same word is used for something that has already come upon someone; in 4:15 it even has the meaning "precede." In both cases the context is eschatological. More is therefore meant than just proximity (4:17). That the expression "Kingdom of God" is not corrected to read "Kingdom of heaven," as elsewhere, shows that Matthew considers the form of the saying fixed. The presence of the Kingdom has already been attested by the Beatitudes in 5:3 ff., the phrase "But now I tell you" in 5:21 ff., the reference to the fulfillment of Isaiah's promises in 11:4, and the actual forgiveness of sins in 9:2. It was already proclaimed in 11:12, as the focus of hostility and oppression to come (the parables about the apparently meaningless labor of the sower or the smallness of the mustard seed in 13:1 ff. will illustrate the potency of the Kingdom for arousing ire).

The irruption of the Kingdom of God is depicted more clearly here than anywhere else. Matthew refers to the "Spirit" on account of verses 18 and 31-32; Luke, who does not include the first passage at all and does not cite the second until 12:10, uses the more primitive and impressive term "finger of God" (Luke 11:20; cf. Exod. 8:19; Ps. 8:6). God, as it were, is already stretching forth his finger from his hiddenness, so that what is to come in the future is already breaking into the present. Just this is for Matthew the work of the "Spirit," whom verse 18 has promised and whom verses 32-33 warn men not to blaspheme against. Matthew thus emphasizes the importance of Jesus' charismatic acts (see the discussion of 9:35).

[29] This is underlined by the image of a strong man being overcome by someone stronger (see the discussion of Mark 3:27) and by the concluding sentence, [30] which appeals urgently to men to decide for Jesus. There are times when one can no longer remain neutral. This goes beyond Mark 9:40 ("Whoever is not against us is for us"); there it is only joining the band of disciples that is under discussion, not confession of Jesus, whose name, according to Mark 9:38-40, the unknown exorcist has just confessed. Ecumenical openness (Mark 9:40) and the unambiguous demand for a clear confession of Jesus (Matt. 12:30) are certainly compatible.

[31-32] Originally the forgivable sin against the Son of Man prob-

ably meant rejection of the earthly Jesus out of ignorance (Acts 3:17), since he is also called the Son of Man (Matt. 8:20; 9:6; 11:19; 12:8; 16:13). The period after Pentecost, in which the Spirit works (John 7:39), is distinguished from this, so that only a deliberate attack on the Spirit is unforgivable. Or does the saying go back to the view of Jesus as the bearer and messenger of wisdom in Q (see the excursus on 23:34-39)? The Son of Man as the one who shows wisdom to be right was already the subject of 11:19. The saying would then mean that men might scorn even the messenger without being irrevocably lost, but not the wisdom which God sends by him, which is also equated with the Spirit of God in Wisdom of Solomon 9:10, 17. Neither interpretation can be assumed for Matthew himself. For him Jesus is identical with wisdom and the Son of Man is already the exalted Judge of the universe, not merely the earthly Jesus (12:40; 13:37, 41; 16:27-28; 19:28; 24:27 ff.; 25:31; 26:64). What is probably meant, then, is that lack of faith is forgivable as long as it is merely a response to a report about the Son of Man, but not when the great works of the Spirit, described in verse 28, take place. Because Matthew also had in mind works of Christ in the post-Easter community, he did not follow Mark 3:30 in making the threat refer explicitly to Jesus' contemporary opponents.

[33] In the Greek text the antithesis is rhetorically formulated "either . . . or . . . ," emphasizing the necessity of a decision. What matters is not the performance of individual good deeds or the avoidance of wicked deeds, but a wholeness that begins with the roots, to which the fruit merely bears witness. [34] The phrase about the brood of snakes strongly underlines the warning against radical evil. Since Matthew applies this phrase in 3:7 (contrary to Luke; cf. the discussion of 11:13) and 23:33 to the Pharisees (and Sadducees), and since verses 32, 34, 36 deal with evil speaking, he is probably directing his attack on their polemic against the proclamation of Christ. This is more likely than the hypothesis that Matthew is seeking to protect himself against false prophets who appeal to the Holy Spirit (vs. 32) but bear bad fruit and speak evil (vss. 33-37). The reference to the heart emphasizes once more that what the mouth utters derives from a man's inmost being and bears witness to it (cf. the discussion of 7:16-18). [35] The same thing is meant by the "treasure" that a man may possess. [36-37] In the final two sentences, Matthew, as is typical

of him, speaks explicitly of the Last Judgment, in which a man's justification or condemnation will depend on what he has said. "Useless" words are not those that are totally neutral, but those that are wicked and ultimately godless (cf. Ecclus. 23:15 ms. S, and the use of "fool" as a term for the godless in Ps. 14:1; Judg. 19:22; etc.); in this context Matthew is referring to blasphemy against the Spirit.

The entire section is dominated by Jesus' saying about the sudden presence of the Kingdom of God. What is extraordinary is not the healings and exorcisms, but the fact that Jesus is so clearly aware of the "finger" of God at work in them. Not in men's decision for God, not even in the proclamation of this decision, but in the authority and power that touches men in Jesus and makes them whole—there God's Kingdom breaks through. This does not abolish its futurity, quite the contrary. It is the coming Kingdom that breaks through here, and without the prospect of a fulfillment to come the promises would be empty. Anyone who sees the Kingdom of God in the healing of two or even twenty madmen must either be mad himself or else be speaking and acting from an authority that knows that God will one day redeem his promises.

The man willing to hear these words of Jesus will live. Those who are healed are not first asked what they believe and what they consider possible or impossible; neither does the increase or decrease of faith alter the fact that the Kingdom has already broken through. Of course this is coupled with perhaps the strongest warning in the whole New Testament (vss. 31-32), and Matthew has yoked verse 28 with it by his choice of the word "Spirit." When a man is no longer willing to be amazed, or at least to leave questions open, but strives instead to account for all the works of God's Spirit in terms of what is already familiar to him, e.g. magic; when he would rather accept belief in the devil or some more modern explanation of the inexplicable than admit the possibility of a real and effective act of God; then this breakthrough of the Kingdom becomes the judgment of God upon him.

The Sign of God (12:38-42)
Cf. Luke 11:29-32; Mark 8:11-12

[38]Then some teachers of the Law and some Pharisees spoke up. "Teacher," they said, "we want to see you perform a sign." [39]"An evil

and adulterous generation demands a sign, and none will be given them except the sign of the prophet Jonah. [40]In the same way that 'Jonah spent three days and three nights in the belly of the monster,' so will the Son of Man spend three days and nights in the depths of the earth. [41]On Judgment Day the people of Nineveh will stand up and condemn this generation; for they turned from their sins when they heard Jonah preach; and there is something here, I tell you, greater than Jonah! [42]On the Judgment Day the Queen from the South will stand up and condemn you; for she traveled from the ends of the earth to hear Solomon's teaching; and there is something here, I tell you, greater than Solomon!"

(Vs. 40—Jon. 2:1 [1:17]. Vs. 41—Jon. 3:5. Vs. 42—1 Kings 10:1-10.)

[38-40] The relationship of this section to the parallel traditions is very revealing. In Luke 11:16, 29-32 the demand for a sign is closely interwoven with the Beelzebul discourse. Matthew therefore is following Q by inserting it here (cf. the introductory remarks on vss. 43-45). Mark, on the contrary, associates this occurrence with the feeding of the multitude; according to John 6:30, too, the feeding is followed by a demand for a sign. Matthew too repeats it in that context, though oddly not in the words of Mark, from whom he borrows the introduction (the question by the Pharisees) and the conclusion (Jesus' departure) in 16:1, 4; in the central section, 16:2a, 4 he repeats 12:39 word for word, except that the sign of Jonah is not explicated in detail, and instead another saying about the demand for a sign (not found in some good ancient manuscripts but similar to Luke 12:54-56) is interpolated (16:2b, 3).

The first part of Jesus' response is composed by Matthew himself in 12:39 as well as in 16:2; otherwise, apart from the addition of "and adulterous" (and "of the prophet" in 12:39) as well as a minor change in the verb, Jesus' answer agrees precisely with Luke 11:29. The expression "so will the Son of Man . . ." (vs. 40) likewise occurs in precisely this form in Luke 12:40, albeit in a totally different saying. This shows that Q probably contained something like the statement in Luke 11:30 ("so too will the Son of Man be a sign to this generation"), although the short recension without any apodosis (Matt.

16:4) suggests that earlier only the cryptic saying about the sign of Jonah was transmitted without any explication. Thus Matthew follows Q, but, like Mark 8:11, involves the Pharisees in the conversation. On the other hand, at the place where he follows Mark (Matt. 16:1-4) he recalls almost these precise words, but without the elaboration, also lacking in Luke 11:29-30, that compares Jesus' stay in the tomb to Jonah's in the belly of the fish. The Pharisees are joined here by the teachers of the Law, in 16:1 by the Sadducees.

[41-42] In verses 41-42, unlike Luke 11:31-32, the inhabitants of Nineveh are mentioned before the Queen of the South. Luke's sequence is in chronological order; Matthew links the Ninevites with Jonah because he preached to them, perhaps in order to state explicitly that the generation that rejects the sign of Jonah, namely the crucifixion (and resurrection) of Jesus, now stands under God's judgment. Originally Jonah was selected as the example, because a story is told of his success in bringing about repentance through preaching, and in a heathen land to boot. A similar statement appears in a Jewish exposition of Lamentations: "I sent a prophet to Nineveh, and he made them repent and turn from their sins. But these Israelites in Jerusalem—how many prophets I have sent to them!" In this form the cryptic saying in verse 39 could have been spoken by Jesus. But as soon as the comparison to the Son of Man (in the form of Luke 11:30) is added, the idea of verse 41 (Luke 11:32) must also be stated, as in the Jewish example. Otherwise the comparison does not work; for "as Jonah became a sign to the Ninevites" by bringing them to repent, so the Son of Man does *not* succeed with this generation. Has Matthew then preserved the correct sequence? If so, then Q would already be saying that Jonah became a sign to a heathen people, but will not become a sign to this generation until the Ninevites put them to shame at the Last Judgment, when it will be too late. In this case the entire thought might go back to Jesus, precisely because it is formulated with as much reserve as in verse 6 (see below).

We are thus dealing with two variants; according to one (Mark 8:11-12), all signs will be denied to "this generation"; according to the other (Q), only the sign of Jonah will be given to "this wicked generation." Matthew then later interprets this sign as referring to the crucifixion (and resurrection) of Jesus. The opposite process, suggesting that Luke eliminated this interpretation only because "three days and three nights" is not precisely correct (but cf. "after three days" in Matt. 27:63; Mark 8:31; etc.), is very unlikely. Such interpretations are often appended, e.g. when the Old Testament is translated into the vernacular and incorporated into the New Testament. The formulation in Mark 8:11-12 is probably an abbreviated version of the Q recension because people no longer knew what the sign of Jonah was. There is no actual contradiction, because according to Q it is not what the inquirers mean by a sign (see below).

[38] "Sign" is not merely another word for "miracle." In the first three Gospels (unlike John 2:11; Acts 2:43; Rom. 15:19; Heb. 2:4) it never refers to healings or miraculous deeds; only Christ himself (Luke 2:34; cf. 12) or the events of the eschaton (Matt. 24:3, 30) are "signs." What Jesus' opponents want is an unambiguous demonstration, an event "from heaven" (Matt. 16:1; Mark 8:11; Luke 11:16). [39] This very desire shows them to be an evil generation; the indefinite article may point beyond the time of Jesus. They are "adulterous" in the Old Testament sense, where idolatry is designated as adultery towards God (Jer. 13:27; Isa. 57:3 ff.; Hos. 1–3).

There probably are concrete ways Jesus' authority might be demonstrated; but just as it would spell the end of love if a husband were no longer content with the daily experience of his wife's love but demanded proof, so the demand for a sign spells the end of faith. Where guarantees are demanded, confidence has vanished. This would make God an object we could master. But what is the sign of Jonah? Is it the sign that Jonah gives or the sign that he himself represents? Luke states merely that the Son of Man himself will be the sign of Jonah. So we should probably understand the sign as explained in Luke 11:32=Matthew 12:41. Just as Jonah's preaching was God's sign to the men of Nineveh, so the Son of Man is God's sign in calling this generation to repentance; the only difference is that the Ninevites did in fact repent, and this generation does not. If verse 41 formed part of the passage from the very beginning, we should think of the Son of Man confronting this generation at the Day of Judgment, even though the Greek future ("will be" Luke 11:30) cannot serve as evidence for the Aramaic original, which probably had no verb at all. We may suppose in any case that at least Q, in the saying about the men of Nineveh, was already thinking of the Last Judgment, when

Jesus would appear to them as the eschatological "sign" they had been demanding—but would condemn them (cf. 10:33).

[40] Matthew is thinking of the Jonah who confronted the Ninevites after being trapped three days in the belly of the fish; he is a symbol of the Son of Man. There is no mention of Jonah's deliverance or of the resurrection of Jesus; but the limitation of the period in the tomb to three days itself shows that Matthew is probably thinking of Jesus as the risen Lord (cf. the discussion of 12:32). [41-42] The people of Nineveh (Jon. 3:5) and the Queen of the South (1 Kings 10:1-13; 2 Chron. 9:1-12) are heathen. Originally, no doubt, this point was stressed, less to the glory of the heathen than to the shame of the Israelites (as in 3:9; 11:21-24). The words "they will stand up" could also be translated "they will be resurrected," but this idea is probably not the one to be emphasized. Twice we hear: "Something greater than Jonah is here . . . greater than Solomon." As in verse 6, the reference is to a greater event, not to a greater individual. What has now appeared is not only greater than the Temple and its High Priest (vs. 6), but also greater than the prophet and greater than the king chosen by God; this is obvious to anyone who has faith, and it need not be stated directly. The combination of king, priest, and prophet occurs also in Josephus as an extraordinary designation for a king of Israel (*Ant.* xiii. 299). Josephus, however, does not speak of anything being "greater."

Thus the purpose of these sayings is to help faith be truly faith. If men want guarantees, they can no longer learn to trust God. They are therefore warned: precisely because Jesus was in the world and, like Jonah in Nineveh, called men to repentance by word and deed, God's Last Judgment will take place. Thus it is both a final warning against the self-satisfaction that closes itself to this event and a final promise: in what Jesus says and does God's Kingdom is in fact already present; it comes to men and awaits their response of faith.

Apostasy (12:43-45)
Cf. Luke 11:24-26

[43]"When an evil spirit goes out of a man, it travels over dry country looking for a place to rest, and finds none. [44]Then it says to

itself, 'I will go back to my house which I left.' So it goes back and finds the house empty, clean, and all fixed up. ⁴⁵Then it goes out and brings along seven other spirits even worse than itself, and they come and live there. And the end of this man is worse than his beginning. This is the way it will happen to this evil generation."

Aside from the last short sentence, we find the same text almost word for word in Luke 11:24-26. This means that it derives from Q. The sequence in Matthew is clearer, however. In the Beelzebul discussion (12:24-30) and in the demand for a sign (12:38-42) the response follows immediately upon the question. The intervening section in Q (Luke 11:24-26) he now introduces, as his addition at the end shows, as a final warning to "this evil generation" (see the discussion of vs. 39). [43] The fate of the single individual mentioned in verse 43 is typical, according to Matthew, of an entire generation. There are times when the temptation to apostasy is repeated a thousandfold. The departure of the demon is vividly depicted (cf. 8:32). The desert is its home (Lev. 16:8, 10, 26). The rabbis interpreted Joel 2:20 as referring to the departure of Satan.

[44] Verse 44 is probably to be understood as a Semitic proverb: "When the demon comes and finds it empty . . . , then . . . ." The parable is directed against incomplete repentance. A heart that has merely been emptied of vices without the entrance of the one who should be its Lord is not proof against a new assault by demons. The reference is not to Jesus' exorcisms but to nominal conversions. Paul, for example, understood that his legalistic religion enabled him to be "blameless" with respect to the requirements of the Law, but led him to a self-proved reliance on his "own righteousness," which was worse than the usual vices (Phil. 3:6, 9). Matthew's thought is not this far advanced; but he sees that the critical danger is rejection of Jesus, which prevents him from taking possession of the human heart. [45] This is shown by the last sentence. The only way to keep air out of a vessel is to fill it, with liquid, for example. Thus Jesus differs from the Pharisees (vs. 27) in that with him the Kingdom itself comes and fills the heart.

very much to see what you see, but they could not, and to hear what you hear, but they did not."

(Vs. 13 = Jer. 5:21. Vss. 14-15 = Isa. 6:9-10.)

Matthew has greatly elaborated this intervening section, which raises serious problems even in its Markan form. **[10]** In the first place, the disciples "come to" Jesus (cf. the discussion of 8:2) and phrase their question more precisely than in Mark. They no longer ask what the parable means; in Mark they are the inner circle and no longer need explanations. The parable form, which Matthew construes as being cryptic, is addressed only to those whose hearts are hardened and who do not understand (vss. 10, 13: "to them"). Neither does Matthew now say that Jesus is alone with his disciples (Mark 4:10). **[11]** Does he have in mind a private conversation out on the lake in the boat? Jesus' response is known to Matthew in a different form, which is also used in Luke 8:10. The plural "secrets" and the word "knowledge" probably are due to the community's thinking in terms of knowing various details of God's plan, especially the events of the eschaton. Matthew himself is probably thinking rather of the themes expressed in the parables, including particularly the Last Judgment, which occupies a special place in his thought. The knowledge that the Christian community knows only a single secret, namely Jesus Christ himself (cf. the end of the discussion of Mark 4:10-12), is no longer clearly maintained. Unlike Mark and Luke, Matthew inserts a word that often is merely equivalent to a colon, but can also mean "because"; the verse might therefore be rendered, "Because the knowledge . . . has been given to you."

[12] The saying about the strange righteousness of God, which, as a Jewish expression has it, fills not the empty vessel but the full one, is cited by Matthew with the addition of "so that he will have more than enough" (cf. the introductory remarks on 25:29), perhaps because he actually has the image of a vessel in mind. At the same time, he does not forget that what the disciples already have is itself God's gift (vs. 11). In Mark this saying does not appear until 4:25, in the context of three others already used by Matthew in 5:15; 10:26; and 7:2.

[13] After the interruption of verse 12, Matthew must change the

Jesus' True Family (12:46-50)
Cf. Mark 3:31-35; Luke 8:19-21

[46]While Jesus was still talking to the people, his mother and brothers arrived. They stood outside, asking to speak with him. [[47]So one of the people there said to him, "Look, your mother and brothers are standing outside, and they want to speak with you."] [48]Jesus answered, "Who is my mother? Who are my brothers?" [49]Then he pointed to his disciples and said, "Look! Here are my mother and my brothers! [50]Whoever does what my Father in heaven wants him to do is my brother, my sister, my mother."

Here Matthew returns to the Markan account, after the interpolation of Q material in 12:31-37 and the use of Q material to expand verses 38-45. Minor points of agreement with Luke against Mark are striking in verses 46-48a, especially omissions. But in the earliest manuscripts verse 47 is lacking, where almost all these omissions are concentrated. They may therefore have come about during the transmission of the text through assimilation to Luke (or assimilation of the Lukan text to Matthew). Both lack the accusation on the part of Jesus' family that he has gone mad (Mark 3:21).

[46] The introduction connects the text more closely with preceding matter than is true in Mark. Matthew's purpose is, on the one hand, to show that even family ties with Jesus do not suffice to separate people from the "evil generation," and on the other to show by counterexample who Jesus' true family are. **[48]** Jesus himself puts the question of who make up his family without explicit occasion. Unlike Mark 3:34-35 (cf. the introductory remarks to that passage), Matthew does not have Jesus refer to everyone present, but only to his disciples. It is they, not all who hear his words, that constitute his family. Romans 8:29 and Hebrews 2:11 speak in similar fashion of Jesus' brothers, though not of sisters and mothers.

[50] In the Greek text, Matthew adds "for" to begin this verse, indicating that all who do the will of God are disciples. This is given even greater emphasis through Matthew's use of "my Father in heaven" rather than "God." Because the Son of God is present in

Jesus, there is now a band of men who are learning to do the will of the Father and thus distinguish the family of God from the evil generation, not, of course, to effect a permanent separation, but in order to work as leaven, as the following parables will indicate (especially 13:33; cf. the sayings about discipleship in 5:13-16).

We can rejoice in the far more daring saying in Mark 3:34-35; it was Matthew who later limited it to the disciples. But we must hear even Mark's version as a call to take doing the will of the Father very seriously, and not interpret discipleship as retreat into a strictly defined sect or a cloister, as many of the Pharisees and the Qumran community did, but as a demand under some circumstances even to sever our ties with father and mother for the sake of the world, which urgently needs our help (cf. the discussion of 10:37; 8:21-22).

The Parable of the Sower (13:1-9)
Cf. Mark 4:1-9; Luke 8:4-8

[1]That same day Jesus left the house and went to the lakeside, where he sat down to teach. [2]The crowd that gathered around him was so large that he got into a boat and sat in it, while the crowd stood on the shore. [3]He used parables to tell them many things.

"There was a man who went out to sow. [4]As he scattered the seed in the field, some of it fell along the path, and the birds came and ate it up. [5]Some of it fell on rocky ground, where there was little soil. The seeds soon sprouted, because the soil wasn't deep. [6]When the sun came up it burned the young plants, and because the roots had not grown deep enough the plants soon dried up. [7]Some of the seed fell among thorns, which grew up and choked the plants. [8]But some seeds fell in good soil, and bore grain: some had one hundred grains, others sixty, and others thirty." [9]And Jesus said, "Listen, then, if you have ears."

For a discussion of the structure of this chapter, see the introductory remarks on 12:1–16:12. On the significance of Jesus' parables, cf. the discussion of Mark 3:23 and the introductory remarks on 4:1-9.

[1] Once more we see an example of Matthew's dependence on Mark: he now has Jesus leave the "house," although in 12:46 Jesus

is still addressing the crowd and has not entered any house. That was stated in Mark 3:20-21; but Matthew omitted the harsh accusation of Jesus' family, although in verse 46 he incorporates the phrase "they stood outside" from Mark 3:31 and now continues his narrative as though Jesus had stayed in a house. [2] More logically, this is the first appearance of the ship in Matthew (see the introduction to 12:15-16). The parable is repeated from Mark with minor changes and omissions. The background of the preceding sections, however, now shows up more clearly how the parable represents Jesus' own fate, the failure of his message and ministry to bear fruit, but also God's good purpose, which is depicted here in a simple metaphor without fantastic details about a coming eschaton.

The Purpose of the Parables (13:10-17)
Cf. Mark 4:10-13; Luke 8:9-10

[10]Then the disciples came to Jesus and asked him, "Why do you use parables when you talk to them?" [11]Jesus answered, "The knowledge of the secrets of the Kingdom of heaven has been given to you, but not to them. [12]For the man who has something will be given more, so that he will have more than enough; but the man who has nothing will have taken away from him even the little he has. [13]The reason that I use parables to talk to them is this: they look, but do not see, and they listen, but do not hear or understand. [14]So the prophecy of Isaiah comes true in their case:

'You will listen and listen, but not understand;
　　you will look and look, but not see,
[15]because this people's heart is hardened,
　　and they have stopped up their ears,
　　and have closed their eyes.
Otherwise their eyes would see,
　　their ears would hear,
　　their hearts would understand,
and they would return to me,
　　and I would heal them.'
[16]"As for you, how fortunate you are! Your eyes see and your ears hear. [17]Amen, I tell you, many prophets and righteous men wanted

Markan text by repeating the words of the question (10*b*). But the crucial alteration is his change of "in order that" (Mark 4:12) to a "because" (but cf. the discussion of vss. 14-15). The hardness of men's hearts is therefore not in accordance with God's purpose; on the contrary, Jesus speaks in parables because their hearts are already hardened. This means also that their hardness of heart is already a reality, not something to come in the future (cf. the discussion of vs. 36).

[14-15] The statement is given in abbreviated form because it is followed immediately by the full quotation, cited word for word according to the Greek Bible (and Acts 28:26-27). In John 12:40 it appears in a form that, like the Hebrew text, ascribes men's blindness to God's own act. Of all the fulfillment quotations to which attention is drawn by a special introduction, this is the only one placed in Jesus' mouth (see the excursus on 1:18-25). This is also the only case, with the possible exception of 1:23, where we find total agreement with the Greek Bible. Some scholars have therefore suspected a post-Matthaean interpolation. In any case, it states that even in men's blindness God's plan is fulfilled, just as human maleficence and God's plan are interwoven, for example, in Judas' betrayal (see the discussion of Mark 14:10). It is possible, however, that the saying, which is usually translated: "Lest their eyes see . . . ," should in fact be taken differently. It could also mean: "Whether their eyes might not see . . . ," in the sense of "In case they still do not see . . . ." This reading would strongly underscore man's decision and responsibility.

[16-17] The beatitude addressed to the disciples is of crucial importance to Matthew. Having expanded the attack on men's hardness of heart and having shown how it is rooted in Scripture, he must now distinguish the situation of the disciples even more emphatically. Here he differs totally from Mark 4:13, where they are fundamentally bracketed with all the rest in their incomprehension, and especially Mark 8:18, where Jesus' scorn, here addressed to the outsiders, is addressed to the disciples themselves. Throughout his Gospel, Matthew distinguishes the disciples, who understand, from Israel, which closes its heart to Jesus (14:33 in contrast to Mark 6:52; Matt. 13:51; 16:12; 17:13; 20:20). They may have little faith (6:30-31; 8:26; 14:31; 16:8; 17:20), but are never totally without faith or totally ignorant (cf.

the discussion of 15:16; 17:4, 8-9, 17, 23).

What is hard to determine is whom Matthew includes among those whose hearts are hardened. On the one hand, the people are distinguished positively from their leaders, although only until 27:25; on the other hand, 21:43 and 22:9 already look forward to the end of Israel as the people of God (cf. the discussion of 13:34-36a). Probably what Matthew means to say is that official Israel rejected Jesus, but this does not exclude the possibility that individual Israelites, e.g. the disciples, belong to the people of God that bears fruit (cf. the discussion of 8:11-12; 21:43; 23:39). This associates the band of Jesus' disciples much more closely with the Christian community (see the discussion of 8:23), while in Mark the disciples' lack of understanding is due to the fact that Jesus has not yet gone to his death and risen again; in other words, the meaning of discipleship has not yet been revealed.

This means in turn that the circumstances of Matthew's own time influenced his description of Jesus' opponents: it is by no means all of Israel that rejected Jesus, and certainly not the unlearned masses scorned by the teachers of the Law who rejected him, but rather the official leadership; Israel as organized in the synagogue has officially divorced itself from the community of Jesus. [16] The Greek text ("As for you . . .") makes a special point of distinguishing the disciples. The saying derives from the source used in Luke 10:23-24. In that context Matthew has replaced it with 11:28-30; he needs it here because the distinction between the disciples and the unbelieving crowd is crucial to him (see the discussion of vs. 19). Contrary to verse 17 and Luke 10:23, Matthew contrasts not seeing with seeing in the absolute sense rather than with seeing particular things. On the other hand, in the very first sentence he mentions ears and hearing, since he is concerned with understanding the parables of Jesus. Originally, no doubt, the emphasis was on seeing the glory of the eschaton; now we are dealing with hearing the word of God. [17] Typically Matthaean (cf. the excursus on 7:13-23 [§4]) is the reference to the "righteous" (Luke 10:24 reads "kings"). There is no mention of the patriarchs or of Moses, because they mark the beginning of God's history, while prophets and righteous men look ahead to its continuation.

The Four Types of Soil (13:18-23)
Cf. Mark 4:13-20; Luke 8:11-15

[18]"Listen, then, and learn what the parable of the sower means. [19]Those who hear the message about the Kingdom but do not understand it are like the seed that fell along the path. The Evil One comes and snatches away what was sown in them. [20]The seed that fell on rocky ground stands for those who receive the message gladly as soon as they hear it. [21]But it does not sink deep in them, and they don't last long. So when trouble or persecution comes because of the message, they give up at once. [22]The seed that fell among thorns stands for those who hear the message, but their worries about this life and their love of riches choke the message, and they don't bear fruit. [23]And the seed sown in the good soil stands for those who hear the message and understand it; they bear fruit, 'some as much as one hundred, others sixty, and others thirty.' "

Matthew has removed the discrepancies in Mark (see the introduction to Mark 4:13-20) and speaks in all four cases of what is sowed on each type of soil, thus equating the seed with each particular type of person. This is suggested by the common Jewish metaphor of the community as a field planted by God (cf. the discussion of 15:13). **[19]** The only remaining discrepancy is the statement, borrowed from Mark, that Satan takes away what has been sowed. This verse also differs from the others in its use of a different tense of the verb from the one used in verses 20, 22, and 23, suggesting that Matthew has in mind a message preached once for all, which applies only to the last, positive example in Mark 4:20.

[18] More important, the emphatic "you" with which the Greek text of verse 18 begins (cf. vs. 16) once more distinguishes the disciples, who "understand" (added in vs. 23), from the multitude, who "do not understand" (added in vs. 19). **[23]** Verse 23 likewise stresses the "bearing" (literally "doing") of fruit; the disciples are therefore among those described in the same terms in 21:43. **[18]** By calling the parable the parable of the "sower" and saying that the "message" (Mark 4:15) is "of the Kingdom" (cf. the excursus on 7:13-23 [§3]),

Matthew places more emphasis on Jesus' role as preacher of the message of the Kingdom.

The interpretation provided here actually reveals no hard secrets; everything it says is utterly simple. It is a secret only because most men do not realize that God's creative Word has come into the world in the simple parable of Jesus, and is awaiting their response.

Wheat and Weeds Together (13:24-30)

²⁴Jesus told them another parable, "The Kingdom of heaven is like a man who sowed good seed in his field. ²⁵One night, when everyone was asleep, an enemy came and sowed weeds among the wheat, and went away. ²⁶When the plants grew and the heads of grain began to form, then the weeds showed up. ²⁷The man's servants came to him and said, 'Sir, it was good seed you sowed in your field; where did the weeds come from?' ²⁸'It was some enemy who did this,' he answered. 'Do you want us to go and pull up the weeds?' they asked him. ²⁹'No,' he answered, 'because as you gather the weeds you might pull up some of the wheat along with them. ³⁰Let the wheat and the weeds both grow together until harvest, and then I will tell the harvest workers: Pull up the weeds first and tie them in bundles to throw in the fire; then gather in the wheat and put it in my barn.' "

Since Matthew has just stressed the need for bearing fruit, it would not be to his purpose to include the parable of the seed that grows even when no attention is paid to it (Mark 4:26-29). For it he substitutes another one that he knows through an independent tradition. As a rule, Matthew incorporates introductions to the parables from Mark or Q as they stand. Since he probably borrowed the parables of the treasure, the pearl, and the net from a tradition that was not merely oral (see the introduction to 12:1–16:12), we may make the same assumption in the case of the four parables of the weeds, the unforgiving servant, the wedding garment, and the virgins, all of which are introduced by the same formula: "The Kingdom of heaven is like [or 'will be like' when the reference is clearly eschatological] a man (king, ten virgins) who . . . ." They are all extensively developed and deal with the apostasy of someone in the community, a problem that appears to be more typical of a certain stratum of tradition than of Matthew himself (cf. the concluding comments on 13:36-43). The incomprehensible presence of evil within the community (see the concluding comments on this section) is also stressed in the other three parables: by the question "How did you get in here?" in 22:12, by the contrast between the amounts owed in 18:23 ff., or by the description of the five virgins as "fools" in 25:2. Matthew has interpolated these parables wherever they were needed.

This parable contains some strange features, above all the enemy who sows weeds during the night. Jesus is perfectly capable of depicting the failure of the sower on a large scale, the rich harvest in grandiose terms, the father's treatment of his lost son movingly; in each case, however, we are dealing with a commonplace occurrence, even though exaggerated. Since the introduction of the Devil into the parable of the sower (vs. 19) is a product of later interpretation, it is possible that here verses 25, 27, 28a were also interpolated by the community. Since Matthew adds or elaborates the account of the Last Judgment in several passages (see the discussion of vss. 42, 50), it is conceivable that verse 30 is likewise in whole or in part a later addition (cf. "harvest workers" instead of "servants"). The whole of time down to the Last Judgment was an age of unrighteousness—or so many Jewish groups believed, including the Qumran community (1QS iii. 17 ff.; iv. 17-19, 24-26).

Jesus of course also speaks of the Judgment, but the parables which urge overzealous converts to wait patiently do not contain elaborate accounts of the Judgment—which would be wholly terrifying. Luke 13:1 ff., where the problem of evil is brought up and men are warned that they face God's judgment, shows how startling Jesus' own efforts to reach the listener are: Jesus calls on *everyone,* no matter how righteous, to repent, or the Judgment will condemn all.

With the omission of verses 25, 27, 28a and 30, or all but the first clause of the last, we would be left with a nucleus that would be appropriate to the time of Jesus (see below). But all of this is hypothetical. The Gospel of Thomas (57) contains a shorter recension, which, however, includes both the enemy and the pulling up of the weeds at the end.

[24] The introduction in verse $24a = 31a$ reads literally that Jesus "put another parable before them"; it occurs only here. It is reminiscent of Moses' putting the Law of God before the people (Exod. 19:7) or of Christian teachers' putting the apostolic tradition before the community (1 Tim. 1:18; 2 Tim. 2:2). The seed is now expressly referred to as "good"; God's goodness in what he does is emphasized. **[25]** But God's actions meet with resistance and provoke hostility. **[26]** The word for "weeds" actually refers to darnel, a poisonous plant often found in wheat fields. **[27]** The two questions asked by the servants underline the incomprehensibility of evil. **[28]** The problem is not solved by the owner's answer, only stated (some enemy planted the weeds). Nevertheless, the entire parable exhibits a great sense of assurance. That the wheat will ripen as the owner intends is not in doubt. **[29]** The critical point is the owner's "no" to his zealous servants who want to pull up the weeds. It seems that this was the practice followed until very recently in the vicinity of Hebron, because the weeds have stronger roots and therefore often uproot the young shoots of wheat when they are pulled out. **[30]** But coexistence is not the final stage. At the harvest, the workers will gather the weeds. Wood is scarce in Palestine, and so dried weeds are used for fuel. This, rather than immediate burning, is probably the fate of the weeds. But the parable concludes with the gathering of the harvest into the owner's barn.

If the nucleus of the parable went back to Jesus, it would represent a strong protest against the tendency of the Pharisees, the Qumran community, and the Zealots to delimit a sect of devout believers. Jesus rejected this practice and kept his circle open. He therefore avoided giving his group a new name, did not adopt a definite title for himself, did not even establish a fixed meeting place or any organization, however loose, for his followers. Quite unsystematically, therefore, he scared off some who wanted to follow him (8:20 ff.) or sent them elsewhere (Mark 5:18-19), while calling others who had not even considered the matter (Matt. 4:18-22). As soon as more weight became attached to any reference to the Judgment, the parable became a warning against taking vengeance rather than leaving vengeance to God. In this sense we find it cited in Romans 12:19 alongside other statements that are reminiscent of sayings of Jesus. The community of course did find evil in its own midst. At first this seemed so inexplicable that it could only be accounted for by the suggestion made in verse 19, that it was the act of an enemy (vss. 25, 27, 28a). Matthew was probably familiar with the parable in roughly this form; his interpretation will appear in verses 36-43.

The Parables of the Mustard Seed and the Yeast (13:31-33)
Cf. Mark 4:30-32; Luke 13:18-21

[31]Jesus told them another parable, "The Kingdom of heaven is like a mustard seed, which a man takes and sows in his field. [32]It is the smallest of all seeds, but when it grows up it is the biggest of all plants. It becomes a tree, so that 'the birds of heaven' come and 'make their nests in its branches.' " [33]Another parable: "The Kingdom of heaven is like yeast. A woman takes it and mixes it with a bushel of flour, until the whole batch of dough rises."
(Vs. 32—Ezek. 17:23; 31:6; Dan. 4:9 [10]-12.)

Mark also cites the parable of the mustard seed at this point. The introduction (vs. 31a) is a Matthaean expression (cf. the discussion of vs. 24). The text itself is a combination of Mark and Q (Luke 13:18-19). From the latter derives the characteristic introduction (literally "like is the Kingdom of heaven [God] to a mustard seed [yeast], which a man [woman] taking . . ."), which is found in all the short parables (see the introduction to 12:1–16:12). The conclusion as well, which speaks of "branches," as described in Ezekiel 31:6 and Daniel 4:12, goes back to Q.

Various Biblical passages influenced the formulation of the parable. In Mark we find the influence of Ezekiel 31:6, where alongside the "birds of heaven" and the "beasts of the field" the "abundance of the nations dwell in its shadow." Q did not spot this veiled reference to the abundance of the nations, emphasizing instead the nesting among or in its branches, a feature that occurs there and in the passage from Daniel, as well as in a Jewish document (see the discussion of Mark 4:30-32). The presently hidden but eternal planting of

God is also spoken of by the Qumran community (1QH viii. 4-9). In Q the mustard bush is called a "tree." This is a case of assimilation to the Old Testament passages, for, although there is a rare mustard tree, it would not be planted in a field.

This first parable was already linked by Q with the parable of the yeast, which exhibits a similar structure. The "bushel" of flour is literally "three measures," a phrase that appears in Genesis 18:6; it would be enough for a hundred people. The Gospel of Thomas includes both parables separately (20 and 96); the Biblical allusion to the birds is retained, but not the three measures. This fact, together with Mark's inclusion of only one of the parables and Q's addition of a new introduction to the second suggests that the two parables were at first transmitted independently and only brought together by the community. This also explains the strange statement that a man takes *a* (!) mustard seed and sows it in his field, which echoes verse 33*a* but also underlines God's purposive activity. Q emphasizes the "growth" of the seed into a "tree" (Luke 13:19); while Mark 4:31-32 (Matt. 13:32) emphasizes the contrast between "smallest of all" and "greatest of all," which does not appear in Q. Matthew combines the two.

[31-32] The meaning hardly differs from that in Mark. In the parable of the mustard seed, emphasis is on the contrast between an insignificant beginning and a magnificent end; [33] the parable of the yeast underlines the fact that God's Kingdom permeates the world, where it has a fructifying and stimulating effect (cf. the discussion of 5:13). This point in turn affects the development of the first parable, [32] retrospectively emphasizing the mention of "growth" (but cf. the discussion of Mark 4:32). Perhaps there is a sense of the contrast between gradual growth and Jewish dreams of a sudden, miraculous inauguration of the Kingdom of God; [33] the term "mixes" (literally "hides") may be reminiscent of the hidden presence of the Kingdom (see the discussion of 11:12), although the word is often used in Greek for "to be in." Perhaps Jesus used the image of yeast deliberately since according to the cult it was unclean, had to be removed before Passover (see the discussion of Mark 8:15), and it generally had negative overtones in Judaism; [32] similarly, in the two passages from the prophets, the image of the tree is used to depict a heathen kingdom (although it is also used for Israel in Ezek. 17:23). Is this meant to

alert the listener through its alienating effect, using unheard-of, icono-
clastic images for the Kingdom of God? Was Jesus perhaps even
thinking of his own band of disciples, the tax collectors and ignorant
fishermen who were wordly and unclean by Pharisaic standards?

In any case, both parables state that since Jesus has come the field
no longer stands empty, the dough is rising, even if the evidence is
invisible or ambiguous. This statement must not be debased by being
made to refer to a church that gradually wins over the majority or a
Christianity silently transforming the world. Jesus is, on the one hand,
exhorting his followers to preach and act unremittingly as he has
taught, and on the other, apprising them that they will not appear to
succeed, no matter how hard they work: they will continually fail and
be oppressed (11:12) until God takes a hand and consummates his
Kingdom.

Jesus Leaves the Crowd (13:34-36a)

[34]Jesus used parables to tell all these things to the crowds; he
would not say a thing to them without using a parable. [35]He did this
to make come true what the prophet had said,

"I will open my mouth in parables;
I will tell what was hidden since the beginning."
[36]aThen Jesus left the crowd and went into his house.
(Vs. 35–Ps. 78:2.)

[34] Matthew follows Mark: verse 34 here corresponds to Mark
4:34; above all, the parables most closely related to verses 31-33—
which might have been put here instead of the passage from Mark—
are not introduced until later (see the introduction to 12:1–16:12). In
what he says, however, Matthew departs from Mark. The statement
that Jesus used parables in speaking to people "as much as they could
understand" is dropped; the "crowd," as Matthew adds once more
(cf. 13:2), simply does not understand the parables. Neither do we
hear that Jesus regularly explained the parables to his disciples. The
disciples understand the parables, and only in special cases do they
ask for more details (cf. vs. 18), e.g. verse 36, where Jesus is staying

in the "house" that separates him and his band from the "crowd." "All these things" now refers to what Jesus has said since verse 3, not, as in Mark, to his entire message, which in Mark revealed indirectly, until the announcement of his Passion (Mark 8:31-32a), when the veil of metaphor is dropped.

[35] In Matthew the Sermon on the Mount precedes, and it is an ethical discourse that should be comprehensible to everyone. The fulfillment quotation added by Matthew comes from a Psalm. The Psalms have frequently been ascribed to prophets; Asaph, for instance (2 Chron. 29:30), is considered a prophet. Some manuscripts even name Isaiah (cf. vs. 14). The quotation here speaks of the revelation of what had previously been hidden: it was a proclamation, but it had to be heard properly to be understood. The Qumran community spoke in similar terms of their "Teacher of Righteousness" (1QpHab. vii. 1-5). Matthew sees here a reference to the imminent separation of the disciples from the crowd, [36a] which is manifested by Jesus' retreat into the house.

Jesus Explains the Parable of the Weeds (13:36b-43)

[36]bHis disciples came to him and said, "Tell us what the parable of the weeds in the field means." [37]Jesus answered, "The man who sows the good seed is the Son of Man; [38]the field is the world; the good seed is the people who belong to the Kingdom; the weeds are the people who belong to the Evil One; [39]and the enemy who sowed the weeds is the Devil. The harvest is the end of the age, and the harvest workers are angels. [40]Just as the weeds are gathered up and burned in the fire, so it will be at the end of the age; [41]the Son of Man will send out his angels and they will gather up out of his Kingdom 'all who have caused people to sin and practised lawlessness,' [42]and throw them into the fiery furnace, where they will cry and gnash their teeth. [43]There 'the righteous will shine' like the sun in their Father's Kingdom. Listen, then, if you have ears!"

(Vs. 41—Zeph. 1:3. Vs. 43—Judg. 5:31; Dan. 12:3.)

Only now is the interpretation brought in; it does not belong to the parable from the outset. It is also lacking in the Gospel of Thomas.

The framework—verse 36*b* and the last sentence in 43 (cf. 11:15; 13:9) —undoubtedly was composed by the evangelist; the idiom "his disciples came to him and said" is of some importance to Matthew (see the discussion of 8:2). Verses 40-43 are clearly Matthaean (see below). Verses 37-39 contain a catalog of correspondences like those found in rabbinic parables. It could be pre-Matthaean, although the clause (lacking in one ancient manuscript) "the harvest is the end of the age" exhibits linguistic peculiarities typical of Matthew (see the discussion of vs. 39). Probably also Matthew's own are the resumptive "the good seed, that is . . ." of the Greek text (cf. 13:20, 22, 23) and the phrase "people who belong to the Kingdom," since the use of "Kingdom" without further qualification is almost exclusively Matthaean (cf. 8:12 alongside 8:11 = Luke 13:28).

[**36***b*] It is typical of Matthew to call the parable merely the parable of the weeds; that is where his special interest lies. [**37**] The interpretation—totally unlike Jesus, but like the rabbis—treats the entire parable as an allegory in which the various cryptic symbols cannot be understood until the key is provided (e.g. Dan. 2:36-45). On the identification of the harvest with the Last Judgment, cf. the discussion of Matthew 9:37-38. That Jesus is the sower, the enemy the Devil, is obvious on its face. Here the Son of Man is Jesus during his earthly ministry; not until verse 41 is he the coming Judge of the world. [**38**] The field is expressly identified with the world, in which there coexist "people who belong to the Kingdom" and "people who belong to the Evil One" through the influence of the Devil. As in verse 19, we should think in terms of "the Evil One," i.e. the Devil, rather than "evil," although the Greek text (literally: "sons of the evil"), which merely refers to membership in a group (cf. the discussion of 8:12), could also mean "evil" in the abstract.

[**39**] The phrase "end of the age" occurs only in Matthew 13:- 39-40, 49; 24:3; 28:20; it is in line with contemporary Jewish thought, which was strongly eschatological. The important point is that the world is moving toward a goal determined by God and must therefore be understood on the basis of its future. [**40**] From verse 40 on, the image of the weeds being burned (see the discussion of vs. 36*b*), i.e. the account of the Last Judgment, dominates the interpretation. [**41**] The Son of Man sends his angels to punish the wicked, not to gather

the chosen as in 24:31. The strange reference to "stumbling blocks" (as the Greek text literally reads), i.e. those who "practise lawlessness," is only comprehensible on the basis of the Hebrew text of Zephaniah 1:3. Of course this does not prove that the author knew Hebrew; the term might derive from the traditional language of the community. In any case, Matthew is fond of the latter expression (cf. the discussion of 7:23), as well as of the term "Kingdom of the Son of Man." In Matthew 16:28 (and similarly in 20:21) we find "his [the Son of Man's] Kingdom" instead of "the Kingdom of God." Since this passage deals with the final Kingdom that will be established when the Son of Man returns, it is impossible to distinguish a "Kingdom of the Son of Man" belonging to the present world from a "Kingdom of the Father" (vs. 43) to come in the future. [42] The expression "fiery furnace" comes from Daniel 3:6; but 2 Esdras 7:36 also uses it to refer to hell. The statement about crying and gnashing of teeth is also Matthaean (cf. the discussion of 8:12). [43] The shining of the righteous is probably taken from Daniel 12:3 (cf. Ecclus. 50:7; Eth. Enoch 39:7; 104:2), where it is said of the wise (Matt. 23:34); but the catchword "righteous" also appears in the context of Daniel 12:3. The appeal to hear shows that even interpretation does not simply reveal the secret. It calls men to faith and action, not just to intellectual assent.

Matthew directs all his attention toward the Last Judgment, which primarily spells condemnation, albeit against the background of the righteous who shine like the sun. If verses 37-39 represent the earlier stratum, they may suggest that both those who belong to the Kingdom and those who belong to the Devil will be preserved. But the interpretation as a whole, especially the verses in which Matthew's special language appears most clearly, has in view the judgment of the "lawless." Since 12:46 Matthew has shown his interest in the separation of the disciples (see the discussion of 12:49) from the crowd (cf. 13:10, 16, 18-19). What is he getting at? Matthew 18:23 ff.; 25:1 ff. apply the term "Kingdom of heaven" to the community in which there are some who are called but then backslide and will be condemned (cf. 22:11-14; 25:14-30). The fish drawn out of the sea by the net, including both good and worthless (vss. 47-48), are also probably a symbol of the community. This holds true, then, for this parable as soon as it is read in conjunction with those other parables (see the discussion of vss. 47-50). But the field cannot simply be equated with the community on the basis of verse 38, which may derive from an earlier tradition.

Now Matthew 12:49-50 emphasizes that all who do God's will are Jesus' disciples. Further, the will of God is to be proclaimed throughout the entire world (28:18-20), so that men everywhere can say yes or no to it and affirm it through their actions (see the discussion of 25:31-46). Thus the Kingdom of the Son of Man encompasses the entire world, to the extent that it is proclaimed everywhere.

But not all men will accept discipleship (cf. 28:17). Matthew himself appears more interested in distinguishing Jesus' disciples from the world than in the problem of a community that includes both good and wicked men, which was the problem dealt with in the parables preserved for his use by tradition (see the introductory remarks on 13:24-30). At its earliest stage, the parable (Jesus' own?) may have been a warning against zealously distinguishing good from evil in human terms. The increased emphasis on the Last Judgment turned it into a warning addressed to members of the community who did not remain faithful to their call. Matthew himself is primarily interested in the notion of the worldwide judgment that separates Jesus' disciples from the world; this also applies within the community (see the introduction to chapters 21–25), but there, according to Matthew, it must lead the community to go after the sinner and, only if necessary, separate from him (18:15-17).

The Parables of Great Joy (13:44-46)

⁴⁴"The Kingdom of heaven is like a treasure hidden in a field. A man happens to find it, so he covers it up again. He is so happy that he goes and sells everything he has, and then goes back and buys the field. ⁴⁵Also, the Kingdom of heaven is like a merchant looking for fine pearls. ⁴⁶When he finds one that is unusually fine, he goes and sells everything he has, and buys the pearl."

These parables exhibit the same structure as those in verses 31-33 (see the introduction to 12:1–16:12). Their language bears the stamp of wisdom literature, where wisdom is referred to as a treasure (Prov.

2:4; 8:18-21; Isa. 33:6) and as a pearl (Prov. 3:14-15; 8:11; Job 28:-17-18). In the Gospel of Thomas they are preserved separately (109 and 76). There the first is a parable about a missed opportunity: a son sells the field he has inherited without realizing that his father has hidden a treasure in it. The second is told in more homely terms: the merchant sells his whole wagonload of goods to acquire a pearl, probably merely because it strikes his fancy. The different introductions in Matthew, where the Kingdom of heaven is first compared to a treasure, then to a merchant rather than a pearl, may point to separate transmission. In the Gospel of Thomas, in each case the point of comparison is the man. There is probably no difference in meaning, although the second may refer to the God who seeks after men.

[44] The "man" is a day laborer, who does not own the field. Whether his action, which is probably unassailable legally, is morally right or not is not at issue. What is important here is the unprecedented and overwhelming discovery of something for which a man will simply go and give up everything. The crucial point is that his great joy makes it impossible for him to do otherwise. [45-46] The point of the second parable is similar. Here, too, the more obviously exaggerated feature that the merchant sells "everything he has" is meant to describe the unique magnificence of the pearl and the appropriate reaction it provokes. Both parables deal with the great joy of the Kingdom of heaven. The real "actors," which initiate and determine the entire action, are the treasure and the pearl, the very things that seem outwardly passive. They are the source of power. And we are told that no sooner does the laborer find the treasure, and no sooner does the merchant find the pearl, than "he goes and sells everything he has . . . and buys" it—and we are not dealing with immensely wealthy men to whom such a price would mean nothing. Thus, the actions of the Kingdom of heaven give rise to the actions of men, just as the call of Jesus at once induces men to leave ship, home, job (4:18-22; 9:9). Thus too, the Kingdom of heaven, which according to verses 32 and 33 seeks to include the whole world, is also an individual matter, and comes to have its effect on the world through the decision of an individual.

The Parable of the Good and Worthless Fish (13:47-50)

[47]"Also, the Kingdom of heaven is like a net thrown out in the lake, which catches all kinds of fish. [48]When it is full, the fishermen pull it to shore and sit down to divide the fish: the good ones go into their buckets, the worthless ones are thrown away. [49]It will be like this at the end of the age: the angels will go out and gather up the evil people from among the righteous, [50]and throw them into the fiery furnace. There they will cry and gnash their teeth."

The structure of this parable is similar, but Matthew adds an interpretation stressing the judgment that overtakes the wicked. Verses 49a-50 agree word for word with verses 40b, 42; the content of verse 49b corresponds precisely to that of verse 41. This concludes the parables, and therefore Matthew places his emphasis here. This cannot have been the original point of the parable, for the Last Judgment as such was so familiar an idea to the contemporary listener that no parable would have been necessary to call it to mind.

Did the parable at one time contain the first sentence only? If so, of course, there must have been something included about "good and worthless" or the like; and the sentence structure of verses 47-48 corresponds to that of verse 44 (31, 33, 45). But even if the reference to separation of the fish formed part of the parable from the outset, the emphasis was probably on the catching of good and worthless fish together in the same net. Thus the parable is basically parallel to the parable of the weeds; in the tradition it may have stood alongside a short recension of the latter, which Matthew replaced with a longer one.

As in the parable of the weeds, the Kingdom of heaven is originally depicted as a mixture of good and evil that man cannot separate in the interests of a "pure church." Thus a warning is stated against any impatience that would lead men in their own right to execute the judgment of God. The Gospel of Thomas has yet a different perspective (8): the fisherman throws all the little fish away and keeps only a single large fish. But this is an interpretation ill suited to the metaphor. It shows how the parables of Jesus continue to develop and influence each other mutually (cf. the single magnificent pearl in vs. 46).

[47] The net is thrown into the lake; the catch is not seen until it is drawn back in to shore. The reference to "all kinds" of fish is necessary for the conclusion, but can hardly be meant to signify the universality of the Syrian community of Jesus as is probably the case in John 21:11. [48] The "worthless" fish are those not fit to eat, primarily those forbidden by the Law. Whether the notion of disciples as fishers of men (4:19) is in the background is questionable. There the emphasis is on "catching" men for the Kingdom of God; here it is on the coexistence of good and evil. [49] Therefore these fishermen are later compared to the angels of the Last Judgment, not to disciples. The two ideas are of course related. Just as Jesus gathers men with his parables, so the disciples gather men with their preaching. But when they gather men for the sake of God's Kingdom, it is with an eye to the coming division. Because they know what will come, they want to give men the opportunity of making the correct decision. That is also the significance of Jesus' parables.

Conclusion (13:51-53)

⁵¹"Do you understand these things?" Jesus asked them. "Yes," they answered. ⁵²So he replied, "This means that every teacher of the Law who becomes a disciple in the Kingdom of heaven is like a householder who takes new and old things out of his treasure." ⁵³When Jesus finished telling these parables, he left that place.

[51] Matthew's conclusion is instructive. Everything depends on "understanding" (see the discussion of vss. 18-23). [52] Matthew obviously sees the disciples as prototypes of the teacher of the Law who becomes a disciple in the Kingdom of heaven (cf. the discussion of 16:19; 18:18). According to Ecclesiasticus 39:3, the teacher of the Law is one who "explores the hidden meaning of cryptic discourses and occupies himself with the riddles of parables." Perhaps Matthew means that "therefore"—because you have understood—there can now be teachers of the Law like that.

By means of a metaphor he emphasizes what concerned him in

5:17-48. The true teacher of the Law has learned from Jesus to see both the old and the new together (cf. Wisd. 8:8)—God's Law, and its new interpretation proclaimed by Jesus and realized in all that he does. Or is Matthew thinking of Jesus' own teaching, and its new interpretation in the "learned" decisions of the community of disciples (16:19; 18:18)? In either case, it is clear that for Matthew the whole collection of parables is a didactic discourse on the Kingdom of God. Such a teacher of the Law is of course no longer a "rabbi," i.e. a "great one," but rather a "disciple" in the Kingdom of heaven, i.e. one who remains a "learner" (the same word in Greek) throughout his life (cf. 23:10). **[53]** For a discussion of the concluding sentence, see the commentary on 7:28.

Jesus Rejected at Nazareth (13:54-58)
Cf. Mark 6:1-6; Luke 4:16-30

[54]And he went back to his home town and taught in their synagogue, and those who heard him were amazed. "Where did he get such wisdom and miracles?" they asked. [55]"Isn't he the carpenter's son? Isn't Mary his mother, and aren't James, Joseph, Simon, and Judas his brothers? [56]Aren't all his sisters living here? Where did he get all this?" [57]And so they rejected him. Jesus said to them, "A prophet is respected everywhere except in his home town and by his own family." [58]He did not perform many miracles there because they did not have faith.

In putting this section next, Matthew follows Mark, except that he omits the episodes in Mark 4:35–5:34, which he has recounted earlier (Matt. 8:23-34; 9:18-26). **[54]** Matthew shortens the account of Jesus' rejection, however; for example, he omits mention of the disciples and focuses on Jesus. In using the Greek imperfect tense, is Matthew thinking of an extended teaching ministry of Jesus? **[55]** It is significant that Matthew himself refers to Jesus ingenuously as "the carpenter's son" (or "construction worker's"; cf. the discussion of Mark 6:3; cf. also the discussion of Matt. 1:16). Perhaps he thinks that the people in Nazareth simply do not know what the reader has known since 1:18-25. Joseph appears as one of Jesus' brothers (instead of Joses; Mark 6:3), and Simon is mentioned before Judas. **[56]** The repetition of the astonished question (vss. 54*b* and 56) shows that for Matthew the emphasis is on Jesus' authority to teach and his power to perform miracles. Therefore he also limits Mark's statement that Jesus was not able to perform a single miracle, by deleting the words "a single" and "able," and linking the statement with the phrase "because they did not have faith," which Mark uses in another context. Such alterations are not, as a rule, deliberate; but they betray the points where the evangelist sensed difficulties in the tradition he was using.

The Death of John the Baptist (14:1-12)
Cf. Mark 6:14-29; Luke 9:7-9

¹It was at that time that Herod, the ruler of Galilee, heard about Jesus. ²"He is really John the Baptist, who has come back to life," he told his officials. "That is why these powers are at work in him."

³For Herod had ordered John's arrest, and had him tied up and put in prison. He did this because of Herodias, his brother Philip's wife. ⁴John the Baptist kept telling Herod, "It isn't right for you to marry her!" ⁵Herod wanted to kill him, but he was afraid of the Jewish people, because they considered John to be a prophet.

⁶On Herod's birthday the daughter of Herodias danced in front of the whole group. Herod was so pleased ⁷that he promised her, "I swear that I will give you anything you ask for!" ⁸At her mother's suggestion, she asked him, "Give me right here the head of John the Baptist on a plate!" ⁹The king was sad, but because of the promise he had made in front of all his guests he gave orders that her wish be granted. ¹⁰So he had John beheaded in prison. ¹¹The head was brought in on a plate and given to the girl, who took it to her mother. ¹²John's disciples came, got his body, and buried it; then they went and told Jesus.

Here, too, Matthew follows Mark, although once again with significant abbreviation. Since Matthew has already included the sending of the Twelve (Mark 6:6-13) in chapter 10, he places the story of the Baptist's death here, directly alongside the rejection of Jesus at

Nazareth, making the fate of the Baptist even closer to that of Jesus. [5] What is said of the Baptist in verse 5 is likewise said of Jesus in 21:46. [12] At the conclusion Matthew has John's disciples report everything to Jesus, just as the Twelve report their experiences to Jesus in Mark 6:30. Matthew 9:14; Acts 19:1 ff.; 1 John 5:6 ff. still betray considerable tension between the disciples of the Baptist and the community of Jesus; but groups of the Baptist's disciples probably joined the Christian community, and may in fact be responsible for the general use of baptism there.

Another point is more difficult. In Mark this episode is inserted to fill the gap between the sending of the disciples and their return; it thus recalls an event in the moderately distant past. [2] Herod, of course, could only have supposed Jesus was John returned from the dead after John's execution. But Matthew [13] says that that execution caused Jesus to flee into the desert, and there Jesus' preaching probably would not have come to Herod's notice. Further, Matthew takes up Jesus' ministry right there as if no flashback had occurred with the story of John. In other words, Matthew did not realize that Mark is telling the story out of sequence. Furthermore, Jesus is still in Nazareth (Matt. 13:58), from which it is impossible to leave "by ship." This made no difference in Mark, because in the meanwhile Jesus had traveled about in Galilee (6:6), sent his disciples out on a mission, and received them on their return.

[1] In particular details, too, we find characteristic changes. The Greek text uses the word "tetrarch" for "ruler," to distinguish Herod from his father (Matt. 2:1). [9] Later Matthew borrows from Mark the title "king," which is not in fact accurate. [2] Matthew omits the conjectures of the people and recounts only Herod's opinion, albeit in almost exactly the words used by the people according to Mark 6:14 (in the best manuscripts). [5] The statement that Herod "wanted to kill" John but was "afraid" uses the same words used by Mark; the latter, however, says that it was Herodias who wanted to kill him and says that Herod was afraid of the Baptist rather than of the people (cf. Mark 6:21, 26). Matthew thus omits Herod's sympathy toward the Baptist and [6-7] his conversations with him (Mark 6:20).

The events leading up to John's execution are told much more soberly and without lurid detail. The usual reading of the beginning of verse 6 is very odd, and can probably only be explained as a borrowing of the correct reading to be found in the Markan context. [9] The king's sadness, albeit expressed in somewhat weaker terms, is striking because Matthew, unlike Mark, states that Herod had long wanted to kill John. [10] Verse 10 reads literally, "He beheaded John," which fits much better into the account of Mark, who has already mentioned the executioner, although "He had him beheaded" must of course be understood following "He sent him." [12] The report of John's disciples links the story with verse 13.

Matthew is concerned to draw a close parallel between the fate of John and that of Jesus (see the discussion of 3:2). Verse 5 explicitly labels the execution of John the murder of a prophet, whereas Mark 6:20 speaks only of "a good and holy man." In Matthew 23:-29-39 Jesus will condemn Israel for killing the prophets and identify himself with the the company of these prophets. And in 17:12 Jesus states openly that he must go the way of the Baptist. What can be dimly sensed in Mark is here depicted in much bolder lines: the way of the Baptist leading to martyrdom will also be taken by Jesus, and his disciples will fare no differently, as already stated in 5:12; 10:17 ff., 34 ff.

Jesus Feeds the Five Thousand (14:13-21)
Cf. Mark 6:31-44; Luke 9:10-17

[13]When Jesus heard the news, he left that place in a boat and went to a lonely place by himself. The people heard about it, left their towns, and followed him by land. [14]Jesus got out of the boat, and when he saw the large crowd his heart was filled with pity for them, and he healed their sick.

[15]That evening his disciples came to him and said, "It is already very late, and this is a lonely place. Send the people away and let them go to the villages and buy food for themselves." [16]"They don't have to leave," answered Jesus. "You yourselves give them something to eat." [17]"All we have here are five loaves and two fish," they replied. [18]"Bring them here to me," Jesus said. [19]He ordered the people to sit down on the grass; then he took the five loaves and the two fish, looked up to heaven, and gave thanks to God. He broke the loaves and gave

them to the disciples, and the disciples gave them to the people. [20]Everyone ate and had enough. Then the disciples took up twelve baskets full of what was left over. [21]The number of men who ate was about five thousand, not counting the women and children.

[13] The Markan narrative is continued. In Mark 6:31, the retreat into the desert was depicted as a period of recuperation for the disciples who had just returned from their mission; here it is due to Herod's threats (see the discussion of vs. 13 above). Mark does not state that "the people followed him"; but the statement is found also in Luke 9:11 and John 6:2. The phrase must have been associated with this episode from very early on. Here, as in Luke, the saying about the sheep without a shepherd (Mark 6:34b) is omitted; it has already appeared in 9:36. [14]Jesus' pity for the people results in healings, as it does also before the second feeding (15:29-31 = Mark 7:31-37), not in instruction, as it does in Mark—once again showing how important Jesus' healings are to Matthew.

[15] "That evening" represents a stylistic difference from Mark; Matthew appears not to have noticed that evening does not come until later, when Jesus is alone, praying (vs. 23 = Mark 6:47); by that time the people are already fed and gone, the disciples "far out" (Matt. 14:24) in the lake. [19] Like Luke, Matthew omits the question asked by the disciples in Mark 6:37b, 38; he states instead in 15:36 that the disciples gave the bread to the people. Despite the mention of fish in the prayer of thanksgiving, we read only of the distribution of the bread; and, contrary to Mark, the fish are also omitted at the end of verse 20. Some analogy to the Lord's Supper in the community has probably colored the account. [20-21] The concluding sentences also differ stylistically from Mark, but are repeated in almost identical words in 15:37-38. This is true most noticeably of the phrase "not counting the women and children"; in Mark 6:44 and John 6:10, as in the English phrase "five thousand men," it is not quite clear whether all the people referred to are males (cf. Matt. 14:35, which reads literally "the males"). The tightening up of the narrative throws Jesus' dominant role into sharper relief; the additions "They don't have to leave" and "Bring them [the loaves] here to me" likewise emphasize that everything depends on Jesus' instructions.

[20] The closer assimilation to the Lord's Supper is in agreement with what we have already observed with respect to 8:23: the story of Jesus and his disciples turns into a reflection of the later community. But it is also stressed that we are dealing with a truly satisfying meal, so that those who are hungry "do not have to leave" to buy provisions, because the disciples "give them something to eat." [13] The direct connection with the death of the Baptist (see above) may contain a reference to what is proclaimed in the Lord's Supper: the Passion.

Human Doubt and Jesus' Power (14:22-36)
Cf. Mark 6:45-56

[22]Then Jesus made the disciples get into the boat and go ahead of him to the other side of the lake, while he sent the people away. [23]After sending the people away, he went up a hill by himself to pray. When evening came, Jesus was there alone; [24]by this time the boat was far out in the lake, tossed about by the waves, because the wind was blowing against it. [25]In the fourth watch of the night Jesus came to them, walking on the water. [26]When the disciples saw him walking on the water they were terrified. "It's a ghost!" they said, and screamed with fear. [27]Jesus spoke to them at once. "Courage!" he said. "It is I. Don't be afraid!"

[28]Then Peter spoke up. "Lord," he said, "if it is really you, order me to come out on the water to you." [29]"Come!" answered Jesus. So Peter got out of the boat and started walking on the water to Jesus. [30]When he noticed the wind, however, he was afraid, and started to sink down in the water. "Save me, Lord!" he cried. [31]At once Jesus reached out and grabbed him and said, "How little faith you have! Why did you doubt?" [32]They both got into the boat, and the wind died down. [33]The disciples in the boat fell down before him and said, "Truly you are the Son of God!"

[34]They crossed the lake and came to land at Gennesaret, [35]where the people recognized Jesus. So they sent for all the sick people in the surrounding country and brought them to Jesus. [36]They begged him to let the sick at least touch the edge of his cloak; and all who touched it were made well.

[23] At the beginning Matthew follows Mark almost word for word. That Jesus stayed behind by himself is stated at once by Matthew in verse 23; Mark mentions the fact retroactively. John 6:15 uses Mark's expression in Matthew's position.

[28-31] The episode of Peter's walking on the water is new. It was composed by Matthew himself, probably on the basis of oral tradition; many of its idioms are typically Matthaean. Verses 28-29, for example, speak of the "water" instead of the "lake" (as in vs. 25 = Mark 6:48). The same alteration can be seen at the end of Matthew 8:32; cf. Mark 5:13. The point of the episode is that the unique power and authority of Jesus live on in the Christian community (cf. the discussion of 10:1). The new episode is intimately linked with the other account; instead of "he got into the boat" (Mark 6:51) we now read that "the disciples get into the boat" (Matt. 14:22); "it is I" (Mark 6:50 = Matt. 14:27) leads to "if it is really you" (Matt. 14:28) and "you are" (vs. 33); the wind mentioned in Mark 6:48 (as well as Matt. 14:24) also plays an important role in verse 30; the fear exhibited by the disciples in Mark 6:50 (and Matt. 14:26) reappears as Peter's fear in verse 30. Thus it becomes clear that Peter is being used once more to illustrate the meaning of discipleship in the ship of the church. The interpolation of course makes Jesus' getting into the ship and the stilling of the storm come later than they do in Mark.

It is possible that an Easter narrative once constituted the background for this story, perhaps the account of Jesus' first appearance to Peter (1 Cor. 15:5; Luke 24:34), which is not depicted anywhere. According to John 21:7-8, Peter leaps into the water to go to the risen Lord, and wades toward him through (not upon) the water. Has this been transformed into an episode in the life of the earthly Jesus? This might be suggested by the fact that Matthew omits Mark's statement that the minds of the disciples remained uncomprehending, and substitutes a contrary statement, which tells how they fall down before him (see the discussion of Matt. 8:2) and confess him to be the Son of God. This confession in fact depreciates the confession of Peter in 16:16, but would be well suited to an Easter narrative.

[34-36] The summary account of Jesus' ministry at Gennesaret likewise follows Mark, though with considerable abbreviation. Mark 6:55 (like 1:34) does not say that "all" the sick were brought (though

Mark 1:32 does). But here, as well as in 4:24, Matthew says that "all" were brought and healed; the point appears to be important to Matthew, probably as an image of the community that brings all its needs before the Lord.

[24] Some manuscripts follow Mark in placing the boat "in the middle of the lake"; others say it was "many stadia [one stadium = about two hundred yards] out" in the lake. The meaning is the same in either case. The "boat" (rather than "the disciples," as in Mark 6:48) is in trouble on account of "the waves" (Mark 6:48 reads "in rowing"); this agrees with 8:24. In both passages we are dealing with an image for the church. Peter's scream corresponds to that of the disciples in 8:25; his lack of faith corresponds to their lack of faith in 8:26. Here, too, Matthew probably looks on the ship as a symbol of the community. [25] Matthew eliminates the feature that Jesus intended to "pass them by" (Mark 6:48); instead he comes to the aid of the disciples.

[26] Their fear is emphasized; they are not without faith, but their faith is small (cf. the discussion of 13:16-17), as the example of Peter illustrates. [28] Peter practically implores the "Lord" to give him an order. The word to "order" or "command" is one of Matthew's favorites; he adds it in 8:18; 14:19 (of Jesus); 14:9 (of Herod); 27:58 (Pilate). Here it emphasizes that everything depends on Jesus' bidding; the disciple does not undertake anything spectacular on his own. [29] Jesus' reply consists of a single word; but that suffices to get Peter to venture everything and bring success to his venture.

[30] But as soon as the reality of the storm and the waves obtrude on the voice of his Lord and drown it out, he begins to sink and can only call to his Lord for help. [31] His cries are answered, but Jesus calls them signs of faltering faith and of doubt. The Greek word for "doubt" suggests "going in two directions at once"; the term used in 21:21 means literally "think asunder," think along two lines; the term in James 1:8 means "to have two souls," as though two souls were struggling within a single breast, the one inclined to go one way, the other another. When faith devotes its attention strictly to the word of Jesus, it may take a realistic view of wind and waves, but must not allow them to distract it. According to Matthew, such faith is prom-

ised everything; but when it begins to vacillate between the command of its Lord and some evident personal danger, it falters.

But we are not dealing simply with "faith and courage in the face of a most arduous undertaking," as Goethe read this story, but with the kind of faith that rivets its attention solely on the word of Jesus; that kind of faith really only begins at the point where Peter fails; for only then is he bereft of all hope but the sight of his Lord and help from him. This, then, is true faith: not the sublime achievement of an especially religious individual, but "single minded" devotion to the Lord, to his bidding and to his help. It can be enforced by necessity, when there is nothing else left to rely on; in fact it is more likely to be found in such a situation. [33] It is striking that after the storm has subsided the disciples for the first time see in Jesus the Son of God and fall down before him. Is Matthew saying that the miracle shows Jesus to be the Son of God? But a similar story was already recounted in 8:26-27, and the raising of a dead woman was even more miraculous.

It is more likely that the confession of Jesus as God's Son appears here because the boat symbolizes the community that confesses Jesus. The contrast between the master and his disciples is even sharper than in 8:23-27, and both sides are emphasized: the power of Jesus and the doubt of the community. Thus the story is a promise for their obedience and a summons constantly to renew their faith, a faith that devotes its attention to the power of the Lord, expressing itself in the prayer "Save, Lord." The crucial points, then, are Jesus' call to follow, the promise he accords to faith, and his saving help in the face of failure.

This is also the way the Gospel will end: the doubting disciples (28:17) are called upon to go out in faith into all the world and are promised the presence of their Lord "to the end of the age." Peter is not depicted as an outstanding hero by virtue of his faith, but as a representative of the disciples in general (see the discussion of 15:15). Old Testament parallels therefore are not so much those passages which speak of God's presence or of wisdom upon the waters (see the discussion of Mark 6:45-52) as those verses from the Psalms about deliverance of the supplicant from waters of distress, e.g. Psalm 18:16: "He grasped me and drew me out of many waters"; 69:1-3: "Save me,

O God [from the waters]"; 144:7: "Stretch forth your hand from the heights, save me and deliver me from many waters." Similar passages are found in the Greek and Latin authors.

The Question of the Law (15:1-20)
Cf. Mark 7:1-23

[1]Then some Pharisees and teachers of the Law came to Jesus from Jerusalem and asked him, [2]"Why is it that your disciples disobey the teaching handed down by our ancestors? They don't wash their hands in the proper way before they eat!" [3]Jesus answered, "And why do you disobey God's command and follow your own tradition? [4]For God said, 'Honor your father and your mother,' and 'Anyone who says bad things about his father or mother must be put to death.' [5]But you teach that if a person says, 'What might have been of use to you from me shall instead be an offering to God,' [6]then he does not need to honor his father or his mother. This is how you disregard God's word to follow your own tradition. [7]You hypocrites! How right Isaiah was when he prophesied about you:
[8]'These people honor me with their lips,
    but their heart is far from me.
[9]It is no use for them to worship me,
    because they teach man-made commandments!' "
[10]Then Jesus called the crowd to him and said to them, "Listen, and understand! [11]It is not what goes into a person's mouth that makes him unclean; rather, what comes out of it makes him unclean."

[12]Then the disciples came to him and said, "Do you know that the Pharisees were offended by what you said?" [13]"Every plant which my Father in heaven did not plant will be pulled up," answered Jesus. [14]"Don't worry about them! They are blind leaders; and when one blind man leads another one, both fall into a ditch."

[15]Peter spoke up, "Tell us what this parable means." [16]Jesus said to them, "You are still no more intelligent than the others. [17]Don't you understand? Anything that goes into a person's mouth goes into his stomach and then out of the body. [18]But the things that come out of the mouth come from the heart; such things make a man unclean. [19]For from his heart come the evil ideas which lead him to kill, commit

adultery, and do other immoral things; to rob, lie, and slander others. [20]These are the things that make a man unclean. But to eat without washing your hands—this does not make a man unclean."

(Vs. 4—Exod. 20:12; 21:17; Deut. 5:16. Vss. 8-9—Isa. 29:13. Vs. 18 —James 3:6. Vs. 19—Rom. 1:28 ff.)

Mark, too, places this discourse here. The changes are illuminating. In the first place, Matthew omits the explanations of Jewish customs (Mark 7:2-4) [5] and the name of the custom censured in verse 5 ("Corban"; Mark 7:11); they are clearly familiar to his community (cf. also the discussion of 26:2). Verse 5 may even be based on a familiar formula: "A curse, if you receive anything of use from me!" In the second place, Matthew tones down the contrast with Jewish religious practice, but without defending the latter. [2] According to Leviticus 22:4-7, priests are required to wash their hands; in this particular case, the disciples of Jesus "disobey the teaching handed down by their ancestors," a weaker statement than the Markan recension, which states that "they do not live by" it. Verse 20 once again refers the whole discourse back to this point. Perhaps in the period of the evangelist these ritual ablutions distinguished the Christians from the Jews (in Syria?). There is also no longer any reference to "much else besides" that Jewish regulations require (Mark 7:4), or to the "traditions of men" (Mark 7:8) and "unclean hands" (Mark 7:5). [11] Both members of verse 11 refer merely to the "mouth," [19] and verse 19 substitutes "slander" for a series of other vices (Mark 7:22). This change and a different sequence result in assimilation to the Ten Commandments. Matthew is thinking primarily of a man's utterances that make him unclean. At the same time, he does not forget that what matters is the heart, as is shown by verses 18 (an addition) and 19 (=Mark 7:21), although Mark 7:19a is omitted. [11] Finally, Matthew says "not" instead of "nothing" (Mark 7:15) and avoids the bluntest expression of the point ("cannot render unclean"; Mark 7:18) and the ironic saying about the privy that makes even unclean foods clean (Mark 7:19). He thus consistently emphasizes the distinction between mere observance of ritual requirements and sins of the tongue in the sense of speaking evil against others. He does not bring up other commandments of the Law for discussion. But he could not have written verse 11 if the community had not considered the Old Testament dietary laws to be binding. That inward, not outward uncleanness is what matters still came as a shock.

[2-8] In the third place, Matthew aggravates the conflict with the Pharisees. He casts the whole episode formally in the mode of a disputation like those that often took place between Pharisaic and Christian scholars after A.D. 70. Therefore he has Jesus respond to the question with an immediate counterquestion (verse 3), raising an even more serious charge against the questioner (Mark postpones this development until verse 8). They themselves transgress the commandment, as verse 4 maintains, where "God" appears as the lawgiver (rather than "Moses"; Mark 7:10). This shows that Matthew still considers the Ten Commandments to be God's Law and binding, although they can be correctly understood only in the light of what Jesus says in response to Peter (vs. 15; see below). Not until it has been demonstrated that the commandment to honor one's parents, cited once more in verse 6, has been transgressed do we come to the charge (vss. 7-9) that Mark introduces the episode with. Thus the disputation concludes with the Scriptural authority from Isaiah that decides the issue.

The word "hypocrites" (cf. the discussion of 6:2) is even more emphatic in verse 7 than in Mark. [12-14] Above all, Matthew distinguishes the disciples of Jesus more sharply from the Pharisees by interpolating an interlude. Obscurity is the price he has to pay. [15] In the question of Peter that follows, the word "parable" in Mark 7:17 refers accurately to the preceding saying about what goes into a man and what comes out of him; this no longer holds true in Matthew 15:15, where it appears to refer to the idea of the blind leading the blind.

The question asked by the disciples, introduced in typically Matthaean style (see the discussion of 8:2), serves to introduce two sayings, the first of which is also preserved in Luke 6:39, and was therefore probably familiar as an independent saying. [14] The Pharisee or devout Jew in general (Rom. 2:19-20) would have presumed that because Israel possessed the Law, it alone among all nations was not blind. But it is this very presumption that Jesus disputes. They have the scrolls of the Law in their synagogues, they can read and interpret them, but this does not guarantee they understand them. In this sense they are blind, although they think that they can lead others who are blind (cf. the discussion of 23:16, 24).

[13] The image of planting actually states that man is not what he achieves or accomplishes, but what God has planted him as. "God's vineyard" was frequently used as a title by Israel (Isa. 60:21; also 5:1 ff.; Jer. 45:4; Ps. 1:3) or by specific groups who considered themselves the true Israel (Ps. Sol. 14:3-4; Jub. 1:16; 7:34; 1QS viii. 5; xi. 8; 1QH vi. 15-17; vii. 10, 18-19; viii. 4 ff.; x. [25-26], 31; CD i. 7; Eth. Enoch 10:16). It would be hard to frame a sharper attack on Israel's faith in its own election: Israel and its ruling class of Pharisees is not the vineyard planted by God but a wild thicket!

[15] In place of the disciples (Mark 7:17), it is Peter who asks for an explanation of the symbolism. In 21:20 the situation is reversed, and in 28:7 Peter is no longer mentioned. This change shows that he basically represents all the disciples (see the concluding remarks on 16:13-20). He receives prominence only when a new understanding of the Law in the community is under discussion (16:19; 17:24; 18:21), although he must in turn make inquiry of Jesus, and thus can only expound Jesus' will. [16] It is exceptional for Matthew to state that the disciples do not understand; but he has turned the statement into a question and thus toned it down: "Don't you understand?" In principle they should understand; but Jesus is not horrified or dismayed (as in Mark) that they don't.

This shows that Matthew was writing at another period and in another situation than Mark. The community of Jesus had already broken with the Jews under Pharisaic leadership. Both groups are therefore more sharply distinguished. On the other hand, the community of Jesus, which included many Jews, was also linked with Israel, its history and its Law. How, then, were this history and this Law to be understood and adopted so that God's true will could be done? The reply is that God never intended sacrifice or ritual obedience as an end in itself, but intended that men should obey him for the sake of other men. Accordingly, Jesus intervenes on behalf of the parents whose son intends to follow the custom of giving to the Temple what would have gone to them; and accordingly, he attacks the dietary laws, which merely protect a man from formal uncleanliness, and he defends people who might be endangered by malicious gossip or incitement to violence. This principle distinguished the community of Jesus from the Pharisaic community (cf. the discussion of 9:13), who, not only in what they did but also in what they taught, actually set up counter-commandments to the Ten Commandments (vss. 5-6*a* are formulated in antithetical style to the Ten).

On the one hand, concentration on the Ten Commandments (vs. 19) has made the answer clearer: only acting contrary to God's will makes a man unclean. On the other hand, the individual and his actions become more central. Jesus made reference to evil within men's hearts, which cannot be blotted out by ritual correctness. The community behind Mark probably added the list of vices that spring from the heart; but they thereby suggested the opposite of what they meant—they suggested just one more set of rules for ritual observance. Mark himself warned against that misunderstanding by stressing the blindness of the disciples toward God's actions in Jesus (see the discussion of Mark 7:1-23).

Does Matthew suppose that the Law is a sufficient guide for men —making them acceptable to God—if understood and interpreted according to Jesus' will? Matthew does reverence the Law; but he alludes to it here primarily to point to the difference between his community and Israel. God requires of all men a perfect fulfillment of the Law; but as Jesus demonstrates, only perfect love can fulfill it, and perfect love is impossible for men (whence, e.g., their tendency to substitute formalism). But as Jesus also shows, what is impossible for men is possible with God (19:19, 26).

Jesus and Israel (15:21-28)
Cf. Mark 7:24-30

[21]Jesus left that place and went off to the territory near the cities of Tyre and Sidon. [22]A Canaanite woman who lived in that region came to him. "Son of David, sir!" she cried. "Have mercy on me! My daughter has a demon and is in a terrible condition." [23]But Jesus did not say a word to her. His disciples came to him and begged him,

"Send her away! She is following us and making all this noise!" ²⁴Then Jesus replied, "I have been sent only to the lost sheep of the house of Israel." ²⁵At this the woman came and fell down before him. "Help me, sir!" she said. ²⁶Jesus answered, "It isn't right to take the children's food and throw it to the dogs." ²⁷"That is true, sir," she answered; "but even the dogs eat the leftovers that fall from their masters' table." ²⁸So Jesus answered her, "You are a woman of great faith! What you want will be done for you." And at that very moment her daughter was healed.

This story agrees in content with its Markan parallel, but it is differently worded and is expanded by an interpolation. The words of Jesus, however, are on the whole the same, as are those of the woman. [22-24] The saying in verse 24 is independent and can easily be removed from this setting (cf. the discussion of 10:6). Matthew is probably trying to make his interpretation of the story clearer; elsewhere, too, he has added the phrases "come and say" (see the introductory remarks on 28:18), "did not say a word" (22:46), and "Son of David" (see the discussion of 12:23; 21:9). The lost sheep are not just one particular group, such as the Pharisees, but all of Israel; Jesus is sent "only" to them (cf. 10:6). The cry "Have mercy on me, sir [or: 'Lord'], Son of David" is found only here and in Matthew 20:30-31 (in Mark 10:47-48 the order is different and the word "sir" is not found). The attempt of the disciples to get Jesus to send the woman away is described in similar terms in Matthew 14:15. Is Matthew also thinking of disciples in his own period who acted this way?

Elsewhere in the episode Matthew abbreviates considerably. [25-26] The changes make Jesus' refusal even harsher; we no longer read that the children must "first" be taken care of (Mark 7:27). At the same time, the response of the woman becomes even more submissive; she even speaks of the "masters' " table. The leftovers (literally "bits of bread") are used to wipe food off the hands. The concluding verse, too, with its reference to the woman's faith and the successful healing, is formulated by Matthew (cf. 8:13); he thus understood the story as similar to that of the officer at Capernaum (see the end of the introductory remarks on that section).

[21] The major changes made by Matthew show how important

he considers the story. By using the terms "Tyre and Sidon" (rather than just Tyre) and "Canaanite" (instead of "Syro-Phoenician"), he introduced Old Testament expressions used to designate the gentiles as distinct from the people of God. As in 10:5-6, 23, Matthew is concerned to show that it is not God who broke the covenant with Israel; Jesus addressed his entire ministry to the people of God and concentrated on them alone. [22] If verse 22 is taken as meaning that the woman "came from that region," then Jesus did not in fact "enter" the territory of the gentile cities, but only went "in that direction." The Greek text can be read either way. God, therefore, has remained faithful to his covenant with Israel; only Israel has for the most part turned its back on the covenant. [23] What happens to the woman, however, is contrary to the disciples' expectations: [28] she experiences healing and deliverance on the basis of her "great" faith (cf. 17:20), which sees in Jesus the Lord and Son of David, that is, the messiah. No injunction to follow the Law is imposed on her. The cry of faith, which resembles that of Peter (14:30; cf. Ps. 22:20; etc.) suffices: "Lord, help me!" Thus Matthew emphasizes both points: God's faithfulness to Israel and the miracle of the faith of the gentiles.

Jesus Feeds the Four Thousand (15:29-39)
Cf. Mark 7:31–8:9

[29]Jesus left that place and went along by Lake Galilee. He climbed a hill and sat down. [30]Large crowds came to him, bringing with them the lame, the blind, the crippled, the dumb, and many other sick people, whom they placed at Jesus' feet; and he healed them. [31]The people were amazed when they saw the dumb speaking, the crippled whole, the lame walking, and the blind seeing; and they praised the God of Israel.

[32]Jesus called his disciples to him and said, "I feel sorry for these people, because they have been with me for three days and now they have nothing to eat. I don't want to send them away hungry, because they might faint on their way home." [33]The disciples asked him, "Where will we find enough food in this desert to feed this crowd?" [34]"How much bread do you have?" Jesus asked. "Seven loaves," they answered, "and a few small fish." [35]So Jesus ordered the crowd to sit

down on the ground. [36]Then he took the seven loaves and the fish, gave thanks, broke them, and gave them to the disciples, and the disciples gave them to the people. [37]They all ate and had enough. The disciples took up seven baskets full of pieces left over. [38]The number of men who ate was four thousand, not counting the women and children. [39]Then Jesus sent the people away, got into the boat, and went to the territory of Magadan.

Matthew begins by echoing Mark 7:31, but without repeating the almost untraceable route taken by Jesus. He also omits the healing of a deaf and dumb man reported by Mark here, possibly because he already recorded a similar incident in 9:32-33 and because the actions of Jesus, which resemble magic, caused him difficulty (cf. the discussion of 9:23-25). He also omits Mark 8:22-26, both on account of Matthew 9:27-34 and because of its content. He inserts instead a summary of Jesus' healings, which serves also to introduce (vss. 30-31) the "people" who are mentioned in verse 32. Mark 7:37 already contained an echo of Isaiah 35:5-6; the addition of the crippled and blind to the dumb makes the reference even clearer. Isaiah 29:13, 18-19, 23 may have furnished the model for the antithesis between those who are healed (vs. 30) and who praise "the God of Israel" (vs. 31) and those who only honor him with their lips (vss. 8-9). The image of Jesus on the hill or "mountain," with the sick laid at his "feet," may be based on the image of the bearer of good news in Isaiah 52:7 (also interpreted by the rabbis as referring to the messiah and the eschaton; Billerbeck III, 10; IV, 952), though John 6:3 also records that Jesus climbed a hill before feeding the multitude.

[31] Once more, unlike the Pharisees, the people are amazed (vss. 1-20). The feeding of the four thousand is recounted almost exactly as in Mark, but somewhat more briefly. [34] The fish are added from the very outset, but their blessing and distribution are no longer described. [36] Although the distribution in verse 36 refers to both bread and fish, the phrase "broke them and gave them," borrowed from Mark, shows that the narrator is thinking only of bread. The disciples' distribution of food to the people is described in the same terms as in 14:19; [38] the rhetorical state-

ment of how many were fed likewise corresponds closely to 14:21. [32] Since Matthew omits the new beginning of Mark 8:1, he locates the feeding on the shore of Lake Galilee (vs. 29). [29] Although there was a gentile population in that region, it is not likely that Matthew intended a contrast with the Jewish location of the first feeding (see the discussion of Mark 8:1, 3). [39] The Dalmanutha of Mark 8:10, an unknown site, is replaced by Magadan, likewise unknown.

The Disciples Distinguished
from Pharisees and Sadducees (16:1-12)
Cf. Mark 8:11-21 (Matt. 12:38-40; Luke 11:16, 29-30; 12:1)

[1]Some Pharisees and Sadducees came to Jesus. They wanted to trap him, so they asked him to produce a sign from heaven for them. [2]But Jesus answered, ["When the sun is setting you say, 'We are going to have fine weather, because the sky is red.' [3]And early in the morning you say, 'It is going to rain, because the sky is red and dark.' You can predict the weather by looking at the sky; but can you not interpret the signs of the time?] [4]An evil and adulterous generation demands a sign, but no other sign will be given them except the sign of the prophet Jonah." So he left them and went away.

[5]When the disciples crossed over to the other side of the lake, they forgot to take any bread. [6]Jesus said to them, "Look out, and be on your guard against the yeast of the Pharisees and Sadducees." [7]They started discussing among themselves, "He says this because we didn't bring any bread." [8]Jesus knew what they were saying, so he asked them, "Why are you discussing among yourselves about not having any bread? How little faith you have! [9]Don't you understand yet? Don't you remember when I broke the five loaves for five thousand men? How many baskets did you fill? [10]And what about the seven loaves for the four thousand men? How many baskets did you fill? [11]How is it that you don't understand that I was not talking to you about bread? Guard yourselves from the yeast of the Pharisees and Sadducees!" [12]Then the disciples understood that he was not telling them to guard themselves from yeast, but from the teaching of the Pharisees and Sadducees.

Matthew still follows Mark; but he obviously understands 15:39 (=Mark 8:10) as meaning that Jesus crossed the lake in the boat alone and there met the Pharisees and Sadducees. [1] The addition of Sadducees here and in verse 6 is contrary to Mark (and Matt. 12:38); in verses 11-12, both Pharisees and Sadducees are added (cf. the introductory remarks on 3:7-10). As a result, almost all the words of Mark 8:13 appear here, but now they have a rather different meaning. [4-5] "He left them and went away" (vs. 4) refers to Jesus; but "the other side of the lake" (Mark 8:13) now applies only to the disciples (vs. 5), who are coming to be where Jesus already is. This means that we no longer read of two trips by Jesus in the boat (Mark 8:10, 13) but only of one, and that the conversation about the yeast of the Pharisees no longer takes place in the boat (Mark 8:14) but on land, after the disciples have returned.

The saying about the sign of Jonah together with its introduction in verse 2a agrees verbatim with 12:39 (except for the addition of "the prophet"); but the reference to Jesus' burial and resurrection is omitted (12:40). The intermediate verses about signs in the heavens rather than "from heaven," as was demanded, are not found in the earliest manuscripts. They were probably added later through the influence of Luke 12:54-56. As in 8:26; 14:29-33, Matthew adds the charge that the disciples have little faith, but eliminates the harsh judgment upon the uncomprehending disciples (Mark 8:18; cf. the discussion of Matt. 13:16-17, 19). [11-12] Instead the warning about the Pharisees and Sadducees is repeated, and it is stated that the disciples finally understand that Jesus was trying to warn them about the "teaching" of the Pharisees and Sadducees. This leaves no place for the healing of the blind man recorded symbolically by Mark in 8:22-26, to show how Jesus' revelation at Caesarea Philippi opens the eyes of his blind disciples for the first time (cf. the discussion of Matt. 15:29-31).

As the thrice-repeated warning shows, Matthew is concerned to make a deep distinction between the disciples of Jesus and the teaching of the Pharisees and Sadducees, i.e., official Judaism as he perceives it. Matthew's verdict is revealed in the episode of the demand for a sign: the band of disciples must be on their guard against a self-conscious religiosity that demands guarantees, when it is God's desire to break in unexpectedly through the fixed notions of their

system. If they do not heed the warning, they will be unfit to follow
him and not remain open to God's actions, which are always new and
often unexpected. The catchwords "know" and "teaching" (vss. 11-
12) pave the way for the following section.

IV
THE ROAD TO THE PASSION
16:13–20:34

In this section, too, Matthew follows the structure of Mark through-out, but incorporates a special tradition in the episode of Peter's confession and, following a hint in Mark, transforms 17:24–18:35 into a set of rules for the community (cf. the discussion preceding 18:1). In addition, he uses the parable of the day laborers (20:1-16) shortly before the final announcement of the Passion to illustrate Jesus' say-ing, recorded by Mark, about the first who shall be last and the last who shall be first. In our discussion of particular details we shall find characteristic additions, omissions, and changes.

God's Revelation in the Confession of Peter (16:13-20)
Cf. Mark 8:27-30; Luke 9:18-21

¹³Jesus went to the territory near the town of Caesarea Philippi, where he asked his disciples, "Who do men say the Son of Man is?" ¹⁴"Some say John the Baptist," they answered. "Others say Elijah, while others say Jeremiah or some other prophet." ¹⁵"What about you?" he asked them. "Who do you say I am?" ¹⁶Simon Peter an-swered, "You are the messiah, the Son of the living God."

¹⁷"Blessings on you, Simon Bar Jonah," answered Jesus. "Because flesh and blood did not reveal this to you, but my Father in heaven. ¹⁸And so I tell you: you are a rock, Peter, and on this rock I will build my community, and the gates of the underworld will never overwhelm it. ¹⁹I will give you the keys of the Kingdom of heaven; what you bind on earth will be bound in heaven, and what you loose on earth will be loosed in heaven."

²⁰Then Jesus ordered his disciples not to tell anyone that he was the messiah.

(Vs. 18 = Wisd. 16:13 [Job 38:17].)

[13] Jesus speaks of the Son of Man here, but does not in the corresponding passage of Mark (8:27-30); and when Mark does use the phrase (Mark 8:31 = Matt. 16:21, where it no longer occurs), it anticipates the Passion. So for Mark the title "Son of Man" implies Jesus' lowliness, humility, and suffering; for Matthew it signifies the reverse—Jesus' universal authority and power, for the time inhabiting flesh.

[17-19] The beatitude addressed to Peter, the saying about founding the community, and the bestowal of the keys are added. That they are preserved only in Matthew does not prove that they are not genuine—the parable of the Pharisee and the tax collector is found only in Luke. There is much evidence that the material goes back at least to the Aramaic-speaking community: the form "Bar [= 'son of'] Jonah"; the Jewish phrase "flesh and blood" for "human being"; finally, the Judaic notions of the gates of Hades—conceived as a person or power—of binding and loosing, and of the keys to the Kingdom of heaven. Above all, the pun "you are Peter, and upon this rock . . ." is pure only in Aramaic, where *kepha* has both meanings; in Greek, *petros* and *petra* are two distinct words.

But can these words derive from Jesus? Even in verse 17 the account of Mark is much more probable. According to Mark, Jesus did not reject Peter's frank confession of him as Christ, but he did not welcome it either. On the contrary, Mark goes on to cite a saying that refers to the suffering (rather than the power) of the Son of Man. But why would Mark have wanted to eliminate the title "Son of God," which is important to him, and Jesus' assent to it? There is certainly no trace of polemic against Peter in Mark (cf. Mark 16:7 and 11:21; 13:3), or anywhere else in the New Testament, even though there was tension between him and Paul (Gal. 2:11-14). Might Matthew 16:17 have been spoken by Jesus at some point or other and introduced here but not into the Markan text? But even in this case Peter's confession must have preceded, perhaps only of Jesus as "Son of the living God" (cf. John 6:69). But how could this have vanished from the tradition? The suggestion that it once stood in place of Luke 22:31(-34) is hardly credible; who would have substituted a mere assurance of intercession on Peter's behalf (despite his denial) for a positive confession of Jesus as Son of God and a blessing pronounced by Jesus? So it would seem that the phrase "Son of the living God" is a post-Easter addition in Matthew.

Likewise, the saying about the community is a post-Easter addition, possibly Matthew's own. In all four Gospels the word "community" (or "church") appears only here and in 18:17. In the post-Easter epistles and in Acts it appears frequently, but always in the phrase "community of God," which translates the Old Testament expression "levy of God," meaning Israel. The New Testament is aware throughout that Jesus, unlike the Qumran community or the Pharisees, does not seek to establish a special community but to call the *whole* people of God back to their Lord. At most communities "in Christ" are mentioned (Gal. 1:22; cf. Eph. 3:21; 1 Cor. 1:2); the only evidence for "communities of Christ" (Rom. 16:16) is insecure, because the clause appears elsewhere in many manuscripts. In any case, the phrase "my community" is impossible in the mouth of Jesus; "my" would have to be a later substitute for "God's."

Jesus is also hardly likely to have used the rabbinic terminology of "binding and loosing" without explaining that he meant by it something totally different from the exposition of the teachers of the Law. Furthermore, though Peter played a leading role in the community at the outset (Gal. 1:18), probably on account of having been the first to see the risen Lord (1 Cor. 15:5), his role did not go undisputed, and James soon took over leadership (Gal. 2:9, 12; Acts 21:18). Even according to Acts 11:2 ff. (cf. 6:1 ff.) the authority Peter has is not based simply on a saying of the Lord. Anyone who would ascribe these verses to Jesus must assume that in the end he merely followed the example of the Qumran community and the Pharisees, concluding that Israel would never hear God's call, and contenting himself with bringing together a band of men who wanted to return to God and giving them a kind of institutional shape so that the group would survive his death. All the rest of New Testament tradition maintains that this was not the will of Jesus or the way he took.

Now verses 18-19 correspond in their content to the Easter account in John 21:15-17 (and 20:23). Originally, therefore, these sayings to Peter might have been associated with such an account (possibly even the account of Jesus' first appearance, 1 Cor. 15:5?). But Jesus' blessing of Peter, in verse 17, presupposes Peter's confession, not some post-Easter meeting. Elsewhere in Matthew, the word "reveal" appears only in sections deriving from Q; and in the entire New Testament, the rare expression "flesh and blood" appears only here and in 1 Corinthians 15:50; Galatians 1:16. All three expressions, however—"Son," "reveal," and "flesh and blood"—appear in Galatians 1:15-16, where Paul tells how God revealed "his Son" (Matt. 16:16) to him and made him an apostle. Is it possible, then, that the confession of Peter (Mark 8:29-30) was already known at Antioch in the form attested in Matthew 16:16-17, so that Paul used those terms, and that Matthew then inserted the post-Easter saying of verses 18-19?

But if these sayings do not derive from Jesus, neither did Matthew compose them. He may be responsible for minor stylistic changes like the inclusion of his favorite terms "and I," "Father in heaven," and "Kingdom of heaven." Elsewhere, however, he avoids Aramaic idioms (Bar Jonah; see the discussion of 9:23-25). If he had composed verses 16-17 himself, he would not have robbed them of their weight by anticipating the name "Peter" in 4:18 and the confession of Jesus as the Son of God in 14:33. These verses therefore probably derive from the early community that identified itself with Peter.

The Syrian church in particular appears to have based its claims on the authority of Peter (see the excursus on 7:13-23 [§6]). Perhaps Galatians 2:11 ff. indicates that Peter left Jerusalem (Acts no longer mentions him as being there after 12:17, except for 15:7), and moved to the Syrian church at Antioch, where he continued his missionary work (1 Cor. 9:5). In verses 18-19 we might be dealing with something like the Syrian church's declaration of independence from the mother church at Jerusalem or from the synagogue. Since verse 19 bases the authority of Peter as rock of the church on his authority to teach in the sense of interpreting the Law, this last possibility seems very likely. In this case the saying would have come into being sometime after A.D. 70 (but see the discussion of vs. 18), when Judaism organized itself once more under the authority of the scholars at Jamnia and thus survived the catastrophe. These scholars claimed sole authority, as indeed they had to, historically speaking, if the distinction of Israel from the gentile world was to be maintained. To oppose them, the church stated that it was to *Peter* that God granted such authority: i.e., they ascribed what actually came about later—Peter's leadership—to the express wish of Jesus. The name Cephas/Peter was of course already part of the tradition. We are not dealing with a Greek name alongside an Aramaic name, as in the case of Saul/Paul, but with a defining epithet.

When did Simon come to be called Cephas? According to Mark 3:16, it was when the Twelve were called; according to Matthew 16:18 (despite 4:18), it was probably after his confession; according to John 1:42, it was when he first met Jesus. This variety illustrates the uncertainty; no one remembers how far back the name goes. There is much to suggest that it was given after Easter. The first appearance of the risen Lord to Simon (1 Cor. 15:5) would have made him the foundation-stone of the entire church. Also reminiscent of the Easter accounts are the sayings, associated here with the giving of the name "Peter," about the future (in other words, post-Easter) building of the church, which the power of death shall never overcome, and about the keys to the Kingdom of heaven. These are echoed in Revelation 1:18 and 3:7. The appearance of the name "Simon" alone in Luke 22:31; 24:34; and John 21:15-17 (cf. Mark 14:37) could suggest that the supplementary name came into use later. But it is not easy to conceive the community's giving him a name unattested elsewhere; and if it does go back to Simon's encounter with the risen Lord, why has this vanished totally from the tradition, although traces remain of a special commission given to "Simon" (Luke 22:32; John 21:15-17)? Furthermore, the additional name appears in all the Gospels during the earthly lifetime of Jesus. Simon evidently held a special position within the disciples even then. Thus in view of the parallel account in Mark 3:17, it still appears most likely that Jesus created the epithets "sons of thunder" and "rock" when he first called his disciples, so as to give them new and prophetic status from the start. But this conclusion by no means eliminates the possibility that the way Matthew 16:18-19 describes the new status of Peter reflects the post-Easter situation.

[14] Jeremiah is mentioned along with Elijah, perhaps because he was the first of the prophets in many Bibles, but more likely because only those who were taken up into heaven by God, like Enoch and

Elijah (Gen. 5:23; 2 Kings 2:11), can return before the end. Such a story is not told about Jeremiah, but according to 2 Maccabees 2:1-9 he hid the ark, the tabernacle, and the altar of incense in a cave before the destruction of Jerusalem so that God could bring them to light at the eschaton; according to 15:12-16, as a constant intercessor on Israel's behalf he appeared to the High Priest in a desperate situation to give him a sword. This means that during the New Testament period he was thought of as dwelling in heaven, even though the expectation that he would be sent to earth as a messenger of God together with Isaiah before the end (2 Esd. 2:18) is probably Christian in origin. Perhaps the Matthaean community also attached particular importance to him because he had prophesied the destruction of Jerusalem. Or is nothing more meant than that many people reject Jesus because they see in him a prophet of disaster and have had their fill of his jeremiads?

[16] The confession of Peter has been augmented by the addition of "the Son of the living God," a formula found only here in the New Testament (cf. 26:63). For Matthew, however, the Son of Man (vs. 13) and Son of God are not opposites; the only question is how "Son of Man" is to be understood. At the crucifiction of Jesus, 27:40 takes up the question of the Tempter: "If you are God's Son . . ."; and 27:43 suggests the influence of Wisdom of Solomon 2:18, where the righteous sufferer is termed "son of God" (or "servant of God"; 2:13). In Mark, the reference to the suffering Son of Man serves to correct the title "Christ"; Matthew uses the titles "Christ" and "Son of God" to explain the ambiguous title "Son of Man." The title "Son of God" finds its ultimate fulfillment in Jesus' Passion (cf. Matt. 3:15 alongside 3:17). Even in 14:33, where divine sonship is associated with performance of miracles, Matthew's main concern is with confessing the Son of God, whose chief attribute is not miracles but a healing love.

[17] The phrase "flesh and blood" describes man as being subject to sickness and death, always limited in strength and knowledge, while "heaven" is the realm of God, not subject to limits. The identification of the crucial event of salvation as knowledge is in line with the thought of Qumran, the epistles to the Colossians and Ephesians, and the non-Pauline appendix to Romans, 16:25-27 (cf. the discussion of Mark 4:10-12). The secret knowledge here, however, is not what

it was in Qumran; here it is knowledge of Jesus' way of suffering.

"Bar Jonah," which means "son of Jonah," is odd, since according to John 1:42 and Gospel of the Nazarenes 14 Simon's father is named John. It is just possible that "barjonah" means "terrorist," although according to Mark 3:18 it is another Simon among Jesus' disciples who is so characterized. Are we dealing with a confusion of two persons? More likely "Jonah" is a short form of "Johanan" (="Johannes" or "John"); despite the prophet of this name, there is no trace of "Jonah" as a proper name in the centuries before and after Jesus.

[18] Despite 4:18, Matthew probably thinks of Jesus as bestowing the name, not interpreting it. What the Father has given him is pronounced by the Son ("And I"). It is he, the Son—not Peter or any other disciple—who will build the church. The period after Easter is undoubtedly meant. The "rock" is Peter himself, not his confession. Only on this interpretation does the pun make sense. This would hold true even if the original Aramaic form had been something like: "I say to you, yes to you, Peter: upon these rocks . . . ." The special status of Peter, before Easter, is attested by the three Gospels that mention only James and John and occasionally Andrew alongside him (cf. John 6:68), after Easter by Galatians 1:18; 1 Corinthians 1:12; Luke 22:31-34; John 21:15-16 (again, only in company with James, now the brother of the Lord, and John). The statement of Paul that there can be no other foundation of the church than Christ (1 Cor. 3:11; cf. 3:21 ff., A.D. 54/55) may contain a polemic against the saying we are discussing. But Matthew, too, imputes no merit to Peter for his strength of faith, since faith comes not from the will or from actions but from God. As the first apostle to experience the miracle of faith, he remains the "rock," even when he turns into a "stone of offense" (see the discussion of vs. 23).

In this sense all the apostles and (New Testament) prophets are the foundation-stone on which the church is built (Eph. 2:20; cf. Rev. 21:14). The Greek word means "rock," only rarely "stone" (see the discussion of vs. 23). Like much of the rest of the ancient Near East, Israel pictured the earth as a hollow mountain towering above the primordial sea, and later as the capstone introduced into the structure of the cosmos by God to keep the floods of the primordial ocean contained. In particular, the rock on the which the Temple was built was thought of as sealing the gateway to the underworld, with the rest of the world extending around it; as such it is also termed the gate of heaven. Thus Isaiah 28:16 speaks of the foundation-stone that God is laying in Zion, from which the waters of God's justice shall pour forth like a "torrent," sweeping away all evil, and upon which the alliance of Israel's enemies with "death and hell" will be broken. But when God becomes a "stone of offense" or a stumbling block, Israel's enemies will overwhelm her (Isa. 8:7-8, 14).

Most important is a prayer from Qumran (1QH vi. 23-28): "Its waves and all its billows crashed against me . . . . The primordial flood roars . . . and my soul arrives at the gates of the underworld." But the worshiper is rescued by being brought within the secure city, founded and built by God upon rock, amid "sheltering gates that vouchsafe no entrance, and secure bolts that do not shatter." Here the images of the flood, the gates of Hades, the city built on rock, and bolts that bar the gate to peril occur together. In addition, 4QFlor. i. 6-7 probably illustrates the transfer of images used for the house of God to the community of those who uphold the Law, although expectation of an eschatological Temple remains alive.

In 4QpPs. 37. 3 (2). 16 we also read of a community being built by the Teacher of Righteousness. A Jewish saying that calls Abraham a rock on which God will build the world contains the Greek word *petra*, and may therefore be an echo of our saying or a polemical countersaying. King Hezekiah, stricken by God, is summoned to the "gates of the underworld" (not hell; Isa. 38:10); God brings men down to them and leads men up again (Wisd. 16:3; cf. 3 Macc. 5:51; Ps. Sol. 16:2; 1QH vi. 24). The places can easily be personified, so that it is not necessary to assume an Aramaic original for "gatekeepers of Hades." It has been suggested that at one time the saying referred not to the church but to Peter, promising him that he would not die before the appearance of Jesus for the Last Judgment (John 21:23). Syriac translations actually read "you" instead of "it"; but in the earliest texts "you" is feminine and addressed to "Zion" as a symbol of the church; later "Zion" was confused with "Simon." The saying therefore states unequivocally that death with all its power cannot put an end to the Christian community.

Although Matthew separates the reference to the death and resurrection of Jesus from our passage (see the discussion of vs. 21), there are echoes of Easter language; Romans 6:9 says that death no longer has any power over the risen Lord; according to Revelation 1:18, he has been given the keys of death and the underworld, but also the key of David (Rev. 3:7 = Isa. 22:22).

[19] In Jewish interpretation, the key of David refers to the teachers of the Law (exiled in Babylon); according to Matthew 23:13, the "keys of the Kingdom of heaven" are in the hands of the teachers of the Law. A contrast is here drawn between them and Peter. He is thus not the gatekeeper of heaven, but the steward of the Kingdom of heaven upon earth. His function is described in more detail as "binding and loosing." Since Isaiah 22:22 is not sufficient to account for even a suspected Aramaic original, the saying must from the very outset have referred to an authority like that of the teachers of the Law. In this context, "binding" and "loosing" refer to the magisterium to declare a commandment binding or not binding, for example, to state that a law against working on the Sabbath is not binding on a priest performing his official duties, but binds those who are not priests. With this of course goes the disciplinary power to "bind" a man if he has transgressed a commandment that applies to him and to "loose" him if not. Everything decided by the "lower court" is confirmed by the "superior court," i.e. God himself. Josephus says of the Pharisees (*Bell. Jud.* i. 111) that they exile and recall, loose and bind. For Matthew, however, there is only one correct interpretation of the Law, that of Jesus. This is accessible to the community through the tradition of Peter and applicable to their practical problems.

Probably we are dealing here mostly with teaching authority, and always with the understanding that God must ratify what Petrine tradition declares permitted or forbidden in the community. At the same time, the expression about being loosed or bound in heaven suggests the authority to pardon a sinner or, if he will not listen, to "bind" him (see the discussion of 5:19). This means that the opening of heaven, the forgiveness of sin, is no longer reserved to the decree of the Pharisaic teacher of the Law. The keys and the authority to use them have been given to the followers of Jesus (for further comments, see the discussion of 18:18). [20] With the concluding verse, Matthew returns to the Markan narrative; because of the interpolation, the disciples must be mentioned again. The last few words explicitly reaffirm Jesus' messianic title, while in Mark it remains an open question how accurate this title is.

For Matthew, then, the major emphasis of this section is on the appointment of Peter to his special ministry. Peter is not described in especially laudatory terms (cf. vs. 23; 14:31) but more as one typical of all the disciples in their ignorance and lack of faith, yet also in their deliverance through Jesus' intervention (see the discussion of 15:15; also of 14:33; 16:21-23, end; 17:24-25; introductory remarks on 18:-21-22). What is said to Peter in verse 19 is applied to all the disciples in 18:18. To say this is not to deny his historically unique position. The unique events during the lifetime of Jesus lay the foundation for what will be repeated continually in the community (cf. the discussion of 8:23). Only on the basis of the tradition that begins with Jesus can the community exercise its authority. Jesus' "successor" can therefore only be the community as a whole. Of course there is room for discussion whether a single leader would be useful to this total community in the performance of its ministry: a pastor or supervisor in the local church, a bishop in a larger region, a Pope in the universal church. But this must be clearly understood to be one form of organization among many, i.e. as something which may be retained at certain times and in certain places, but which should be replaced by other forms elsewhere (cf. the excursus on 7:13-23).

Jesus Speaks about His Suffering and Death (16:21-23)
Cf. Mark 8:31-33; Luke 9:22

²¹From that time on Jesus Christ began to show his disciples that he must go to Jerusalem and suffer much from the elders, the chief priests, and the teachers of the Law, and be put to death, and be raised to life on the third day. ²²Peter took him aside and began to rebuke him. "God forbid, Lord!" he said. "This must never happen to you!" ²³Jesus turned around and said to Peter, "Get away from me, Satan! You are a stumbling block to me, because these thoughts of yours are men's thoughts, not God's!"

[21] Matthew does not follow Mark in linking the announcement of the Passion directly to the preceding episode with "and," but says "from that time on," referring to the whole period to follow. He explicitly mentions the "disciples," whom Mark does not speak of until later; the announcement is therefore no longer a public proclamation. But just as Jesus' public preaching started with the words "From that time on he began . . ." (4:17; cf. also 22:46), so now the proclamation of his Passion begins the same way. It is also noteworthy that he does not adopt the Markan term "teach." Teaching is primarily public and ethical in nature, whereas "show" refers to revelation of divine mysteries, like those that Revelation 1:1 says are entrusted by God to Jesus "to show his servants what must take place." Perhaps this also accounts for the appearance of the full title "Jesus Christ," found only here and in 1:18, although some manuscripts do not include it. There is also more emphasis on Jerusalem than there was in Mark. "On the third day" is more accurate than "after three days" (Mark 8:31; also Matt. 12:40); it probably derives from the language of the community, from their liturgy or a confession of faith (1 Cor. 15:4; cf. also the discussion of Matt. 17:9).

[22] Matthew places special emphasis on Peter, going beyond Mark to quote his objection directly. The Greek of the first sentence is highly elliptical: "Gracious to you, Lord!" As parallels show, the probable meaning is "God forbid!" The translation "God will protect you from it" is unlikely. [23] Jesus' rebuke about the "stumbling block" or "offense" (*skándalon;* cf. the discussion of Mark 6:3) is also not found in Mark. Now the sayings about the "elect stone" laid as a cornerstone in Zion (Isa. 28:16), which can also become a "stone of stumbling" (*pétra skandálou;* Isa. 8:14-15) play an important role in the early community. They are independently yoked together in Romans 9:33 and 1 Peter 2:6-8 (cf. also Ps. 118:22-23 in Matt. 21:42). Elsewhere, too, the same quotations and images are applied at one point to Jesus, at another to the disciples (cf. 1 Cor. 3:11 and 1 Pet. 2:6 with Matt. 16:18; Heb. 1:5 with 2 Cor. 6:18 and Rev. 21:7; Rev. 2:26 with 19:15; John 12:38 with Rom. 10:16; John 8:12 with Matt. 5:14; see also the concluding remarks on Matt. 18:10-14). Thus the image in verse 18 (Peter as rock) has probably influenced the image in verse 23 (Peter as stumbling stone), just as Christ himself is both a foundation-stone and a stone of stumbling.

The double nature of the community of Jesus can already be observed in Peter. It is chosen by God, endowed with the gift of new knowledge, and under way toward the Kingdom of heaven; at the same time it continues to live in peril of temptation and even under threat of judgment. It has not been taught about the "deep secrets of Satan" (Rev. 2:24); these it experiences in its own disobedience, above all in its resistance to a theology—or, better, a practice—of the cross. Just as Peter is called back to discipleship, where he must learn to think God's thoughts, so too is the community. Once more Peter represents every disciple. The way is paved for a theology of the cross arising from experience, like Paul's theology of suffering and defeat.

Discipleship (16:24-28)
Cf. Mark 8:34–9:1; Luke 9:23-27

[24]Then Jesus said this to his disciples, "If anyone wants to follow after me, he must deny himself, take up his cross, and follow me. [25]For whoever wants to save his own life will lose it; but whoever loses his life for my sake will find it. [26]Will a man gain anything if he wins the whole world but loses his life? Of course not! Or what could a man give to regain his own life? [27]For the Son of Man will come in the glory of his Father with his angels, and then he will 'repay everyone according to his deeds.' [28]Amen, I tell you, there are some among those standing here who will not taste death until they have seen the Son of Man come in his Kingdom."
(Vs. 27—Ps. 62:12; Prov. 24:12.)

[24] Here Matthew follows Mark almost verbatim; but he presents the material as instructions for the disciples, not as an address to the crowd. Only the disciple, according to Matthew, decides to follow Jesus, thus distinguishing himself from the crowd. Mark stresses the appeal to all; only later is it possible to see who obeys and who does not. In Matthew, on the other hand, the saying is linked with Jesus' rebuke to Peter in verse 23: temptation and renewed discipleship alternate constantly in the life of the disciple.

[25] Matthew speaks of "finding" one's life rather than "saving"

it because he is also familiar with the saying in the form it takes in 10:38-39. He is thinking of men's amazement at the fullness of life in the coming Kingdom. [26] The future tense in verse 26, instead of the present, used by Mark, also reveals an eschatological perspective. For this reason also the following verse is appended directly with "for"; the coming of the Son of Man to judgment is the reason for this appeal.

[27] The warning that the Son of Man will deny anyone who has denied him on earth (Mark 8:38) is omitted because the same saying (in its Q form) has already appeared in Matthew 10:33, and because these words are addressed only to the disciples. Instead, Matthew uses an Old Testament quotation (Ps. 62:12; Prov. 24:12; frequently cited in the New Testament) to make the point that men's actions will be requited. Since in Psalm 62:12 this refers only to the reward of the righteous, Matthew may be thinking of the same thing in this section, addressed to the disciples, therefore writing "deeds" instead of "works." This would view the life of faith as a unity, not divisible into so many individual acts (cf. the discussion of 3:8; 7:16-18).

The saying about the appearance of the Son of Man has become a main clause rather than a subordinate clause, [28] and the concluding verse is no longer separated from it as in Mark 9:1. This shows how the entire section builds up to the Judgment by the Son of Man. He is mentioned once more at the conclusion; [27] the "holy angels" (Mark 8:38) have become "his angels" (vs. 27; cf. 13:41; 24:31; 25:31; Matthaean redaction in each case); the "Kingdom of God" has become "his Kingdom." Jesus therefore shifts his role from crucial witness at the Last Judgment (cf. the excursus at Mark 8:27-33) to that of Judge and Lord of God's Kingdom. Whether Matthew expects these events to take place before the death of the last disciple of Jesus is not clear; possibly he takes the saying about "not tasting death" in the sense that the disciple of Jesus can die secure in the knowledge that death has been overcome and that he will be raised.

At the very beginning (vs. 13) and the very end (vs. 28), Matthew has introduced the Son of Man to provide a framework for the entire section. The question about the Son of Man (vs. 13) is finally answered by reference to the judgment that awaits even the disciples and the reward that faithfulness will receive (cf. the discussion of 13:47-50).

**God's Answer to the Announcement
of the Passion (17:1-9)**
Cf. Mark 9:2-8; Luke 9:28-36

¹Six days later Jesus took with him Peter and the brothers James and John, and led them up a high mountain by themselves. ²As they looked on, a change came over him: his face became as bright as the sun, and his clothes as white as light. ³Then behold, Moses and Elijah appeared to them, talking with Jesus. ⁴So Peter spoke up and said to Jesus, "Lord it is a good thing that we are here; if you wish, I will make three booths here, one for you, one for Moses, and one for Elijah." ⁵While he was talking, a shining cloud came over them and a voice said from the cloud: "This is my beloved Son, 'with whom I am well pleased'—'listen to him!' " ⁶When the disciples heard the voice they were so terrified that they threw themselves face down to the ground. ⁷Jesus came to them and touched them. "Get up," he said. "Don't be afraid!" ⁸So they looked up and saw no one else except Jesus. ⁹As they came down the mountain Jesus ordered them, "Don't tell anyone about this vision until the Son of Man has been raised from the dead."

(Vs. 2—Exod. 34:29-30. Vs. 5—Ps. 2:7 [2 Sam. 7:14]; Deut. 18:15; Isa. 42:1.)

In the account of the Transfiguration, the changes Matthew makes are clear. [1] Is John introduced as the brother of James because he was less well known to the Matthaean community than the martyr James (Acts 12:2)? [2] The transformation of Jesus is described as a glorious brightness. The images of the sun and light replace that of the whiteness of new cloth (Mark 9:3), and the radiance of his face is particularly emphasized (as in Luke 9:29). Such radiance appeared on Moses' face after his encounter with God on Sinai (Exod. 34:29-35; also mentioned by Philo and Josephus); but Jesus' skin is not mentioned as in the case of Moses, and a closer parallel is probably the expectation that at the resurrection the faces of the righteous would shine like the sun (2 Esd. 7:97; Syr. Bar. 51:3;

in rabbinic literature *passim;* cf. Judg. 5:31). Above all, the risen Christ is described in similar terms in Revelation 1:16. [3] Moses is mentioned first (as in Luke 9:30), corresponding to the sequence of Biblical history. That the episode was originally an appearance of Elijah, to which Moses was added later (cf. the discussion of Mark 9:4), can now be seen only from the retention of "appeared" in the singular.

[4] The conversation with Jesus, which Mark mentions only after the fact, is for Matthew the actual content of the vision. The disciples address Jesus as "Lord" (see the discussion of 8:2), and even the addition of "if you wish" shows that they are far from foolish, as Mark 9:6 asserts (omitted here). [5] Even the cloud is represented as a cloud of light (Rev. 14:14); it is not a natural cloud, but simultaneously reveals and conceals the presence of God himself. The voice of God is emphasized in the Greek text by the Biblical phrase "and behold" (see the discussion of 8:2). More precisely than in Mark the voice repeats the exact words spoken at Jesus' baptism (3:17), but adds (with Mark 9:7): "listen to him" (cf. Deut. 18:15). As in 28:19-20, Matthew probably has in mind here Jesus' ethical instruction, rather than the preceding announcement of the Passion, to which Luke 9:31 makes special reference.

[6-7] Only in Matthew is the reaction of the disciples (cf. Mark 9:6) described in terms taken from the Old Testament (Isa. 6:5; Ezek. 2:1; Dan. 8:17; 10:9-10, 15-19; Rev. 1:17; cf. Eth. Enoch 14:14, 24-25). Matthew does not base his account on stories associated with Moses but on Old Testament passages that touch on the mystery of the eschaton and resurrection. We often read in the Old Testament that men are abolished with fear at the sight of God but are told not to be afraid—usually, however, in the context of prophetic or apocalyptic experiences. The verb "get up" is used in just this way when Jesus raises the dead, e.g. in 9:25; it is also used this way by extension in healings (8:15) and in the short baptismal hymn in Ephesians 5:14. We also read that Jesus "touches" the sick or dead in 8:3; 9:29. Only here and at his appearance as the risen Lord (28:18) do we read that Jesus "comes to" the disciples (see the discussion of 8:2); in both cases he comes to them as Lord over death, raising them up and giving them back true life. Probably Matthew is trying to depict by anticipation

what will one day happen to the disciple when his Lord comes to him as the risen Christ and restores him to life.

[8-9] The disciples lift up their eyes instead of just "looking about" (Mark 9:8) because they have fallen to the ground, which they do not do in the Markan account. Of course the "vision" (as Matthew calls it; cf. the use of the same word in Dan. 2:19; Acts 10:17; etc.) vanishes; but as in 28:20 Jesus himself remains (as Matthew emphasizes). Matthew also follows good Jewish usage in speaking literally of Jesus' "awakening" rather than "rising" from the dead (Mark 9:9). The same is true in 16:21; 17:23; 20:19; even in the usual sense of "stand up" Matthew avoids the verb (he uses it only here, in 9:9, and 26:62; Mark uses it sixteen times). Once more, the statement about the disciples' lack of understanding (Mark 9:10) is omitted (cf. the discussion of 13:16-17).

As the interpolation in verses 6-7 shows, Matthew is primarily interested in how these disciples, who stand as prototypes for all later disciples, experience the Transfiguration. Their falling to the ground and being "raised" by Jesus, as well as the introduction of the light symbolism, makes Matthew's account more suggestive than Mark's of what will happen at the resurrection, when Jesus will "come to" men and "touch" them, taking away all fear forever and giving them life.

Elijah and the Suffering Son of Man (17:10-13)
Cf. Mark 9:9-13

[10]Then the disciples asked Jesus, "Why do the teachers of the Law say that Elijah has to come first?" [11]" 'Elijah' does indeed come first," answered Jesus, "and 'will restore everything.' [12]But I tell you this: Elijah has already come and people did not recognize him, but treated him just as they pleased. In the same way the Son of Man will also suffer at their hands." [13]Then the disciples understood that he was talking to them about John the Baptist.
(Vs. 11—Mal. 3:23[4:5].)

[11] The structure of the conversation as Jesus and the disciples come down from the mountain is clearer than in Mark (cf. the discus-

sion of Mark 9:9-13). The future tense in "will restore" (Mark 9:12 uses the present) corresponds to the tense found in the Greek Bible, though the manuscript evidence for it is not absolutely certain. This tense would suggest that the Baptist (vs. 13) will yet do this; but Matthew probably has in mind that "the way he was treated" (vs. 12; cf. the Septuagint text of Gen. 40:14 and one manuscript of Dan. 11:7) has prevented John from doing so. Above all, however, the order is reversed: first we are told that Elijah has already come, but, as Matthew adds in explanation, was not recognized; only then do we hear of the suffering of the Son of Man, on analogy to the suffering of Elijah. [13] Thereupon the solution to the riddle is explicitly stated (as it already was in 11:14), namely that John the Baptist is Elijah returned; we are also told that the disciples understood this, in contrast to the people who "did not recognize him." Thus the disciples, who understand, oppose the teachers of the Law, who do not.

Jesus Heals an Epileptic Boy · and Instructs the Disciples (17:14-21)
Cf. Mark 9:14-29; Luke 9:37-43

[14]When they returned to the crowd, a man came to Jesus, knelt before him, [15]and said, "Sir, have mercy on my son! He is epileptic and has such terrible fits that he often falls in the fire or in the water. [16]I brought him to your disciples, but they could not heal him." [17]Jesus answered, "You unbelieving and perverse generation, how long must I be with you? How long do I have to put up with you? Bring the boy here to me!" [18]And Jesus admonished him, and the demon went out of him, so that the boy was healed at that very moment. [19]Then the disciples came to Jesus in private and asked him, "Why couldn't we drive the demon out?" [20]"It was because you have so little faith," answered Jesus. "For Amen, I tell you this: if you have faith as big as a mustard seed, you can say to this hill, 'Go from here to there!' and it will go. And nothing will be impossible for you. [[21]But only prayer and fasting can drive this kind out.]"

As in 8:28-34; 9:18-26, Matthew abbreviates the Markan text considerably. For the most part the text is shortened at the same points as in Luke, though not in the same way except in verses 16b ("they could not") and 17 ("Jesus, however, answered and said, 'You unbelieving and perverse generation' "). It has been suggested that two forms of the same story are woven together in Mark 9:14-29; what Matthew and, to a great extent, Luke provide corresponds quite closely to the first version of the account. It was therefore obviously still being told in this short form.

[18] Verse 18 reveals, however, that Matthew was also familiar with the Markan recension. Only in Mark does Jesus direct his admonition (correctly) to the demon just before it leaves the boy; only Mark mentions the demon before this point. In Matthew the admonition is actually directed to the sick boy. The healing is described very briefly, in terms reminiscent of Matthew 8:13. The faith of the man (Matthew uses his preferred Greek word which actually means "human being" and can apply to any reader) is indicated by his kneeling before Jesus and calling him "sir" (literally "Lord"; cf. the discussion of 8:2), as well as by his cry for help, "have mercy," which is also inserted in 15:22 (cf. 9:27). Mark describes the boy's sickness in some detail; Matthew merely refers to it briefly as epilepsy (literally "lunacy," a term whose etymology reflects the theories of ancient medicine; Matthew alone uses the word, here and in 4:24).

[16] The inability of the disciples to heal the boy is also mentioned, but not their dispute with the teachers of the Law. Indeed, the teachers of the Law (Mark 9:14) are no longer mentioned, for [17] Jesus' bitterness is directed against the people as a whole in Matthew's opinion, not just against the disciples, who are not brought in until verse 19 (cf. the discussion of 13:16-17). In any event, Matthew expands Jesus' exclamation, adding the phrase about the "perverse generation," taken from Moses' lament over Israel (Deut. 32:5).

Even more than Mark, Matthew takes the story as nothing more than an occasion for a discourse on faith. He therefore concentrates on the faith the disciples have experienced, omitting the lack of faith on the part of the teachers of the Law as well as the magnificent portrayal of the father's nascent faith, threatened by doubt (Mark 9:22-24). [19] The disciples who "come to" Jesus (see the discussion of 8:2) [20] are accused by him of having "little faith" (some manuscripts, influenced by vs. 17, say "no faith"). Although for Matthew the faith of the disciples is a fundamental principle, their faith is endangered when faced by too great a challenge, so that their attention starts to vacillate between Jesus and the approaching challenge or danger (see the discussion of 14:31 and Mark 11:23).

The whole story leads to Jesus' saying that faith is like a mustard seed, which resembles the saying found in Mark 11:22-23 = Matthew 21:21. This probably represents its earliest form (see the discussion of Mark 11:23), which was also known to Paul (1 Cor. 13:2). Jewish parallels speak only of the "mountain-moving ingenuity" with which the teachers of the Law split hairs to interpret it. The metaphor of the "mustard seed" is found also in Luke 17:6; the reference to a "mountain" appears in Mark 11:23, the "sea" in both those passages but not here. In Greek a tree or mountain rising out of the sea serves as an image for something that is impossible. Here Matthew may be thinking of the miracles to come at the eschaton (Isa. 40:4). If Matthew 17:20 is in fact the earliest form of this saying, it was appended later to the story of the cursing of the fig tree; in this case Luke 17:6 is an intermediate form between the two statements, in which the reference to the mustard seed may already suggest the possibility that faith can grow (Luke 17:5). In any case, Matthew is familiar with the saying through the tradition of his community, and lets it influence the saying in 21:21 as well ("Amen, I tell you this: if you . . ."). [21] At the end some copyists have followed Mark 9:29 in adding the reference to prayer and fasting, because they considered it important for the life of the church in their day.

Matthew thus cites the story in its Markan context, but turns it into a lesson about faith. The subject matter is no longer universal, the nascent faith of the man who for the first time approaches Jesus, but the ever-endangered faith of the disciple. At this point we find the saying about faith like a grain of mustard seed. What is required of the disciple is therefore not that his faith be especially impressive, but that it be a faith, however small, that looks to Jesus in "simplicity" and expects everything from him. Then "nothing will be impossible for you," as Matthew puts it in emphatic contrast to verse 16, using exactly the same verb. For Matthew, once more, faith very much implies power and authority to perform charismatic healings (cf. the excursus on 7:13-23 [§2]). Matthew may even think that the small faith of these disciples has given place to a greater faith since the promise of the risen Lord (28:20); but he nonetheless speaks of temptations that endanger the community (see the discussion of 13:41 ff. and chapters 21–25). Did he perhaps omit Mark 9:14*b*-16 because the dialogue between the Pharisees and the disciples of Jesus had been broken off by his time?

The Second Announcement of the Passion (17:22-23)
Cf. Mark 9:30-32; Luke 9:43-45

[22]When they all came together in Galilee, Jesus said to them, "The Son of Man is about to be handed over to men [23]who will kill him; but on the third day he will be raised to life." The disciples became very sad.

The introduction to the second announcement of the Passion is abbreviated. **[22]** The idea that Jesus wants to remain hidden (Mark 9:30) is omitted. The identity of those who "came together" is not specified; probably the disciples are meant, since they have just been referred to. The phrase "in Galilee," which does not really fit, comes from Mark 9:30. Or are we to think in terms of popular messianic expectations (cf. Luke 9:43; John 6:15), which Jesus countered by announcing his Passion? Luke is familiar with this announcement in a striking and brief form, which might go back to Jesus himself and represent the original version of the more elaborate announcement of the Passion: "The Son of Man will be handed over into the hands of men [Aramaic: 'sons of men']." The influence of this form appears in Matthew: the form of the verb agrees with Luke 9:44 against Mark. **[23]** The prediction of the resurrection (see the discussion of 17:9), however, which is not found in Luke 9:44, is recorded in the form found in Matthew 16:21, and the statement that the disciples "became very sad" likewise occurs (with a different subject) in 18:31. In Mark 9:32, we read: "But they did not understand what this teaching meant"; according to Matthew, they understood quite well (see the discussion of 13:16-17).

Payment of the Temple Tax (17:24-27)

[24]When Jesus and his disciples came to Capernaum, the collectors of the double drachma came to Peter and said, "Does your master not pay the double drachma?" [25]"Of course," Peter answered. When Peter went into the house, Jesus spoke up first, "Simon, what is your opinion? Who pays duties or taxes to the kings of this world? The citizens of the country or the foreigners?" [26]"The foreigners," answered Peter. "Well, then," replied Jesus, "that means that the citizens don't have to pay. [27]But we don't want to offend these people. So go to the lake and drop in a line; pull up the first fish you hook, and in its mouth you will find a stater. Take it and pay them for you and me."
(Vs. 24—Cf. 2 Chron. 24:6.)

On the place of this section in the structure of the whole Gospel, see the following section.

Since every verse contains Matthaean idioms (on vs. 25, cf. the discussion of 18:12-13, introductory remarks), Matthew probably composed this episode himself on the basis of oral tradition. **[24-25]** It is possible that at one time the story mentioned only Peter's response to the tax collectors (vs. 24 and the beginning of vs. 25), as authority for remaining faithfully within the Jewish cultic community. In its present form, it combines the fundamental liberty of the community of Jesus with a readiness to follow the prevailing norms of Jewish law in externals like payment of the Temple tax. This position probably represents Matthew's perspective (see the discussion of 24:20). The essential points of the story must have come into being before the destruction of the Temple, since afterwards the tax was collected only for the benefit of the Romans. If there was also a Jewish tax as well, which is not impossible, it would not have been called a double drachma; and Roman taxes are not under discussion, since "kings of this world" is used metaphorically within the parable, like the phrase "king of flesh and blood" found in the writings of Jewish teachers. The point is that just as these kings do not tax their own citizens (or, as the text reads literally, "sons"), in contrast to subject provinces, so the King in heaven does not tax the citizens (or "children") of his Kingdom.

It is highly unlikely that the Matthaean community refused to pay taxes to the state (cf. Rom. 13:1-7). Furthermore, to urge that community to pay such taxes is hardly the point here, since there is no mention of the other eleven disciples and the stater (vs. 27; see the discussion of vs. 24 below) is sufficient only for Jesus and Peter. This point, too, suggests a pre-Matthaean tradition, since both 17:22 and 18:1 imply the presence of all the disciples.

[27] It is questionable whether verse 27 formed part of the episode from the very beginning; coming after the actual point of the narrative (vs. 26), it introduces a miracle as a second climax. It is conceivable that first the freedom of the community from the Jewish Law was emphasized, while later, but still before Matthew, the community (Antioch?) added verse 27 to say that in practice this freedom could be renounced.

The allegorical saying about the freedom of God's children could go back to Jesus (see the discussion of 5:9). [24] But then the original occasion would not be clear, since the episode as it stands is patently the product of the post-Easter community: the tax collectors address their question to Peter rather than Jesus because in the community Peter must serve to interpret the will of Jesus (16:19; see the concluding remarks on this passage). The tax collectors consider a negative reply possible, and in fact that is precisely Jesus' answer in verses 25-26. Jesus is not claiming a special privilege for a specific class. Even the monastic community at Qumran, which came into being as a protest against the Temple at Jerusalem and its priesthood, paid the Temple tax without objection. The double drachma is a Phoenician coin collected as Temple tax (cf. Exod. 30:11-16; Neh. 10:33-34). The stater is a Greek monetary unit, which at Antioch and Damascus equaled precisely four drachmas, the Temple tax for two persons. This fact, too, points to the historical site of the community in Syria. The statement that the tax is collected where a man lives betrays knowledge of the Jewish practice. The knowledge that it was collected a month before Passover really tells us nothing about the life of Jesus; even if the episode took place exactly as narrated, it would have been inserted here by Matthew for purely structural reasons, and would therefore not prove that Jesus was still at Capernaum a month before Passover (and even if so, in the year of his death or an earlier year?).

[25] Peter's quick "yes" is called in question by Jesus; Jesus' disciples are no longer foreigners but citizens of the Kingdom, sons of the King, and therefore free. [26] The contrast between the son, who is free, and the servant, who is not, is almost without parallel in Judaism but is peculiar to all of primitive Christianity (Rom. 8:21; Gal. 3:23–4:7; John 8:31-36; Heb. 3:5-6). At the same time, the disparate documents of the New Testament all agree that Jesus remains the Son in a special sense (see the discussion of 5:9). Only after the distinction between free and slave is established can one ask whether there may be reasons for doing of one's own free will what one is no longer required to do.

[27] The last sentence gives a positive answer. Whether the point is an actual mission to the Jews, the conversion of individual Jews, or merely avoidance of unnecessary friction cannot be determined. The motif in the miracle comes from the realm of fairy tale; one is reminded of the story of Polycrates, who casts his ring into the sea to propitiate the gods and gets it back in the fish served for his dinner. Similar stories are told by the rabbis. Behind the story, however, stands the idea that although God subjects his Son to the Law with all that the Law implies, including the cross (Gal. 4:4-5), he is at the same time the Lord who does everything for his Son and himself pays what the Law demands. Thus his band of disciples, too, may hope for God's gift, which is ever new.

This short episode is important to Matthew because it emphasizes the total and fundamental freedom of the Christian community from the Jewish Temple community, while maintaining the principle that one must not offend one's Jewish contemporaries in matters that are not central to the faith (see the discussion of 18:6). There is a negative legalism that is no better than positive legalism when it supposes that fundamental freedom must be demonstrated at all costs (cf. 1 Cor. 9:19 ff.; also 8:1 ff.; Rom. 14). Theologically it is important that we are dealing with a practical question affecting the conduct of the community, and that this question can only be answered by reference to Jesus himself, the one Son who makes his disciples free sons of God.

The Structure of Chapter 18

The very fact that problems of the community are brought up here, between the second and third announcements of the Passion, is instructive. Negatively, it means that Matthew does not associate these questions with the missionary discourse in chapter 10; in other words, he is not interested in regulations for specific functionaries, but in what applies to all Jesus' disciples. Positively, it means that the catchwords "child" and "these little ones" in Mark 9:36, 42 constitute the point of departure. At first Matthew follows the thread of Mark. The location and the mention of the "house" in Mark 9:33 have already been included in Matthew 17:24-25. **[17:24-27]** The question of the Temple tax, however, is discussed before the conversation about who is the greatest; in Mark 9:34 that conversation follows without the Temple tax episode. But that episode is obviously so important to Matthew that he uses it as an introduction to the whole chapter. **[1-5]** The conversation about being great (18:1-5) is reshaped in such a way that the disciples now appear in a good light (see the discussion of 18:1). In addition, an "Amen, I tell you" saying is introduced, which is appropriate here (18:3) although it does not appear in Mark until 10:15. Since an echo of it is also heard in John 3:5-7 (see the discussion of Matt. 18:1-5), it was clearly also preserved as an independent saying.

[6-9] The sayings about giving offence (Mark 9:42-50) are supplemented by the addition of a saying that is also associated with the first saying about offence in Luke 17:1-2. **[10-14]** This introduces the theme of "one of these little ones," which Matthew develops in verses 10 and 14, borrowing the short parable of the lost sheep, which also occurs in Luke 15:3-7, and adapting it to the present context by giving it a new interpretation, so that it refers to the obligation to go after one of the brethren who has strayed. It concludes once more with an "Amen, I tell you" saying that describes God's final verdict, preceded by two conditional clauses.

[15-18] The same structure reappears in the very next section (18:15-18), which sets forth the procedure to be followed by the community when one of its members has fallen into sin. Probably the

community used this and similar sayings to define the legal system through which the Spirit of God orders the Christian community (cf. the introductory remarks on 5:19). Since verse 17 speaks of gentiles and tax collectors, a combination possible only in Jewish Christian communities, not in that of Matthew himself (cf. 21:32, 43), at least this verse must be based on tradition. The only real parallel is the traditional saying in 5:46-47. As a former Pharisee, Paul speaks negatively of the gentile way of life, but never of the gentiles themselves, and 3 John 7 already means "non-Christians" by the term *gentile*.
[21-35] The regulation mentioned in verses 15 and 22 corresponds to the one in Luke 17:3-4, which comes directly after the saying about giving offence (vss. 6-7 = Luke 17:1-2). Thus Matthew develops the rule that is also preserved in Luke 17:3-4, takes up its second half once more in verses 21-22, and illustrates it by means of the parable of the unforgiving servant, which he links with the theme established in verse 21 (forgiveness) by means of the concluding saying in verse 35.

We can therefore make the following observations: (1) In 17:24-27 Matthew makes the entire next chapter a treatment of fidelity to Judaism and the new freedom of the Jesus community. (2) Matthew takes the two parables of the lost sheep and the wicked servant who will not forgive and sets them clearly in a framework defined by his theme ("one of these little ones," vs. 10; forgiveness of a brother, vs. 21) and a concluding saying that picks up the wording of the theme (vss. 14 and 35). (3) The sayings of Jesus in Luke 17:1-4, which in Luke also are linked with the saying from the Markan context that Matthew incorporates in verse 6, appear here in verses 7, 15, and 21. The initial structure is thus furnished by Mark; but it is continued by the sayings of Jesus associated in Q with the first saying (Luke 17:1-4). (4) The urgency of an "Amen, I tell you" saying (usually followed by conditions and then God's eternal verdict) is pointedly brought to bear on the parable of the lost sheep and the regulation governing treatment of a sinful brother. CD xiii. 9-10 shows that both themes go together; there, too, the overseer must concern himself with those who go astray, just as a shepherd concerns himself with stray sheep —but this duty to bring back the lost is just as much a duty to "loosen all the fetters of their chains" (cf. vs. 18*b* here).

Who is responsible for the elaboration of the traditional material?

The controversy about the Temple tax was probably introduced by Matthew, as stylistic arguments suggest. As can be demonstrated in verses 21 and 35, the framework surrounding the parables also goes back to Matthew, though his theme is defined in verse 21 by the saying in Luke 17:4, in verse 10 by the saying in Mark 9:42 or Luke 17:2 (=Matt. 18:6). Whether a certain similarity in structure (see the discussion of 5:19) indicates that verses 3-5, 12-13, 15-18 are of pre-Matthaean origin is very dubious. The conditional clauses have very different functions. At least the structure of verses 1-5 goes back to Matthew. It is also reasonable to assume that Matthew used his own words to formulate the parable in verses 12-13, which was already fixed in its main features, and perhaps he also supplemented the bylaws obtaining in his community, recorded in verses 15-17, by adding the principle in verse 18. The parable of the debtor (appended by Matthew to vss. 21-22) derives from a special tradition.

Being Childlike (18:1-5)
Cf. Mark 9:33-37; Luke 9:46-48

[1]At that moment the disciples came to Jesus, asking, "Who is the greatest in the Kingdom of heaven?" [2]Jesus called a child, had him stand in the midst of them, [3]and said, "Amen, I tell you, unless you repent and become like children, you will never enter the Kingdom of heaven. [4]The greatest in the Kingdom of heaven is the one who humbles himself like this child. [5]And whoever welcomes in my name one such child as this, welcomes me."

[1] Following the interpolation about the Temple tax, Matthew returns to the text of Mark. But he reshapes this section by substituting verses 3-4 (see above) for the principle that the greatest one must be the servant of all (Mark 9:35), which reappears in Mark 10:43-44=Matthew 20:26-27. The result is an actual conversation, like that found also in Matthew's revisions of miracle stories (see the introduction to 8:1-4): the introduction brings on a questioner, whose question is quoted in direct address; [2] Jesus responds with an instructive action (a healing, for example, in the miracle stories) and verbal instruction based precisely on the question (cf.

vss. 1*b*, 4*b:* "the greatest in the Kingdom of heaven").

[3-4] The first of the newly incorporated sayings exists in four versions: Matthew 18:3; Mark 10:15; John 3:3, 5. Common to all are the introduction "Amen, I tell you, unless . . ." and the phrase ". . . will never enter the Kingdom of heaven" (except John 3:3; see below). Since John never speaks of the Kingdom of heaven except in 3:3, 5, the expression undoubtedly derives from a saying in his source material, i.e., verse 5. John 3:3 is thus the Johannine restatement, which speaks only of birth from above and the "seeing" of the Kingdom of God that is taking place even now; the traditional saying in verse 5 referred to baptism and entrance into the eschatological Kingdom of God. It corresponds in large measure to Matthew 18:3. The metaphor of becoming a child (Jesus' own metaphor?) in time came to be associated with baptism, as similarly in 1 Peter 2:1 ff., and was interpreted by the community in the light of their doctrine of baptism as referring to birth through water and the Spirit. Whether Matthew 18:3 or Mark 10:15 is the earlier is hard to decide. Although the rabbis speak of "accepting" the Kingdom of God, i.e. obedience to the Law (Billerbeck on 11:29 A a), and Matthew emphasizes repentance and says also in 5:45 that the disciples are to "become" children of God, the Markan version, "Whoever does not accept the Kingdom of God . . . ," is better explained as an assimilation to 9:37 = Matthew 18:5 ("Whoever welcomes [literally: 'accepts'] one of these children . . ."). It is not really possible to "accept" something and then "enter" it. Furthermore, the saying in Matthew can be traced back to an even earlier Aramaic form. Jesus' mother tongue has no word for "back" or "again," but has to paraphrase: "repent and (=again) become a child," where the word translated "repent" means literally "turn back." Thus Jesus himself might have said, without any emphasis on the notion of repentance, that whoever cannot "become a child again" cannot enter the Kingdom of God.

[1] The location, a house at Capernaum (Mark 9:33), was already mentioned in Matthew 17:24-25. There follows directly the question of the disciples as to who is the greatest. There is no longer any mention of their quarrel about earthly greatness; according to Matthew, they approach Jesus with respect (see the discussion of 8:2) and

ask to be instructed about what it means to be great in the Kingdom of heaven. Their question is thus the result of true devotion (see the discussion of vs. 4). [2] As in Mark, Jesus performs a kind of symbolic action, placing a child before the disciples. He calls the child to him, rather than "taking" him as in Mark, and it is no longer stated that he put his arms around him, because the purpose of comparison is now different. [3] Matthew adds the saying about becoming like children, which Mark does not cite until 10:15; it is better suited to the disciples' question about greatness than is the saying about welcoming children (Mark 9:37 = Matt. 18:5).

Matthew's purpose is undoubtedly to emphasize repentance in the sense of return to childlike thought, will, and action. [4] This is shown by his use of the saying, to explain what it means to become a child, that one should humble himself. This expression was very popular in Judaism at the time of Jesus (cf. the discussion of 23:12), although it does not really fit the more radical image of becoming a child, for children do not humble themselves: they are already little and aware of their littleness, so that out of gratitude (or fear) for security they accept what those who are larger and stronger can give them. Now Matthew has not forgotten that being little is itself a gift; he adds "like this child," thus linking this verse with what precedes. His purpose is therefore not simply to recommend a way of achieving greatness in the Kingdom of heaven. Only the man who can accept humility from his Lord (the Greek text uses the same word in 11:29) can humble himself. But what Matthew is really stressing is the challenge to live one's life vividly and consciously, in all that one does, with childlike lack of self-concern.

With the phrase "the greatest in the Kingdom of heaven" he comes back to the disciples' question, and characterizes it once more as a proper one. Its answer has been given through Jesus. It is typical of Matthew that question and answer focus on the coming Kingdom of God, which will reward the community for its proper conduct (cf. the discussion of 19:27). The reply stands in sharp contrast to those given by teachers of the Law; they, for example, call academic teachers "rabbis," i.e., "great" ones. Jesus' band of disciples, by contrast, remain amateurs and as helpless as children. They must consciously and deliberately live as children, for only children are flexible and open to learning new ideas (see the discussion of 21:14-16; 23:8-12). [5] This could also constitute the transition to the recommendation that children be welcomed, which, with its emphasis on ethical conduct, is in line with Matthew's concern to illustrate what repentance means in practice. But it is not recommended as a meritorious work, as it is by the rabbis, or as a way of securing recruits, as in the Qumran community.

Our section may be based on an actual saying of Jesus. He may have had in mind that men might learn once more to say, "Abba, Father," to realize their dependence on God, to entrust their entire lives to him and to expect everything from him. Thus the saying stands on a level with the Beatitudes addressed to the poor and humble (5:3, 5; 11:25). The translation into Greek placed more emphasis on the repentance leading to such an attitude, in this very way expressing Jesus' point that repentance is not a religious exercise but a turning to the Father. Matthew underlines the fact that such repentance must also involve men's thoughts and actions. Mark, too, may have sensed this in his choice of the active verb "accept." Jesus' saying about return to childlikeness was understood by the community as a reference to the new birth given men by the waters of baptism and the Holy Spirit, thus following that strand of Jesus' thought that speaks of what befalls men rather than what they accomplish. John, finally, incorporated this saying into his conversation between Jesus and Nicodemus, setting it in the sharpest contrast possible to the scholar, who supposed that by his own intellectual powers, by his ingenious theology, he could attain what in fact he could only receive as a gift, like a child. John thus understood and put more pointedly what Jesus had probably once said more ingenuously and without all the theological reflection of the Christian community during its first decades.

Offense (18:6-9)
Cf. Mark 9:42-48

[6]"If anyone should cause one of these little ones who have faith in me to stumble, it would be better for that man to have a millstone tied around his neck and be drowned in the deep sea. [7]How terrible

for the world that there are offenses! Offenses will always come—but how terrible for the man through whom offense comes! ⁸If your hand or your foot causes you to stumble, cut it off and throw it away! It is better for you to enter life without a hand or a foot than to keep both hands and both feet and be thrown into eternal fire. ⁹And if your eye causes you to stumble, take it out and throw it away! It is better for you to enter life with only one eye than to keep both eyes and be thrown into the fire of hell."

The conversation about the stranger who is performing exorcisms (Mark 9:38-40) is omitted, because Matthew cannot conceive of a true charismatic working outside the community of Jesus (cf. the discussion of 7:15 and 12:30). The problem is also sensed elsewhere; a papyrus, for example, contains this: "Whoever is far from you today will be near to you tomorrow." Mark 9:41 has already been incorporated in 10:42, in the context of the mission of the Twelve.

[7] In the tradition of Q (Luke 17:1-2), a prediction of the offenses that would necessarily come, i.e. the temptation that would beset the entire world just before the end, was linked with the admonition from Mark 9:42 "not to cause one of these little ones to stumble [or: 'to take offense']." This does not really fit. On the other hand, the exclamation "How terrible for the world!" in Matthew 18:7 is appropriate to this prophecy of eschatological terrors. The one through whom these terrors come was thus originally a figure like the Antichrist (2 Thess. 2:4-5), or, within the context of Judaism, a pagan king like Antiochus Epiphanes, who persecuted Israel and attempted to exterminate the Jews. The curse upon him was then generalized and applied to anyone who caused "one of these little ones" to stumble (vs. 6), and linked with this warning, which was probably already current independently. Matthew includes the apocalyptic saying in verse 7 because it elaborates what he says in verse 6.

[8-9] The three sayings that follow in Mark 9:43-47 he reduces to two by juxtaposing hand and foot. In the second he writes "life" instead of "the Kingdom of God," thus assimilating it more to the first than does Mark (cf. the introductory remarks on Matt. 5:29-30). But he does not mention hell until the final member. He omits the terrify-

ing quotation in Mark 9:48 about the worm that never dies and the fire that never goes out, although for him, too, the fire is "eternal" (vs. 8; Mark 9:43: "unquenchable"). He also omits the obscure sayings about fire and salt (Mark 9:49-50).

[6] The expression "these little ones" follows the image of the children more directly than it does in Mark. The term undoubtedly refers to the disciples (cf. the discussion of 11:25 and the excursus on 7:13-23 [§5]); they are described not only as "having faith," but, notice, as "having faith in me." This is the only passage in the first three Gospels that speaks of faith in Jesus. Many stories clearly associate faith with Jesus (8:13, 26; 9:2, 22, 28-29; 14:31; 15:28; 16:8), for instance when those seeking to be healed or finding themselves in distress demonstrate their faith by resting all their hope for help in him (see the introductory remarks on 8:1-4; 8:2; 8:18-27), above all when even a heathen expects him to break through all previous rules and restrictions (8:5-13). In formulating this verse, however, Matthew has borrowed the idiom of the later community. At the end of verse 6 the warning is if anything stated more sharply than in Mark. It takes on its special tone because in 17:27 Jesus has just cited a counterexample. Matthew is thus interpreting his tradition in the light of discussions like those suggested in 17:24-27 and attested in Romans 14:1 ff.; 1 Corinthians 8:7 ff.; 10:25 ff. Everywhere the "little ones" or the "weak" are to be protected.

[7] The saying that follows practically places all this in an eschatological context. When men are made to stumble in their faith and thus run the risk of losing their salvation, there takes place a "scandal" (the Greek word) or offense reminiscent of the final attack by God's enemy before the end. So seriously does Matthew take the question of faith or unfaith, but also the vulnerability of the "little ones" of Jesus. [8-9] He therefore repeats the hard sayings about cutting off hand and foot and taking out an eye, which he has already cited in similar form in 5:29-30. He undoubtedly takes them literally, not as symbols of excluding lapsed members of the community, for there is no trace in Matthew of the Pauline image of the Christian community as the body of Christ.

Responsibility for a Brother (18:10-14)
Cf. Luke 15:3-7

[10]"See that you don't despise any of these little ones. For I tell you that their angels in heaven always behold the countenance of my Father in heaven. [[11]For the Son of Man came to save the lost.] [12]What do you think? What will a man do who has one hundred sheep and one of them goes astray? Will he not leave the other ninety-nine grazing on the hillside and go to look for the lost sheep? [13]And when it happens that he finds it, Amen, I tell you, he feels far happier over this one sheep than over the ninety-nine that did not get lost. [14]In just the same way your Father in heaven does not want any of these little ones to perish."

[10, 14] The catchword "one of these little ones" (vs. 6) appears once more; it stands like a parenthesis at the beginning and end of this section. The reference to "my/your Father in heaven" likewise occurs in both verses of the framework (cf. the introductory remarks on chapter 18). [12-13] The framework interprets the parable, which is also found in somewhat different form in Luke 15:3 ff. In contrast to those who imperil the little ones, the disciples of Jesus are called on not to despise them, because God does not want a single one of them to be lost. That this refers to the practical conduct of the community is shown by the context of verses 6-9 and especially 15-20.

Comparison of the two forms of the parable suggests that on the whole the Lukan recension is the earlier. The introduction "What if one of you . . ." appears to be typical of Matthew (cf. the introductory remarks on 12:11), while "What do you think?" appears only in John (11:56) and Matthew (six times: 17:25; 21:28; newly inserted in 22:17, 42; 26:66). It is also easier to account for the change from "in the desert" (Luke 15:4), which of course is meant to suggest a steppe with a little grass, to "on the hillside" (Matt. 18:12) than the reverse process. Luke 15:6 keeps the description of the man's happiness within the parable, while Matthew 18:13 sounds like a didactic summary of the whole.

With his changed form of this parable, Matthew makes a point different from Luke's: above all, in the appended interpretation (vs. 14) Matthew does not follow Luke 15:7 in bringing out the point of God's joy, but speaks admonishingly of the "will of God" which must also be binding on the community. Should we see in the background an Aramaic saying that spoke of God's "pleasure," which was then translated in one case as his "joy," in the other as his "will"? The more likely explanation is that Jesus himself merely told the parable (roughly Luke 15:4-6), Luke singled out the catchword for repetition in his interpretation, and Matthew adapted it to suit his general purpose.

[10] Judaism expects that the righteous will one day behold the countenance of God (2 Esd. 7:98; Rev. 22:4; 1 Cor. 13:12). Most of the rabbis assume, however, that the angels cannot see him. At most this privilege is granted to the very highest order of angels, the "angels of the countenance" (Eth. Enoch 40; Greek Bar. 11:4, 9; Luke 1:19), just as only the most trusted confidants of the king can behold his face (2 Kings 25:19). That God sends his angels to protect the righteous is Old Testament doctrine (e.g. Ps. 91:11); after the time of Christ, the rabbis interpreted this to mean that every righteous man has many personal guardian angels. This notion of a personal guardian angel makes its first appearance in Tobit 5:2, perhaps on the basis of Persian ideas, perhaps because the souls of the dead were pictured as angels (cf. Acts 12:15), which then gradually came to be thought of as angelic counterparts to particular individuals. All of these angels were on earth, however, not in heaven. At the time of Jesus, only the angels of entire nations were said to be in heaven (Ecclus. 17:17; Dan. 10:12 ff.; cf. Rev. 2:1; etc.). Elsewhere when angels are spoken of as in heaven, they are never assigned to individuals. The closest thing to personal guardian angels on earth were propounded at Qumran, where it was said that angels were in their midst (1QSa ii. 8-9), but were not assigned personal charges—at most they were to have special care of the weak (1QH v. 20-22). Personal guardian angels were said to be in heaven—but only in later Jewish writings (Greek Bar. 12–13; Apocalypse of Paul 7–10; Targ. Pseudo-Jonathan Gen. 33:10; 48:16). Precisely because this idea is far from universal, it is doubly significant that Matthew assigns such angels—ones that already behold the coun-

tenance of God—to the little ones that are so easily despised and overlooked by men. We are not dealing with the pretty little cherubs of popular art; angels are cosmic powers through which God rules the universe or intercessors who bring before God all the evil that befalls men (Tob. 12:15; Eth. Enoch 104:1). The little ones are so important that God's universal sovereignty is for their benefit: their plight is seen, their prayer is heard.

[14] This means, to drop the imagery, that God himself takes their part and stands alongside them with his beneficent will. [12-13] The parable of the sheep corresponds to the facts: in Palestine flocks were of moderate size, guarded by the owner himself. His leaving his flock untended was not an obvious response; David, for example, found someone else to care for his sheep before he left (1 Sam. 17:28). The conclusion is solemnly emphasized with "Amen," because it is not obvious; the rabbis generally maintained that God is happier over a righteous man than over a sinner who repents (Billerbeck II on Luke 15:7 B)—only in one case are the righteous warned that they themselves will not stand where the penitent one day will. Even the Christian community did not consider this principle self-evident, as the Gospel of Thomas (107) shows: it stresses that the lost sheep was an especially fat one, "the largest." This change totally perverts the meaning of the parable; that a single particularly devout person is worth more than ninety-nine average Christians is precisely the position Jesus attacks.

[14] The interpretation emphasizes God's will (see above). Here, as in verses 6 and 10, emphasis is on the individual. In a certain sense the worth of the individual is maintained because God is personally concerned with each of the "little ones." But the individual remains isolated as long as he "strays"; our parable itself, not to mention verse 15, shows that in this very situation salvation is not to be expected from his own individual conscience but from the brother who goes after him.

This parable illustrates the fact that a parable of Jesus must say different things in different situations. Originally it described God's great joy over one who was living separate from his people and is now restored. It depicted an action, not just an attitude. It was therefore not meant to describe God's eternal grace but to give account of how he comes at a specific moment, seeking after the outsider, the one who has been written off. When Jesus tells the parable it is clear that this is taking place at the very moment, in his preaching and in his ministry. Whether the parable was originally meant as an invitation or as a defense of Jesus' conduct against the attacks of his opponents (as Luke 15:1 ff. takes it) can no longer be determined.

Matthew, of course, was familiar with the idea that in Jesus' whole ministry God was going after his people like a shepherd (9:36; 15:24). He could thus have understood the parable in this sense. But there were situations in his community in which it was no longer sufficient merely to speak of this principle. Among the "little ones" of Jesus there were some who were lost, and no one from the community went out after them; yet the community went right on praising God for going out and rescuing all the lost. In such situations the parable in its original meaning no longer had anything to say; it may even have supported the community in its inertia. Matthew therefore set it in a totally new context. And it suddenly spoke with a fresh voice. The comparison of the community's leader to a shepherd is not new (Ezek. 34:1 ff.; CD xiii. 9). In Matthew, however, responsibility can no longer be evaded by being delegated to a holder of some particular office (cf. the discussion of vs. 15); his parable is meant to jar the community as a whole (cf. vss. 15-18 and the excursus on 7:13-23 [§5]). If God is unwilling to lose a single one of these little ones, someone in the band of his disciples must get up and go after the one going astray. **[10, 14]** As the framework shows, Matthew did not forget that a disciple can only go after his brother with the necessary love and perseverance because he has learned from Jesus the depth of God's concern for him and all his brethren. **[11]** Late manuscripts have interpolated an additional verse from Luke 19:10, recalling the Lukan parable to emphasize the point even more. Here, however, Matthew's interest is in admonishing his own community.

A Brother Who Sins (18:15-18)
Cf. Luke 17:3-4

¹⁵"If your brother sins, go to him and show him his fault. But do it privately, just between yourselves. If he listens to you, you have won

your brother back. [16]But if he will not listen to you, take one or two persons with you, so that 'every accusation may be upheld by the mouth of two or three witnesses.' [17]But if he will not listen to them, then tell the whole thing to the community. And then, if he will not listen to the community, treat him like a heathen or a tax collector. [18]Amen, I tell you: what you bind on earth will be bound in heaven; what you loose on earth will be loosed in heaven."

(Vs. 16=Deut. 19:15; 2 Cor. 13:1.)

Luke 17:3 (=Matt. 18:15) contains the same catchwords as Luke 17:4 (=Matt. 18:21): "sin—repent—forgive." Originally, therefore, the two verses stood together (cf. the introductory remarks on chapter 18). The wording differs somewhat between the two recensions, but we are clearly dealing with the same saying.

[15] A similar statement is already found in Leviticus 19:17: "You shall not hate your brother in your heart; you shall show him his fault and not bear sin for his sake." In Judaism, "neighbor" refers primarily to shared nationality, "brother" to shared religion; "brother" therefore designates a member of the religious community. At the time of Jesus, there was generally only a very restricted obligation to win back one who had gone astray; often the comfortable theory was espoused that self-restraint was better. Only in the close-knit community of Qumran were all called upon to take responsibility for an erring brother (1QS v. 25–vi. 1; CD ix. 2-4, with three stages similar to those described here). It is noteworthy that the passage speaks only of sin in general, not of a particular sin against the one who offers correction. Every disciple of Jesus is therefore charged with responsibility for each of the brethren (as in 1 Thess. 5:11, 14-15). The straying one's honor is to be maintained by an initial conversation without witnesses, and the expression "win back" shows that what matters is the sinner, not a "pure community."

[16] At the second stage, too, there is no mention of anyone in an official capacity. The disciple of Jesus has only his fellow disciples, not an "overseer" as at Qumran. There are thus undoubtedly rules governing life in the community, but no institutional hierarchy. Those

who receive the word cannot yet be distinguished from those who proclaim the word; whoever has received the word must impart it to his brother when the latter has need of it. The presence of one or two of the brethren is meant to protect the sinner; the admonisher may well be wrong, or someone else may find the right words when he cannot. The addition of the legal dictum from the Old Testament suggests a degree of consolidation. Was the community still aware that Numbers 35:30 and Deuteronomy 17:6 were regulations governing imposition of the death penalty? Be that as it may, the principle is also cited quite generally in 2 Corinthians 13:1 and 1 Timothy 5:19.

[17] Even when the sinner deliberately "ignores" (the literal meaning of the Greek word) what the entire community says and is condemned, no leader of the community appears; the last word is given to the totality of the brethren—[18] or better, to God himself, who at the Last Judgment validates the sentence already pronounced by the community. How these proceedings were actually carried out is hard to say. The dictum in verse 18 probably envisions that the verdict be merely pronounced and then left to God to carry out (cf. the introductory remarks on 5:19). [17] But verse 17 presupposes something more, probably the severance of all ties with such a brother (as in 2 Thess. 3:14).

[18] The last sentence promises the whole community what was promised to Peter in 16:19. In the present context, "binding" and "loosing" refer to the sinner, and represent conviction and acquittal. This clearly holds true for John 20:23 as well, where all the "disciples" likewise receive the authority of the Spirit to denounce sins or to forgive them. Since John never speaks of the Twelve except in 6:67, 70 and in the traditional formula "one of the Twelve," this statement applies to all the faithful, like all the farewell discourses preceding it. One might therefore say that Matthew 16:19 refers more to the teaching magisterium, 18:18 to church discipline. But the same words are used to express both; in Matthew's mind, therefore, the community is merely exercising a function that was entrusted to Peter merely as an example for all. For the Matthaean community, Peter still represents the authority that transmits Jesus' new interpretation of the Law and makes the life of the community possible in actual practice; Peter

is succeeded, however, by the entire community, which draws upon his authority to determine in each new case what is sinful and what is not (see the concluding remarks on 16:13-20). Thus 1 Corinthians 5:1-5 is a closer parallel than Qumran.

The problem of Sin was only gradually perceived in the community. According to Paul, it was expected even in exceptional cases like that described in 1 Corinthians 5:1-5 that the sinner would enter into salvation. Nevertheless, there was no confession of "sins" among the faithful, even though Paul mentions many instances when the community's acts fell short of the community's faith. These cases are taken very seriously as "lapses," but are always still clearly distinguished from the "sin" (always singular) in which the nonbeliever lives. This means that life is seen as a single whole, which, with all its obedience and all its failures, all its actions and all its experiences, is devoted either to God or to everything else under the sun, and is thus as a whole either "righteousness" or "sin." Only in James 5:16 do we find a confession of sins on the part of someone who is sick, since sickness was then thought to be a punishment for sin (John 9:2-3; cf. 1 Cor. 11:30); even there, however, it is not the rule (vs. 15). The statement in 1 John 2:2-3 is almost cancelled by 3:6, and Hebrews 6:4-6 finds sin within the community most exceptional. Only the fifth petition of the Lord's Prayer holds fast to the idiom of the Old Testament, with its repeated prayers for the forgiveness of past sins (cf. the discussion of Matt. 6:12). Nevertheless the whole New Testament is aware that there is such a thing as a failure that makes it impossible to go on living by what God gives. But such failure needs not so much to be forgiven as to be recognized and healed. It is clear that the only way this can happen is by return to the one whose gift opens the possibility of new life. The New Testament knows nothing of any regularly repeated confession of sins, as though the whole drama of salvation had always to begin all over again. Paul says instead that we must learn again and again to walk in the Spirit by which we already live (Gal. 5:25), or to realize in our conduct toward our fellow men what already holds true for us "in Christ" (Phil. 2:5-7).

In 18:15-18, Matthew, too, looks upon sin as an exception; but the depth of his concern about winning back one of the brethren shows how seriously the community took those aspects of everyday life that were out of harmony with the gospel; this concern distinguished the Christian community from the sectarians, and from many Pharisees as well, who dreamed of a perfect community. At the same time, however, the community did not accept sin as being natural, but fought it; this distinguishes it from modern denominations with their confessions of sin every Sunday. The real goal is the winning over of the sinners, so that all disciplinary measures taken amount in fact to an offer of salvation; but this offer is to be taken so seriously that everything possible must be done to make sure the brother hears what is being said (also in 1 Cor. 5:5; 2 Thess. 3:14; 1 Tim. 2:4; 2 Tim. 2:24-26; Tit. 1:13).

The statement about "binding," however, shows how dangerous the effects of traditional language can be. If a specific commandment is called binding, this means of course that it is binding in the eyes of God. And the community is given authority to declare command-ments binding. But this does not mean that they cause it to be binding, only that they *interpret* it so. Above all, the power to bind does not mean that an ecclesiastical inquisition can damn people for eternity. The statement that as new situations arose Peter and the community could determine what was permitted and what was not made it possi-ble to surmount inflexible legalism; but such legalism can hardly be avoided when one speaks of "binding" a person. What Matthew probably has in mind is that anyone who promises salvation to an-other also becomes a judgment upon the individual who rejects the offer, so that the disciple of Jesus is necessarily also a preacher of judgment (see the concluding remarks on 10:1-16). This interpreta-tion is supported by the whole context (vss. 10-14, 21-22), which deals with responsibility toward one's brother, love for him, and forgive-ness. There is not the slightest mention of keeping the community pure, which is a secondary goal in 1 Corinthians 5:6-13; 2 Timothy 2:21. Furthermore, the procedure is far less legalistic than at Qumran, where what amount to ecclesiastical penalties and limited excom-munication obtained. Even though God's great act of love in Jesus is not mentioned until the end of the chapter, it forms the background even here; more is involved than a law requiring "purity" of the community. This can be seen from the fact that the words which bind the brother in sin can be pronounced only by the community as a whole, after many attempts to win him back, whereas the declaration of forgiveness can be pronounced in private conversation (vss. 15, 21-22).

Christ in the Community (18:19-20)

[19]"Once again: Amen, I tell you, whenever two of you on earth agree about anything they pray for, it will be granted them by my Father in heaven. [20]For where two or three come together in my name, I am in the midst of them."
(Vs. 20=Cf. 28:20.)

The next saying is linked by means of catchwords: the phrase "two or three" (vs. 16) reappears, and the precise correspondence between what is done "on earth" and what takes place "in heaven" links verse 19 with verse 18. The juxtaposition probably antedates Matthew, since he hardly ever uses catchwords as an organizing principle. This may be another "Amen" saying, but the "Amen" is omitted in many manuscripts (as in 19:24 alongside 19:23).

[19] At least ten males must be present for corporate worship in Judaism; for the disciples of Jesus, however, such rules are abolished: it is promised that the prayer of even two worshipers will be heard (cf. 21:22 [the same Greek verb occurs at the end of 21:21 as in 18:19]). In the present context, the idea is that what the community decides to bind or loose will be ratified by God; "anything" probably refers, as in 1 Corinthians 6:1, to a "dispute" between members of the community. The authority of the community's words is thus the authority they gain through prayer. It is assumed, of course, just as in 7:7-11, that the community prays according to God's will, as Jesus taught his disciples to pray in the Lord's Prayer.

[20] Even more worthy of note is the promise of Jesus' presence. Jesus speaks as though he had already ascended to heaven. The disciples come together in his "name." The name of Jesus (cf. the discus-

sion of 6:9) is like an authority standing over the community; it is often linked directly with the operation of the Spirit (1 Cor. 6:11; cf. 5:4; Acts 4:7). In his name the word is preached and demons are driven out (Matt. 7:22), in his name men are baptized (see the discussion of 28:19), his name is spoken when men confess their faith (24:9; Acts 4:17-18; Heb. 13:15). Here, then, it is the exalted Lord who speaks (see Matt. 28:20). And his statement denies importance to the presence of an institution, the size of the community, the sanctity of the place, the blessing of an official functionary, or visible success in the world. It is only the presence of love that confers the presence—and the power—of Christ on the community. The power of Christ's presence is attested in Acts (e.g. 4:9-12), in the letters of Paul (e.g. 1 Cor. 5:3-4), in John (e.g. 14:12-14), and in Revelation (e.g. 2:1). Here we find the eschatological fulfillment of all the hopes and yearnings of the Old Testament: the presence of the God who is unknown has been replaced by the presence of the man who is known, who can be called by name, the presence of Jesus Christ himself. Jesus now takes the place of the Law, as described by a Jewish saying: "When two men sit together and words of the Law are between them, then the presence (of God) is dwelling among them." The final verse of the Gospel promises this presence of Jesus to those who keep his commandments; here the Gospel makes clear how central prayer is to these commandments.

Loss of Grace (18:21-35)
Cf. Luke 17:4

²¹Then Peter came to Jesus and asked, "Lord, how many times can my brother sin against me and I have to forgive him? Seven times?" ²²"No, not seven times," answered Jesus, "but seventy times seven. ²³Because the Kingdom of heaven is like a king who decided to check on his servants' accounts. ²⁴He had just begun to do so when one of them was brought in who owed him ten thousand talents. ²⁵The servant did not have enough to pay his debt, so his master ordered him to be sold as a slave, with his wife and children and all that he had, in order to pay the debt. ²⁶The servant fell on his knees before his master. 'Be patient with me,' he begged, 'and I will pay you

everything!' ²⁷The master felt sorry for him, so he forgave him the debt and let him go. ²⁸Then that servant went out and met one of his fellow servants who owed him a hundred denarii. He grabbed him and started choking him. 'Pay back what you owe me!' he said. ²⁹His fellow servant fell down and begged him, 'Be patient with me and I will pay you back!' ³⁰But he would not; instead he went and had him thrown into jail until he should pay the debt. ³¹When the other servants saw what had happened, they were very upset, and went to their master and told him everything. ³²So the master called the servant in. 'You wicked servant!' he said. 'I forgave you the whole amount you owed me, just because you asked me to. ³³Shouldn't you have had mercy on your fellow servant, just as I had mercy on you?' ³⁴The master was very angry, and he handed the servant over to the torturers until he should pay back the whole amount. ³⁵That is how my heavenly Father will treat you if you do not forgive your brother, every one of you, with your whole heart."

[21-22] There follows in verses 21-22 a variant of the second of the two sayings brought together in Luke 17:3-4. In somewhat fuller form the saying also occurs in the Gospel of the Nazarenes (15), where conflation of the Matthaean and Lukan forms lends it even greater force: a man must forgive up to seventy times seven times (Matthew) in one day (Luke). Following the elaboration of verse 15 in verses 16-20, the theme must be reintroduced. True to his usual form, Matthew has Peter come forward (cf. the discussion of 8:2). We can see both points once more: in questions of doctrine Peter comes to the fore (cf. the discussion of 16:19 and 18:18), but Peter himself is still learning and must rely on Jesus' instruction. He asks how often "a brother must be forgiven." Matthew uses the same phrase to conclude the parable.

The introduction (vss. 21-22 = Luke 17:4) and the parable itself he incorporated from the material before him; the parable is not even about repeated forgiveness, so that it is not strictly appropriate. The parable is extensively developed, and was probably familiar to Matthew as part of his special tradition (cf. the discussion of 13:24-30). The point of the parable is strongly underlined by the similarity of verse 26 to verse 29, the conclusion of verse 30 to verse 34, and the expression "one [emphasized] who owed him" (vs. 28) to that in verse 24 ("one [emphasized] . . . who owed him"). Because the relation between master and servant corresponds so precisely to that between servant and fellow servant, the meanness of the servant is incomprehensible, while the punishment imposed by his master at the end is intelligible and appropriate.

[21] We now have a different situation: sin against the inquirer is the subject of discussion. Peter has learned in the school of Jesus that forgiveness must take the place of vengeance; but he is still asking about limits (cf. the discussion of 5:21-48), and has therefore departed only quantitatively, not qualitatively, from the Jewish principle that a man may be forgiven once, twice, or thrice, but not four times (albeit with reference to God's forgiveness). [22] Peter is still counting, but at least up to seven. Jesus' answer, however, abolishes all limits, whether it is translated "seventy times seven" or "seventy-seven times." The words are reminiscent of Lamech's song of revenge (Gen. 4:23-24), which sings of vengeance multiplied by the same factor. The world bearing the stamp of Adam's fall is restored to wholeness through the disciples of Jesus.

This applies only to the Matthaean recension, which is clearly assimilated to the Greek Old Testament. Unlike Luke 17:4, the Matthaean version makes no mention of repentance on the part of the brother. The Testament of Gad 6 calls for even the unrepentant to be forgiven. A man never reaches the limits of love (Rom. 13:8a).

[23] As is often true in Jewish parables, God appears as a king, [24] but the parable is deliberately exaggerated because God's actions far surpass all human actions. The sum amounts to about fifty million denarii; when one considers that a denarius was the normal daily wage of a worker (see the discussion of 20:2), and that Herod's total annual income amounted to only nine hundred talents, and the taxes imposed on Galilee and Perea together only two hundred, the size of the debt becomes clear: it is enormous, almost inconceivable even for the governor of an entire province. The sum is made up of the highest number used in arithmetic and the largest monetary unit employed in the ancient Near East. That the servant is "brought in" might mean that he is already lying in prison, having been unmasked as a swindler. [25] The sale not only of a debtor but of his entire family was not in

accord with Israelite law; it is common knowledge, however, that foreign kings acted in this manner (2 Kings 4:1 [children, but not the man's wife]; cf. Isa. 50:1; Amos 2:6; 8:6; Neh. 5:1-13). Jewish law set up many protective barriers and permitted a man to be sold only to make good a theft.

[26] The servant's falling to his knees reveals his extremity, as does his promise to repay everything, which he cannot possibly do. His master's mercy (see the discussion of 20:34) is unparalleled. He grants not just postponement but total remission of the debt. The Greek term for the latter is itself strange. Its literal meaning is "loan" —perhaps because all a man has is lent him by God? Possibly, however, the expression had a more general sense in Aramaic. [28] The debt owed by the fellow servant is five hundred thousand times less than the debt just cancelled. This is why the morally proper and legally unimpugnable demand "Pay what you owe" rings so vicious and grotesque. [29] And once more the scene is repeated. But the reaction of the servant is different.

[30] By the standard of what has just taken place it is scandalous and shocking. It was unusual for a man to be imprisoned for debt in Palestine, though not in other countries around the Mediterranean. [31] It is easy to understand why the other servants are upset; the same words ("were very upset") are used in 17:23 to describe the reaction of Jesus' community to his death. [32-33] The only possible consequence is the condemnation of the servant by the king. It is stated in the form of a question, so that the guilty servant himself must reply, and with him those who hear the parable. [34] Torture, too, was forbidden in Israel; but it is known to have been practised in neighboring countries and even at the court of Herod. The concluding statement reveals the hopeless position of the servant: how can he ever hope to repay the gigantic sum? The wording corresponds precisely to that used by the servant toward his fellow servant.

The parable of the weeds, which is related in form, made use of extraordinary and exaggerated features to show that the Kingdom of God cannot be defined in any human images; such exaggeration is even more apparent here. God's inconceivable act of mercy, which contradicts all human notions of justice, is so displayed that the listener can only stand in awe and amazement. So incomprehensibly great is God's goodness toward man, his strange righteousness that restores instead of destroying. When God's goodness comes alive in Jesus' preaching and ministry, transforming the world, only creation itself is comparable. Paul speaks the same way about the righteousness of God, which is beyond our power of comprehension in making the sinful man a son of God, even while seeking to reform his entire conduct toward his fellow men (Phil. 2:1-13; Rom. 12:1; 2 Cor. 8:7-9; cf. the excursus on Matt. 5:6).

Thus this chapter concludes with a parable that states in brilliant, almost garish colors that the community can live on the basis of God's inconceivably great grace—not only can, but must. Matthew himself, in his concluding sentence, merely underscores this admonition to the community, and its alternative—destruction in the Last Judgment. Throughout the entire chapter, Matthew is concerned to help the community really live as the community of Christ. The righteousness of the community is to be greater than that of the Pharisees (5:20); it is not sufficient just to proclaim freedom from the Law (17:24-27). Only when the heart has become new and man has become childlike can he live as a disciple of Jesus (18:3).

Matthew is well aware of the danger that besets the little ones of Jesus in their lives; many have already been lost. And so he can only warn against causing offense, appeal to men to go after those who have gone astray, to exert every effort to help those who have fallen into sin come back, but never to be vindictive about insults or injury, remembering always the great forgiveness of God and extending such forgiveness to others. For when the forgiveness that has been received is not shown to others, it no longer has meaning for the heart and God takes it back. [35] The phrase "with your whole heart," which also appears in the commandment to love God (22:37), is also used in Jubilees 35:13 and elsewhere: it keystones the whole passage, and indeed the New Testament. God's forgiveness is not for decoration but for use.

Marriage (19:1-12)
Cf. Mark 10:1-12

[1] When Jesus finished saying these things, he left Galilee and went into the territory of Judea, on the other side of the Jordan

River. ²Large crowds followed him, and he healed them there. ³Some Pharisees came to him and tried to trap him by asking, "Is it allowed a man to divorce his wife for any reason he wishes?" ⁴Jesus answered, "Haven't you read that in the beginning the Creator 'made them male and female,' ⁵and said, 'For this reason a man will leave his father and mother and unite with his wife, and the two will become one flesh'? ⁶So they are no longer two, but one flesh. Man must not separate, then, what God has joined together." ⁷The Pharisees asked him, "Why, then, did Moses give the commandment for a man 'to give his wife a divorce notice and send her away'?" ⁸Jesus answered, "Moses gave you permission to divorce your wives because of your hardness of heart. But it was not this way from the beginning. ⁹I tell you, then, that any man who divorces his wife, except for unchastity, and marries another commits adultery."

¹⁰His disciples said to him, "If this is the way it is between a man and his wife, it is better not to marry." ¹¹Jesus answered, "Not all apprehend this word, but only those to whom it is given. ¹²For there are eunuchs who were born that way, and there are eunuchs made that way by men, and there are eunuchs who have castrated themselves on account of the Kingdom of heaven. Let him who can do it accept this teaching."

(Vs. 4—Gen. 1:27. Vs. 5—Gen. 2:24; Eph. 5:31. Vs. 7—Deut. 24:1. Vss. 8-9—Cf. Matt. 5:31-32; Mal. 2:15.)

[1] The formula at the beginning here shows that Matthew understood chapter 18 as a unit; this clause always occurs as the conclusion of major discourses (cf. the discussion of 7:28). He immediately returns to Mark by mentioning the location of the next episode, but omits the "and" between "Judea" and "on the other side of the Jordan River," so that the reader might suppose there was a Judea beyond the Jordan, which there was not. The order of the two regions was already reversed in Mark, so that Matthew may have been intending to correct the text to read that Jesus went to Judea, and crossed the Jordan to get there. [2] Unlike Mark, Matthew does not just say that large crowds came together, but that they followed Jesus. He thus

distinguishes between the people and the officials who reject Jesus; not until 27:25 do the people take the side of their leaders. Finally, Matthew describes Jesus as healing rather than teaching; Jesus' healing ministry is extremely important to him.

[3-9] The wording of the conversation on marriage corresponds largely to that in Mark; but its structure is entirely new, and now follows the model of a Jewish disputation. [3] The change in form also changes the content. That the Pharisees are trying to trap Jesus is stated at the very beginning of the sentence, not at the end, as in Mark. If the translation above is accurate, their question is now a typical question of how to interpret the Law, like those discussed at the time by Hillel and Shammai, the leaders of the two major schools of interpretation: is "any reason a man wishes" sufficient grounds for him to divorce his wife (cf. the discussion of Mark 10:2)? If this reading is correct, the question no longer concerns the legitimacy of divorce itself, as it does in Mark; this is assumed to be self-evident. It is possible, however, that the phrase means "for any reason whatsoever," as it does when associated with a negative (24:22); in this case Matthew would not differ fundamentally from Mark. [4-6] In any case, however, Jesus' response stands at the very beginning; the Old Testament Law remains in effect, but it must be understood as interpreted by Jesus.

It nevertheless includes a radical rejection of divorce on the basis of Genesis 1:27 and 2:24 (cited by Matthew according to the text of the Greek Bible). [7] The discussion that follows is formally correct: one passage of Scripture is cited against another, and Jesus' opponents bring up the commandment about a divorce notice. [8] Jesus does not reject the commandment, but terms it nothing more than a permission granted on account of their hardness of heart. It did not obtain "from the beginning," as he says, repeating the catchword from verse 4. This phrase also occurs at this point in the Markan account. In Mark, Jesus' opponents twice ask what is "permitted" and Jesus asks what is "commanded"; here, on the contrary, the opponents gleefully cite the "commandment" of Moses (vs. 7), which Jesus evaluates merely as "permission," a concession, thus devaluing it (vs. 8).

The argument that in cases of conflict the earlier annuls the later is also used in Galatians 3:17, and Jewish Christians declared that all the commandments proclaimed after the incident of the golden calf (Exodus 32) are without force (Didascalia vi. 16. 1 = Apostolic Const. vi. 20. 1; Ps. Clem., *Recog.* i. 35-36). **[9]** The conclusion of the dialogue follows Mark 10:11, with an interpolated introductory formula: "I tell you," which is reminiscent of Matthew 5:22, although the "I" here is not so heavily emphasized against the Old Testament commandment. Mark 10:12 is omitted because in Judaism a woman cannot divorce her husband. Instead divorce is conceded in case of unchastity (one of the best manuscripts uses exactly the same words as Matt. 5:32), thus basically reinstituting the tradition of the strictest teachers of the Law from the school of Shammai.

The dialogue is thus organized much more logically as a disputation: Jesus' appeal to the creation story, which implies a radical attack on the presupposition about divorce, is countered by the Pharisees with a different passage from Scripture, which Jesus thereupon terms a mere concession. All this of course weakens the point made in Mark. Above all, the concession of divorce in cases of unchastity, added by Matthew, represents a return to the thought and practice of his opponents. On the other hand, the contrast is heightened by the fact that Jesus' opponents presuppose from the outset the self-evident possibility of divorce, and Jesus disputes this very point.

[10-12] The appended conversation with the disciples is found only in Matthew. According to Mark 10:10 it took place inside the house; but Matthew has omitted this verse, so that according to him Jesus is on his way somewhere, and verses 11-12 are given as instruction to the disciples. Jesus' saying is twice called a mystery that must be given to man by God, because he could not understand it by himself. Verse 11 would be more appropriate to the end, and it has been suggested that Matthew may have set it at the beginning and at the same time replaced it with the concluding clause (end of vs. 12) to make clear from the outset that the saying applies only to the disciples. In any case, Matthew uses the disciples' question in verse 10 just as he does in 19:25, to link these sentences with the preceding material; in addition, the Greek word translated "the way it is" in verse 10 is the same as the word translated "reason" in verse 3. Contrary to the obligation to marry imposed on the devout Jew (but cf. Wisd. 3:13-14), celibacy is here recommended in certain cases.

The contemptuous term "eunuch" is striking. Eunuchs are excluded even more strictly than tax collectors from the people of God; God's Law expressly forbids them entrance into the community (Deut. 23:1). A castrated animal cannot even be offered as a sacrifice (Lev. 22:24). Jesus thus takes the side of those who were scorned and written off by everyone. It is possible that opponents applied this term to Jesus himself and perhaps also some of his disciples because they were unmarried. An unmarried Jewish rabbi defended himself by saying, "What shall I do? My soul cleaves to the Law; let others keep the world going!" (Billerbeck on vs. 12 C).

The final statement is deliberately shocking (cf., for example, 5:39); even if Jesus or his community had heard of the self-mutilation practised by other nations, the words would be unthinkable as a literal recommendation. The saying thus takes up the contemptuous expression and declares that, contrary to the Law of Moses, it might be God's will to call to his service persons unfit for marriage, that there are even those who deliberately choose celibacy for the sake of God's will (cf. also the remarks toward the end of the discussion of 5:32). The meaning would be totally different if "this word" (vs. 11) referred to the preceding passage (vss. 1-9). Then it would mean: if others can bear even mutilation or self-mutilation, how much more you should be capable of marital fidelity. But this reading is very unlikely, because it would have to be restated once more at least in a concluding sentence.

The whole section shows how unlegalistic Jesus is. He can speak with equal ease of the mystery of indissoluble marriage and of the mystery of celibacy, and both sayings can be genuine sayings of Jesus. He commands neither marriage nor celibacy; either can be a state in which to serve God. It is therefore "given" to many to see the meaning of celibacy. The idea is almost Pauline. Paul, unlike official Judaism, placed a high value on celibacy; but, unlike the monks of Qumran, he did not suggest that it be required. It is a charisma, a special gift allowed to certain individuals (1 Cor. 7:7). There is thus no hint of any double moral standard. Neither is there any reference to an ideal of poverty or to the virtue of asceticism (see the discussion of 19:21). Jesus shares with his whole nation the unbroken affirmation of God's good creation, which is also the basis of marriage, even though the Kingdom of heaven, that is, the world of God to come, can cast light on celibacy. Generally, men testify their approval of God's creation by marriage and bringing up their children; some, however, are especially called to prefigure the end and goal of creation, God's new world in which men and women will not marry (22:30).

Jesus Blesses Little Children (19:13-15)
Cf. Mark 10:13-16; Luke 8:15-17

[13]Then some children were brought to him so that he might place his hands on them and pray, but the disciples scolded them. [14]Jesus said, "Let the children come to me, and do not stop them, because the Kingdom of heaven belongs to such as these." [15]He placed his hands on them and left.

This brief episode is narrated more objectively than in Mark, although few changes are made in its wording. Jesus is not simply to "touch" the children but to lay his hands on them and pray for them. Matthew thus understands blessing as intercession based on authority. Perhaps he has in mind the blessing of children by the elders in Palestine on the Day of Atonement; more probably, a popular custom has here been given a Christian interpretation. Jesus' displeasure with his disciples and his putting his arms around the children are omitted, as is the saying about being childlike to enter the Kingdom of God (Mark 10:15), already incorporated in 18:3; but the expression "such as these" reminds us that having the attitude of a child toward God is not simply a matter of age, but depends on the gift of being able to encounter God like "one of these little ones," without any demands or reservations.

Discipleship and Freedom from Possessions (19:16-30)
Cf. Mark 10:17-31; Luke 18:18-30

[16]Once a man came to Jesus. "Master," he said, "what good thing must I do to receive eternal life?" [17]"Why do you ask me about what is good?" answered Jesus. "There is only One who is good. Keep the

commandments if you want to enter life." [18]"What commandments?" he asked. Jesus answered, " 'Do not murder; do not commit adultery; do not steal; do not bear false witness; [19]honor your father and mother'; and 'love your neighbor as yourself.' " [20]"I have obeyed all these commandments," the young man replied. "What else do I need?" [21]Jesus said to him, "If you want to be perfect, go and sell all you have and give the money to the poor, and you will have treasure in heaven; then come and follow me." [22]When the young man heard this he went away sad, because he was very rich.

[23]Jesus then said to his disciples, "Amen, it will be very hard, I tell you, for a rich man to enter the Kingdom of heaven. [24]I tell you something else: it is much harder for a rich man to enter the Kingdom of God than for a camel to go through the eye of a needle." [25]When the disciples heard this they were completely amazed. "Who can be saved, then?" they asked. [26]Jesus looked straight at them and answered, "This is impossible for men; but 'for God everything is possible.' "

[27]Then Peter spoke up. "Look," he said, "we have left everything and followed you. What will we have in return?" [28]Jesus said to them, "Amen, I tell you thus: when the Son of Man sits on his glorious throne at the new creation, then you who have followed me will also sit on twelve thrones and judge the twelve tribes of Israel. [29]And everyone who has left houses or brothers or sisters or father or mother or fields for my name's sake, will receive a hundred times more and inherit eternal life. [30]But many who are first will be last, and last first." (Vss. 18-19—Exod. 20:12-16; Deut. 5:16-20; Lev. 19:18. Vs. 26—Gen. 18:14.)

Here, too, Matthew follows Mark with characteristic changes. [28] A new element is the promise to the disciples that they will sit on twelve thrones. The same promise occurs in expanded form in Luke 22:28-30. Matthew links this saying with verse 27 by means of the term "follow" (cf. 5:13, 14; 10:17, 26; 11:2, 20; 15:14). Thus the Twelve are distinguished from "everyone who" has given up much for Jesus (vs. 29). Matthew is probably also responsible for the reference to the Son of Man sitting on his glorious throne, which clashes with the more primitive role of Jesus as witness at the Last Judgment (see the excursus on Mark 8:27-33). The throne image is not found in Luke 22:30; but Matthew uses almost the same words for it in 25:31 and here in verse 28*a*, each time in a different construction ("throne" in the genitive instead of the accusative; cf. Luke 22:30) from that used in verse 28*b*, which agrees in its essentials with Luke 22:30. In 13:41, too, Matthew has introduced the Son of Man in an eschatological role; in 24:3, 27, 37, 39 the "coming" of the Son of Man refers to the eschatological day; and in 16:27 and 24:31 the angels at his appearance become "his" angels.

The term "new creation" or "rebirth" betrays Greek influence. This term does not appear in Luke 22:30, which speaks instead of the "Kingdom" that God has "bequeathed" to Jesus and its festal banquet. Luke's terminology suggests as its background the Jewish covenant, since in Greek "bequeath" derives from the same root as "covenant"; and the goal of this covenant is the restoration of the twelve tribes in the Kingdom of God, depicted as a banquet (cf. Isa. 25:6-8). Matthew is the first to make explicit mention of the twelve disciples. Apart from the expression "my Kingdom," which is not textually secure, covenant images might well go back to Jesus, precisely because they do not envision a separate community, but rather all Israel as the covenant people won back to God.

The introduction in Luke (22:28) with its reference to "perseverance" (cf. Luke 8:15; Acts 14:22; 11:23; 13:43) amid "temptations" (Acts 20:19; Luke 4:13; 8:13) is probably Luke's own; but whether the images of banqueting and judging, which cannot take place simultaneously, were linked from the very beginning remains in doubt. Luke expressly links banqueting and judging (22:15-18, 25-30); in Mark no specific mention is made of judging, but Jesus' prediction of the final banquet (14:22-25) comes between two judgment-like pronouncements (14:17-21, 27-30). In any case, Matthew borrowed only the notion of the twelve disciples sitting on their thrones. Revelation 3:21 promises all the faithful that they will sit upon the throne of Christ, just as he sits with God upon his throne; this passage is probably also an echo of our saying. The suggestion that it constitutes the original form is very unlikely, because the imagery has grown very blurred, although the parallel between the gift of Jesus to his disciples and that of the Father to Jesus (Luke 22:29) is preserved. In Testament of Job 4:6-7; 33, as in Luke, we find the themes of perseverance in temptations and enthronement as a reward; but here we are dealing with a Christian adaptation of Jewish tradition. Whether this was pre-Lukan is also uncertain.

[16] Matthew's changes can be sensed at the very beginning, less in the "behold" of the Greek text and the "coming" of the inquirer (see the discussion of 8:2) than in the new form the question takes. Matthew avoids the Markan form of address, "good master," substituting instead "master, what good thing . . ." (in Greek "master, what good" instead of "master good, what"). Thus he escapes the difficulty of Mark 10:18, where Jesus appears to deny his own goodness. [17] The response of Jesus is altered to match; it can only be explained as a transformation of the Markan recension: "Why do you ask me about what is good?" instead of "Why do you call me good?" That men must not only avoid sin but must also do good has been a familiar principle to the Jew since Amos 5:14-15; Micah 6:8; it was also adopted by the community of Jesus (Rom. 12:2; Gal. 6:10; cf. Matt. 7:11-12; 12:35). The statement that there is only One who is good, namely God himself, likewise makes sense only in Mark, not in Matthew; for if someone does what is good, which is in fact the will of God, certainly that is not in conflict with the principle that only God himself is good. Therefore although he generally tends to abbreviate, Matthew must state the concern of the inquirer once more. "If you want to enter life." At the same time, the inquirer's seriousness of purpose is tested (cf. vs. 21). Matthew states explicitly that the man must "keep" the commandments (John, too, often uses the term); it is one of Matthew's major concerns.

[18] The rich young man inquires further than he does in Mark, asking which commandments Jesus means; this is perhaps meant to suggest that the man has something higher in mind than the Ten Commandments; or are they to be distinguished from cultic regulations? The extra commandment "Do not cheat" (Mark 10:19) is left out; [19] but the commandment to love one's neighbor (Lev. 19:18) is appended (see the discussion of 5:18), as is also done in Jewish catechisms (cf. Didache 1–2). [20] Only in Matthew and only at the

point where Mark has the inquirer say that he has kept the command-ments ever since his "youth" does he appear as a young man. Here, too, the Matthaean version is a recasting of the Markan. According to Mark 10:21, Jesus tells him that he still lacks something; here the young man himself asks what he lacks.

[21] Mark states that Jesus looked at him and loved him; Matthew omits any mention of Jesus' emotions. Instead he makes the discus-sion that follows depend on the condition "if you want to be perfect." This clause has been especially conducive to the misunderstanding that there is a superior grade of discipleship, that of perfection, which is not necessary for salvation but can expect a special reward (cf. the excursus on the Sermon on the Mount following Matt. 7:29 *a* §1). The preceding verses 10-12, understood as extolling ascetic celibacy, have contributed to the misunderstanding. This would be in line, say, with the requirement imposed by the monastic community of Qumran, where the novice had to give up all his possessions when he entered the community. But according to 5:20, 48 perfection is the "more" that Jesus expects of *every* disciple, namely love of one's neighbor. This love is learned and inculcated by following Jesus. The question asked by the young man concerning what he still needs, and above all the continuation in verses 23-24, make it clear that we are still dealing with the question of eternal life itself, not the question of a special rank within it.

Jesus did not demand of all people that they literally follow him, giving up home and possessions; neither did he single out those who did follow him in this sense and make them a class superior to the rest. All one can say is that a special form of service is required of some and to them it is granted, giving them greater responsibility and a richer ministry.

[23] Only Matthew introduces what Jesus has to say about the rich with "Amen, I tell you . . ." (cf. the introductory remarks on 5:18). [24] The disciples' shock and the repetition of the sentence (Mark 10:24) are omitted; [25-26] otherwise Matthew abbreviates only slightly, with the result that the camel "enters" through the eye of the needle in the Greek text, just as the rich man enters the Kingdom of heaven (Mark 10:25 reads "goes through").

[27] A new element, however, is the explicit question about re-

ward and the special promise made to the Twelve: **[28]** that they will sit upon twelve thrones. This corresponds to the question about who is the greatest in the Kingdom of heaven asked by the disciples in 18:1 and understood positively by Matthew. They will be installed as regents over Israel, which itself will be restored at the eschaton to its full complement of twelve tribes. What about Judas? Does Matthew solve the problem the way Acts 1:21-22 does? Did Luke 22:30 omit "twelve" (before "thrones") because in his account Judas has just been unmasked? Certainly there is no thought of an "institution of twelve" that is to continue within the community. When James dies a martyr's death (Acts 12:2) he is not replaced. As in the case of the "judges" of Israel, "judge" can refer to continuous leadership. Unlike Luke, however, Matthew probably does have in mind the judgment at the beginning of the new eon. He says nothing about any eternal throne for Jesus; this notion would cause him difficulties, since it would imperil the reign of the one God who will one day be "all in all" (1 Cor. 15:28). The throne of the Son of Man is the judgment seat (Matt. 25:31; cf. 16:27; 13:41), and the notion of God's people participating in the Judgment is attested in 1 Corinthians 6:2 (cf. Dan. 7:22; Wisd. 3:1, 8). The image of twelve thrones may simply originate from the idea that those who have shared Jesus' fate by following him on earth will do so also at the climax of history. There may be echoes of Daniel 7:9, since some rabbis were of the opinion that the thrones mentioned there were meant for the great leaders of Israel. Revelation 20:4 probably refers to heavenly elders, that is, angelic power. The closest parallel is a passage from Philo in which the twelve patriarchs are represented as cosmic regents in heaven (*Questions on Exodus*. ii. 114; a similar notion appears in The Testament of Judah 25; in neither case can Christian influence be ruled out).

The idea of a "rebirth" goes back to the Stoic school of Greek philosophy, which expected a universal conflagration to be followed by a new world in an ever-repeated cycle. Greek-speaking Jewish writers use the term for the restoration of Israel after a time of distress (Josephus) and for the restoration of the earth after the Deluge (Philo). There is no corresponding Aramaic or Hebrew word. Matthew therefore borrowed the word from the language of Hellenistic Judaism, perhaps in order to anticipate the reference to the coming eon (Mark 10:30). It is hardly likely that it includes a conscious reference to a new creation (as in 1QS iv. 25), since Matthew speaks of the end of the eon (see the discussion of 24:3) but never of the end of the world. The notion of the rebirth of an individual (Tit. 3:5) only came in gradually and cannot be found in the Judaism of this period. [29] Closely related is Luke 12:8 (cf. Matt. 10:32), where the "I" of the earthly Jesus is also formally distinct from the "Son of Man," even though the two are essentially identical. The promise given especially to the Twelve applies in similar fashion to all the followers of Jesus. Matthew differs from Mark in omitting the promise of reward on earth and referring only to eternal life. The expression "for my name's sake" succeeds better than Mark in including both those who accompanied the earthly Jesus and the post-Easter disciples. The actions of the former serve as a model for the latter (cf. the discussion of 4:17).

It is striking how Matthew inserts the requirement to love one's neighbor into the Ten Commandments. He interprets the invitation to follow Jesus as a challenge to learn this kind of love. It is the fulfillment of the commandments that gains a man entrance into the Kingdom of heaven (see the discussion of 5:20). But only in following Jesus can one learn what it means to love one's neighbor and thus to fulfill the commandments; there is promised in return a rich reward, to be realized when Israel attains its goal and lives as a new nation of twelve tribes under the regency of Christ and his twelve disciples. Even though this last idea may be alien to us, it expresses what Jesus was probably meaning to say in his choice of the Twelve (cf. the excursus on Mark 6:7-13): God remains faithful to his own actions; history is not a hopeless, meaningless confusion. This means that all suffering and striving, all hope and despair will not be forgotten, but will find their reward. But, as in the Old Testament and above all in the coming of Jesus, this fulfillment will again and again appear surprisingly different from what men expect.

The Surprising Righteousness of God (20:1-16)

¹"The Kingdom of heaven is like the owner of a vineyard who went out early in the morning to hire some laborers to work in his

vineyard. [2]He agreed to pay them a denarius for the day and sent them to work in his vineyard. [3]And about the third hour he went out and saw some men standing in the market place doing nothing, [4]so he told them, 'You also go to work in the vineyard, and I will pay you what is right.' [5]So they went. He went out again at the sixth and at the ninth hour and did the same thing. [6]About the eleventh hour he went out and found other men still standing there. 'Why are you wasting the whole day here doing nothing?' he asked them. [7]'It is because no one hired us,' they answered. 'Well, then, you also go to work in the vineyard,' he told them. [8]When evening came, the owner of the vineyard told his foreman, 'Call the laborers and pay them their wages, starting with those who were hired last, and ending with those who were hired first.' [9]The men who had begun to work at the eleventh hour came and received a denarius each. [10]So when the men who were the first to be hired came to be paid, they thought they would get more; but they too were given a denarius each. [11]They took their money and started grumbling against the employer. [12]'These men who were hired last worked only one hour,' they said, 'while we put up with a whole day's work in the hot sun—yet you paid them the same as you paid us!' [13]He answered one of them, 'Listen, friend, I have not cheated you. Did you not agree to do a day's work for a denarius? [14]Now, take what is yours and go home. It is my will to give this man who was hired last as much as I have given you. [15]Don't I have the right to do as I wish with what is mine? Or is your eye evil because I am generous?' [16]So the last shall be first and the first last."
(Vs. 15—Cf. 6:23.)

The parable has been inserted here as an illustration of the last sentence (19:30), although its original significance was quite different. It may be asked whether this parable was already associated, by tradition, with that saying (repeated 20:16). But it should be noted that Matthew has once before (18:14, 35) taken a saying, introduced a parable with it, then restated the saying another way at the end. Matthew may have a special purpose in changing the sequence found in 19:30, so that now the "last" are mentioned first. We must therefore first inquire what the parable by itself means, and only then what point Matthew is using it to make.

[1] The narrative follows the rhythm of daily labor in Palestine. "Working hours last from the dawning of the sun to the rising of the stars," we read in rabbinic literature, and Psalm 104:22-23 says the same thing. There is no glorification of labor—the burden of the day's toil and the hot south wind are mentioned in verse 12—that is simply the way things are. [2] The wages mentioned are the amount usually paid (Tob. 5:14-15 and rabbinic literature) and specified in contemporary labor law. The formalities are described explicitly, so that no one can doubt that everything is procedurally correct. [3] Demand meets supply in the marketplace: unemployment was a part of Palestine then as now. [4] In the case of the second group, the employer does not fix upon a specific sum, but in general terms upon what is proper. [5] The process is repeated twice more; [6] but only in the case of those hired just before the end of the working day is the brief conversation quoted; here, obviously, we have the point of emphasis. The hiring of laborers so late in the day is not impossible; it might be done, for example, in the case of an abundant harvest just before the rainy season with its danger of frost at night. It is, however, unusual. No promises are made to the last group either, but the lateness of hiring gives it special prominence. The employer does not question their reason for not working; but it is evident they were not yet in the marketplace at the sixth or the ninth hour. It is simply left open whether their coming this late to find work is their own fault.

[8] According to Leviticus 19:13 and Deuteronomy 24:15, a laborer must be paid on the evening of the day he has worked, so that the poor will not starve. The last hired are the first to be paid. This point is simply necessary for the story, because otherwise the first would not see how much the last received. [9] It has been suggested on the basis of an obscure rabbinic statement (Billerbeck on vs. 8) and Roman labor law, which was not in force in Palestine, that the law required the last to be paid a full day's wages; but verses 11-12 make this out of the question. Equal pay for unequal work is totally unexpected and objectionable. [10-12] It enrages those who have not only done twelve times as much work, but have had above all to bear the heat of the day. They are indignant that the owner has made those who came last of all "equal to them." Had they not witnessed this,

they would have gone home content with their wages. **[13]** The owner of the vineyard is obviously present when the laborers are paid; otherwise we would have to assume that in their indignation they proceeded to his home to call him to account. While the laborers speak without using any forms of address, not to mention titles of courtesy, the owner addresses one of them as one would address a person whose name one does not know but with whom some sort of relationship exists, calling him "friend" and pointing out to him the unassailable legal situation. That he should give the last an equal amount is strictly a matter of his own generosity; there is no need to account to anyone for his decision. **[15]** "With what is his" or "on his own property" he can do as he likes. The parable closes with the contrast between the "evil eye" (the literal meaning of the Greek; see the discussion of 6:23) of the indignant laborer and the generosity of the owner.

This is probably the real point. It is true, of course, that as early as verse 10 all expectations are shattered. One might say that the parable disposes of the concept of wages or reward by applying it. Even this, however, is not the crucial point. There is no polemic against the concept; in a certain sense God's goodness is even expressed in terms of a reward. That the laborers are hired and thus receive what they need for themselves and their families is itself a good deed toward them; and there is of course nothing wrong with their expecting to receive their denarius. It is comparison that creates trouble. This is why the argument in verses 11-15 is described in such detail. On this point, too, the parable remains open. Whether the grumblers allow themselves to be convinced by the owner and learn to recognize his generosity is not recorded. That is the question Jesus leaves his listeners with: whether they can learn from him to see with the eyes of God and no longer with their own "evil eye." It is God's will to employ men; he sees what they do and does not forget it; he even gives them a just reward. All this is itself an expression of his goodness. But the man who imports his own ideas of what is right and just cannot understand this. To measure God's goodness by the standards of men's works does not do justice to either. Anyone who fails to understand that God gives infinitely more than a just wage also fails to understand that the reward given by God is an expression of his goodness.

A Jewish parable in a funeral oration of A.D. 325 speaks of a king who summons a particularly competent laborer to walk for several hours with him; in the evening, to the indignation of the rest, he pays him full wages on the grounds that he accomplished more in two hours than the others did in an entire day. If the speaker was familiar with Jesus' parable, he used it to express the exact opposite: to each according to his deserts, even though the standards are not always transparently clear to human eyes. In addition, this parable is an exposition of Ecclesiastes 5:11: "Sweet is the sleep of the laborer, whether or not he has plenty to eat"; in other words, the Jewish parable purports to interpret a Scriptural passage that holds true always and everywhere: labor itself is much of its reward.

In Jesus' parable, however, the point is precisely reversed—good "works" earn no reward and are not in themselves rewarding; whatever reward they meet with is God's gift—and indeed in this parable the strange righteousness of God in giving gifts actually *takes place*. It takes place as Jesus tells the story: tax collectors and prostitutes come to him and find entrance into the Kingdom of God. This is as concrete as the denarius in the parable, where matters are not allowed to rest with an inward emotion on the part of the owner. Thus this parable comes very close to that of the two sons, of whom the one who was lost shares in the banquet, while it remains an open question whether the moral elder son can even find his way to the banquet hall (Luke 15:11-32); but it also comes very close to what Paul terms the righteousness of God. This righteousness sees and acknowledges the good works that men do (Matt. 20:10*b;* Luke 15:31). But this righteousness is of such a strange sort that it is lost when men claim it by right, when they compare their own performance with that of others instead of concentrating on the goodness of the Lord, before which all accomplishments vanish (Matt. 20:12-15; Luke 15:29-30, 32; Phil. 3:8-9). Thus the incomprehensible goodness of God itself becomes a stumbling block to the man who refuses to give up his human ideas of justice and merit. It does not matter how long and how hard a man has worked, only that he was recruited and heeded the call.

[16] Matthew uses the saying about the first and the last as a setting for the parable. In 19:30, this saying means that those who here and now possess everything may one day come after those who now

give up everything and follow Jesus. The same saying occurs in Luke 13:30 after the announcement of judgment upon Israel and the promise to the gentiles. In the tradition, therefore, the saying describes the fact that those who are rich in this world can be lost at the Judgment, and those who are poor can be saved. In 20:16, Matthew underlines what is merely a secondary feature by means of the saying, namely the fact that those who came last are paid first. By this he is not saying that his disciples will one day receive their reward, while Israel will not. This interpretation would not fit the parable, where all receive the same reward, nor would it fit the following section about the Passion of Jesus and his dismissal of the idea that disciples will receive greater rewards (20:17-28). Probably Matthew is saying that the disciples will cease to be among the last and come to be among the first, but that they may also be once more among the last if they do not recognize the goodness of God—if they do not rejoice from the heart over the "little ones" whom God calls, in other words, if they cannot live as a community according to the principles inculcated in chapter 18.

Some manuscripts add at the end the saying from 22:14, "Many are called, but few are chosen." This would merely put the potential threat into words, and the conclusion of the parable would cease to be an open question and become practically a condemnation of the multitude. So interpreted, the parable would no longer solicit men to understand God's goodness, only caution them against expecting too much from it. Rather than give this depressing tone, Matthew leaves the question of rewards open; in verse 16 he even puts in first place the unexpected generosity that is shown to the last-hired.

In Jesus' mouth the parable is a warning against "grumbling" (the same term is used in Luke 5:30; John 6:41 ff.; 1 Cor. 10:10), the kind of attitude that exclaims indignantly over tax collectors and prostitutes, "You have made them equal to *us?*" By the time of Matthew the community recognized the principle of acceptance as being almost self-evident, since even the gentiles had entered into the community. On the other hand, an attitude of disdain did crop up in the community—toward those who drifted away (18:14), and the community was not alway sedulous in forgiving them (18:21, 32-33). Thus Jesus' story came to speak with an always pertinent voice; that it still does so is the sign of a good parable.

The Third Announcement of the Passion (20:17-19)
Cf. Mark 10:32-34; Luke 18:31-34

[17]As Jesus was going up to Jerusalem he took the Twelve aside and spoke to them privately, as they walked along. [18]"Listen," he told them, "we are going up to Jerusalem, where the Son of Man will be handed over to the chief priests and the teachers of the Law. They will condemn him to death [19]and then hand him over to the gentiles, who will make fun of him, whip him, and crucify him; and on the third day he will be restored to life."

[17] This third announcement of the Passion is told as it is in Mark, though without the significant Markan introduction (see the introductory remarks on Mark 10:32-34). Only the statement that the episode took place "as they walked along" (literally "on the way")—like Mark, Matthew may already be thinking of the way of the cross—is borrowed from Mark; but it is inserted at a different point. [19] The announcement that the resurrection (see the discussion of 17:9) will take place on the third day rather than after three days agrees with 16:21 and 17:23. It is significant that Matthew replaces "kill" with "crucify"; only here (and in 26:2) does this term appear in the announcements of the Passion. The primitive confession of faith speaks of Jesus' death (1 Cor. 15:3; cf. Rom. 6:10; also 1 Pet. 3:18; Acts 3:15 alongside 4:10 and especially 5:30); the manner in which he died took on importance for Paul on theological grounds: according to Deuteronomy 21:23, the man who is "hanged on a tree" (Gal. 3:13; cf. Acts 5:30) is accursed by God. Therefore Jesus has really taken the place of the sinner accursed by God, identified himself totally with him, and won him back his place with God. It is doubtful whether this idea is in Matthew's mind; possibly he mentions the manner of Jesus' death because it is typically Roman, and the gentiles (= Romans) are mentioned here (but cf. also 26:2).

True Greatness (20:20-28)
Cf. Mark 10:35-45

[20]Then the mother of Zebedee's sons came to Jesus with her sons, and fell down before him to ask him for a favor. [21]"What do you

want?" Jesus asked her. She answered, "Promise that these two sons of mine will sit at your right and your left in your Kingdom." [22]"You don't know what you are asking for," Jesus answered them. "Can you drink the cup that I am about to drink?" "We can," they answered. [23]"You will indeed drink from my cup," Jesus told them, "but I do not have the right to choose who will sit at my right and my left. These places belong to those for whom my Father has prepared them."

[24]When the other ten disciples heard about this they became angry with the two brothers. [25]So Jesus called them all together to him and said, "You know that the rulers have power over the people, and their leaders use violence against them. [26]This, however, is not the way it shall be among you. If one of you wants to be great, he must be the servant of the rest; [27]and if one of you wants to be first, he must be your slave—[28] like the Son of Man, who did not come to be served, but to serve and to give his life as a ransom for many."

[20] Apart from its beginning, this story is practically identical with its Markan counterpart. By means of his characteristic "then," Matthew links it more closely with the announcement of the Passion. For someone to come to Jesus and fall down before him is also typically Matthaean (see the discussion of 8:2). The most important difference, however, is that it is the mother, not the disciples themselves, who asks the favor. This shows that there were women, too, among the followers of Jesus (Luke 8:1 ff.; Mark 15:40-41 = Matt. 27:55-56), although their names are not definitely recorded (cf. the discussion of 27:56 and the introductory remarks on Mark 16:1-8). Matthew 27:56 equates "the mother of Zebedee's sons" with Salome (Mark 15:40). The disciples themselves are thus exonerated of greed for glory (see the discussion of 13:16-17), while their mother joins the circle of Israelite mothers (1 Samuel 1; 2 Maccabees 7; cf. Luke 1:39-45).

Was Matthew perhaps sensitive on the question of primacy among disciples because Peter—the leader in Matthew's community—had been both singled out and rebuked by Jesus (16:17-19; 14:31 and 16:22-23)? A certain rivalry between Peter and the "beloved disciple," probably meaning John, is revealed in John 21:21 ff. (cf. 13:23-26; 18:15 ff.; 19:26-27; 20:4, 8; 21:7). [21] Perhaps Matthew substitutes "your Kingdom" (cf. the discussion of 13:41; 16:28) for "glory" (Mark 10:37) because the image that follows is more suggestive of places of honor at the festal banquet than of thrones, as in Matthew 19:28.

[22] Jesus addresses his reply to the two disciples rather than to their mother; this shows how Matthew corrected the Markan text at the beginning but then went on to borrow it unchanged. The image of the baptism by death is omitted, perhaps because John did not suffer martyrdom with James (see the introductory remarks on Mark 10:35-45). A man who had not actually been martyred could also be thought of as having partaken of the cup of Jesus' Passion (cf. Rev. 1:9). [27] In writing "your servant" instead of "the servant of all" (Mark 10:44), Matthew has in mind the brotherly service one member of the community owes another, as detailed in chapter 18. [28] The saying about the Son of Man as servant is not introduced as reason, the way it is in Mark 10:45 ("for"), but as a model ("like"), in such a way that this servant role makes it possible for the disciples to follow the same way. The identity between the two ways is more strongly emphasized.

Here, as in the small alteration in verse 27, we see the special meaning Matthew attaches to this section. It concludes the entire period in which the disciples are to learn what it means to live in the community of Jesus. Matthew 18 described how the community could live as a free congregation of brothers without having any members placed in positions of superiority and control, held together only by brotherly service, imposed upon all, and the authority of the prophetic spirit and charismatic healing. The way of life of Jesus' disciples is thus the way of life of Jesus himself; according to Matthew it must always be so. But the life and death of Jesus are subsumed under the single concept of service. Some manuscripts contain an addition to verse 28: "But you must seek to grow from littleness to (true) greatness and from being greater to being lesser." Other manuscripts add a negative to the last phrase: ". . . and not (to be brought down) from being greater (through arrogance) to being lesser." This is then followed by the parable about the guests who look for the best places at the banquet, in other words a parallel version of Luke 14:8-10. For centuries, then, the parable itself continued on its course, being appended to other sayings of Jesus through new introductions. In this form, admittedly, the parable seems to be recommending a method of achieving true greatness, namely through self-abasement, thus coming closer to the advice of the rabbis than the words and ministry of Jesus.

Two Blind Men Follow Jesus (20:29-34)
Cf. Mark 10:46-52; Luke 18:35-43

[29]As they were leaving Jericho a large crowd followed Jesus. [30]Two blind men who were sitting by the road heard that Jesus was passing by, so they began to shout, "Son of David! Have mercy upon us, Lord!" [31]The crowd scolded them and told them to be quiet. But they shouted even more loudly, "Son of David! Have mercy on us, Lord!" [32]Jesus stopped and called them. "What do you want me to do for you?" he asked them. [33]"Lord," they answered, "we want you to open our eyes!" [34]Jesus had pity on them and touched their eyes; at once they were able to see, and followed him.

The last episode before the entry into Jerusalem is also told as in Mark, albeit in remarkable agreement with Matthew's own 9:27-31. [30] In both accounts there are two blind men, perhaps because here the acclamation of Christ is especially emphasized, by the titles "Lord" and "Son of David," as well as the exclamation "Have mercy on us!"—such statements of faith, strong as they are, are made still stronger by coming from the mouths of two witnesses. [29] As in 9:27-31, the introductory verse speaks of "following" [33] and the conclusion of "eyes being opened"; but the two expressions appear at different points in the narrative. Certain idioms are therefore fixed, although the evangelist is still for the most part shaping his material freely. In 20:29-32 and 34b, in contrast to 9:27-31, the influence of the Markan tradition can be discerned.

[29] No name is mentioned, nor are the blind men characterized as beggars (Mark 10:46); [30-33] neither is Jesus called a Nazarene, though he is still addressed three times as "Lord," a term reserved by Matthew for believers (see the discussion of 8:2). [34] This means that Matthew took the phrase "they followed him" to mean that the men joined Jesus as disciples. This is probably also why he omitted the

phrase "on the road," introduced by Mark as a conscious echo of 10:32, so that the "following" would not be interpreted as going with Jesus through the streets of Jericho.

[30-31] "Son of David" appears also in Mark 10:47-48; Matthew has already used the phrase in 9:27; 12:23; 15:22. The reason it is placed at the end of the sentence in the Greek text may be that the acclamation "Lord have mercy on us!" had already become a fixed liturgical formula. The extended narrative in Mark 10:49b-50 is omitted, with the result that the encounter between Jesus and the blind men becomes more central.

[34] Jesus' pity is explicitly mentioned. It corresponds to the second word in "Have mercy on us." But, as in 9:36; 14:14; 15:32; 18:27, a different word, characteristic of the late portions of the Old Testament, is selected rather than the word used in the liturgical formula. Only here is it applied to the Son of David. It is strange that no mention is made of the faith of the blind men, which is brought out in 9:28; instead, as in 9:29, Matthew tells how Jesus touched their eyes, although elsewhere he follow the opposite procedure, focusing attention on the conversation about faith and omitting bodily manipulations. Thus what Jesus does becomes the center of attention.

Obviously Matthew's knowledge of this brief episode is based on a special tradition. It is important to him as the last episode in Jesus' ministry before the Passion on account of the threefold acclamation of Jesus as Lord and the twice repeated cry "Lord, have mercy on us (Son of David)," which probably had already been incorporated into the liturgy of the community. This acclamation results in Jesus' having mercy on the blind men, and carrying out the act of deliverance that makes disciples of those who turn to him for help.

V

THE DAYS IN JERUSALEM
21:1–25:46

On the whole, Matthew follows the outline of Mark. Even more than Mark he depicts Jesus as the gentle king whose coming was foretold (21:4-5), emphasizing at the same time that this does not go unnoticed (21:10). By placing the cleansing of the Temple immediately after the entry into Jerusalem, the evangelist moves the cursing of the fig tree and the fulfillment of the curse (which now takes place at once) to the following day. As a consequence, this episode no longer surrounds the narrative of the cleansing of the Temple. For Matthew, the cursed fig tree is no longer a symbol of the rejection of Israel but a sign of the power of prayer that is grounded in faith (see the discussion of 21:-21-22). For this reason there is also no reference to the opening of the sanctuary to "gentiles" (see the introductory remarks on 21:13). On the contrary, the people (Jews) are depicted as having a certain appreciation of Jesus, albeit insufficient (see the discussion of 21:10-11), and a contrast is drawn between the children who acclaim him and the official leadership (see the discussion of 21:14-17). Jesus' animosity is directed against the mercenary greed rampant in the Temple. More than in Mark, the question of whether Israel accepts or rejects Jesus is left open. Matthew is more concerned with Jesus' teaching in the Temple than with his cleansing of it.

The parable of the vineyard and its tenants Matthew places within a frame of two others, greatly increasing its emphasis. The first parable speaks of a man, the second of a landowner (only in Matthew), and the third of a king. The first speaks of the Baptist, the second of Jesus, the third of the disciples. All three are closely linked with each other and with the question of authority. This shows up even in the external structure. "You did not believe him" occurs in 21:25 and 32 (here Matthew's own formulation), linking the first parable with the question of authority. That Israel might lose its chance to enter the "Kingdom of God" (everywhere else Matthew says "Kingdom of heaven") is stated in 21:31; and Matthew repeats the point in 21:43. In addition, 21:28 and 33 both speak of "vineyards." Thus the first and second parables are connected. The statement that God "sent his servants" and "sent other servants" is phrased the same way in both 21:34, 36 and 22:3, 4, linking the second and third parables.

More important are the material connections. The section dealing with the question of authority makes a point of leaving everything open: the planned attack upon Jesus is transformed suddenly into a *trial* in which the leaders of Israel are examined, ending with an open question (21:27). The first parable is the fundamental *verdict:* what "tax collectors and prostitutes" have understood, the leaders of Israel have not recognized (21:32). The second parable brings the *sentence,* formulated by the listeners themselves (21:41) and adopted by Jesus (21:43): the gentiles shall take the place of Israel. In the third parable, finally, the *execution* of the sentence is depicted (22:7). But this is still not the climax, for the whole development has another end in view, namely to warn the community that they face the threat of this same judgment if they act as Israel did (22:11-14).

That the evangelist is really thinking along these lines is confirmed by the subsequent repetition of the trial schema. The disputations in 22:15-46, especially the final one about the Son of David, represent the *trial* of Israel, which once more ends with an open question (22:45-46). The great series of curses in 23:1-32 constitutes the *verdict,* and 23:33-36 the *sentence:* the punishment for the murder of all innocent men will fall upon them. In 23:37–24:2 the sentence is *executed:* with Jesus, God himself leaves the city, as is visibly demonstrated by the destruction of the Temple (an event already in the past for Matthew and his readers).

Once more, however, this is not the end. In 24:3 ff., it is true, the coming of the Son of Man is clearly set apart and depicted as the victorious advance of the liberator who comes to set his community free from the "tribes of the earth," who weep and lament (see the discussion of 24:30-31); but the major emphasis, as in the prophets (Amos 5:18; Jer. 6:14-15), is on the appended warning to the *community,* which might experience an identical fate with the "hypocrites" of 23:13 ff. (24:11-12; 24:37–25:46; cf. the discussion of 24:51). In exactly the same way Matthew repeated earlier threats of judgment upon Israel (3:8, 10; 8:12) as warnings to the community (7:19; 13:42). From 24:27 to 25:31 the coming of the Son of Man dominates everything that is said. Therefore it is no more possible for the Christian to presume on his position with respect to the Jew (Rom. 11:17-24) than for the Jew to do so with respect to the gentile (Rom. 2:17-29) or the devout with respect to the less devout (Rom. 14:10).

The Entry into Jerusalem (21:1-11)
Cf. Mark 11:1-10; Luke 19:29-38

¹As they approached Jerusalem, they came to Bethphage, at the Mount of Olives. There Jesus sent two of his disciples on ahead ²with these instructions: "Go to the village there ahead of you, and at once you will find a donkey tied up and her colt with her. Untie them and bring them to me. ³And if anyone says anything, tell him, 'The Master needs them'; and he will let them go at once." ⁴This happened to make come true what was spoken by the prophet:
> ⁵"Tell the daughter of Zion,
>   Behold, your king is coming to you.
> He is gentle and rides on a donkey,
>   and on a colt, the foal of a donkey."

⁶So the disciples went ahead and did what Jesus had told them to do: ⁷they brought the donkey and the colt, threw their cloaks over them, and Jesus got on. ⁸A great crowd of people spread their cloaks on the road, while others cut branches from the trees and spread them on the road. ⁹The crowds walking in front of Jesus and the crowds walking behind began to shout, "Hosanna to the Son of David! Blessings on him who comes in the name of the Lord! Hosanna in the heights!"

¹⁰When Jesus entered Jerusalem the whole city was thrown into an uproar. "Who is he?" the people asked. ¹¹"This is the prophet Jesus, from Nazareth of Galilee," the crowds answered.

(Vs. 5—Isa. 62:11; Zech. 9:9. Vs. 9—9:27; 20:30-31; 21:15; Ps. 118:26.)

[1] In verse 1, Matthew omits the obscure location (Mark 11:1) and the feature that no one had ever ridden on the colt (Mark 11:2). [3] In verse 3 he omits the phrase "back again," so that the text no

longer states that Jesus will send the donkey back when he is done with it, but only that the owner will place his donkeys at Jesus' disposal as soon as the disciples ask for them. Thus Jesus' command is made to sound more authoritative: everything is put to the service of the King at his entry. Matthew likewise eliminates Mark 11:4-6a, which describe how everything miraculously foretold by Jesus takes place just as predicted; instead he inserts a formula emphasizing the absolute obedience of the disciples.

[2, 7] The most striking change is the mention of a donkey and its colt in verse 2, and especially in verse 7. Now Matthew has inserted Zechariah 9:9 in verses 4-5 as a prophetic quotation (cf. the excursus on 1:18-25 [§2]). Taken literally, it speaks of a donkey and (the "and" appears only in the Septuagint) a colt (Gen. 49:11 likewise), but only because Hebrew writers often use hendiadys (cf. for example Ps. 2:1-5; 33:10-12; also Num. 21:28; Deut. 32:2; 1 Sam. 2:6-7; Isa. 47:1). Matthew has thus made the Markan reference to the prophetic passage explicit and at the same time emphasized its literal fulfillment, although it is hard to picture how Jesus is supposed to ride on both—first on one and then on the other? Something similar has taken place in 27:34 (see the discussion of Mark 15:23) and John 19:23-24 (see the discussion of Mark 15:24).

The interpolated quotation calls Jesus "king." Matthew changes the acclamation in verse 9 to correspond; [9] it no longer hails the "kingdom of David" but rather Jesus personally, calling him "Son of David," as 20:30-31 has already done, and saying that he is "gentle" or "humble" at his coming. Perhaps Matthew omitted the adjectives "righteous and victorious" from the quotation deliberately. Even Psalms of Solomon 17:37 is aware that the messiah will not trust in horse and rider or in military levies; this applies even more to the peaceful king of Isaiah 11:1-9 (cf. 42:1-4). The statement made here, however, goes even further. Jesus, who promised salvation to the wretched and humble in his Beatitudes, now stands at the beginning of his own humiliation (Passion) story.

[5] At the beginning of verse 5, a promise from Deutero-Isaiah (62:11), which likewise speaks of the "daughter of Zion," has replaced the first words of Zechariah 9:9, perhaps because the author is quoting

from memory, perhaps because the passage from Isaiah particularly underlines the consoling fulfillment of promises made to the city of God (depicted as a woman). This would be consonant with rabbinic hermeneutics, in which a passage containing the same word as another serves to interpret the latter. It is also possible that the two passages had already become fused in the liturgy of the community, just as various texts of the words of institution are fused in our eucharistic liturgies.

[10] The excitement of the whole city of Jerusalem is mentioned explicitly (cf. the beginning of verse 5; also Ruth 1:19), perhaps as a deliberate contrast to King Herod's alarm in 2:3. Matthew likes stressing that all Jerusalem or all Israel is affected by the presence of Jesus. [11] It is true, however, that the jubilant crowd accompanying Jesus does not get beyond the testimony that he is a prophet. Or is the reference perhaps to "the prophet" promised in Deuteronomy 18:18?

Matthew places his emphasis on the character of Jesus, who termed himself gentle and humble (11:29-30), and is therefore the promised King for all the little ones, the poor and humble, who expect everything from God (5:3-5). Thus he introduces the Passion narrative. The obedience of the disciples is also part of the story: they follow Jesus' instructions to the letter and thereby contribute to fulfilling the promise.

God's Judgment on the Cult of Israel (21:12-22)
Cf. Mark 11:11-25; Luke 19:45-48

[12]Jesus went into the Temple and drove out all those who bought and sold in the Temple; he overturned the tables of the moneychangers and the stools of those who sold pigeons, [13]and said to them, "It is written, 'My house will be called a house of prayer.' But you are making it a 'thieves' cave!' " [14]The blind and crippled came to him in the Temple and he healed them. [15]The chief priests and the teachers of the Law became angry when they saw the wonderful things he was doing, and the children shouting and crying in the Temple, "Hosanna to David's Son!" [16]So they said to Jesus, "Do you hear what they are saying?" "Indeed I do," answered Jesus. "Haven't you ever read,

'From the mouth of children and sucklings you have prepared praise for yourself?'" [17]Jesus left them and went out of the city to Bethany, where he spent the night.

[18]On his way back to the city, early next morning, Jesus was hungry. [19]He saw a fig tree by the side of the road and went to it, but found nothing on it except leaves. So he said to the tree, "You will never again bear fruit!" At once the fig tree dried up. [20]The disciples saw this and were astonished. "How did the fig tree dry up so quickly?" they asked. [21]Jesus answered, "Amen, I tell you this: if you believe and do not doubt, you will be able to do what I have done to this fig tree; not only this, you will even be able to say to this hill, 'Get up and throw yourself into the sea,' and it will. [22]If you believe, you will receive whatever you ask for in prayer."

(Vs. 13—Isa. 56:7; Jer. 7:11. Vs. 15—Ps. 118:25. Vs. 16—Ps. 8:1-2.)

The most striking change is the transfer of the Temple episode to the day of Jesus' entry. According to Mark, it took place on the following day, after a night spent at Bethany. There is no way to resolve the contradiction; Matthew probably wanted to depict a more logical sequence of events (cf. the introductory remarks on Mark 11:1-11 and on 11:12-26). Thus only two days elapse between Jesus' entry and the debate about authority, rather than three as in Mark. The latter also treats "those who sell and those who buy" as two groups, merchants and pilgrims; Matthew lumps both groups together, perhaps because he is thinking only of the merchants, thus criticizing more harshly a practice based on motives of profit. Matthew omits the incomprehensible prohibition against carrying any kind of vessel through the Temple (Mark 11:16); and his addition of verses 14-16 and omission of reference to the gentiles (Mark 11:17) effects a shift of accent. In Mark 11:17, the Biblical quotation refers to what will take place according to God's plan; in Matthew 21:13 it refers only to what should be, but has been corrupted by Israel's cult. The Gospel of the Nazarenes (25) speaks at this point of the radiance in Jesus' eyes, before which everyone fled.

The difficult clause in Mark 11:13, "because it was not the right time for figs," is also omitted. In verses 20-22 Matthew abbreviates

slightly and omits Mark 11:25 because the saying has already occurred in Matthew 6:14-15. The phrase "If you believe" is reminiscent
of 17:20, and the appended warning against doubt recalls 14:31. That
doubt is a particular hindrance to prayer (vs. 22) is also stated in
Ecclesiasticus 7:10; James 1:6-8; 1 Timothy 2:8.

The passage in verses 14-16 probably goes back to the evangelist.
The quotation follows the Septuagint precisely; the term used for
"wonderful things" also comes from the Septuagint; and the acclamation "Hosanna" is formulated the same way it is in verse 9. The
coupling of "blind and crippled" (vs. 14) is also a Matthaean addition,
as it is in 15:30-31 (based on 11:5?—see the discussion of vs. 14 below).
Jesus' "teaching" is omitted (Mark 11:17a-18) and his "healing"
substituted (see the excursus on 7:13-23 [§2]). The healings are superfluous for verse 16; all that is needed is the children who continue the
jubilation of verse 9.

Since this is also the only passage in the first three Gospels to
mention a healing in Jerusalem, it must be especially important to
Matthew. The word "came," the phrase "Haven't you ever read," and
the proof by Scripture are typically Matthaean. The schema is that of
Matthaean disputations: an action by Jesus (or the disciples)—pro-
tests by his opponents—response based on Scripture (cf. 9:9-13). But
Matthew did not invent the episode. The fact that neither the children, who are introduced in a subordinate clause, nor the teachers of
the Law exhibit any reaction to the cleansing of the Temple, which
Matthew has just recounted, suggests that this little story was once
an independent account and may even have been linked with verses
10-11 before the cleansing of the Temple was interpolated—an event
that according to Mark did not take place until the next day. Above
all, Luke 19:39-40 contains a similar episode: a protest by Pharisees
against the noise of Jesus' followers, and Jesus' reply. In Luke, however, Jesus' reply is different. Since the Aramaic words for "children"
and "stones" are almost identical *(bnaiyā/abnayā)*, it is reasonable to
suppose that oral tradition spoke of children and of a response by
Jesus along the lines of Luke 19:40 ("If these are silent, the stones will
cry out"). In this case Lukan tradition would have interpreted "children" as a term for the disciples, and Matthew would have substituted
a Scriptural quotation for the response of Jesus. Perhaps he was even

thinking that the quotation ended ". . . for the sake of your [God's] enemies" (Ps. 8:2). In any event, the official rejection of Jesus by the authorities now stands in sharp contrast to his jubilant acceptance by the children. That official rejection here stands in place of the decision to kill Jesus in Mark (11:18) and leads to Jesus' retreat from the city.

[14] The healing of the blind and crippled is especially important to Matthew, probably on account of 2 Samuel 5:8, according to which the blind and crippled are excluded from the Temple. According to Matthew 11:5, their healing already demonstrates that the eschaton promised by Isaiah has come; now their exclusion from the Temple community is annulled. Perhaps Matthew is even thinking that it is the "Son of David" (21:15) who repeals the ordinance of David disqualifying the crippled and blind—an ordinance which also applied at Qumran, where the crippled, blind, deaf, dumb, insane, and deformed were excluded (1QSa ii. 5-7). Psalm 8, which deals with man's shortcomings and their erasure by God, is interpreted as referring to Jesus' healing work also in 1 Corinthians 15:27; Ephesians 1:22; and Hebrews 2:6-9. Knowledge of God has already been promised the "little ones" in Matthew 11:25. They recognize God's coming in Jesus and God's "wonderful works," while the official "builders" reject the "wonderful" stone, Jesus (21:42). The theme of Jesus' rejection starts here—linguistically and metaphorically intertwining the ideas of disciples-as-little-ones and Jesus-as-Temple-stone, each to be rejected by men, and exalted by God.

Thus this text is imbued with a tone of great seriousness: Jesus leaves the Temple, and with him God himself departs. Even though there is no mention of any formal decision to kill Jesus, it is clear that the chief priests and teachers of the Law, with their rigid and inflexible expectations of the Kingdom of David, have irrevocably missed their chance to hail the true "Son of David," who is recognized by the more responsive little ones. The business of the Temple will continue—another forty years—but the Temple is an empty shell, without the presence of God.

At the same time, our text is imbued with great joy: as Jesus leaves, the rejoicing of the little ones accompanies him, and within the Temple are the blind and crippled, now healed, who earlier had been excluded, to whom Jesus has now opened the house of God. The clock can no longer be turned back, and the children who realize this prove themselves better realists than the authorities, who see at most a drop of water on a hot stone. **[21-22]** This makes it all the clearer that the strong faith to pray spoken of in verses 21-22 is not mere religiosity; it is granted to whoever, like a child, has not yet committed himself totally, but can rely completely on God in whatever concrete situation he finds himself, and expect everything from him (cf. the discussion of 14:31). This is symbolized, as verse 20 explicitly states, by the immediate drying up of the fig tree.

The Question about Jesus' Authority (21:23-27)
Cf. Mark 11:27-33; Luke 20:1-8

²³Jesus came back to the Temple; and as he taught, the chief priests and the elders of the people came to him and asked, "By what authority do you do these things? Who gave you this authority?" ²⁴Jesus answered them, "I will ask you just one question, and if you give me an answer I will tell you by what authority I do these things.

²⁵"Whence was the baptism of John? From heaven or from men?" They started to argue among themselves, "What shall we say? If we answer, 'From heaven,' he will say to us, 'Why, then, did you not believe John?' ²⁶But we if say, 'From men,' we are afraid of what the people might do, because they are all convinced that John was a prophet." ²⁷So they answered Jesus, "We don't know." And he said to them, "Neither will I tell you, then, by what authority I do these things."

Matthew has made minor changes. It is noteworthy that in verse 23 he omits the "teachers of the Law" (Mark 11:27). The only new element is Jesus' teaching in the Temple (vs. 23; Mark 12:35 is therefore omitted in Matt. 22:41), which now provides occasion for the opponents' question, rather than the cleansing of the Temple, as in Mark. In Matthew, the cleansing of the Temple is separated from this debate by a rather extensive interpolation (vss. 14-17). It is Jesus' authority to teach that is now expressly questioned. Matthew 21:26 avoids the anacolouthon in Mark 11:32.

Yes and No to the Father (21:28-32)

[28]"Now, what do you think? There was a man who had two sons. He went to the older one and said, 'Son, go work in the vineyard today.' [29]'I don't want to,' he answered, but later he changed his mind and went to the vineyard. [30]Then the father went to the other son and said the same thing. 'Yes, sir,' he answered, but he did not go. [31]Which of the two did what his father wanted?" "The older one," they answered. "Amen, I tell you," Jesus said to them, "the tax collectors and prostitutes are going into the Kingdom of God ahead of you. [32]For John came to you showing you the right path to take, and you would not believe him; but the tax collectors and the prostitutes believed him. Even when you saw this you did not change your minds later on and believe him."

[31] The parable itself probably goes back to Jesus, though of course not the Matthaean introduction (see the discussion of 18:12-13), which concludes with Jesus' question (vs. 31a). The juxtaposition of "tax collectors and prostitutes" in verse 31b is unique, and nowhere else does Matthew speak of the "Kingdom of God" (rather than the "Kingdom of heaven"). He therefore found the saying in fixed form in his sources. It might belong to the parable, but it might also be an isolated saying of Jesus that Matthew placed here because he found it germane either to the parable or to the saying about John the Baptist.

[32] In any case, Matthew uses verse 32 to link the whole section with verses 25-27 by borrowing from the latter the theme of the Baptist and the expression "you would not believe him"; he repeats the verdict once more, and echoes the words of the parable: "You did not change your minds later on." As Luke 7:29-30 shows, Matthew had before him a saying to the effect that the "tax collectors . . . justified God" (the Greek root is the same as in "right" [Matt. 21:32]), while the Pharisees rejected God's purpose. Matthew phrases the saying with this in mind, although the association with the parable of the man who says "yes" but gives the lie to his words by failing to keep his promise does not really fit; for Jesus' opponents have already said "no" to John, not "yes." Once again the parallel between the

ministry of the Baptist and that of Jesus is expressed (see the discussion of 3:2). If the parable is Jesus' own, it was addressed to the situation of Pharisees versus tax collectors and originally ended with Jesus' simple assent ("You have judged correctly").

Some ancient manuscripts, as in the translation above, mention the son who refuses first; this is a logical sequence for the father's actions. Others no less ancient begin with the son who agrees. This, too, is possible; in this case the father would have asked his second son when he discovered that the first had in fact not gone. This would be descriptive of God's history with his people: official Judaism said "yes" to God, but in fact did not do the will of the Father; then came the tax collectors and prostitutes (or gentiles), for whom the situation was reversed. But the very patness of this application suggests that the original order of the parable was reversed when it came to be interpreted this way.

Even more noteworthy is a manuscript that mentions the son who refuses first, but has the opponents in verse 31 say, "The second," as though all that mattered were whether one agreed to do something, not whether it was actually done. The best one can do with this reading is to suggest that because their hearts were hardened they deliberately gave the wrong answer so as to avoid the point of the parable; in this case, however, one would expect Jesus to accuse them of doing so. It is possible that this strange form of the parable led to the inversion of the two sons (so that the one who refused came second), because only with this change was the answer "The second" logical. Probably, then, the parable originally ran something like the translation above.

The parable itself is clear and simple. Of course the only possible answer is that the first (i.e. the son who said "no") did the will of his father, while the second used fine words—he politely called his father "sir"!—but didn't do anything. Who is meant? Originally the parable referred to those who thought they were believers, fulfilling the will of God, but were not, while those who felt excluded from Israel actually were fulfilling the will of God: in other words, the devout who rejected Jesus on the one hand, the tax collectors and prostitutes on the other. That these should enter the Kingdom of God is the miracle at which the angels in heaven rejoice (Luke 15:7, 10), and even the Father himself (15:23-24). Matthew, too, takes the parable this way in verse 32.

Before the coming of John the Baptist, the Pharisees had said "yes" to God, and formally accepted his Law. But this formalism is precisely how they have failed to do his will. It is likely that after Easter there also entered in the notion of the Jews, who had rejected Jesus, and the gentiles, who accepted him and are in a sense prefigured in the tax collectors. In the context of verses 25-26, however, Matthew is trying to say that the people had already made the wrong decision when they rejected John the Baptist, although 3:5 has a rather different message.

"To believe" or "to have faith" thus means to say "yes" to the "right path," as the text puts it in Old Testament terms (Job 24:13; Prov. 8:20; 16:31; 17:23; 21:16). The notion is not of a "faith" that assents merely intellectually, emotionally, or verbally, saying "Lord, Lord!" (or "Sir!") (Matt. 21:30; 7:22). For Matthew "faith" does not imply acceptance of the Baptist as bringer of salvation, but rather of the God he preached. How concrete Matthew's thought is appears in his use of the present tense: ". . . are going into the Kingdom of God ahead of you." The decision is already made; in Jesus the Kingdom of God has in fact come upon them. Like 7:24-27, the parable is a harsh judgment upon those who say "yes" verbally and intellectually without seeing that the will of God is realized in their lives; at the same time it is an urgent call to such realization. This distinguishes the parable of Jesus from the Jewish parable that urges humility, in which four say "no" because they are not sure they can do what is required, while the fifth says "yes" but does not perform, thus laying himself open to the special wrath of the king. What Jesus says brings infinitely more comfort: there really are obedient disciples among those who would never claim to be. His words are therefore an invitation to tax collectors and prostitutes, and to the reader. The next parable will speak of the Son who says "yes" to the will of his Father—and *does* it.

The Parable of Israel's Rejection of Jesus (21:33-46)
Cf. Mark 12:1-12; Luke 20:9-19

³³"Listen to another parable," Jesus said. "There was a landowner who planted a vineyard, put a fence around it, dug a hole for the

winepress, and built a watchtower. Then he rented the vineyard to tenants and left home on a trip. ³⁴When the time came to harvest the grapes he sent his servants to the tenants to receive his harvest. ³⁵The tenants grabbed his servants, beat one, killed another, and stoned another. ³⁶Again the man sent other servants, more than the first time, and the tenants treated them the same way. ³⁷Last of all he sent them his son. 'Surely they will respect my son,' he said. ³⁸But when the tenants saw the son they said to themselves, 'This is the heir; come, let us kill him, and we will get his inheritance.' ³⁹So they grabbed him, threw him out of the vineyard, and killed him. ⁴⁰Now, when the owner of the vineyard comes, what will he do to those tenants?" Jesus asked. ⁴¹"He will certainly kill those evil men," they answered, "and rent the vineyard out to other tenants, who will give him his share of the harvest at the right time." ⁴²Jesus said to them, "Haven't you ever read what the Scriptures say?

'The very stone which the builders rejected
    has become the cornerstone.
This was done by the Lord;
    how wonderful it is in our eyes!'

⁴³"And so I tell you," added Jesus, "the Kingdom of God will be taken away from you and be given to a people who will produce the proper fruits. ⁴⁴[Whoever falls on this stone will be broken to pieces; and if the stone falls on someone it will crush him to dust.]" ⁴⁵The chief priests and the Pharisees heard Jesus' parables and knew that he was talking about them, ⁴⁶so they tried to arrest him. But they were afraid of the crowds, who considered Jesus to be a prophet.

(Vs. 33—Isa. 5:1-2. Vs. 42—Ps. 118:22-23; Isa. 28:16; Rom. 9:33.)

[34-36] The parable itself is told much as it is in Mark. Instead of individual servants, Matthew mentions a group of servants in verse 34 and another group in verse 36, because he is thinking of the prophets of the Old Testament; Mark does not bring out this interpretation until 12:5 b. Jeremiah 7:25-26 already bemoans the fact that God's repeated sending of prophets has been fruitless. Only Matthew mentions "stoning"; he is probably thinking specifically of the stoning of the prophets (vs. 35; 23:37). In verse 39 the Markan order is

reversed: the heir is thrown out, then killed, possibly because Jesus was first led out of Jerusalem (the vineyard of God), then killed outside the city (Heb. 13:12). **[41]** In verse 41 the use of a classical Greek idiom (literally "evilly kill those evil men") and the pious reference to Psalm 1:3 ("he will deliver his fruit at the right time") are noteworthy; **[43]** in verse 43 also Matthew underlines the importance of "bearing fruit." Verse 34 repeats that the whole harvest belongs to the owner. The servants are to collect not merely "a share of the harvest" (Mark 12:2) but the "harvest"; in addition, Matthew calls it "his [the owner's] harvest," not merely the harvest "of the vineyard" (Mark 12:2). God requires the whole because it is his property.

The message of the parable is stated explicitly: God's Kingdom will be taken from Israel and given to a people that "produces the proper fruits" (cf. the introduction to chapters 21–25). This represents a typically Matthaean extension of the term "give" (literally "deliver") in verse 41, which is more appropriate to the parable. There is more at stake than recognition of the owner and his claim to his harvest; what matters is that the fruits of the harvest be "produced" (3:8, 10; 7:19; 13:26; cf. the discussion of 22:11-13). Unlike Mark, Matthew has the listeners themselves pronounce the verdict (vs. 41).

The new people comprises all nations, as 28:19 will show. Therefore Matthew does not use the word, hallowed by Biblical tradition, that designates Israel as the people of God (e.g. 21:23), but one that usually refers to the gentile nations. The community is therefore not simply the new Israel, but a new people of a special sort. **[45]** After such a clear statement as verse 43, which rejects *all* who have failed to do God's will, verse 45 is not really appropriate—it implies Jesus is speaking only of the chief priests and Pharisees. This verse was borrowed (and altered) from Mark, and was probably taken by Matthew to mean that the leaders of the people "know" that Jesus is rebuking not just Israel in general but them in particular. Along with the chief priests Matthew mentions the Pharisees, who do not appear in Mark 11:27. This combination occurs only in Matthew and John. Historically speaking, it is not quite accurate (see the discussion of Mark 1:22 and 8:31); it is probably occasioned by the fact that in the period of Matthew the Pharisees were the only representatives of

Judaism who still played an important role, though people were still aware that the "chief priests" were the authorities who had condemned Jesus.

[46] The masses have nothing more than a vague notion that Jesus is a prophet whose importance is equal to that of John (vs. 26). Verse 43 states explicitly, in fact, that the people as a whole bear no fruit. Verse 44, which develops the symbolism of the stone on the basis of Daniel 2:34-35, 44-45, is not found in some manuscripts. It should actually follow verse 42. Although the image of building is found together with that of farming in Jeremiah 1:10; 1QS viii. 5; 1 Corinthians 3:9; Colossians 2:7, the "stone" is out of place following verse 43; it was probably added by certain copyists on the basis of Luke 20:18. The saying about the cornerstone, from Psalm 118, was adumbrated in Matthew 16:18; here it is combined with another saying about a stone (see the "stone of offense" discussion on 16:18 and the introductory remarks on Mark 12:1-12). In 1 Peter 2:6-10 and Romans 9:25-26, 32-33, also, the idea of a new people of God (vs. 43) is linked with the quotation about the elect foundation-stone (vs. 42) and the stone that causes men to stumble (vs. 44); in those places, however, it is Isaiah 28:16 and 8:14-15 that influence the text, not the passage from Daniel. It is clear, therefore, that this was a frequent theme in primitive Christianity. Much as Matthew is thinking of the transfer of the Kingdom from Israel to the new people of God, his emphasis on the production of fruits always confronts this new people with the question, are they really bearing fruit?

The Parable of God's Rejected Invitation (22:1-14)
Cf. Luke 14:16-24

¹Jesus again used parables in talking to the people. ²"The Kingdom of heaven is like a king who prepared a wedding feast for his son. ³He sent his servants to tell the invited guests to come to the feast, but they did not want to come. ⁴So he sent other servants with the message: 'Tell the guests, "My feast is ready now; my steers and prize calves have been butchered, and everything is ready. Come to the wedding feast!"' ⁵But the invited guests paid no attention and went away: one went to his farm, the other to his store, ⁶while others

grabbed the servants, beat them, and killed them. ⁷The king was very angry; he sent his soldiers, who killed those murderers and burned down their city. ⁸Then he called his servants. 'My wedding feast is ready,' he said, 'but the people I invited did not deserve it. ⁹Now go to the highways and invite to the feast as many people as you find.' ¹⁰So the servants went out into the streets and gathered all the people they could find, good and bad alike; and the wedding hall was filled with people.

¹¹"The king went in to look at the guests and he saw a man who was not wearing wedding clothes. ¹²'Friend, how did you get in here without wedding clothes?' the king asked him. But the man said nothing. ¹³Then the king told the servants, 'Tie him up hand and foot and throw him outside in the dark. There will be crying and gnashing of teeth.' ¹⁴For many are called, but few are chosen.''

The content and message of the parable are identical in Matthew and Luke, but the two recensions differ greatly in structure and detail. There is hardly any verbal agreement. [1] Each evangelist composes his own introduction. Typically Matthaean is the introductory formula with the mention of "parables"; Matthew makes the same addition in 13:10, 13 (cf. 34). Unlike Luke, Matthew states that the man who gives the feast is a king and the occasion is the wedding of his son. This introduction may at one time have belonged with verses 11-14.

[11-14] The latter passage was probably originally an independent parable. It is hardly likely that it was added by Matthew, for it contains purely symbolic features, not merely an allegorical description of how the unworthy are punished; and verse 14, which Matthew did add (q.v.), is not appropriate to the parable. But it would not be correct to state that the evangelist's only interest is polemic against Israel. The subject matter of the warning in verses 11-14 fits into his overall conception (see the introduction to chapters 21–25). On the other hand, these verses, which have no parallel in Luke, cannot have belonged to the first parable from the outset, for in the present context it is incomprehensible why the motley crowd that had been going about their business on the streets should be wearing wedding clothes when they are invited to the feast completely without warning. It has

been suggested that every guest was also given festal clothing (cf. Gen. 45:22; Judg. 14:12 ff.); but there is no evidence for such a custom in the time of Jesus—it would have been extremely exceptional and Matthew would have mentioned it. Furthermore, the Greek word for "servants" is not the same here as the one used in the first parable. In verses 11-14 then, we have a parable *opposite* (in form) to that in 1-10; we are dealing incontrovertibly with a royal invitation and with the originally intended guests. Since "king" and "wedding" symbolize the Lord of the Last Judgment and the time of salvation (cf. the discussion of 18:23; Mark 2:19; also Rev. 19:9), everyone realizes that we are dealing with the Last Judgment and with the time of salvation, which will be missed by everyone who does not prepare himself for it (cf. Matt. 25:1-10). That the wedding feast is prepared for the king's "son" makes it especially clear that Matthew is thinking of the culmination of history in Jesus. It is possible that these eschatological features did not find their way into the parable of the invitation until the two parables had been combined.

There is, however, a Jewish parable in which the two motifs are associated. Rabbi Jochanan (d. *ca.* A.D. 80) is said to have told the story of a king who invited his servants to a feast. The clever ones got dressed up while the foolish ones went about their work. When the feast was suddenly announced, they showed up in their working clothes. Later this is described in detail: the painter went to his whitewash, the potter to his clay, the smith to his coals, the laundry-man to his laundry, until finally the king declares: "They shall not eat of the king's feast." This recalls the parable of the ten virgins as well as the parable of the wedding clothes, and it shows how such images were adopted and elaborated by (Jewish) Christians and by Jews and influenced each other mutually, although we cannot make out all the steps.

[3] The use of "servants" in the plural is surely due to the evangelist; it corresponds to 21:34-36 (see the introduction to chapters 21–25) and is to be explained, just as in that passage, as depicting God's history with his people, culminating in the destruction of Jerusalem. If the Greek form "the invited guests" is taken literally, the guests had already been invited, as Luke 14:16 also states. It is possible, however, that Matthew is thinking in terms of

Semitic idiom and means "the guests to be invited."

[4] Be that as it may, verse 4 speaks of a second invitation. Since this second mission of the king's servants leads to final rejection, and since we are told that everything is ready, Matthew here is probably already thinking of the disciples, who invite men in the name of Jesus. This was not possible in 21:36, since the parable culminates in the sending of the son and his murder. Here, however, we are dealing from the very outset with the "wedding" of the "son" of the "king" (cf. also the discussion of 23:34). The repeated invitations place great emphasis on the unwillingness of the guests (mentioned already in vs. 3) and the patience of the king.

[5] Luke 14:18-20 says that the reason the guests do not come is that they have things they consider more important; they might even intend to come later, after they have taken care of their affairs. In Matthew, however, the invitation is flatly rejected in verse 3 without any reason being given, and verse 5 says merely that, since they would rather not come, they go about their usual jobs. Here, too, Matthew depicts the refusal in clearer and more fundamental terms.

[6] That there are still "others" who actually slay the servants sent to invite them (as in 21:35) is hardly comprehensible within the context of the parable; neither does this feature have any parallel in Luke. Only Josephus (*Ant.* ix. 265) tells a similar story, from the time of Hezekiah. [7] Verse 7 proceeds in the same vein. Here the story becomes totally incomprehensible, but the description is reminiscent of punishments sent by God (Isa. 5:24-25). The wrath of the host is mentioned by both evangelists; but it is impossible to conceive of the king coming with his army not only to slay those who had been invited but to burn down their city (not "cities"), and doing all this while the feast stands ready for the newly invited. The parable deals with ordinary citizens, who buy fields and use oxen, not with men who rule entire cities. After this punishment, furthermore, the verdict of the king in verse 8 is pointless. Verses 6-7 are thus clearly an interpolation in the narrative, which earlier passed directly from verse 5 to the wrath of the king (beginning of vs. 7) and then to verse 8. Here the events of A.D. 70—the taking and burning of Jerusalem by Roman armies—have colored the language of the parable. There is no special mention of the Temple, which was destroyed in the year 70, but only

of the city, probably because the vengeance of a "king" upon a "city" of murderers is a stock motif of many Near Eastern narratives.

[8-10] In the Lukan parable the servant goes out twice to invite new guests, first into the town, then into the countryside; this feature is probably meant to represent the missions to the Jews and to the gentiles. In Matthew the servants go out only once, to the crossroads, in order to invite "good and bad alike" (vs. 10, see also vs. 14). In this way, each evangelist says, the host's hall was filled.

[11-14] The parable of the wedding clothes, perhaps with verse 2 as its introduction, is clearly an admonition to the community. In the parable of the feast, verses 6-7 cannot have been interpolated until after the parable came to speak of a king—probably, in other words, after the parable had been combined with verses 11-14. Since the entire structure of chapters 21–25 (see their introduction) focuses on admonishing the community, it was probably Matthew himself who combined the two parables (or even composed the second), at the same time inserting the reference to the destruction of Jerusalem as a terrible warning for the community. The threat in verse 13 b as well as the expression "outside in the dark" undoubtedly goes back to him (cf. 25:30; 8:12; also 13:42, 50). At one time the parable of the feast probably concluded as verse 10 now does, though without the specific reference to a wedding hall. Originally it may have been taken as referring to the contrast between the Pharisees and the "people of the land," whom they looked down upon; soon, however, it came to be taken as referring to the contrast between Jews and gentiles. As soon as this change had taken place, it became natural to include the persecution of Jesus' messengers (vs. 6) and God's judgment (vs. 7), as in 23:34-36.

A third form of the parable occurs in the Gospel of Thomas (64). As in Luke, there is no mention of any king or wedding. The invitation is described more briefly, the excuses in more detail. The latter include collection of debts by merchants, purchase of a house, and collection of rent; evidently the narrator is no longer living in a rural environment (Luke 14:18-19) but in an urban one. The servant is also sent into the streets to invite guests, but the point of the parable is now to warn the listener against commercial transactions that preclude entrance into the Kingdom of heaven. Even this much-altered form of the parable shows that, except for his repeating of the second invitation, Luke remains closest to the original form of the parable. It probably goes back to Jesus himself.

[1] This parable, too, Matthew inserts here because it illustrates the rejection of Jesus by Israel, and at the same time warns the community against the same mistake. [2] The changes emphasize the joy of the occasion: it is a royal wedding feast (cf. the discussion of 25:1). [3] The word for "invite" also means "call." Paul uses the same word to describe the power of the gospel, which "calls" people to God. The point is therefore God's call to salvation. The general invitation already issued is now about to bear fruit, but amazingly no one takes it seriously. Once again the host issues his invitation in terms as concrete as possible. The expression used by Matthew refers to the noon meal, which was occasionally eaten in Palestine in imitation of the Roman practice, rather than the customary evening meal mentioned in Luke 14:16-17. [5-6] The refusals become unequivocal, and judgment follows.

[7] The point, at least in Matthew, is not merely that acceptance of the invitation should take precedence over everything else. The devout Israelites decided unequivocally in favor of God's Kingdom, and were ready to give up all earthly gain in return. But at the very moment when the feast they have been looking forward to comes to them in the invitation of Jesus, they do not notice it. They think there is plenty of time for everything they want to take care of; afterwards they can still get to the feast. That is, assuming they really want to get there. But in fact they do not, for now that everything stands ready, now that it is time for them to come, their unwillingness is revealed. [8] The invitation, however, is still extended. [9-10] Good and bad alike are called, because the host wants to see his hall full.

[11-14] The parable that follows shows that the guests do not simply remain as they are. The "wedding clothes" mean something like a new mode of existence (cf. Rev. 19:8: "the righteous deeds of God's people"; also Isa. 61:10). Paul, too, uses the image of the baptized Christian putting on Christ (Gal. 3:27) or the new man (cf. Col. 3:10) like a garment that covers him completely. That this new mode of being is to be festive, not a dreary new legalism, has already

been made clear by Matthew 9:14-15 = Mark 2:18-19. **[14]** With the concluding statement Matthew cautions against the false security which thinks God's salvation is "in the bag." In a similar vein we read in 2 Esdras 8:3: "Many have been created, but few shall be saved." (RSV) There is a difficulty, however, in that elsewhere "called" and "chosen" are synonymous. But we can also say, for instance, "You can gain someone's love and still not have it," because love must be lived and realized afresh each day. Thus Matthew is trying to say that one can sit in the banquet hall without joining in the feast because he is sitting there "without wedding clothes"; in other words, he is not totally there in his heart. "Called" means taking up the initial invitation (vss. 3-8), "chosen" means persevering to the end (24:22, 24, 31). What is meant therefore is that anyone who is called by God must not look on this call as something that is his by right; he must live it anew each day. When this call no longer shapes a life and makes it festive, it has vanished without a trace. The statement is thus not really an interpretation of the parable, in which only a single individual is "not chosen" (contrary to vs. 14), but a homiletic application.

In Jesus' mouth the parable was probably an invitation to joy, an incomprehensible, glorious offer of grace in images as concrete as possible. At the same time, however, it stated that those first invited do not find their way to the feast, while those outside in the streets quite unexpectedly come to the feast. Perhaps the original point of the parable, especially if the wedding was not yet part of it, was that those who were invited intended to come to the feast after taking care of their business without realizing that the decision had to be made then and there. In this case the parable would be addressed to those who would like to be present when the Kingdom of God comes one day in glory, but do not realize that it is already present for them in Jesus' invitation. Some have sought to deny that Jesus spoke the parable on the grounds that he did not first invite the devout and only afterwards the tax collectors. This is true, of course, but the temporal sequence should not be pressed. The notion that those who had already heard God's invitation in the Law and weekly worship, in other words the devout, were the "first" to be called is a natural idea; it need not have originated after Easter, nor need it refer to the sequence of first Jews then gentiles.

It is true, however, that the incorporation of a multitude of Jewish disciples into the gentile Christian community left its mark on the tradition: in Luke, in the doubling of the invitation to the strangers; in Matthew, in the reference to the events of the year 70. Naturally the message of the gospel must be addressed to each new situation; this takes place in all authentic preaching. It is necessary and proper that experiences should be referred to in which faith sees God at work. There is a danger, however, of reducing the parable to a description of Israel's apostasy. Then we would have the situation of Mark 4:15 repeated: the listeners naturally include themselves in the second group, those who found their way to the banquet hall. Therefore Matthew has to employ a second, appended parable to reaffirm that the invitation and warning in the parable are still operative after the year 70: only the man who does not suppose he has accepted the invitation once and for all now that he has been baptized, but rather lets the invitation stamp his entire life, will continue to sit at the feast. Here, too, we can see Matthew's special concern (cf. the introduction to chapters 21–25): it is Jesus' own band of disciples (who know how great and glorious the invitation is) who must heed the warning not to lose what has been given to them. The absolute authority with which the king acts in verses 1-10 is equaled by that with which he acts in verses 11-14.

The Pharisees' Question about Paying Taxes (22:15-22)
Cf. Mark 12:13-17; Luke 20:20-26

[15]The Pharisees went off and made a plan to trap Jesus with questions. [16]Then they sent some of their disciples and some members of Herod's party to Jesus. "Teacher," they said, "we know that you tell the truth. You teach the truth about God's way, without worrying about what people think, because you pay no attention to a man's status. [17]Tell us, then, what do you think? Is it permitted to pay taxes to the Roman Emperor, or not?" [18]Jesus was aware of their evil plan, however, and so he said, "You hypocrites! Why are you trying to trap me? [19]Show me the coin to pay the tax!" They brought him a denarius, [20]and he asked them, "Whose face and inscription are these?" [21]"The

Emperor's," they answered. So Jesus said to them, "Well, then, pay to the Emperor what belongs to him, and pay to God what belongs to God." [22]When they heard this, they were filled with wonder; and they left him and went away.

[15] Matthew has to conjure a quarrel with the Pharisees (see the discussion of 21:45). Therefore in verse 15 he emphasizes their role more than Mark does, in verse 16 speaks of their "disciples," and in verse 17 adds a peculiarly ironic Matthaean flourish (see the introductory remarks on 18:12-13: "What do you think?" here is a mockery of Jesus' pet opener). In verse 18 he substitutes "evil" for "hypocrisy," and then in turn appends the term "hypocrites" (see the discussion of 6:2). For Matthew the four disputations constitute a single unit. Except for the question asked by the Sadducees, which could not possibly be placed in the mouth of the Pharisees, these disputations have become a single controversy between Jesus and Judaism in its Pharisaic form. The concluding statement in verse 22b comes earlier in Mark, at 12:12, directly *before* the passage on taxes to Caesar. The Pharisees' exit sets the stage for the onset of the Sadducees (vs. 23). For a discussion of the doctrine of the two kingdoms, see the excursus following 7:29, *a.* 2.

The Sadducees' Question about Rising from Death (22:23-33)
Cf. Mark 12:18-27; Luke 20:27-40

[23]That same day some Sadducees came to Jesus. (They are the ones who say that people will not rise from death.) [24]"Teacher," they said, "Moses taught: 'If a man who has no children dies, his brother must marry the widow so they can have children for the dead man.' [25]Now, there were seven brothers who used to live here. The oldest got married, and died without having children, so he left his widow to his brother. [26]The same thing happened to the second brother, to the third, and finally to all seven. [27]Last of all, the woman died. [28]Now at the resurrection, whose wife will she be? All seven of them had married her." [29]Jesus answered them, "How wrong you are! It is because you don't know the Scriptures or God's power. [30]For at the resurrection men and women will not marry, but will be like the

angels in heaven. [31]Now, as for the resurrection: haven't you ever read what God has told you? He said, [32]"I am the God of Abraham, the God of Isaac, and the God of Jacob.' This means that he is the God of the living, not of the dead." [33]When the crowds heard this, they were amazed at his teaching.

(Vs. 24—Deut. 25:5-6 [Gen. 38:8]. Vs. 32—Exod. 3:6.)

Matthew has here allowed the Sadducees, who denied any resurrection, to state their position in a logical and apparently conciliatory way. This is perhaps because by the time of Matthew they no longer played any role in Judaism. The quotation in verse 24 has been somewhat modified, probably so as to follow Genesis 38:8 in the Greek Bible (there is also an allusion to this story in Matt. 1:3). The conclusion mentions the amazement of the crowds, who are distinguished from Jesus' opponents (see the discussion of 27:25). The verse agrees almost word for word with Mark 11:18, which Matthew omits from its original context.

The Pharisee's Question about the Great Commandment (22:34-40)
Cf. Mark 12:28-34; Luke 10:25-28

[34]When the Pharisees heard that Jesus had silenced the Sadducees, they came together, [35]and one of them, a teacher of the Law, tried to trap him with a question. [36]"Teacher," he asked, "which is the great commandment in the Law?" [37]Jesus answered, " 'You must love the Lord your God with all your heart, with all your soul, and with all your mind.' [38]This is the greatest and first commandment. [39]The second is like it: 'You must love your neighbor as yourself.' [40]On these two commandments depend the entire Law and the prophets."

(Vs. 37—Deut. 6:5. Vs. 39—Lev. 19:18. Vs. 40—Cf. Rom. 13:8-10.)

[34] The teacher of the Law mentioned in Mark 12:28 need not have been one of the Pharisees (see the discussion of Mark 1:22). Matthew mentions Pharisees explicitly and speaks of a full-scale assembly (see the discussion of Matt. 22:15). In addition he changes

what is said in Mark 12:28: the teacher of the Law no longer approves the good reply Jesus gave the Sadducee, being thus encouraged to ask his own question; instead, the Pharisees note, probably with satisfaction, that Jesus has stopped the mouth of their opponents. [35] Matthew agrees with Luke in his use of the term "teacher of the Law" (in Matthew belonging to the Pharisaic party), in calling the question a trap, in having the questioner address Jesus as "teacher," in omitting the response of the questioner, and in the details of verse 37. In Luke, however, it is the questioner who furnishes the answer from the outset; Jesus commends him for it. Was this important story recounted orally in different versions and used in catechesis, for example, so that this form influenced both evangelists? What was still a genuine question in Mark has here been reduced to a mere trick to entrap Jesus—an important change.

[40] Matthew accordingly omits the final commendation of Jesus on the part of the questioner, who takes up Jesus' response and makes it his own (Mark 12:32-34), and Matthew transfers Mark's conclusion to a later point, verse 46. It is inconceivable to Matthew that a Jewish teacher of the Law should ask Jesus a question with honorable intent or give an answer that Jesus could commend; the battle lines have been clearly drawn and open dialogue broken off. In the quotation cited in verse 37 Mark follows the Greek translation a bit more closely; possibly Matthew's form was current in his community. Did he omit the beginning (Mark 12:29) because it represents the confession of faith of Judaism, repeated daily by every devout Jew?

[39] He explicity places the commandment to love one's neighbor on an equal footing with the commandment to love God, and adds that "the entire Law and the prophets" "depend" (literally "hang") on these two commandments (see the discussion of 5:18), perhaps the way a door hangs on its hinges. Then righteousness as a whole depends on the fulfillment of these two commandments; and these two are not important simply, as the rabbis assert, because all the other essential commandments come from them. No, they are (together) the "great" commandment because they are the *only* ones that need be obeyed. And, of course, the questioner asks [36] only about the "great" commandment, i.e., the "greatest"; and [38] Jesus' answer makes it clear that that commandment is "the great and first one."

In addition, Matthew, by introducing the term "Law," sets Jesus clearly apart from Pharisaic pettifogging. **[37-39]** This accounts for the omission of the statement that there is one God (Mark 12:29) which here is not at issue: the whole point is the contrast between Pharisaic legalism and the ethics of love for God and one's neighbor. Jesus not only limits the necessary commandments to two, but by fusing those two he also prescribes how to perform the first: only the first commandment is called "great," but the second is equal to it, for one can love God only by loving one's neighbor.

Thus Matthew unerlines the fundamental difference between Pharisaic observance of the Law and Jesus' call to love one's neighbor. Not through legalistic observance of particular commandments but through a sense of love for one's neighbor, expressed in concrete actions and embracing all of life, is the Law fulfilled. That is the "better righteousness" (5:20).

Jesus' Question about the Son of David (22:41-46)
Cf. Mark 12:35-37; Luke 20:41-44

[41]When the Pharisees gathered together, Jesus asked them, [42]"What do you think about the messiah? Whose son is he?" "He is David's son," they answered. [43]"Why, then," Jesus asked, "did the Spirit inspire David to call him 'Lord'? Because David said,

[44]"The Lord said to my Lord:

Sit here at my right side,

until I put your enemies under your feet.'

[45]If, then, David called him 'Lord,' how can the messiah be David's son?" [46]No one was able to answer Jesus a single word, and from that day on no one dared ask him any more questions.

(Vs. 44—Ps. 110:1; cf. 1 Cor. 15:25-26.)

[41] According to Mark 12:35, Jesus "was teaching in the Temple," addressing the crowd and referring to what the "teachers of the Law" say. Here, however, the question is addressed to the assembled Pharisees. **[42]** Thus the passage becomes a part of the whole disputation and the question is made much more direct. "What do you think [see the introductory remarks on 18:12-13] about the messiah?" no longer serves merely to introduce a discussion about how to interpret a passage from Scripture; it demands a response to the most important question of all. At the same time, it is not some earlier teachers of the Law but those who now stand face to face with Jesus who reply. **[45]** In verse 45 Matthew (like Luke) substitutes the word "how" or "in what way" for Mark's "to what extent" (Mark 12:37). It is possible that this discussion emerged at a time when Jesus' Davidic descent was not certain or was not generally recognized, although there is much evidence to the contrary (see the discussion of Mark 12:35). At any rate, Matthew and Luke are seeking to emphasize more clearly than Mark that Jesus' Davidic descent is not the question; the problem is how Jesus can be both Son of David and David's Lord. **[46]** Matthew reserves until this point the statement that people ceased to ask Jesus any more questions (Mark put this earlier, after the "great commandment" discussion, in 12:34), because he considers this conversation also part of the disputation with the Pharisees. Matthew thus underlines the impotence of Jesus' adversaries to make reply and sets the scene for the condemnation discourse in chapter 23. Jesus remains victor without resort to violence.

Matthew thus sees the entire period beginning with Jesus' entry into Jerusalem as a time of conflict with the leaders of Israel. The entry leads directly to the cleansing of the Temple. The next day begins with the cursing of the fig tree, and the question of authority shows that Israel's decision has gone against Jesus just as it went against the Baptist. This is underlined by the parables of the two sons and the great feast; in Matthew's view, these, like the parable of the vineyard, depict Israel's rejection of God throughout the entire course of God's history with his people, down to the execution of his Son and his destruction of Jerusalem, seen as his retribution. The question of authority was put by state officials; the disputations (22:15 ff.) are dominated by the Pharisees. They are Jesus' real opponents. Thus the groundwork is laid for the great discourse in chapter 23.

Jesus Condemns Jewish and Christian Pharisaism (23:1-39)
Cf. Mark 12:37b-40; Luke 11:39-51; 13:34-35

¹Then Jesus spoke to the crowds and to his disciples. ²"The teachers of the Law and the Pharisees," he said, "sit in the seat of Moses.

[3]So you must obey and follow everything they tell you to do; do not, however, imitate their actions, because they do not practice what they preach. [4]They bind up heavy burdens and place them on men's shoulders, yet they aren't willing even to lift a finger to help them carry these burdens. [5]They do everything just so people will see them. They make their phylacteries wide and their tassels large! [6]They love the first place at feasts and the first seats in the synagogues; [7]they love to be greeted with respect in the market places and have people call them 'rabbi.'

[8]"You must not be called 'rabbi,' because you have only one teacher and you are all brothers. [9]And you must not call anyone here on earth 'father,' because you have only the one Father in heaven. [10]Nor should you be called 'leader,' because your one and only leader is the Christ. [11]The greatest one among you must be your servant. [12]Whoever makes himself great will be humbled, and whoever humbles himself will be made great.

I. [13]"Woe to you, teachers of the Law and Pharisees! Hypocrites! You lock the door to the Kingdom of heaven in men's faces, but you yourselves will not go in, and neither will you let people in who are trying to go in!

I a. [14]["Woe to you, teachers of the Law and Pharisees! Hypocrites! You take advantage of widows and rob them of their homes, and then make a show of saying long prayers! Because of this your punishment will be all the worse!]

II. [15]"Woe to you, teachers of the Law and Pharisees! Hypocrites! You cross sea and land to win one convert; and when you succeed, you turn him into a child of hell twice as bad as you yourselves are!

III. [16]"Woe to you, blind guides! You teach, 'If a man swears by the Temple, that is nothing; but if he swears by the gold in the Temple, he is bound.' [17]Blind fools! Which is more important, the gold or the Temple which makes the gold holy? [18]You also teach, 'If a man swears by the altar, that is nothing; but if he swears by the sacrifice on the altar, he is bound.' [19]How blind you are! Which is more important, the sacrifice or the altar which makes the sacrifice holy? [20]So then, when a man swears by the altar he is swearing by it and by all that is on it; [21]and when a man swears by the Temple he is swearing by it and by God who dwells in it; [22]and when a man swears by heaven he is swearing by God's throne and by the one who sits on it.

IV. [23]"Woe to you, teachers of the Law and Pharisees! Hypocrites! You tithe mint, dill, and cumin, but you neglect the really important things of the Law, such as justice and mercy and faith. These you should practice, without neglecting the others. [24]Blind guides! You strain a fly out, but swallow a camel!

V. [25]"Woe to you, teachers of the Law and Pharisees! Hypocrites! You clean the outside of your cup and plate, while the inside is full of violence and licentiousness. [26]Blind Pharisee! Clean what is inside the cup first, and then the outside will be clean too!

VI. [27]"Woe to you, teachers of the Law and Pharisees! Hypocrites! You are like whitewashed tombs, which look fine on the outside, but on the inside are full of dead men's bones and all kinds of uncleanness. [28]In the same way, on the outside you appear to everybody as righteous, but inside you are full of hypocrisy and lawlessness.

VII. [29]"Woe to you, teachers of the Law and Pharisees! Hypocrites! You make fine tombs for the prophets, and decorate the monuments of the righteous, [30]and you say, 'If we had lived long ago in the time of our fathers, we would not have shared with them in the blood of the prophets.' [31]So you actually bear witness that you are sons of those who murdered the prophets! [32]You, too, fulfill (only) the measure of your fathers!

[33]"Snakes, sons of vipers! How do you expect to escape the judgment of hell?

[34]"And therefore I tell you: I send you prophets and wise men and teachers; you will kill some of them and crucify them, and others you will whip in your synagogues and chase them from town to town. [35]As a result, all righteous blood that has been spilled upon earth will be upon your heads, from the blood of righteous Abel to the blood of Zechariah, Barachiah's son, whom you murdered between the Temple and the altar. [36]Amen, I tell you: all this will befall this generation!

[37]"Jerusalem, Jerusalem! You kill the prophets and stone the messengers God has sent to her! How many times have I wanted to gather your children, as a hen gathers her chicks under her wings, but you would not let me! [38]See, 'your house will be completely forsaken.'

³⁹From now on you will never see me again, I tell you, until you say, 'Blessed is he who comes in the name of the Lord.' "
(Vs. 31—Cf. Exod. 20:5. Vs. 35—Gen. 4:8, 10; 2 Chron. 24:20-22. Vs. 38—Jer. 22:5; 12:7. Vs. 39—Ps. 118:26.)

At this point Mark inserts some of the sayings attacking the teachers of the Law that occur in Matthew in verses 6-7; others, associated with these sayings both here and in Luke 11:39-52, albeit in a different sequence, he places in the setting of Jesus' journey from Galilee to Jerusalem. Neither the sequence of the sayings nor their setting is fixed by the tradition. This discourse, like those previously examined, undoubtedly goes back to Matthew's work as compiler and editor; naturally this statement does not exclude the possibility that Matthew incorporated genuine sayings of Jesus (such as vss. 12, 23 with the exception of the last clause, and 27-28?). He has brought together quite disparate material. Verses 2-7 are addressed to the crowd, 8-12 to the disciples, 13-33 to the teachers of the Law and Pharisees, and 34-39 to the people as a whole, especially the inhabitants of Jerusalem. Above all, the discourse presents totally different and contradictory positions (see the concluding summary).

[1-7] The introduction is linked to what precedes by means of "then," which is typical of Matthew's style. It distinguishes both the disciples of Jesus and the crowd (see the discussion of 27:25) from the "teachers of the Law and Pharisees" (see the discussion of 22:34). Verses 2-3 have no parallel, but were not composed by Matthew himself, for they contradict his general position (15:3 ff.; 16:11-12; 5:21-48; see below). They date from a period when the Christian community was still trying to live strictly according to the Jewish Law. The addition of "and the Pharisees" holds true only for the time after A.D. 70; previously they had no actual authority in questions of doctrine. Matthew himself, however, may have made the addition. On the other hand, these words would hardly be possible after *ca.* A.D. 85, when Judaism pronounced its curse upon heretics, especially Christians, in words that were repeated at every service of synagogue worship. Verse 4 is also found in Luke 11:46 in a condemnation discourse parallel to verses 13-33, although very different in form; only the vivid phrases about the "burdens" that "they themselves"

aren't willing to lift a "finger" to help with established themselves firmly. In comparison with verses 2-3, the teachers of the Law are viewed in a more critical light: they impose burdens on men that are beyond their strength (a similar statement appears in Acts 15:10).

Yet another view appears in verse 5a. Here the teachers of the Law are not accused of ignoring the Law in their actions, but rather of doing as much as possible, though only for their own glory. Since the verse is formulated in almost exactly the same way as the Matthaean introduction in 6:1, it probably derives from the evangelist himself, who uses it to introduce the sayings he borrows from Mark. The details in verse 5b may also derive from Matthew's own everyday observation; they illustrate more precisely what might be meant by "long robes" (Mark 12:38). The sequence of 6b-7a agrees with Luke 11:43, showing that the second half of this saying was also preserved independent of Mark and was incorporated into the Lukan discourse from this independent tradition (see above). The word for "love" in verse 6, which is not found in Mark, has been replaced by another word in Luke 11:43; but it appears in Luke 20:46, where Luke cites this saying a second time, in a form that otherwise agrees totally with the wording in Mark. This shows how such sayings could be handed down in different variants, and could be recorded by the evangelists now in one form, now in another.

[8-10] The end of verse 7 leads into verses 8-10. Here Matthew has linked two different groups of sayings. With verse 8 we come to an admonition addressed to the disciples; here Matthew is less concerned to debate with Judaism than to regulate the Christian community. The group of sayings is itself not homogeneous. The second half of verse 8 translates "rabbi" as "teacher," while in verses 9 and 10 different (but equivalent) words are used. The first saying might go back to Jesus, maintaining that God is the only Teacher of Israel (Jer. 31:34), perhaps even in the form: ". . . for one is great [rab(bi)]: God." This might be the reason why the saying speaks of "brothers" rather than "disciples" (="pupils").

The second saying might also be a saying of Jesus. Originally, however, as its divergent formulation shows, it derived from another situation, being a warning against appeals to Abraham as the father of Israel (cf. 3:9), instead of entrusting oneself to God as one's only

Father. The saying is strangely worded: the Greek text reads literally, "You must not call here on earth 'father.' " It can hardly be taken to mean, "You must not call anyone among you 'father.' " If the saying once read, "You must not call Abraham your father," this would explain why it is only in this verse that we find the phrase "your father."

The two sayings would then have been brought together after Easter and applied to the new situation of the community (cf. 1 John 2:27), with the third, newly composed, saying added to clarify that the others are a warning against love of titles. The present form is certainly an outgrowth of the Christian community; for there is no trace of the absolute use of the title "the messiah (= Christ)" in the Judaism of the period, and its use as an honorific begins after Easter. In the mouth of Jesus we find it only in Mark 9:41, where Matthew 10:42 retains the earlier form; in Mark 12:35, where it does not refer directly to Jesus; in Mark 13:21-22, where it is employed by false teachers after Easter; and in Luke 24:46, likewise after Easter. Even in John it appears only once (17:3). In addition, these verses presuppose that Christians will claim such titles (cf. Matt. 13:52; 23:34). There was therefore to have been something like a democratic community rule, based not on jockeying for high position, but on actions for others (see the excursus on 7:13-23 [§2]). This section (vss. 8-12) stands in sharp contrast to the approval of the teaching authority of the Jewish rabbis in verses 2-3.

[11-12] In verses 11-12 Matthew himself adds two frequently cited sayings; verse 11 (cf. the introductory remarks on Mark 9:33-37) is formally quite close to 20:26 (and possibly Luke 22:26), while verse 12 is like 18:4 and especially Luke 14:11; 18:14. Matthew thus expatiates in more general terms on humility—placing the three previous sayings in a broader framework. He takes a similar course in 5:20 for 5:18-19, in 5:23-24 for 5:21-22, in 6:14-15 for 6:9-13, in 18:18-19 for 18:15-18, etc.

[13-33] With verse 13 we come to a series of seven curses or "woes" (not counting vs. 14). Mark 12:38-40 includes none of these; Luke 11:38-52 includes six, but in a different sequence and in many cases with different wording. In Luke 11:43 and 46, for example, we find two curses that Matthew (and Mark) cite without putting in the

curse form. On the other hand, Matthew 23:25 uses this form, whereas Luke 11:39 does not. Sayings attacking the Pharisees were thus assembled in various ways to make up series of curses. Series of seven appear to have been especially popular; Luke actually has seven, although he introduces the first without the word "woe," and, by means of an interpolation between the fourth and the fifth, distinguishes artificially between three curses upon the Pharisees and three against the teachers of the Law. Matthew 23:13-33 clearly includes verses 16-22 (a secondary saying) to make up seven.

[13] The first curse is formulated differently in Luke 11:52: the legal experts have taken away "the key of knowledge" (see the discussion of Matt. 11:25). Luke describes only the consequences in terms similar to those used by Matthew. Matthew, with his reference to the Kingdom of God, probably comes closer to the original wording. There is a papyrus that cites this saying in a form similar to that of Luke, but in contrast to Jesus' commandment to be clever as serpents.

[14] Verse 14 is not found in any of the ancient manuscripts; it was added by a copyist on the basis of Mark 12:40.

[16-19] The third section, verses 16-22, is striking. Only here is the formula "teachers of the Law and Pharisees! Hypocrites!" lacking; what follows is unusually lengthy and corresponds to what has already been said in (15:14 and) 5:33-37, although the wording is totally different. Verses 16-19 exhibit parallel structure: it is absurd to maintain that to swear by what is lesser is binding, while to swear by what is greater is not. A similar point is made by the stricter rabbis and in CD xvi. 7-8. [20-21] Verses 20-21 repeat explicitly and in reverse order the conclusions already suggested by the rhetorical questions. The conclusion of verse 21 has been influenced by verse 22; instead of "what is on it" it speaks of "God who dwells in it." [22] Verse 22 picks up 5:34 and reverses the argument: even apparently inoffensive oaths involve God. Here we can still hear the voice of Jesus: God cannot be evaded. The term "fool," however, which appears in verse 17, is the same as that forbidden by Jesus in 5:22. The Temple is still assumed to be standing, nor is it under attack; this points to the time before A.D. 70.

[23] In the fourth curse, Matthew and Luke agree only on the first elements in the lists of three things to be avoided and three things to

be practiced: the "tithing of mint" and the doing of "justice"; in addition, they agree on the principle that one should do the latter without neglecting the former. Luke's mention of "all other vegetables" destroys the ~ting of the saying, which speaks only of absurd trifles; in addition, he Christianizes the familiar Jewish trinity of justice, mercy, and faith by adding "love of God." Several manuscripts of Luke go even further, eliminating the statement that tithing should not be neglected, because it was no longer practiced in the Christian community. This saying likewise derives from Jewish Christianity prior to A.D. 70, when tithes were still offered at the Temple and the administration of civil justice was still in Jewish hands. Extreme Pharisaic legalism (see below) is defended, so long as the more important commandments are not forgotten. [24] Verse 24, which begins like verse 16 (= 15:14) with "blind leaders of the blind," appends the striking image of swallowing a camel.

[26] The fifth curse, verse 26, which begins with "blind Pharisee" (singular!), appends a piece of positive advice—clean the inside of the cup. This is the only place such a note is struck; but it is reminiscent of Luke 11:41. The original form of the saying is hard to determine. Luke 11:39 contrasts the "outside of the cup" with "what is inside you"; a reference to the inside of the cup is almost impossible. Since all the rabbinic passages merely stress the importance of cleansing the inside, the saying was probably originally directed against a cleansing that is concerned only with externals like cups and plates, not with the heart within. This is also suggested by the reference to the Creator, who made both "outside" and "inside" (Luke 11:40). It is true that Luke himself no longer understood the saying correctly, since he returns in verse 41 to what is inside the cup and recommends giving it to the poor in order to become clean. Matthew certainly is not thinking of men's hearts, but rather of the contents of the plate and cup, which are unclean because acquired unjustly in the sight of God. His addition in verse 26 is out of place in the curse, since it suggests improvement.

[27-28] The form of the next curse diverges markedly from Luke 11:44. The phrase "on the inside are full of . . ." appears in the same words in verse 25; the contrast between the inside and the outside of the Pharisee appears in Luke 11:39-40. The community therefore

probably framed a curse on the basis of a metaphor about "white-washed tombs," and this while it was still generally accepted that contact with the remains of the dead made people unclean. Verse 28 could be Matthaean, although the words for "inside" and "outside," as well as their use, differ from verse 26, which is definitely Matthew's own.

[29-32] The final curse argues rather too ingeniously that those who seek to disclaim all responsibility for the crimes of their fathers admit thereby that they are their fathers' sons and thus share in their guilt; Luke 11:47-48, which does not use the "woe" formula, says only: "The fathers murdered the prophets, the sons build their tombs (thus proving themselves accomplices)." Here, too, Luke appears to preserve the earlier version. Verse 33 is probably Matthew's conclusion to the series of curses; it is reminiscent of 3:7.

[34-36] Verses 34-36 correspond to Luke 11:49-51. In Luke, however, this passage is spoken by the Wisdom of God. Originally this must also have been true of the Matthaean saying. This is shown by the use of the third person (Luke 11:49), which would be inappropriate in a discourse addressed by Jesus to the crowd. Above all, the use of "therefore" as a connective makes sense only in Luke, because he continues: ". . . the Wisdom of God said." This is the only sense in which it can be taken in Matthew (cf. the translation). "Wise men and teachers" are also appropriate to a wisdom saying; they never appear together elsewhere in Matthew (see the excursus below on vss. 34-39). The saying corresponds formally to an Old Testament oracle of disaster, such as frequently follows a series of "woes" (cf. Isa. 5:18-24, also 8-10). Here the same sequence already appears in Q. The past tense ("Wisdom said") in Luke 11:49 shows that originally Jesus was not claiming to speak as Wisdom but was citing an earlier saying of Wisdom in which she appeared as the speaker (before creation; Wisd. 7:27; 10:1 ff.?) and surveyed the course that God's history with his people was to take. The reference to "this generation" was probably added in Q because Jesus had come to be considered the final messenger, his death the final summary of the fates of all the messengers of God's Wisdom. Luke placed the apostles alongside the Old Testament prophets and included the course of history after the death of Jesus. Matthew, however, has Jesus speak as incarnate Wisdom, and there-

fore changes the future tense ("I will send") into the present ("I send"). In all three categories he is thinking of New Testament messengers. Verse 34b reflects the experience of the Christians, as is shown above all by the term "crucify." Nowhere outside the New Testament do we find personified Wisdom linked in this way with the violent fate of the prophets.

[37-39] The saying addressed to Jerusalem occurs in almost exactly the same words in Luke 13:34-35; it therefore derives from Q. The same key words appear as in the preceding saying: "send," "prophets," "kill." This may be why Matthew placed the saying here. It, too, was probably once spoken by Wisdom. "How many times" is much more appropriate to Wisdom than to Jesus, who, according to both Matthew and Luke is now making his first appearance in Jerusalem (with the exception of the infancy narratives). In Greek, Hebrew, and Aramaic, "wisdom" is feminine; so is the Greek word for "bird," here translated "hen." The image is appropriate, as is that of "gathering under her wings." The concluding excerpt is also appropriate in this context (see the excursus below on vss. 34-39).

Baruch 4:1 states that Wisdom is the Law of God, and then in 4:12 Jerusalem begins a lament: "I am forsaken on account of the sins of my children, because they have departed from God's Law." This is closely related to the lament that the children of Jerusalem have rejected Wisdom and Jerusalem is therefore forsaken (Matt. 23:37-38). Finally, everywhere else Matthew uses a different Greek form of "Jerusalem"; the form here, therefore, is certainly traditional. It is true that here the sending of the messengers lies in the past, while in verses 34-36 it lies in the future; but verses 35-36 agree for the most part with the retrospective view of verse 37 and the glimpse of the judgment to come in verse 38.

The connection between the two sayings (vss. 34-36 and vss. 37-39) is not intimate, but their material relationship is clear. Both might have been associated with each other and with the series of curses even in Q (the first of the sayings appears with the curses in Luke; Matt. 23:34-36 = Luke 11:49-51). Luke had to introduce the second saying at a later point, since he does not use Jerusalem as a setting for this discourse. The phrase "to her" (rather than "to you") in the first sentence indicates a Jewish milieu; the expression translated "how" occurs frequently in the Greek Old Testament; and stoning is the Jewish method of execution, while Jesus was not stoned. Jesus might have borrowed such a saying of Wisdom; but he would probably have interpreted it as referring to God himself, who wishes to gather Israel under his wings; it is more likely that the community, with justice, saw the fate of Jesus represented in such sayings (see the excursus below on vss. 34-39).

Verse 39 at least was added after the saying was interpreted as referring to Jesus, for Jewish literature contains no hint of any return of Wisdom with the messiah. Matthew himself added the phrase "from now on"; its purpose is to state explicitly that the judgment depicted in verse 39 is taking place in the very moment Jesus is leaving the Temple. "From now on" God will be present where two or three are assembled in the name of Jesus (18:20) and will see his commandments observed among all the nations of the earth (28:19-20). Verse 39b (=21:9) must refer to the second coming of Jesus, not to the entry into Jerusalem.

[1] Even in the introductory verse Matthew shows that he has a twofold purpose. First, he wishes to address the "crowds," that is, speak as a missionary for Jesus in the conflict between the community of Jesus and Judaism, which in his period was dominated by the Pharisees. Second, he wishes to speak to the disciples, that is, summon the community to proper conduct, according to the norms of Jesus (as in Luke 20:45; cf. the discussion of Matt. 5:1).

[2] The claim of the Pharisees to occupy the seat of Moses means that Moses is looked upon as a teacher and that he can be understood only as interpreted by the Pharisees and teachers of the Law. [3] This is not disputed; on the contrary, Jesus calls on men to follow this teaching. But the Pharisaic teachers are accused of not practising what they preach. This statement contradicts 5:21 ff. and 15:1 ff., where it is not the Pharisees' conduct that is attacked, but their teaching (15:5-9). The Pharisee described by Jesus in the parable of the Pharisee and the tax collector (Luke 18:9-14) does indeed practise what he preaches, doing more than the Law demands. And here we hear the voice of a strict Jewish Christianity that liked to live according to the teachings of the Pharisees and placed the major

emphasis on actual practice (many rabbis took a similar position). Matthew is able to include these statements because he interprets them according to 5:17-20.

[4] This is shown by the next saying. The heavy burdens are the multiplicity of individual commandments; here we hear the voice of a reformed Judaism or of a group of Jewish Christians for whom the Law as interpreted by the Pharisees was no longer a source of joy and the gift of God, but a burden. The monks of Qumran or the consistent Pharisees, who took the Law especially seriously, frequently conjured up in their contemporaries a sense of despair like that experienced by Luther as a young man. A principle was therefore sought that would summarize all the individual commandments and make it possible to live according to the Law without presupposing familiarity with all its individual commandments and their interpretation—which of course were accessible only to the theologian. This attempt at simplifying can be sensed in Jewish documents of this period (2 Esdras). Within the community of Jesus, his radically new approach (see the discussion of 5:21 ff.) had led to the realization, even before Paul, that although Israel's obedience to God's commandments was important in itself and set Israel apart from the gentiles, it did not make Israel righteous in the sight of God. According to Galatians 2:15-16, Paul assumes that this was known even to Peter (cf. James 2:10). The second half of the statement, like its Jewish parallels, probably means that the teachers of the Law do not follow it themselves; it can hardly mean that they are unable to help others to come to terms with it.

[5] Unlike verse 3, verse 5 implies that the teachers of Law and Pharisees did what the Law required. The problem is that they did it in order to be commended by other men. At this point we hear the voice of Matthew himself, as in 6:1. This shows how he can combine the very diverse traditions of verses 2-3, 4, and 6-7: teachers of the Law and Pharisees imposed enormous burdens on men with their numberless regulations, but, admirable as their respect for the Law was, they failed to realize God's purpose in his Law. Their concern was always to fulfill every commandment precisely, so that others might appreciate how obedient they were. They overlooked the cognizance of God, whose notion of how the Law should be fulfilled cannot be defined in simple terms. A similar view can be detected in the

background of Romans 2:28 ff. (cf. the discussion of 6:1). Matthew speaks of tassels and phylacteries instead of long robes (Mark 12:38) because he accuses the Pharisees not of vanity but of being overly precise in their religious observances; they were concerned only with what was visible to the eyes of men and misconstrued obedience as an achievement to be measured by human standards.

Small boxes containing the text of Exodus 13:1-16; Deuteronomy 6:4-9; 11:13-21 were laced to the left upper arm near the heart and about the forehead, because Deuteronomy 6:8 states that the commandments of God should be bound upon the hands and about the forehead. They were often worn like amulets—which is what the word means in Greek. Numbers 15:38-40 requires tassels on garments in recollection of God's commandments. Their length was a matter of dispute among the various schools. The verse in Matthew does not criticize the custom, but only the motive of making a show with especially wide laces or long tassels. **[5-6]** A similar accusation is already found in Mark 12:38-39; it appears also in the form of a curse in the Lukan attack on the Pharisees (Luke 11:43). **[7]** Matthew's censure of the love of titles establishes a connection between his attack on the Pharisees and the admonition he directs at his own community; the Christian community, he implies, must be absolutely egalitarian —titleless—if it is to avoid Pharisaic pride, and foster the honest concern for others that Jesus bids.

[8-10] The Christian community is fundamentally a brotherhood. God is their Father and Jesus their Teacher; there can never be any competition for this authority. Its uniqueness must be attested by total renunciation of honorifics, a refusal to pursue what is only for God and Christ. This is fully consonant with a proper sense of the dignity of age (15:4-6), though not with the use of "Father" or "Presbyter" (="Elder") as honorifics. By etymology, "Rab(bi)" means "(my) great one"; at the time of Jesus it was not limited to "teachers." The exclusive emphasis on teaching is typical of Matthew and his tradition. "Father" was not used frequently as an honorific form of address, but it is attested by 2 Kings 2:12; 6:21; 13:14; Acts 7:2; 22:1 and contemporary examples. Neither is it to be used of the "fathers" sacred to Israel's history; the disciples of Jesus must not live in the past.

[11-12] Matthew makes it abundantly clear (see the introductory remarks) that mere renunciation of titles is not enough; Jesus states a criterion of rank that abolishes all distinctions of merit as men can judge them. All venerations—whether official or tacit, communal or simply the self-approval within an individual—indicate the subject's actual remoteness from God's esteem (Job 22:29; Prov. 29:23). Behind Matthew, therefore, there stands a community that knows only one hierarchy, this paradoxical hierarchy of God (cf. the discussion of 18:4 and the excursus on 7:13-23 [§5]), which also applies to Christian teachers of the Law (13:52; 23:34).

[13] The first curse speaks of the power of the keys entrusted to the teachers of the Law (see the discussion of 16:19). The Kingdom of God is pictured as a room to be entered. Perhaps at one time the saying referred to those who declared that entrance into the Christian community was irreconcilable with Judaism and thus Judaism stood in the way of the Christian mission. Elsewhere Matthew speaks of the Kingdom of God in future terms (see the discussion of 13:41); he uses this saying to suggest that the way of Pharisaic legalism does not lead to the coming Kingdom of God. On the term "hypocrite," see the discussion on 6:2.

[15] Verse 15 is evidence of intensive Jewish missionary activity, a possibility usually ignored. A convert (or "proselyte") is a person who accepts Judaism and has himself circumcised as a sign of his obligation to obey all the commandments. That Judaism was attractive to many is attested by several Greek writers, and also by the "God-fearers" (Acts 10:2, 22; 13:16, 26; 17:4, 17; 18:7), who attended the synagogue more or less regularly but did not become converts. The Christian mission, which did not demand circumcision or observance of the cultic regulations, must have been felt as competition. Behind this verse may be the fact that gentiles converted to Judaism might well have been more fanatic than those who converted them. Perhaps the translation in verse 15 should read "even more divided" —the word rendered "twice" corresponds precisely to that for "single," and can also mean "twofold," "divided."

[16-22] The next curse, which differs formally, shows by example that casuistry is ruled out, in other words, it is impossible to consider

every conceivable case individually. Verse 21 speaks directly of God because casuistical fencing is at bottom an attempt to escape from God; yet God is always present, oath or no oath.

[23] The point of verse 23 is that the "better righteousness" Jesus desires (5:20) encompasses the weighty things of the Law: justice, mercy, and faith. Micah 6:8 and Zechariah 7:9-10 summarize the crucial commandments in similar terms. The first word literally means "judgment," and refers to the just verdict that maintains the cause of the weak and oppressed. Old Testament justice is not formal Roman justice, according to which all citizens were equal before the law—an equality that in practise favored the rich. The primary purpose of Old Testament justice was protection; it therefore actually favored the weak. "Justice" and "mercy" are therefore much more closely related than they are in our usage. The last word also means "fidelity," and can therefore refer to both the proper attitude toward God (faith) and toward one's neighbor (fidelity).

[24] The Pharisees' failure of fidelity is made vivid by an extravagant image. The conscientious Pharisee not only included everything in his garden in observance of the commandments in Leviticus 27:30; Numbers 18:12; Deuteronomy 12:6; 14:22-23, so as not to omit anything; he even strained everything he drank through a cloth because some insects are unclean and must not be swallowed. The camel is not only huge, but also, according to Leviticus 11:4, unclean. Such obedience is magnificent: not only does the Pharisee pay his taxes to the state and his regular Temple assessment, but he also tithes conscientiously for the support of the poor and the Temple. But even the Jewish trinity of justice, mercy, and fidelity point to something more central: condemnation of unfairness, mercy towards all, and fidelity in the practice of religion or in one's conduct toward one's fellow men. In these three Matthew sees his entire program outlined. The "better righteousness" with respect to the Old Testament Law of God was already mentioned programatically in 5:20. It can be summarized as "mercy" or "love of one's neighbor" (see the discussion of 5:18). It can be lived only through faith in the one who has authority to reinterpret God's Law and who lived this Law as the messiah of lowliness—thus giving his disciples an example of its fulfillment (see §5 of the retrospective summary).

Scrupulous legalism does not give "justice" to the lowly; at best it throws them a sop. It does not yet include "mercy," which sees others; it is, finally, not "faith," which expects everything from God. God is trapped instead in the scrupulous observance of particular regulations, so that he can no longer encounter men as a living God with gifts that are always new, and demands that are always changing. In this saying we can hear how the community struggled with the problem of legalism. The original saying assumed that the strict tithing of the Pharisees was absolutely proper, but pointed out that there were more important commandments. As Matthew reports it, however, in the context of the entire Gospel, the far more radical perspective of Jesus shed new light upon it. Luke gave it yet another interpretation, referring to love of God, understood as the requirement of giving to the poor (11:41). Finally the statement that tithing should not be ignored was itself eliminated (see above).

[25] The beginning of verse 25 refers to the cleansing of dishes; the second half is obscure. Matthew suggests that the food and drink have been acquired by injustice and avarice. What is inside does not really belong to those who are enjoying it; their abundant food and drink shortchanges others. [26] It is the justice with which the food and drink in them is acquired, not cultic washing, that makes cups and plates "clean" in the eyes of God. Possibly, however, there may already be a hint of the metaphorical interpretation that looks upon the Pharisee himself as the "vessel" that is unclean within.

[27] Matthew does not actually express that notion until the next section. Tombs were whitewashed regularly before Passover to warn pilgrims not to render themselves unclean by careless contact. [28] The only important point is the contrast between outward appearance, against which 6:1 ff. has already sounded a warning (cf. 23:5), and inward filth. "Hypocrisy and lawlessness" (see the discussion of 6:2 and 7:23), here probably felt to be equivalents, is a typically Matthaean phrase summarizing what God condemns. Originally the polemic may have been even more bitter: just as a whitewashed tomb may look elegant while rendering anyone who walks over it unclean, so contact with the Pharisee and his teaching, imposing as they may appear, can separate anyone from God.

[29-30] The tomb of David is mentioned in Acts 2:29; Jewish

documents also speak of tombs, about which something like a cult of the saints was beginning to form. But warnings also went up: "The righteous do not need elaborate tombs; their monuments are their deeds." Stories are told of how the prophets were martyred: how Isaiah, for example, was sawed in two and Jeremiah stoned; the Old Testament is unacquainted with these stories (but cf. the discussion of vs. 37), but they are known to Hebrews 11:36-38 and certain Jewish writers. On the "righteous," see §4 of the excursus on 7:13-23. Once more the attempt to evade God is censured, the desire to gloss over history and disown the deeds of one's fathers.

[31] The very fact that one wants to know nothing of it shows how evil is the past from which one springs; one does not erase it by turning one's back. Or is the attack merely directed against the superficiality of their devotion, which sets up monuments? The saying may be based on a Hebrew pun like those popular among teachers of the Law: *bōnim* means "builders" or "witnesses"; *bānim* means "sons"; and the word for "monument" is related to that for "life" or "soul." Matthew may mean that in their very appeal to the prophets they exhibit the same hardness of heart that those prophets attacked in their fathers. [32] If the concluding sentence is read as an imperative, the tone becomes one of scalding irony: bring the sin of your fathers to fruition by doing what they left undone (vss. 34-35)! [33] The summary, echoing the Baptist's proclamation of judgment, cuts off all escape.

[34] Jesus' implicit message is always repentance. This upbeat emphasis would predominate here if the "therefore" could be linked directly with what follows, making the disasters to come only contingent. But probably they should be taken in a harsher and more fateful way: "Therefore (it is inevitable): . . . ." Even so, Matthew sees a causal connection between the two sections, and there is thus always a latent hope. In what follows he has in mind Christian prophets, wise men, and teachers of the Law. That he does not mention apostles or even elders shows that he comes from a community organized along different lines, in which the Christian message is shaped by the accustomed forms of Judaism: interpretation of Scripture and collection of wisdom aphorisms. What is astonishing—precisely because it has precedent—is that prophets have come to proclaim God's message for

the new age (cf. the excursus on 7:13-23). They are all sent by Jesus to call Israel to repentance. But the opportunity is squandered; the messengers sent by Jesus are persecuted.

[35] God's judgment is as a consequence inescapable, a judgment that writes an end to all history. Matthew may even be thinking of 27:25. There is an ancient notion that spilled blood cries out until it is avenged (Gen. 4:10; Job 16:18; Isa. 26:21; Ezek. 24:7-8). About the first murder mentioned in the Bible there is no dispute. "Zechariah" undoubtedly refers to 2 Chronicles 24:20-22, i.e., the last murder mentioned in the Bible. In the Hebrew text the name of the victim is Zechariah and he is a priest, thus accessible to murder within the precincts of the Temple (2 Chron. 24:21). Almost all the Greek versions, however, call him Azariah. Above all, the latter is a son of Jehoiada, while Zechariah, son of Barachiah, is the literary prophet, whose slaying is nowhere reported. Since Luke 11:51 contains nothing more than the phrase "from the blood of Abel to the blood of Zechariah," it is reasonably certain that Matthew is mistaken. This is much more likely than the suggestion, which has been made, that the reference is to another Zechariah, the son of Baruch.

[36] Does Matthew use "this generation" to refer only to the generation living at the time of Jesus' Passion and the destruction of Jerusalem, or does he interpret it in the light of 27:25 as referring to all Israel, which rejects Jesus (see the discussion of 24:34)?

[37] The Old Testament speaks of God in the imagery of a bird protecting its young (Deut. 32:11; Isa. 31:5; Ps. 36:7). Converts to Judaism were also described as having been taken "under the wings of the Shekinah [=the presence of God]." Jesus thus comes to occupy the place of God himself (see the introductory remarks on vss. 37-39). The point of the passage is that God becomes concretely real on earth and that this takes place in Jesus. Then God does not simply require men to come to him; he takes the initiative himself and desires to assemble those who are his own. This action of his "has become flesh" in Jesus (John 1:14). The Old Testament does not expect God to assemble his people until the eschaton (Ps. 102:21-22; 106:47; 147:2; Isa. 52:10; 2 Macc. 1:27; cf. Matt. 24:31). But once again Jerusalem refuses, as it had already done at the time of Jeremiah 7:25-27.

[38] Whether "house" refers to the city of Jerusalem or the Tem-

ple makes no material difference. **[39]** The use of the conjunction "for" in the Greek text shows that Matthew's purpose is to say: with the departure of Jesus, God has departed from his house, fulfilling the divine judgment announced by the prophets (Jer. 12:7; cf. Ezek. 8:6; 11:21; Eth. Enoch 89:56; Syr. Bar. 8:2; 2 Esdras 16:37). Not until Jesus returns (see the excursus following 25:46) will the period of God's absence come to an end. Taken precisely as it stands, verse 39 should mean that it is the Pharisees and teachers of the Law who will hail his return. But the conclusion is set apart so distinctly from the discourse against the Pharisees that it actually addresses all Jerusalem (vs. 37), announcing that God will desert the city until they rejoice in his return. Perhaps there is a faint hint here of something like what is found in Romans 11:25: a final return to God of all people. We are not specifically told, however, whether all the people or merely some among them will hail his return; furthermore, 21:9 shows that one can rejoice while still in ignorance, without realizing what one is doing. Or do we have a situation like that in 5:26, where a condition is imposed that can never be met?

A retrospect shows how skillfully Matthew has taken diverse traditions and woven them into a single whole. Polemic runs the entire gamut: from full acceptance of the teaching of the Pharisees, who merely fail to practice what they preach (vss. 2-3) or at least fail to observe the important things of the Law (vss. 23-24), through the complaint that what the Pharisees require is impossibly difficult (vs. 4) and the charge that they themselves do good works, but only to gain the admiration of men (vss. 5-7), to the more radical attack on ridiculous (vss. 16-22) or purely outward legalism (vss. 25-38), culminating in the accusation that the Pharisees bar the Kingdom of God to themselves and all their followers (vss. 13, 15) and are therefore the real murderers of the prophets (vss. 29-32). If one is looking for polemic against theologians, it is unnecessary to go outside the Bible.

The intensity of this judgment discourse must be understood first against the background of Matthew's own time. The young community, persecuted by the Jews and threatened with scourging and crucifixion (vs. 34), had to look out for its very life. On the other hand, it faced a Judaism that itself could only survive the catastrophe of A.D. 70 by observing the strictest discipline. From the human perspective,

Judaism survived only because the Pharisaic teachers of the Law reduced the whole of life to strict regulations, thus preserving the ancient tradition. On the other hand, the young Jesus movement, which had experienced the presence of the Spirit, the rebirth of prophecy, and the great liberation to love, could only distinguish itself as vigorously as possible from this attitude. Conflict was inevitable.

What runs unmistakably through the entire discourse is the warning against trying to evade God, against trying to "get around" him. The threat arises whenever anyone seeks in all seriousness to serve God, but only in order to "master" him. Precisely because men would like to be certain that they are not deviating from him and his will, they seek to make him available and tractable. But this is an attempt to circumvent the living God, who repeatedly wishes to say something new to us in the face of our perfect discipline, expecting something new, something greater of us.

Similar charges were also leveled within contemporary Judaism, but only against individual figures and practices, not against the system itself. We must admit that the picture here of Pharisaic piety is one-sided and therefore misleading; it nevertheless remains true that Matthew, like those Jewish voices, is seeking to call men to self-knowledge and repentance. At this point he is also addressing his own community, as we can see from the interpolation in verses 8-12, but above all from the resumption of the Judgment motif in chapters 24–25 (see the introduction to chapters 21–25). Thus this discourse, too, must be read in the context of the entire Gospel; Matthew's bitter attack is also upon home. Any other interpretation turns it into an un-Christian judgment upon others.

Jesus as the Wisdom of God. Ever since Judaism came to think of God as sitting enthroned far off in heaven and ceased to speak of his direct appearance upon earth, the Wisdom of God was frequently mentioned. It was conceived as a person (as early as Prov. 8:22 ff.; 9:1 ff.; cf. Prov. 9:3 with Matt. 23:34), although the term actually referred to God's wise actions upon earth. Ecclesiasticus 24:4-17 tells how Wisdom went forth from God, sought refuge in vain among all the nations, and was finally welcomed in Jerusalem. Ethiopian Enoch 42, however, tells of Wisdom's return to heaven disappointed. Instead of the "Wisdom" of God, men also spoke of the "Logos" or "Word" of God. This made it easier to identify Wisdom with the Law (Ecclus. 24:23; Bar. 4:1). Such statements helped primitive Christianity to understand Jesus' coming from the Father, his ministry on earth, and his return to the Father as the wise and beneficent action of God himself (cf. John 1:1 ff. and 1 Cor. 8:6; Col. 1:15 with Prov. 8:22-23; Ecclus. 24:12). In Q Jesus is already looked upon as Wisdom's messenger (see the discussion of 11:25; 12:32; and the introductory comments on 23:34-39), together with the Baptist (see the introductory comments on 11:19c).

Among the first three evangelists, however, only Matthew identifies Jesus with Wisdom. What in Luke 11:49 is said by Wisdom is said in Matthew by Jesus; and only in Matthew is the threatened departure of God's Wisdom, that is, God's presence upon earth, equated with the departure of Jesus from the Temple (see the discussion of vs. 39 above). According to Luke 7:31-35, God's Wisdom reveals itself in the ministry of the Baptist and of Jesus; they are seen as two parallel bearers of Wisdom, and are recognized by Wisdom's "children." Matthew, on the contrary, seeks the "works" of Wisdom in the works of Jesus, thus identifying him with Wisdom (see the discussion of 11:19). Matthew 11:25-27, where Jesus is simply the bearer of God's Wisdom, which he reveals to men, has its parallel in Luke; but verses 28-30, where Jesus himself adopts the voice and role of Wisdom, are found only in Matthew. Unlike John or Paul, Matthew never speaks of Jesus' dwelling with the Father before his birth (see §1 of the retrospective summary); but he shares their realization that in Jesus God's own wise and saving activity has become incarnate on earth.

Above all, this line of thought opens the possibility of coming to terms with the Law. If God's Wisdom, Word, and Law have, so to speak, become flesh in Jesus, there can be no question of tossing the Law overboard (5:17-18); on the contrary, it is only in Jesus that the real purpose of the Law is revealed (5:20, 21-48; 11:28-30). In revealing this purpose, Jesus not only teaches the Law but fulfills it, i.e. carries it out. Thus his disciples are the true teachers of the Law in the time of fulfillment, teaching and doing God's will (5:13-16; 13:52; 23:34; cf. the introductory comments on 27:3-10).

God's Judgment on Israel (24:1-3)
Cf. Mark 13:1-3; Luke 21:5-7

[1]And Jesus left the Temple and went away. And his disciples came to him to show him the Temple's buildings. [2]"You see all these things, don't you?" he said. "Amen, I tell you, not a single stone here will be left in its place; every one of them will be thrown down."

[3]As Jesus sat on the Mount of Olives, the disciples came to him in private. "Tell us when all this will be," they asked, "and what will be the sign of your coming and of the end of the age?"

This introduction to the discourse on the end of the world follows Mark closely. But Matthew has left out the story of the widow's offering (Mark 12:41-44) in order to connect 24:1-2 closely with chapter 23. Thus Jesus' departure from the Temple is appended directly to 23:38-39. All the disciples, not just one as in Mark, "come to" Jesus (see the discussion of 8:2), illustrating how some have chosen to follow him while others have deserted. The summary phrase "all these things" is Matthaean, as in 24:8, 33; and 23:36. For Matthew the destruction of the Temple is God's judgment on Jerusalem for killing the prophets, as the introductory formula "Amen, I tell you" emphasizes. In it the judgment pronounced by Jesus in 23:34-38 is fulfilled. But 23:39 has already referred to the final coming of Jesus.

Verse 3 is characteristically transformed by Matthew. Once more it is all the disciples who "come to" Jesus; the expression "in private" no longer refers to the four distinguished by Mark from the rest, but to the entire band of disciples, in other words, the whole community of Jesus, separated from the people of Israel. Unlike Mark, Matthew makes no more mention of the Temple; above all, he clearly distinguishes the question "When will all this be?" which probably still refers to the destruction of the Temple, from the much more important question, which now differs from its Markan counterpart: "What will be the sign of your coming and of the end of the age?" Matthew thus clearly distinguishes between the judgment upon Israel for rejecting Jesus, which can be seen in the destruction of the Temple in the year 70, and the second coming of the Son of Man, which will inaugurate the Last Judgment. It is between these two events that the community of Jesus lives, here represented by the disciples. For a discussion of the term "coming," see the excursus following 25:46. The idea of a consummation and of an age hastening to its end derives from Daniel 12:4, 13 and from Jewish apocalyptic in general, whose speculations were devoted entirely to the coming world of God.

The Coming of the Judge of the World (24:4-36)
Cf. Mark 13:4-32; Luke 21:8-33

[4]Jesus answered, "Watch out, and do not let anyone fool you. [5]Because many men will come in my name, saying, 'I am the messiah!' and fool many people. [6]You are going to hear of wars and rumors of wars; take care, do not be terrified! For 'it must take place,' but it does not mean that the end has come. [7]For 'nation will rise against nation and kingdom against kingdom,' and there will be famines and earthquakes everywhere. [8]All these things are like the first pains of childbirth.

[9]"Then they will hand you over to affliction. And they will kill you, and you will be hated by all nations for my name's sake. [10]Many will fall away at that time; they will betray each other and hate each other. [11]Then many false prophets will appear and fool many people. [12]And because lawlessness will abound, many people's love will grow cold. [13]But whoever holds out to the end will be saved. [14]And this Good News about the Kingdom will be preached through all the world, for a witness to all nations; and then will come the end.

[15]"You will see 'the abomination of desolation' of which the prophet Daniel spoke, standing in the holy place." (Let the reader understand what this means!) [16]"Then those who are in Judea must run away to the hills. [17]The man who is on the roof of his house must not take the time to go down and get his belongings from the house. [18]The man who is in the field must not go back to get his cloak. [19]How terrible it will be in those days for women who are pregnant, and for mothers who are nursing! [20]Pray to God that you will not have to run away during the winter or on a Sabbath! [21]For there will be at that time a great 'affliction, far more terrible than any since creation,' nor will there be any to surpass it. [22]And if those days were not shortened, no

flesh would be saved; but for the sake of his chosen people, God will shorten those days. [23]Then, if anyone says to you, 'Look, here is the messiah!' or 'There he is!'—do not believe him. [24]For false messiahs will appear and 'false prophets'; they will perform great 'signs and wonders' for the purpose of deceiving God's chosen people, if possible. [25]Listen! I have told you this ahead of time. [26]Or, if people should tell you, 'Look, he is out in the desert!'—don't go there; or if they say, 'Look, he is in the chambers!'—don't believe it. [27]For the Son of Man will come like the lightning which flashes across the whole sky from the east to the west. [28]Wherever there is a dead body the vultures will gather.

[29]"But immediately after the affliction of those days 'the sun will grow dark, the moon will no longer shine,' 'the stars will fall from heaven, and the powers of heaven will be shaken.' [30]Then the sign of the Son of Man will appear in the sky; then all the tribes of the earth will weep, and they will see the Son of Man coming on the clouds of heaven with power and great glory. [31]The great trumpet will sound, and he will send out his angels to the 'four winds,' and they will gather his chosen people 'from one end of heaven to the other.'

[32]"Let the fig tree teach you a lesson. When its branches become green and tender, and it starts putting out leaves, you know that summer is near. [33]In the same way, when you see all these things, know that the time is at the door. [34]Amen, I tell you, this generation will not pass away until all these things take place. [35]Heaven and earth will pass away; my words will never pass away. [36]But no one knows when that day and hour will come—neither the angels in heaven, nor the Son; the Father alone knows."

(Vs. 6—Dan. 2:28. Vs. 7—Isa. 19:2; 2 Chron. 15:6. Vs. 15—Dan. 9:27; 11:31; 12:11. Vs. 16—Ezek. 7:16. Vs. 21—Dan. 12:1. Vs. 24—Deut. 13:2-3. Vs. 29—Isa. 13:10; 34:4. Vs. 30—Zech. 12:1, 12-14; Dan. 7:13-14. Vs. 31—Isa. 27:13; Zech. 2:6; Deut. 30:4. Vs. 35—Cf. 5:18; Isa. 40:8.)

[4-8] The first section of the eschatological discourse corresponds totally to Mark. In verse 5, Matthew makes the statement more precise: "I am the messiah." For him, too, the coming of false teachers

is not yet the end, but simply the "first pains of childbirth." **[9-14]**
He does, however, reshape the section about persecution in verses
9-14. The crucial alteration is his inclusion of Mark 13:9-13 previously, in the missionary discourse (see the discussion of Matt. 10:17-
25). Here, therefore, he only borrows the key phrase "they will hand
you over (and kill you)" (Mark 13:9a, [12b]) and immediately appends the saying about the hatred to be shown the disciples (Mark
13:13), although this saying has already been included in Matthew
10:22; now, however, it is changed **[9]** so that they are hated by all
the other "nations." This is what distinguishes the afflictions of the
eschaton from those of the present.

But the theme of hatred from others is only touched on; the real
distress will come from within the community itself. It will involve
more than just the conflict of brother against brother or parents
against children (Mark 13:12 = Matt. 10:21). Those who have "fallen
away" are now **[10]** to be in conflict with faithful Christians (cf. the
discussion of 11:6; also 13:21, 41, 57; 15:12; 16:23; 17:27; 18:6-7;
26:31, 33). This is the straying from the faith predicted by Daniel
11:41 (only in the Septuagint!) for the eschaton, shortly before the
intervention of the archangel Michael and the resurrection of the
dead. **[11]** It is occasioned by false prophets, already inveighed against
by the end of the Sermon on the Mount; those false prophets will bring
their "lawlessness" to fruition at the eschaton (see the discussion of
7:23; 13:41).

[12] "Lawlessness" does not mean apostasy from Pharisaic literal-
ism in obeying all the commandments of the Mosaic Law, but a way
of life that refuses to recognize any divine law, which is identical for
Matthew with a way of life in which one's neighbor no longer has any
legal claim. The result is therefore described as love grown cold. This
can mean love for God or for one's neighbor; for Matthew the emphasis is on the latter (see the discussion of 5:18). False doctrine is
accordingly not erroneous theology, but an attitude that in practice
does not display love.

Salvation depends on holding out to the end; the words correspond to Mark 13:13. Now, however, they no longer refer to holding
out in the midst of persecution, but in the face of false teachers, who
no longer take God's commandment of love seriously and mislead

"many" (the word occurs three times in vss. 10-12).

[14] Only now does Matthew insert the statement about the preaching of the gospel from Mark 13:10, while altering it so as to guarantee that the reference to Jesus' preaching of love for one's neighbor will be noted (see the excursus on 7:13-23 [§3]). That this preaching will be a "witness to all nations" before the end comes should probably be taken in the sense of 25:31 ff.: love for one's neighbor must be preached to all nations, for love is the standard by which they will one day be judged.

[15-22] In the section describing what will take place in Judea, Matthew once again follows Mark throughout. [15] But he adds that the prophecy of the "abomination of desolation" is to be found in Daniel, so that the caution in parenthesis will refer the reader unambiguously. The reference to the Temple is also more explicit (cf. Dan. 9:27). In the Hebrew Bible, Daniel is not included among the prophets; this arrangement makes its first appearance in the later Greek translation. [17] The expression "must not take the time to go down and get" is better put than its Markan equivalent: the man on the roof will have to come down in any case; what he must not do is go back into his house.

[20] What is most striking is the prayer hoping that people will not have to flee (vs. 16=Mark 13:14) on the Sabbath; Mark 13:18 mentions only the winter. To prohibit flight on the Sabbath even amid the calamities of war would be to interpret the Law in the strictest way possible; normally such circumstances would exempt people from Sabbath restrictions. It is hardly possible Matthew himself is still thinking in such strict terms; it is also unlikely that this passage merely means that people cannot purchase supplies on the Sabbath or that those fleeing on the Sabbath would be recognized at once as Christians because Jews can go only "a Sabbath distance" (Acts 1:12). This means that Matthew is drawing on a tradition that insisted on the strictest possible observance of the Law. Matthew borrowed this tradition because the Sabbath was still kept in his community—not according to the rigorous demands of the Law, but probably as Jesus himself kept it. The Sabbath was not broken except in cases of real necessity; only the law of love always took precedence over the law of the Sabbath (see the discussion of 12:9-14).

[22] The reference to God's merciful shortening of the days of affliction is borrowed from Mark. The Matthaean interpretation in verse 13 lends it new weight: the most dangerous temptation is the loss of love. At this very point men must rely on God's mercy to see them through.

[23-25] The prediction of false messiahs and false prophets also follows Mark throughout, except that Matthew speaks of "great" signs, thus emphasizing how dangerous they are. [26-28] But he adds significant weight to this warning by appending new material. Since this material is found also in Luke 17:24 and 37, we are evidently dealing with a common tradition (Q?). To begin with, Matthew 24:27 is precisely parallel to 24:37 (and 38-39) in the Greek text: "For just as . . . , so will be the coming of the Son of Man." The corresponding passages are also put close together in Luke, although the wording differs somewhat (17:24, 26-27, 30). This is probably how Matthew found the material in the tradition he had before him. The admonitions to be watchful, however, which come next in Q, belonged at the end of the discourse, where Mark already had similar material (Matt. 24:37-42—Mark 13:35 is included in vs. 42). Luke omitted the warning against false prophets from his section (Luke 21:5-33) corresponding to Mark 13:1-31, and inserted it in another eschatological discourse (Luke 17:23-37, where 17:23-24 = Mark 13:21-23). In other words, Luke sensed that the warning was an intrusion into the sequence.

In Matthew the intrusion is even more elaborate than it is in Mark. The coming of the Son of Man is not mentioned until after verse 29, which should follow 21(-22) directly (cf. "those days" in vs. 22 with "after the affliction of those days" in vs. 29). But Matthew is concerned to describe the false prophets, so he adds greater detail. He has in mind figures like those depicted by Josephus (*Bell. Jud.* ii. 261). A certain Egyptian led thirty thousand men into the desert, where they hoped for a repetition of the miracles that took place during Israel's journey from Egypt to the Promised Land; he appeared with his followers on the Mount of Olives, where the messiah had long been expected to appear, in order to conquer Jerusalem for God's Kingdom. The result was a pathetic defeat: the prophet took flight, while almost all his followers perished in an engagement with the Romans.

[26] This story explains the reference to the "desert," while the reference to the "chambers" remains obscure; Luke says merely "here and there." Perhaps what is presupposed is the Jewish teaching that the messiah will live in hiding until the day he siezes power (cf. John 7:27). Fanatics of all ages have tried to define the Kingdom of God and identify it with a particular program, usually revolutionary. Jesus, to be sure, knew that the coming Kingdom was breaking into the life of the present, often in revolutionary ways; but a given social movement could never be identified with the Kingdom of God, for that Kingdom exists not as institutions in a fixed place but as acts of individual love everywhere. That of course does not rule out institutions and communal endeavor; but it leaves no room for fanaticism. The ultimate sovereignty must be God's, i.e. the desire to help men, not control them.

[27] The image of lightning stresses the universal scope of Jesus' coming; the picture is that of a horizontal lightning bolt, conceived by the ancient world as illuminating the whole earth, east to west, at the same moment. Such will the "presence" of Jesus be on "his day" (Luke 17:24). He will appear in divine omnipotence as Lord and judge of the whole world. Whether the image is also meant to express the suddenness of his coming is not certain, though likely. Two points are being made: God's sovereignty will be universal; it is not the private concern of a few devout individuals, but a total new creation of the world. And it will come suddenly, in such a way that it will be impossible to observe it from a safe distance; it might break in today, for example.

[28] The final saying, about the vultures, is more difficult to interpret. In Luke 17:37 it comes at a different point, in the context of the Judgment, when one will be taken, another left behind. There, too, the image is intended to show how nonsensical it is to ask where the Son of Man will make his appearance. In Africa, for example, one can see the branches of the trees fill with vultures wherever lions have dismembered an antelope, so that there is no need to ask where the corpse is. Not only will there be no mistaking it when Jesus, the real messiah, comes again—it will report like horizontal lightning—but

the end of the age is attested even now: false messiahs and prophets are converging like vultures at the end-time of humanity. Thus Matthew ends the interpolation (vss. 23-28) by hinting the imminence of the end (the corpse) and reminding his readers about the false prophets.

[29-31] The appearance of the Son of Man is once more described, in parallel to the Markan account, though with interesting changes. Matthew emphasizes that the second coming will occur "soon" or "immediately" after the affliction; elsewhere he omits this word, which Mark uses frequently. The only counterexample is Matthew 27:48; in Matthew's special material it appears only in 14:31; 25:15; 4:22. Here it replaces Mark's vague expression "in those days," which in other places Matthew shows a distinct liking for (e.g., 3:1). On the one hand, therefore, Matthew is warning against the false prophets who state that Christ has already come; on the other, he is strengthening men's hope that the coming will be soon.

[30] What is "the sign of the Son of Man" that will "appear in the sky"? Should we take this to mean "the sign, i.e., the Son of Man," so that there would be no distinction between the sign and the appearance itself? This would fit with verse 3; but in this verse (30) that is almost inconceivable, since it is explicitly stated that the Son of Man is seen only later. The church very early thought of the sign as a cross appearing in the sky. When Didache 16:6 speaks of the "sign of spreading," it probably refers to the opening or "unrolling" of the heavens, not the outspread arms of Jesus hanging from the cross. But chapter 1 of the Ethiopian Apocalypse of Peter says explicitly: " . . . while my cross goes before my face." That is how our verse was interpreted at that time. A Christian interpolation into the Apocalypse of Elijah (32) also speaks of the "sign of the cross." In the middle of the second century, we read in the so-called Epistle of the Apostles: ". . . while my cross [Coptic text: 'the sign of the cross'] goes before me" (16); the Gospel of Peter (39) says that on Easter morning three men—two angels and Jesus—emerged from the tomb, followed by a cross. But our text does not make any mention of a cross.

The explanation is probably much simpler. [31] Matthew also mentions the great trumpet that, according to 1 Thessalonians 4:16, announces the coming of Christ, and is already associated with the

Day of the Lord in Isaiah 27:13. Now we read in Isaiah 18:3: ". . . as when a [military] sign is raised on the mountains, as when the sound of the trumpet is heard"; in Jeremiah 4:21: "How long must I see the [military] standard, and hear the sound of the trumpet?" (RSV); in Jeremiah 6:1: "Blow the trumpet in Tekoa, and raise a [military] signal on Beth-haccherem" (RSV); and in Jeremiah 51:27: "Set up a [military] standard on the earth, blow the trumpet among the nations" (RSV). Everywhere except Jeremiah 4:21, where the translator has completely misunderstood the passage, we find the same words as in Matthew 24:30-31 for "sign, signal, standard," and for "trumpet." These same terms occur also in Jewish liturgical prayers, for instance in the tenth of the Eighteen Benedictions, which were already recited regularly in the first century of the Christian era, and in almost identical words in the modern New Year's liturgy: "Sound the great trumpet for our liberty, set up the standard to gather our outcasts, and gather us from the four corners of the earth." At Qumran "trumpets" (1QM ii. 15–iii. 11) and "standards" (iii. 12–iv. 17) likewise play an important role. Thus, the two always appeared together in the Bible used by the community of Jesus, and Matthew is merely trying to say that the standard of the messiah will be raised and the trumpet blown when he comes to establish God's Kingdom finally upon earth. Even Matthew is probably not thinking in terms of visible standards or audible trumpets in the sky, but is merely trying to say that God's final victory will come like a liberating army to a nation on the point of disaster. The terminology may even suggest that the events of the eschaton will transcend description in words and must be expressed through the symbols of sign, standard, and music.

[30] Even more interesting is the insertion of a quotation from Zechariah 12:10. In the Hebrew text, we read: "They will look on him whom they have pierced and mourn for him, as one mourns for an only son . . . ." The Christian community very soon discovered this text and interpreted it as referring to the death of the "only Son" of God, as in John 19:37, where the "piercing" refers to the spear wound. Since, however, Zechariah 12:10-14 speaks of the lamentation of all the tribes of the earth, it soon came to be interpreted as referring to the lamentation of the world at the Last Judgment (see Revelation 1:7, where Daniel 7:13 is also brought in). The same two passages, in the

opposite order, are associated in Matthew 24:30; the quotation from Daniel is already found in Mark 13:26. Revelation 1:7; Mark 13:26 and Matthew 24:30 use another word for "see" than the one used in Daniel; the term they choose rhymes with the word for "weep" or "lament" (Matt. 24:30: "kopsontai [see] . . . kai opsontai [weep]"). It is therefore possible that the two passages were combined even before Mark in the oral instruction of the community, and that this led to the rhyming of the first two words; the Greek translation of Zechariah 12:10 as we have it uses yet another word. This might explain the use of the phrase "they will see" to introduce Mark 13:26 and Revelation 1:7 and account for the motif of "piercing" in Revelation 1:7, which also occurs in Zechariah 12:10; in Revelation it probably refers to the nails used to crucify Jesus.

Such Biblical texts were often transmitted orally. This explains why Mark 14:62 and Revelation 1:7 (most manuscripts) read "with the clouds," as does one manuscript of Daniel 7:13, whereas Matthew 24:30 and one manuscript of Revelation 1:7 read "on the clouds," like the more reliable translation of Daniel 7:13; and finally, Mark 13:26 reads "in the clouds." A complete (handwritten!) copy of the Bible cost a fortune; such copies were very rare. Bishop Melito, for example, had to journey from Sardis to Palestine to find one. Oral transmission of catchphrases is therefore more than probable. In any case, Matthew attaches great importance to the idea of the Last Judgment and the great terror that will come over all nations when the Son of Man appears; Mark at this point focuses only on the gathering-in of God's chosen people. For Matthew, too, of course, this notion furnishes the comforting conclusion (24:31; cf. the discussion of 23:37).

[32-36] The parable of the fig tree corresponds, with minor exceptions, to the wording found in Mark 13:28-32. [33] In verse 33, however, Matthew substitutes "all these things" for the "this" of Mark 13:29, so that verse 33 must refer to the same events as verse 34. Perhaps he wants to make both verses refer merely to the preliminary signs (cf. vs. 8) and thus get around the difficulty that the second coming itself had not taken place within the first generation (cf. the discussion of Mark 13:30). Since, however, the same change in wording is also found elsewhere (see the discussion of vs. 2), it probably does not signify such a reinterpretation: "all these things" refers not

only to preliminary signs but also to the Last Judgment itself. [34] Jesus' statement is not patently false because by "this generation" Matthew means not just the first generation after Jesus but all the generations of Judaism that reject him (see the discussion of 23:36).

[35] Verse 35 is omitted in one of the earliest manuscripts; since, however, Matthew is here following Mark almost word for word, and since the verse occurs in Mark, its omission here is probably only an oversight on the part of the copyist. [36] In verse 36, a series of manuscripts have omitted "nor the Son," because a later period found any ignorance on Jesus' part offensive.

The Call to Keep Watch (24:37-51)
Cf. Mark 13:35; Luke 17:26-36; 12:39-46

[37]"For like the days of Noah, so will be the coming of the Son of Man. [38]Just as in the days before the Flood, people ate and drank, men and women married, up to the very day Noah went into the ark; [39]yet they did not know what was happening until the Flood came and swept them all away. That is how it will be when the Son of Man comes. [40]At that time two men will be working in the field: one will be taken away, the other will be left behind. [41]Two women will be at the mill grinding meal; one will be taken away, the other will be left behind. [42]Keep watch, then, because you do not know what day your Lord will come. [43]Remember this: if the owner of the house knew the time when the thief would come, he would stay awake and keep watch, and not let the thief break into his house. [44]Therefore you must always be ready, because the Son of Man will come at an hour when you are not expecting him.

[45]"Who, then, is the faithful and wise servant, whom his master has placed in charge of the other servants, to give them their food at the proper time? [46]Blessings on that servant if his master finds him doing this when he comes home! [47]Amen, I tell you, he will put that servant in charge of all his property. [48]But the wicked servant says in his heart, 'My master will not come back for a long time,' [49]and he will begin to beat his fellow servants, and eat and drink with drunkards. [50]Then that servant's master will come back some day when he does not expect him, and at an hour he does not know. [51]The master

will cut him to pieces, and make him share the fate of the hypocrites. There he will cry and gnash his teeth."
(Vs. 38—Gen. 7:7. Vs. 43—1 Thess. 5:2.)

The conclusion of the discourse has been reshaped. The parable that concludes this section in Mark (Mark 13:34-36) does not appear in Matthew until 25:13-30, where it is highly elaborated; only in 24:42 do we find an echo of the Markan conclusion. For the rest, Matthew here brings together short parables and parabolic references that are found in Luke in two different eschatological discourses; Matthew lumps them together here because they are so closely consonant with the parables that follow (chapter 25). Mark 13:37 is no longer necessary, because Matthew 24:1 mentions the presence of all the disciples, not just four.

[37-39] Luke expands the comparison of Christ's coming (see the excursus after Matt. 25:46) to the Flood by inserting a second comparison to the time of Lot. This is probably a later addition, because Luke 17:31 warns against turning back (=Matt. 24:17-18), and this warning recalls Lot's wife, who was turned into a pillar of salt when she looked back. [38] According to the rabbis, carefree "eating, drinking, and marrying" without a thought of God's judgment was typical of Noah's contemporaries; Ethiopian Enoch 65:10; 106:18 also speak of injustice and godlessness. The inhabitants of Sodom and Gomorrah, on the other hand, are reproved not for their carefree way of life but for committing the most terrible abominations (Gen. 19:4-9; Jub. 16:5-6; 20:5; Wisd. 10:7). On the other hand, the two righteous men Noah and Lot, and the associated punishments of the Flood and the rain of fire, are already linked in 2 Peter 2:5-7 (similarly already in Wisd. 10:4, 6; 3 Macc. 2:4-5; also Ecclus. 16:7-8; Test. Naph. 3:4-5; Philo, *Moses* ii. 263. [Jub. 20:5]), whereas 1 Peter 3:20 mentions only Noah. The construction is clear in Matthew: the description is given first in general terms, then in specific detail: "Just as . . . , so . . . ." Luke, on the contrary, begins with the general statement (17:26); he then introduces the details about Noah, somewhat abbreviated, in an independent clause. He takes the opposite approach in the second example, beginning with the details about the time of Lot, which

accumulate to form an awkward "as" clause; then, like Matthew, he adds a "so" clause referring to the coming of the Son of Man. **[39]** Matthew himself probably introduced the term "parousia" into verses 37 and 39, just as he did in 24:3, 27; an echo of the original formulation can still be heard in verse 38*a:* "in the days of [Noah or the Son of Man]."

[40-41] In Matthew 24:40-41, as in Luke 17:34-35, the saying about the separations that will occur at the Last Judgment is appended: one person will be taken, another left. In both Gospels the first example concerns two men, the second two women; in Matthew the two men are working in the field, which harmonizes with the example of the women grinding meal, whereas according to Luke they are sleeping "on that night," which suggests that Christ will come at night. This notion may go back to parables like Mark 13:35; Matthew 24:43, or even to the expectation throughout Judaism that eschatological salvation would come during the night of Passover.

[42] The exhortation to keep watch, because the day (in Mark as in Matt. 24:43 [Q]: "the hour") when "your Lord" (in Mark: "the master of the house") will come is unknown, leads into the parable of the thief. **[43]** The entire content of verses 42-51 also appears in Luke 12:39-48; there it is preceded by a parable distantly related to Matthew 25:1-13 and a warning against piling up riches, which appears in Matthew in the Sermon on the Mount (Matt. 6:19-21 = Luke 12:33-34). This warning was probably already connected with Luke 12:39 ff. in Q, because both sections speak of "thieves" and (according to the text preserved in Matthew) of "breaking in." This would mean that Matthew took the saying about piling up riches—which was independent—and patched it, as he did many others, into his Sermon on the Mount. The parable of the thief agrees almost word for word with Luke 12:39-40, except that Matthew introduces the catchword "keep watch" into verse 43 in order to link it more closely with verse 42.

[45-51] The parable of the good servant and the wicked servant likewise appears in both Gospels in approximately the same form, except that Luke turns the servant into a majordomo set in charge of the other servants (Luke 12:42; but merely "servant" in 12:43, 45, 46); so in his version it is not really appropriate for his master to reward him by placing him in charge of everything. Luke is probably thinking of leaders of the Christian community, whose responsibilities are greater than those of the regular members; this is why he inserted Peter's question in 12:41 between the two parables, which were right together in Q. In Matthew, despite verse 45, the "servant" is more nearly the equal of his "fellow servants" (vs. 49).

[51] The term "hypocrites" (see the discussion of 6:2) and the threat of "crying and gnashing of teeth" (see the discussion of 8:12) derive from Matthew himself. An expanded form of this last parable is found in Gospel of the Nazarenes 18. There the wicked servant is recast into the parable of the three servants (= Matt. 25:14-30), so that one multiplies the talents entrusted to him, another buries them, and the most wicked squanders them on prostitutes and women who play the flute. This shows how the subject matter of such parables continued to develop and be retold in every conceivable variation.

[37-39] The comparison to the period of Noah sees men as lost not because they are abysmally wicked, as in Genesis 6:5 ff., but because they are thoughtless and take no heed of coming judgment. What men are doing—eating and drinking and marrying—is itself unexceptionable; but they are doing them without taking account of the reality of God, that is, God's approach to them. This is their disastrous "ignorance." The contrast with Jewish apocalyptic thought, which attributed such terminal evil to fallen angels (Gen. 6:1-4), is striking. The warning is addressed not to men who are flagrantly wicked (as it were demons) but to respectable citizens who have forgotten the reality of God. This means that the parable is directed against the very men who hear it, not just some wicked third party.

[40-41] Unlike Mark and Luke, Matthew uses the idea of pairs of people separated by the sudden Last Judgment, to make the discourse seem a warning before which no one can stand secure. Of two people engaged in the same occupation, one will be accepted, the other cast aside. This is how God's judgment will come upon his own community. [42] Matthew speaks of the "day," not the "hour" (of the night), although the latter would have gone better with what follows; this is because it is not so much his purpose to emphasize that Christ

could come any time, as that one must live one's life in the shadow of the coming Judgment, whether it is near or distant (cf. the introductory comments on Mark 13:28-37).

[43-44] The parable of the owner of the house and the thief emphasizes not the joyful nature of Christ's coming, but his coming in judgment. According to 1 Thessalonians 5:2-4, the Day of the Lord comes like a thief for the unbeliever, but not for the believer, who is prepared (cf. 2 Pet. 3:10). Not until Revelation 3:3; 16:15 is the image of thief applied to Jesus himself, coming to judge the world. The form preserved in 1 Thessalonians 5:2-4 is probably the earliest. The image of a thief is appropriate for the day of God's judgment. The implication of disguise is also a reminder that God *is* Jesus the man, so that Judgment is not merely to come, but has already begun. Thus the parable, which originally referred to the Day of Judgment in general, now has "Christological significance": Jesus replaces the "Day." Here, too, it is not the immoral conduct of the owner of the house but his carelessness that brings about his downfall. "Watching" is not simply joyous expectation of the coming glory; it is taking seriously the imminence of disaster. The same point was made without benefit of parable in the reference to the Flood.

[45-51] The final parable, too, warns the reader against a languishing expectation, and consequent indifference; he is rather to conduct himself properly during the entire interim until the coming of the Lord, above all in relations with his "fellow servants." Whether the coming is to be in the immediate or the more distant future matters only in that the latter assumption [48] might lead to negligence and a failure to believe practically in the Last Judgment (vs. 48; cf. 25:5, 19; 2 Pet. 3:4, 9). The New Testament never speaks of divine intoxication, as Philo does; only Ephesians 5:18 comes close to this usage. [49] Elsewhere "drunkenness" (vs. 49) symbolizes the recklessness that no longer thinks in "sober" terms of responsibility in the eyes of God (cf. 1 Thess. 5:6-8; Luke 21:34; 1 Cor. 15:34; 1 Pet. 1:13; 5:8; Isa. 28:1 ff.; Joel 1:5).

[50] Once again the point is the reference to the certain judgment that will distinguish the faithful "servants" from the wicked (see the discussion of 10:24). [49] The wisdom that is commended is not intelligence, but the ability to have a proper understanding of reality,

including God's coming (see the discussion of 25:2). The Old Testament also speaks of the wise and the foolish in the sense of the devout and the godless. The true realist, therefore, is the one who takes God into account (cf. 7:24; 10:16; 25:2 ff.; Luke 16:8). It is characteristic of Matthew to exhort a sober wisdom that does not suppress rational understanding but rather makes use of it for to Matthew, Jesus is the Wisdom of God (see 11:25, and the discussion of 23:34). The only important difference between Matthew's text and that of Luke is the reformulation of the commission "to give them food at the proper time." Since the wording is almost identical with Psalm 104:27, the idea is possibly that the believer acts in his own life as the responsible steward of God.

[51] This very fact exposes him even more grievously to the danger of failure, which would equate him once more with the "hypocrites" of 22:18 and 23:13-36 (see the introductory comments on chapters 21–25). The idiom "share the fate of" (literally "give him his portion with") and the image of "cutting to pieces" occur in a similar passage in 1QSii. 16-17 and probably derive from Psalm 37, where the land is given to the righteous, but the wicked man is "cut off from the midst of" (1QS ii. 16) it. Was this taken too literally (cf. Acts 1:18), or is being "cut to pieces" a Persian mode of punishment (Billerbeck)? The crass threat of punishment which already forms part of the parable in Q is further enhanced in Matthew by the reference to "crying and gnashing of teeth," which points to damnation at the Last Judgment (cf. the discussion of 8:12). In contrast to the preceding parable, however, the commendation and rich reward of the wise and faithful servant come first. Neither does the parable speak simply of two servants, as though it were possible to distinguish so easily who is good from who is wicked, for example the believer from the nonbeliever, or the Christian from the Jew. Both possibilities remain open to one and the same servant. If the parable was spoken by Jesus, it may have been originally a promise and only by implication a warning; but Matthew emphasizes the latter feature by introducing the servant of verse 48 as "wicked" (Luke 12:45 leaves him neutral; he will become wicked" if he . . ."), and urging the community not to follow his example. Even in Matthew, however, the life of the disciple

receives its depth and richness from the Lord's coming, which is a promise as much as a warning.

The proximity of chapter 24 to chapter 23 is important. Chapter 23 pronounces judgment on Pharisaic Judaism in harsh and oppressive terms; chapter 24 pronounces judgment in equally harsh terms —but this time on the community of Jesus. Matthew stresses the alikeness of the two groups by sending the "wicked servant" of the "lord" or "master"—in other words, the unfaithful disciple of Jesus —to the same fate as the "hypocrites." Persecution at the hands of Jewish or pagan authorities is not a sign the troubles of the eschaton have begun; it is part of the daily routine of a disciple of Jesus. What is a sign that Judgment has begun is any temptation to live a life heedless of the commandment to love. Such a life would of course be a state of intoxication blind to reality, the reality of God's judgment. Jesus was concerned lest his disciples surrender to the world, with the result that his coming would have no effect—a loveless world left to itself would quickly be Judgment enough.

The Parable of Readiness (25:1-13)

[1]"On that day the Kingdom of heaven will be like ten girls who took their lamps and went out to meet the bridegroom and the bride. [2]Five of them were foolish and five were wise. [3]The foolish ones took their lamps but did not take any extra oil with them, [4]while the wise ones took containers full of oil together with their lamps. [5]The bridegroom was late in coming, so the girls began to nod and fall asleep. [6]But at midnight the cry rang out, 'Here is the bridegroom! Come and meet him!' [7]The ten girls woke up and trimmed their lamps. [8]Then the foolish ones said to the wise ones, 'Let us have some of your oil, because our lamps are going out.' [9]"No, indeed,' the wise ones answered back, 'there is not enough for you and for us. Go to the store and buy some for yourselves.' [10]So the foolish girls went off to buy some oil, and while they were gone the bridegroom arrived. The five girls who were ready went in with him to the wedding feast, and the door was closed. [11]Later the other girls arrived. 'Lord, Lord! Let us in!' they cried. [12]But he answered, 'Amen, I tell you, I do not know you.'

[13]"Keep watch then, because you do not know the day or the hour."

This parable is found only in Matthew, although some passages from it are echoed in Luke (24:10-12; cf. Luke 13:25), and the admonition to keep watch at the conclusion of the Markan discourse (Mark 13:33-37) is related. At one time it may have belonged to a special collection of parables (see the introductory comments on Matt. 13:24-30). Since Luke 13:25 looks like nothing more than a fragment, in which the "master of the house" is simply a piece of traditional imagery, it is more likely that our parable has influenced the Lukan saying than the other way around; cf. the development from Mark 2:19 to 2:20 or from Mark 13:35 to Matthew 24:42. Whether the parable goes back to Jesus himself or not depends on whether the delay of the bridegroom's arrival until midnight was an integral feature from the very beginning. If the idea of midnight is essential, the parable probably originated in the community, which of course realized that Jesus was not coming to judge the world as soon as they first expected. If the delay till midnight (vss. 5-6) was a late addition, the parable might be ascribed to Jesus himself.

According to verse 1, the subject is the Kingdom of heaven, not the coming of the Son of Man, as Matthew interprets it by means of verse 13 (see below) and the phrase "on that day" in verse 1, which is typically Matthaean and links it with 24:44-51. The bridegroom, who symbolizes God in Isaiah 62:5, would then be an allusion to God's time of salvation, as in Mark 2:19. The community does not appear yet as the bride (Rev. 21:9; 22:17; 2 Cor. 11:2; Eph. 5:25-27); in Jesus' words in Mark 2:19a, the community is represented by the wedding guests. It is true that the girls are more like the "bride," and Matthew (as well as Mark 2:20) identifies the bridegroom with Jesus by means of the terminology used in 25:11-12, which is reminiscent of 7:22-23.

In the vicinity of Bethlehem as late as the turn of the century torches were used to illuminate wedding processions at night. These consisted of sticks wrapped with rags soaked in olive oil, with which girls would dance until the flame went out. The word used in our parable almost always means "torches"; in John 18:3 it is even used to distinguish them from lamps. If this is what is meant, the girls did not light their torches until verse 7, since they burn for only about a quarter of an hour. At the last minute more oil has to be poured over them so that they will at least continue burning until the end of the torch dance. In this case all of verse 1 merely sets the stage. The ten girls wait with the bride and light their torches as soon as the bridegroom comes, in order to welcome him and perform their dance. So interpreted the parable could go back to Jesus; it would call men to be ready to respond to God's glorious invitation. Only the discovery that Jesus' coming was far in the future led the community to introduce the elaboration of verses 5-6. Such an interpretation is possible; if it is correct then verse 8 would have to mean: "Our torches will go out too soon."

In Judith 10:22 and all the papyrus remains that have been discovered the Greek word means "lamps," as it probably does in Acts 20:8 and a Greek translation of Daniel 5:5; a rabbinic passage also speaks of lamps (that is, copper bowls filled with oil and rags and fastened to a pole) borne on a bridge. Therefore at least in the present form of the parable verse 8 refers to lamps that are about to go out because the bridegroom is so long delayed. The community asked itself, perhaps on the basis of a parable of Jesus, what it meant to wait for the second coming after several decades had passed, and it is the exalted Lord who gives the answer. The concluding sentence (vs. 13) is reminiscent of Mark 13:35 (Matt. 24:42), combining the "day" (Matt. 24:42) and the "hour" (Matt. 24:44; cf. Mark 13:35). It did not belong to the original parable, because it is off the point (see below).

[1] "Then"—at the coming of Jesus (24:50)—will be seen the true state of affairs, which is now still hidden (future tense; cf. the discussion of 13:43). The Kingdom of God is comparable to the wedding banquet, not the ten girls; we must therefore interpret the verse as meaning: "What happens in the Kingdom of heaven is like what happens to ten girls" (cf. the discussion of Mark 4:26). For Jesus, a banquet is the most typical image for full communion with God in the coming Kingdom (cf. Matt. 8:11; 22:1-14; Luke 12:37; 14:15-24; 15:23-24; 22:30; Matt. 26:29; Acts 10:41; also Isa. 25:6-8). A wedding is the most obvious occasion for a banquet; Jesus also uses a wedding

to symbolize the fulfillment of history (see the introductory remarks on Mark 2:18-22). The second half of verse 1 could be taken as a summary title. Probably, however, it already marks the beginning of the narrative, which continues directly in verse 2; the girls are awaiting the coming of the bridegroom, perhaps near the house of the bride, with their lamps burning.

[2] Once again, to be wise or foolish is not the same thing as having a high or low IQ (cf. the discussion of 24:45 and 5:22). Perhaps the narrator still hears an echo of the Hebrew terminology, where "wise" means "seeing" or "with eyes open." Those who are wise are those whose eyes are open to what is yet to come and do not live simply for the day. [3-4] They take along an emergency supply of oil, thinking beyond the immediate present.

[5] The bridegroom is extremely late in coming; this is unusual but not impossible. Here the situation has colored the narrative. It is true that "sleeping" is sometimes used to symbolize unreadiness (1 Thess. 5:6; Rom. 13:11; Eph. 5:14); here, however, it plays only a narrative, not a symbolic role (the wise girls also fall asleep!), explaining why the girls do not see that their lamps are burning low. [6] The hour of midnight is merely to suggest a long vigil; sayings like Mark 13:35 may have influenced the terminology. The cry is not the wailing of Matthew 24:30, but within the framework of this parable the joyous outcry of those who see that the one they have been waiting for is finally coming.

[7] The girls "trim their lamps" and notice that they are about to go out; this presupposes that they are already lit, although the wicks must be trimmed and oil added. The order to go to the store because there is not enough oil for everyone is not meant ironically, since it is carried out. [10] In a rural village it would have been possible to buy something even around midnight, because everyone would be up and about for such a celebration. Neither the refusal of the wise girls to share their oil nor the possibility of getting more from the store should be interpreted allegorically. The only point that matters for the story is that the foolish girls are not there when the time comes. [11-12] That the doors are shut is only to be expected; the response of the bridegroom and his harsh refusal follow from the situation: God's judgment will be equally unequivocal and irreversible.

[13] The parable concludes with a general admonition to keep watch. It is true that in the parable keeping watch (as opposed to falling asleep) does not play any role (see the discussion of vs. 5); what matters is readiness for a lengthy period of waiting. But "keeping watch" is already used by extension to refer to such readiness, which does not ignore the passing of time but does live for the future as well as the present. The concluding clause suggests that the "day" might come much sooner than expected; this does not contradict 24:45-51 for it is the *wicked* servant who is counting on a long delay (vs. 48). The reference to midnight, however, implies that the wait might equally well be long—men's faith must at any rate be prepared to endure any length.

This ambiguity is a major point of the parable. It is a sign of understanding the parabolic form when we see that the same image leads to different conclusions in different situations (cf. the discussion of Mark 3:23 and 4:13-20). When Jesus calls on his disciples to keep watch, he is calling on them to take the reality of God so seriously that they can come to terms with its sudden appearance at any moment within their own lives, precisely because they know that this reality will one day come unboundedly in the Kingdom of God. This attitude can of course turn into fanatical abstention from earthly labor on the grounds that the end will come within a few months (2 Thess. 2:2; 3:11-12), or into negligence on grounds that the end has still not come and that it is impossible to live for decades in the glow of imminent eschatological hopes. When this happens, the same appeal takes on the opposite meaning: men must not cling to such hopes at all costs; they must remain faithful for decades or even centuries. And it is the same Lord who gives his community the same admonition, "Keep watch," even when it means one thing to some and something else to others (cf. the introductory remarks on Mark 13:28-37).

The Parable of Responsibility (25:14-30)
Cf. Mark 13:34; Luke 19:11-27

¹⁴"For it will be like a man who was about to leave home on a trip; he called his servants and put them in charge of his property. ¹⁵He gave to each one according to his ability: to one he gave five talents,

to the other two, and to the other one. Then he left on his trip. ¹⁶The servant who had received five talents went at once and invested his money and earned another five. ¹⁷In the same way the servant who received two talents earned another two. ¹⁸But the servant who received one talent went off, dug a hole in the ground, and hid his master's money. ¹⁹After a long time the master of those servants came back and settled accounts with them. ²⁰The servant who had received five talents came in and handed over the other five talents. 'Lord, you gave me five talents,' he said. 'Look! Here are another five talents that I have earned.' ²¹'Well done, good and faithful servant!' said his lord. 'You have been faithful in small things, so I will put you in charge of large things. Come on in and share my happiness!' ²²Then the servant who had been given two talents came in and said, 'You gave me two talents, Lord. Look! Here are another two talents that I have earned.' ²³'Well done, good and faithful servant!' said his lord. 'You have been faithful in small things, so I will put you in charge of large things. Come on in and share my happiness!' ²⁴Then the servant who had received one talent came in and said, 'Lord, I know that you are a hard man; you reap harvests where you did not plant, and gather crops where you did not scatter seed. ²⁵I was afraid, so I went off and hid your money in the ground. Look! Here is what belongs to you.' ²⁶'You bad and lazy servant!' his master said. 'You knew, did you, that I reap harvests where I did not plant, and gather crops where I did not scatter seed? ²⁷Well, then, you should have deposited my money in the bank, and I would have received it all back with interest when I returned. ²⁸Now, take the money away from him and give it to the one who has ten talents. ²⁹For to every one who has, even more will be given, and he will have more than enough; but the one who has nothing, even the little he has will be taken away from him. ³⁰As for this useless servant—throw him outside in the darkness; there he will cry and gnash his teeth.' "

[14] Verse 13 was formulated to echo the conclusion of the eschatological discourse in Mark (13:35); Mark 13:34 sets its stamp on the introduction to this parable. The sentence is incomplete in both Gospels and needs some sort of addition, such as "The Kingdom of God is like . . . ." In the Greek text, Matthew begins this parable with

"for," thus linking verses 13 and 14 even more closely. He therefore understands the parable in the sense of verse 13 (cf. the introductory comments on 24:37-51). In its Matthaean form, it is by and large quite clear. [15] The enormous sum entrusted to the servants is striking (see the discussion of 18:24); even the last servant receives one hundred times as much as the servants in Luke. The sum undoubtedly increased in the course of tradition, in order to underline the greatness of God's mercy, as in 18:23 ff. The allotment according to ability, in contrast to the equal distribution in Luke, is likewise probably a later development based on the notion of the manifold gifts of God. [19] The isolated statement that the lord returns "after a long time" (vs. 19; not in Luke) may be due to the experience of the community.

[21, 23] The addition of "Come on in and share my happiness!" in verses 21 and 23, as well as the throwing of the servant [30] "outside in the darkness, where he will cry and gnash his teeth" (vs. 30), which also have no parallel in Luke, are expansions that fall outside the narrative of the parable and point to the Last Judgment. The same holds true for the contrast between "small" and "large," since the ten talents in verse 20 already amount to more than the entire sum distributed at the outset. The formulation of verse 30*b* is Matthew's own (see the discussion of 8:12). Verse 30 should follow verse 28 immediately, but represents a duplication in any case: the earthly punishment, which makes sense within the framework of the parable (vs. 28), has added to it the punishment of hell (vs. 30).

[29] The intervening saying (vs. 29) is an isolated one preserved in similar form in Mark 4:25 and Gospel of Thomas 41; as Luke 19:26 shows, it was associated with this parable prior to Matthew and Luke, and only the addition of "and he will have more than enough" is characteristic of Matthew and his tradition (also Matt. 13:12). [28] It is probably the insertion of this dictum, which states that to him who has even more will be given, that led to having the wicked servant's money not only taken away from him but given to the one who had made the most profit. In Luke this additional reward is ridiculously small in comparison to the ten cities already entrusted to the servant's care. But the statement in Luke 19:25 that this servant already has ten minas is intended to place even greater emphasis on the startling nature of this principle of God.

Luke alone states that the man—now a nobleman—goes to be made king and then "comes back" (a typically Lukan expression) to destroy his enemies. This feature is undoubtedly a later addition, occasioned by the interpretation of the parable as referring directly to the coming of Christ and recalling events at the accession of Archelaus (4 B.C.), who was recognized as king at Rome and took terrible vengeance on the Jews who stood in his way. Luke also paints the incompetent servant in blacker colors. **[18, 25]** Rabbinic law says that whoever immediately buries property entrusted to him (Matt. 25:18, 25) is no longer liable because he has taken the safest course conceivable; the man who merely binds it up in a cloth is punished (Luke 19:20; Billerbeck on vss. 14-18). The form taken by the parable in the Gospel of the Nazarenes 18 is clearly moralizing (see the introductory remarks on 24:51).

[14] The lengthy absence of the lord is important for this parable, because it makes it possible for the servants to be entrusted with real responsibility in the interim. **[15]** Matthew also stresses that the gift and responsibility are commensurate with the ability of each servant. Even the least competent still receives ten thousand denarii (cf. the discussion of 20:2); the lord has a very high opinion of his servants' abilities. **[16-17]** Two of the servants take a risk, which of course could entail the loss of everything entrusted to them, because they know that what their lord has given them must be actively at work, must live, must effect something new. **[18-19]** The third can only think of absolute security. For a long time the situation remains constant, and the different courses of action taken by the servants seem to have no consequences. But the day of reckoning comes.

[20] The first tells how much profit he earned with the funds given him by his lord (Luke puts it more elegantly: how much profit the funds earned); **[21]** he is rewarded, not with a well-endowed pension, but with even greater responsibility (cf. 24:47). A Jewish saying strikes a similar note: "The reward for fulfilling the Law is (more) fulfilling the Law" (Billerbeck on 5:19 A). It is true, however, that the reference to happiness anticipates the eschatological joy that Christ will give his disciples. **[22-23]** The second servant is treated similarly.

[24-25] The third shows as soon as he opens his mouth that he is not interested in his lord's advantage but in saving his own skin. He is by no means a scoundrel or even negligent like the servant in Luke 19:20. He neither expects his lord to be away for a long time (24:48) nor to return soon (25:3-5). But he is a man who cannot venture his own person, who cannot risk his own prosperity for the sake of his lord. This makes him a wicked servant, because indolence in the service of this lord is wicked. [27] If he felt unfit for his work he should at least have let others work with the funds given him. [28-29] Now what was given is taken away. A saying that also appears in another context is used to describe the remarkable law of God's righteousness: where God's gift has already borne fruit, God gives in superabundance; where it has remained fruitless, it is lost completely. This means that God's gift can never be passively possessed; it is like a muscle: it must be worked and stretched or it withers. [30] The last sentence takes leave of the parable and points to God's judgment upon the servant who will not let God's gift to him bear fruit.

A single parable can still be discerned behind what both Matthew and Luke record; apart from the minor additions mentioned in the introductory remarks, that root-parable agrees for the most part with what we find in Matthew. It could easily go back to Jesus himself. Probably the chief emphasis was originally on the gift God gives each man, which must be made use of now, because in the coming Judgment the man will be lost who seeks to secure his own state instead of using what God has given him to benefit his Lord, i.e., others. The man who is ready to extend and risk his life will find it, not the man who wishes to secure it (Mark 8:35). Whoever is anxious about his own continuance and fails to notice that this anxiety is causing him to let the gift of his Lord lie fallow, or who even thinks he is in the right and accuses his Lord of injustice, like the day laborers in 20:12 or the elder brother in Luke 15:29-30, has committed the error of the third servant.

Jesus may have concluded the parable with verse 27. The lord's absence is to remind the disciples that they must act on their own responsibility and initiative. The parable is aimed at those devoted to their own personal security, devoted to the vindication of their own righteousness, rather than being devoted to God, which means being devoted to other people, taking active (and risky) steps to help them.

Jesus is saying that a religion concerned only with not doing anything wrong in order that its practitioner may one day stand vindicated ignores the will of God.

It was Q who added the interpretive statement that whoever has will have more given to him (vs. 29 = Luke 19:26). Q is therefore concerned to emphasize that men will be judged according to their conduct (cf. Matt. 16:27). There too, the major point was probably God's order to *use* his gifts: men must not seek anxiously for security, but venture themselves for God. Of course the community now took Jesus' preaching along with his entire life and death as normative, using them to interpret God's injunction and to define the criteria by which God would one day judge the world. At what point they came to identify the "lord" of the parable with the dead and returning Christ remains dubious. Luke certainly placed great stress on the absence of the lord and used 19:11 to make his interpretation of the parable clear: Christians know that the coming of Christ is far in the future. But thanks to the preaching of Jesus they are fully familiar with the will of God for this interim period, although the explicit command of the lord appears only in Luke 19:13 b. The responsibility entrusted to them, for which they will one day be accountable, is all the greater.

For Matthew, too, the parable refers clearly to Jesus and his coming, as is shown by its placement between 25:1-13 and 31-46. Matthew considerably elaborated features that bring to mind the Judge of the world, who apportions to men eternal happiness (vs. 21 end, 23 end) or damnation (vs. 30). In addition, he added the information that the first two servants were "faithful," the third "bad" and "lazy," although one may ask whether burying the money was not more work than a trip to the banker. The "fear" felt by this servant (also in Luke 19:21) may have reminded Matthew of passages like 8:26 and 14:30-31. He is thus concerned to emphasize that the believer not only hears but transforms what he hears into action. This is also why he introduces the parable with the word "for," linking it to the injunction to keep watch because no one knows the day or hour. It is hardly legitimate to read into the sequence the notion that verses 1-12 place more emphasis on religion and contemplation, verses 14-30 on ethical activity. Both parables are meant to warn the community against the illusion of thinking themselves saved; its members must recall God's injunction (love your neighbor) each and every day, because they do not know when they will be called to account.

The Final Judgment (25:31-46)

[31]"But when the Son of Man comes in his glory and all the angels with him, he will sit on his royal throne, [32]and all the earth's people will be gathered before him. Then he will divide them into two groups, just as a shepherd separates the sheep from the goats: [33]he will put the sheep at his right and the goats at his left. [34]Then the King will say to the people on his right, 'You that are blessed by my Father: come! Inherit the kingdom which has been prepared for you ever since the foundation of the world. [35]For I was hungry and you fed me. I was thirsty and you gave me drink. I was a stranger and you received me, [36]naked and you clothed me; I was sick and you visited me, in prison and you came to me.' [37]The righteous will then answer him, 'When, Lord, did we ever see you hungry and feed you, or thirsty and give you drink? [38]When did we ever see you a stranger and welcome you, or naked and clothe you? [39]When did we ever see you sick or in prison, and visit you?' [40]The King will answer back, 'Amen, I tell you: whenever you did this for one of the least of these brothers of mine, you did it for me!' [41]Then he will say to those on his left, 'Away from me, you that are under God's curse! Away to the eternal fire which has been prepared for the Devil and his angels! [42]For I was hungry but you did not feed me. I was thirsty but you did not give me drink. [43]I was a stranger but you did not receive me, naked but you did not clothe me; I was sick and in prison but you did not visit me.' [44]Then they will answer him, 'When, Lord, did we ever see you hungry, or thirsty, or a stranger, or naked, or sick, or in prison, and did not serve you?' [45]Then the King will answer them back, 'Amen, I tell you: whenever you refused to help one of the least of these, you refused to help me.' [46]And 'these' will be sent off 'to eternal' punishment, but the righteous 'to eternal life.' "

(Vs. 31—Dan. 7:13; Zech. 14:5. Vs. 46—Dan. 12:2.)

Some scholars consider this account of the judgment of the world as a direct discourse from the mouth of Jesus; others consider it wholly a Matthaean invention. Whatever it is, it is not a parable. Only the term "the King" is a common metaphor, and only in verses 32-33 do we find a comparison ("just as a shepherd separates . . .") for what is done by this King. This observation argues against tracing the passage back to Jesus, who, so far as we can still tell, depicted the coming Kingdom and the Last Judgment only in images and metaphors. Despite Matthew 10:40-42, which speaks of Jesus' messengers, and 18:5, it is not certain that Jesus practically identified himself with the poor. Above all, the vision of "all earth's people," although not impossible for Jesus in the light of Matthew 8:11-12, is hardly to be expected outside the context of an attack on Israel's complacency.

On the other hand, not all the material derives from Matthew; he would hardly have spoken in the introduction of the Son of Man and then gone on to speak of the "King." The superscription is purely Matthaean; in its first half, it repeats Mark 8:38 almost verbatim (cf. Matt. 16:27), except that the "glory of the Father" has now become "his glory" (that is, the glory of the Son of Man); the introductory "when" and the entire second half correspond totally to Matthew 19:28, apart from the word "then," which is one of Matthew's favorites. In addition, only Matthew is acquainted with the notion of Christ's enthronement (19:28). In the form preserved to us, Christ is the Judge; this is stated directly in verse 31 and suggested by the use of "Lord" as a term of address and the solidarity of the Judge with "the least of these brothers of mine." It is true that "brothers of mine" is not added in verse 45 or, according to some ancient manuscripts, in verse 40. The role of the messiah as Judge is almost without parallel in Judaism; at most, it may be suggested by Ethiopian Enoch 61:8, but we do not know how old this passage is. Since God is also addressed as "Lord" (e.g. Isa. 6:11 in Hebrew; frequently in Greek), before the superscription (vs. 31) was added, God may have been thought of as the Judge.

In the Old Testament, God is called "King" in eschatological contexts (Isa. 24:23; 33:22; Zeph. 3:15; Ob. 21; Zech. 14:16-17; cf. Psalms 47, 93, 96–97, 99), though always with additional qualification, e.g. "our King," "King Yahweh." Could the present description then go back to a Jewish source? In one such source we read: "My children, when you have given food to the poor, I account it as though you had given food to me" (Midrash Tann. on Deut. 15:9). Our text, however, goes further: it does not say "as though." Probably, therefore, as certain details suggest (see below), it is of Jewish Christian origin and referred to Christ from the very beginning. In Judaism, too, the messiah occasionally appears as King (Zech. 9:9 = Matt. 21:5; Ps. 89:18, 27; Ps. Sol. 17:35; possibly also Ezek. 37:22, 24; for a discussion of New Testament passages, see below). That he exercises God's royal sovereignty is stated by Micah 5:1; 1 Chronicles 17:14; cf. 1QSb v. 20-21. In addition, the promise contained in 2 Samuel 7:12-16 (cf. Ps. 2:7; 89:20, 26-27), which held for the reigning king of Israel, was applied to the messiah at the time of Jesus (Acts 13:33; Rev. 1:5). Ezekiel 34:17-30 might have furnished the model for our passage. But it speaks only of the "prince," not the king (34:24); and this prince separates the strong sheep from the weak, hardly the sheep from the goats (34:17?). The point is the promise of the one shepherd who replaces the incompetent shepherds.

[31] The introduction has nothing new to say; every term in it has already appeared elsewhere. Its sole purpose is to bring to mind these familiar expectations, to which the account that follows refers. [32] "All the earth's people" can mean not only the gentile Christians but in fact all mankind. They will be "gathered" or, more precisely, "herded together"; the term, typical of Matthew, describes what a shepherd does. What is probably meant is that the sheep will be separated from the goats, although the latter term can also mean "rams," usually in the sense of he-goats. This separation is characteristic of flocks in Palestine; the animals graze together during the day but are separated at night, since the goats prefer warmth, the sheep fresh air.

[33] Like the righteous, the sheep stand on the right. The narrator sees in them the more valuable animals, or he may be thinking of their white color in contrast to the black color of the goats, or of the identification of the people of God with a flock of sheep (2 Sam. 24:17; Ps. 77:20; Isa. 63:11; Jer. 13:20; Ezek. 34:2 ff.; etc.; in Hebrew there is no clear distinction between sheep and goats).

The earliest Christians rarely referred to Jesus as King (see above). The term is conceivable on the basis of the inscription on the cross (Mark 15:26) and the role which this title played at the hearing before Pilate (Mark 15:2); it was probably eschewed, however, on account of its political significance. Apart from Matthew 21:5 (cf. Luke 19:38), it is found only in John 1:49 (cf. 6:15; 18:37) and in Revelation 17:14; 19:16 (cf. 15:3), where it refers to the eschatological Christ. The statement that the Kingdom of God has been prepared since the creation of the world underlines the certainty of the promise; the idea that something we expect to be fulfilled at some future time is already present with God is typically Jewish.

[35-36] The righteous are promised their reward on account of certain acts of charity, the ones listed of course being only examples. The end of verse 35 reads literally "you herded me"; but in Aramaic and in the Septuagint this word means "receive with hospitality." Only against this background does the statement make sense. It is important to note that two acts of charity highly regarded by the rabbis, lament for the dead and their burial, are not mentioned; visiting of prisoners takes their place. Jesus is not worried about "acts of charity" toward the dead, but with people who need help. [37-39] Totally unparalleled, however, is the ignorance of the righteous about what good works they have done for the King. The man vindicated is the one who knows of no good works he could claim to his credit. Something of this surprise has already appeared in 7:21-23; 20:8-9, 16.

[40] Only the response of the Judge reveals to them that they encountered him in that unprepossessing man, exposed to danger, oppressed, at his wits' end—in all the many insignificant people they can no longer remember. Christ's identification with human beings, especially the poor, needy, and persecuted, is implied in 10:40-42 and also in Acts 9:4; 22:7; 26:14: anyone who persecutes Jesus' disciples persecutes Jesus himself. What is unusual in this passage is that the promise is spoken to all the poor, not just Christian missionaries. This does not mean that Christ simply merges into his disciples or into the poor of this world. Even when identified with them he remains their Lord, who encounters them as Judge. We are therefore dealing neither with mysticism, in which the line between God and man is blurred, nor with Stoic identification of God with all mankind, but with an act

of charity to a particular individual who may not be appealing or sympathetic. The text reads literally "a single one of these"; but Hebrew makes no distinction between the number "one" and the pronoun "one" (i.e., anyone at all). The second meaning is more likely. The word "these," which is also in fact superfluous, might also be an echo of Semitic idiom.

[41] The other group is condemned to eternal fire (see the discussion of 5:22). Does the added phrase "for the Devil and his angels" mean, as it does in Revelation 19:20-21; 20:9-10, that they alone remain there eternally, while those who are condemned to the fire are annihilated there (cf. however Matt. 25:46 and the discussion of 10:28)? Only the judgment is recorded, not its execution or the torments of hell. [42-44] The condemned, too, are totally surprised; they are not aware they have done anything wrong. Perhaps it is even legitimate to observe that the former speak merely of "coming to" him, whereas the latter speak in more "religious" terms of "serving" him. [45] They, too, are told that Jesus came to them in the "least." They are condemned not for doing anything wicked but for having failed to do good. [46] The concluding verse underlines the separation once more, with an echo of Daniel 12:2. Even if "eternal punishment" could be understood as meaning an eternally irrevocable decree of annihilation, the parallel phrase "eternal life" makes eternal torment the more likely meaning. It is possible that the original parable spoke only of annihilation, and Matthew added the notion of torment.

It is clear that those who stand at the bar of the Last Judgment are not merely Christians but all mankind. But what is the criterion by which they will be judged? Are the "least of these brothers of mine" Jesus' messengers? The similarity to the "least" in 10:42 and 18:6-14 is striking, and the expression "one of these" is the same in both places. Matthew states, furthermore, that Jesus' disciples are his brothers (12:49; 28:10). This could also explain the visiting of prisoners, which goes beyond Jewish parallels: those imprisoned for their preaching are visited by the newly converted members of the community (2 Tim. 1:16-17, etc.); tribulations like those cited here are also listed in 2 Corinthians 11:23, 27, 30, where Paul's missionary labors are depicted. In this case, men's "yes" or "no" to the worldwide preaching of these messengers, as displayed in their actual treatment of them, would be the criterion for vindication or condemnation at the Judgment. This interpretation is quite possible.

Against it one may say that Matthew (as well as Mark 9:42 and Luke 17:2) always uses the phrase "these little ones" for the disciples, never any variant; why then would he use another expression here? Further, in 10:14 Matthew is primarily concerned with the *words* to be spoken by Jesus' messengers, not with the kind of reception they meet (that is the concern of Luke—see 9:4-5; 10:7-12). Above all, would Matthew have taken the acts of charity crucial for the Judgment and confined them to those done for disciples—after having, in the commandment to love one's enemies, specifically condemned such distinctions (5:43-48)? Elitism is the possible meaning here; but more likely Matthew construes the words of the Judge in a broader sense.

Are we then to exercise human sympathy and compassion merely because Jesus himself awaits us in everyone who is poor, homeless, alone? That reduces, in effect, to an ethics of reward and punishment. Now Matthew does place great emphasis on seeing that God's will is not merely heard but in fact done (cf. 9:13 and 12:7). But he stresses with equal emphasis that the self-congratulatory man who thinks he has done all that is required does not do God's will (20:11-12). Conversely, the truly obedient man does not make his good deeds a matter of record (6:3)—not before God (6:7), not even (and this is most striking) before himself (25:37-39). What Jesus' parable is saying is that men must love one another not because he tells them to with threats and promises—not from a regard for themselves, however subconscious—but with a spontaneous sympathy that regards only the other person's good. But how can men love those they find unlovable? Matthew is of the opinion that the only way one can learn to fulfill the law of love is from Jesus (see §3 of the Retrospect). Only the man who has received forgiveness—from Jesus (9:2, 9-10, 13; 11:28-30) or from any man (18:27: the "greatest of these" are also Jesus)—learns to forgive (18:28-35), and to encounter others with compassion (9:2-8, 35-36a). But since Jesus forgives and loves *all* those willing to accept his love (21:15, 31; 9:9, 27-30; 11:25-30, etc.), everyone can love his fellow man.

The parable in 20:1-16 maintains contrary to righteousness based on works that God's reward does not depend on the measure of a man's deeds, but remains a free gift; our section emphasizes in the face of a merely intellectual or emotional "faith" that only acts of love will carry weight before the bar of God's Judgment. So much stress is placed on this notion that the assumption of a spoken message is not even mentioned. One can say that, as in the case of the criminal on his cross (Luke 23:42-43), there can be a genuine, if incomplete, faith that consists only of a trusting cry for help; but there can also be a genuine, if incomplete, faith that consists only of carrying out God's will toward the poor and lowly; the man who has such faith worships God and enriches himself though he intends neither. The extent to which all acts of charity display true compassion will not be revealed to all until the Last Judgment.

These (20:1-6 and 25:31-46) are the two limiting statements of the New Testament, which protect us against righteousness through works on the one hand and righteousness through intellectualized theology on the other; they make it untenable to boast of one's deeds and sneer at "plaster saints" and the practice of silence and prayer, or, on the other hand, to despise "secular" charity that does not include a confession of faith. In either direction the disciple of Jesus must never let anxiety about his own perfection, the development of his own personality, get the upper hand; what matters is the life he lives for others. The very rigor of the Judgment, which calls every man's conduct into question, serves to magnify God's grace and mercy. The man who knows this can only turn to the one who promises rest to the burdened and riches to the poor (11:25 ff.; 5:3 ff., 21-48).

The Return of Christ. Matthew places the three parables in 24:45–25:30, and the revelation discourse in 25:31-36, emphatically in the context of the second coming ("parousia") of Jesus (Matt. 24:30-31). A word for "parousia" does not occur in Judaism; it is peculiarly Greek. Strictly speaking it means "presence"; then it comes to mean the sudden reality of presence: "coming," "arrival." In this sense it appears in papyri that speak of the visitation of a ruler. In the New Testament, the word makes its first appearance in Paul; it occurs four times in Matthew 24, as well as James 5:7-8; 2 Peter 1:16; 3:4,

12; 1 John 2:28. It always designates Jesus' eschatological coming, never his birth. The usual translations, "return" or "second coming," are inaccurate; for the New Testament, there is only one "coming" of Jesus: his coming at the end of the world.

Jesus undoubtedly expected a final irruption of the Kingdom of God and a Last Judgment. He submitted to the baptism of John, and although he parted company with John over the question of fasting (see the introductory comments on Mark 2:18-22), he never disputed John's message, which preached the imminence of the eschaton and the coming of the Judge, even though he differs from John in also seeing the irruption of God's Kingdom into the lives of men as happening now (cf. the excursus on Mark 1:15). Nevertheless, though he believed in a future (as well as present) eschaton, it is hardly likely that Jesus ever spoke of his own eschatological appearance. Mark 13:24-27 is borrowed from the Greek translation of the Old Testament, and at least the last verse is not found in its present form in the Hebrew Bible. These words, as they now stand, were therefore certainly not spoken by Jesus. Mark 8:38 must of course be taken into consideration—in it Jesus associates Judgment with a return on his part (cf. the concluding section of the excursus on the Son of Man at Mark 8:27-33). But the passage most likely to record a genuine saying of Jesus is Mark 14:62, and it too may originally have referred to Jesus' exaltation to the divine realm rather than his return to earth. We have observed that Matthew 25:14-30 and 31-46 in their original form probably spoke of God's Judgment, not the coming of Jesus. In the vast majority of the parables or sayings that speak of God's future Judgment, there is no reference to the coming of Jesus (Mark 2:18-22; 3:28-30; 4:1-9; 8:35-37; 9:42-48; 10:17-31; Matt. 5:21-22; 6:1-18; 7:1-5, 24, 27; 8:11-12; 10:15; 11:20-24; 12:42; 13:24-30 [vs. 41 differs], 41-50; 18:18, 23-35; 20:1-16; 22:1-14; Luke 12:16-21, 57-59; 13:1-9; 15:1–16:9, 19-31; 18:9-14).

In itself the notion of the return to earth of someone exalted to God's presence is not unusual in this period (Mark 9:11-12; cf. 6:14-16; the Qumran sect may also have expected their Teacher to return at the end of time [CD vi. 10-11]). But nothing is ever said of any second coming on the part of Jesus, only of his coming. Further, the relatively rare references to his coming are nowhere associated with the prophecies of his death and resurrection. Nevertheless when the community learned to speak of Jesus' coming to judge the world, it did not say anything fundamentally different from what Jesus had already said. Jesus simply assumes as a matter of course that God will judge the world according to the norms defined by Jesus' preaching and general conduct. In Jesus God becomes real for man. This simply means that the God whom men will encounter at the Last Judgment will have the lineaments of Jesus. Thus Jesus himself may well have made the statement that when God comes to judge the world Jesus will be God's witness, intervening for or against each individual and thus determining the verdict (Mark 8:38; see the excursus on the Son of Man at Mark 8:27-33). The crucial point is whether men will let Jesus open their eyes to God so that their lives may be ruled by him. If their lives are not so ruled, they themselves will judge them, finally, as not worth living; if they are so ruled, their owners will find them eminently worthwhile. Thus Jesus expresses, and lives, the standard by which all in the end judge themselves—whence the idea that in the final judgment it is Jesus who judges men.

We can see as early as Paul how the expectation of God's coming to judge the world turns into the expectation that Jesus will come to judge the world (Rom. 14:10/2 Cor. 5:10; both notions occur together in 1 Cor. 4:4-5). Whoever takes seriously the idea that in Jesus God himself encounters men can no longer simply think of two distinct persons standing side by side like two individual human beings; he understands that God is one with Jesus. This is probably also what John means when he speaks of the unity of God and the Word (1:1), the Father and the Son (10:30), or what Paul means when he says that at the end Jesus Christ will subordinate himself totally to God, that God may be "all in all" (1 Cor. 15:28). According to Paul and John, then, it is only for the time that sinful man separates himself from God that God steps outside himself, so to speak, to encounter man, who is alienated from him. The statement that the Son will one day subordinate himself totally to God maintains the truth that in Jesus we encounter none other than God. The other statement, that he is sent as Savior and Judge, maintains the truth that God always encounters man as something as yet unknown; he never simply merges into the experience of love or responsibility (cf. the excursus on Father, Son, and Holy Spirit at Matt. 28:19).

VI

THE PASSION AND RESURRECTION OF
JESUS
26:1–28:20

In the Passion narrative, too, Matthew basically follows Mark. But we can also observe an oral tradition, in the main running parallel to Mark but occasionally diverging and supplanting the Markan account. We find minor points of agreement with Luke (Matt. 26:68 = Luke 22:64; Matt. 27:58-59 = Luke 23:52-53; Matt. 28:8 = Luke 24:9; and compare the account of Judas' fate in Matt. 27:3-10 with Acts 1:16-20). But above all, we find substantial points of agreement with John (Matt. 26:2, 3 = John 12:1; 11:53; Matt. 26:7-8 = John 12:3-5; Matt. 26:25 = John 13:27; Matt. 26:52 = John 18:11; Matt. 27:29 = John 19:2; Matt. 27:37 = John 19:19; Matt. 27:57 = John 19:38; Matt. 28:9 = John 20:19). There are also interpolations. Some can be traced back to the community's study of the Old Testament; this applies particularly to the stories about Judas (Matt. 26:15; 27:3-10). Others, like the episode of the guards at the tomb, betray subsequent development or attempts to meet Jewish attacks on the credibility of the resurrection; still, however, they contain a relatively early form of the Passion narrative, with no hint of any anointing by the women (as also in John 20:1; see the introductory comments on Matt. 28:1-4). Other material is early, probably earlier and more trustworthy than the Markan version: the name Jesus Barabbas (27:16-17?), the scarlet robe (27:28), the form of the Eli/Elijah saying (27:47), and the saying about the Temple (26:61). Everywhere, finally, we can observe the influence of the Markan text, even when the two versions do not parallel each other (see the discussion of 27:15, 32, 50, 55, 60).

Here, too, we can see Matthew's theological purpose. Jesus' mastery of the situation is underlined: his saying is fulfilled (26:2; cf. 27:63; 28:6; and the discussion of 26:24); by his own free will he does

God's will and goes to his Passion (26:42; cf. the discussion of 26:1-2, 50). In an almost Johannine way he knows that his time is come (26:18; cf. the discussion of 26:10). The title "Christ" already appears in 27:17, 22; contrariwise, it is omitted in 27:42, but probably because Matthew still knows that "Christ" and "king" mean the same thing. The resurrection is no longer felt to be an insoluble mystery; it is even suggested before it takes place (27:52-53). The Passion leads to the enthronement of Christ as Lord of the universe (cf. the discussion of 26:64, 12, 18, 50; 27:53); there are already hints of the Johannine perspective (John 3:14-15; 12:28, 32; etc.; also Luke 9:51).

Accordingly, the contrast between Jesus and Jesus Barabbas is developed more extensively, to emphasize the notion of vicarious suffering (Matt. 27:15-23). The Passion of Jesus convulses the whole earth and causes the dead to rise, thus marking the end of this world and the beginning of God's new world. This event is closely connected with the rending of the Temple curtain, which represents the end of the Jewish cult (27:51-53). For Matthew, then, the Passion also marks the decisive split with Judaism. Up to this point the masses of the common people, in contrast to the official authorities, have followed Jesus willingly; now they go over to the side of their leaders and accept responsibility for putting Jesus to death (27:24-25). Doubts about the resurrection of Jesus, which in Matthew's opinion is a matter of public knowledge, are merely the result of unwillingness to believe (28:11-15).

Finally, the Passion is depicted as the way of the righteous sufferer; not only does it direct the way Jesus' disciples are to go, it also makes it possible for them to follow him (cf. the discussion of 26:42, 52-54; 27:43). The Passion narrative, and with it the Gospel, concludes with the enthronement of Jesus as Lord of the universe and his commission to his disciples to call all peoples to obedience to the commandments of Jesus (28:18-20). None of this is worked out in theological terms; the reticence, indeed the coldness of the Passion narrative is maintained. The bare events, recounted in the most economical terms, must carry Matthew's message. Narrative account and gospel message are still for the most part identical.

The Plot against Jesus (26:1-5)
Cf. Mark 14:1-2; Luke 22:1-12

¹And it happened, when Jesus had finished teaching all these things, that he said to his disciples, ²"In two days, as you know, it will be the Feast of Passover, and the Son of Man will be handed over to be crucified." ³Then the chief priests and the elders of the people met together in the palace of Caiaphas, the High Priest, ⁴and made plans to arrest Jesus secretly and put him to death. ⁵"We must not do it during the feast," they said, "or the people will riot."

The brief statement in Mark 14:1-2 has been greatly expanded. Matthew wants to point out what is uppermost at the very outset of the Passion narrative. [1] The formula that regularly concludes all the great discourses (see the discussion of 7:28) is expanded to say that Jesus had finished teaching "all" these things. Nor is anything said about his setting forth once more. The time of teaching, and thus of decision for or against him, is past. What follows is the time of Jesus' Passion; what takes place in it is understood only by his disciples, to whom he addresses the next saying. [2] The reference to "unleavened bread" (Mark 14:1) is omitted (cf. the introductory comments on Matt. 15:1-20); but see 26:17. Above all, what was nothing more than a date in Mark is put by Matthew into the mouth of Jesus himself, thus giving it greater significance (cf. the discussion of 26:27).

On the Passover itself the Son of Man is handed over to be crucified. To whom he is to be handed over is not specified; it is possible that Matthew is already thinking of Jesus' death as the sacrifice of the Passover lamb. This notion is certainly attested in Paul (1 Cor. 5:7) and very likely also in John (19:36; cf. Exod. 12:46; Num. 9:12 and John 1:29, 36; also the discussion of Mark 15:25, 42 and the introductory comments on Mark 14:12-16). The full solemnity of the title "Son of Man," in association with the traditional terminology of sacrifice (Rom. 4:25, in an early formula; 1 Cor. 11:23; Mark 9:31; 14:41; Luke 9:44; 24:7; Acts 21:11) and the Matthaean reference to the crucifixion (see the discussion of Matt. 20:19) seeks to stress that Jesus himself sets the entire process of the Passion in motion by what he says.

[3] The close relationship between the words of Jesus and the meeting of the authorities is underlined by the Matthaean "then." In contrast to Mark, Matthew mentions the elders of the people (although the genitive is lacking in one ancient manuscript), not the teachers of the Law; perhaps he is already laying the groundwork for the *people's* acceptance of responsibility for Jesus' death (27:25).

[4] Now, however, the people are still on Jesus' side, so that the authorities are even afraid that a riot might ensue (=Mark 14:2). [5] Matthew goes beyond Mark in knowing the name of Caiaphas (also in 26:57=John 18:13). John 11:49 not only agrees with Matthew that Caiaphas was chief priest, but also in saying that an actual assembly was held by the authorities to reach a decision, although in John it takes place before Jesus' entry into Jerusalem. The palace of the High Priest, which is also mentioned later (26:58), appears here already as the location of the assembly.

Jesus Anointed at Bethany (26:6-13)
Cf. Mark 14:3-9; Luke 7:36-50

⁶But while Jesus was in Bethany, at the house of Simon the leper, ⁷a woman came to him with an alabaster jar filled with expensive myrrh, which she poured on Jesus' head while he was sitting at table. ⁸The disciples saw this and became angry. "Why all this waste?" they asked. ⁹"This could have been sold for a large amount and the money given to the poor." ¹⁰Jesus knew what they were saying and said to them, "Why are you bothering this woman? It is a fine and beautiful thing that she has done for me. ¹¹You will always have poor people with you, but I will not be with you always. ¹²What she did was to pour this myrrh on my body to get me ready for burial. ¹³Amen, I tell you, wherever this gospel is preached, all over the world, what she has done will be told in memory of her."

[7] The story of the anointing is somewhat abbreviated. We are not told that Jesus is sitting at table until verse 7, because in Greek the accumulation of circumstantial phrases in Mark 14:3 is grammatically almost impossible. Instead we find the typical statement that the woman "came to" him (see the discussion of 8:2). The Greek word

translated "expensive" is not the same one used in Mark 14:3. John 12:3 uses both words together. **[8]** According to Matthew it is the disciples who are upset, although they do not let fly at the woman as "some" do in Mark 14:4-5; in John 12:4-5 it is Judas. **[10]** Jesus replies to what the disciples are saying among themselves (as Mark 14:4 states); his omniscience is stressed (cf. the discussion of Matt. 9:4). The difficult statement "She did what she could" (Mark 14:8) is left out. **[12]** Elsewhere the dialogue between Jesus and his disciples is abbreviated (vss. 8-9, 10-11); in verse 12 it is somewhat expanded. This is the focal point. The anointing of a dead body can be understood as a typically Jewish "good deed" (vs. 10; but cf. the discussion of 25:35-36); Matthew may already be thinking of it as the anointing of the King of the universe (see the introductory comments on chapters 26–28). Once again Mark's reference to the gospel or good news is expanded in typically Matthaean fashion (cf. the excursus on 7:-13-23 [§3]).

Judas Agrees to Betray Jesus (26:14-16)
Cf. Mark 14:10-11; Luke 22:3-6

¹⁴Then one of the Twelve—the one named Judas Iscariot—went to the chief priests ¹⁵and said, "What will you give me if I hand Jesus over to you?" "But they offered" him "thirty" silver coins. ¹⁶And from then on Judas was looking for a good chance to betray Jesus.
(Vs. 15—Zech. 11:12.)

[14] The woman who anoints Jesus is the only one who understands what is taking place. The contrast between her actions and the actions of Judas and the authorities is further heightened. Verse 3 placed special emphasis on what she did; here Judas' betrayal, introduced by the typically Matthaean "then he went," is placed immediately after the anointing. **[15]** Above all, Judas is greedy, as he is depicted in John 12:6; he is out to "sell" Jesus (in contrast to Mark 14:11). What Mark narrates in indirect discourse has been turned into direct discourse (cf. Matt. 14:1-2 and the discussion of 26:27). The precise sum is mentioned; the community found it in their Bible, which, as they thought, had described the life of Jesus before the event, and specifically in a passage from the prophet whose influence has already been felt on the narrative in 21:4-5 (Zech. 11:12; cf. the discussion of Matt. 27:3-10). Some manuscripts, not especially good, read "staters" or "silver staters" rather than "silver coins"; it is hard to determine whether this was the original reading or represents a later assimilation of our passage to the text of Zechariah. In any case it is a ridiculously small sum. According to Exodus 21:32, it is the amount a man must pay if his ox has killed a slave belonging to another man; at the time of Jesus, the sum was worth only about a tenth as much. In addition, the verb can mean either "pay" (as it probably does in Zech. 11:12) or merely "offer" (as it probably does here). [16] The phrase "from then on" further underlines the fact that the prospect of payment is the actual motive behind Judas' treachery.

Preparations for the Last Supper (26:17-20)
Cf. Mark 14:12-17; Luke 22:7-13

¹⁷On the first day of the Feast of Unleavened Bread the disciples came to Jesus and asked him, "Where do you want us to get the Passover lamb ready for you to eat?" ¹⁸"Go to a certain man in the city," he said to them, "and tell him: 'The Master says, My hour is near; I wish to celebrate the Passover at your house with my disciples.' " ¹⁹The disciples did as Jesus had told them and prepared the Passover meal. ²⁰When it was evening, Jesus and the twelve disciples sat down to eat.

[18] The abbreviation of the Markan account makes a striking difference in its meaning. The miracle of Jesus' prophetic knowledge and its literal fulfillment are eliminated. The disciples are sent to "a certain man" (a similar idiom occurs in Ruth 4:1; 1 Sam. 21:3; 2 Kings 6:8), someone known to them. [19] Instead of the statement that they found everything just as Jesus had said, we now read that they obediently carried out all Jesus' commands (cf. the discussion of 1:24; 21:6). [17] This is in line with the way the disciples "come to" Jesus deferentially at the very outset (see the discussion of 8:2), expressly stating that they want to get the Passover lamb ready for him ("for you").

[18] The authoritative "The Master says" is borrowed from Mark; it is followed, however, by a new statement: "My hour is near" (cf. Rev. 1:3; 22:10). The Greek word means "the appointed time" (i.e., appointed by God); thus Jesus' death and resurrection are interpreted as a single eschatological event, precisely determined in advance by God. The expression "celebrate the Passover" comes from the Old Testament (Josh. 5:10, etc.); for Matthew, however, it no longer refers to the Jewish Passover, but rather to the celebration already fixed in God's plan, the first Paschal feast of the New Covenant. [20] Mark 14:17 says that two disciples are sent on ahead, and that Jesus then comes "with the Twelve"; this inconsistency is eliminated; now we read only that Jesus was at table "with the twelve," all of whom were presumably sent on ahead (see the discussion of 24:1, 3).

Identification of the Traitor (26:21-25)
Cf. Mark 14:18-21; Luke 22:14, 21-23

[21]And while they ate, Jesus said, "Amen I tell you, one of you will betray me." [22]The disciples became very upset and began to ask him, one after the other, "Surely you don't mean me, Lord?" [23]Jesus answered, "One who dips his bread in the dish with me will betray me. [24]The Son of Man will die as it is written; but how terrible it will be for that man who will betray the Son of Man! It would have been better for that man if he had never been born." [25]But Judas, who betrayed him, spoke up. "Surely you don't mean me, Rabbi?" he asked. Jesus answered, "So you say."

[22, 25] The other disciples address Jesus as "Lord"; according to Matthew, Judas says only "Rabbi" (25, 49), like those who do not believe. In Matthew's own time this probably still distinguished Christians from sympathetic but non-Christian Jews. [23] In Mark we read only that one of those who eats from the same dish as Jesus will betray him; Matthew speaks of someone who has just dipped his hand in the dish. This is a more specific reference to Judas; in John 13:26-27, where Jesus himself dips the morsel and gives it to Judas, the reference is unambiguous. Both Matthew and John also refer to Judas as "the one who betrayed him" or "the one who was to betray him" (here and

27:3; John 6:71; 12:4). The agency of Jesus in his own doom is already being stressed by Matthew, albeit not so clearly as by John. With his own mouth, so to speak, Jesus sets in motion the preordained course of events; **[24]** and the threat borrowed from Mark (9:42) is lent even greater weight because it was already pronounced in similar terms in 18:6-7 as a warning. Verse 25 goes beyond anything Mark says, clearly and specifically referring to Judas as the one who betrayed Jesus.

The Promises of the Last Supper (26:26-29)
Cf. Mark 14:22-25; Luke 22:15-20; 1 Corinthians 11:23-25

²⁶But while they were eating, Jesus took bread, pronounced the blessing, broke it, and gave it to his disciples. "Take and eat it," he said; "this is my body." ²⁷Then he took the cup, gave thanks, and gave it to them. "Drink it, all of you," he said; ²⁸"for this then is my 'blood of the covenant,' which is poured out for many for the forgiveness of sins. ²⁹I tell you, I will never again drink of this fruit of the vine until that day when I drink it anew with you in my Father's Kingdom." (Vs. 28—Exod. 24:8; Zech. 9:11; Jer. 31:31 ff.)

[26] After the interpolation of verse 25, Jesus is no longer the sole speaker; therefore "Jesus" has to be inserted as the subject here. The original Words of Institution have been somewhat expanded in liturgical use. **[27]** Alongside "take" from Mark, we now find "eat," a precise parallel to the command to "drink" with reference to the cup. These were probably the words used by the minister who distributed bread and wine to his brethren in Matthew's community, inviting the participants forward to eat and drink.

The second command is an interesting example of how a new saying of Jesus comes into being. Up to the point where "they drank" is changed to "drink" (both in the same tense in Greek), the sentence is identical with Mark 14:23; but a narrative statement has been transformed into a saying of Jesus (likewise in 26:2, 39, 42; the same thing happens with other speakers in 26:15, 66; 27:21). Here the change took place under the influence of the Eucharistic celebration, in which the minister distributing the bread and wine stands facing the recipient and addresses him. Eating and drinking are thus turned into an obedient discharging of Jesus' command, [28] on the basis of a newly inserted "then" before the reference to the blood of the covenant.

The added phrase "for the forgiveness of sins" was omitted by Matthew in his account of John's baptism (Mark 1:4); in the story of the paralytic, however, he speaks not only of Jesus' authority to forgive sins, but also that of the community (Matt. 9:8). The word translated "for" (as likewise in 1 Pet. 3:18; 1 John 2:2; Heb. 5:3; 13:11) has been assimilated in Greek to the wording of Isaiah 53:4, a passage that speaks of the Servant of God who suffers for our sins. In Isaiah 42:6; 49:7-8 the Servant of God himself is referred to as God's "covenant" with his people, and according to Jeremiah 31:34 the forgiveness of sins is part of the "new covenant." Matthew thus looks upon the death of Jesus as the basis for the forgiveness of sins, albeit in such a way that the forgiveness is exercised by the community (18:18 as well as 9:8) and that only the man who forgives others can receive forgiveness (see the discussion of 6:14-15 and 18:35).

Matthew thus probably sees Jesus going to his death less as an atoning sacrifice to God's obduracy—although this idea does appear in 20:28 and 26:28—than as a pioneer, who opens the way of a new life to those who follow him (cf. the use of "like" in 20:28; also section 1 of the Retrospect). [29] Looking forward to the eschaton, Jesus speaks not only of the Kingdom of God (Mark 14:25) as the Kingdom of "my Father," but also of drinking "with you." Matthew thus emphasizes the table fellowship between Jesus and his disciples at the end of time; the only other passage that so stresses this notion is Luke 22:30. When Matthew goes on to have Jesus say that he will "never again" drink of "this" wine, he may mean that Jesus is already renouncing the festive cup, consciously taking the first step toward his death.

Jesus Predicts Peter's Denial (26:30-35)
Cf. Mark 14:26-31; Luke 22:39, 31-34

[30]And when they had sung a hymn, they went out to the Mount of Olives. [31]Then Jesus said to them, "This very night all of you will

fall away because of me; for it is written, 'I will slay the shepherd and the sheep of the flock will be scattered.' ³²But after I am raised to life I will go to Galilee ahead of you." ³³But Peter spoke up and said to Jesus, "Even though all the rest fall away because of you, I will never fall away!" ³⁴Jesus said to Peter, "Amen, I tell you, this very night, before the rooster crows, you will deny me three times." ³⁵Peter answered, "Even if I have to die with you, I will never deny you!" And all the disciples said the same thing.

(Vs. 31—Zech. 13:7.)

[31] In the prediction of Peter's denial, Matthew emphasizes the bond between Jesus and the disciples more than Mark does, possibly through the addition of the "flock" in the quotation from Zechariah, but especially through the phrase "because of me," [33] with its corresponding "because of you" in Peter's reply. In verse 35, too, the phrase "with you" is expressed more emphatically than in Mark 14:31. Peter's self-confidence is likewise underlined by the addition of "I will never fall away." Coming as it does after the appointment of Peter as the foundation-stone of the community, which even death cannot overcome (Matt. 16:18), Jesus' prediction is so devastating that the Scriptural citation showing that such things must come may be felt as a kind of excuse. [34] As in verses 74-75, Jesus' prediction speaks of the rooster's crowing only once, not twice as in Mark.

Jesus' Exemplary Agony (26:36-46)
Cf. Mark 14:32-42; Luke 22:40-46

³⁶Then Jesus went with his disciples to a place called Gethsemane, and he said to them, "Sit here while I go over there and pray." ³⁷He took with him Peter, and Zebedee's two sons. Grief and anguish came over him, ³⁸and he said to them, " 'My soul is saddened to the point of death; stay here and watch with me.' " ³⁹He went a little farther on, threw himself face down on the ground, and prayed, "My Father, if it is possible, let this cup pass me by; but not what I want, but what you want." ⁴⁰Then he returned to the three disciples and found them

asleep; and he said to Peter, "How is it that you three were not able to watch with me for one hour? ⁴¹Keep watch, and pray so that you will not fall into temptation. The spirit is willing, but the flesh is weak." ⁴²Again a second time Jesus went away and prayed, "My Father, if it is impossible for this to pass me by without my drinking it, your will be done." ⁴³He returned once more and found the disciples asleep; they could not keep their eyes open. ⁴⁴Again Jesus left them, went away, and prayed the third time, saying the same words. ⁴⁵Then he returned to the disciples and said, "Sleep on and rest. Behold, the hour has come, and the Son of Man is handed over into the hands of sinners. ⁴⁶Get up, let us go. Behold, the man who will betray me is near."

(Vs. 38—Ps. 42:6, 11; Jonah 4:9.)

[36, 38, 40] Once again the bond between Jesus and his disciples is underlined by talk of Jesus' going "with them" and the twice repeated "with me" (cf. "to the disciples," in vss. 40 and 45). [37] The statement that Jesus was beset with "grief" is weaker than the "distress" of Mark 14:33; the change is due to assimilation [38] to the saying in Psalm 42. [39] To "throw oneself face down upon the ground" (literally "upon one's face") is a Biblical idiom (e.g., Gen. 17:3, 17). The first prayer represents a coalescence of the two Markan sayings about the hour passing and the cup being borne past (as the Greek reads literally). The Aramaic term "Abba" is omitted; it had probably fallen into disuse in the Matthaean community, in contrast to the Pauline community (Rom. 8:15; Gal. 4:6; see the discussion of Mark 14:36). [40] In Mark 14:37, Jesus rebukes Peter by asking, "Simon, are you sleeping?" Here the question is omitted, and the following sentence is rephrased in the plural, being addressed to all three disciples rather than to Peter alone. [41] The disciples are called on to keep watch; for Matthew, the phrase takes on special gravity from the extended sense emphasized in 24:42; 25:13.

[42] The second prayer is a new composition. Unlike the first, it begins at once with submission to God's will, and leads up to the third petition of the Lord's Prayer, which is cited verbatim (6:10). Thus Jesus' withstanding of temptation becomes the prototype and basis for

all praying in the community. In the Greek, "this" can refer to the cup, but the expression is probably kept general so that it can stand for everything God imposes on men. **[43]** The saying about the disciples' incomprehension (Mark 14:40) is omitted; it is strikingly reminiscent of the saying about Peter in the story of the Transfiguration, which is also omitted (Mark 9:6; cf. also the discussion of Matt. 13:16-17). **[44]** Matthew instead recounts a third episode of prayer which can only be inferred in Mark, thus smoothing out the narrative. "The same words" spoken this time by Jesus, as in the second prayer in Mark 14:39, are not the plea to be saved from death but the submission to God's will. **[45]** The word "behold" (see the discussion of 8:2) further emphasizes this readiness on the part of Jesus, which shows that he has overcome temptation. **[46]** The inversion of the Markan word order ("Near is the man who will betray me") corresponds to the statement "Near is the Kingdom of heaven" (3:2; 4:17; 10:7), and is probably intentional.

Thus Matthew describes how Jesus, in the course of praying, achieves a submission to God's will, at the same time seeking the companionship of his disciples because he wants to help them follow in his footsteps, inculcating in them the petition of the Lord's Prayer found only in this Gospel—"your will be done."

The Arrest of Jesus (26:47-56)
Cf. Mark 14:43-52; Luke 22:47-53

⁴⁷And while he was still speaking, behold, there came Judas, one of the Twelve, and with him a large crowd carrying swords and clubs, sent by the chief priests and elders of the people. ⁴⁸The traitor had given the crowd a signal: "The man I kiss is the one you want. Arrest him!" ⁴⁹When Judas arrived he went straight to Jesus, and said, "Hail, Rabbi," and kissed him. ⁵⁰Jesus answered, "My friend, what you are here for, let it take place." Then they came up, arrested Jesus, and held him tight. ⁵¹And behold, one of those who were with Jesus reached out his hand, drew his sword, and struck at the High Priest's slave, cutting off his ear. ⁵²Then Jesus said to him, "Put your sword back in its place, for all who take the sword will die by the sword. ⁵³Don't you know that I could call on my Father for help and at once

he would send me more than twelve legions of angels? ⁵⁴But in that case, how could the Scriptures come true that say it must happen in this way?" ⁵⁵At the same hour Jesus spoke to the crowd, "Did you have to come with swords and clubs to capture me, as though I were an outlaw? Every day I sat down and taught in the Temple, and you did not arrest me. ⁵⁶But all this has happened to make come true what the prophets wrote in the Scriptures." Then all the disciples left him and ran away.

[47] The narrative follows Mark. The reintroduction of Judas, which suggests that the story was once told outside the context of verses 14 and 25, is borrowed from Mark. Once more the elders are referred to as the elders "of the people," and the teachers of the Law are omitted (see the discussion of 26:3). [49] When Judas accosts Jesus, Matthew adds the usual form of salutation in Greek (as he does also in 28:9). [50] Jesus' response, in the form of a question, is new. It is Jesus who instigates the action. Mark may have omitted this saying on account of its obscurity, while it continued to be preserved by oral tradition. It can be translated: "Is that what you are here for?" More probably we are dealing with an elliptical idiom (there are certain parallels for such an idiom) which means: "What you are here for, let it take place." Taken in this sense, it would express Jesus' readiness to meet the fate that stands before him; it would almost amount to a command setting the succeeding course of events in motion.

[51] The introductory formula "and behold" (see the discussion of 8:2) makes a special point of the sword episode. "Reaching out one's hand" is a Biblical idiom (Gen. 22:10; Judg. 3:21; 15:15; 1 Sam. 17:49). It is not just anyone who sets out to defend his master, but a disciple of Jesus (cf. also 26:2). [52] Above all, Matthew inserts a fundamental saying of Jesus, introduced, as so often in his Gospel, by "then." It commands Peter to put his sword back in its sheath (as in John 18:11). It is certainly incorrect to follow Luther in reading into this verse an approval of taking up the sword. On the contrary, Jesus maintains his own position, thus becoming the prototype for his followers, who renounce violence and prefer to suffer injustice (5:39). Reaching for the sword cannot really protect them, but only evoke a

violent response to which they will ultimately fall victim. At the same time, Jesus is not faking or swaggering in his renunciation of force. He actually commands a power that could put a final end to all other power; but this he renounces (cf. 4:1-11).

[54] This is based on a Scriptural reference to the effect that "it must happen this way." Revelation 1:1 uses the same formula to describe the eschatological events that must take place according to God's will. Thus Jesus' Passion takes its place among those events which must come to pass according to God's plan in order that his Kingdom may be consummated. [55] The next verse is introduced by a new beginning formula—"at the same hour"—which acts as a kind of seam between the interpolation and the Markan text, to which Matthew now returns. Jesus' authority to teach is emphasized by his sitting, since, as Matthew is well aware, Jewish teachers sit while giving instruction. [56] Matthew again underlines Mark's reference to Scripture by adding a formula that recalls his several quotations (see the excursus on 1:18-25). As is often the case, he goes on to say that we are dealing with prophetic Scriptures. As Law the Scriptures are still in force; but to the extent that they are prophetic, they have found their fulfillment in Jesus. The strange episode of the young man who runs away naked (Mark 14:51-52) is omitted. Instead, Matthew emphasizes that all those who deserted Jesus and fled were "disciples."

Matthew's interpolation has turned the story of Jesus' arrest into a fundamental statement about the use of force (see the excursus following 7:29, a. 2). Fulfilling the Sermon on the Mount, Jesus backs up his teaching by the actual deeds of his Passion. This lays the foundation for real obedience: the conduct of man derives from that of Jesus, or, ultimately, from that of God himself. Men repeatedly demand that God send his angelic legions, visible or invisible, to eradicate all evil through the forces of heaven; God refuses. God's pathway through history, as Scripture teaches and as "must happen," is not the conquest of all resistance; it is instead reflected in Jesus' way of the cross. Men can never agree in their prayers about where the evil to be destroyed is to be found; they turn on each other instead, each trying to get the best of the other in prayer. This is a significant consideration, but does not solve the most difficult problem. This problem is not solved until men understand that God refuses in principle to impose his will by force, seeking rather the response of faith.

Faith must be as free as love, which can never be forced, but perishes where it is demanded by force. Therefore true faith comes into being at the very point where God is most powerless: face to face with the cross of Jesus. Matthew is well aware (as his accounts of various healings show, for example) that prayers are heard in response to human importunity; and the spectacle of Jesus' importunity here can help build up a weak and nascent faith. On the other hand, Matthew is also aware that God is never constrained, not even by importunity, and that genuine love of God is free—i.e. it does not arise from God's promises or threats. Jesus' love for God here *is* genuine —it does not hinge on God's favorable response; but his faith in God is also genuine—he knows that God can save him, but that God's will is better than even salvation.

The Confession of Jesus and the Denial of Peter (26:57-75)
Cf. Mark 14:53-72; Luke 22:54-71; John 18:12-28

[57]But those who had arrested Jesus took him to the house of Caiaphas, the High Priest, where the teachers of the Law and the elders had gathered together. [58]Peter followed him from a distance, as far as the courtyard of the High Priest's house. He went in and sat down with the guards, to see how it would all come out.

[59]And the chief priests and the whole Council tried to find some false evidence against Jesus, to put him to death; [60]but they could not find any, even though many false witnesses came forward. Finally, however, two men stepped forward [61]and said, "This man said, 'I am able to tear down God's temple and three days later build it back up.' " [62]The High Priest stood up and said to Jesus, "Have you no answer to give to this accusation against you?" [63]But Jesus kept quiet. Again the High Priest spoke to him, "In the name of the living God, I adjure you to tell us if you are the messiah, the Son of God." [64]Jesus answered him, "So you say. But I tell you this: from this time on you will see 'the Son of Man sitting at the right hand of the Almighty,' and 'coming on the clouds of heaven.' " [65]At this the High Priest tore his clothes and said, "Blasphemy! Why should we need any more witnesses? Behold, now you have heard his blasphemy! [66]What do you

think?" They answered, "He is guilty, and must die." [67]Then they spat in his face and beat him with their fists; and others struck him [68]and said, "Prophesy for us, Messiah! Guess who hit you!"

[69]Peter was sitting outside in the courtyard, when a servant girl came to him and said, "You, too, were with Jesus the Galilean." [70]But he denied it in front of them all. "I don't know what you are talking about," he answered, [71]and went on out to the entrance of the court-yard. Another servant girl saw him and said to the men there, "He was with Jesus the Nazarene." [72]Again Peter denied it, and answered, "I swear that I don't know that man!" [73]After a little while the men standing there came to Peter. "Of course you are one of them," they said. "After all, the way you speak gives you away!" [74]Then Peter began to curse and to swear, saying, "I do not know that man!" Just then a rooster crowed, [75]and Peter remembered what Jesus had told him, "Before the rooster crows, you will deny me three times." He went out and wept bitterly.

(Vs. 64—Dan. 7:13; Ps. 110:1.)

The alterations of the Markan account are minor but interesting. **[57]** As in verse 3, we find the name of Caiaphas. The listing of teachers of the Law and elders (without the phrase "of the people") follows Mark more closely than does verse 3; but there is no mention of "all the chief priests." Matthew probably thinks of them as being already assembled, waiting for Jesus. **[58]** Mark 14:54 and John 18:18 say that Peter was trying to get warm; Matthew and Luke omit this detail. The Greek word can mean "palace" or "courtyard"; according to Matthew 26:69, however, Peter is sitting outside in the courtyard.

[59] Matthew indicates from the outset that the authorities' pur-pose is to gather "false" evidence that would formally meet the legal requirements and suffice for a death sentence. **[60]** But unlike Mark, Matthew speaks of "two" whose testimony agreed, and therefore must be true. **[61]** This means that the saying about the destruction and rebuilding of the temple is not a false accusation (Mark 14:57, 59), but an accurate statement of what Jesus said. Since Zechariah plays an important role in Matthew (21:5; 24:30-31; 25:31; 26:15, 31; 27:9), he probably has in mind the messianic "branch" mentioned in Zechariah 6:12, who will build the new temple, an event for which men had been waiting since Ezekiel 40 ff. In Matthew, however, the saying does not include the characteristic Hellenistic phrase "(not) made with hands," and this suggests that the Matthaean form is earlier (cf. the discussion of Mark 14:58). On the other hand, the saying is probably a Matthaean addition to point out that Jesus merely said he could do this, not that he would do it. Thus Matthew emphasizes Jesus' divine authority without turning him into a kind of revolutionary against the Temple and the priesthood.

[63] Since Matthew usually abbreviates the Markan account significantly, it is striking that the High Priest asks his question with the formula adjuring Jesus to answer in the name of the living God (cf. 16:16). For Matthew the decision obviously rests on the question of whether Jesus can correctly be called the Christ and the Son of God (cf. the discussion of 16:16). Except in special cases, such a formula was commonly used only when a witness was being sworn; the notion of Jesus as (blood) witness for God before all the world (1 Tim. 6:13) may therefore already be in the background. Matthew phrases Jesus' affirmative answer as "So you say," not "I am," as does Mark, probably because Jesus thus places responsibility for the oath on the inquirer rather than accepting it himself (5:33-37; 23:16-22). The change is hardly meant to suggest that the title "Messiah" is valid only for Israel. Jesus may well be implying that the High Priest has no idea what he is actually saying. The same expression is also used in 27:11 (= Mark 15:2), where it is to be taken as evasive.

Not until the next sentence does Jesus lay bare the deepest mystery, as the addition of "But I tell you" shows. It is he who is enthroned at God's right hand, and is so "from this time on." Matthew is fond of this locution (vss. 16, 29); but "from this time on" is not precisely accurate, for Matthew means "soon," at least with regard to Jesus' coming on the clouds of heaven (Matthew replaces the "with" of Mark 14:62 with the "upon" used in Dan. 7:13). But Matthew's overall meaning is that "from this time on" they will see only the *triumphant* Son of Man, to whom all power in heaven and earth is given (28:18), and who will return to judge the world (25:31). Thus in a manner faintly reminiscent of John the torment of Jesus is seen as not only necessary for, but in fact a part of, his enthronement as Lord at the right hand of God (cf. the introductory comments on chapters 26–28).

Only Matthew records the verdict of the High Priest, which condemns Jesus to death: **[65]** "Blasphemy!" In contrast to the High Priest (vs. 63), however, and to Peter (vss. 70, 72, 74), Jesus has taken no oath. **[66]** Only in Matthew is the death sentence pronounced in direct discourse (cf. the discussion of vs. 27). Matthew, however, omits the detail that "everyone" consented (cf. John 7:50-51 and the discussion of Matt. 27:1). In Matthew's abbreviated account it looks as though the members of the Council themselves spat on Jesus and struck him; the various groups are not well defined. According to Mark 14:65, however, only the servants slapped his face. Abbreviation of the statement in Mark has turned "spitting and blindfolding (his face)" into "spitting in his face." **[68]** This change renders the next verse obscure. Up to the addition of "Messiah" or "Christ," it agrees verbatim with Luke 22:64, and elucidates the remarkably abrupt imperative "Prophesy!" in Mark 14:65. Is Matthew suggesting that Jesus name the man who is striking him?

[69] Peter's first denial is recounted in somewhat abbreviated form. In it we find the derogatory term "Galilean" applied to Jesus; it may have suggested that he was a potential revolutionary (cf. Acts 5:37; also 1:11; 2:7; and Justin, *Dial.* cviii. 3.). Now, however, **[70]** it is spoken "in front of them all," albeit in a form that is still evasive. **[71]** According to Matthew the second question is asked by another servant girl, according to Mark by the same one. Matthew, unlike Mark, states that Peter has withdrawn into the entranceway, where it is dark. Now, in direct opposition to Jesus' teaching, he takes an oath (cf. the discussion of vs. 65), unambiguously denying Jesus. **[73]** The charge of being a Galilean (Mark 14:70) Matthew explains by saying that Peter's speech betrays him as a potential follower of Jesus. If anything, Matthew places even more stress on the curse. Thus Peter withdraws from any association with Jesus; the charge that he had been "with Jesus" (Mark 14:67) is repeated by Matthew (vss. 69, 71; cf. the discussion of 26:29, 36, 38, 40). According to 26:35, however, in contrast to the Markan recension, Peter has already insisted that he is ready to die "with Jesus." **[75]** On the crowing of the cock, cf. the discussion of verse 34. Peter's remorse is strongly emphasized in the statement that he wept bitterly (cf. Isa. 22:4; 33:7). It agrees verbatim with Luke 22:62, but its textual support is not absolutely secure.

Without making any major changes, Matthew emphasizes the divine authority of Jesus: he could destroy the Temple and rebuild it, and his Passion is the way to enthronement, so that those who condemn him will know him as Lord of the universe and coming judge. Veiled beneath impotence, in the outcast of Nazareth there is taking place God's saving judgment of the world; the one who renounces all violence and willingly accepts execution is appointed Lord of all the world. In John, this theme will become the focus of the Passion narrative. At the same time, Matthew even more than Mark holds up Jesus as an example to inspire his community, Peter as an example to warn them, since they are repeatedly required to confess their faith boldly (Acts 2:29; 4:31; Phil. 1:20; Eph. 6:19).

Jesus Taken to Pilate (27:1-2)
Cf. Mark 15:1; Luke 23:1

¹Early in the morning all the chief priests and the elders of the people made their plan against Jesus, to put him to death. ²They put him in chains, took him, and handed him over to Pilate, the Roman governor.

[1] In contrast to 26:57, verse 1 states that "all" (the word is not in Mark) the chief priests took part in the council; the elders are once more called elders "of the people," but the teachers of the Law are omitted (see the discussion of 26:3). More important is the observation that Matthew is probably not speaking of a (new?) consultation, as does Mark 15:1, but of a death sentence determined at break of day, as is stated in an idiom with Latin overtones. In any case, Matthew appears to have in mind an immediate continuation of the account in 26:66-68; the suggestion that this is the first time all the members of the Sanhedrin assembled is improbable in the light of 26:59 ("the whole Council"). [2] The title given Pilate is not his official title; it refers to his military authority.

The Death of Judas (27:3-10)

[3]When Judas, the traitor, saw that Jesus had been condemned, he repented and took back the thirty silver coins to the chief priests and the elders. [4]"I have sinned by betraying an innocent man to death!" he said. [5]"What do we care about that?" they answered. "That is your business!" Judas threw the money into the sanctuary and left them; then he went off and hanged himself.

[6]The chief priests picked up the money and said, "This is blood money, and it is against our Law to put it in the Temple treasury." [7]After reaching an agreement about it, they used the money to buy Potter's Field, as a cemetery for foreigners. [8]That is why that field is called "Field of Blood" to this very day.

[9]Then what the prophet Jeremiah had said came true: "And I took the thirty silver coins, the amount the people of Israel had agreed to pay for him, [10]and it was used to buy the potter's field, as the Lord commanded me."

(Vs. 9—Zech. 11:12-13; Jer. 18:2-4; 19:1-15.)

Judas' fate is recorded in three variants. Besides our text we have Acts 1:18-20 and the account of Papias (fragment 3; around the middle of the second century). Acts states that he stumbled and burst open, so that all his insides spilled out. Therefore the field where he met his death was given the name "Field of Blood." This strange description has probably been influenced by the account of the end of the wicked in Wisdom of Solomon 4:18-19: "They then become a despised corpse . . . , because he [God] will dash them speechless to the ground." Matthew also speaks of the Field of Blood, but gives a different explanation of its name: it is the field bought with the blood money returned by Judas. The most fantastic account is that of Papias, who tells how Judas was afflicted with dropsy and became so grotesquely swollen that he could no longer squeeze through openings where a cart could pass with ease, and his eyes became so enveloped in flesh that he became blind, and even a physician with his instruments could no longer penetrate to them. He then died in great pain;

the place where this took place was laid waste, and to this very day conveys such a stench that a man can pass only if he holds his nose.

It is still possible to trace the development of this legend. Acts 1:20 is based on two passages of Scripture, the first of which is Psalm 109:8 ("May his days be few," RSV). Reading on, the community discovered that the curse soaked into his body like water (Ps. 109:18; cf. Num. 5:22), and took this statement literally. The other passage was Psalm 69:25 ("May their place become a desolation, and may no one dwell there"). The community took this verse to refer to the field where Judas met his death, and elaborated the description in the manner found at the conclusion of Papias' account. In the same Psalm we read two verses earlier that their eyes are to be so darkened that they cannot see, and again the community visualized this in concrete terms. Some scholars have suggested reading "headlong" (Greek *prēnēs*) in Acts 1:18 as "swollen" (from *pimprēmi*, "swell up"); the suggestion cannot be supported on linguistic grounds, but the phonetic similarity may have contributed to the development of the story in Papias.

Thus Luke and Matthew are still familiar with the story of a field near Jerusalem called the Field of Blood, associated with Judas. The next step was the discovery of Zechariah 11:12, where we find the more specific information that the blood money given Judas according to Mark 14:11 consisted of "thirty silver coins" (Matt. 26:15). [5] The following verse of the Hebrew text in Zechariah reads: "I cast them into the treasury in the house of the Lord"; Judas was therefore said to have repented and given back the reward he received for his wickedness (vs. 5). In Greek, the forms for "cast" and "receive" could be either first person singular or third person plural, so that the passage could refer either to Judas or to the priests. [9-10] Verses 9 b and 10 constitute an independent translation of the conclusion of Zechariah 11:13; there, however, the clause giving the price, etc., precedes the statement "I [or: 'they'] took the thirty silver coins." What did they do with the money? The original text in Zechariah undoubtedly stated that they cast it into the Temple treasury. Possibly the rejected idea of putting it into the Temple treasury (vs. 6) goes back to a text that preserved this original meaning.

A minor scribal error, affecting a single letter of the Hebrew text, resulted in the reading "for the potter." This recalled the potter's house to which God commanded Jeremiah to go (Jer. 18:2 ff.) and suggested the other episode in which he had to buy a "field" for seven shekels and ten "silver coins" and "place" the deed in a pot (Jer. 32:6-14). Since complete Bibles were extremely rare (see the discussion of 24:30), people had excerpts containing important passages and learned other sections more or less by heart. Thus it was easy for various Biblical quotations to be conflated, and it is understandable that the community finally assigned the entire quotation in verses 9 *b*-10 to Jeremiah. This was roughly what happened to Jeremiah, as they recalled the story, and so it also had to be the case for Judas' death.

The final phrase, "as the Lord commanded me," comes from yet another source: Exodus 9:12, which describes the sixth plague, boils caused by soot. The association may be due to the form the quotation from Zechariah has in the Greek Old Testament. The translator could make no sense of the expression "to the potter," already corrupt in the Hebrew text, and rendered it "into the furnace." As Scripture was then interpreted, it was reasonable to connect "furnace" and "soot"; this association made it possible to incorporate the quotation about the command of the Lord. [8] Since the striking name "Field of Blood" had already been explained by means of the account of Judas' death, the community concluded that before the purchase it had been called "Potter's Field" (vss. 7-8). Thus the entire story, in all its essentials, is a product of the Old Testament read as prophecy. As far we can tell, Genesis 37:28, which states that Judah (Greek: Judas) sold his brother for twenty silver coins, was never drawn upon. The story thus came into being by stages, under the influence of first one and then another Greek or Hebrew text. Matthew incorporated it by and large as he found it; the Potter's Field plays no role in his narrative.

[3] The introduction with "when" and the characterization of Judas are typical of Matthew. He thus associates the remorse of the traitor with the death sentence passed by the Council, just as he found the remorse of Peter associated in Mark with the trial before the Council. Chronologically this episode cannot belong here, since the Council are on their way to Pilate with Jesus. [4] Legally speaking, the proceedings against Jesus should be reconsidered and Judas

should be brought to trial for giving false evidence. Neither course is taken, however. **[5]** Is the courtyard still open to the general public, making it possible for Judas to throw the money into the Temple? Perhaps such an act is in line with a Jewish custom for cancelling an agreement. Or is it only a repetition of the prophecy (see above the introductory comments on vs. 5)? Judas, who has betrayed the Son of David, hangs himself like Ahithophel, who betrayed David (2 Sam. 17:23); thus he himself executes the sentence the Council refused to pass against him.

[6-8] Those who have just condemned Jesus contrary to all law while refusing even to consider their own self-incrimination are scrupulous in treating the trifling sum of money according to the principle laid down in Deuteronomy 23:18, which, to be sure, speaks only of the wages of a harlot or a sodomite. The unclean money is used for an unclean purpose, the purchase of a cemetery for foreigners, presumably gentiles. **[9-10]** The conflated quotation that gave rise to the entire story is cited by Matthew at its conclusion, introduced with his special formula (see the excursus on 1:18-25).

This section thus illustrates how legends were already coming into being even in the New Testament period. But this is not the crucial point. Matthew's final use here of his accustomed formula for the fulfillment of Scripture shows how important this episode is to him, obviously because it serves to warn the disciple of Jesus about the judgment he faces if he does not remain a faithful follower. The fate of Judas in his remorse stands in harsh contrast to that of Peter in his remorse, of which we have just heard. Perhaps Matthew's purpose is even to suggest that the man who wants to make amends on his own even to the point of executing his own sentence will not find salvation, whereas the man who can only break down and weep, expecting nothing more of himself and his efforts but recalling only what his Lord had said, remains within the realm of salvation.

The King of the Jews Is Sentenced to Death (27:11-26)
Cf. Mark 15:2-15; Luke 23:2-5, 17-25

¹¹Jesus was brought before the Governor, who questioned him. "Are you the king of the Jews?" he asked. "So you say," answered Jesus. ¹²And when he was accused by the chief priests and elders, he

said nothing. [13]So Pilate said to him, "Don't you hear all these things they accuse you of?" [14]But Jesus refused to answer a single word, so that the Governor was greatly surprised.

[15]At every Passover Feast the Governor was in the habit of setting free one prisoner, anyone the crowd asked for. [16]At that time there was a well-known prisoner named Jesus Barabbas. [17]So when the crowd gathered, Pilate asked them, "Which one do you want me to set free for you? Jesus Barabbas or Jesus the so-called messiah?" [18]He knew very well that they had handed Jesus over to him because they were jealous. [19]While Pilate was sitting on the judgment seat, his wife sent him a message: "Have nothing to do with that innocent man, because in a dream last night I suffered much on account of him." [20]But the chief priests and the elders persuaded the people to ask Pilate to set Barabbas free and have Jesus put to death. [21]But the Governor asked them, "Which one of these two do you want me to set free for you?" "Barabbas!" they answered. [22]"What, then, shall I do with Jesus the so-called messiah?" Pilate asked them. "Crucify him!" they all answered. [23]But Pilate asked, "What crime has he committed?" Then they started shouting even more, "Crucify him!" [24]When Pilate saw that it was no use to go on, but that a riot might break out, he took some water, washed his hands before the people, and said, "I am innocent of this blood. This is your doing." [25]The whole crowd answered back, "His blood be on us and on our children!" [26]Then Pilate set Barabbas free for them; he had Jesus whipped and handed him over to be crucified.

Here Matthew departs more than elsewhere from Mark. Obviously the episode of the hearing before Pilate has undergone considerable elaboration in the course of transmission. In John, the "ecce homo" ("behold the man") and the crucial debate about Jesus' kingship (see the discussion of 25:33) have been transferred to this section. Of the five brief scenes that make it up, the first, the accusation, follows Mark most closely. Even so, Pilate is called by his official title (vss. 2, 11, 14-15, 21, 27; 28:14; never in Mark). The contrast with Barabbas has been consciously expanded. In the third scene, the interruption of Pilate's wife is new. The sentencing of Jesus once more follows Mark, whereas the Governor's washing his hands in the last scene is not recounted anywhere else. Whether more is involved than orally transmitted elaborations of the Passion narrative cannot be determined. Linguistic features in verses 24-25 suggest Matthaean formulation.

[11] Jesus is mentioned by name once more because of the interpolation on the death of Judas. The title "king of the Jews" (=Mark 15:2) in the mouth of a gentile from the west corresponds to the same title in the mouth of gentiles from the east at the beginning of the Gospel (Matt. 2:2). [12] Matthew adds the "elders" in order to show that representatives of the people are involved in bringing charges against Jesus (see the discussion of 26:3). His additional stress on Jesus' silence (vss. 12 and 14) is also deliberate. [14] He was probably thinking of the example of the suffering Servant of God in Isaiah 53:7. The amazement of the Governor is also further emphasized by the addition of "greatly" (cf. Isa. 52:15?).

[15] The contrast with Barabbas is framed more loosely. The release of a prisoner at Passover is described more clearly than in Mark as a fixed custom, and the catchword "crowd" (Mark 15:8) appears in Matthew at the outset (vs. 15). [16] The Greek text of verse 16 reads literally: "They had . . . a prisoner." Does this peculiar formulation refer to the crowd just mentioned in verse 15, who could choose between him and Jesus, or to the Romans, who have not been mentioned? The crime of Barabbas is not specified; instead, he is called a "well-known" or "infamous" prisoner; the Greek word means a man held for interrogation and not yet brought to trial. [17] The demand of the people is omitted (Mark 15:8); Pilate takes the initiative. According to Matthew, Barabbas ("son of Abbas") is also called Jesus, assuming that the few manuscripts that contain this reading are correct. Since it is more reasonable to assume that the name "Jesus," later felt to be holy, was dropped than that it was added, this may record the earliest recollection. The reading is supported by the fact that Jesus is expressly called "the so-called messiah" or "Christ" (vss. 17, 22; not vs. 20) in order to distinguish him from another Jesus, namely "Jesus (the) Barabbas" (the article is found even in manuscripts that no longer contain the name "Jesus"). In this case Jesus the son of Abbas is contrasted to Jesus the so-called messiah, as Pilate puts it, and the very first question of the Governor

is framed as a clear either/or. [18] Unlike Mark, Matthew states that all the people, not just the chief priests, handed Jesus over to Pilate.

[19] Like John 19:13, Matthew mentions that Pilate is sitting on his official seat as judge—the gesture heightens the contrast between his titular authority and his actual impotence. A "pavement" like that mentioned by John has been uncovered by excavations at the Antonia, a fortress adjacent to the Temple; but the palace at the western edge of the city is a much more likely location. The omen of the Governor's wife further heightens the grotesqueness of the decision against Jesus Christ and for Jesus Barabbas. The expression "in a dream" is typical of the infancy narratives (1:20; 2:12, 13, 19, 22). As in those, Matthew probably sees here God's personal intervention in behalf of Jesus. As a gentile, she speaks merely of "that just man," but thus confirms his innocence. Similar stories appear in many legends, and it is possible that this feature preserves a record of the Christian community's conviction that Jesus was innocent. Later stories mention the woman's name, Procula Claudia; in the Greek and Ethiopian Churches she is even considered a saint. The so-called Acts of Pilate recount Pilate's lengthy and unavailing efforts to dissuade the Jews from their purpose; finally Pilate himself becomes a Christian saint.

[20] Once again the either/or is explicitly stated: to choose Barabbas means to send Jesus to his death. [21] According to Matthew, Pilate repeats the crucial question once more in these same terms: "Which of these two . . . ?" The people answer his question explicitly. [22] Only then comes the question about the fate of Jesus, who is once more called "the so-called Christ." The Greek text reads literally "Let him be crucified!" instead of "Crucify him!" (Mark 15:13); the change may have been made unconsciously because Pilate does not actually carry out the crucifixion or because it contains a stronger echo of the confession of Jesus as the man "who was crucified" (28:5).

[23] Matthew stresses again that the people "all" shout for Jesus' death; the tense used in the next verse indicates that they do so repeatedly. [24] According to Deuteronomy 21:6-7, the leaders of a city in the vicinity of which a man has been slain are to use the ritual of handwashing to disavow the crime. Since Psalms 24:4; 26:6; and 73:13 show that the expression is almost proverbial, and since it also is found among the Greeks, it is not inherently impossible that Pilate

did so; but it is inconceivable that he would have made a public spectacle of his own illegal decision and the impotence of Rome in the face of demands by a subject populace. This feature therefore is in line with the general tendency increasingly to absolve the Romans and blame the Jews. As early as Luke the uninitiated reader could not but conclude (from 23:25-26) that the Jews crucified Jesus, especially because the soldiers do not "come up" until verse 36. Justin has a Jew say, "We crucified him." In the Gospel of Peter, the command to put Jesus to death is issued by Herod, Pilate has to ask Herod for Jesus' body; and it is the Jews, not the Romans, who hand over the corpse to Joseph for burial. That a gentile woman receives God's revelation while the people of God reject it is in line with chapter 2 of Matthew, with the confession of the officer at the foot of the cross (27:54), and with the faith of the other officer at Capernaum (8:10).

[25] "The whole crowd"—all the people, not just their leaders— unequivocally reject Jesus, after the manner of a legal formula (Josh. 2:19), calling down Jesus' blood on themselves and their descendants in case of a miscarriage of justice. Only here and in verse 64 does the Passion narrative use the solemn term that distinguishes the people of God from the gentiles (cf. the discussion of 21:43). It occurs also within quotations that speak of the blindness of the people with respect to Jesus (13:15; 15:8). But in 27:20 and 24 the same expression ("crowd," "many people") is used that elsewhere refers to those who follow Jesus (4:25; 8:1; 12:15; 14:13; 19:2; 20:29), or wonder at him and extol him (7:28; 9:8, 33; 12:23; 15:30-31; 21:8-9, 11), as well as the crowd feared by Herod (14:5) and the Jewish authorities (21:26, 46; cf. also the introductory comments on 3:7-10). Now, however, the people of God's own covenant call on him to bring judgment down upon them, so terrible is their blindness (see the discussion of 13:16-17). The only thing that makes the verse defensible is Matthew's repeated warning to the Christian community not to go the same way. As his interpolated account of the fate of Judas has just shown, he takes quite seriously the possibility that the Christian community, too, could fall victim to God's judgment (cf. the introductory comments on chapters 21-25). Hebrews 12:24 speaks of the blood of Jesus in different terms. [26] In the second half of verse 26, which otherwise follows Mark verbatim, Matthew inverts the word order, so that the

Greek text begins, "Jesus, however . . . ," thus placing Jesus directly alongside "Barabbas."

Thus at the conclusion the contrast between the two Jesuses is emphasized one last time. This contrast is the actual focus of the episode. But there is less stress on the idea of Jesus' suffering on behalf of the sinner or the criminal—although this notion has also influenced the account—than on the incomprehensible choice made by the blind people of God's covenant. The only ray of brightness in this story is God's revelation to the gentile woman and her response. In her we find a hint of why Jesus must go his agonizing way, silent as the Servant of God in Isaiah, to whom Matthew 12:17 ff. has already clearly referred. Those whom no one would have expected are brought within this covenant through Jesus' way of suffering, and open themselves to the God who has sought them out. What the pagan magi, to whom God likewise appeared "in a dream" (2:12), already suggested is clearly revealed: God is present to help those very people who do not yet know him. That is his amazing way of upholding his covenant. To say this does not exhaust the possibilities; but perhaps it can help us see that there is vicarious suffering which opens a new way to many, even though it need not be expressed in terms of sacrificial atonement.

The Soldiers Mock the King of the Jews (27:27-31)
Cf. Mark 15:16-20

27Then the soldiers of the Governor took Jesus into the Pretorium, and the whole cohort gathered around him. 28They stripped off his clothes and put a scarlet robe on him. 29Then they made a crown of thorns and placed it on his head, and put a reed in his right hand; then they fell on their knees before him and mocked him. "Hail, King of the Jews!" they said. 30They spat on him, and took the reed and hit him over the head. 31When they had finished mocking him, they took the robe off and put his own clothes back on him. Then they led him out to be crucified.

[28] In the episode of the soldiers' mockery Matthew follows Mark at all points. The scarlet robe is referred to by a word that means

the cloak of a lictor, a member of the "military police." This is probably an accurate historical reminiscence. **[29]** The explicit statement that they put the crown of thorns on his "head" appears also in John 19:2; even Zechariah 6:11, in a messianic passage (cf. Heb. 10:21), may have influenced the wording. Only Matthew has anything to say about the reed, which resembles a royal scepter but is also used to strike the helpless prisoner (as likewise in Mark 15:19). The mocking obeisance of the soldiers in Mark 15:19 (not in all manuscripts) is mentioned earlier by Matthew, so that mockery and physical abuse are more clearly distinguished and are recounted in sequence.

The Crucifixion of Jesus (27:32-37)
Cf. Mark 15:21-26; Luke 23:26, 33-35 *a*, 38

³²But as they were going out they found a man from Cyrene named Simon, and they forced him to carry Jesus' cross. ³³They came to a place called Golgotha, which means "The Place of the Skull." ³⁴Then "they gave" him wine "to drink," mixed with "gall"; and when he tasted it, he would not drink it. ³⁵When they had crucified him, "they divided his clothes among them by lot." ³⁶And they sat there and kept watch beside him. ³⁷Above his head they posted a notice of his crime: "This is Jesus, the King of the Jews."
(Vs. 34—Ps. 69:21. Vs. 35—Ps. 22:18.)

[32] Simon of Cyrene, no longer a familiar figure to the Matthaean community, is mentioned more briefly than in Mark. **[34]** Mark 15:36 (=Matt. 27:48) speaks of vinegar being given to Jesus to drink after he is already nailed to the cross. The community saw in this act the fulfillment of Psalm 69:21. Since, however, the parallel half verse (see Matt. 27:48) also mentions gall, Matthew assumed that Jesus was given gall to drink the first time. Thus, clearly echoing the Psalm passage, he has replaced the narcotic wine given before execution as an act of mercy (Mark 15:23), with the mocking drink of gall, which Jesus does not refuse until he has tasted it and recognized its malicious intent. This text is therefore a result of the same process observed in 21:7. The Gospel of Peter (16) likewise has an observer say, "Give him gall with vinegar to drink." Thus Matthew depicts the crucifixion primarily in terms of mockery.

[35] Unlike Mark, he does not mention the crucifixion itself in a main clause but in a participial phrase, represented in translation by a subordinate clause. The most recent excavations suggest with reasonable certainty that the upright of the cross remained fixed like a medieval gallows, and that nails were driven not through the victim's palms but through his wrists, with a single nail driven through both heels placed together.

[36] Matthew goes on to say that the soldiers kept watch over the crucified victim, probably to prevent attempts to free him. The statement is hardly likely to serve the purpose of John 19:33-34 (see the discussion of vs. 49), emphasizing the reality of Jesus' death in the face of speculations that Jesus' own person had already departed from his body and "ascended" into heaven (Gospel of Peter 19; cf. 1 John 4:2-3; 5:6). In the inscription on the cross Matthew has inserted the name of Jesus, like John 19:19, as well as the statement that it was the soldiers (in an act of mockery?) who posted it on the cross.

Jesus Is Mocked on the Cross (27:38-44)
Cf. Mark 15:27-32

³⁸Then two bandits were crucified with Jesus, one on his right and the other on his left. ³⁹People passing by "shook their heads" and hurled insults at Jesus: ⁴⁰ "You were going to tear down the Temple and build it back up in three days! Save yourself, if you are the Son of God! Come on down from the cross!" ⁴¹In the same way the chief priests and the teachers of the Law and the elders mocked him: ⁴²"He saved others but he cannot save himself! Isn't he the King of Israel? If he will come down off the cross now, we will believe in him! ⁴³He trusted in God; let God save him now, if he is pleased with him; for he said, 'I am God's Son.' " ⁴⁴Even the bandits who had been crucified with him insulted him in the same way.

(Vs. 39—Ps. 22:7; 109:25. Vs. 43—Ps. 22:8.)

[40, 43] Among those who mock Jesus on the cross, Matthew includes the "elders" (cf. 26:3; 27:12-20). What is more important, he

phrases their words like the question of the Tempter (4:3, 6): "If you are the Son of God . . . ." An echo of the Passion Psalm (22:7) is heard in Matthew 27:39 (=Mark 15:29); now the next verse is added: "He trusted in God; let God save him now, if he is pleased with him," which echoes the next verse of the Psalm (22:8). The word for "trust" does not come directly from the Psalm, but from Wisdom of Solomon 2:17-20, where the righteous man, insulted by all, calls himself God's son (without the article, as here) and God's servant. The passage continues: "If the righteous man is God's son, he will protect him and deliver him from the hand of his adversaries." The subject is the righteous man in general, but the words are extremely close to what is said here about Jesus (cf. the "removal" of the righteous man and his role at the Last Judgment in Wisd. 4:7, 10, 16; 5:1-5). More than Mark, therefore, Matthew sees Jesus here as the righteous sufferer mocked by the world. With his entire life he has done precisely what scorn is here heaped on him for: he has "trusted in God," thus keeping the first commandment. That he does so even more fully in his death those who mock him do not understand. They refuse to trust in God; therefore they demand proof from God, and demand to have it "now," that is, when *they* find it necessary. Therefore they are blind to the fact that in this very place and at this very moment, when they think God is absent, he is present.

The Death of Jesus as the Revelation of God (27:45-54)
Cf. Mark 15:33-39; Luke 23:44-47

⁴⁵But from the sixth hour on the whole country was covered with darkness until the ninth hour. ⁴⁶At about the ninth hour Jesus cried out with a loud shout, "Eli, Eli, lama sabachthani!" That means, "My God, my God, why did you abandon me!" ⁴⁷Some of the people standing there heard him and said, "He is calling for Elijah!" ⁴⁸One of them ran up at once, took a sponge, soaked it with "vinegar," put it on the end of a reed, and tried to make him "drink" it. ⁴⁹But the others said, "Wait, let us see if Elijah is coming to save him!" ⁵⁰Jesus again gave a loud cry, and gave up his spirit. ⁵¹And behold, the curtain hanging in the Temple was torn in two, from top to bottom. The earth shook, the rocks split apart, ⁵²the graves broke open, and many bodies

of the saints who had fallen asleep were raised to life. [53]They left the graves; and after Jesus rose from death they went into the Holy City and appeared to many. [54]But when the officer and the soldiers with him who were keeping watch over Jesus saw the earthquake and everything else that happened, they were terrified and said, "He really was God's Son."

(Vs. 46—Ps. 22:1. Vs. 48—Ps. 69:21.)

Once again Matthew follows Mark closely. The time of day, which was omitted in verse 35 (Mark 15:25), is included here, probably because it suggests the literal fulfillment of Amos 8:9 (see the introductory comments on Mark 15:33-39). [46] Jesus' cry is given in Hebrew: "Eli, Eli." This is an instance of accurate tradition, because only in Hebrew is the confusion with Elijah possible, not in the Aramaic form "Eloi" given by Mark. The translation is also phrased differently, in part echoing the Greek Old Testament. The saying and its translation in this form were probably both known to Matthew from the tradition of his community.

[48] The offer of vinegar to drink, perhaps bitter soldiers' wine, was probably conceived of originally as an act of mercy; [49] now the accompanying words of the guards turn it into an act of mockery. According to Matthew it is not the soldier offering Jesus the vinegar who mocks him but the others. As a result, the command "Wait," literally "Let" (shortened from Mark's "Let me"), is now meant to stop the soldier from what he is about to do instead of urging the others to let him do it. The mockery is probably intensified by Matthew's substitution of "save" for "bring down" (Mark 15:36); in verses 40, 42 this is what is expected of the Son of God. In a few manuscripts the spear wound from John 19:34 is inserted here (cf. the discussion of vs. 36); in these manuscripts the sequence of the Johannine "blood and water" is reversed, probably to correspond to the sequence of baptism and the Lord's Supper, the two sacraments symbolically alluded to (cf. 1 John 5:6). In Matthew, however, Jesus is still alive at this point. The statement about the "other one" who stabbed Jesus in the side may have been added in the margin by a reader because verse 48 speaks of "one" who offered him something to drink.

[50] Jesus' death is also formulated somewhat differently; it is now no longer a loud cry that Jesus "gives up," but his spirit. This strengthens the impression, already present in Mark, that to the very end Jesus refused to desert the one who appears to have deserted him, thus showing that contrary to all appearances God is indeed present. Into God's hands, as Luke 23:46 states explicitly, Jesus "gives up" his spirit. According to the Gospel of Peter (19), "his strength" departs from Jesus on the cross, which is interpreted as his being received into heaven (despite what is said in the introductory comments on 28:5-7).

[51] The signs following Jesus' death are a new element. The eschatological events that have taken place in the death of Jesus are invisible to those who stand there mocking and to the disciples, who are not standing there; here they become visible to everyone as symbols. God with his new world breaks into the old world, just as in 1 Kings 19:11 his appearance caused the earth to quake and the rocks of Horeb to split. Mark 15:38 uses the same verb to describe the rending of the Temple curtain; here it is further highlighted by the addition of "and behold" (see the discussion of 8:2). While the bystanders look on unmoved, mocking and uncertain, the very rocks reel and shatter.

[52] What is more, graves open and men are restored to life. Latin and Greek writers are familiar with earthquakes and even the appearance of men long dead in the wake of great events; this passage, however, speaks of physical resurrection. The wording is even reminiscent of the great resurrection passage in Ezekiel 37 (vs. 12), which, however, merely serves to symbolize the spiritual renewal of Israel. Three times the use of the passive suggests that God himself is at work. Jerusalem with the Mount of Olives is the place where the resurrection is one day to begin; here the bones of all the Israelites will assemble, wherever they may lie buried. Therefore aristocratic Jews have their tombs located there so as to be first at the resurrection (cf. Matt. 27:60). The "saints" in the Bible are all the members of the people of God, here the devout Israelites who died before Jesus. This would of course be a huge number, so that there may be lurking in the background the expectation, occasionally found in Judaism, of a special resurrection for the patriarchs and the Jewish martyrs. Ignatius, Epistle to Magnesia, ix. 2, speaks especially of the prophets;

the so-called Acts of Pilate has in mind the patriarchs.

[53] These resurrected "saints" wander through the city and appear to people as public signs against their mockery and lack of faith. The phrase "after Jesus rose from death" is very strange. It can hardly have been written in its present form by Matthew; had it been, it would have belonged in verse 52. Furthermore Matthew would have recounted these events in chapter 28, possibly in the context of the great "earthquake" in 28:2. Since verse 54 states that the soldiers of the watch see the miraculous signs, it is impossible to account for the phrase as a mere anticipation of something that took place later. Either the original reading was "after they rose from death," as attested by certain individual late manuscripts, or the comment is a later addition. In this case, which is much more likely, we are dealing with a correction. Jesus is the first of all men to be raised to life (1 Cor. 15:20; Rom. 8:29; Col. 1:18); therefore it is impossible for any of the dead to rise before him. The notion that Jesus went to the underworld directly after his death and there set the Old Testament saints free to share in the resurrection (1 Pet. 3:19; 4:6) can hardly be ascribed to Matthew; neither would it solve the problem of Jesus' rising after them (28:1-6). It has also been proposed that at one time Jesus' death was thought of as a direct apotheosis from the cross to God, like that of Enoch and Elijah (Gen. 5:24; 2 Kings 2:11; cf. the discussion of Matt. 27:36, 50 and the introduction to chapters 26–28), but that Matthew was not aware of this, and verse 53 was corrected to conform to the idea. But this hypothesis remains mere speculation without evidence to support it.

[54] The confession of Jesus as Son of God has been borrowed by Matthew from Mark 15:39, but with certain changes. In the first place, it is placed in the mouths of all the soldiers of the watch. Above all, however, the interpolations in verses 52-53 mean that what the soldiers "see" is no longer the quite unspectacular death of Jesus, but the violent earthquake and its consequences. Thus this confession loses its force in comparison to the Markan account. One might even ask why, in the face of such obvious miracles, all Jerusalem does not speak in this vein—a thought that already occurred to the author of the Gospel of Peter (see the discussion of vss. 62-66).

Matthew borrowed from Mark all the features describing Jesus' suffering, including the shout that God had forsaken him and the cry marking his death. None of this is devalued. The special mark of this death, in fact, is suffering through the sense of having been abandoned by God. Unlike Mark, however, Matthew already reveals glimpses of the victory God has achieved. Not only the darkness but the earthquake, open graves, and dead men walking the streets show that what has taken place here is in the truest sense of the word earthshaking. Death has already been robbed of its power and the course of the world has been interrupted. And this is not even limited by the irreversibility of time. God, who stands above time, includes in the new life here coming into being even those who have long been dead. Thus the question posed by Matthew's account is not whether these bizarre events are credible or not, but whether we can follow the evangelist in seeing as he does the death of Jesus as the epochal event from which to date a change in our way of living, seeing the final power of love over death.

The Burial of Jesus (27:55-61)
Cf. Mark 15:40-47; Luke 23:49-56

⁵⁵There were many women there, looking on from a distance, who had followed Jesus from Galilee and had served him; ⁵⁶among them were Mary Magdalene, Mary the daughter of James and mother of Joseph, and the mother of Zebedee's sons.

⁵⁷When it was evening, a rich man from Arimathea arrived; his name was Joseph, and he had also become a disciple of Jesus. ⁵⁸He went to Pilate and asked for the body of Jesus. Pilate gave orders for the body to be given to Joseph. ⁵⁹So Joseph took it, wrapped it in a new linen sheet, ⁶⁰and placed it in his own new grave, which he had had dug out of the rock. Then he rolled a large stone across the entrance to the grave and went away. ⁶¹But Mary Magdalene and the other Mary stayed there, sitting facing the grave.

[55] Like Mark, Matthew records that of the disciples only women were witnesses to the crucifixion. But he speaks from the very outset of "many" women, while Mark 15:41 does not mention "many

other women" until later. As a consequence, we now read that the whole group of women had followed Jesus, albeit "from Galilee," not "in Galilee" (as in Mark), so that strictly speaking all that is claimed is that they joined him for the journey to Jerusalem. **[56]** The third woman Matthew mentions is "the mother of Zebedee's sons"; Mark 15:40 speaks of Salome. These might be the same woman; Matthew 26:37, for example, says "sons of Zebedee" instead of "James and John" (Mark 14:33; for a discussion of their names, see the introductory comments on Mark 16:1).

Joseph of Arimathea is called "rich"; Isaiah 53:9 states that the Servant of God will have his grave among the rich. As in John 19:38, Joseph is called a disciple of Jesus, while Mark says with more reserve that he was looking forward to the Kingdom of God. **[58-60]** The burial itself is recounted more succinctly; the details echo Luke. Emphasis is placed on the purity of the linen and, as in John 19:41, on the newness of the grave (cf. Luke 23:53). Both features indicate that Jesus is given the resting place that is his due, even though only a few women and one male disciple, not heretofore singled out, care for his remains. Only Matthew makes it clear that we are dealing with a grave that is Joseph's own (cf. the discussion of vs. 52). But he omits the statement of the other evangelists that Joseph himself took the body of Jesus down from the cross. The fact that the stone sealing the tomb was large is anticipated on the basis of Mark 16:4. **[61]** The abbreviated expression "the other Mary" compensates for the inconsistency of Mark at the first mention of the women (here vs. 56). In the Greek text it is striking to notice that the verb is singular: does this suggest a reminiscence that Mary Magdalene alone was at the tomb (John 20:1; cf. the introductory comments on Mark 16:1-8)?

The Guard at the Grave (27:62-66)

[62]But on the next day—that is, the day following the day of preparation—the chief priests and the Pharisees met with Pilate [63]and said, "Sir, we remember that while that liar was alive he said, 'I will be raised to life after three days.' [64]Give orders, then, for the grave to be safely guarded until the third day, so that his disciples will not be able to go and steal him, and then tell the people, 'He was raised from

the dead.' This last lie would be even worse than the first one."
65"Take a guard," said Pilate to them; "go and guard the grave as best
you can." 66So they left, and made the grave secure by putting a seal
on the stone and leaving the guard on watch.

It is a historical fact that people charged Jesus' disciples with
having stolen his body. According to Matthew 28:13-15, such charges
were still being made in the time of the evangelist. Justin confirms the
charge, speaking of Jewish missionaries who actively disseminated it.
Presumably, therefore, there was considerable Jewish propaganda
against the Christian message of Jesus' resurrection. This charge Matthew's community intended to refute; such a purpose would explain
this story. Of course it was not simply made up out of whole cloth.
On the one hand, non-Christians considered how to account for the
empty tomb, and suggested that the body had been stolen; on the
other hand, the Christians asked themselves how these others could
have fallen into such an erroneous assertion, and suggested that there
was a Jewish conspiracy against belief in the resurrection of Jesus.
This suggestion slowly turned into a rumor, and the rumor turned
into a narrative to which men gave full credence.

Other considerations may also have played a part. There are many
accounts of how devout believers escaped from closely guarded and
hermetically sealed prisons, usually with the help of an angel who
opens the locked doors (cf. Acts 12:3-10). About 100 B.C., for example, the Jewish writer Artapanus tells how Moses was imprisoned by
Pharaoh, but all the doors of his prison opened of their own accord;
some of the guards died, the others fell into a deep sleep and did not
wake up until later, to discover their weapons broken. It is conceivable
that the story in 28:2-4 (see the introductory comments) of how an
angel comes down to roll away the stone, which is out of place in its
present context, together with 27:62-66 and 28:11-15 contains an early
account of Easter, in which the resurrection itself must have been
described. The Gospel of Peter (see above) could be dependent on this
account. This hypothesis is vulnerable to the objection that Matthew
would then have been personally familiar with a description of the
resurrection but failed to use it, and that the Gospel of Peter was even
more reticent. Furthermore, the word for "watch" or "guard" in 28:4

is the same as in 27:36, although a different word is used in 27:65 and 28:11. This shows that the (oral?) tradition in 28:2-3 did not assume the presence of any guard, but merely was trying to make the rolling away of the stone more vivid (Mark 16:3-4). In this case Matthew, following the models mentioned above, used verse 4 to establish a connection with the guards that were present according to his tradition, at the same time having the angel sit on the stone (28:2) in order to make the transition to the Markan account (28:5-10).

The story soon became popular. A Jewish Christian addition in The Testament of Levi 16:3 brands Jesus a "liar," as does Matthew 27:63. Above all, the Gospel of Peter shows how the tradition continues to proliferate. Here we not only find the name of the officer of the watch, we are also told how "teachers of the Law, Pharisees, and elders" along with the soldiers roll the huge stone in front of the tomb, secure it with seven seals, and join the soldiers in keeping watch; the entire scene is observed by all the people from Jerusalem and its environs.

Now Acts 10:41-42 summarizes the point made by all the resurrection narratives: Jesus appeared only to believers. This represents a deliberate refusal to prove the resurrection in the face of unbelief. Faith dies from proofs, just as true love perishes when it demands proofs of another's love. If God had first to prove himself in men's eyes, he would no longer be God. Therefore there can be signs of the resurrection, which the believer accepts with gratitude, but never proofs that would convince unbelief. And so this story marks the first step along a road that runs counter to the witness of the Bible.

[62] It is hard to believe that the Jewish authorities would go to Pilate on the Sabbath, which is described rather strangely as the day following the "day of preparation" (Mark 15:43). According to John 18:28, they are so afraid of becoming unclean that they do not even dare to enter his palace the day before. [63] Here Pilate is addressed as "lord" in the Greek text (see the discussion of 8:2). The phrase "after three days," which Matthew corrects everywhere else to read "on the third day," shows that Matthew is borrowing a traditional account. Perhaps Matthew has in mind 12:40, when the Pharisees, though not the chief priests, were present in Jesus' audience, or even 26:61 (John 2:20-21). [64] Matthew has obviously heard speculation that disciples stole the body (28:15); it shows that the fact of the empty

tomb was not disputed, but rather its explanation. "The [not: 'his'] disciples" is terminology used by the later community. [65] Pilate's remark that they should guard the tomb as well as they could sounds ironic. There is a suspicion of how ridiculous the enterprise is from its very outset. [66] The lion pit into which Daniel was thrown was also sealed (Dan. 6:17). Christian art associated the two events; whether Matthew already did so can no longer be determined.

The story creates enormous difficulties because it tries to do something that is by definition impossible: to prove the resurrection of Jesus objectively to those who do not believe. In a certain sense the modern discussion is on a similar plane. What is now historically beyond dispute, however, is not the empty tomb but the fact that a series of people were convinced that they had seen the risen Lord (1 Cor. 15:5-8), with the result that a group of terrified fugitives became a host of messengers who, disregarding all danger to themselves, proclaimed this risen Lord with total conviction and within a few decades won men from throughout the known world to be his followers. Today, too, that fact is largely undisputed, but not its explanation. Of course modern men are not so naive as to accuse the disciples of stealing Jesus' body. This would have meant that they fled Jerusalem in confusion and terror only to undertake a daring coup a few hours later. But it is possible to see in the disciples' experience of the risen Lord a mere visual and auditory hallucination, explicable in purely psychological terms and not necessarily based on anything more than the unconscious conviction that Jesus, who had already convinced the disciples while he was on this earth, could not be irrevocably dead. Faith sees that the motive behind Matthew's "proof" narrative is quite as nugatory as the motive behind the psychological account. And accordingly, faith can make something even out of Matthew's wrongheaded narrative. Through these very verses there still resounds something of the laughter of God, which breaks through not only tombs that are barricaded, but all the mental manipulations of men (Ps. 2:4).

The Victory of God (28:1-10)
Cf. Mark 16:1-8; Luke 24:1-11

¹Late on the Sabbath, when the first day of the week was beginning, Mary Magdalene and the other Mary went to look at the grave.

²And behold, there was a strong earthquake; an angel of the Lord came down from heaven, approached, rolled the stone away, and sat on it. ³His appearance was like lightning and his clothes were white as snow. ⁴The guards were so afraid that they trembled and became like dead men. ⁵The angel spoke to the women. "Do not be afraid!" he said. "I know that you are looking for Jesus, who was crucified. ⁶He is not here, for he has been raised, just as he said. Come here and see the place where he lay. ⁷Quickly, now, go and tell his disciples, 'He has been raised from the dead, and behold, he is going to Galilee ahead of you; there you will see him!' Behold, I have told you this." ⁸So they left the grave in a hurry, afraid and yet filled with joy, and ran to tell his disciples. ⁹And behold, Jesus met them and said, "Hail." They came up to him, took hold of his feet, and fell down before him. ¹⁰"Do not be afraid!" Jesus said to them. "Go and tell my brothers to go to Galilee, and there they will see me."

[5-7] While the message of the angel agrees for the most part with Mark, the introduction and conclusion of this section diverge significantly from the Markan account. The introduction betrays a later stage of development. Not yet, however, is the resurrection itself described, as it is in the Gospel of Peter, where witnesses are named who see how the stone rolls away of its own accord as two men descend from the heavens and leave the tomb with a third, whose head already towers into the heavens, followed by a huge cross. But even according to Matthew the tomb was sealed and guarded. [1-4] Therefore a miracle must take place if the women are even to see the open tomb. Of course the two traditions—that of the guards and that of the women—do not go well together, because everything recounted in verses 5-10 has to take place while the soldiers are unconscious (see the introductory comments on 27:62-66).

[8-10] The conclusion of the section tells how the angel's command was carried out. This was necessary because according to Matthew the disciples went to Galilee on the basis of this command. For a discussion of the historical question, see the excursus on Mark 16:1-8. The conclusion here agrees in content and to some degree in form with Luke 24:9. Whether Jesus' encounter with the women was recounted in a similar way in the original ending of Mark's Gospel

we do not know (see the discussion there). The repeated command not to be afraid would be more appropriate following Mark 16:8.

On the other hand, several linguistic peculiarites show that Matthew at least revised the material. A certain similarity to the Johannine tradition is strikingly apparent, although in John only one Mary goes to the tomb. Like Matthew, John says nothing of any anointing of Jesus' body (see the discussion of vs. 1). His Mary, too, meets Jesus, albeit not on the road (despite John 20:2) as in Matthew 28:10; she, too, is sent by Jesus "to his brothers" (a feature peculiar to John and Matt. 28:10). This may be connected with Psalm 22, which plays an important role in the Passion narrative; Psalm 22:22 reads: "I will proclaim your name to my brothers." It may also be associated with the notion of Jesus as the firstborn of many brothers (Rom. 8:29; Heb. 2:11). In any event, the expression is rooted in the pre-Matthaean and pre-Johannine community.

[1] Matthew's transfer of the women's visit to the evening of the Sabbath is noteworthy. For the Jew, whose day begins with evening, this marks the beginning of the first day of the week. For someone who had grown up in the sphere of Hellenistic Roman civilization, the first day would begin the following morning. Luke 23:54 uses the same verb to designate Friday evening. Perhaps the original account stated only that the resurrection took place when the Sabbath was over or when the first day of the week was dawning, so that one might think in terms of Saturday evening, another of Sunday morning. The suggested translation "later than the Sabbath" is grammatically impossible, apart from the fact that no one would have used such a strange expression. At most it might mean "after the conclusion of the Sabbath"; but that, once again, would be Saturday evening. Thus Matthew probably sets the visit to the tomb on Saturday evening and the resurrection of Jesus during the night before Sunday. Matthew says nothing about the women's desire to anoint the body (Mark 16:1; Matthew also reduces the women from the three in Mark to two, consistent with Matt. 27:61). Anointing would be a problem, to say the least, first because of the huge stone, and also after the passage of an entire day in the corrosive Near Eastern heat. The guards Matthew assumes to be present would also make such anointing impossible.

[2] Instead, the two women are turned into witnesses, if not of the resurrection itself, at least of the attending events, which are further emphasized by the use of "and behold" (cf. the discussion of 8:2). The strong earthquake recalls the theophanies of Exodus 19:18 and 1 Kings 19:11-12 or Psalm 114:7: "Tremble, O earth, before the Lord [Jesus, to the Christians]. . . ." Here, too, it is the appearance of the Lord in his angel that causes the earthquake. The next clause, in fact, begins with "for," thus indicating cause. Above all, it is now the "angel of the Lord" (the phrase appears only in 1:20, 24; 2:13, 19; Luke 1:11; 2:9; and Acts) who rolls away the stone and sits like a conqueror upon it. Does the narrator have in mind that this opens the way for the resurrection of Jesus, which is invisible to everyone?

[3] The angel is described in greater detail than in Mark. "White as snow" describes "the Old One" (i.e. God) in Daniel 7:9 and the exalted Christ in Revelation 1:14. In the latter passage, Christ is also described in terms taken from the description of the angel in Daniel 10:5-6. Daniel 10:6 is also the source of the statement, not incorporated in Revelation 1:14, that his face was like lightning. A similar description is found in Luke 24:4 and occurs earlier in Luke 9:29 in the Transfiguration narrative (cf. Matt. 24:27). All the elements thus recall the signs expected to accompany the coming of the Lord at the end of the world and the irruption of the Kingdom of God.

[4] Probably we are to think that the emergence of Jesus from the tomb, which is not described, took place while the guards were unconscious; the same word is used to describe their "trembling" as is used to describe the trembling of the earth in 27:51 (similarly in 28:2). There is a grotesque element in this guarding of the tomb: those who seek to hold the dead man prisoner fall to the earth as though dead before him, who lives.

[5] The "young man" of Mark 16:5 is not explicitly called an "angel" until Matthew's account; his role is amplified not only by what he does in verse 2 but also by what he says. He "knows" what the women are looking for, and his command (vs. 7) sends them running to the disciples: "I have told you" (not Jesus, as in Mark 16:7). [6] Because of a transposition, the words "crucified" and "risen" do not occur juxtaposed, as they do in Mark 16:6; instead, the phrase "just as he said," which in Mark does not appear until the end of the angel's message, recalls Jesus' prediction of the resurrection.

The command to inform the disciples of Jesus' resurrection comes before the reference to Galilee, just as in the Markan text. Peter is no longer singled out from the disciples, since the special appearance to him (1 Cor. 15:5; Luke 24:34) has vanished from Matthew's tradition.

[8] According to Matthew, the women do not enter the tomb, as Mark 16:5 would have it; accordingly, they now do not go "out," but "away." According to Matthew as well as Mark they are filled with fear, but Matthew also describes them as being filled with joy. In the New Testament joy is especially characteristic of the Easter event (John 16:20-22; 20:20; Luke 24:52 [cf. the Christmas salutation in Luke 2:10]). Therefore Matthew also differs from Mark in telling how they hasten to do what they are bidden. The appearance of Jesus is again emphasized by the formula "and behold," but even more so by the approach and reverence of the women (see the discussion of 8:2). Jesus' salutation is the common Greek form (as in 26:49; in John 20:19, 26, on the other hand, we find the salutation "peace" that is common in Hebrew and Aramaic). Jesus' appearance is conceived so realistically that the women can grasp his feet. But this feature is not yet meant to counter false notions of the resurrection; it grows quite naturally out of the narrative. Jesus' command that the women go and tell his "brothers" (see above) is the same as that of the angel; it, too, begins: "Do not be afraid."

Matthew's account is already moving in the direction of presenting the resurrection as an objective, provable event (cf. the discussion of 27:62-66). Nevertheless, Matthew shows the hesitancy characteristic of the whole New Testament to name *witnesses* to the resurrection. Indeed, Matthew thinks of Jesus as coming out of the tomb while the guards are unconscious, but it is doubly noteworthy that the women, who observe everything else, cannot see this. At bottom Matthew knows that only the *words* interpreting what happened—in this case the message of the angel—can lead to understanding, not the observation of phenomena, however remarkable. Thus the entire event holds no meaning for the guards and those who posted them. Matthew's account of what happened is still a proclamation and a call to faith; it has not been transformed into a legendary demonstration negating the need for faith.

The Resurrection Cannot Be Proved or Disproved (28:11-15)

[11]But while the women went on their way, some of the guard went back to the city and told the chief priests everything that had happened. [12]The chief priests met with the elders and made their plan; they gave a large sum of money to the soldiers [13]and said, "You are to say that his disciples came during the night and stole his body while you were asleep. [14]And if the Governor should hear of this, we will convince him and you will have nothing to worry about." [15]The guards took the money and did what they were instructed to do. To this very day that is the report spread around by the Jews.

This continues the tradition discussed in 27:62-66. It is striking that the soldiers do not report to their superiors but rather to the chief priests—perhaps they do so because they got their orders at the insistence of the latter. Once more the chief priests and elders are mentioned, but not the teachers of the Law or the Pharisees (see the discussion of 26:3). Once more a sufficient sum of money is dispensed to solve everything. Apart from its use in the parable of the three servants (25:18, 27), the expression for money appears only in the stories of Judas' betrayal (26:15; 27:3-9). Just as money betrayed Jesus into the hands of the authorities, so now it is to silence his resurrection. How the soldiers are supposed to have noticed that the disciples were stealing the body while they were fast asleep is hard to explain (cf. the introductory comments on vss. 1-4). Above all, to ask them to say they had fallen asleep while on watch and allowed what they were guarding to be stolen is asking them to sign their own death warrant. A mere promise to intercede on their behalf would never have satisfied Roman soldiers, even though bribery was traditional in the Near East. The concluding statement, however, reveals the origin of the whole story about the guards: Jewish propaganda, with which the Matthaean community was still beset. Verse 15 is the first in which Matthew uses the expression "Jews" in his own voice (elsewhere it is used only by gentiles): that he does so indicates that Christians and Jews have already gone their separate ways.

The charge that the disciples stole the body was untenable; but the way the Christian community countered the charge was worse. The most dangerous element in the counterattack was the Christian community's arrogance—its self-righteousness in assuming that the resurrection of Jesus was an obvious historical fact, which only the malevolent could deny—its assumption in other words, that unbelief was merely willful refusal to accept what was secretly believed to be true. In assuming so arrogant a stance the community was forgetting that faith is a gift of grace, unmotivated and above all unmerited; and certainly such an assumption of self-righteousness was out of keeping with the forgiveness preached by Jesus. Nevertheless, though not excusable it is understandable. The Old Testament speaks of people outside the community commissioned by God to confound it, for example the prophet Balaam (Num. 22:5); here, indeed, the community is confounded—but by itself rather than the outsiders. Passages like Romans 2:15 also sense something of such an idea.

Of course none of this has been thought out theologically. No one had yet realized that the resurrection of Jesus, which had taken place in the hearts of the faithful, does not have to be objectively demonstrable to all. The community was naive to try to account for all the extraordinary facts. Nonetheless, we can also see that through its words there speaks an unshakable faith, for which the resurrection of Jesus is so clearly the basis of all joy, of all life and death, that it can no longer even imagine harboring doubts. Perhaps this shows that a faith that is too unshakable, unfamiliar with any sense of doubt, is in particular danger of giving false explanations, thus losing those who are closest to having faith (25:31-46!).

The Presence of the Risen Lord with His Community (28:16-20)

[16]The eleven disciples went to the hill in Galilee where Jesus had told them to go. [17]And they saw him and fell and worshiped him, even though some of them doubted. [18]Jesus drew near and said to them, "I have been given all authority in heaven and on earth. [19]Go, therefore, make disciples of all peoples and baptize them in the name of the Father and the Son and the Holy Spirit, [20]and teach them to obey everything I have commanded you. And behold, I will be with you always, to the end of the age."

(Vs. 18—Cf. Dan. 7:14.)

The concluding episode was undoubtedly familiar to Matthew from the tradition of his community. It is almost impossible to determine, however, to what extent its wording was already fixed and to what extend it is due to Matthew's hand. It has even been suggested that Matthew composed the entire section himself. Many feautres in it are related to his ideas: the reign of the exalted Lord (cf. the Kingdom of the Son of Man in 13:41) with the purpose of making men "disciples" (27:57, a Matthaean insertion); the injunction to teach Jesus' commands (the Sermon on the Mount); the contrast between the restriction of Jesus' ministry to Israel (10:5-6; 15:24) and the worldwide mission of the post-Easter community (8:11; 12:21; 25:31-32); the aid given by Jesus (8:25; 14:30).

[18] It is significant that the only evidence (and it is faint) that Jesus is not speaking from heaven but is walking the earth is an unequivocally Matthaean idiom, used only by him and frequently inserted by him into the traditional material he draws on ("Jesus drew near and said to them"). For its part, however, the tradition spoke only of a heavenly appearance, like that experienced by Paul. This is how the resurrection appearances were probably all pictured in the earliest period, since 1 Corinthians 15:5-8 makes no distinction whatsoever between the experience of Paul and that of the Easter witnesses before him. Jesus' resurrection was conceived in this period as a direct translation from the tomb to heaven.

[16] The site of the appearance, but especially the hill, which Matthew does not mention previously, and perhaps also the ambiguous reaction of the witnesses, formed part of the tradition from the beginning. To be sure, the motif of doubt has been considered a late addition, indicating problems within the community; it was thought best not to dignify these doubts by recognizing them: therefore, according to this theory, all reassurances about the reality of the risen Lord were omitted and only his words are cited. The wording is strange. The text reads literally, "They, however . . ."; or, if others were mentioned previously, it reads, "The others, however, doubted." This either means that all the disciples doubted even though they worshiped, or it means that along with the eleven there were others present who doubted. Both possibilities are hard to conceive, although the former would be theologically pleasing and might recall such

passages as Judges 6:11-24; 13:8-23. Might there lie in the background an account which recorded only the doubts of the disciples? It is possible that Matthew himself added the statement that they worshiped Jesus (as in 8:2; 14:33). This would mean that he took the statement to mean that some of the eleven worshiped, while others doubted. In this case the motif of doubt (see the concluding remarks) would have a firm place in the historical tradition: an appearance of the crucified Jesus was the last thing the disciples expected.

[18, 20] We may now consider what Jesus says to the disciples. The initial and concluding sayings (vss. 18*b*, 20*b*) are the most likely parts belonging to the narrative in its earliest form, with the possible exception of the phrase "end of the age," which is a correction on the part of the evangelist in 24:3. The resurrection thus is the beginning of Jesus' reign, which will last until the end of the world, at which time the Kingdom of God will dawn. This is also the interpretation of Mark 14:62 (=Matt. 26:64) and 1 Corinthians 15:24-28, where the coming of the Son of Man on the clouds of heaven and the final subordination of Son to Father bring the Son's reign to a close. Elsewhere, too, there is evidence for the association of Jesus' exaltation (in the resurrection) with the eschatological fulfillment of history. This is probably the earliest understanding of Easter, corresponding to what the first witnesses to the resurrection experienced: the one who was scorned by the entire world and died a martyr's death has been exalted by God to reign in heaven; he will one day return, at the inauguration of God's Kingdom.

[19a] It is not easy to determine how early the notion of proclaiming this reign and institutionalizing it became associated with the resurrection. The two are linked in the later hymns of the community: 1 Timothy 3:16; likewise Romans 16:26 and in the later, non-Pauline postscript to Romans; also Colossians 1:23, 27; and Ephesians 3:6. Undoubtedly, witnesses to the resurrection, probably from the very first day (as in Gal. 1:16), understood their encounter with the Lord as including a commission to proclaim his resurrection to others. It is undoubtedly true that a long and bitter struggle was fought in the primitive community before the idea of the gentile mission was accepted.

That pagans were also called to salvation was suggested by Jesus'

own words and actions (8:11; 15:21-28), and even by the practice of
the Pharisees (23:15). The prophets, too, had expected that at the
eschaton nations would flock to Zion. As the mission of the Pharisees
(23:15) shows, this led to the idea of going out into the gentile world
to invite the gentiles to accept circumcision and become members of
Israel. Verse 19a would therefore not be impossible for the period
immediately after Easter.

Even before Paul, and concurrently with his mission, disciples of
Jesus were going out among the gentiles; communities in Syrian Antioch and in Rome came into being without his help. It was not the
earliest community proper, but rather Greek-speaking Jews of Jerusalem who went to Samaria and Syria; but the notion of a universal
gentile mission does not appear until relatively late, in the passages
mentioned above, as well as in Mark 13:10 (= Matt. 24:14), and even
then it is still not connected with the exaltation of Jesus. In the very
earliest period, then, we should think at most of a proclamation that
Jesus had risen from the dead, which would move the gentile world
to join Israel for the eschatological pilgrimage to Zion. Of a proclamation to Israel there is here no mention at all.

[19b] We do not know the origins of baptism. Most likely a sizable
group of John's disciples who joined the community of Jesus after
Easter brought it with them; in any event, it is always assumed in the
New Testament that everyone is baptized. Everywhere except here
baptism is spoken of as being in or through the name of Jesus (Acts
2:38; 8:16; 10:48; Rom. 6:3; 1 Cor. 1:13, 15; 6:11; cf. 10:2), so that the
addition of the threefold name represents a later development. Now
Eusebius, one of the early Fathers, when speaking before the Council
of Nicea (A.D. 325) regularly (twenty-one times) cites our passages in
a shorter form: "Go and make disciples of all people in my name
teaching them . . ."; it is not clear whether "in my name" goes with
the preceding or following phrase.

Justin cites Isaiah and apostolic tradition as the basis for the
threefold name without any reference to our passage. It can hardly be
doubted that Matthew himself wrote the text as it stands in all the
manuscripts, for as early as the end of the first century the Didache
(7:1, 3), strongly influenced by Matthew or his tradition, bears witness
to the same baptismal practice, although also still mentioning the

earlier form of baptism in the name of Jesus (9:5). Passages like those mentioned below in the excursus on Father, Son, and Holy Spirit show how easy it was for the name of Jesus to be expanded into Father, Son, and Holy Spirit. Thus Matthew probably bears witness here to the baptismal practice of his (Syrian?) community, which need not be that of other communities, e.g. in Palestine or Asia Minor. Whether Eusebius was still familiar through oral tradition with a preliminary stage of Matthew 28:19 is very uncertain; it is equally possible that he is using an abbreviated quotation of our verse, just as today we often use an abbreviated form of the Ten Commandments.

[16-20] The present form of the account yields a rational sequence of narrative, statement of authority, command, and motivation for the command, similar to that found in the so-called messenger formula of 2 Chronicles 36:23. For a discussion of how Matthew and his community understood the account, see the conclusion of this section.

[16] The disciples are referred to, with historical accuracy, as numbering "eleven," while the full "twelve" mentioned in 1 Corinthians 15:5 implies the notion of the fulfillment of all promises (Matt. 19:28; Luke 22:30; Rev. 21:14; cf. the excursus following Mark 6:7-13). They all represent (cf. the discussion of Matt. 10:2) "brothers" (28:10) of Jesus. Mountains have been the sites of God's revelation (5:1; 14:23; 17:1) ever since the Old Testament (Sinai and Horeb). Galilee, the site of Jesus' earthly ministry, is stressed once more.

[17] The disciples' worship, expressed in characteristically Matthaean terms ("fell"; see the discussion of 8:2), is commensurate with Jesus' authority, as claimed in verse 18. For the way Matthew understands doubt, cf. the discussion of 14:31. [18] The Matthaean idiom "draw near" has connotations of Jesus' coming to the aid of those who doubt. The way this saying is formulated recalls Daniel 7:14, which says of the Son of Man: "And to him were given power and all nations . . . and all glory, so that they might serve him." This shows that the exaltation of Jesus on Easter was viewed in the light of eschatological expectations. To be sure, no other motifs from Daniel 7 are present, and the coming of the Son of Man with the clouds of heaven, promised in Daniel 7:13 (Matt. 24:30; 26:64), is still in the future, so that the connection with Daniel is not absolutely certain. It is noteworthy,

however, that Jesus is given no new title, e.g. *Kyrios* ("Lord"), as he is in Philippians 2:9-11, a hymn written down some twenty years earlier. For a discussion of Matthew's understanding of what this means, see the concluding remarks. "Heaven and earth" is the all-inclusive formula of the Old Testament; it also appears in Matthew 6:10, in the petition of the Lord's Prayer that is unique to the Matthaean community.

[19] How much emphasis is placed on "going" is a matter of debate. Unquestionably "make disciples" contains the main verb, to which everything that precedes and follows is subordinate (literally: "going . . . baptizing . . . teaching . . ."). At some preliminary stage the expression "go" might therefore derive from Semitic usage, where it merely denotes the beginning of an action (cf. 9:13). But Matthew also uses the verb to describe how the disciples go forth on the mission Jesus commands them to undertake (10:6-7), and he attaches great importance to the theme of the "way" in any case. It is therefore probable that he finds Jesus' commission to go out into the world significant. The association of a participle in this tense with a main verb in the same form is in fact typical of Matthew, so that he might even have added it of his own accord.

The gentile nations or people have already been referred to, not only in Mark 13:10 (=Matt. 24:14) but also in Matthew 10:18. Now the rule of Christ over the entire world is associated with universal discipleship, as in the hymn in 1 Timothy 3:16. For a discussion of baptism and the threefold name, see below. The idea of a name as the sign of someone's presence had already appeared in the Old Testament. Where God's name is called upon, where the name of the king is proclaimed, there the one called by name becomes present, together with his power or his aid. The formula "in the name" reads literally "upon the name"; it is probably to be explained as a Greek idiom, where it is used in commercial and banking circles in the sense of our "to the account of." In Greek, soldiers also take an oath "upon the name of . . . ," and psuedonymous documents are written "upon the name of . . . (Paul, for example)."

Father, Son, and Holy Spirit appear here in juxtaposition. The way has already been paved for this usage through passages such as

1 Corinthians 12:4-6; 2 Corinthians 13:13. It is also reminiscent of John 14:16-17; 1 John 5:5-6; 1 Peter 1:2; Revelation 1:4-5, where the seven spirits are the Spirit of God sent to the seven communities, etc. Narratives like that of Jesus' baptism, in which God sends the Holy Spirit to the Son, are closely related. But our passage goes beyond these, because all three are brought together in a single name, which is crucial to what is said. Naturally we are not yet dealing with any developed doctrine of the Trinity. Just as the Holy Spirit is given by the Father (in 3:16 Matthew adds "God's," in 10:20, "your Father's"), so the Son is sent by the Father (10:40) to reveal the Father (11:27). As in those passages, so here all power is "given" him by the Father. Behind the threefold formula stands the conviction that in the Son as well as in the Spirit God himself becomes present, without any restriction or diminution.

This notion implies a conception that is even more profound. The Christian community understood that when a man has once encountered God, he can no longer see him in isolation, as ultimate being or the principle of nature, say, but can only look upon him as one who acts, who comes to meet us, who seeks us out. Simply to speak of God in isolation, of the dry and abstract "one God," is to show that one does not yet understand who God really is. It is correct to state that he is the one God confessed by Israel (Mark 12:29, not incorporated by Matthew; but cf. Mark 10:18 [=Matt. 19:17]); but it is still to misunderstand God not to realize that he comes to us and seeks us out with his love. John expresses this idea by saying that God is love or God is Spirit (1 John 4:8, 16; John 4:24). But these terms do not refer to our human love or our human spirit, which could only be called divine by extension. Therefore both after Matthew and in his period the Christian community spoke of the Son who was already present with the Father before creation. In speaking thus the community was likewise trying to say that God is never an isolated, lifeless God, some kind of ultimate principle of being; it insisted particularly that from all eternity God opens himself to us by seeking us out, by loving us. God is thus already in his own being favor and love; and the love revealed in Jesus of Nazareth, not to speak of the love men have for each other, derives from the original act of love, from God.

To put it in more modern terms: the juxtaposition of the three modes in which God encounters us describes him as the subject and author of all the favor and love that has encompassed the world from all eternity and will continue to do so for all eternity. God is thus protected against our misunderstanding him: we do not already know him as some isolable concept, so that Jesus merely gives us additional information about him; neither may we think that a God who was originally dispassionate was suddenly transformed into a loving God because of the Fall. God is always immediate and more than intellectual—he is the instant experience of love and relationship between men; but he is more than that, for he is also the assurance of future love, and of love both to us and from us greater than in our present power. Both aspects are stressed: in the Son and in the Spirit God comes to us totally; at the same time, he remains the God who confronts us and is yet the expectation of still more. According to one of the most famous mathematical logicians of the modern era, Whitehead, the doctrine of the Trinity is one of the greatest achievements of the human intellect (cf. also the excursus following 25:46).

[20] Matthew is concerned that the disciples teach and do everything that Jesus taught. Jesus gave his commandments in the course of his earthly ministry; the community must not confuse them with a post-Easter gospel speaking only of the Lord of the universe and thus ignore the quotidian actions commanded by him (cf. the excursus following 7:13-23 [§3]). The enduring presence of Jesus, once more emphasized by "and behold," therefore has two aspects. All power and authority are indeed given to him, so that he will be with his disciples to support them. At the same time, this is true only where they daily acknowledge and experience his presence in his commandments. This is of course not the last word; the "end of the age" will inaugurate something greater still, already spoken of in 22:1-14 and 24:4–25:46.

The unique features of this Easter account can be seen when it is compared to the others. It has several points in common with them: the disciples see Jesus, they doubt (Luke 24:37-38, 41; John 20:25 [cf. 14-15]; 21:4; Mark 16:11, 13-14), and Jesus speaks to them and sends them forth. But the differences are readily apparent. In Matthew the disciples see Jesus suddenly, without his appearing by coming into their midst (Luke 24:36 [cf. 15]; John 20:19, 26; 21:4). He is enthroned in heaven and is suddenly seen by the disciples; the statement that he comes to them upon the earth is Matthew's addition. Therefore it is only here that we read of the worship of the disciples, of the proclamation of the authority given Jesus as Lord of the universe, of his presence with the disciples, and of the end of the world, when all that has happened will be brought to its goal as determined by God. There is no trace of certain features which appear in almost all the other accounts: references to the reality of Jesus' corporeal presence (Luke 24:39; John 20:20, 27; cf. 21:6), his table fellowship with the disciples (Luke 24:30, 41-42; Acts 1:4; 10:41; John 21:9-10, 13), and his vanishing at the end (Luke 24:31, 51; Acts 1:9; Mark 16:19). Instead, Jesus remains with his disciples until the end of the world.

Therefore their mission is also conceived differently (cf. Luke 24:47-48; Acts 1:8; John 20:21; Mark 16:15). The Spirit is not given to the disciples (as in Luke 24:49; Acts 1:4, 8; John 20:22-23); neither are they commanded to preach the gospel. They are, of course, to go out into the world, but for the purpose of making disciples of all peoples and teaching the commandments of Jesus. This is something different from the blessing in Luke 24:50 or the more closely related promises of charismatic gifts (Mark 16:17-18). It is not in the new preaching of the post Easter community but in the commandments he taught during his earthly ministry that Jesus will be present with his disciples and establish his rule among all nations, in order that God may reign as Lord here on earth until he one day comes to establish his eternal Kingdom.

Fundamentally, then, this passage speaks less of the mission of the Christian community than of its life in discipleship, which is to be above all an example. In contrast to Mark, Matthew places little stress in his Gospel on "preaching" and "evangelizing"; the "gospel" is defined more specifically as the message proclaimed by Jesus (see the excursus on 7:13-23 [§3]). Such concepts as "discipleship," "keeping the commandments," and "going" take the place of preaching. Instead of the unverifiable Spirit, Matthew speaks of the presence of Jesus. Baptism is less a ceremony that imparts salvation; "for the forgiveness of sins" is a formula associated with the Lord's Supper, which accompanies the disciples throughout their lives (Matt. 26:28).

Baptism, on the other hand marks simply the beginning of a life of obedience, in which the disciples will remain through their lives both teachers and students in the Kingdom of God (cf. 13:52). Faithfulness will be rewarded with salvation. Thus Matthew dismisses his readers with the promise that Jesus will not desert his disciples until all is fulfilled.

The promise stated at the outset has been fulfilled; Immanuel ("God with us"; 1:23) is present, and the promise made to Abraham for his offspring (1:1 ff.) has become true in Immanuel; he has become a blessing for all peoples (Gen. 12:3). It is possible, if one wishes, to speak of this passage as the enthronement of Jesus, if it is made clear that the primary interest of the account is the commission given the disciples, i.e. the community. The primitive Christian community thought of the resurrection of Jesus as his exaltation; this passage therefore presents a clear contrast with the typical enthronement psalm, in which there would appear an acknowledgment of this new Lord of the universe by all nations (Phil. 2:10-11; 1 Tim. 3:16). Matthew 28:18-20 is to be understood as the instructions and promise of one who has ascended his throne. The instructions are to bring about the fulfillment of the promise—they are, in the period between Jesus' earthly ministry and the end of the age, to impart his spirit to all people, so that all nations will acknowledge him as Lord.

Retrospect

1

One of Matthew's most striking innovations appears in the confession of Peter. The title "Son of Man," by which Mark 8:31 connects the crucial events of Jesus' life with his Passion, death, and resurrection, is appropriate for the eschatological Judge (Matt. 25:31); but, as 16:13 shows, Matthew still finds the title ambiguous. Only the terms "Christ" and "Son of God," which he considers essentially equivalent, really state who Jesus is. Therefore Peter's statement is commended as a direct revelation from God (16:16-17). The incorporation of the temptation narrative (4:1 ff.) prevents misunderstanding Jesus' messianic role as that of a political revolutionary; and the rebuke to Peter, who cannot understand the path of suffering Jesus must take, is stressed even more by Matthew than by Mark (see the discussion of 16:23). The path taken by Jesus is that of the humble (11:28) and gentle (21:5) messiah. In what sense, then, is he the Christ?

The reorganization of the material in chapters 5–11 is striking in comparison with the retention of the Markan structure in chapters 3–4 and 12–28. The change must have been highly significant to Matthew (see the introductory comments on 4:17–11:30). In chapters 5–7 and 8–9, Jesus is presented as messiah in his message and his ministry. His messianic dignity is thus based primarily on his teachings and his saving acts. This collocation is undoubtedly based on the prophecy in 11:5 (see §2 below). But the interpolation of the missionary discourse addressed to the disciples in chapter 10 shows that Jesus' authority in word and deed continues in the persons of his disciples (10:1, 7). He is the messiah in that he gives to all who follow him the possibility of fulfilling God's will in word and deed.

Thus the image of the Servant of God, silently proclaiming his message and working as a charismatic healer, stands at the center of the Gospel (12:15-21; cf. the discussion of 27:14); his life of wandering from place to place can be understood as an anticipation of the life his disciples will lead (see the excursus on 1:18-25 [§3]). Matthew probably hit upon this statement by identifying Jesus with the figure of Wisdom or the Logos, already familiar in Judaism (see the excursus on 23:34-39). In Paul and John the same identification also describes the Son of God's life in heaven before his birth; Matthew's statement is simpler than these: perhaps it reflects his reaction against such doctrines as simply too much for a Jew to accept, or perhaps his is simply an earlier stage of theological reflection. Whatever the case, Matthew is concerned to show that the "gospel" preached after Easter does not differ from the preaching of the earthly Jesus (see the excursus on 7:13-23 [§3]). Matthew is suspicious of any doctrine of Christ that sees in him only the exalted *Kyrios* or Lord (Phil. 2:9-11; 1 Cor. 12:3); therefore this title does not appear in 28:18-20, where it would be appropriate, and in 7:22 it is placed in the mouth of the hypocrites, while the polite term "lord," equivalent to "sir," addressed to the earthly Jesus is a real sign of faith.

The earthly Jesus, thus, is a forerunner, pioneering the new way for his disciples. Therefore the Gospel concludes by saying that the exalted Jesus will remain present in his commandments, which his disciples will continue to proclaim, and thus conquer the world (see the discussion of 28:20). Therefore great emphasis is placed on the faith that the disciples will require to act with authority (see the discussion of 14:31; 17:20; 21:21-22). Therefore the disciples must not be blind like other men, as they are in Mark, but fundamentally understand the message of Jesus (compare, for example, 13:16-17; 14:33; 16:17; 18:1; 20:20 with the corresponding passages in Mark).

2

What, then, is the relationship between the Christian community and Israel? According to 11:2-6, Jesus fulfills the predictions of the prophets. Long before Matthew, Christians understood the Old Testament as the book that predicted the fate of Jesus and his disciples. There must even have been Christian equivalents of the Jewish teachers of the Law, who collected and assembled such references (see the introductory comments on 27:3-10). The parallels between the account of Jesus' infancy and the story of Moses had been discovered even before Matthew (see the introductory comments on 2:1-12). Matthew himself reinterpreted Jesus' birth under persecution as the realization of God's preordained will, introducing an especially large number of quotations from the prophets at this very point (see the excursus on 1:18-25). The very incorporation of the infancy narratives, but above all the genealogy that precedes them, which exhibits an almost mathematical regularity in God's history that runs from Abraham (not Adam, as in Luke 3:38) to Jesus, indicate that for Matthew the Old Testament is fulfilled in the story of Jesus. The continuity of God's history with his people is not interrupted.

This means, for Matthew, that God keeps faith with Israel. Only Matthew goes so far as to say that God sends Jesus to Israel alone (10:5-6; 15:24). Of course the Baptist's harsh words to the descendants of Abraham (3:7 ff.), coming directly after the initial story of Jesus, which itself begins with Abraham (1:1), show that descent from Abraham guarantees nothing to a people who will not hear. And Matthew reshapes Jesus' discourses in Jerusalem (see the introductory comments on chapters 21–25), to show God struggling for Israel not once but twice, and Israel's "no" to him twice. Only after Israel as a whole has finally rejected God's offer (27:25; see the discussion of 13:13) is the way open to the calling of the gentiles, which is presented in 12:21 and 28:19 as the actual goal of God's saving work (see 1:5-6; 2:1; 4:15; 8:11; 25:31-32; and the discussion of 1:3).

Even here, however, Matthew maintains that the Christian community does not simply take the place of Israel. The hallowed word "people," which is reserved for Israel, is not applied to the Christian community, although it is a "nation" that bears the fruit God had expected Israel to bear (see the discussion of 21:43). Matthew is not interested in this holy (or unholy) history for its own sake, but because of the hope (for Israel) and the warning (for his community) it implies. Pre-Matthaean tradition already spoke of the rejection of Israel and the election of the nations (Mark 12:1-12; Luke 14:16-23). Mark used the cursing of the fig tree to emphasize God's judgment upon the cult of Israel even more than Matthew does; the Lukan conclusion to the parable of the banquet, "None of those who were invited will taste of my banquet," refers even more bluntly than Matthew to the destruction of Jerusalem (see Matt. 22:7). Matthew still leaves open the possibility of hope even after judgment (see the discussion of 23:39). But the main point for Matthew is that all this serves to warn the Christian community.

In principle, the disciples of Jesus understood this (see §1 above); but they still had little faith and were therefore subject to temptation (14:30-31). At the very point where the disciples are commended and distinguished from those who do not understand (13:13-17) there follows the parable of the weeds, which is an explicit caveat against a too-ephemeral faith (Matthew substitutes this parable for one in Mark which depicts men as sleepers, constitutionally incapable of strengthening their faith: Mark 4:26-29). Matthew himself probably authored the strong warning of judgment to come, in his interpretation of the parable (Matt. 13:40-43, cf. 49-50). The depth of his concern to warn the community about the coming judgment is also revealed by his frequent use of the phrase about wailing and gnashing of teeth (8:12), addressed to the community (the phrase derives from Q, where it refers to Israel); see 13:42, 50; 22:13; 24:51; 25:30. Above all, the total structure of chapters 21–25 (see the introductory comments) leads up to this warning.

The emphasis on the Pharisees in the debates at Jerusalem (see the discussion of 22:15) and the story of the soldiers appointed to guard the tomb (see the discussion of 28:15) demonstrates the degree of Matthew's involvement in the continued debate with Judaism. As his placement of the question about Temple tax at the beginning of his "community rules" section (17:24-27) shows, he is deeply concerned the Christian community not be a stumbling block to Israel, but, if possible, an instrument of their salvation. The consistent distinction (prior to 27:25) between the Jewish people, who still remain open to Jesus and his message, and their leaders, reveals the same attitude.

3

The dispute about the Temple tax emphasizes the fundamental liberty of the children of God in two directions: they are free of the obligation to pay it, but they are also free to pay it for the sake of others. This poses the problem of the Law. Even before Matthew, Jesus' criticism of the Law was significantly qualified. This change appears in the Sayings Source as well as in the catechetical tradition of the community. The least point of the Law will not be done away with (5:18 = Luke 16:17). What is wrong with Jewish religiosity is its motive: a desire to appear virtuous in the eyes of others (Matt. 6:2-6, 16-18; 23:5). Pharisaic scholarship would be quite in order if men really acted according to its precepts (23:2-3).

Matthew incorporates such statements because for him Jesus has not annulled the Law but fulfilled it. Jesus' "I, however" does stand in contrast to the law of Sinai, as Matthew himself stresses, putting the words of Q into the form of antitheses (5:21-48). But the Law is not broken or changed, it is given life because in the teaching and life of Jesus and his community there is realized for the first time the *purpose* of God's Law. In Jesus the Wisdom of God, which is often identified with the Law (Ecclus. 24:23; Bar. 4:1; etc.), is incarnate (see §1 above and the excursus on 23:34-39). The Wisdom of God is his commandment to love—this commandment contains the entire Law and the prophets (see the discussion of Matt. 5:18)—and Jesus, in his healings and death, shows that this commandment can be fulfilled (see the excursus following 7:29).

The commandment to love is the standard by which all peoples will finally be judged (25:31-46). This means that the commandment to show mercy under all circumstances transcends the Sabbath, as Matthew makes clear by his interpolation in 12:1, 7, but also, according to Matthew, when there is no question of showing mercy the Sabbath must absolutely be kept (see the discussion of 24:20). Therefore Matthew reinterprets the conclusion of the Sermon on the Mount, turning the whole into an attack on the false prophets whose "lawlessness" consists in their neglect of love (see the introductory comments on 7:13-23; 24:11-12).

4

Thus the Christian community is understood as the band of disciples in which Jesus lives on because it observes and teaches his commandments (28:19-20). Matthew therefore inserts the regulations governing the life of the community at the point where care for "these little ones" appeared in the Markan text. This is the most important responsibility of the community. Accordingly, Matthew interprets the parable of Jesus that spoke of God's seeking and helping love as an admonition to the community to go after any brother in danger as a shepherd goes after a sheep (18:10-14); he codifies a general admonition into specific guidelines for the conduct of the community (18:15-18). Similarly, he takes the parable of the unforgiving servant as a strong warning to the community against endangering brotherly intercourse through unreadiness to forgive. Again, his only commentary on the Lord's Prayer is a blunt warning against intransigence (6:14-15). And still again, in the parable where rewards are given even to those who came at the very end, he places primary emphasis on the warning against envy (20:1-16). He takes this concern over fellowship so seriously that he even takes an obscure saying about the disasters of the eschaton and applies it to anyone who endangers one of "these little ones." That is how vehemently Jesus takes their side!

Only a community that lives in love can be salt to the rest of the earth, light to all men, a city on a hill. Such a community reveals the Father in heaven to the world through its good works (5:13-16). The interpolation of chapter 10 between the exposition of Jesus in chapters 5–9 and the fulfillment quotation in 11:2-6 (see §1) shows that these good works consist in the continuation of Jesus' ministry on the part of his disciples, who prophetically proclaim the Kingdom of God and exercise the authority to heal (10:1-7; cf. the excursus on 7:13-23).

Perhaps it is Matthew's purpose to depict Jesus himself as the prototype of such charismatics (see §1). But the important point, as the conclusion of the Sermon on the Mount (see §3) and the talk of the "gospel" or "good news" (see §1) insist, is that the teaching of Jesus not be forgotten. This teaching is given to the community above all through Peter, who not only recorded the sayings of Jesus but also interpreted them for the post-Easter period (see the discussion of 16:19). Nevertheless, although his position at the headwaters of tradition remains unique, he stands as a model for all the disciples of Jesus, who receive the same commission and the same promise (18:18). They recognize only the paradoxical hierarchy of 18:4 and 23:11-12. Nowhere do we find specially appointed leaders of the community or other functionaries; an institutional hierarchy is explicitly rejected (23:8-10; see the discussion of 23:7). Authority to speak and to act derives from the life of the community; it is not institutionalized.

5

And yet what Matthew writes is still a Gospel. Despite some tendencies in that direction, he did not fall into casuistry, the attempt to lay down ever more detailed regulations that would apply to every conceivable case, stating what a man must do to be obedient. Discipleship is an undivided whole that demands far more than the observance of certain precepts, however strict; this point is made by Matthew himself. Therefore the promise of "God is with us" (1:23) is fulfilled in the "I will be with you" of the risen Christ (28:20). This certainly does not mean that the disciples will be protected from all assaults. Matthew sees in the boat pounded by the waves a symbol of the community (see the discussion of 8:23 and 14:24); he looks on persecution as the normal state of the community, not something reserved for the eschaton (see the discussion of 10:17-25 [concluding remarks] and 5:10). But he looks upon such discipleship as a gift. Although he associates the Baptist very closely with Jesus and puts the same message in his mouth (3:2), the Baptist remains merely a forerunner (3:3), whereas Jesus in this message (4:17) is the light itself that shines on those who dwell in darkness in Galilee of the gentiles (4:15-16).

In the Beatitudes Matthew tries to show that Jesus' teachings are not simply words of wisdom timelessly true, but rather constitute an authoritative promise, and thus a present proclamation of the eschaton (see the discussion of 5:3-12). Only through participation in the authority of Jesus do the disciples exercise authority (9:1-8; 10:1, 7, 24-25). Thus it is the way taken by Jesus himself that creates for the community the possibility of living in discipleship (see §1). Therefore

Matthew places an interpretation on the "messianic secret" entirely different from Mark's. No longer does it mean that no one understood Jesus before his Passion and resurrection; according to Matthew, it means that Jesus carried out his ministry silently, as the Servant of God, to save the weak (see the concluding remarks on 12:15-21). The interpretation of Jesus' death as a ransom for many (20:28), which Matthew borrowed, is not really the focus of his theology; and only the Eucharistic liturgy of his community contains the addition, "for the forgiveness of sins" (26:28; cf. 1:21). When he links the forgiveness of God with the forgiveness of one's brother, repeated, if necessary, seventy times seven times (18:22, 35; also 6:12, 14-15), he is thinking of God's repeated forgiveness, which in the fullness of its riches can be described only in images that almost defy comprehension (see the discussion of 18:24). This inconceivably great forgiveness is not purchased, but rather exemplified, by Jesus.

Other passages also stress the fact that such discipleship bears the marks of being an outright gift: the commendation of the disciples (13:16-17), which is a new interpolation on the part of Matthew; and the promise of an easy yoke and a light burden to those who are tired from bearing heavy loads (11:28-30). This is expressed most movingly in the term Matthew uses for a disciple of Jesus (Matthew makes it his own even though he did not invent it; cf. Mark 9:42): "one of these little ones." Thus the Christian community, threatened by its own lack of faith, can turn again and again from the ambiguity of doubt to simple trust in him who alone will come to their aid: Jesus, who is truly the Son of God (Matt. 14:31-33) and will be with them to the end of the world (28:20).

INDEX
OF NAMES AND SUBJECTS
German original compiled by Gotthold Holzhey

Numbers after entries refer to explanations of the respective Scripture passages. The special excursuses that follow expositions of individual passages are noted by the capital letter E.

(2d pt.); 5:6 (2d pt.); 5:3-12, concl.; 5:18 (1st pt.); 6:10, 11, 13,
33; 7:15, 21-23; 7:28 f. E "Sermon on the Mount" [a. 4; b. 6];
8:24; 9:13; 10:17 ff.; 10:23 (1st pt.); 10:17-24, concl.; 10:34 (2d
pt.); 11:2-6, 4, 5, 10, 27; 12:23 (2d pt.); 13:11, 39; 16:14, 18;
17:6, 7; 18:6; 19:1-12, concl.; 19:28 (2d pt.); 24:4 ff.; chapter
24, concl.; chapter 25, concl.; 25:31-46 E; 26:29, 54; 28:3, 19*a*;
28:18 (3d pt.); 28:16-20, concl.
Evangelical counsels (see **Sermon on the Mount**)
Evil: 4:2-4 E; 5:37-39; 6:13; 7:9-11, 12; intro. to 7:13-23 E [7];
7:13, 14; 12:34; 13:18 ff.; intro. to 13:24-30; 13:27 ff.; 13:24-30,
concl.; 13:37; 26:47-56, concl.
   struggle against: 7:28 f. E "Sermon on the Mount" [c. 2]
Evil One (see **Satan**)
Exaltation of Jesus: 8:17; 25:31-46 E; 26:63; 26:57-75, concl.;
28:18 (1st pt.); 28:18-20 (2d pt.); 28:18 (3d pt.); 28:16-20,
concl.; Retrospect [1]
Exorcism (see **Demons**)
Eye: 5:29, 30; 6:22-23; 20:15
   for an eye: 5:38
   of God: 20:15
   tearing out: 18:8, 9

Faith: 4:5; 5:3 (2d pt.); 5:8; 5:9 E; 6:9-13, concl.; 6:19-34, concl.;
7:28 f.; 7:28 f. E "Sermon on the Mount" [a. 3, 7; b. 1, 2; c. 2,
4, 5]; 8:5 ff.; 9:27 ff.; 11:3, 4, 5, 6; 11:2-6, concl.; 11:19*c* (2d
pt.); 11:25; 12:22-37, concl.; 12:39; 21:38-42, concl.; 22:1-14;
23:23 (1st pt.); 23:24 (2d pt.); 24:45 (2d pt.); 25:31-46, concl.;
26:47-56, concl.; intro. to 27:62-66; 28:1-10, concl.; 28:11-15,
concl.; Retrospect [1]
   Apostasy from: 7:6; 12:43 ff.; 24:9 f.
   freedom of: 7:28 f. E "Sermon on the Mount" [c. 4]
   in God and Jesus: 1:23 E; 5:45; 6:26 ff.; 6:19-34, concl.;
   7:21-23; intro. to 8:1-4; 8:5 ff.; 9:22; 9:27-34, concl.; 14:31 ff.;
   17:14-21, concl.; 18:6
   healing and: 8:5-10; 9:1 ff., 18 ff.; 12:22-37, concl.; 15:22-24;
   17:14 ff.; 17:14-21, concl.; 18:6; 21:21-22
   love and: 7:28 f. E "Sermon on the Mount" [c. 6]

James: 17:2; 19:28 (2d pt.)
Jerusalem: intro. to 5:21-48
    destruction: Introduction [5]; intro. to 4:1-11; 10:17; 16:17-19;
    22:7 (1st pt.); 23:37 (2d pt.); 23:1-39; Retrospect [2]
    Jesus in: intro. to chapters 21–25; 21:1-11; 21:1 ff.; 27:52 ff.
    Jesus addresses: 23:37-39 (1st pt.)
Jesus (see the appropriate topic, e.g., **Exaltation of Jesus; David,**
    son of)
Jewish Christians: 7:6
Jewish mission: 22:8-10 (1st pt.); 23:15 (2d pt.)
Jews: 2:19, 20; 3:7-10; 4:2-4, 8-10; 5:3 (2d pt.); 5:13 (2d pt.);
    13:16, 17 (1st pt.); 15:13; 21:43
    Christian community and: 15:2; 15:1-20, concl.; 16:17-19;
    17:24, 25; 17:24 (2d pt.); 17:24-27, concl.; intro. to chapter 18;
    18:4 (2d pt.); intro. to chapters 21–25; 22:41-46, concl.; 23:1-7
    (1st pt.); 23:15 (2d pt.); 23:1-39, concl.; Retrospect [2]
    covenant people (see **Covenant**)
    election: 1:2, 11; 8:5 ff.; 10:5-6 (2d pt.); 15:13; 19:28 (2d pt.);
    intro. to chapters 21–25; 21:43; 22:1-14, concl.; 24:1-3; 27:25,
    52; Retrospect [2]
    gentiles and: 8:5 ff., 11-12, 28 ff.; 10:1 (1st pt.); 10:5-6 (2d pt.);
    10:34 (2d pt.); 12:41, 42 (2d pt.); 15:25, 26; 16:18; intro. to
    chapters 21–25; 21:32; 21:28-32, concl.; 22:11-14 (2d pt.);
    22:1-14, concl.; 23:4 (2d pt.); 27:24 f.
    Jesus and: intro. to 4:17–11:30; 13:16, 17 (1st pt.); 15:15 (2d
    pt.); 15:21-28, 25, 26; intro. to chapters 21–25; 21:33-46;
    Retrospect [2]
    Samaritans and: 10:5-6 (2d pt.)
John the Baptist: 3:1 ff., 7 ff., 8; 4:12 ff.; intro. to 11:2-6;
    11:12-15, 16-19; 11:13; 14:1-12; 14:1 ff.; 17:11; 28:19b
    and Jesus: 3:1 ff., 13 ff.; 3:13-17, concl.; intro. to 4:17–11:30;
    4:17 ff.; intro. to 11:2-6; 11:7 ff., 13, 18, 19; 11:7-19, concl.;
    12:33-35; 14:1-12; intro. to 14:1-12; 14:1-12, concl.; 21:32;
    Retrospect [5]
    disciples of: 3:14-15; intro. to 4:17–11:30; 9:14; intro. to
    11:2-6; 28:19b
Jonah: 12:38-40; 12:38 ff., 39; 16:4, 5, 17

Name: 6:9

    assembly in Jesus': 23:37-39 (1st pt.)

    of God: 5:22; 6:9; 28:19

    of Jesus: 1:21, 23 E; 1:18-25 E [3]; 1:21; 6:9; 18:20; 19:29

Nazarene: 1:18 (2d pt.); intro. to 2:13-23

Nazareth: 1:23 E; intro. to 2:13-23; 2:23; 4:13; 13:55

Neighbor: 5:23; 18:15

Nonviolence (see **Violence**)

Oath (see also **Swearing**): 5:33-37; 5:33 ff.; 7:28 f. E "Sermon on the Mount" [c. 4]

Obedience: 5:33-37, concl.; 7:28 f. E "Sermon on the Mount" [a. 1]; 23:5 (2d pt.); 23:24 (2d pt.); 26:47-56, concl.

    to God and Jesus: 1:23 E; 3:7-10; 4:3, 4; 4:1-11, concl.; 5:9 E; 5:29, 30; 5:43-48, concl.; 6:10; 8:5 ff.; 15:1-20, concl.; 21:1-11, concl.

    of Jesus: 3:15 E; 4:2-4; 4:1-11, concl.; 5:17-20, concl.; 8:1-4, concl.

Offense: intro. to chapter 18; 18:6-9; 18:7 (1st pt.)

Office (see also **Leaders**): intro. to 7:13-23 E [6]; 16:13-20, concl.

Old Testament (see **Fulfillment of the Scriptures**)

Opponents of Jesus (see also **Chief priests; Jews; Pharisees; Teachers of the Law**): intro. to 12:1-16, 12; 12:31, 32; 13:16; 21:45

Parables: intro. to 12:1-16, 12; 13:1-9; intro. to 13:24-30; intro. to 13:31-33; 13:34 ff., 44 ff., 47 ff.; 18:21, 22 (2d pt.); 19:16 ff.; 20:1 ff.; 21:28-32, 33-46, 33 ff.; 22:1 ff.; 22:11-14 (2d pt.); 25:1-13, 1 ff., 14-30, 14 ff.; 25:14-30, concl.

    interpretation: 13:10-17, 10 ff., 18 ff., 34*a;* intro. to 13:36 ff., 51 ff.; 20:1-16, concl.; 21:28-32

Parousia (see also **Eschatology**): intro. to 7:13-23 E [7]; 10:17-24, concl.; 13:41; 16:27; intro. to chapters 21–25; 23:37-39 (1st pt.); 23:39 (2d pt.); 24:1 ff., 28 ff., 32-36, 37-39; 24:51 (2d pt.); intro. to 25:1-13; 25:13; 25:1-13, concl.; 25:28 (1st pt.); 25:14-30, concl.; 25:31-46 E, concl.; 26:63; 28:3; 28:18, 20 (2d pt.)

of Jesus: 7:24-27, concl.; 10:32, 33 (2d pt.); 12:41, 42 (1st pt.); 12:40; 16:18, 21, 28; 17:1-9, concl.; 17:23; 20:19; 25:31-46 E, concl.; intro. to chapters 26–28; 26:17 ff.; 27:53; intro. to 27:62-66; 27:62-66, concl.; 28:1 ff.; 28:1-10, concl.; 28:11 ff.; 28:11-15; 28:11-15, concl.; 28:16 ff.; 28:16 (1st pt.); 28:18; 28:16-20, concl.

Resurrection appearances: 16:17-19; 17:6, 7; 27:62-66, concl.; 28:8-10, 9, 17; 28:16-20, concl.

Return of Jesus (see **Parousia**)

Revelation: intro. to 11:25-30; 11:26; 16:17

  of God: 1:18-25 E [2]; 5:22; 10:27 (1st pt.); 11:26 ff.; 11:25-30, concl.; 16:13-20; 27:45-54

Revenge: 5:38; 6:4; 16:27; 18:21 (2d pt.)

  renunciation of (see also **Violence**): 5:21-48; 5:38 ff.; 7:28 f. E "Sermon on the Mount" [b. 6]

Reward: 5:12; intro. to 5:21-48; intro. to 6:1-18; 6:1 ff.; intro. to 6:19-34; 10:1-16; intro. to 10:40–11:1; 19:21; 20:15; 25:31-46, concl.

  merit and: intro. to 6:1-18; 6:2 ff.; 7:28 f. E "Sermon on the Mount" [b. 1]; 9:14 ff.; 11:19 (2d pt.); 20:15; 25:31-46, concl.

Rich (see **Wealth**)

Righteous, the: 5:3 (2d pt.); intro. to 7:13-23 E [1, 4, 5]; intro. to 10:40–11:1; 13:17 (2d pt.); 13:36b-43, concl.; 18:10 (1st pt.)

  and the unrighteous: 5:45; intro. to 7:1-6

Righteousness: 3:15 E; 5:6 (2d pt.); 5:10; 5:20 (2d pt.); 5:17-20, concl.; 5:43-48, concl.; 6:1; intro. to 6:1-18; 12:43 ff.; 18:18 E; 20:15; 23:23 (2d pt.)

  before God: 5:43-48, concl.; intro. to 6:1-18

  fulfillment of: 3:13 f.; 3:15 E

  new (better): intro. to 4:17–11:30; intro. to 5:21-48; 6:9-13, concl.; 18:21-35; 23:24 (2d pt.)

  of God: 1:3, 5, 6; 3:14, 15; 3:15 E; 5:6 (2d pt.); 5:17-20, concl.; 6:33; 7:1-6, concl.; 7:7, 8; 11:26; 12:19, 20; 18:21-35; 20:1-6; 20:15, 16 ff.; 25:28, 29 (2d pt.)

  of Jesus: 4:1-11, concl.

  of the Pharisees and teachers of the Law: 5:20 (1st pt.)

  way of: 3:1 ff.; 21:28-32, concl.

Jesus: 8:1-4, concl.; 8:18; 12:5 ff., 22 ff., 29 ff.; 27:38 ff.;
  Retrospect [1, 5]
  prophets: 10:24; 21:24-36
Service: 6:24; intro. to 7:13-23 E [5]; 11:25-30, concl.; 20:28;
  20:20-28, concl.; 23:28 (2d pt.)
Sheep: 7:13-23; 7:15; 7:13-23 E [7]; 10:5-6 (2d pt.); 10:16;
  15:22-24; 18:12, 13 (2d pt.); 25:33
Shepherd: 10:5-6 (2d pt.); 18:12 f. (3d pt.)
  leaders (see **Leaders**)
  sheep and: 18:12 f. (3d pt.)
Significance of Jesus for the world: Introduction [5]; 1:3, 5, 6;
  intro. to 2:1-12; 2:2; 2:1-12, concl.; 2:13-23, concl.; 5:16 (2d
  pt.); 8:5-13, concl.; 10:5-6 (2d pt.); 12:21, 30; 13:36b-43, concl.;
  13:45, 46, 47; 28:19; 28:19a
Signs: 12:38-40; 12:43 ff.; 27:51
  Jesus as: 12:39
  of Jesus: 24:1 ff.; 24:30 (1st pt.)
  and wonders: 12:38
Sin (see also **Forgiveness of sins**): 1:21; 5:4 (2d pt.); 6:16; 7:28 f.
  E "Sermon on the Mount" [a. 6; b. 1]; 8:17; 9:1 ff., 9 ff.;
  12:31, 32 (2d pt.); 18:15 f.; 18:18 E; 18:21 (2d pt.); 20:19
  against the Holy Spirit: 12:31, 32 (2d pt.)
Slavery: 7:28 f. E "Sermon on the Mount" [c. 4]
Smugness: 3:7ff.; 5:4 (2d pt.); 5:32; 5:43-48, concl.; 7:28 f. E
  "Sermon on the Mount" [a. 6]; 8:5-13, concl.; 12:38-42, concl.;
  22:11-14 (3d pt.)
Sobriety: 24:25 (2d pt.)
Sodom and Gomorrah: 10:15; intro. to 11:20-24; 11:23, 24; 24:38
  (1st pt.)
Son: 12:17-21, 18
  of God: Introduction [4]; 1:18 (2d pt.); 1:23 E; intro. to
  2:13-23; 2:13-23, concl.; 3:7; intro. to 4:1-11; 4:2-4; 4:1-11,
  concl.; intro. to 4:17–11:30; 4:25; 5:9 E; 14:28-31, 33; 16:17-19,
  16; 17:27 (3d pt.); 22:11-14 (1st pt.); 24:30 (2d pt.); 26:67;
  27:38 ff.; 28:19 E; Retrospect [1]
Son of David (see **David, son of**)
Son of Man (see also **Suffering; Judge**): 8:20; 9:1 ff.; 10:32, 33

INDEX OF EXCURSUSES